DAUGHTER OF FIRE

Daughter of Fire

A Diary of a Spiritual Training
with a Sufi Master

IRINA TWEEDIE

THE COMPLETE UNABRIDGED EDITION

Blue Dolphin Publishing
1986

Original Title: *The Chasm of Fire*
Copyright © 1979 Irina Tweedie
First abridged edition published by
Element Books
Longmead Shaftesbury
Dorset SP7 8PL England
ISBN: 0-906540-01-1

The Complete Unabridged Edition: *Daughter of Fire*
Copyright © 1986 Irina Tweedie
Published by Blue Dolphin Publishing, Inc.
P.O. Box 1908, Nevada City, CA 95959

ISBN: 0-931892-05-8 cloth
      0-931892-04-X soft

Library of Congress Cataloging-in-Publication Data
Tweedie, Irina, 1907-
  Daughter of fire.

  Previously published as: The chasm of fire. c1979.
  1. Tweedie Irina, 1907- —Diaries. 2. Sufis—Diaries. I. Title.
BP80.T92A33 1986   297'.42 [B]   86-72368
ISBN 0-931892-05-8
ISBN 0-931892-04-X (pbk.)

Printed in the United States of America by
Blue Dolphin Press, Inc., Grass Valley, California

9 8 7 6 5 4 3 2

To the Lotus Feet
of my Revered Teacher

The Path of Love
Is like a Bridge of Hair
Across a Chasm of Fire
                    —an early Christian mystic

Give me freedom to sing without an echo,
Give me freedom to fly without a shadow,
And to love without leaving traces.

"We must shut our eyes and turn them inwards, we must look far down into that split between night and day in ourselves until our head reels with the depth of it, and then we must ask: 'How can I bridge this self? How cross from one side to the other?' . . . . A gulf bridged makes a cross; a split defeated is a cross. A longing for wholeness presupposes a cross, at the foundations of our being, in the heart of our quivering, throbbing, tender, lovely, love-born flesh and blood, and we carry it with us wherever we journey on, on unto all the dimensions of space, time, unfulfilled love, and being-to-be.

"That is sign enough. . . . The beating and troubled heart can rest. In the midnight hour of the crashing darkness, on the other side of the night behind the cross of stars, noon is being born."

—Laurens van der Post
Venture to the Interior

Chapter Titles

PART TWO

THE WAY OF NO RETURN

Foreword

THIS BOOK IS AN ACCOUNT of spiritual training according to the ancient Yogic tradition.

"Keep a diary," said my Teacher, "one day it will become a book. But you must write it in such a way that it should help others. People say, such things did happen thousands of years ago—we read in books about it. This book will be a proof that such things do happen today as they happened yesterday and will happen tomorrow—to the right people, in the right time, and in the right place."

I preserved the diary form. I found it conveys better the immediacy of experience, and for the same reason I use throughout the first person singular: it happened to me, I am involved in it day by day.

When I tried to write it in an impersonal way, rather like a story, I found that it lost its impact.

The first draft of the manuscript was begun in September 1971, in Tongue, Sutherland, Scotland, nearly ten years after having met my Revered Teacher. I could not face it before, could not even look at the entries. It was like a panic; I dreaded it. Too much suffering is involved in it; it is written with the blood of my heart. A slow grinding down of the personality is a painful process.

> Man cannot remake himself without suffering.
> For he is both the marble and the sculptor.
>
> Alexis Carrell,
> *Man the Unknown*

Suffering has a redeeming quality. Pain and repetition are fixative agents.

The reader will find it very repetitive. Naturally so. For it is the story of a teaching. And teaching is constant repetition. The pupil has to learn the lesson again and again in order to be able to master it, and the teacher must repeat the lesson, present it in a different light, sometimes in a different form, so that the pupil should understand

and remember. Each situation is repeated many a time, but each time it triggers off a slightly different psychological reaction leading to the next experience, and so forth.

I hoped to get instructions in Yoga, expected wonderful teachings, but what the Teacher did was mainly to force me to face the darkness within myself, and it almost killed me.

In other words he made me "descend into hell," the cosmic drama enacted in every soul as soon as it dares to lift its face to the Light.

It was done very simply, by using violent reproof and even aggression. My mind was kept in a state of confusion to the extent of being "switched off." I was beaten down in every sense till I had to come to terms with that in me which I kept rejecting all my life. It is surprising how the classical method of training, devised perhaps thousands of years ago, is similar to the modern psychological techniques; even dream analysis has a place in it.

Somewhere in one of the *Upanishads*—I don't remember which one—there is a sentence which puts our quest for spirituality in a nutshell: "If you want Truth as badly as a drowning man wants air, you will realize it in a split-second."

But who wants Truth as badly as that? It is the task of the Teacher to set the heart aflame with the unquenchable flame of longing, and it is his duty to keep it burning till it is reduced to ashes. For only a heart which has burned itself empty is capable of love. Only a heart which has become non-existent can resurrect, pulsate to the rhythm of a new life.

". . . Ye have to die before ye can live again. . . ."

It is my sincere and ardent desire that this work should be a pointer on the Way, at least for some of us. For as a well-known saying goes: "We are both the Pilgrim and the Way."

I.T.

Whenever the pronoun "He" or "Him" is used in the text with a capital letter, it always refers to God and never to the Teacher.

PART ONE

ACROSS THE CHASM OF FIRE

1

*Second Birth**

2nd October, 1961
COMING HOME . . . MY HEART WAS SINGING. This feeling of joy seized me
as soon as I left the train.

The large railway station was like so many others I happened to see
during my travels in India—the steel rafters, the roof blackened by
smoke, the deafening noise of hissing railway engines, one train just
pulling out with much heaving and clatter, the usual crowd of
squatting figures surrounded by their belongings, patiently waiting
for the departure of some local train, coolies fighting for my luggage,
the flies, the heat. I was tired and very hot, but somehow, and I did
not know why, I loved this station; just the feeling of having arrived
made me feel glad.

Drawn by an old horse, the *tonga* (a two-wheeled carriage) was
plodding along for already more than forty minutes, on the way to
Aryanangar, the district of my destination. This part of the town
seemed fairly clean, even at this time of the day; it was nearly 5 p.m.,
and still very hot.

I felt light, free and happy, as one would feel when coming home
after a long absence. Strange . . . this wonderful sensation of coming
home, of arriving at last. . . . Why? It seemed crazy. I wondered,
how long am I destined to stay here? Years? All my life? It mattered
not; it felt good. That was all I knew for the moment.

We were trotting along a wide avenue flanked with trees. Large
bungalows, gleaming white, set well in the gardens behind stone walls
and iron fences, announced in large letters the names of banks,
insurance companies, engineering firms—large concerns known all
the world over. A main post office to the right, a large hospital to the
left, then a large bazaar covering a wide open space—passing glimpses
into the side-streets lined with shops and barrows, goods displayed
on the pavements, and all the noise, all the typical smells composed

---

*According to a very ancient Eastern tradition, the disciple is born, when for the
first time the glance of the Teacher falls on him.

of fried oil and garlic, spices and incense of the bazaar. I sniffed the air
. . . it was good.

It was just one more Indian city, such as I had seen many a time
before; and still . . . and still, this glorious feeling of coming home,
there was no earthly reason for it . . . it seemed crazy.

True, I came to meet a great Yogi, a Guru, and I expected much
from this encounter. But surely this was no reason to feel so light, so
childishly happy. I even caught myself laughing aloud and thinking:
For the rest of my life it will be . . . and immediately I was amazed at
this idea. You are getting potty, old girl, I said to myself; that's it:
potty. But never mind, life was so good—it was such fun to be alive,
to breathe, to move, to be a bit mad and . . . to have arrived!!

We were just passing a large cotton mill, then a railway crossing. I
noticed the time on a tower clock; it was half-past five. We still went
on and on. How slow the horse was, and so thin—all the ribs were
sticking out from under a dry parchment-like skin. The driver was
very thin, too; he must be tired also, and he looked hungry like his
horse. I had a sudden feeling of guilt, for my suitcases were heavy—
they nearly filled out all the space in the precariously wobbling two-
wheel vehicle. I sat sideways, rather uncomfortable, clasping the
handle of one of the suitcases to prevent it from falling off at every
jerk. The fact that I was tired and felt very hot were details—they
mattered little, for I was coming home. . . .

After many repeated inquiries from the street-vendors and
shopkeepers on our way, my *tonga* driver delivered me at last to my
destination. It was a low, sprawling terracotta-red bungalow set in
the midst of a large open garden, with flower beds in front, and
plenty of trees in the back, and trees spaced here and there all
around. The street was fairly wide, a tiny post office standing in a
garden amongst palm trees was just opposite, and next to it I noticed
a bakery. After a hot, dusty journey it looked like heaven, all so fresh
and peaceful.

But my joy was short-lived. Mrs. Ghose, the proprietor, told me
that she had no accommodation free. She said that she wrote to Miss
L. about it and seemed surprised that I knew nothing about it. "But I
will take you to Miss L.'s friend, Pushpa; there you are sure to find a
place to stay for the time being."

She climbed into the *tonga* beside me and, seated practically on top
of my suitcases, was already giving rapid instructions to the driver in
Hindi. This time the horse needed plenty of encouragement, and we

started off again. Mrs. Ghose, stout and middle-aged, gathering her voluminous sari around her, kept talking rapidly, something about tenants and some letters, but I hardly listened. Was worried. L. had given me to understand that the place for my stay was assured, and here I was, not knowing where I would spend the night. There were no hotels in the vicinity, so much I knew from what she had told me. After a day's and a night's journey, I badly needed a rest.

I was still occupied with my thoughts when she suddenly ordered the driver to stop. "Here lives Miss L.'s Guruji." She turned to me, "Would you like to meet him?"

I did not like meeting anybody at this particular moment; my dress was covered with dust, my hair sticky with perspiration—all I wanted was a cold shower and a cup of tea. It was the most unsuitable moment to meet anyone, least of all an important personage like a Guru! But my protests were of no avail; she was already disappearing through a wide wooden gate leading into a rather dry-looking garden with several shrubs and a few trees. In the background stood a long white bungalow—a door was at each end of it, and a large, tall doorway with wooden shutters in the middle, leading presumably into an inner courtyard.

Before I even had time to recollect my thoughts, three bearded Indians emerged from the door opposite the gate and were advancing towards me followed by Mrs. Ghose. All three were elderly; all three were dressed in white. I stood up, jumped down from the *tonga* and, joining my palms in the Indian way of greeting, looked at each of them in turn, not being sure which one was the Guru. The oldest and the tallest of the three, who looked exactly like a prophet in a nativity play—long, grey beard, blazing dark eyes—walked ahead of the other two, and, as if in answer to my thoughts, pointed to the one walking closely behind him. This was the Guru.

Next moment he stood in front of me, quietly looking at me with a smile. He was tall, had a kindly face and strange eyes—dark pools of stillness they were, with a sort of liquid light in them, like golden sparks.

I just had time to notice that he was the only one to wear wide trousers and a very long *kurta* (a collarless Indian-style shirt) of immaculate whiteness; the other two were clad in rather worn *kurtas* and *longhi,* (a straight piece of usually cotton material tight around the waist and reaching to the ankles).

My mind had hardly time to register it—then it was as if it turned a

somersault, my heart stood still for a split second. I caught my breath
. . . wild cartwheels were turning inside my brain and then my mind
went completely blank.

And then it was—it was as if *something in me* stood to attention and
saluted. . . . I was in the presence of a Great Man. . . .

"There is no accommodation for me with Mrs. Ghose," I said
quickly, looking at him confused and insecure. I was aware that I was
saying it just to say something, anything, for I felt helpless,
completely lost. Deep down in me there was a sort of complete
terror, a kind of excitement, and at the same time I felt annoyed with
myself for feeling shy and confused like a child.

"Miss L. wrote to me that you will be coming," he said, and his
smile deepened. It was a pleasant, baritonal voice; it suited well the
general aura of peace which seemed to surround him.

Mrs. Ghose stepped forward and began to tell her story all over
again, that she wrote to Miss L., that she had nothing free, but
perhaps the letter went astray, etc., etc. He nodded slowly:

"You will be able to stay with Pushpa, and," he added, **"I expect
you tomorrow at 7 a.m."**

Some more polite words were exchanged; he asked me about my
journey, but I hardly had any recollection of it, could not think,
hardly understood anything.

Shortly afterwards we arrived at Pushpa's place. It was a large two-
story house with a very small garden. She herself was pleasant
looking, plump with a pretty face. She came to meet us, her father-in-
law following her, an impressive figure, dignified, all in white, with a
large Alsatian dog at his heels. Mrs. Ghose once more began her
explanations.

Soon I found myself installed in the guest room on the ground
floor; it had a bathroom attached to it and a ceiling fan. In front of the
two windows was a high brick wall covered with a luscious flowering
creeper, and the light filtering through the leaves covering the
windows made the room look green and cool.

The bliss of a cold shower, a short rest, then a lovely Indian meal
with the whole of the family seated around a large round table in the
dining room. The Alsatian dog was also present under the table at
Babuji's (Grandfather's) feet, licking himself and smelling to high
heaven; but again, it was only a detail, and it too fitted somehow into
the frame of the whole experience and was accepted as such by me.

3rd *October*

HOW WELL I SLEPT under the humming fan, but could not go to him at seven in the morning as he told me.

Breakfast was at 9 a.m. All the family kept piling questions on me, about England, my travels, about myself—everybody had something of special interest to ask—and it was only after ten when, at last, I was free to go. Pushpa sent her boy-servant to show me the way.

Already, when passing through the garden gate, I could see him seated in his room in a very large chair opposite the open door, from which he could see part of the garden and the entrance gate. He looked steadily at me coming towards him. With a brief nod he acknowledged my greeting.

"I expected you at seven," he said, fingering his *mala* (a kind of rosary much used in the East). **"It is not exactly seven now."**

I explained that the breakfast was late, and that I could not get away earlier.

He nodded. **"Yes, it would have been discourteous,"** he remarked, and told me to sit down.

The room was silent. He seemed to pray, bead after bead of the mala sliding through his fingers. I looked around. It was a corner room, not large, rather narrow. Another door to the right flanked by two windows was also leading into the garden. Two large wooden couches *(tachats)* were standing along the left wall which had two recesses built into it, filled with books. A row of chairs and a small divan for the visitors stood facing the tachats with the backs to the windows and the side door, leaving only a narrow passage to the third door at the opposite end of the room. It was covered by a green curtain and led to the next room from which one could reach the inner courtyard. All was clean and orderly—it could easily be a student's room. The sheets, cushions and covers on the tachats were spotlessly clean. He was dressed all in white—wide pajama trousers as they used to wear them here in the north of India—but his *kurta* was unusually long, rather like a robe, as I noticed it yesterday.

His name, executed by naive infantile hands, hung in three frames on the wall over the tachats. One was in cut-out felt, clumsily and unevenly cut, the other embroidered in cross-stitch, the third in printed letters in Indian ink—things children as a rule give to their parents or relations on birthdays or similar occasions.

While looking at the frames, I mused over this name and was glad that I saw it written before me and did not need to ask him or anybody else. I remembered vividly how I told L. in a sudden panic that I did not want to know his name when she was giving me his address, in my tent, in Pahalgam, in Kashmir. It was baffling, and I had no explanation why I felt that he had to remain without a name, without even a face for me.

L. told me that the fact of not wanting to know his name had a deep meaning, but refused to clarify the point.

"You will know one day," she said rather mysteriously. And here it was: right in front of me, written three times, hanging on the wall. But I still did not know why she refused to explain and why I had such a fear.

"Why did you come to me?"* he asked, quietly breaking the silence.

I looked at him. The beads in his right hand were resting on the arm support of the chair, and all at once, as if waiting for this very question, I felt a sudden irresistible desire to speak, an urgency to tell everything, absolutely, about myself, my longing, my aspirations, all my life. . . .

It was like a compulsion. I began to speak and talked for a long time. I told him that I wanted God, was searching after Truth. From what I had learned from L., I knew that he could help me and told him what I understood about him and his work from L.'s descriptions.

I went on and on and on. He kept nodding slowly, as if the torrent of my words was a confirmation of his own thoughts, looking at me, no, rather through me, with those strange eyes of his, as if to search out the very intimate, the very hidden corners of my mind.

"I want God," I heard myself saying, "but not the Christian idea of an anthropomorphic deity sitting somewhere, possibly on a cloud surrounded by angels with harps; I want the Rootless Root, the Causeless Cause of the Upanishads."

"Nothing less than that?" He lifted an eyebrow. I detected a slight note of irony in his voice. He was silent again, fingering his mala.

I too was silent now. "He thinks I am full of pride," flashed through my mind. Indistinct feelings of resentment surged from the depth of my being and went. He seemed so strange, so incomprehensible.

---

*The traditional question of every Oriental Teacher to an aspirant or a would-be disciple. According to Spiritual Law the human being must clearly state his case himself. The Teacher will do nothing against the free will of the individual.

As he looked out of the window, his face was expressionless. I noticed that his eyes were not very dark, rather hazel-brown with small golden sparks in them as I had noticed yesterday.

I began again telling him that I was a Theosophist, a vegetarian, and . . . **"Theosophist?"** he interrupted inquiringly. I explained. **"Oh yes, now I remember, long ago I met some Theosophists."** Again the silence fell. He closed his eyes. His lips were moving in silent prayer. But I still went on explaining that we don't believe that a Guru is necessary; we must try and reach our Higher Self by our own efforts. **"Not even in a hundred years!"** He laughed outright: **"It cannot be done without a Teacher!"**

I told him that I did not know what Sufism was.

"Sufism is a way of life. It is neither a religion nor a philosophy. There are Hindu Sufis, Muslim Sufis, Christian Sufis—My Revered Guru Maharaj was a Muslim." He said it very softly with a tender expression, his eyes dreamy and veiled.

And then I noticed something which in my excitement and eagerness I did not notice before: there was a feeling of great peace in the room. He himself was full of peace. He radiated it; it was all around us, and it seemed eternal—as if this special peace always was and always would be, forever. . . .

I looked at his face. He could be said to be good-looking in a masculine sort of way. There was nothing feminine in his features— the rather strong nose, the very high forehead. The grey beard and mustache gave him a dignified and distinctly Oriental appearance. His hair was short-cut, Western style.

"How shall I address you? What is the custom?" I asked.

"You can call me as you like, I don't mind. People here call me 'Bhai Sahib,' which in Hindi means 'Elder Brother'."

So, "Bhai Sahib" is going to be for me too, I thought. That's what he really is: an Elder Brother to us all.

"When I arrived, I had a feeling of coming home; and now I cannot get rid of the impression that I knew you before. That I knew you always. Bhai Sahib, where did we meet last time?"

"Why ask?" He smiled, **"Some day you will know yourself. Why ask? But we met before, not once, but many a time, and we will meet many times again; that much I can tell you."**

At 11:30, he sent me away.

"For the first few days (he put a special emphasis on the word ONLY), **you will not stay here for long periods at a time. Be back after 6 p.m."**

I left and took with me the haunting memory of his face, full of infinite sweetness and dignity, and this impression remained with me for quite a while. Who is he? I felt greatly perturbed.

2

Perplexities and Premonitions

WE HAD LUNCH. Much talk at the table, all the family present. Grandfather is lovely, quite a character. So fair-skinned, he looks European, always dresses in white, a silent man of very few words.

After lunch I went to have a rest in my room. Everybody else did the same, as is the custom in every hot country. The room was cool and tranquil, full of green light like a secluded greenhouse. Only the soft swish of the ceiling fan, an occasional car passing by, and the usual noises and voices of an Indian street. I stretched out luxuriously, the pleasant sensation of cool air on my skin, thinking over lazily this morning's conversation.

It was then I suddenly realized that I did not remember his face . . . I could not recollect what he looked like! It gave me such a shock that I literally gasped. His garment, his mala, his hands, the room and the furniture, I remembered well—and a good part, though not the whole, of our conversation; his slender feet in brown strap-sandals; wait a moment—the feet, those sandals—where have I seen them before? Oh yes, in a dream long ago; I was looking at them, trying to follow their rhythm, when a tall Indian, whose face I did not remember, was leading me in a dance on a stony desert road. They were the same feet, the same sandals. But his face, seen only a few hours ago, I could not recollect. . . .

I realized that I remembered a body, *and no face!* Got such a fright that I sat up on the edge of my bed—am I dreaming? Am I mad? What is it? Who is this man? Did he mesmerize me, or am I going round the bend? Was very disturbed. Lay down again, *forcing* my mind to remember, but to no avail. The more I tried, the more I became confused.

Just to do something, to pass the time, I got up and wrote a short letter to L., just a few lines, that I met him, and hoped that she would be here soon.

I could hardly wait till 6 p.m. When I arrived, he was sitting cross-legged in his chair in the garden talking to some men seated around on chairs. I felt very relieved. Of course, how stupid of me! Here he is in the flesh, looking very real and solid like everybody else. And sure enough he *had* a face, and he was laughing at this very moment, for he was telling a funny story in Hindi. Everybody laughed, and I was looking fixedly at him. I could not understand how I could be so foolish, to forget something so obvious. I did not want to have the same experience again; it was far too disturbing. I wondered, how far can I trust my mind, my memory. So I looked at his features, to impress them well in my mind. (Little did I know then, that never again would I be able to forget his face.)

After a while he turned to me and said in English: **"I would like you to keep a diary, day-by-day entries of all your experiences. And also to keep a record of your dreams. Your dreams you must tell me, and I will interpret them for you. Dreams are important; they are a guidance."**

4th October

WENT TO BHAI SAHIB in the morning after breakfast, and in the evening after six. My judgment? I still do not know. I cannot even think properly. As on the first day, when I was annoyed with myself, my brain kept getting empty and I could hardly think coherently. Now too, especially when I am at his place, the thinking process seems to slow down considerably. Thoughts come and go, lazily, slowly, just a few, and far in between. I see people come in, touch his feet, sit down quietly, and fall into a deep state, completely oblivious to their surroundings. I was told that this is the state of *Dhyana*, but what this *Dhyana* is supposed to be he did not tell me. He only smiled and said that I will know it myself one day . . . I have heard this one before, so it seems.

Perhaps after all, it is of no importance if he is a great Guru or not. Perhaps it does not even matter to be able to understand who he is. If he can teach me how to abstract the senses (*indrias*, in Sanskrit)— because this is what the *Dhyana* seems to be—to be able to meditate like this, oblivious to everything, I wouldn't ask for more. After all, it is supposed to be a desirable state to which all Yogis aspire; and it is the most difficult state to achieve, especially for us in the West. For us who are used to living and functioning on the mental level, to be beyond it seems a utopia, a sheer impossibility. But here I see it done, so seemingly easily, so effortlessly—and what's more, he told me that I will be able to do it too, one day. Can hardly believe it. I will never be able to do it, so it seems to me.

Bhai Sahib was telling us about his father who died years ago in January, the celebration which is going to be on that day, the anniversary of his death.

"But until then we will go. . . ."

A kind of panic seized me: my mind began to reel and then went blank. . . . I could not understand one word of what he was saying, heard the sound of his voice, but the words had no meaning—it was just a sound, nothing more. Something in me *knew* the meaning of what he was saying, but it was *not* the brain, and I was very frightened.

"Did you get my idea?" he concluded.

"I did." I lied. "But Bhai Sahib, it is a frightening thought, for it seems to be a journey of no return. And a journey which has no return is always terrifying. The personality is afraid, because it knows that the 'I' will go, that *it has to go*. There comes a time in our life when we have to burn all the bridges behind us, or they are burned for us, which is the same thing. Because the little self will be afraid, it will put up a terrific fight for its life."

All the while I was speaking, I was amazed at my answer, because I really did not hear one word of what he had told me. Still, my answer must have been the right one, for he smiled gently without comment, nodded, and began to speak to others in Hindi.

5th October

ON THE FIRST MORNING, three days ago he had said, **"If you say to a human being: sit in this *Asana* (posture), or that one, meditate in this way or that, you are putting the human being in prison. Leave the man alone, and he will find God in his own way."**

But is he not trying to put me in prison? This fact of my mind not working? What is the meaning of it??

Asked him this morning if it was true, as I read in one of Mr. Leadbeater's books, that the *Atma*, when in incarnation, assumes the features of the physical body and can be seen, more or less one foot above the head of the person; and the eyes are the same as the physical eyes?

"The eyes and the forehead are the same; and yes, it is true, it can be seen above the head of the person."

Then I asked, why on the second day of our meeting he wanted to know if I was free, completely free, had no dependents, neither relations to look after, nor any obligations to bind me.

"You know that I am free; so why did you ask?"

"Yes, I know of course that you are free. But I wanted a confirmation from yourself. Sometimes in this physical world we have to behave and speak as if we knew nothing."

It seemed a strange answer. But I did not ask further.

Looking at me thoughtfully, he said slowly: **"It takes time to make a soul pregnant with God. But it can be done; IT WILL BE DONE. . . ."**

This too seemed a strange statement. I kept very still, looking at him, and wondering.

Later a young man came whom I have already seen here, a handsome, tall Indian with a severe face; he could be about thirty, so I thought. This time he brought his little girl with him; she was three-and-a-half, as he later told me. A pretty child with enormous eyes, like deep pools of innocence. It is strange and wonderful that all the children of all the nations are beautiful. Why do people change so much when they grow up?

The young man touched Guruji's feet bowing down very low, sat down and fell immediately in deep Dhyana, as usual, sitting there perfectly motionless, unconscious of everything, his child standing between his knees, playing quietly with a flower.

"He is a very evolved human being," said Bhai Sahib, as soon as the man had left.

"He works on the railway and comes here when he can."

The old man, whom I thought looked like a prophet in a nativity play (by the way, his name is Munshiji), came in with a list in his hand, asking questions. The servant was called in. Bhai Sahib's wife* came with a dish of rice and a long discussion began in Hindi. His wife does not speak English at all.

---

*Sufis lead the normal life of a householder, and marriage for them does not represent a barrier to reaching the higher states of consciousness.

3

Doubts

6th October, 1961

DOUBTS KEPT COMING into my mind. Many doubts. Such ordinary surroundings. Such ordinary people around him. Is he a Great Man? There seems to be no glamor of a Great Guru, a Great Teacher, about him, as we used to read in books. . . . He was so simple, living a simple, ordinary life. Clearly, he took his household duties seriously. I could see that he was the head of a large family, six children, and his brother and his family living also in the same house, all sharing the same courtyard. And I saw also other people there, a few other families—the place was full of comings and goings, full of all kinds of activities, not to count his disciples of whom there seemed to be many.

Decided to speak to L. about it. She will soon be back. She had to remain in Kashmir because of a religious congress in which she took part.

In the meantime I resolved to stay away as much as possible.

Went there after 6 p.m. He was writing letters seated cross-legged on his tachat. I tried to read a book I brought with me. Soon he looked up and asked me if I felt uneasy, if I felt any pain. Told him that if my foot is not better, I will not come tomorrow. My foot was hurting, could hardly walk because of the infection I brought with me from Amritsar. There was a painful sore in between the toes, an inflammation giving me much trouble. I suspected the pools of water one had to cross before entering each temple were the culprits, but I did not tell him so. Besides it was only a suspicion; it could be anything. He made some sympathetic noises. While speaking, I secretly hoped that he would cure it instantly. Did not mention it, but had this idea at the back of my mind. He looked at my foot. **"It will come right by itself,"** he said, as if aware of my thoughts. **"Rest is useful,"** he added and continued to write. Did not stay long and went home.

9th October

PUSHPA'S HOUSE is roomy and comfortable. Ceiling fans are in every room. With the excuse of the small infection on my foot, did not go to the Guru.

But I went this morning. He was talking nearly all the time about his Guru and how much money he spent on him. I wonder if the old man knows my thoughts about him and talks like that because of it. I have now every possible suspicion about him. Stayed for a very short while.

In the afternoon it was raining heavily, so did not go either. Will try to keep away from him until L.'s arrival. So much hope shattered. . . . Did I expect too much, perhaps? It seems all so commonplace, so banal, so ordinary. And he hardly bothers to answer my questions:

"You will know one day."

Why and how? What prevents him from explaining? What an attitude!

Went to a classical concert with Pushpa's husband and daughter. To a *Gita* class on Sunday morning. Nothing special; the *Gita* class was held by a Ramakrishna Swami of Ramakrishna Mission Order. But the concert was lovely, and the tape recordings of wonderful Indian classical music which Pushpa's husband played to us in the afternoon were exquisitely beautiful. Otherwise boring days. Plenty of worldly chit-chat. Endless waiting for meals never served punctually, and a feeling of great loneliness . . . dark endless longing, and I do not know for what. Much disappointment and much bitterness.

Who are you? Are you what L. told me: a Great Teacher, a man of great spiritual power, or just one of so many pseudo-gurus one meets here in India at every step?

Are you a Teacher at all? You seem to have many disciples—I saw plenty of them already in the short time I have been here. From what I heard from L., you must be a great man. But are you??

10th October

IT WAS RAINING in the morning. Went about 5 p.m. Nobody was there. Then the professor of mathematics arrived and sat with us. Later Bhai Sahib suggested to us that we might like to go to a discussion which was held in the park. A platform was erected for this purpose. Plenty of learned Hindus were attending. I refused. Told him that I wanted to be punctual at the *Kirtan* (singing of devotional hymns) which was held at Pushpa's place at 7 p.m.

Left with the professor of mathematics who was also coming to the *Kirtan*. Walking along he asked me what this discussion was supposed to be about. I said, about the *Avatar* (Divine Incarnation) of Ram; there is a theory that he was the only real incarnation of Vishnu (the second person of the Hindu Trinity; the Preserver) and nobody else. Then I began to tell him about my doubts. Is there any purpose to go to Bhai Sahib at all? Is it not a waste of time? He listened with great seriousness.

"If you are convinced that your Guru is always right, that he is the only great man, then you will progress. Your Guru may not be great at all, but you think that he is, and it is your faith which will make you progress. It is the same with Ram: what does it matter if he is the only incarnation of God or not; for the man who believes it, he is. So why discuss? I refuse to participate in intellectual acrobatics."

I agreed with him. "What disturbs me most with Bhai Sahib," I went on, "is the fact that he does not answer questions. Every time I want to know something, he will say: **'You will know it one day yourself.'** Now, who can tell me if I really will know? Maybe I never will; so why not simply answer it? I want to know NOW, not sometime in a hypothetic future! I begin to wonder if I am wasting my time!"

"You know," he said, "just to give an example, for instance, a son of a rich man inherits the wealth of his father, and then he will have more than you and me. Now, here it is the same in this place. This man has a certain power which will reveal in time something very wonderful within yourself. It happened to others; it happened to me. I have been here for the last twelve years, I speak from experience. I don't know how it happens; I have no explanation for it. I even don't know how one can inherit such a thing, but it is a fact. Stay here for a month, and you will be in a state L. is, and we all are, and then you will think differently. L., when she came years ago, spoke as you do now."

I said that I was sure that it would take longer than one month.

"Of course it takes years," he agreed, "but after one month you will be able to form a judgment."

I told him that I decided at any rate to stay here until March, and he answered that it would be wise to do so. "I have seen strange and wonderful things happen to human beings. It is as I tell you; and Dhyana is definitely NOT a mediumistic trance; it is a yogic state, and has nothing to do with mesmerism either."

We were entering Pushpa's gate. The veranda was brightly lit;

many people were already there. "Dhyana is complete abstraction of the senses, *Indrias*, in Sanskrit; it is a Yogic state, as I have just told you."

We entered the room; the music started. I was in deep thought. So, that was it. Somehow, I felt that this conversation represented a turning point. An intelligent man, an intellectual, with a balanced mind, normal, reasonable, gave me his opinion. I liked and trusted him from the first moment I saw him, a few days ago. In my heart I felt I should give it a try, accept the situation as it presents itself, and see what will happen. . . . Why not? Lights were burning in front of the pictures of Rama, Shiva and Parvati (Hindu deities). The room was crowded, everyone seated on the floor. Kept looking at the faces full of devotion while my heart kept rhythm with the ancient melody—"Hari Rama, Hari, Hari. . ." and I was thinking and thinking . . . and was still thinking deeply when back in my room, hardly aware of howling dogs roaming the streets and the evening noises of a busy Indian street.

"Is Dhyana just sleep?" I asked.

"If you think that it may be sleep, then it is sleep; if you think it is not, then it is not." His face was stern. But there was like a faint suspicion of a wicked little twinkle in his eye, a hidden laughter.

Not much of an answer, I must say. Quite in keeping with his general attitude.

12 October

THOUGH EVERYBODY keeps telling me that the climate here is not a good one, I find it healthy and invigorating. It seems to agree with me. I am always well where the sun sees me. My body needs the sun. The food at Pushpa's place is excellent. I am eating too much, sleep well, am hungry, my health is good. The foot healed completely in the last few days.

Arrived about 5 p.m. Nobody was in the room. Sat down in my usual place in the chair opposite his tachat. His wife came in, searching something in the recess amongst the books. Then he came in. I don't remember how we came to talk about Dhyana, but probably I began, because it kept worrying me. As soon as I came into his room, the thinking process slowed down and I felt sleepy. I told him so and he translated it to his wife. She said that I was not the only one—it happens to her too; as soon as she lies down, she falls asleep.

"I never sleep during the day," he remarked.

"How can you keep awake in this place?" I wondered, "I feel sleepy as soon as I sit down!"

He laughed. Then he began to tell me that in 1956 he was very ill, desperately ill, and many people came who could be of some help, in one way or another. But they all sat there fast asleep, and his wife used to say: "What did they all come for? Just to sleep here?"

"So Dhyana does mean to be asleep after all? Is Dhyana and sleep the same thing?"

"No. It is not. It could be similar at the beginning. But if you remain too long unconscious without being conscious somewhere else, then you are not normal, then something is wrong with you."

"Do you mean to say that one becomes conscious somewhere else when unconscious on the physical plane? You may remember that I asked you several times about it, but you never answered!"

"Of course!" He laughed merrily. **"It comes gradually, little by little. It takes time. But before you can do it, you must forget everything. Leave everything behind."**

I said that it seemed to be a frightening thought. He laughed again softly and gave me a look of kindly amusement. Could not see why he found my answer so funny. . . .

"How do you swim?" he began again after a silence. **"You throw water behind and behind you, that's how you propel yourself. Spiritual life is the same; you keep throwing everything behind, as you go on. This is the only way; there is no other."**

"Is there not a danger to become stupid by forgetting everything?" I wondered.

"Why?" he retorted, **"If you have ten rupees in your bag, and you get 10,000, you will forget the ten rupees, will you not? The ten rupees are still there, but you don't think of them anymore, isn't it?"**

I could see what he meant and also that he was right. Later I was telling him about a discussion we had with L. about spiritual life, and that she was of the opinion that I could not go on further alone by myself, or progress more than I had already, for she said that a Guru was absolutely necessary.

"A Guru is a short-cut—a short-cut and a sharp-cut. But not a Guru; a friend, a Spiritual Guide. I have nothing to teach."

"What do you mean by a System?" He used this expression often in conversation; it seemed an unusual one to me, was not quite sure if I understood its meaning.

"A System is a School of Yoga, or a Path to Self-Realization—the meaning is the same. We are called Saints, but it is the same as Yogis—in Wisdom there is no difference. The color of our Line is golden yellow, and we are called the Golden Sufis or the Silent Sufis, because we practice silent meditation. We do not use music or dancing or any definite practice. We do not belong to any country or any civilization, but we work always according to the need of the people of the time. We belong to Raja Yoga, but not in the sense as it is practiced by the Vedantins. Raja means simply: Kingly, or Royal, the Direct Road to Absolute Truth."

"And why is it that one cannot go on by oneself any further and would need a Guru?"

"Because by yourself alone you can never go beyond the level of the Mind. How can you vacate?"

"You mean to empty the mind, to clear it from any thought?" I asked, not being sure what he meant by "vacate."

"Yes, how can you vacate, clear out your mind, if you are constantly working through the mind? How can the mind empty itself of itself? You must be able to leave it, to forget everything. And this, one cannot do alone. For the mind cannot transcend itself."

"Will I ever be able to do it, for I am afraid of this idea," I said doubtfully. He laughed again, looking at me sideways.

"If you are ill, who does the work? Others, of course! If you are unconscious, be sure, there will be many people to look after you!"

I said that it may be true in theory if, for instance, I can easily be robbed in deep *Samadhi* (a superconscious state, a merging into the Universal Consciousness).

"No," he retorted, "then you are not in Samadhi. If you are in Samadhi, you go to your Creator, and the Creator will look after you. And even if you are robbed, it is not because you were in Samadhi, but because it was your destiny to be robbed, and it is of no importance to you once you have reached this state of consciousness. When we travel together, you will see that I take nothing with me— I am not afraid."

"But if you travel and have no money, somebody has to travel with you and keep the money and be careful that it is not lost, otherwise you both will be in trouble," I insisted.

"Yes, that could be true, but not necessarily so. Perhaps I could travel free, or the money will be forthcoming. God works through many channels. At any rate, I affirm, that he who is in Samadhi, nothing happens to him, and if it does, he does not care." He fell silent. **"You have your knowledge,"** he said thoughtfully after a while. **"You will forget it all. You** MUST **forget it, before you can take any further step."**

I wondered if this is what the scriptures mean—one should forget all books, leave all acquired knowledge behind; only then one can make the big leap into the Unknown beyond the mind. He agreed.

"There are only very few people in the world nowadays who can teach you the Sufi method. The Sufi method represents complete freedom. You are never forced. To put somebody in Dhyana—it can be done—but it would only show that my will is stronger than yours. In this case it would be mesmerism, there is nothing spiritual about that, and it would be wrong. When the human being is attracted to the Spiritual Guide and wants to become a Shishya **(disciple), there are two ways open to him: the Path of** Dhyana, **the slow, but the easier way; or the Path of** Tyaga **(complete renunciation), the Road of Fire, the burning away of all the dross, and it is the Guide who has to decide which way is the best suited in each individual case. The Path of** Dhyana **is for the many, the Path of** Tyaga **is for the few. How many would want to sacrifice everything for the sake of Truth? The** Shishya **has every right to test the Guide; but once he is satisfied and accepts the Guide"**—here he laughed his young and merry laughter—**"then the Guide can take over, and the disciple has no free will for a while."**

He contradicts himself, I thought, but said nothing. Then he began to speak about his Guru, the Great Sufi. **"He is always with me,"** he said.

"Do you mean that you see him?" I asked.

He had a tender, faraway look: **"If I say that I see him with these physical eyes, I would by lying; if I say that I don't see him, I also would be lying,"** he said after a brief silence. I knew what he meant: he could reach him in his higher states of consciousness.

Well, perhaps, it is a good thing after all, that I came here . . . and I was thankful for the opportunity of this long conversation.

15th October

WENT TO GITA CLASS this morning. Of no interest. When I arrived at Bhai Sahib's place, he was asleep. His lean figure in white *dhotie* (a loose garment the men wear which is tied on the waist) looked strange and contorted. I sat down quietly, in the corner near the door on the tachat which stands along the wall behind his own. Later a young man came and, noticing that the Guru was asleep, sat down and closed his eyes. He was from Delhi and was here for the first time, Bhai Sahib told me afterwards. I was sitting cross-legged. All was still. Some noises from the street—a child was crying somewhere in the courtyard. Then I became aware of a great power in the room. A tremendous power. For the first time, I felt like this; it was like being in a power-house. I scarcely could breathe; the force was terrific. I had a great disturbance in the throat; the heart was beating, beating and aching . . . and the beat was irregular. Seem to have lost the sense of time.

After a while, perhaps one hour or so, Bhai Sahib sat up, looked around with glazed eyes, and then sat motionless in deep meditation. Cross-legged, looking ahead with unseeing eyes . . . the force in the room seemed greater and deeper, increasing all the time—the room was vibrating, humming with it. One literally could HEAR it like a great sound, high and low at the same time. I remembered how L. looked when she was in deep Samadhi, but this was a different thing altogether. . . .

I sat with closed eyes, trying to endure it . . . it was difficult to bear, this tremendous force. The mind?—it was hardly present at all. Lost somewhere, swallowed up, dissolved, or rather absorbed by the charged atmosphere of the room. Opened my eyes after a while and saw that he was looking directly at me. It gave me kind of a jerk, like an electric shock. The expression of his eyes . . . it did frighten me, but I immediately realized that he was not really looking at me at all. His eyes were wide open, unseeing, empty eyes—he was not in this world at all . . . this was quite evident. I began to feel so sleepy that I had to fight with all my might against falling asleep.

After a while his wife came in and told him that tea was ready. He took the small towel which he always carried with him and went out. Not a word was spoken. The young man, who until then was sitting there silently, now said something to me. I could not reply, could not utter one word. Too great was the peace, the seemingly eternal stillness.

Went home, fell on my bed, and plunged in a deep sleep.

16th October

WENT TO HIM in the morning. I did not speak, neither did he. He kept walking up and down on the brick elevation in front of the house, repeating his prayers, mala in his hand.

17th October

ARRIVED IN THE EVENING about six. *Durga Pooja* (devotional service in honor of the goddess Durga) was going on in Deva Singh Park opposite the house, across the street. From a large marquee, brightly illumined by colored lights, loud music was pouring out a rhythmic sing-song of devotional prayers. He was not in the garden but somewhere in the street, so I was told. Something had happened, a fight, or a disturbance of some sort, and he was talking to a police officer.

His wife and the women of Bhai Sahib's household stood in a group discussing the event. A bright lamp was fixed on a branch of one of the trees in the garden. Thousands of moths and insects were dancing madly around it. What was attracting them so much to the brightness of the light to be in such an ecstasy? And I was thinking what a glorious thing it must be to be a tiny moth in the Hands of God, and to die like this in utter ecstasy in the blaze of His light. . . . What force was driving them? It must be a very powerful force or instinct, because though half-burned, they seemed not to be deterred from returning again and again in a mad ecstatic dance until they fell to the ground in the last convulsions of death.

To die burned by Thy Light . . . what a wonderful death!

Jagan Nathji, the professor of mathematics, came walking through the gate, and all the women suddenly disappeared into the passage which leads into the inner courtyard.

Bhai Sahib came stalking in with big steps followed by gesticulating men in dhoties. The atmosphere became more and more charged with excitement and everyone seemed to be shouting except him. Some more men came in. Could not bear the noise; it was jarring on my nerves. Stood up and went into the room. Sat alone in the dark in his big chair. Had much disturbance in the throat. Something must be wrong with the throat *Chakra* (a psychic center). I had better ask him about it, when an opportunity arises.

Soon the chairs were brought in; all men filed into the room, and I left. It was too much for me. It was raining softly. The air was so fragrant, as only the air of India can be. All the year round shrubs are flowering in the gardens around. I walked swiftly, lifting my face to the moist air, breathing deeply.

To vanish dancing in the Light . . . a heavenly thought. . . . To die in the explosion of Thy firework of glory, to burn oneself out in the blaze of Thy Light. Gentle drizzle on my skin. As on the crest of a wave, the whole of my being was carried away in a powerful longing. It was something new—a new chord, echoing, reverberating in the depth of my being. A yearning to vanish in Thee. . . . I stopped dead, then slowly went home.

18th October

WENT IN THE EVENING. Did not speak. Neither did he. He was writing letter after letter, and his wife kept coming and talking and interrupting him. There is no privacy in India. How difficult it must be for him; never alone, interrupted, disturbed at all times during the day, even when in deep meditation. I wondered how he could bear it; but perhaps he was used to it, being Indian himself, and did not mind it at all?

I saw that at Pushpa's place it was the same story: one could not have any conversation without being constantly interrupted by servants walking into the room wanting this or that, or asking questions on household matters. Children wanted attention; one never had any peace at all; there was always incessant coming and going and noise and movement.

19th October

CAME IN THE EVENING. Still cannot speak. At Pushpa's place am also very silent. Read most of the time. Do not feel like speaking at all.

Soon after me a man came in and began to talk to him in Hindi. After a while Bhai Sahib turned to me, introduced the man as a professor of history, and told me that he would like to talk to me. Did not feel like talking at all, but could not refuse, and he seemed a nice person. After a few preliminary exchanges of polite sentences he told me that he knew exactly my state of mind. I retorted slightly ironically that if he did, why did he not explain what was that state? He said that I am thinking that what I see here is mesmerism, or sleep, and keep doubting if it is a good thing, or just nonsense, and if I should remain here or go away. Told him that this was in fact my actual state of mind at present. An interesting conversation followed, of which I hardly remember anything, which is a pity. At the end I asked as a conclusion what would be the right attitude according to him.

"First, faith; absolute faith in the Guru. One must have faith that he knows the right road which will lead to the Truth. Without absolute faith in the Guru, it is impossible to achieve anything." He was speaking seriously with utmost conviction. "When one should feel sleepy, one should relax, close the eyes and wait for something. Mind you, for a long time you may wait, and nothing will happen. It is here, where faith will help you. Feel deeply that you are in the Presence of God, and wait, full of alertness and surrender for His Grace. Then you will not fall asleep, not really, and one day the Grace will strike you."

I asked him how long it takes, as a rule, for such a thing to happen.

"I think not more than two years," he answered. "This is the average."

"Do you mean to say that I have to stay here all the time? Endure the heat of the plains? I surely will die!"

He sat up straight. "By no means. I feel you should not stay at Bhai Sahib's place too long at a time. A little in the morning and a little in the evening. Then go away and come back after one week or two, go away for a few months in summer when the heat becomes unbearable, and so on."

I could not agree with him. If I decide to stay here for the training, to go away from time to time would be a waste of time! Surely if I want spiritual life, the only important thing would be to take the greatest advantage of the opportunity, in spite of the difficult circumstances.

20th October

WENT IN THE EVENING. His wife was talking non-stop all the time. There was nobody except myself. It is all so empty and banal. Who is he? How would I know? Perhaps a sign will be given to me? I knew that it happens sometimes that a sign is given. . . .

Feel restless and afraid. He could put me in a state where I could give all my money away, or do something mad, like caressing those dirty children, masses of whom one can see in the streets—as it happened to L. when she felt such love, as she told me one day in Kashmir.

How can I trust him? Have faith? How is it possible? What shall I do? This man has power. There is no doubt about that. And those strange heart conditions, and new surge of feelings: what does it all mean?

4

More Doubts

DID NOT GO. Better wait for L.'s arrival. She wrote a short note that she will be arriving on the 29th. The Conference was delayed, and then she has to go to Delhi before coming here. I had better not go at all until she is here. What's the use?

And still . . . still, somehow I feel that he can take me "there," where love is, and stillness, and the mind is not. . . .

25th October, 1961

LOOKING AFTER PUSHPA'S GARDEN. Re-arranging flowers. Planting. Watering. Being frantically active. Better not to think. Work and work, just that. Such a disappointment, the whole affair. . . .

We went with Pushpa to the nursery twice and got lovely crotons, orange trees and cactuses. Planting, planting and planting. The flat roof will be a desert garden; all the cactuses and shrubs, which do not need much water and can stand a great amount of heat, were carried upstairs. The servants don't like me—I make them work. The rubbish has been cleared away by the gardener with the cooperation of the coolie. Suggested to Pushpa to have parties on the roof. She seemed to like the idea. Frantic with activity. Not to think. Not to think. At any cost . . . so much had I hoped. How hot and deep is the disappointment. Oh please, my mind: stop thinking!!

On my last day before I had left Amritsar, I remember the tourist guide took me in the morning to see an historical *Gurdwara* (temple of the Sikh religion) dedicated to the twelve Sikh Martyrs slaughtered by the Muslims. We came in when the prayers were already in progress, seated ourselves on the *dharri* (thick cotton carpet) amongst the worshippers, and waited till the Order of the Day was written out on the blackboard. The guide translated it from the Punjabi:

"Is there somebody who can take me to the Lord?
I will go to him, touch his feet and kiss his hands,
And serve him faithfully, him, who can take me to the Lord."

There are moments in life when we become aware, as if in a flash, that the finger of Destiny is catching up with us. This was such a

26

moment. I remember clearly I suddenly felt cold, became afraid, and did not know why. It was just that I know now—the finger of Destiny touched my heart. I KNEW this message was for me. "I will not go to him," a sudden panic flashed through my mind. I will go to Ceylon as originally intended, and then return to England to my work at the T.S. Library. But I chased this thought away. My heart was full of hope. I thought it must be a good omen; those words of the Order of the Day were meant for me, for I was going to someone who, I felt sure, could help me on the Road to the Truth.

Of course, we all know that we have to do our work ourselves. He will be able only to point out the way, create the right spiritual conditions, to make the work easier for us. But to walk, to get there, we must do it ourselves. The toil we have to do alone.

There is a kind of power at his place—it is a fact, I am quite sure, not just imagination. Very disturbing. I keep away, waiting for L. She must help me to clear some points. And if she cannot . . . then I will go to Madras, have a look at South India and Ceylon, and then forget the whole affair. IF I CAN. But it will not be so easy, if at all possible. Only at the idea of going away, something in me keeps crying. It is so deep that I hardly am conscious of it; it is just on the threshold of comprehension. It is like a homesickness. A great yearning. Homesickness for our Real Home? For the Home of all of us, human beings, and the Home of everything else, as well, in this Universe. . . . Oh, You who know all hearts, help me to sort it out! Help me to see the Right Road! I am like one who is wounded, so sore, and a small voice within keeps crying all the time. Such a restless state. So I work, work and work, and wait for L.

Transplanted forty-six pots yesterday, and they were large. Hard work. Must get some sticks, preferably bamboo sticks, and some netting for the creepers.

There IS, there MUST BE, the Road to the Real Home. And because I cannot trust him, the only person who could help me, I CANNOT TAKE IT. For a little light I pray, a little spark of light, just to see the right direction, the next step!

The heart keeps beating very fast as if in fever, very often missing out beats, and when this happens a kind of suffocation is felt in the throat. I stopped drinking tea since Pahalgam, when this condition began. It coincided with L.'s arrival at my tent. It makes me wonder now. . . . But now it is gradually getting much worse . . . palpitations and pain in the heart, and a kind of pressure as if of a stone.

26th October

WAITING FOR L.

27th October

WAITING FOR L. and working in the garden as hard as ever. How lovely are the sunrises seen from the roof—the pink, ethereal sunrises of the Indian plains, and full of peace, the sunsets in the haze of the heat. How lovely you are, India, even here, where the skyline on the far horizon looks like the skyline of London's East End: smoking, tall, factory chimneys, just peeping out behind the trees of the park.

28th October

WOKE UP in the middle of the night. Have restless nights lately.

Crammed with confused dreams. Woke up with the sentence resounding in my ears, and seemed still to hear it while waking up, "There is no other Way at all to go." The *Upanishad* flashed through my mind while waking up completely. Which *Upanishad?*—could not remember. It seemed unimportant. No other way. Only this was important. It was as if somebody else was thinking it, not me. Felt tired, so tired . . . no other Way . . . no other Way for me. . . . And the idea of leaving, of having to go from here all of a sudden, like a shock, filled me with unspeakable terror. A victim must feel like this before being killed, the finality of it. Then I knew to my profound dismay THAT I COULD NOT GO. Will NEVER be able to go. And it had absolute finality, like the very act of dying.

30th October

L. CAME ON SATURDAY in the morning. I was on the roof in my gardening pajamas working with liquid cow-dung. Had a long talk with her after her bath and several more discussions since then. She did not prove to be of much help. She could not understand why I was so afraid to lose all my money. Apparently he refuses money, L. saw him doing so. He accepts money, but to give it away—this is also true, "But why on earth do you assume that he will force you?"

"Because I feel that he has some kind of terrible power; it disturbs me. It does not seem human. I feel that he can do anything with me, anything at all, that I am completely helpless in his hand, and more so because I have discovered that the very thought of going away fills me with a kind of desperation for which I have no rational explanation."

She gave me a strange look and suggested that it might be a test, for it seemed to her that money represents such an important factor in my life. But I dismissed this explanation as not at all convincing, or not one that I could easily accept. Told her how disappointed I was. I even cried. Did hope that she would ask him for an explanation as to what happens to my mind—and what about the heart condition? Actually I asked her to do so, but not in front of everybody; perhaps when she is alone with him, and there are no interruptions.

But apparently she asked him as soon as somebody had left, in the brief interval before somebody else arrived, so they were interrupted. All that he had said, so she told me, was that I am suffering from a too restless mind, and fearful imagination. But, she added, she quite understood my state of mind, the state of doubt and disturbance. Perhaps in my place she would feel the same. I could see that she was distressed and felt sorry for me. She was a friend, but could I trust her? I have a sneaking suspicion that she had a talk with him, but got instructions not to tell me the result. One of her remarks made me think so: when I told her that it seems impossible to have trust and confidence in him, she answered in her simple, serious way, that at the beginning it is not so necessary to have implicit faith and confidence; it is necessary later. But in the meantime there will be proofs of many happenings; I will discover many things, and then may have the confidence.

"Stay for a while," she said, "and see what happens."

At the beginning it is not necessary. . . . Will that mean, could that mean, there would be, or could be, a continuation? Even an end, someday? I gave up. Could not think. Seemed too great an effort.

Pushpa's husband has flu, so we did not go to the *Gita* class. L. took some poems in Urdu to Bhai Sahib from the little Parvine, the charming and delicate girl I had met at Kamla's house in Shrinagar. These devotional poems were supposed to be lovely, so I hoped to hear the translation, at least of some of them. I was telling myself that this was the only reason why I wanted to go. But of course, the real reason was that I wanted to be in his atmosphere again. I missed it so much. Ten days had elapsed; it was such a long time. . . .

The stupid Shastri was already sitting there. I had time to warn L. what a fool he was and a vain one into the bargain. And true enough, Bhai Sahib soon asked him to show off his knowledge and chant some verses from the Vedas.

He chanted little and explained much in Sanskrit and bad English, clearly for our benefit, and L. said afterwards that it had no sense whatsoever, neither his Sanskrit nor his English comment. I got so impatient with this fool—his screechy voice, like a parrot's, jarred on my nerves—that I went out into the garden for a while to take some fresh air. It was cool, the sky was cloudy, the wind blew in my face. Was walking up and down under the trees, breathing deeply. The garden was still; nobody was about. When Shastri had left, there was much amusement about his self-importance, and L. was commenting on the Nest of the Bull, the passage she asked Acharya to explain, but he could not. I became aware of a great disturbance in the heart. It positively kept stopping, and each time I had a feeling of suffocation. It was very tiresome.

In Pahalgam, after meeting L., it began. It came back with renewed force, but this time it was different. It most certainly had to do with Bhai Sahib's presence, or perhaps only with his place? At this moment he was talking to his wife who came in and stood at the door. I took the opportunity to ask L. if I could ask him what to do about the heart activity. Of course, she said, I should ask him. I did as soon as his wife had left. He said that there is a physical heart and a non-physical one, and when the latter is activated, the former is bound to feel it.

"Nothing will happen to you," he smiled. **"Don't fear, no harm at all. I am here to see to that."**

The conversation was still turning around Shastri Acharya and his chanting. After a while Bhai Sahib turned to me and asked: **"Now you have no disturbance at all, is it so?"**

I realized to my astonishment that my heart was quite all right. **"It is because I have it now,"** he smiled kindly.

"Oh no!" I exclaimed, "give it back to me again, please! I don't want you to have it, it would be unfair to you!"

"Am I a juggler," he smiled his still quiet smile, **"to let it go backward and forward?"**

He really was laughing now, obviously amused. But I asked him seriously to give it back to me again.

"I challenge you to do it; I want to see if you can do it; I want to believe that you have the power to do so!"

"Give it back to her doubly!" L. exclaimed. "It will serve her right!"

The conversation was resumed, once more, about the Vedas and

the Nest of the Bull, the passage L. was so baffled about. Then silence
fell. When I happened to look at the Guru, he was far away.

"Look, oh, look at him!" I whispered to L. "Do look at this
expression on his face; like carved stone, antique and cruel; it looks
as old as humanity!"

All of a sudden, I got the heart trouble again, and not only that, but
giddiness and headache as well. But I told L. that I still did not
believe that it was he who could do it; perhaps it was just a
coincidence that it ceased and came back once more. She looked
disgusted, and said that I was much worse than the doubting
Thomas, and being unnecessarily difficult, and so on. Sitting in his
customary cross-legged position, Bhai Sahib was rocking himself
gently . . . he was in Samadhi. Watching him I was telling L. in
French, that his face was so Oriental, Chinese or Tibetan. A face one
seemed to have known always. . . .

"Do you know how you look when in Samadhi?" I asked when he
looked up after a while, opening his eyes. "Tibetan, yes, Tibetan, and
as old as the hills!"

"**Tibetan?**" He repeated it slowly; his voice was strange, monotonous; and looking straight at me: "**Tibetan; if you know it, why do
you still doubt?**"

It took my breath away. I knew what he meant and silently I bowed
to him with joined palms.

After that L. and I left for lunch.

5

A Sign

31st October, 1961

LAST EVENING we went for a walk, the three of us, he, L., and myself. I hoped to see the Ganga (Ganges), but it was getting dark already and I feared that we would not see much. He was walking very fast, and we could hardly keep pace with him. In the meantime he was telling L. how he intends to teach her what to do when a pregnant woman comes and wants a male child. "Is it a Mantra?" I ventured to ask.

" **No, not at all, just a hint, a hint only, and the child will be a male without any doubt.**"

L. has been with him for the last thirteen years, on and off, when she comes to India. I was intrigued that such things could be done and hoped to learn more about it, but they were discussing now how most people come to the Saint to ask mostly only for worldly things.

We arrived at the *Ghat* (elevated bank of the river where ritual bathing takes place and also cremation) and saw in the darkness that there was hardly a river at all at that point. At this time of the year the Ganga apparently flows at a distance of about two miles from here. Like nearly all Indian rivers she changes her course from time to time. In the light of the rapidly fading dusk one could just detect puddles of stagnant water amongst banks of sand stretching far into the distance. We turned back. He was talking to L., I was listening distractedly. Suddenly I was struck by one of his sentences:

"...**We, who are pledged to the service of humanity.**"

I pricked up my ears. This was the sign I was waiting for. . . . I was sure. I knew the meaning of that, I thought, with gladness and relief. It means that he belongs to the Hierarchy, the Great Brotherhood who helps the evolution of mankind. Tried to reflect upon it, but they began to talk about the states of Dhyana, and L. kept teasing me, making comments about my fear of it.

We went for a moment into the Deva Singh Park opposite his house, where a stage was erected for the Ram Lilas Play (a festival in honor of Ram). He had a short talk with one of the young men, then we all sat in the garden in front of the house. A few people came, mostly men from the neighborhood. I asked L. what time it was—it was getting late. It was eight, and L. got up.

"I am leaving you," she said with a smile.

"**Can you leave me?**" His voice had a hidden laughter in it.

"It is time to go for our supper," L. answered.

"**No**," he shook his head; "**I mean . . . can you, could you leave me?**"

"No, never!" She said with emphasis.

He turned to me: "**And you, could you leave me?**"

"Oh, yes, I can!" I realized my reaction came too quickly. Suspiciously so.

"**TRY**," he said it very quietly, looking me straight in the eyes, and I nearly said to him: "Switch off the Light!" as I sometimes said laughingly, because when he has this strange, unearthly light in his eyes, I cannot look at him; it seems too much; it is like a physical pain. . . .

We left. I felt disturbed and asked L. what would she make of this last remark of his.

"I am not quite sure; but did you not say yesterday that your greatest trouble seems to be that you know that you won't be able to go away? I think his remark alluded to that."

She could be right. I too am inclined to think that it was exactly what he meant.

"I did not tell him anything about our conversation," she continued. "I never tell anything." I said that I believed her.

So, it means that he KNEW. He knows that I cannot go away anymore. This morning I did not go to his place because I wanted to make entries into my diary and was also waiting for Pushpa's gardener who did not come. The pots for the seedlings must be prepared. L. went there alone.

When she came back, she was telling me that he said to her that I did not want Dhyana, so I am not going to have it. "I was annoyed," she said. "What's the use of going there? Just for conversation?"

Listened to her and wondered . . . did I want Dhyana? Somehow I recoiled from the idea of becoming unconscious; this is perfectly true. Was it because I did not trust him completely? Was this the reason for being uneasy about it? Did he speak to L. like this because he intends to put me on the other road, The Path of *Tyaga*, complete renunciation?

Not once, but several times, I told him that I want to become like him, to have Samadhi in full consciousness, which is, of course, the highest Yogic state. Make the highest Ideal your Goal and then try to reach it, I remember, I said. He answered gravely:

"In order to become completely conscious on all the levels of being, we have to go through a period of unconsciousness. How will we transcend the physical plane otherwise? Complete abstraction of the senses, complete elimination of the thinking process, represents a temporary loss of consciousness."

So, I think that I will come to KNOW Dhyana, but my Path will be a different one. But I said nothing to L. about it.

1st November

WHEN L. AND I REACHED his place this morning, he was already in the garden. L. began to walk with him up and down. They were immersed in a deep discussion, I think on the subject of *Kundalini* (an aspect of Cosmic Energy, which according to Yogic tradition resides at the base of the spine)—the book she intended to publish. I was sitting inside the room on the tachat, in the usual corner, near the door leading into the garden. He came in after a while. L. was in the inner courtyard. I heard her laughing with the children.

Asked him about the meaning of the last word he said when we were leaving last evening. Told him that a few days ago, in the morning, still between wake and sleep, I realized with a certain shock that I will not be able to go away. Could he have meant the same thing? He laughed gaily and said that it was precisely what he had meant.

"It is your Higher Self who is preventing you from leaving, who told you to stay."

He took some writing paper from the recess and began to write letters. I sat still for a while. L. came in. A conversation began in the course of which L. was saying that the disciples of Socrates bitterly complained that they were at a disadvantage: that it is not fair to them that in his presence their mind does not work and they cannot discuss properly, as it is expected from them. Just like me, I thought. Well, that settles it . . . I stay. Felt a kind of relief; a decision had been taken.

"Some force has been used on you, something had to be forced, and it will go on, not only now, but for years, for always, while this physical body lasts."

I asked how was it that I did not notice it, and when was it?

"**It was one day when we were left alone for a while, quite at the beginning.**" His eyes seemed to pierce through me.

"And why should you feel or notice it?" L. asked. "What does the mind know beyond its range of cognition?"

"**This force which has been used on you,**" he continued, "**will make you doubt, will cause disturbances of many kinds, but it was necessary.**"

I sat there wondering . . . and the heart kept hammering wildly in its cage of ribs.

Perhaps the Road will be free now? The Road to Freedom will open?

IN THE EVENING L. was asking questions on how the Guru gives to the disciple, according to the Sufi System; and is it the same in all the Yoga schools? Apparently, yes. It is done through *Prana* (life force; etheric energy) and mainly through the Heart Chakra. In all great schools it is the same.

Early in the afternoon, after lunch, seated in the veranda, I was reading *La Vie de Mme. Gayon,* a French mystic, a book which I borrowed from L. Shortly before we had to go to Bhai Sahib, Jagan Nathji came. He sat down and began to speak about Bhai Sahib and my doubts which I had mentioned to him a week ago. I asked again what is on the "other" side of Dhyana, and he confirmed that it is NOT sleep. Only at the beginning it may be so, or it may seem so, but not later. He spoke with great admiration of Bhai Sahib; clearly he tried to do his best to help me.

I suspected that he dropped in this afternoon for this very purpose. I was moved. He was such a kind person!

In the fading evening light in his room L. sat in deep Dhyana. I was watching for more than one hour; she did not stir. He was lying on the tachat and his disciple Panditji, a village Brahmin (he was one of the three who came to meet me when I first arrived; the other, the tallest, was Munshiji—it was he who gave me the impression of a prophet from a Nativity play), was massaging his feet. A few days ago he told me that Panditji has been with him for the last two years, serving him, and only now he got the Initiation according to the Sufi Tradition.

"**He is in a good state,**" he added. One could easily see that. He had the eyes of bliss. Now, slowly, methodically, he was massaging Guru's feet for over one hour. By now the room was in near darkness. The light of the street lamp partly shaded by the trees in the garden, dimly illumined the room through the open door. Sat there full of deep peace. It was such an Oriental scene: the *Shishya* massaging Guru's feet. L. in deep Dhyana, kitchen noises and voices coming from the inner courtyard. Someone with a lovely tenor voice passed in the street. . . . Life was good. . . .

2nd November

W AS ALONE with him this morning. L. had to stay at home to correct the proofs of her latest book which arrived from France. Sitting on the tachat he was—I opposite him on a chair—with half-closed eyes fingering his mala. He fired question after question at me concerning my life and myself. Ideas kept rushing clearly and sharply into my mind, could not help being flattered that he seemed to show interest in me. Then L. came. Discussion turned to her book and the states of Kundalini.

"It is of no importance if you believe in the existence of Kundalini or not: Kundalini IS. Kundalini is not sex impulse alone; but sex-power forms part of Kundalini. As a rule, this Energy at the base of the spine is more or less dormant. By our System it is awakened gently; it will not give you much trouble."

"Not much," he added thoughtfully, looking at me. "With L. it was different. Her Kundalini was awakened by Hatha Yoga practices. That's why she has much trouble. I do what I can to help her, but," he shrugged, "it is in the Hands of God."

"When awakened by Hatha Yoga, it becomes a great problem. It is a difficult way. One has to know how to take it up and take it down again through all the Chakras, and it is troublesome. But with us, we begin to notice it only when it reaches the heart Chakra; it means peace, bliss, states of expanded consciousness. We awaken the King, the Heart Chakra, and leave it to the King to activate all the other Chakras."

In the evening L. came for a little while and left soon. I remained seated in my corner of the tachat. He was in the big chair. Slowly, one by one, the beads of his mala slid through his fingers. Even outside all was still. The garden seemed to sleep, hardly any sound of the traffic; the street was silent. He stood up and went out of the room for a short while, returned, and this time came to sit on the tachat and went into a deep state of Samadhi. I noticed that he was in a different posture than usual, not cross-legged, but seated on his heels, and was facing me who was in the corner near the door. As a rule from this place I can see only his profile when he speaks to people seated on the chairs opposite his tachat.

He stared at me with unseeing eyes, a strange smile playing on his lips. My heart made one big leap to the throat in sudden fear. . . . I never saw him like that before. His face seemed to be composed of sheer energy, difficult to describe. Devic perhaps? Certainly a human face can never have this expression. . . . The feeling of dynamism, of tremendous power, increased more and more. I just sat there, the mind was not working much. Thoughts came and went in a kind of slow motion, all sorts of insignificant thoughts. The idea occurred to me that perhaps he may be doing something to my higher vehicles, but as I did not feel anything, so, I thought, perhaps I am mistaken.

Time was passing, maybe one hour or even more—my head was swimming. Began to think that I could go home and write some letters. He seemed in a very deep state; will slip out without disturbing him. A calendar hung on the opposite wall. Could not remember which day was today. On the 2nd of October, I came here, seven years after I had learned about Theosophy for the first time. Exactly seven years . . . strange. . . .

An ant was crossing the floor, it was black, very large, about one inch long. Many insects grow to an outsize here in India. Was watching it for a while till it disappeared under a chair.

"What thoughts are in your mind?" His voice startled me.

"Nothing in particular, just a few silly thoughts."

"Go home and lie down," he ordered. **"Speak to nobody, try to rest; give your mind a rest."**

Did not feel that my mind needed a rest, but got up ready to go. "For how long shall I rest?"

"Oh, half an hour or so, or even more if you can." His voice was full of indifference, quite casual. I understood that something very special had happened, but what? There was no way of finding out. Mind was peaceful, very few thoughts of a fuzzy, indistinct kind. Body was peaceful too. . . .

In our room L. was working on her proofs, all the lights were on. She looked up in surprise for she did not expect me home so soon. I told her that he had sent me home with the order to lie down. "Oho," she said and continued to work. I expected some kind of comment, but she ignored me.

After supper went to our room immediately and was trying to sleep. Soon realized that I was keyed-up . . . it was like a humming, a constant vibration in the whole of the body, like a nervous tension without actually being nervous. Told L. that I won't sleep tonight. And I didn't. The whole night I turned restlessly about. But there was no tiredness, strangely enough. Felt elated, excited, but otherwise fine. Not sleepy at all, full of energy in the morning.

3rd November

WHEN DRESSING and having my bath I was turning over in my mind what to say, for I decided to have an earnest talk with him.

Gave cowdung to all the chrysanthemums. Watered them. Did all sorts of jobs. And felt on top of the world.

6

One of the Hierarchy

"**AND HOW DO YOU FEEL THIS MORNING?**" he asked as soon as I sat down.

"May I ask something?"

"**You may ask,**" he smiled.

"What happened last night?"

"**What do you mean by that?**" he smiled faintly.

"You must know what I mean."

"**Oh, you mean what had happened on the inner planes? I was out of my body and know nothing.**"

Told him that I did not sleep. He said that he also did not sleep, and added that he usually sleeps only for twenty minutes, not more than half an hour. I knew from L. that the rest of the night he is in deep Samadhi. Told him how fine I felt this morning and explained the meaning of the English expression: "keyed-up," like strings of a musical instrument which were given a few turnings of the keys to be able to respond to a higher pitch of a sound or note. He nodded. "**It is like that,**" he said simply. I suspected that something unusual had happened, but as I did not feel anything at the time, so I thought I was mistaken.

"**Very wonderful things did happen yesterday and this morning.**" He said it slowly, looking out of the window. "**But the physical vehicles cannot have any cognition of it.**"

In the afternoon I was alone with him. L. was still busy with her proofs. He was seated cross-legged on the tachat writing letters. When I came in, he gave me one of his faint smiles and continued to write. I waited for an opening, and when he sealed up two envelopes and looked up, I offered to post them on my way home. He nodded.

"**They must go today, someone is in need of help.**"

Then I told him what a relief it was for me to know that he belongs to the Great White Hierarchy: his sentence when we were returning from the Ganga, "**We who are appointed to the Service of mankind,**" gave me the clue.

"**Hierarchy?**" He lifted his eyebrows.

39

Clearly, he did not know what I meant. Though his English was very good, slightly biblical, perhaps because he had hardly any opportunity to practice it, he did not know every English expression. Besides, it was a Greek word, at any rate. I explained what I knew from books about the Great Brotherhood and its function in the world to help with the evolution of mankind. He sat motionless, looking at me. His face was expressionless. I took a deep breath; how my heart was pounding—one cannot think clearly when this happens! I could see that he was listening with the utmost attention.

"And who are they?" He glanced at me sideways with a stern expression. A swift feeling of terror came and went . . . but the abruptness of the question made me laugh.

"Why are you laughing?" He looked hard at me.

I leaned forward: "Because I do not need to answer this one! Here is one of its members right in front of me!"

He smiled. Then quite unexpectedly, he threw his head back and laughed his boyish laughter. How young he can look, I thought, how amazingly young and gay.

"Yes," he said still smiling, **"but we usually do not mention these things, it is not done."** (Later, each time I happened to mention to his disciples the subject of the Hierarchy, they changed the subject.)

He poised carefully and deliberately the point of the pen on the sheet of paper before him and continued to write. Great stillness was in the room: only the scraping of the pen, the swoosh of the ceiling fan, and the wild pounding of my heart.

At last he finished, put the writing material into the recess and reclined, stretching himself comfortably on his back and crossing his hands on the pillow supporting his head.

"Hmm."

I knew I could speak. Told him that I was doubting so much who he was, and if I can, if I should, trust him. Now I know that I can, and I am glad. I brought a book with me, "The Mahatma Letters" (*Mahatma Letters to Mr. Sinnet*, London: Fisher Unwin, 1924) and wanted to show it to him. Explained that it contained letters of the two great Beings who inspired Mme. Blavatsky, the founder of the Theosophical Society. They were in their physical bodies eighty years ago. Mme. Blavatsky was trained by one of them, Master M., in Tibet for twelve years.

One day, after a lecture on the subject of those letters, myself and two friends decided to see the originals which are preserved in the British Museum. On the 2nd of November, 1956, we went to see them. Seated there in the hush of the reading room, reading the yellow pages of the original letters, I suddenly had a vision of high mountains covered with snow, deep valleys and great solitude. I KNEW that once, long ago, I worked for those Masters, and I pledged myself to work for them again. And placing the two forefingers of my right hand on Master K.H.'s signature—as one does when swearing an oath—I offered myself for ever, for always, and though I knew that one is not allowed to make any conditions, I said to him that because I pledge myself completely, without any reserve of any kind, I feel that I have the right to ask for one thing: DON'T LET ME FORGET IT EVER ANYMORE! For in this life I forgot, and lead a useless, empty life of the world, wasting my time!

"And now, Bhai Sahib, I will never be able to forget it, for I met you. Deep down I feel that there is no other way for me at all to go, as it is said in the *Upanishad*. I trust you now. I will not resist anymore—will try not to resist you consciously, at any rate. Unconsciously, of course, I cannot know. . . ."

"I will take care of this," he said with a strange enigmatic smile; he closed his eyes.

"Do with me everything you deem necessary to make me fit for the work, because I well realize, as I am now, I am useless for the work you may want me to do."

He turned to face me with a smile: **"I told you I was out of my body last night. All I can say is that you are being prepared for this work."** Suddenly his face assumed the strange expression he always has when functioning on a different plane of consciousness; the bottomless look in his eyes, the inward look, which does not see things of this world.

"Do you remember your previous life?"

"No."

The reflection of endless infinitude in his eyes, beyond space, divorced from time, seemed to penetrate right through my very being.

"But it must have been a bad one, because I came with bad tendencies into this one."

"We all have plenty of bad tendencies," he said, and then as if speaking from very far away, his eyes completely veiled with a kind of blue mist, he added very, very slowly: **"The time may come, I don't say that it will come, BUT IT MAY COME, when you will have powers and will know many things."**

I said that I suspected I was evolving on Hatha Yoga lines because in this life, elderly as I am, my body could do all the exercises relatively easily without ever having learned them, and I love doing them.

"That's why you forgot everything!" Again this young boyish laughter. I knew what he had meant. But for some reason I felt hurt.

Told him once, I remember, that I was afraid of clairvoyance, and if one is afraid of something, there could be a suspicion of a past memory in the unconscious, of something gone wrong. One is never afraid without a reason lurking behind it.

To have any kind of powers can lead one astray.

There was a time when I lived with this book, *Mahatma Letters.* I don't remember how often I read it. And I brought it with me to India. I took the book out of my handbag and opened it, showing him the pages where parts of the letters and the signatures of the Masters are reproduced. He took it, put on his reading glasses, and looked intently at Master M.'s letter. Then turned the page slowly and looked intently at Master K.H.'s letter. His face bore a strange expression, very alert and as if listening.

"This one," he said, pointing at Master K.H.'s signature, **"this one is greater than the other."**

I was thinking that, for all the opinions I have heard, it seemed to be the reverse. L., who is an expert in graphology, when I told her about it, did not agree with his opinion. It seemed to her that Master M. has more genius. But it is a well-known fact that from the spiritual point of view, it is not absolutely essential to be a genius. How many greatly spiritual people were great without being geniuses in the proper sense of the word.

"You told me that you understand that you will have many difficulties and are prepared to face them. So, you do it from your *own free will.* **Remember that. You will suffer injustice and will be hurt where it hurts most. Where you are most afraid of being hurt. You do realize that?"**

I said that I did. I knew what I was doing, but I also feel that I HAVE NO CHOICE.

Then he asked me why I pledged myself; was it a vision?

"If you mean by a vision that I saw or heard something with my senses, no. But if you mean by a vision a clear mental image and a certitude without any possibility of doubt, then, yes."

"This must be a link from a previous life . . . not necessarily the last." He said it thoughtfully, narrowing his eyes to a slit. Again his face assumed this special expression which so much fascinates and even slightly frightens me.

4th November, 1961

WAS THINKING this morning that seven years ago, on the 23rd of October, for the first time I came to 50 Gloucester Place, the Library of the Theosophical Society. I remember the door was painted green. It is still green today.

Seven years later, also in October, I met my Teacher. And on the 2nd of November, 1956, I went to see the originals of the Mahatma Letters in the British Museum. Now, on the 2nd of November—is it just a coincidence?—according to what he told me, something was done to affect my evolution. Strange. . . or is it?

Slept badly and restlessly, but it was much better than the previous night. The effect of whatever it might have been, seemed to wear off, on the physical plane, at least.

When reading a book sitting in the veranda after lunch, quite out of the blue, a strange sweetness pervaded my heart. It was such a subtle feeling. As soon as I tried to analyze it, it kept vanishing, reappearing again, peeping out from behind my thoughts. This feeling, so light, so elusive, had nothing to do with my environment, and it had nothing to do with him either. At least not directly. It goes beyond him, to something infinitely sweet, so infinitely dear. . . closer to me than breathing. I caught myself thinking. Yes, that's what it is. . . and it is just like the beginning of falling in love. Falling in love with what??

6th November

"HOW DOES ONE GET LOVE, Bhai Sahib? How does one get humility?"

"How do you smell the scent of flowers? There is no effort from the part of the flower, neither from your side; you just smell it, effortlessly."

"L. told me that since she knows you, she always sleeps well; I hardly slept for the last three nights."

"The way of training is different; the time will come when you will say: I did not sleep for years."

"Can one see *Prana?*"

"Yes, but not with the physical eyes. In Dhyana the flow of Prana

is reversed, but not so in sleep. Reversed, in the sense that all the sensorial energies are intraverted, absorbed in the heart, instead of being extraverted. It is a movement within, instead of without, as in the waking state of consciousness, or in sleep. For the first few times the Teacher has to do it and put the *Shishya* in Dhyana; later he learns how to do it himself. *Realizing Atman is one thing, but to realize Brahman is something else."*

"Can it be done in one life?"

"It can be done, AND IT IS DONE in one life. From the moment the training has begun, the progress continues. Sometimes one gets the Realization on one's deathbed. When I misunderstood you yesterday and thought that you were sixty-five and not fifty-five as you are in reality, I had a doubt in my mind. . . ."

"What doubt, Bhai Sahib?"

"You see, of course, it is not appropriate to tell people how long they are going to live. . . ."

"Oh, Bhai Sahib!" I interrupted, "please do not make the training much longer, now that you know that I am ten years younger! Do not give me the realization on my deathbed!"

"No, for those who are pledged for work, it is done quicker. You know, of course, that all the Karmas have to be burned up; I told you that before; you will have to suffer injustice, you will be attacked, it will hurt."

"Yes, I know, and I am prepared for it!"

Speaking of a well-known Indian Saint, now deceased, he said: "He was not a maker of Saints. There are very few in the world who are makers of Saints. He was not a Master of Consciousness; he was the Master of the Unconscious, but he could not translate it into daily life."

"I had a dream, Bhai Sahib; may I tell you? I was in Pushpa's car, her husband was driving. We came to a bridge on which was a huge heap of furniture. Ugly, old, dusty, heap of furniture. The car had to go over it in order to cross the bridge. But the heap was too steep, the car could not take it. So, the driver turned the car to the left into a narrow lane, the entrance of which was barred by a large lorry. Putting the car into a low gear, he slowly approached it, very slowly and deliberately perforated the radiator of the lorry standing in front with a pointed bar sticking out of our car. Out of the perforated hole petrol began to pour swiftly. Pushpa was holding a vessel under it. 'Good,' I said; 'this petrol will serve for our car to go over the bridge.' And I woke up. Old furniture will mean the old conditioning which has to be overcome?''

"The convenience is not yours, the car belongs to Pushpa. It means she is helping you by letting you stay in her house. She is helping you in this way. With the petrol taken from another car, the one in which you are traveling will be able to cross the bridge. Soon," he added, "there will be no furniture on the bridge and the car will cross over easily."

Tuesday, 7th November, 1961
Divali, Festival of Light

TODAY WE WENT to the *Samadhi* (here meaning "grave, place of rest") of his father, seven miles from Kanpur. With a large lorry we went. It was fun. The whole of his family, many other people, neighbors came too—all in the lorries a policeman arranged for our transport. The Sufi's tomb in a white mausoleum of simple and sober proportions is rather large, open on all sides, supported by columns. The floor is paved with red tiles. It was all lit with candles and small butter lamps. All around are fields, groups of trees in the distance. The sky was still pink after the sunset, softly pink with grey clouds. A strong, spicy fragrance was in the air, typical of the Indian plains. Many people were here. Old disciples of the Guru and far too many children. The atmosphere was very good but not so dynamic as sometimes in Guru's place. Too many people and too much disturbance, children running about making noise. L. said that I think this way because I don't understand. The grave of a Sufi is a highly magnetic place.

After coming back we sat in Guru's garden for a while. During supper I nearly fainted at the table; everybody commented on me getting so pale—was afraid to fall down—it would have been very awkward. But it passed soon.

8th November

BECAME AWARE of much peace, lately. It came gradually like a thief. I hardly noticed it at first. It is a different kind of peace from the one experienced for the last few years. Before, it used to be a feeling of peace, plus joy, all laughter, and life was good. Now, it is like a deep, still pool, full of silence and darkness. Very deep and very, very silent. It is such a neutral feeling that I quite understand that it could be a background to anything at all—for instance, joy can be impressed upon it, or love, or spiritual dryness, or loneliness.

Anything can go with it, any other feeling or state without even disturbing it. It has no color, seemingly no substance, no other feeling except a stillness, a tranquil peace. It makes me think of the depth of the ocean, always calm, even when huge waves are raging on the surface.

Slept well last night. Was it because L. told him the evening before that I nearly fainted? But we thought that he did not hear what she was saying. A crowd of people came pushing in and she was interrupted.

7

Echoes from the Past

9th November, 1961

SLEPT WELL. Very well. I wonder if the effect of what the Guru gave me a few days ago is wearing off? Peace is with me though. In the last few days, when I could not sleep, I was in a sort of half-state which seems to be the preliminary state of Samadhi, and is called the "Sleep of the Powerful" in the Scriptures . . . so L. told me. It was filled with images, mostly of him, or his face, but chiefly only his eyes—all sorts of confused dreams which seemed so real, so intense, larger than life. And there was great restlessness of the physical body. But in the mornings there was no tiredness whatsoever, quite on the contrary, great energy. Every morning I went on the flat roof to do the yogic exercises at dawn, *Surya Namaskar* (ritual prostration before the rising sun) and the rest, and watched the sun rise serenely behind the feathery crowns of distant palm trees.

As soon as a noisy, talkative man had left, and we remained alone with the Guru, I took the opportunity to ask him about the ice-cold feeling on the top of my head each time when doing the *Bhoot* exercise (standing on the head).

"Do you take something after the exercises, as I told you to do when you began to do them a few weeks ago?" he asked. I said that I didn't. Milk and butter on an empty stomach disgusts me.

"Then take a cup of hot tea with a bit of butter in it, to prevent the dryness of the brain."

In nearly all books on Yoga they speak of "dryness" to be avoided—I wonder what it means? It certainly must have a meaning, which we people in the West don't understand. Personally I don't believe for a moment that the so-called brain-dryness can be prevented or relieved by a bit of butter in a cup of tea. . . .

"You think your Kundalini is asleep, but it can wake up at any moment."

He looked straight through me, with this unseeing look of his, when he is not looking at the physical body. It is like a bottomless dark pool, eyes covered by a bluish veil, eyes which do not seem to see.

I had better have this tea with butter after all; one never knows. . . .

Then he began to sing. I love it. It is so disturbing. I do not know why. He has a pleasant voice and always sings in Persian or Urdu. As soon as his voice fills the room, it is as if I am transported to another plane of being. The brain stops working. I do not seem to listen with the mind, but with something else. These songs of his, monotonous and in a language I don't understand, disturb something very deep in me. It is like trying to get hold of long-forgotten memories, buried in the remotest past—glimpses which are awakened by his voice and are somehow connected with him. It is as if I knew this sound so well, that it was part of me, of the "me" which I could not get hold of, or ever understand. Memories, so vague, so dim, so fleeting, like the whiffs of mist I saw amongst the pines on the slopes of the Himalayan hills. When one tries to pin them down, to concentrate on them, they dissolve into nothing just like the mist; it always disappeared before it reached you, because it was so tenuous that when it was all around you, you could not see it anymore.

He translated the song: **"When you are burning with thirst, do not search for water, remain thirsty."**

It made me smile. Since yesterday I have a burning desire for Truth. Deep. Strong. Endless. As never before. It goes on and on and on, the whole of my being streaming forth into an endless river of longing.

He began another song, a long sad one. In the refrain, repeated softly and as if with resignation, the name of Mustafa occurred again and again. The melody was beautiful, as vast as the sands of the desert.

"When Lord Mohammed's followers came into power, Mustafa (another name for Mohammed) **was buried without a** Kaftan (a long outer garment). **Why? The answer came 1200 years later. It was given by a Sufi Saint, Sarmad. The ruler Aurangzeb Alambhir said to him: 'What sort of a man are you; you have nothing to put on, look at you—you are naked! But I am a King. I can dress the whole nation if I wish; my own garments are rich and wonderful!'**

"Said Sarmad: 'Who made you a King and me a beggar is the same God! Those who are defective, those who are sinners, are supplied with clothes and worldly possessions, but those who are Saints, do not need all this, for they are Beloved of God!'

"The body of Mohammed threw no shadow. His body was not really physical, so, it had no shadow.

"'Suf' means 'wool.' Wool is warm. If the heart is warm, then there is love. When you see a Saint whose heart is soft and warm, he is a Sufi. The Teaching is given according to the state of evolution of the disciple and according to his temperament and conditioning. As he progresses, more aspects of the Truth are revealed."

10th November

WHEN ASKED, told him that I sleep well. He laughed.

"Well, L. told me the other day that you nearly fainted; I had to do something about it."

I protested violently. Said that it was nothing to speak of, and I like this in-between state which left no tiredness in the morning. I was full of energy—please, I wanted it back. I reproached L. for telling him, was furious and nearly quarreled with her, telling him that if he does not give me this state back, he will find me sitting at his doorstep at four in the morning. He shook his head in silent disapproval. L. was annoyed with me and said this is not the way to speak to the Guru.

Later, about midday, there was such a wonderful fragrance in the air, like flowering trees, some wonderful scent coming from afar, and all around in the garden. . . a gentle breeze full of oxygen, like a lovely, fresh perfume. I drew his attention to it. He ordered me to go around in the garden and try to find out from where it came. But everywhere I went, it was eluding me; there was only the kitchen smell, or of toilets, or of dust.

"Come with me: is it here or here?" he kept asking. But it was nowhere, it was gone. He wanted to know what kind of fragrance it was, and added that he could smell it too, and had I ever noticed it before?

Told him that I smelled it in Kushinagar, the place where Lord Buddha died, and also at *Samadhi* of his Revered Father, the other day. Then I was thinking that it was the smell of the Indian plains. But never had I smelled it in his garden before.

In the evening we were alone, he, L. and myself. He asked L. how she spelled her first name and the surname. She wrote it in block letters; he looked at it for a long time with closed eyes and then told her a few things about her future. Afterwards he asked me for my maiden name, and I too had to write it down in block letters, and he had some trouble how to pronounce my surname, Karpow.

"Why do you want our names?" laughed L. "You can know by other means everything about us!"

"Why should I use my *Siddhi* (yogic power) if I can do it simply by

analyzing your names?" he asked, giving her one of his sideways looks.

He was right. According to spiritual Law one should never use one's Power if it can be done by ordinary means. Slowly, as if speaking with difficulty, he asked me how long I intend to remain in the Theosophical Society. "For ever after," I said, and it seemed even strange that this question should arise at all. Life without T.S. seems unthinkable. I seem to be part of it, quite naturally.

"Yes," he continued slowly as if lost in thought, **"it seems to me that you are intended to, I do not say that it will be, or you shall, or are going to do it, but you are intended to do much work. Very much work. Great work is in store for you. There is much work for you to do . . . yes . . . and you are going to be very old."**

12th November

WE TOOK THE RIKSHAW to the Allan Forest. L. and I. For the whole morning. It is a lovely forest. A small lake with huge pink lotuses in full flower. My body walked like an automaton, like in a dream. The "dreamfeeling" lost completely when in Darjeeling and since then, was here again, stronger than ever. We sat on the grass on a small hill, later near the lake. We talked about the Path, Guruji's environment which is not an easy one for a Western woman, about Dhyana and the like.

"Dreamfeeling? Glimpses from the *Buddhic* plane. It is created by the inability of the mind to reconcile them with the life on the physical plane," explained the Guru when asked. A kind of teething trouble of the mind, I thought. . . .

13th November

AFTER MY YOGIC EXERCISES, for the first time, I took a bit of butter and a cup of hot tea. Had to admit that it made a lot of difference. It gives a pleasant feeling of well-being in the whole of the body. Guru knows what he is talking about.

14th November

"If I knew how painful Love is
I would have stood at the entrance of the Lane of Love;
I would have proclaimed with the beat of the drum:
Keep, keep away, keep away!
It is not a thoroughfare, there is only one way in,
Once entered, I am helpless, I stay here. . . .

But you who are outside; look out!
Think before entering; how painful it is,
Full of sorrow, to walk the Lane of Love!"

HE LOOKED RADIANT, seated cross-legged on the tachat singing this Persian song, beating the time on his thigh with the palm of his hand. L. told me afterwards that Sufis rarely speak directly; they will tell a story or sing a song, or tell a parable. It is their way of Teaching. And teaching stories are used by all the Sufi schools.

"He for instance would speak to me and mean you," she said; "one has to learn how to listen. A Teacher has no right to test a disciple or subject him to any trouble, or test, without a previous warning. The warning is never given directly. Often the disciple does not understand it or is made to forget. But the warning is always given, for Sufis believe in the free will of the individual. The human being must consent—his consenting gives the Teacher the right to act according to the necessity and the needs of the disciple, who himself, by consenting, draws down the Grace."

It made me think. . .was still thinking before falling asleep at last. Are those songs for me or for L.? The one of the painfulness of love . . . I wonder.

8

Effortless Path

THIS MORNING WHILE WE WERE DRESSING, I heard L. grumble and mumble to herself in sheer frustration.

"What's the matter, old girl?" I asked.

"It is very bad for a philosopher not to be able to think," she said, and we both laughed. "And just imagine: people sitting for hours trying to control the mind, to make it blank, to still the thought process; and we, we have to make an effort to think!"

She was right. What a System! I thought. Thanks to God, or my *Samskaras* (karmic seeds), or to whomsoever it may be: what a good fortune to have come here!

Went to his place. L. was to join me a bit later. An old man was already sitting there, and he and Bhai Sahib were taking about *Jinns* (Mental Elementals; according to Sufi beliefs a parallel evolution to men). The old man who was sitting opposite the Guru was saying that sometimes Jinns come to a Saint to be trained.

"To be trained in spiritual things? What for, if they themselves are spirits?" I was amazed.

"Not only in spiritual things, but also to read or write or some other knowledge belonging to this world," he said.

"Is it true?" I asked the Guru.

"Sometimes it happens," he smiled.

"Do you have some Jinns whom you train?"

He smiled this enigmatic smile of his when he does not want to answer and changed the subject.

16th November

"IN OUR SYSTEM the Realization is achieved in one life. One need not come back. You have been here for six weeks. Do you notice how much progress you have made?"

"The mind does not know about it, so how can I know?"

"I didn't ask your mind, I asked YOU."

I thought for a while. "Bhai Sahib," I said, "there is a difference. I always thought that I wanted Truth badly enough; but now it is like a burning fire inside me, a longing, like an obsession."

He smiled kindly. Told him that I saw a lot of violet color when I was in his place. Violet flashes of color, even when my eyes were closed.

"**You have a pure heart; there are two ways of lower and higher clairvoyance: *Pitriyan* and *Devayan*, respectively. You belong to the higher one.**" He looked out of the window thoughtfully. The light of the greenery, the foliage, the shrubs, was reflected in his eyes, and his skin looked greenish; a face not really of this world.

"I suffer lately from heat-waves; it usually starts in between the shoulder blades, radiates over the thorax, never lower than the stomach, then mounts to the head making my forehead perspire. It never lasts long, perhaps half to one minute. Is the Heart Chakra responsible for it?"

"**Perhaps it is, but maybe it is not. As a rule, I don't tell which Chakras are activated and which are not. The whole of one's life would not be long enough to open all the Chakras. In our System it is done by Dhyana. I, myself, have changed the System somewhat. I did it with the knowledge of my Superiors, of course, my Revered Father and my Revered Guru Maharaj.**

"**I discovered new Chakras; in the Scriptures not all the Chakras are mentioned. Not all the occult knowledge is given out at one time. Humanity progresses. The Teaching, once secret, is now for everyone. At one time, in the past, rich people were not supposed to know about it, but nowadays everyone is taught who wants to know and is earnest about it. *Sannyasis*, for instance, work mainly through the Brow Chakra. There is not much love in *Sannyasis*. In our System the Heart Chakra is mainly used. Of course, when the Heart Chakra is open, such force, such power is flowing through it, that one forgets everything.**

"**One day, my Revered Father got an order from his Guru Maharaj to go and search for Saints and Yogis and ask them one question: 'Can you give me something without an effort from my part?' 'No,' everyone of them answered; 'we cannot. Nobody can. Go away.' He left our home just in the clothes he was wearing, taking nothing with him, leaving his wife and children. And when he returned, several years later, he had the same clothes on, or at least they looked the same to us. Have you heard of a System like ours, where the *Shishya* does not need to make any effort at all?**"

He looked at me with a smile and I had to admit that I never heard of any.

"No effort needed; just come here and sit. Everything is done for you. Why make an effort? Effort does not lead anywhere. If one is a real Guru, a Sat Guru, and knows how to write on the back of the hearts. . . . The Spiritual Guide does not make conditions; he is like a loving mother. The child can be angry, can run away. The mother does not take it very seriously. She cares for it just the same, and does not love it less, because of it. *Shishyas* can and do sometimes leave the Guru, but the Guru is never supposed to do so.

"And where can the *Shishya* run away? Where can he go? *Guru* and *Shishya* relationship is forever. If one is pledged to one Guru, where can one go? The Guru is like an experienced rider; and the experienced rider makes the horse go where he wants.

"But *Shishyas* are not slaves. They are free. But even when the personality wants to run away, it is difficult for it to do so: the Higher Self knows better. . . .

"Ours is the System of freedom. But the majority does not like it. People want contortions, Hatha Yoga, discipline, mind control, meditations. They are not happy otherwise, they think nothing is being done. Here, I do not ask you even to pray. Just sit here with me. Even speech is not necessary. Only something one has to explain, sometimes. We live in the epoch of the mind. Mind, Manas, is the ruler. Most of the people are not satisfied; they will not accept anything unless at least some kind of explanation is given. Our System has never been widespread; it is for the few. And it is from heart to heart, and the Goal is reached in one life. But how many want the Truth? Are prepared to surrender to the Truth? Not with everyone is it possible. But IT CAN BE DONE."

17th November

WHEN ALREADY IN BED, chatting with L., a sudden happiness pervaded me wave after wave—so light, so completely unconnected with anything belonging to the world.

Woke up as bright as a bead. This special happiness was gone, but the body felt good and very fit. Exercises on the roof. Bath. Gardening. Watered the lawn. After a hasty breakfast went with L. to the Guru.

He was dictating his correspondence to Panditji. We saw him tearing the receipt of a money order into small pieces. When L. made a smiling remark about the smallness of the pieces of paper, he said with a shrug, that some people apologize so much for nothing, so nobody should be able to read it.

"I refused this twenty rupees at first; it was in October. Because they told me for what purpose this money should be spent. I am not a slave. I won't be made a slave of anyone. If they haven't got enough faith in me that I will spend this money rightly, they can keep it. I surrendered somewhere; I am completely free.

"A Master is a Master and nobody should tell him what and what not to do. I cannot be limited. In our System we do not want slaves. Surrender is NOT slavery. Surrender is Freedom. And *Shishyas* are NOT slaves, for they learn how to surrender. . . ."

18th November

"HAVE I UNDERSTOOD correctly that in other Systems the Chakras are awakened one by one, and the life-span of an individual proves to be too short for this process to be accomplished? So it can never be completed in one life? Is it so?"

"In our Yoga System the ultimate result is achieved in one life by Dhyana. Only one Chakra is awakened: the Heart Chakra. It is the only Yoga School, in existence, in which LOVE IS CREATED by the spiritual Teacher. It is done with Yogic Power. The result is, that the whole work of the awakening, of quickening, is done by one Chakra, which gradually opens up all the others. This Chakra is the Leader, and the Leader is doing everything. If you want to buy a part of my property, do you go to the property? Certainly not, you come to me. You deal with the proprietor. And in our System we deal only with the Leader.

"I told you once that we belong to Raja Yoga. But when you try to study Raja Yoga from books you will be told: do this, do that, concentrate, meditate, sit in this posture. Today it is obsolete. Times have changed. The world is progressing; those methods have been outgrown. They are dead. But our System is alive; it has preserved its dynamism for it is changing with the times."

19th November

WAS A BIT depressed this morning. Everything seemed to be so difficult, not worth while attempting even.

When at Guru's place I saw a very old man sitting there, and he was trying desperately to keep awake while the Guru was talking to him non-stop. It was really pitiful to watch how he hardly could keep his eyes open. Out of politeness he just could manage to be sufficiently awake to nod from time to time or mumble something in assent. And clearly even this was a great effort. He was in a deep state, and the Guru kept tearing him out of it quite ruthlessly; it seemed cruel to the poor old thing!

"Bhai Sahib, you were quite cruel!" I laughed when the man had left.

He lifted his eyebrows. **"Why? He has to learn how to come out of it quickly, up and down, so to say, in and out. The consciousness has to be able to return rapidly and efficiently. The time comes for some people, not for all, when the state of Dhyana becomes so sweet that they are inclined to spend too much time doing it. We are in physical bodies; we are not intended to pass our life in an unconscious state!"**

I kept quiet. I had better get used to the idea that whatever he does is done for a purpose—and stop criticizing!

There are four kinds of Saints:

1. MASJU—always merged, mostly under vibration (unconscious, under Love).
2. SALIK—on the Path of *Dhyana,* conscious and unconscious; progressing (Love to some extent).
3. SALIK BIL MASU—*Dhyana* with Love, becoming warm (unconscious).
4. MASU BIL SALIK—burning with flames, fully conscious in unconsciousness (Love predominant).

I asked many questions for the sake of asking, some of them futile, some silly. I did it just to taunt him. He said I should not do it; it is *sankalpa-vikalpa,* (projections, distractions of the mind, restlessness of thought); it is bad and nothing has ever been solved by the Mind. L. told me that I was discourteous, and he is far too patient with me.

"Opportunity may come once in a lifetime. If missed, who knows how long you will have to wait for another one. Lives perhaps; who knows? I feel you are missing an opportunity. Be careful not to miss the boat." Her eyes, very blue, very serious, had a sad expression. To miss the boat . . . a feeling of exasperation seized me: I MUST, I simply MUST . . . somehow, I must stop, must accept . . . but how? I did not know. . . .

20th November

LAST EVENING I fell asleep when sitting in the usual corner on the tachat in Guru's room. Nobody saw me. It was so still and quiet and dark. L. was in deep Dhyana. I did not sleep for the last few nights, but felt no tiredness, no sleepiness in the evening, just as it was at the beginning. L. always told me that the tiredness is the result of fighting the "Thing"—I presume she means the impact of Spiritual Power.

I am as fresh as could be in the morning. The brain is clear. Feeling full of energy.

There are four different stages of progress:

1. SALOK—enters the Arena; the danger is the Manas, Mind, i.e. doubts, etc.
2. SARUPA—to become like THAT, danger of Satan (pride).
3. SAMI—so near that one cannot say if they are one or two. Danger *Devas*, they revolt so that the human may not be their master. In other words, that would mean all the illusions from which people suffer: clairvoyance, vision of Devas.
4. SAYUJ—perfectly united so that all the stages become one in Oneness. Danger of soul. They think that they have realized everything, and reject God and the Master (inflation, according to C. Jung).

First comes Realization, later Consciousness (full knowledge of Realization). For instance: I am in Delhi. That is the realization of the fact of being in Delhi. But you may not know Delhi—only if you know the town, street by street, have you a complete knowledge of it. In the mystical states there is at first fulgurant contact, very fugitive; later, continuous absorption which is a permanent state; and the third is SWABHAVA state, where the experience becomes part of one's nature. SAHAJA—one dwells in one's proper nature and one is master of it. This is Effortless Samadhi according to the Vedantins.

Sufis calls the first state: HAL; the second: MAKAN; and the third: FANA FI 'L-HAQQ.

21st November

DREAM: I remember only the end of it, when I and either my sister (or L.?) came into a very large empty room which was closed until now and full of dust. We sat on the mats, or rugs, and in the room were a few smallish animals which I knew were "deer-spiders." They had the body of a tiny deer, not larger than a weasel, but in the place where should have been its head they had tentacles, like octopuses, and wicked eyes. I knew they were very dangerous, and I was afraid of them as they tried to come nearer. But my sister (or L.) was telling me that it is enough to swoosh them away with my shoe, and they will go away. I did as I was told and they did go. Later we came back into the same room, after many happenings of which I remember nothing, but this time I did not see the deer-spiders and said so to my companion. But suddenly I saw one coming right at me intending to attack me. I grabbed it at the back of the neck, as one does with snakes, pressing its head to the ground. "Give it to me," said an old man with a beard coming towards me. I said I could not, because if I let it go, it will bite me, but he did not listen and got hold of the animal. And as I let it go, it swiftly turned round, got hold of my finger and, while the old man was tearing it away, half of my finger came with it, the teeth of the animal tearing at it savagely. It did not hurt, but looked rather bad.

INTERPRETATION: **"Something savage and dangerous has been taken away, wounding you. Things do happen, and how will you know that they are happening? You are told so in a dream."**

Didn't he say a while ago that some force had to be used on me?

Couldn't that be the meaning of the dream? Slept well again. Told him though that, if he does not sleep at all, it is not proper for me to sleep either.

"Maybe . . . later—not yet," and he smiled. I always knew, when I said something which pleased him, by a radiant smile half-hidden in his beard. . . .

Dusty furniture. Large room full of dust, never opened before; wicked animals, old man with a beard . . . hmm . . . very significant from the Jungian point of view. . . .

22nd November

ONCE HE SAID that love is created or produced in the heart of the disciple by the Yogic Power of the Guru.

"How is it done?" I asked. L. was dressing after her bath and stood in front of the mirror powdering her face.

"I don't know," she said simply, examining her forehead closely.

"But how can I be made to love him? He is a stranger to me! I respect him, he intrigues me, I find him intensely interesting; but love? No, there is none of that, and how is it to be understood?"

She was outlining her lips with lipstick with deliberate slowness. "Well," she said, looking at my reflection in the mirror and wiping off a small smudge from the corner of her mouth, "well, the disciple progresses through love. Love is the driving force, the greatest Power of Creation. As the disciple has not enough love in him to have sufficient of the propelling power to reach the Goal, so love is increased, or 'created' simply by activating the Heart Chakra."

"But how can I love him just like that?" I was puzzled. She

narrowed her eyes to a slit and for a while said nothing, just looking at me in the mirror.

"Are you sure," she said, "are you sure that you will love him?"

I stared at her, "But," I began. . . .

"Are you QUITE sure that it is him that you will love?"

The electric kettle began to boil; she turned quickly away and began to make tea. What did she mean? Could it mean that the love is not really to the Teacher, or only apparently so? So, that would mean . . . I understood. And all went very still in me. Very, very still. . . .

"What was it? Because something WAS," I said to him as soon as he entered. But he turned and stood at the open doorway, looking at the pink, soft, sunset sky. Tall and erect, he seemed quite young seen from the back.

"What it was? Just as you have felt!" he said, entering the room, and sat down in his big chair.

I came about five p.m. L. was to come a bit later. His wife was in the room with the grandchild. When they had left, an idea occurred to me that he might be doing something yogically, of which my mind can know nothing. I proved to be right. It came like a flood of "something," hitting me—it was almost physical. Nothing definite, just a feeling. The rhythm of breathing changed briskly, the heart seemed to go mad—racing, then missing beats, then going slow, stopping, then racing again. It was definitely uncomfortable; my head began to swim and I felt giddy. Tried to compose myself looking at the pink sky, all aglow with the setting sun. The door into the garden was open; a small breeze was rustling in the leaves. All the time I was wondering, what exactly was done to me? He went out of the room after a while. When he came back, I asked him what it was but did not get a proper answer; he just mumbled something into his beard and sat heavily into his big chair. I told him what I had felt. He only smiled. Told him that lately, in the last ten days, L. and I checked our pulse-rate; it was always around sixty, and a few nights ago mine was much slower, so slow that I began to wonder.

"Last week you told me that you wanted a miracle. You said that it will give you faith, will stop your doubts. What was my answer? That you would not have believed them anyhow; besides, miracles are not 'produced' on command, to satisfy a curiosity. But how many miracles did happen to you since you are here? If you sleep or

not, it makes no difference; the body is not tired, and in spite of the
very low rhythm of the heart, you feel no tiredness either, but are fit
and full of energy. My normal pulse rate is around 110; a doctor, if
he would examine me, will think that I have a high fever, but I have
not."

I said that probably later on my heart will also beat very quickly
and I will not sleep at all, or very little, as he does; I was told that after
a while the disciple's vibrations are adjusted to those of the Teacher,
even on the physical plane. He nodded.

"If I understood you correctly the other day, the teaching is given
according to the stage of evolution of the *Shishya* and according to his
temperament. Truth is only partially revealed, more and more as the
progress goes on. So, if I believe in Karma and Reincarnation, you
will talk to me accordingly; to L., who does not believe in either, you
do not mention them at all."

**"It is of no importance if one believes in these things, and if one
believes or not in the Great Hierarchy; Karma IS, Evolution IS;
humanity is taken along in progress. If they believe in certain things
or not, it makes no difference. I never mention those things to Miss
L., what's the use? It is not at all important what one believes in our
System of Freedom."**

In a sudden glow of affection, I told him how glad I was that I came
to him, that it was the most wonderful thing that could happen to
me, and whom have I to thank for it?

"Thank your Higher Self!" he said, but somebody came at this
moment, and we were interrupted. Must ask him on a next occasion
what exactly did he mean?

When L. came this evening, we went for a walk, the three of us, the
Guru, L. and I.

"Recently you have said that we are not even asked to pray, but
can we pray?" He said one can if one wants to. Told him that I will
write down the prayer I did for years and show it to him, but he said
that the prayer is not with words—NEVER. When asked again, he said
that prayer is perfect Unity with God, and only this is real prayer.
When going home, I told him I felt hopelessly discouraged—even do
not know how to pray, so it seems. . . . The state of Dhyana is what
spiritual progress is all about. I feel like a child left outside the fence
when a circus performance is going on inside. Dhyana seems to be a
ring-pass-not, which one has to cross on the way to God.

As we were passing Pushpa's house, I stopped at the gate to go inside where the *Kirtan* was already in progress; they continued to walk on. I stopped to look at them walking along in deep conversation. Somehow it seemed symbolical; they were going away, leaving me alone, to join a crowd of singing people, a ceremony which had no meaning for me . . . felt very low and deeply discouraged.

9

The Mystical Sound

WE HAD A LOVELY TIME this morning and much laughter. To get some additional explanations, L. brought her notes on *Kundalini*, and Guru's witty remarks and her comments were very amusing. But I had better leave it out. I must write here only what happens to me directly, and make exceptions only if it affects me personally or has to do with my experiences.

He sent us away before twelve. I lay down on my bed for a short rest, as I usually do when coming from his place. Listening within, I noticed a vibration. It was like a motor going inside me, vibrating in the whole of the body; but this description is not quite correct: it is perhaps like a SOUNDLESS supersonic Sound; the feeling was like after a great row, a strong tension, an excitement without excitement. Parallel to that went a tremendous longing for IT, for that which is Nameless. And in this longing was peace . . . only infinite peace. . . . I know, it sounds rather complicated, but it is the best I can do when trying to describe it.

When L. came back from the post office, she told me that it is the famous Mystical Sound, "DZIG," the preliminary step to Dhyana. I was fascinated . . . was watching it going, inside me . . . such a new experience.

In the evening a man was sitting opposite the Guru telling him his troubles, of which he had many. When he had left, the Guru began to sing. I was sitting there, the "sound" going on inside me with a tremendous longing—but for what? I was not quite sure. . . . Waited for an opportunity to ask. He sang in Urdu and translated it:

"I will come to you in the shape of a Nightingale,
Many branches are on a tree, on each branch I will be . . .
The nightingale is here, there, everywhere . . .
When you will hear it, you will know that I am here,
The nightingale who at all times is everywhere . . ."

The room was dark, full of peace, filled with his voice. It seemed to me that he was singing it for me. I have to love him, I thought. The

Shishya has to love the Guru. One can only progress through love
. . . and love for the Guru is Love for God. He began another song:

"I am here and I am there and I show myself in different shapes.

And you may wonder what or who am I and you will not
understand . . .

But in time the answer is given . . .

I am here and I am there and it is all the same,

Everywhere all the time, am I alone . . ."

This one I did not understand and was still pondering over it when
he began another song:

"There must be a complete surrender even physically,

Surrender of everything without reserve and without regret,

If you want to see the Real Shape of the Guru.

Either the Guru has to come down to you,

Or you must go to him, but a complete surrender is needed,

If you want to see the real shape of the Guru!"

"Did you get the idea?" he asked. Perhaps, I ventured, it was the
answer to my request the other day, to let me see him as he really is.

"Yes, either you are a guest on my plane, or I am on yours, but at
first, a complete surrender is essential, complete surrender, begin-
ning from the physical body and on all the levels."

Told him that I understood, and even told that to L. a few days
ago, that my physical body is going to be subjected to much strain
and I am quite prepared for it, ready for everything which will be
necessary to be "taken in gallop," the expression he used when
talking to me a few days ago.

"Don't say that you are ready for it; rather say that you are trying
to do it; it is better."

"Yes, Bhai Sahib," I answered, and my heart was so full of
gratitude.

"If one is pledged, pledged for spiritual life and work, there must
be no reserve, a complete surrender on all the planes, when one
enters the Arena. What is a pledge? It is a promise, never to be
broken, never."

"It lasts for ever and ever and ever," I said softly, thinking how I
swore my promise with my fingers on the signature of the Master,
that fateful day in the British museum—a day that seemed so long
ago and yet so near, as if it was yesterday. . . .

Later an incident happened. One individual who had been living
on him for years without working, a lazy, dirty fellow, came in

abusing him loudly. He answered in a gentle, pacifying tone of voice, and when L. began to tell him off for his disgraceful behavior, I could not control myself any longer, took my shoe off and wanted to bag him on the head. Only Guru's gentle voice restrained me, asking me to sit down. The fellow was shouting abuses, it was all very disturbing, and it spoiled our lovely evening.

24th November

IT WAS LIKE A BURNING FIRE inside my heart today. The longing for God. . . .

"Do you think I speak just for the sake of talking?" he said to L. on account of some matters concerning them. **"Oh, no! Every word is said on purpose with meaning! And speaking of Love: Love can never be hidden: NEVER! It is something which cannot help to shine!"**

L. was annoyed with me. She said, in Guru's household nobody could sleep in the night, because the man whom I threatened with my shoe swore to kill the Guru and me, and was shouting all night. She said that I am too impetuous, and don't know how to behave in Guru's presence.

This man is a Brahmin. He is a school-teacher by profession, but he is not balanced in his mind. He is very ugly and looks like an orangutan, small, hairy, very long arms like an ape, and his face too is ape-like. L. told me that he lost his job years ago because of his Communist activities, and his emotional age is a boy of twelve. He has been living with Guru's family for several years already, and he does not work. I asked L., how is it that Guru's premises are full of most objectionable people? She said that this is the Sufi way. All those who are without work, who are rejected by society, the awkward, the too loud, too weak in mind, too sick in body, he will give them refuge and hospitality. So many people live in his courtyard, and one or two thatched huts are even in the garden.

"Poor wife of his! She must be a saint herself to put up with such conditions!"

"Yes," said L., "it cannot be easy to be the wife of a Sufi Saint!"

We had a brisk walk in the park, in the evening. He was completely unconscious, walking swiftly with long strides. We could hardly keep up with him. L. told me that, when we are with him, we should try to remain on the outside, to protect him from the traffic, for he is quite unconscious in his physical body.

"Can *Devas* become human beings? I read somewhere that in order to reach the ultimate goal, they have to go through the human evolution?"

"How can they? *Devas* are made of Light and Light only. How can they become humans? Human beings are made of four elements, of five, if you include ether *(Akash)*; *Jinns* are made of Light, Fire and Air, and they are more powerful than the *Devas* who, as I have said, are made of Light only. *Devas* are a different evolution. *Devayan* is a Path which humans take on the way to Perfection. *Devas* also take it, but are stopped at *Nirodika*, half-way through. Only man can go further on the Path of *Devayan*. *Pitriyan* is not a path; man comes back and back again on the wheel of return.

"One day I saw for the first time a *Jinnee*. I was only a boy and remained late, for I was massaging my Revered Guru Maharaj's feet. About midnight he said to me: 'Go, my boy.' I went out of his room—it was this room where we are sitting now—and I saw many of them outside. I was terrified. 'Why are you afraid?' laughed Guru Maharaj. 'He is your slave! You are more than him.' *Jinns* are very powerful, and beyond good and evil as we understand it. Like the *Devas*."

DREAM: My overcoat was stolen. A man came to me and said, "It is not stolen; come with me and you will get it."

"You must know how to interpret this one," he said. He spoke with a stony, severe expression. His eyes were half-closed, cold, looking very far.

"But I can't!" I exclaimed, "how can I?"

"What could it mean that an overcoat is taken from you? Was it an old coat?" he asked, not changing his severe expression.

"No, a new one, of good material, and I was sorry because I thought that it was stolen and I needed it." He made a grimace of disgust.

"How can you be so dense? What is a coat? A cover, something to cover your body. The cover has been taken away from you." His face was as stony and as stern as ever. I said that I still couldn't understand.

"Do not insist; it is as I say. You believe in Karma. When you are on the Path earnestly and seriously, your Karmas are taken away from you. Either you have to suffer them, as I already have told you the other day, in your physical life, or they will come to you in dream. One second of dream-suffering is like three years of real suffering in life. When you are on the Path, you are speeded up, and you pay for them in your dreams. If you stay away from the Path, once decided, all the Karmas you will pay in full in your daily life. But once on the Path, the Grace of God reaches you, catches up with you, and the mental Karmas will go away in dreams.

"Emotional sufferings are cleared up by the suffering Love causes, but the Physical Karmas one has to suffer in the physical body. We are not supposed to have another one, if we are with the Teacher. So, clearly, all has to be cleared in the present one. There is a place where Karmas cannot reach if it so pleases God. His Grace is infinite, and Karmas fall away from you.

"Every dream has a different interpretation according if the dreamer is a man or a woman. For instance, if a man dreams that the roof of his house is falling in and the house is roofless, it means that he is going to be without work. If a woman dreams the same thing, it means that she is going to be a widow."

I suddenly remembered that L. told me not long ago that she dreamed she had lost her underwear in the middle of a street and was very embarrassed. I told him about it.

"If this is dreamed by somebody on the spiritual Path, it means that the person in question is nearing the ultimate illumination, but if a worldly person dreams it, it means that she is VERY worldly. Did you dream it?"

I said, "No, a friend of mine."

"You are deceiving me!" he exclaimed, and seemed very angry. I assured him that I was far from deceiving him. I only did not mention L.'s name because I did not know if I was entitled to do so, for the dream was not mine.

"You are deceiving me!" he repeated.

I was annoyed. It was unjust.

"One day when I was still young, my Rev. Guru Maharaj asked me: 'How much money have you got?' Thinking that he meant how much money I had on me, I said: '200 rupees! Everything has been stolen from me except those 200 rupees!' He laughed merrily—why was I such a fool as to think that he meant the money I had at that moment?"

"Oh, but it is unjust!" I exclaimed, "If he is a Saint and knows everything, why didn't he know that you misunderstood him? He took advantage of the situation, and I think it is most unjust!"

"**This is a silly remark,**" he said, this time really annoyed, and went out. L. said that I was wasting her time; she has to ask important questions on the subject of Kundalini.

"Don't argue so much," she said; "it is a wrong attitude, try to understand."

But I was furious, and I told him so as soon as he came back. It is so difficult to understand him; he expresses himself in such an obscure way; it is most frustrating!

"I express my thought clearly enough, but more often than not you pretend to misunderstand me and, as for me, it is a sheer agony to try to understand you! You speak in mysterious parables, and often you contradict your own statements!"

"**I contradict myself,**" he said ironically. "**I really don't know what I am talking about! What a pity!**"

L. told me impatiently that my attitude is wrong and I will achieve nothing by it.

He sent me away soon afterwards because he wanted to give her some explanations on Kundalini. I left really angry. And what is all this mystery about? Why can't I hear it? Felt humiliated.

10

Love is Produced

WAS DISTURBED AND UNHAPPY. I knew that I displeased him, and it made me worry. Also I couldn't see how, for a long stretch, I could accept the squalid surroundings and sit there for hours. Accept his injustice, the dirty beggars, the smelly, noisy crowd which assembles here during the Bandhara (a public ceremony: "the opening of the gates of grace"), as L. told me. My heart was very heavy. When L. came in the evening, I was already sitting outside, brooding my unhappy thoughts and watching the delicate sunset in greys and soft pinks, fading gradually in the sky.

"You are here? Come inside please!" I heard his voice, went in and sat with L. He was talking to his wife and baby grandchild. Then he took his blanket, and we sat outside. Curled up in his chair, his feet stretched out on the opposite one, huddled in his white blanket, he began to speak.

"When my Rev. Guru Maharaj was alive, so many people came to him only to hear him speak. He had such a beautiful voice, and he could explain so well that nobody ever misunderstood him; no doubt was left in the heart of anybody." He turned to me, **"I realize that my English is not perfect,"** he continued, **"I do not pretend that I never blunder; I am not a master of your language."**

I told him that his English is very good; it is his obscure way of expressing himself which confuses me; English is not my own language either. It is difficult for me to accept anything unless I understand it. But here I not only don't understand most of the time, but he misunderstands me and accuses me of deceiving him; it becomes a hopeless situation.

"You ask me a question. I give you a straight answer, and you get annoyed with me!" I concluded.

"I am not a God, only if I concentrate on a thing, I know it, but this is not always possible."

"But in this case it is completely hopeless for I cannot reach you, neither on the mental nor intuitional level." I felt dejected. He fell silent.

Then he told us a story of a King and a Saint. When the King had the desire to see the Saint, he had no time to go and see him, so that the Saint one day came to see him. The King was on the rampart inspecting his soldiers and wanted to come down when he saw the Saint approaching, but the Saint climbed up to him on a rope. This story meant to give an illustration of how, if the disciple is ready, the Master comes to meet him. While he was speaking with a soft, gentle voice, such tenderness was in his faraway face, that all the time I had a feeling of a great and mysterious meaning of it all. . . .

"The thing which keeps worrying me, and I absolutely cannot understand, is how to love the spiritual Teacher. One cannot say to a human being just like that: LOVE! or, LOVE NOT! How can one order such a thing! It simply cannot be done! Love just IS or IS NOT. I respect you immensely—I am fascinated by you—but love? Certainly not, I surely don't love you at this moment."

"Love is produced . . . is produced ALWAYS," he repeated. "The Shishya cannot love like this by himself. For here is not a question of a human love. It is something entirely different. And the relationship with the Teacher is a very difficult one. So love is produced, and it goes on."

26th November

WENT WITH PUSHPA to a nursery this morning owned by a rich cloth merchant. We took an eye-full of so much beauty. What a lovely garden, bougainvilleas, crotons, roses, a riot of colors—glorious the thousands of pots of huge chrysanthemums for the exhibition, already prepared, standing in rows, roses of all colors and sizes, and flowering creepers, so many, so colorful, so exotic! A tropical paradise, and the fragrance was overpowering.

In the evening Professor Batnagar came as we arrived. We had a lively conversation on the System, on God and other confusing things. He is good looking, very intelligent, a learned and refined type of Hindu, and he is a brilliant speaker. I told him that I cannot swallow the idea of the Grace of God, and he started to tell me his version—which was all wrong, a limited conception of an even more limited Godhead than even the Orthodox idea of it. I was sitting on the tachat and, when I unintentionally looked in his direction, I suddenly saw Bhai Sahib looking at me with this strange expression of love and tenderness . . . the eyes which do not see and which each time give me something like an electric shock. He does something to me, I thought, and a few times during the conversation I noticed his unblinking look, and was quite sure that something was done, even if for the moment I did not feel anything. But there was a premonition and deep fear. . . .

27th November

LAST NIGHT at about 10 or 10:30, I suddenly became worried. A kind of fear or anxiety, without any apparent reason came over me, and it was mounting and increasing by leaps and bounds. At last I couldn't bear it any longer and told L. about it. She became worried too, and asked me if I felt something had happened to the Guru. I could not explain, but I was sure that it had to do with him. This morning a depression persisted, dull and heavy. Later L. went to his place about eight, while I was attending to the chrysanthemums. When back she said that he was not in, but everything seemed to be O.K.

As I was combing my hair in front of the large mirror, all of a sudden my heart began to race like mad, my head began to spin, and much noise was in the ears—as if all the oceans of the world were roaring inside my head. Everything began to look like a faraway dream, and not real at all. Went to breakfast. People speaking, eating, walking . . . were like empty dolls without substance. Nothing had a meaning. Had to concentrate, had to try to collect my thoughts, in order to understand and to be able to co-ordinate my movements. It was as bad as that. Went to the Guru before L. He was sitting outside with his mala, praying silently. Went to sit behind him in the shade.

"When have you decided to go to Benares?" he asked. I said that I did not know, have not decided on the date as yet.

"When is Good Friday this year?" he wanted to know. Could not answer properly, got mixed up, was looking up the date in the year '61, instead of '62.

"Hoo, hoo, you cannot think clearly," he said good-humoredly. I said that I could not. Then I asked him what happened to him last night, about ten or later, and told him about the strange depression I felt.

"My physical body is all right," he said, and said no more, but smiled a faint, as if an inward smile. When told what I had felt this morning, he remarked:

"The Manas has been suspended, and only Buddhi remained."

So, I knew that some kind of force had been used, probably he was fed-up with my doubting and arguing. And I was sure that something was wrong yesterday, even if his physical body was all right.

"I went for a walk before five this morning, and I have been walking until half an hour ago. I felt an acute pain in my back for about twenty minutes."

L. looked up.

"I gave Pushpa a sitting, and she told me that she fell and hurt her back." He and L. compared the time. It was at the same time.

"You see, you meditate with her, and there is a link already!" he exclaimed. Then he told us how one must have trouble in order to be able to progress. **"In our System we live in the world, have worries about money, family, and the like. How do you progress without worries? If you are worried, you make an effort, you make a leap."**

I said that if people have no worries, he will create them for his disciples.

"Well, I will not make it so that you should break your arm or leg, but the greatest worry will be when one begins to love the Spiritual Guide. Then really the worry begins. At the beginning there are no worries, the Teacher wants the disciple to remain; but as soon as the disciple loves him, as soon as there are no doubts, the troubles commence for the disciple. He will feel like crying . . . why, why does the Master not notice me, does not speak to me—is he angry? Why is he here and I am there, and so on! Before this time comes, one should run away quickly," he added looking at me. **"What do you feel exactly?"** he interrupted himself, suddenly looking sharply at me.

"Well, all the oceans and all the seas of the world seem to be concentrated in my head. Walking down the street, when coming to you, I had just enough consciousness left in me to keep to the right side of the road and try not to be overrun by the traffic. Crossing the road I could not see where I was going. I thought it was dangerous. I could see only when I looked right in front of me—right or left I could not see clearly, as it seemed to be obliterated, like in a mist. If I see an object—for instance, this chair in front of me—between the image of the chair as seen by me, and the conscious realization that it is a chair and not something else, there is an interval of a fraction of a second. I have to concentrate on a particular noise, or picture, or any other object or sensation to be able to name it. In connection with it, I remember, that in the works of J. Krishnamurti, it is said somewhere that we should abstain from naming the things around us. If we can manage that—in between the picture of an object, say a rose, and the naming of it, which classifies it as a rose and not as a dog or a chair—if in between this interval of seeing and remembering which will become longer and longer, it may happen that in that moment, one day, the illumination would come." He nodded.

"You spoke of a miracle a few days ago," he said very slowly, **"have you still the courage to speak of miracles? The roar of all the oceans is in your head; or the mind is not there at all; or you don't sleep without being tired; your thinking process in my place is slowed down so much that you 'sleep'; there is a peace not of this world in you, which you cannot explain, or a longing so strong that life is not worthwhile living, upheavals, premonitions. Tell me, are those not miracles? Great and important miracles?"**

His voice was soft and very gentle as if full of deep compassion. I lowered my eyes and felt small . . . smaller than a grain of sand. Then L. asked him a few questions on Kundalini and different Pranas, and their functions, all things of which I understand nothing, even if my brain works properly. In the state it was at this moment I did not even understand what she was talking about. . . .

In the evening I went there and was first as usual. When he asked me how I felt, I told him that my mind was still not working properly, but in the afternoon when I was writing my diary it was not too bad. He again asked me when I was going to Benares. Checking on the calendar hanging on the wall near the door, I suggested that perhaps I could go on the 4th of December, which is a Monday. He said that he has to go to Allahabad, and he never travels alone; he will come with me, will be met at Allahabad, and I could proceed to Benares.

"I will let you know by tomorrow," he said.

I asked him if my brain will be still so numb and inefficient, while I had to travel, because if so, it may prove to be very uncomfortable.

"It will be noted down in my diary."

"Do you mean to say that you will note down in your diary when you have to give me back my wits?" I laughed, and he only nodded. That made me laugh even more, and we both finished by being amused, laughing at this incredible idea, when seen from the point of view of the ordinary world.

He was grinning into his beard while writing something on a piece of paper which later he gave to his son with some added instructions in Hindi.

I asked some questions: "Why does the memory not work well at all? Does the memory belong to the mind?"

"The memory does not work well because Manas (Mind) has been suspended, and though the memory does not belong to the mind, strictly speaking, for it has a different center, still, it has to work *through the mind*. This Path of our System is not at all troublesome; it is the easiest Path. It only seems difficult when there is confusion."

Well, it seems clear, that there has been plenty of confusion in my mind in the last few days, even weeks. . . .

Later, in conversation: "TO ENTER THE ARENA IS TO ACCEPT THE PATH OF THE MASTER.

"The world is for us as we create it: if you say there is a *Bhut* (spirit) in the tree, then there will be a *Bhut* for you.

"This is all Manas. But what is Manas? Nothing! Manas is *Maya* (illusion). You want everything, but are not prepared to make sacrifices, to pay the price. Here they sit and say: 'I was intelligent, now I cannot even think, where is my memory, what happened to me?' People are not prepared to give anything up. If you want to go anywhere, you will have to take the plane or the train—you are expected to pay the fare, is it not so?

"Be always a friend of the Almighty, and you WILL NEVER DIE! Prayer should be done always, even ordinary prayer should be done, but of course, the only REAL prayer is merging, ONENESS with God, only this is a true prayer. Once we have reached this point within us, we do not need anymore factional support."

According to the Sufi System there are three activities of the brain: Manas (mind); Memory (working through the Manas); Unconscious (where all the memories of the heart are kept). The Unconscious is independent of Manas.

L. told me last night that there was some trouble after all, but not a physical one for the Guru. Bhai Sahib told her that between 10 and 10:30 p.m. he was on the way back from visiting a woman who had an accident. She came under a car and was badly but not seriously hurt. L. suggested that probably he took upon him her fear, as it easily can be done, and he does it often, so she said.

"I am strong," he would say with a smile, "I can take it."

I wondered if what she was telling me was correct. If it was, that could be a serious thing for me, for I will get it all secondhand, so to say. As the time goes on, one is more and more identified with the Guru, and I see trouble looming ahead. So much more, because I get all sorts of worries and troubles lately from the people who come to him. I seem to pick it all up. That surely is bound to become more uncomfortable in the future.

And I keep wondering what will be done, what will happen about this question of love. . . . Love will be produced. So he said. Produced . . . but how? I wonder. . . .

29th November

HE WAS TALKING to L. about someone in France. **"And now,"** he continued, turning to me, **"let's leave L.'s case aside. Why are you here? You stayed here for the last two months, you did not receive anything, I gave you nothing, and still you are here. Why?"**

"Because I think that it is the right thing to do," I answered.

"No!" he retorted. **"You stay because your heart wants you to do so. There is something in the heart, a substance, which makes you do so."**

"You are right; that's why from the very beginning I could not go away and was so disturbed by discovering this fact. I value freedom so much and hate to be forced to do anything. There is a mystery hidden somewhere, and my mind was much frightened. I suspect that the mind was afraid, for it knows that it will be the loser, but the mind is strong and it will give trouble. Only it looks to me that you are knocking it out altogether." I smiled doubtfully. But he only laughed his kind-hearted laughter.

Later he said to L. speaking of somebody: **"Your attitude has to force the Master, your life has to be lived in such a way that he sees that you are in earnest and is FORCED to accept you."**

1st December

"DO CHRISTIANS BELIEVE IN EVOLUTION?" he asked.

"Some do," answered L.

"Does science believe in evolution?"

"Yes," said L., "science does, but for plants, animals, etc., even many scientists believe that man has been created."

"How does one prove to an atheist the existence of God? By letting him experience it?"

"Yes, I suppose, this will be the only way to make him believe in God." This is for me, I thought. He speaks to L., but it is meant for me. He knows that I believe in evolution, and that I don't really believe in God.

2nd December

IN THE AFTERNOON did not remember what happened in the first half
of the day, who was there for lunch, what kind of food we had. A
complete blank. L. told me that nothing of importance happened. I
was feeding the squirrels (chipmunks), who for the first time took
the nuts from my hands, and Veena, Pushpa's daughter, went to the
test match with her father.

Wrote to Benares for accommodation, and to Adyar; will be going
to the T.S. Convention. Leaving for Benares on Tuesday with the
Guru. He goes to Allahabad which is on the way, so we will travel
together.

Sitting in the darkness after sunset in my usual place, I prayed.
How easy the prayer is now! Never could I pray like this before! My
mind is still, transparent, as though paralyzed, and my heart flies
away like a trembling bird . . . flies away into the peace of . . .
God?—or just peace??

3rd December

I DREAMED that the storm was approaching from the sea. Huge black
clouds rolling on and on, nearer and nearer. I began to close the
windows on the side of the approaching storm, but left open those
on the opposite side of the house, thinking that they are safe because
facing the sun; the sky was still blue and clear on this side of the
horizon.

**"The dream is incomplete. Not much use telling you what it
could mean, because it will only mislead you. I have told you that
the past will come up in dreams now, as the time goes on. 99½% of
the Karmas will be dealt with in dreams; the remaining half
percent, of course".** . . . he fell silent looking into the far distance.
Into my past? Or into my future? I thought, observing his calm, the
serene brow, the perfect stillness.

The sky was so blue, so beautiful this morning, so fragrant was the
air. Winter is lovely in the Indian plains. Deep is my love for you,
beautiful India, so manifold, so incomprehensible, darkly mysterious for us from the West.

"Bhai Sahib, what is being done to my heart? It goes completely
mad. Stops beating, races, stops again, goes slow, and is fluttering
like a bird caught in a cage."

We were sitting outside; he had his mala sliding slowly through his
fingers; his lips were hardly moving in silent prayer.

"Please do remember that I will have to travel. I would not like anything to happen while I am away. If it does, I leave everything—the Convention, the tax-office, the bank—and take the first train to you!" He smiled.

"Of course when you go away, things can happen when you are far from me. To a Sufi Saint came a disciple and said to him: 'I wish this night will never end, and there shall be no morning for me tomorrow!' The Saint, touched by so much love, did not pray for it, but there was for days no morning for the disciple, no sun rose for him."

"But I do not understand what it has to do with me being afraid of something happening when I am away; though it certainly is a lovely story," I said. "The mind seems not at its best just now." He smiled again.

"All I wanted to say is that many things could happen if one loves. When L. had left here for the first time years ago, such currents of love were coming that even the people here used to ask me about her and how she is."

But do I love? It does not seem so. So, I just wondered. . . .

11

Benares and Adyar

LATER ON, REFERRING TO PRAYER and the answer he gave me some time ago that prayer with words is of no use at all, and I said I was so discouraged, that for the time being I stopped all praying. Only now I came back to it. He said that he does not explain well enough sometimes, perhaps it has to do with the language. Prayer with words is all right, if it is accompanied by the prayer of the heart.

"If the heart is praying, it is all right! If your heart has heard your prayer, God has heard it!" says a Persian song.

"Mohammedans pray five times a day. But many repeat it only mechanically. What's the use of it? Try to understand me, what I really mean, do not stick to words, then we will overcome the language barrier."

"It may come later, Bhai Sahib; for the moment it seems to me you are asking the impossible. But since the mind does not work at its full speed, prayer goes wonderfully well, as never before." Again this smile, so very still. He closed his eyes.

Looking at him, I kept wondering why his eyes were full of tears when he was telling me the story of the Saint and the disciple who did not see the morning. Perhaps it was his own experience, in connection with his beloved Guru Maharaj, as he reverently calls him.

I sleep well, but my sleep is full of colorful dreams which I forget immediately. The only thing I know is that he is present in all my dreams. Told him last week about it. He said nothing, only smiled as he does so often. Never have I dreamt of anybody to such an obsessing extent. Even if I forget or don't remember, I know nevertheless that he is always in my dreams, in ALL my dreams, so naturally as he would belong there, as if he were always part of my dream-life, in the very depth of myself.

9th December,1961

BENARES WAS LOVELY. Full of shimmering light, bustle and sunshine. Had the same room as last year, in Shanti Kunj, and my meals at the girls' hostel. The Guru didn't come with me; when my rikshaw

77

stopped at his gate on the way to the station, to pick him up, he was in bed with an attack of pain in his back.

The reason for my going to Benares was to get my zink trunk which some members of the T.S. had stored for me. Did not go anywhere, not even to the Ganga. Did not do anything either, but walked in the compound and stayed only two days. Have found a marked difference in myself. I seem to have lost all interest in everything. When taking part in conversation, I have to make an effort to follow because it interests me so little. And the mind is not flexible, not very sharp. Have neither the desire to go back nor to remain, but have much peace. When walking in the grounds, looking at the trees, the flowers, the lovely transparent sky, had moments as if all of a sudden the thought was completely suspended in nothingness; just looking, just feeling; the same dream-quality which I had so often when a child alone with nature, and which I had lost completely after my school days, was here again, sharp and clear. Only this time it was deeper, clearer, almost frightening to the mind. It comes without warning in fleeting moments, and every time it happens, for a second or more—who knows?—I am lost in it, but then it is immediately drowned in a kind of fear; the mind panics in this state of blissful non-being, and I caught myself making desperate efforts to remember where I was, and to link this state to the memory which disappeared somewhere for the time being. Naturally, I succeeded to remember quickly, but the blissful state was gone. Since my childhood I know, and have always known that, in my dreams, in the night, this state in its pure quality, without fear, is there so naturally and belongs to me, in what I called "my other life," my dreams. It is a strange experience to get glimpses of it in my waking state.

11th December

BACK IN KANPUR saw Bhai Sahib only twice for a short time, stayed only two days before leaving for Madras. This morning, quite out of the blue, got a flat. It was really offered to L., but it is too small for her; she expects a friend from France. Two tiny rooms, whitewashed, clean. It is in a house belonging to some Indian Christians. Seem to be nice people, but several families live in the courtyard, and there are many children. My door also leads into the courtyard, so I expect that there will not be much privacy. But I took it in a flash, had no choice, and from the 1st of January I can move in. When I told the Guru about it, he approved. He had seen it; he went to see it with L.

last evening. Now, when I come back, there will be no worry about accommodation. One obstacle for my stay here has been removed.

"**No, no,**" he said quickly, "**no obstacles whatsoever!**" Once more he told me not to make any engagements after coming back. "**The flat is good for the moment. We will do a lot of work there,**" he said, and that was enough for me.

13th December

AND SO IT CAME. . . it tiptoed itself into my heart, silently, imperceptibly, and I looked at it with wonder. It was still small, a light-blue flame, trembling softly. It had the infinite sweetness of a first love, like an offering of fragrant flowers with gentle hands, the heart full of stillness and wonder and peace.

I was looking out of the window on the landscape sliding by; groups of mango trees, sugar-cane plantations, rocky, low hills, then flats again, endlessly. The train was taking me South, and it was eleven hours late. Was lazily reflecting on what some fellow-passengers had just told me, that Kerala was so lovely, and it was just the right time of the year to visit Cochin. My original intention was to see the South this winter, and it seemed rather a pity that I won't be able to do it. For I well knew that I will stay in Kanpur, for God knows how long a time. Money can be transferred from London to anywhere in India. I should really go, I thought. It would be so agreeable, exciting in fact, to see new places, the colorful tropical South. Rich in vegetation and wild life, but people are so poor, worse off than in the North, if such a thing could be possible.

But I knew that I was cheating myself, knew that I will never go. COULD NOT GO. This "something," the powerful drive which for years made me do things which I just had to accept, to obey, because I could not help doing so, this "something" made me sell my house in order to be free, made me go to India, and finally brought me step by step to Kanpur, to undertake the longest journey, the greatest adventure of my life; and it will not let me go anywhere but back to Kanpur, back to a future full of dark, half-admitted fears.

It was then, that I noticed the little blue flame, burning softly inside my heart.

"**Love will be produced,**" you had said. And since then, I kept wondering how it will come to me. Will it be like the Voice from the Burning Bush, the Voice of God as Moses heard it in the days of old? Will it be like a flash of lightning and thunder out of a blue sky, making the world around me a blaze of glory? Or will it be, as L. suggested, that you will produce Love in general, Love for everything, and the Teacher will be included in it? But I told her that it could not be so—not for me, to be able to surrender completely, to sweep away all the resistance; it must be big, tremendous, complete, without reserve, without limit—the conditionless, absolute forgetting oneself.

But what I felt now was not so. . . it was just a tender longing, so gentle, so full of infinite sweetness. Like all laws governing this universe, Love will follow the way of least resistance. In all my life I never knew the feeling of love flashing suddenly into my heart. It always came softly, growing timidly, like a small blue flower at the side of the road, so easily crushed by the boots of those who may pass by. And if there was love in my life in the past, it always grew slowly, steadily, increased until it became big, large, sweeping like a tidal wave, sweeping everything that stood in its way and at last filled all my life. So it was in the past, and this time too, it is coming to me in the same way. . . I suppose, because our hearts are made in a certain way, and we cannot help being what we are.

Slept the whole afternoon, and when in the evening I looked again into my heart, it seemed to me that there was nothing there, only a subtle feeling of peace. So I thought that I was mistaken after all; it was not love, just imagination, an error of judgment. It must have been a mistake.

16th December

BUT IT WAS NOT. On the contrary, I noticed that it silently grew when I wandered in the lovely compound here in Adyar. My first impression of Adyar was that it is so small. When I came here for the first time, more than two years ago, I arrived from the crammed-in England. Then Adyar seemed so vast to me. But now, after hundreds of miles of rolling hills and endless landscapes, seemingly reaching beyond the horizons, Adyar was tiny, a really small place. The people who live in it are still the same, as everything else was still the same. I always found it so strange, to find people and places just the same as you had left them, even after many years. Strange and incredible it seems, especially when for you so many things have changed, and the world is not the same again. It always fills me with astonishment how it could be that there is so little change in people and mentality.

Here too, all seemed to be the same just as I had left it. But even if it seemed small to me, Adyar was as lovely as ever, and so fragrant, with many flowering shrubs and trees. Looking up to the deep blue sky, the white clouds, as it was my habit, I sent a quick thought of greeting to the Infinite Life, to all this wonderful blue. But every time I did it, I saw your face clearly outlined against the azure of the sky— perhaps not exactly your face, but the expression of it—as I have seen it when you smile, first with your eyes, and then it deepens to vanish into the beard; or the faraway look and the blank expression, when still and composed, you slide the beads of your mala through your fingers; or the face, as if cut out of stone, hard, severe, as old as the hills, as ancient as humanity. The unseeing eyes, wide open, flashing a dark light, the face which made me nearly jump out of my skin with fright when I first happened to see it, and which looks so Eastern, Chinese, or Tibetan, and which, since then, I saw often and learned that you look like this when in deep Samadhi, out of your body.

To my surprise, it was always your face with its various expressions between me and my thoughts of the Infinite Life, no, rather as if they were part of the Infinite Life itself, never to be separated again in my mind. Then, only then, I knew for sure that I have lost myself in you and that never, never will I get my heart back again. "For my heart was lost in Heaven and remained there with the stars." I remembered the line of poetry, but did not remember who wrote it. And when I took some books and articles on Sufism from the Adyar Library, this flame grew so big that it set my heart aflame, flooding it with joy!

When I came to you, a little more than two months ago, I did not know anything about Sufism. Nothing of its glory, its tradition, its boundless freedom, its never ending love! It was like a revelation, and I realized how much I had missed by not knowing it before. Even the little I have learned about it—for we have not many books on Sufism at present in our Library—filled me with enthusiasm. And once more I thanked my good star (or my destiny?) for guiding me to you.

18th December

"LIGHT WILL COME TO THEE from Longing," says Darya Khan. I don't know anything about the Light, but I certainly have Longing. It is strong, even, constantly going on like a call from far away.

Went to the Garden of Meditation this afternoon to hear good Western music which I missed so much all those last years in India. I nearly cried and was much moved. The quality of listening seems to be different. And the sky was full of feathery, pink clouds.

Adyar is full of delegates for Convention. To avoid the inconvenience of sharing a room with other delegates, Norma offered me their outhouse on the edge of the casuarina wood on the beach. A *charpoy* (a rope-bed) was put in, I found some long sticks lying about, put up my mosquito net and was comfortable. Norma was sending me a cup of coffee and a *chappathi* every morning with her servant. The place was lovely, isolated. There was an old-fashioned sink and water, for in the olden days it was used as a wash-house. The sound of the pines (casuarina is a poverty-stricken pine growing on the sandy beaches), and the sound of the surf all day and night. Actually, in Adyar one is everywhere within the sound of the sea. Especially in the night, one can hear the ceaseless coming and going of the waves.

The sandy beach is very shallow; one can walk far out, and the water is still only to the knees. The long, tall waves roll on majestically from afar in steady succession. Just before they curve over when breaking down, crested with white foam on the top edge, right inside the curve, it is green, translucent, the light of the rising sun behind them. And right there in the curve, in the liquid green, there was your face. . . .

Your face looked at me from every lotus flower; it was inside the hibiscus flowers, in every one of them; in the dark water of the pond itself, it was quietly looking at me. . . then I knew that there was no escape, that I have reached the end of my road. And where I will be going from now on, there can be no return for me.

No, I knew nothing about the teaching of Sufism. I am like a blank sheet of paper for you to write the creed of your glorious System with letters of Love. Will you forgive me for fighting you for over two months? If you knew the hearts of men, as I am sure you do, you must have known how much distrust, how much doubt there was in it. (Perhaps it still is? and still will be?) But I know that you have forgiven me already, because you understood. **"To make a Saint takes no time,"** you had said, **"but who is prepared to sacrifice everything?—that this world should be nothing, non-existent for you anymore. Who is prepared to accept it?"**

I think I do. For the process had already slowly begun before I met you. Gradually I seem to lose interest in everything. Nothing pleases me. Not the beautiful surroundings, nor interesting people, lectures, friends. Lectures are only words, and so many of them meaningless anyhow. People have so little love, are incased in themselves. Even the loveliness of the landscape is nothing if I have to be separated from you.

"For a bearded man came with his song and made me blind to the beauties of the world." You translated to us this Persian couplet.

"When one is a maker of Saints and knows how to write on the back of the hearts"—I remember you saying this to us one day. You know how to do it, Bhai Sahib. I throw my heart at your feet, and when you tread on it, never mind! Write on the back of my heart one letter: one letter only: that of Alif. Write it with living fire, to be consumed at your feet with eternal longing. I will leave it there; will never ask it back again. It does not belong to me anyhow. It always was yours. Only this time owing to my conditioning, to my Western education, I forgot it. I did not recognize you, Bhai Sahib. I was blind and did not see that the Feet of the Great Lover, the Creator of all Love and your feet were one and the same. . . .

You said to us that complete surrender is necessary. But now I read that more than that is required. The condition of self-annihilation is demanded from the disciple in your System. Self-annihilation in the Master.

> "The latter ascertains by his own powers whether the 'Union' is perfected. If this is so, the disciple is passed to his Teacher's Master, the Spiritual Influence of the original Founder of the 'Path,' or System, to which they belong. This Founder, of course, is long since deceased, and for a time the disciple can only come into conscious relation with him by the aid of his first Teacher. In time the consciousness of the disciple becomes so absorbed in this great Master, as to possess all his Spiritual Powers. He is then passed still higher up his chain until he reaches 'self-annihilation in the Prophet.' By the Prophet is here understood, not Mohammed, as man, but as the 'Primal Element,' the First Intelligence, the Word. Beyond lies only the last, the final stage—'Union,' 'God,' 'Truth,' what you will, words are meaningless; it is beyond all telling, and the Sufi says: 'From him who has made the journey, no news returns.'"

> —from the text of J.M. Watkins, on Sufism.

So, this is the Goal of Sufism. Then how could you say, as you told us again and again, that it is an effortless Path? Why do you choose to deceive your disciples? But you will not deceive me. I never believed in such a thing, and I told you so. Maybe it could be effortless for those who are content to sit with you for years, get a bit of Dhyana,

because they are not prepared to pay the whole price, are afraid to go
further. But if one goes out for the Whole Thing, and is prepared to
give up everything for it, to put everything on one card, without
reserve, how can that be effortless???

Like birth, Creation is a painful process. To be able to create, one
has to destroy first. Destruction is synonymous with pain. I saw
people who have been for the last forty years with you, and they are
still petty, full of the small self. I do not want that. Sings the Persian
poet:

"He is my own little self, my Lord, he knows no shame;

But I am ashamed to come to thy door in his company!"

If you want a great thing, the Greatest Thing, you must pay a great
price. What greater price can you pay than your life, your innermost
being?

To reach the Goal, you have to be turned inside out, burned with
the fire of Love, so that nothing should remain but ashes, and from
the ashes will resurrect the new being, very dissimilar from the
previous one. Only then can there be real Creation. For this process
IS destruction, creation AND Love. Another name for Love is Pain
and Effort.

"Life means Longing. Progress is only possible through
Longing. And as the Path of Progress is infinite, there should be
infinite Longing. Thus Longing becomes itself a form of the
Infinite, to be desired for its own sake. This is why the Mystics
idealize Longing. The other name for Longing is Love.

"Longing is to the Soul what water is to the soil. Even as the
earth needs water to soften its particles, so that seed may
sprout, the human Soul needs sorrow to make it fertile.
Without longing, without sorrow, softening your Soul, there
can be no progress, no germination of the seed. That is the law
of the spiritual life as of the physical. And, therefore, while yet a
Soul strives, while yet he is imperfect and subject to tempta-
tion, as everyone of us is in this life, he must have longing and
sorrow, which arise from the memory of the Beloved, to guard
him from the danger of self-complacency and lead him safely to
the Goal. Longing not only supplies an incentive to life, but it
makes you mild and humble. And humility is a very necessary
factor of spiritual life. It is but a child of Longing. Both live
together. Humility and Longing imply imperfection. And the
uncertainty of perfection in human life is what makes Longing
and Humility necessary for a spiritual aspirant. And so Madan,

a Sindi singer says: 'Even after thou hast attained, continue to fear, oh Madan!'"

—from the Spirit of Sufi Culture, Akbat Ashram, Tract No.12, September 31, by A.H. Jaisinghani

Therefore, never tell me again, that it is an effortless Path. Never. But give me sorrow, pain and longing.

Let me become like yourself. And do not tell me as you did once: **"Why like me? Why not higher? There is no limit, you know!"**

"Well, I think this never will be possible, Bhai Sahib. Because if one day, by your Grace, I will be where you are now—you, yourself, will be much, so much further ahead. Sufis do not believe in standing still. You said it yourself. Says the great Ibn' Arabi: "No recoiling movement or devolution can in any sense be applied to the Will. It knows no standstill, no stepping back. This process is eternal, and as we are part of His Creation, part of His Will, it is easy to see that as individuals we cannot ever realize Him completely."

So how can I be more, or even like you? You will always be ahead of me. But I will be always grateful if you will grant me inspiration from your Light, if you stretch out your hand to help me to go on to complete the journey the human Soul can undertake—"The night journey across the sea to get the pearl of Great Price," to quote Carl Jung.

                                              19th December

IT IS WINDY TODAY. All night the sea roared. Yesterday the river was like a mirror; clouds stood motionless in the sky. As soon as I am alone, the feeling of unreality becomes so strong. I wonder why, as if everything around me were only a dream—a crazy, empty dream. Cannot explain the reason for it . . . there is of course this long-ing. . . .

Walking alone in the moonlight last night, thinking about Adyar and how different my reaction to it is now since I last saw it, a thought did strike me: what would happen, if, for one reason or another, I couldn't go back and had to stay here for ever? My heart was seized with terror and bleak despair, so much so that I was astonished at myself. As bad as that, is it? I thought. It became so clear to me that I could not go back to my previous life anymore. There is nothing to go back to. Emptiness, a no-man's land. The only thing that matters now is you, and my future tied up with you—it seems to me forever now. Perhaps it always was. Blind and deluded, I did not know it.

12

Flight Into The Unknown

THERE IS A QUALITY IN ME growing slowly, which I try to pin down without success. It is more noticeable and acute when I am alone, wandering about in the grounds, FEELING things around me, and trying to analyze this feeling. There are, for instance, those water lilies, here in the Garden of Remembrance, a lovely place near the river from where one can see a bit of the sea and the shore.

In a few small ponds around the six-pointed star they grow, the lotuses, beautiful, huge, pink or white with yellow centers. Beds of colorful zinnias, flowering shrubs and trees around, insects, grass—everything NEAR me—has an immediate rapport with me, is part of me, intimately, absolutely, quite naturally in a mysterious way. It is a sense of complete being, with no effort. They are near and dear to me, but in a detached way, if one could put it so, and there is hardly a thought in my mind, very little of it, just feeling. It seems to be an automatic process—it just happens, I don't produce it deliberately. All things further away are non-existent. Things like trees are more in the distance, the sky, the river, the sea. To become aware of them I have to make a kind of effort, to shift my consciousness when looking at them and concentrating on them. This takes a slight effort. But as soon as I do it, they form part of me too, are included in this feeling of "belonging" to each other and me. And so I wander about, wondering, looking at a world which is changing, and knowing, of course, that nothing has changed, only me. Adyar is just as it always was. It is I who am discovering a new quality, new values; they surge up, are uncovered from the depths somewhere in me, but they were always there; they must have been. . . .

Strange destiny that I didn't meet you before, Bhai Sahib . . . lived for so many years an empty, useless life. For it is you, and you alone, who can help me now to learn how to love a King. The Great King of our hearts.

That's why I would die of heartbreak if I couldn't go back to you, Bhai Sahib, to your drab surroundings, to the smoky town, the noisy street, the dusty garden, for in some inexplicable way, you and the King in my heart merge in one endless longing.

86

The voice of the wind in the casuarina trees. The voice of the birds. Dancing shadows on the glittering water of the pool covered with round, waxy leaves of lotuses. Sitting on the water like stars. Pink ones. White ones. And the exquisite pale yellow ones, the petals half-transparent.

The wind from the sea smelling of oxygen and salt. Free are you, wind, but I am not free any more, bound by the chains of Longing for ever. Never will I be free again. The yearning inside me, deep, dark, restless. How full of pain is your "effortless Path," Bhai Sahib!

"The world is full of beautiful things until an old man with a beard came into my life and set my heart aflame with longing and made it pregnant with Love. How can I look at the loveliness around me, how can I see it, if it hides the Face of my Lover?" This you sang on the eve of my departure and were laughing while translating it to us.

Long breakers, rhythmical, unceasing sound of the surf. . . .

21st December, 1961

THE BAY OF BENGAL is to the East. How the wind from the sea smells of salt. The lotuses seem more numerous this morning and lovelier than ever. Fascinating to see how they flower: you see buds deep down in the water, leaves half-folded, standing upright, tense, as if longing, waiting to reach the surface of the water, to come out into the air, to the light. Green, round and crisp they are. Flowers reclining gently, opening just under the surface, the first few petals already above the surface, the chalice itself still submerged, filled with water. Verily, the lotus is the noblest of all flowers! Every other flower, if left in water for a few days, will decay, but not so the lotus. Here they stand, stars from heaven, of the glossiest pink the purest white, the palest yellow or deepest blue. All this loveliness rising from the mire of the river bed or the pond, the perfect symbol of the Soul, tense with eagerness to reach the Light.

Since I opened my eyes this morning, I was lying awake full of still joy, because I had booked my train reservation yesterday, for Friday, 29th December. At the back of my mind there was this joy while I was walking away from the station office, the ticket tucked safely away in my bag. Now it is sure that I am going back to you soon. To the drab Kanpur. The whole Universe full of beautiful things cannot keep me away now, for I have the ticket. I will not stay till the end of the Convention.

22nd December

DREAM: Got into a train, then noticed that it was only an engine with a driver who nearly drove it into a wall, but then managed to turn it round without damaging the wall. When arrived, I remembered that I had left my jacket behind—it was a yellow one like a short coat. "I have put it on a tree," said a little boy, "I'll get it for you!" I saw my jacket hanging on a branch of a tree, and the boy ran up the branch to get it, but instead of giving it to me—for I was standing nearby on the top floor of a building, the tree was practically touching it—he threw it down and jumped from the tree, flying like a bird. I was astonished how gracefully he swooped down, but most annoyed because I knew that there was a purse full of small change in the pocket which surely will be lost now! When I got the jacket, sure enough, the purse was missing, and I was most upset. Asked where the police station was to report the loss, but was told it is far away, across the fields—I had no time to get there, the train was to depart. Met a man in the meantime who was from the police and, while complaining to him about the loss, woke up.

23rd December

YESTERDAY KEPT DOUBTING all the time if you are the "Master of the three worlds," as L. once told me, quoting from the Scriptures, and if you can take me to the highest Goal. The mind kept mocking me, telling me that you are not, and that I will be wasting my time.

Could not sleep because of the mosquitoes and the roar of the sea. Finally got up in the middle of the night, fastened the mosquito net more securely, but the blighters kept coming inside because the wind kept moving it. The jungle around was full of unfamiliar noises, and there was all the time the sound of the surf and of the wind in the trees. Missed the sunrise this morning, was even too tired to think.

Sitting alone amongst the pines, I was sick with yearning. Doubt, my mind, doubt . . . go on doubting. What's the use of it?. . . If he can take me to the supreme Goal or not . . . if he is the right Teacher or not . . . it was he who has set my heart on fire. And it longs endlessly. And I have no peace anymore. Counting the days to go back. The powerful pull makes me sick in my heart; even the food tastes dreadful. And always this dream-quality, a kind of giddiness accompanied by a slight pain in the region of the heart which seems to make the surroundings so unreal.

24th December, Christmas Eve

I DON'T SLEEP WELL. The roar of the sea is obsessive. I know that from now on the sound of the waves will be synonymous with Longing in my memory. Like the Longing, this sound goes on, an obsession. Never ending, on and on, all night, all day.

Was surprised to find the atmosphere at the E.S. meetings so charged. Had forgotten it rather. Later, walking alone, was thinking of my discovery that in the whole of the Universe there is nothing else but the Lover and the Beloved. This is the Truth; they are the only two, the only reality is this. God and His Creation—and the Creation loves God, and God loves His Creation. Nothing else has a meaning but that alone, and the more I think of it and turn it over in my mind, the more I discover how true it is, and how everything absolutely is this duality which ultimately will be resolved in Unity. When this day will come to me, then I will be born again.

In Norma's flat on the first floor, gramophone records of a symphony concert were played. I sat under a tree, listening. Just in front of me was a flaming crimson bougainvillea, and a shrub full of large, yellow, bell-like flowers. In between the branches of casuarina pines, one could see a large, white cloud, bulging like a balloon. The sky was of a milky blue, and there was such peace . . . the rich tone of a full orchestra—Sir Thomas Beecham was conducting the sound of the sea. There was the feeling of being free. Alive. Deep, deep in my heart, a dark premonition of some doom approaching. A somber future, the Great Unknown. . . .

25th December

IT IS CHRISTMAS DAY. Sitting in the casuarina grove for hours on the soft sand, reading *The Reality of Religion*, which Norma lent me. This morning got up tired, in spite of having slept well. Sat on the shore to see the sunrise. It rose from the water amongst the mist and low clouds, and I felt so restless and sad. Nothing pleases me. There is only one desire—to go back soon. Nothing has meaning—"and all the beautiful things in the world. . . ." Oh, let's leave it at that. . . .

Last night went to Norma about 8 p.m. to hear some music, Beethoven's fourth piano concerto. We were sitting in the veranda facing the beach and the sea, watching the moon just risen, low on the horizon, yellow and large. The sea was dark. Then Wagner's introduction to *Parsival* was played, then the Good Friday music, and the *Liebestod* from *Tristan and Isolde*, and Siegfried's journey on the Rhine from *Götterdämmerung*. It all seemed so unbelievably lovely. The sea, the moon, the beach, patches of moonlight on the white sand, fresh fragrance of the sea and of flowers, and I was experiencing in myself a curious phenomenon: I was LISTENING WITH THE HEART. Yes, it was just so; the music was reaching me through the heart. The mind was still. The heart was wide open to receive the sound, and the sound went into it. The sound was, but the mind was not there . . . never experienced anything like that! Of course it was a magnificent recording directed by Toscanini, but even so, I could not explain how I could listen with the heart. Of course, I could switch over and listen with the mind too, but then it was as it used to be before—enjoying the music, appreciating it—and this gives much enjoyment too. But if I just listened, through the heart, just listened, and no thinking was involved in it, then the heart sang with the violins, it WAS the trumpet call, it WAS the woodwinds, and I WAS THE MUSIC.

Nobody like the great Arthuro Toscanini could make the sound of the strings appear so tender, the woodwinds so full of longing, and the brass instruments were a cry from the innermost depth of the heart. Amazed, I watched myself. It was a new experience, quite an outstanding one, and it occurred to me that perhaps this was the true way of experiencing music. No appreciation, no thinking, but BEING it, being the sound itself, the longing and the love of it, following every shade, every nuance, every inflection, every mood. It remains to be seen if it is possible with every kind of music, with less perfect performances, if I, myself, could keep up this state.

Was emotionally so worn out I thought I would not be able to sleep, so I sat on the beach alone in the moonlight, a cold wind in my face. Thinking and longing, and longing and thinking, and being restless and sad—counting the days to go to my future with hope, premonitions, and fear.

On the 29th, at 4:45 p.m., left northwards to commence: "The night journey over the sea to get the Pearl of Great Price" (C. Jung).

On the last evening of my stay in Adyar, Joyce came and we sat under a tree and listened to a concerto of Vivaldi played upstairs in Norma's flat. The night was very dark, no moon. We spoke of so many things, sitting on the beach afterwards—of the future, and what it may bring, of Adyar, of her and me—and I was happy, because I was leaving.

The journey was tedious. The train was hours late, so I missed the connection and had to wait ten hours in Jahnsi to catch the Lucknow express at 1 p.m. Arrived at Pushpa's place at 7 p.m. Nobody was home. Had a bath and hair-wash—Indian trains are so full of smoke. On my bed was lying a letter. It was from my sister Mila. As soon as I picked it up, I felt trouble was inside. And a big trouble. Mila had been very ill for the last two years, suffering from progressive paralysis. She will have to sell her house, and she is asking me to help towards father's lodgings because she will have to take a flat for him and herself. Was sitting on the bed worrying when L. came in and told me that Bhai Sahib was worried all the time about a letter which was to arrive for me. Told L. about the situation and that I will help, of course. My father had been staying with my sister for the last sixteen years. She always bore the burden herself without asking us to contribute. Now it is my duty to help. I am sure my younger sister will also do the same.

1st January, 1962

WENT WITH L. in the morning. He smiled and I was glad to see him. "Bhai Sahib," I said, "I came back to be at your orders."

"Yes, yes; sit there!" he said, with an impatient movement of his head in the direction where I had to sit. I sat down.

My new flat could be comfortable, so it seems. Only the toilet is a bit far, and all these children in the courtyard; it remains to be seen how it will work. But it is clean and has quite a good atmosphere. It is nice to be able to cook one's own meal.

2nd January

FELT A BIT DISAPPOINTED yesterday, for he did not speak to me, actually ignored me completely. He went out with his wife and L. for a walk and returned with a rikshaw. I sat alone in the garden; they all went inside. After a while I approached the door of his room asking if I could come inside; it begins to be rather cold in the evenings; the air felt damp. He did not answer.

He was lying on his tachat, his hands crossed under his head looking at the ceiling. I sat down. Then all his family came in and began a never-ending chatter, children making such a noise; it was very trying. This *baraonda* (pandemonium) went on and on; the wife began to massage his feet, then the young police officer took over. Poor L. was trying very hard to be in Dhyana. I got more and more restless. To make things even worse, the boys put the radio on. A female voice, harsh and vulgar, began to howl a song from a film. Then Bhai Sahib began to sing. It was too much for both of us. I saw L. crying, but she said nothing. The voice of a Saint and of a prostitute competing with each other! I got up, wanting to leave, but he said in general, not really talking to me directly, that *Prasad* will be distributed, so I understood that I had to stay. Sat down again. But the noise of the radio grew louder and louder, everybody talking their heads off, especially the wife and the police officer; they seemed to be discussing some local event which amused everybody. I got up and left abruptly—could not bear it a moment longer!

L. told me when she came, I was already in bed, that he was annoyed; I had behaved discourteously, so he said.

3rd January

HE IGNORES ME COMPLETELY. When I come in and salute him, there is no response, as if I did not exist. Well . . . here I am, I was prepared to be accepted as his disciple, hoped to get teaching, and he does not even notice me!

4th January

I MUST DO SOMETHING ABOUT IT . . . must speak to him. He must know that I returned to become his disciple. And he behaves in such an irritating way.

13

The Challenge

AND HE IS NOT WELL. Coughing much, and he is weak; one can see it very plainly. I had better tell him my intentions, as I should have done as soon as I returned. Better to tell him exactly what I want; that is: to get some tuition and to be accepted by him. I arrive here with a notebook, prepared to take notes, but he speaks mostly Hindi, so it is not much use.

About midday, L. left with his grandchild to buy him a toy. He got up at once in order to go inside. Just managed to catch him: "Bhai Sahib, I would like to speak to you!"

He reluctantly sat down again. It was clear that he was irritated, though he tried to look polite. But I too was annoyed. I simply HAD to speak to him, so I really did not care. We were in the garden, he seated near the wall beside the door of the large room, I was opposite him on a chair. "Bhai Sahib," I began, "I came back to be at your orders and your command."

"Yes, yes," he interrupted me hurriedly, "I know, I know."

In this moment my heart stopped, my head began to spin, my breath came out in gasps; this time I was even more annoyed with myself, to be such a fool and behave like a stupid girl in his presence; also I saw that he wanted to go. Anger rose in me.

"You who are a maker of Saints, and know how to write on the back of human hearts, write on the back of my heart one letter—one letter only—that of Alif! Write it with living fire, to be consumed at your feet with eternal longing!"

I stopped. Looking at him, I thought it was a good speech. I quoted his own words, and I said my own bit; it should have made at least some impression on him.

"Yes, yes," he repeated impatiently. His face was expressionless, stony and cold.

I really got angry now. We were sitting outside, he in his old brown winter coat, his back to the wall. It was a cool day of hazy sunshine. I leaned forward. "I challenge you to produce love," I said, and I laughed. I must have sounded defiant, for I was angry.

He kept looking right ahead, his face had no expression. And then, with a voice which seemed not to be his own, but sounded as if coming from very far—from across eternities, flashed suddenly through my mind—he said: **"Many people have challenged me, about many things, many people. . . ."**

"And so? Do you accept the challenge?" I insisted, I was still laughing. I saw him stiffen. He looked suddenly as old as humanity, as ancient as the hills, when with this very empty faraway look of his, the face hollow as if desiccated with age, very slowly, very softly, with a small thin voice he said in a kind of sing-song: **"I accept the challenge. . . ."**

"Khanna!" (food) called out his wife, appearing at the door. He got up. **"You can go; I am going to have my lunch."** His voice was his usual; he went in and closed the door behind him. He had tears in his eyes.

I sat alone for a while and felt the cool wind on my cheeks. Fresh January day in the plains, I thought mechanically. Had a poignant feeling of great meaning. Felt uneasy for some reason. Something was set in motion. Could it be a milestone, a turning point? Then I, too, got up and went home to cook myself something to eat.

In the afternoon, L. and I were sitting inside the room. He came in rapidly; his face was wet; he had a towel on his shoulder. His wife came in too.

"Mrs. Guru," I began; I wanted to tell her something, and he usually translates it to her. He was proceeding to hang his dhotie on the hanger near the door when he turned round sharply: **"It is most improper and disrespectful to call my wife Mrs. Guru, most improper! What will the people think if you happen to call her so in public? They will say: you do not know how to behave properly!"**

I was dumbfounded, and said that I had no intention to be disrespectful; I simply did not know her name, so how shall I call her, what is her name?

"It will be even more improper to call her by her name," he said sternly, standing in front of me. **"Guru Mata, you have to call her; this is due to her! And it means the same as Mrs. Guru,"** he added, turning away.

I said it was perfectly O.K. with me and did not mind how to call her. I understood that I obviously had done something very wrong according to the Indian code of behavior. Why the same expression should be right in Hindi, but wrong in English, was a mystery to me; still, I will do as he says.

5th January, 1962

"WHAT DO YOU KNOW about the Sufi Tradition?" he asked in the afternoon. In the morning he did not speak to us at all, only in Hindi; many people were present, mostly from the province. My small notebook was hidden in my handbag just in case.

"Not much," I answered. "Only what I have read in a few books when in Adyar. And as far as I understood, in the Sufi literature, surrender, as he used to emphasize, is not the end: a complete self-annihilation in the Master is required. The Master will ascertain by means of his powers if the Union is complete, and then will pass the disciple to his Master who is not in the physical body anymore. At the beginning the disciple cannot communicate with the Master's Master directly without the help of his first Master, but later he will learn how to do it by himself, and at the last stage the pupil is passed on to the Prophet, not as Mohammed, as man, but as God, the Supreme Essence."

He listened attentively, nodding his assent from time to time and murmuring: "Yes, yes, correct."

"But this is such a tremendous Goal, it will require a supreme effort of the whole being—how can you say that it is effortless? How can such a thing be effortless when it is beyond even any possibility of imagination?"

"You will see later, how effortless it is," he said softly; his face had the infinite compassion, and I felt disturbed, for I instinctively knew that it was I who was the object of his compassion.

"You were explaining to me your idea of merging into the Master," he said later, sitting himself beside me on the tachat. I said that I did not know if this was the merging, only the Sufi book speaks of the complete annihilation into the Teacher.

"Yes, I know," he continued, "that is difficult; it takes time, and for that purpose you must completely change your attitude. Your attitude is wrong! Completely wrong! I never criticized my superiors!"

"What is meant exactly by attitude? The right attitude of the mind?" I ventured, hoping to get some clear definition.

"No, of the heart. The right attitude of the heart! Mind is nothing!"

"Then help me. Give me longing, intense longing, and sorrow, and fear, and love. The other name for longing is Love," I said.

"Yes," he said slowly, "yes, Love and Longing are one and the same thing; they are synonymous." He kept nodding with a vacant faraway look, as if seeing something very far in the distant future.

Somebody came in, and he began to talk in Hindi. I sat there puzzled. He turned to me: **"You will know later what I mean."**

All the while sitting near L., I kept thinking what he exactly meant by the wrong attitude. Suddenly, I understood. It was like a flash.

"Yes?" he inquired, turning towards me as if I had said something.

"I have got it!" I said.

"And what have you understood?"

"What I seem to have understood is that, if I want the whole thing, I must behave accordingly. To follow the tradition the pupil has to obey implicitly." I smiled at him.

"Yes, this is good enough; it is the beginning," he smiled back. He sent me away earlier than L. When I was leaving, I saw this beautiful smile I loved so much and had missed all those days. . . .

6th January

DID NOT SLEEP LAST NIGHT, was thinking and thinking. I must change radically.

"Please don't think that I am displeased with you, if I speak to you like this; if I am really displeased, you can sit here for years and you will get nothing."

I got nothing in those last few days, and my heart was so full of longing, so full of desire to go on. I really must try to swallow everything, must change completely. This morning I decided to behave as everybody else. I got up when he came in and will do that from now on. I saw that his best disciples do it. It seemed to me that he gave me an ironic smile, but perhaps I was mistaken?

In the evening after talking all the time in Hindi, he suddenly turned to me: **"Mrs. Tweedie, how are you?"**

"Thank you, I am well."

"Did you sleep well?" he inquired.

I said that I did not sleep since midnight at all.

"And why?" he wanted to know.

"Thinking," I said.

"Thinking what?"

Told him that I was reflecting on his words about me changing my attitude. He kept nodding. **"Yes,"** he said slowly, **"Plenty to think about, isn't it?"** He did not speak to me anymore, but when I was leaving there was again this lovely smile like a warm greeting on my way home.

7th January

MR. CHOWDREY and another disciple were already in the room when I came in. They usually are both in Dhyana. I sit quietly in my corner and begin to wait, listening to hear his step. He sweeps in quickly, blanket under his arm, mala wrapped around his wrist. Tremendous drive and dynamism are like a secret spring hidden somewhere in the recesses of his being. He looks so young. With elastic steps he crosses the room and sits himself on the low tachat. After that he usually does his mala, or chants Persian songs, or sometimes verses from the *Ramayana*. Or just chats with Chowdrey and the other fellow. To me he does not speak. But it is like a secret bond, a feeling of unity, a kind of complicity—of something that only he and I know—like a tuning of the whole of my being into him. Nothing is said. A smile and a nod when I leave. That's all.

He told us that he is leaving for Lucknow. Before he left in the afternoon, he told us to come as usual, every day, the same as when he is here.

"If you come only when I am here, it means that you are selfish, wanting to get something. Service is attitude of the heart."

I told him that it will be difficult to sit here without him, because of the boys throwing stones at us. He will tell his wife, he said. Will he not disturb his wife with such trivial matters? I said, hoping to get out of the unpleasant duty to sit here alone.

"My wife will not mind," he said, **"we like guests. Guests for us are sacred. We always have guests having food with us permanently, five, six, people, every day. No, you are welcome, why should my wife mind? Our culture is different; we are never disturbed."**

So, I came and sat there amongst fighting, dirty kids.

8th January

HIS BROTHER WAS SITTING with us in the morning in deep Dhyana. Suddenly I noticed that my heartbeat changed. It was quite noticeable and quite sudden. It went powerfully, very rapidly, like a big powerful pump, on and on, and I listened to it thoughtfully. It was an ordeal to sit in the garden exposed to the curiosity of the urchins playing around my chair, and smelling most dreadfully. Had to complain to his brother, but could not complain constantly. As soon as he had left, they did it all over again.

9th January

IN THE LATE AFTERNOON he is supposed to come back. L. came to sit with me for one hour in the morning.

10th January

TRIED TO TUNE INTO his thought-process. One simple thought is not too difficult to catch, but the complete thought-process is very difficult. It seems to me that even if he thinks about ordinary everyday things, he is on a much higher level. But today I tuned into him for a fraction of a second in longing. There is this longing in me for the last few days. It goes with the more rapid heartbeat. Powerful and strong like a pull, and sometimes it is as if the whole body is being drained away, flowing away in the intense longing, leaving a kind of languor behind. I just sat there as usual, praying to Him to give me more of it, of this longing, for I can stand a lot more. More longing, more fear, strong and endless, and it should be like a liquid fire in my veins instead of blood. It was then that, for one split-second, I reached him in longing somewhere. He was in deep Samadhi, and I was with him in an infinite bliss, infinite pain of non-ending longing. . . .

11th January

"CAN YOU MAKE THIS LONGING STRONGER?," I asked, bending forward. He shook his head.

"No, this is not my method of training. I do it by and by . . . gradually. An exception was made for my elder brother by my Rev. Guru Maharaj. I do it differently. One cannot give food intended for six months at one go. Little by little. . . ." Later he said: "Never worry; leave the worry to me," he laughed kindly. "Bodies are different . . . need different kinds of nourishment. Some need laughter; then they shall go where there is laughter. Some need solitude. . . ." I knew that he meant L. and me. She needs laughter and reproached me because according to her I have no sense of humor. I know I need solitude.

12th January

DAY AFTER DAY to sit in these squalid surroundings amongst the screaming, noisy horde of dirtiest children, all running about the place, roaming freely everywhere . . . at times beyond endurance. Twice I cried in sheer despair. But the most frustrating fact is that I do not get even one question answered. As soon as I ask a question, everybody present begins to discuss it, expressing their opinions in which I am not in the least interested, for I wanted HIS answer. He will sit there, listening to everybody, smiling politely, until in sheer despair I will say that it was after all I who had asked the question and wanted his answer, and as I do not get it except as a lot of useless arguing from everybody else, I won't say anything anymore. And he just turns to me and smiles at me in the most maddening way.

Since 3 a.m. I could not sleep but my tummy did not trouble me as it did of late. The bathroom is far away across the courtyard and it is difficult to go there in the middle of the night. By the time I dress and reach there and come back I am so completely awake that I cannot fall asleep anymore. I mentioned it to him in conversation. By the way, I noticed that as soon as I mention a trouble, or a minor difficulty to him, behold, the difficulty is no more! Of such instances I had quite a few already. Sometimes I notice it only when it is gone already. Yes, it is of no use to be resentful and fight against the circumstances and create a barrier; I will not change India, nor the people, nor his environment. It is much better to make up my mind to bear them patiently. So much more, because I had ample proof that in no matter what beautiful surroundings I am, I don't see them; I long to be in his presence, I saw it happen in Adyar.

"Criticize yourself, criticize yourself constantly, and you will get somewhere."

13th January

WHEN I WAS COMING in the morning, I saw the kids again easing themselves on the pavement just in front of the gate. They all had a green diarrhea . . . must be a kind of disease, perhaps contagious. I knew that I had to tell him one day or another, and not only for my sake. I decided that it had to be done . . . it represents a danger for everyone, but I did not think that the opportunity will present itself so soon. He swept in, with his light step, blanket under his arm. He was smartly dressed because his daughter, who lived somewhere in the North, was expected sometime about mid-morning. He chatted with his disciples, and seemed to sparkle.

Seen from where I was sitting, his Indian style hat (*topi*), looked like a cardinal's hat. I saw his profile, his beard, the lively expression when speaking and laughing, and for the first time I noticed a special light around him. A kind of luminosity. I kept staring at it. Durghesh, his daughter, arrived with some members of his family who went to meet her at the station and they all went inside. L. and I, we were sitting outside when he came out and sat down with us in the sun.

"Bhai Sahib," I began in a low voice.

"Yes," he said and from his expression I knew that he was aware that I was about to tell him something disagreeable. Told him then that all the children ease themselves right in front of the gate, every morning; I see them when I arrive. The garden smells like a latrine and it is difficult to avoid the excrements when trying to enter the gate. One has to be careful to step over them. L. said that it was very true and most disgusting. He was surprised. I suggested that he should ask Poonam, his youngest daughter . . . and in this moment Poonam came out and when asked told him a long story in Hindi. He was very annoyed and said that he will see that it should not happen again; he has three outside toilets (the toilets inside the courtyard are for the use of his family only), and he called the kids and began to tell them off. His wife came out and there was a lively discussion in Hindi. A sweeper-woman came in, whose child had just died; she was weeping and the Guru was talking to her exclaiming every moment: "Hari Ram!" In between I tried to tell him that we did not see such conditions in our country . . . human beings living like animals, most undignified and a distressing spectacle. Such conditions I have only seen in Old Delhi where Pakistan refugees live and it seems the same here in his front garden! And I have to sit here . . . it is like sitting in a toilet; children urinate even near the chairs where we sit. L. is also here, but her case is different—she is half-conscious most of the time, but I have to sit here in full consciousness, have to endure it. It is a psychological torture.

"Yes, yes," he was speaking quickly, as if impatient. "You told Pushpa, all those were my children, and you have committed a great blunder!"

I said, "Yes, I confess, I did, quite at the beginning."

"Every fool can tell you that all of them cannot be my children," he said angrily.

"But if they all play together how was I to know who is and who is not! It is a known fact that Hindus have very numerous families; at first I thought they were all yours; later I knew they were not and I told Pushpa that they belong to some dirty people who live in your courtyard!"

I could see that he was irritated, but I continued to speak as quickly as possible to be able to tell him all I wanted before some interruption came, and L. helped me by telling that people from Europe would judge wrongly . . . we do not know the conditions in India. Bending down he swept his grandchild who was sitting on the floor into his arms and went outside the gate into the street. The sweeper-woman with a bucket of water got busy near the gate. After a while he came back. There was no frown on his brow . . . he was smiling kindly. I was glad that I told all I wanted to tell even at the cost of him being angry; perhaps it will be a help to others who come here and he will send these dreadful people away. But I doubted. . . . He sat with us for a long time, talked a lot and was very kind. The feeling of power was tremendous; I felt as tense as a string.

In the evening he was not well. We sat till 8:30, and when I went home was worried for him. From what he said, it seems that it was not his own fever, but somebody else's, he took upon himself. We want him well for the sake of all of us. Many people came, the stupid old swami also. He talked with them; I was glad just to sit there. At home had some food, went to bed and prayed for him . . . and praying fell asleep. Woke up several times in the night and everytime I opened my eyes I saw his face. A great vibration was in the whole of my body.

14th January

THIS MORNING he looked wonderfully well, the bluish light from the window on his bronze skin made his face look noble, even regal. I prayed for him.

Later, when we were all sitting outside, he told me not to go to bed immediately after a meal, but walk up and down in the room, or pray, or meditate for a while.

"As soon as you lie down, sleep comes; this is not good; try to meditate and fall asleep while meditating."

14

The Four Doors

MEDITATED LAST NIGHT as ordered. It went like fire, and never before could I pray as I did. Now, the prayer seems to come from the heart, without effort seemingly, and it is the pouring out of the Soul to God. . . .

Could not sleep well, was awake from 2 a.m. Each time I pray I see his face clearly before me, as if I am praying to him. Is it because my God has no attributes? Infinity of Life, the Eternal Immutable Law? Is it because he is the mediator between IT and me, that I see his face and seem to pray to him??

16th January

I AM REDUCED to the state that I see his mental picture everywhere. Not for one second am I alone. It is a strange feeling. A fire is burning somewhere deep inside the body, but cannot locate it. Even a feeling of heat is felt, and wherever I look I see him in everything, as if he were all-present and the whole world was him. Strange. . . .

This morning he did not come out at all. I was sitting alone and felt annoyed. When L. came, she went inside, and when she came out, she said that he will not come out at all, so we decided to go to Allan Forest.

Half an hour later we went by rikshaw. It was a lovely, sunny day. We had a pleasant, peaceful afternoon. L. was telling me about his Guru Maharaj whom she met one year before he died. He was very small, delicately built; he was over ninety and nearly blind.

"Old age for me could never represent beauty; we in the West are far too much conditioned by the Greek concept of beauty which is youth and vigor," she was saying. "And still I found him so beautiful. Could not speak to him for he did not know English; all I wanted was to become his disciple. But he said, pointing to Bhai Sahib who acted as interpreter: 'He is my boy, he will look after you!' I was not too happy, for I wanted him to be my Guru, but one year later he was dead."

18th January

HE CAME OUT as though lit with internal light this morning. I have never seen anything like it. He seemed to sparkle, though his health is not good; he is weak and does not eat for days. I just look and look . . . this light—from where is it coming? It seems to radiate from his skin and is all around him as well.

VISION: (this morning between sleep and waking) His face in blinding light; the beard standing out like living flames; the eyes unseeing, terrible, the eyes of deep Samadhi—and this face is smiling at me . . . like an irresistible call, this smile, and I throw myself into it, like a swallow when it is diving in flight. For a split-second there was a moment of the most perfect, most unbelievable bliss, hard to bear . . . as if the utmost bliss and the utmost pain were one, the very same thing, not to be separated, and clearly I knew that there is no difference between absolute happiness and absolute pain. It is only our reaction to it. My heart was still beating wildly when I became completely conscious and the vision was gone. When completely awake, I was full of amazement . . . wondering. Like a moth, I thought. Oh, like a moth to be dissolved in Light, to disappear forever! The bliss of non-being: is it THAT???

19th January

HE CAME OUT THIS MORNING all dressed in white and sat down. My mind became blank with the suddenness of a switch turned off. L. arrived and sat there quietly. Nobody spoke. His lips pressed tightly; he looked far away.

"**What happened last night?**" he asked suddenly, looking me straight in the eyes. He startled me.

"I don't remember," I stammered, "no memory at all; but please do tell me!" I said it timidly, for his face was so cold and severe. He shook his head.

"**Such things are not told, if you don't remember. But Manas helps sometimes,**" he added thoughtfully, and then closed his eyes.

And sometimes it doesn't, I thought. Felt completely dazed, could not keep my thoughts together—like frightened mice, they seemed to dash about. Manas. . . . How right he is: Manas is nothing! For there IS something else; so tremendous, so wonderful, and Manas is helpless—it knows nothing about it.

Then he proceeded to tell us how one merges into one's Teacher, when two Souls become one.

"When I was young with my first wife, I rarely had any intercourse with her. Every night I merged into my Revered Guru Maharaj. There can be no greater bliss imaginable than when two Souls are merging into one with love. Sometimes the body is also merged. How is it done? Well, the Soul pervades the body, you see, that's how it is done. The body partakes of it, is included in it by reflection, so to say. And no bliss in the world is greater than this: when you are One with your Teacher."

20th January

THERE IS THIS QUESTION OF SURRENDER. I wanted to know more about the merging; it was not at all clear to me. How can one achieve the physical surrender on higher planes of consciousness? He always said that physical surrender is essential as well. I cannot imagine how it can be done? How can one understand the possibility of reconciliation of the dense physical and of the atmic level?

"Please help me, I feel so confused," I pleaded. I was lost and discouraged, thinking and thinking, getting nowhere, trying to understand something which seemed completely beyond understanding.

He listened smilingly, lightly fingering his mala.

"I did not want to mention it to you before," he said quietly. "Some things one should not mention freely, until the time comes for it. As you have said yourself, the surrender of the body can be achieved much deeper, more intimately and more completely than in the sexual union. In sexual union there will be always two. How can there be oneness? But it is done and it can be done. I told you yesterday, the Atman, or the Soul pervades the body, is present in every cell, every atom of the body. So you see, spirit merges into spirit; there are not two bodies as on the physical level—but one. That's why it is so complete. Physically, naturally there will be always two in union; but not so in the spirit. There is nothing to understand really . . . so simple." He smiled.

"But how will the mind reconcile it? To understand it seems impossible!"

"Manas will be able to reconcile it, by and by. Let time come."

I had to be content with that. He looked so well today, no tiredness, his face shining with golden glow, dressed in white, the eyes full of light, difficult to look into, and difficult to bear his gaze.

People began to arrive. Plenty of people. Much talk and laughter, some were sitting as usual in deep Dhyana. He was full of fun and sparkle, laughing and joking. He had a great sense of humor; he could laugh at himself and at others, but in such a way that it never did hurt—he never hurt anybody's feelings.

It was a windy day. White clouds were chasing each other. He sat on his chair, legs drawn up, chin resting on his knees—the conversation was mostly in Hindi. Suddenly he turned to me:

"Supposing there are four doors leading into the Spiritual Life: one of gambling, one of drink, one of theft and one of sex. And supposing you are told that you have to pass through one of them in order to reach spirituality; what would you do?"

He looked at me with a radiant smile. I had to avert my eyes: he was surrounded by blinding light; even his white garment seemed to emanate light. My heart made a helpless jump against the ribs, then stopped. I caught my breath. The mind became completely empty . . . I looked at him helplessly.

"He did ask you a question about the doors, and you have not answered it!" said L. He looked at me expectantly; I felt all the eyes on me.

"I don't know the answer, my dear," I answered, trying to control my wild breathing.

He repeated it again: **"Well, what will you do, tell me, if it is only through these doors that you can reach your God."** He laughed now outright, looking straight at me.

It always creates a difficult situation—I cannot even think when he looks at me, and to speak, well, I am conscious that I make a muddle of it. This time the effort to be coherent seemed superhuman.

"Well," I hesitated, "I suppose that if I have to take the door of gambling I will have to gamble first, in order to pass through it; if it is the door of drink, I suppose I have to get drunk; if of theft, I have to steal something, and if . . ." and here I stopped. There were many people sitting, looking at me, mostly men, listening to every word.

"And if it is the door of sex?" he asked with a wicked little twinkle in his eyes and just a suggestion of a smile.

"Well, I suppose I will have to do it too," I said quickly. I was really perplexed, not knowing what he was driving at. He threw his head back and laughed heartily, greatly amused. I don't know why I had a sudden feeling of a foreboding. His laughter . . . why? . . . somehow it made me shiver.

Then he told us that we are all going to a concert tonight. **"Dress smartly,"** he addressed L. and me. **"So will I. We Sufis are lovers of beauty. Because we have renounced the world, it does not mean that** we should look miserable. But neither do we want to stand out and attract undue attention. We do not wear special robes, because that might create a barrier between other people and us. We behave like others and dress like others. We are ordinary people, living ordinary lives. We are smart with smart people, simple with simple ones, but we never give a bad example. We will always lead a life of the highest morality. We will always obey the law of the land in which we live; but in reality we are beyond the laws of men, for we obey only the Law of God. We surrendered somewhere; we are completely free!"

A rikshaw stopped at the gate. A young man, of the type one meets here often nowadays—cocky, satisfied, sure of himself, half-educated, vain—came in and sat near Guru. I cannot stand this type. Unfortunately, one meets far too many of this kind nowadays in modern India. Immediately, without losing a moment, he began to interrogate Guruji as to who we are, what we are doing, how long we will stay, etc. Then he turned to L. and began the same story. I got more and more irritated because he began a regular interrogation, about her degrees and qualifications. The cheek of it!—to her who has a Doctor's degree in Sanskrit from the Sorbonne University in Paris, has published books on this subject, of which, I was sure, this young cockerel had not the haziest idea! I could not restrain myself any longer and told him in a rather irritated way that, after all, we are much older than him, that it is most improper to ask about our affairs—it is not his business at all. If he comes here for the sake of spiritual life, why is this idle curiosity? Why does it matter to him anyhow? It is indiscrete and a sign of bad education! He was taken aback and began to apologize. Guru seemed distressed; L. said quickly that she did not mind at all to answer personal questions, and a tense situation ensued. She told me later that the Guru was upset because I was not polite to his guest.

I arrived back at 4 p.m. L. was there already, looking very smart. He was fingering his mala, with the horrible youngster sitting beside him talking non-stop.

I took time to dress before coming. For years already, I did not fuss so much about my outer appearance. It was as if I was young again once more, when to look one's best is of the utmost importance. The black velvet blouse with real guipure lace, the golden-green taffeta skirt, my best Italian sandals. Took time to groom and lacquer my hair, and put a drop of the last remainder of my French perfume. We went by rikshaws; I was sitting with his brother, he went with the youngster, L. was with his eldest son in the third.

The concert was lovely. L. sat next to him and I beside her. Never, oh never, have I enjoyed music so much in all my life! Lately, I seem to listen differently, with the heart and not with the mind at all. I BECOME the sound, the music itself. Was it because of the high musical standard, or was it me in my receptive mood; I don't know. A paroxysm of pure joy was ringing in my soul. Glorious. Endless. Ragas (musical scales) were sung by a young woman in a black sari studded with golden stars. Hers was the softest, the loveliest voice, full of devotion. Then came an exceptional Sarod player, who was a master of his instrument; the Sarod seemed to sing almost with a human voice. Sarod (wind instrument) is such a rich instrument, of infinite possibilities; and his technique was superb.

Lastly came a male singer, very good he was, lovely voice, but it was better not to look at him, only to listen. He showed off, grimaced, made faces as if he were struck by sudden idiocy; his mouth crept sideways, the eyes popping out. The concert was transmitted through the network of All India Radio. The invitation cards were collected at the door by a police officer in gala uniform. Bhai Sahib looked very smart—Indian style tight trousers, long raw silk jacket with a high collar buttoned right down. Next day Prof. Radesham kept teasing me because I looked so "devastating," according to him, in my cocktail outfit. We went home by car. Pushpa's father-in-law gave us a lift. Had a very light meal and, with my head still full of lovely Indian music, went to bed.

15

The Dweller on the Threshold

IT WAS THEN, AT THIS MOMENT, just when I stretched out comfortably pulling the blankets over me, that to my surprise I felt a vibration, a SOUND in the lower part of my abdomen. I sat up in surprise. No, I was not mistaken—it was a sound, and I listened to it . . . never felt anything like that before. It sounded like a soft hiss, and felt like a gentle tickling, as if of butterfly wings, a kind of flutter, or rather a spinning sound like a wheel. Very strange. A suspicion flashed through my mind that perhaps it was leading to some kind of trouble, but what? There was a deep, dark fear, but where? It was so foreign to my body, so unusual, so out of the blue. . . .

It did not take me long to discover. Without the slightest indication that it may be coming, I was flooded with a powerful sexual desire. It was just the desire, to no object in particular, just the desire, per se, uncontrollable, a kind of wild, cosmic force. I sat there helpless, shaking with fear. Good heavens, what is happening? Tried to listen, TO FEEL from where this vibration came—where was it exactly? Then I knew: it was at the base of the spine, just above the anus—I could feel it there distinctly. It must be the *Muladhara Chakra!* (psychic center at the base of the spine). I went ice-cold with terror. This was the *coup de grâce!*—I thought . . . he activated the *Muladhara Chakra* at the base of the spine; and he left the Kundalini there, to cook myself in my own juice. . . .

The most terrifying night of my life began. Never, not even in its young days, had this body known anything, even faintly comparable, or similar to this! This was not just desire—it was madness in its lowest, animal form, a paroxysm of sex-craving . . . a wild howling of everything female in me, for a male. The whole body was SEX ONLY, every cell, every particle was shouting for it, even the skin, the hands, the nails, every atom. I felt my hair standing up as if filled with electricity, waves of wild goose-flesh ran over my whole body, making all hair on the body stand stiff . . . and the sensation was painful.

But the inexplicable thing was that even the idea of any kind of intercourse was repulsive and did not even occur to me. The body was shaking. . . I was biting my pillow not to howl like a wild animal . . . I was beside myself—the craziest, the maddest thing one could imagine, so out of the blue, so sudden, so violent!

The body seemed to break under this force. All I could do was hold it stiff, still, and completely stretched out. I felt the overstretched muscles full of pain, as in a kind of cramp; I was rigid, could not move. The mind was absolutely void, emptied of its content; there was no imagery, only an uncontrollable fear—primitive, animal fear. And it went for hours. I was shaking like a leaf . . . a mute, helpless trembling jelly, carried away by forces completely beyond any human control. A fire was burning inside my bowels. The sensation of heat increased and decreased in waves. And I could do nothing . . . was in complete psychological turmoil.

I don't know how long it lasted, or whether I slept out of sheer exhaustion, or if I had fainted. The whole body was shaky and trembling in the morning. The cup of tea tasted bitter. Felt like vomiting.

21st January, 1962

WHEN AT HIS PLACE kept looking at him full of fear. I seemed to be all right now. The horrible vibration was gone. The body seemed normal, only very weak. The horrible youngster was sitting with him talking. He answered from time to time, but clearly he hardly listened—he was mostly in a deep state. I sat down and looked around; everything was as usual. If the body were not so weak and feeling as if wounded, it would be difficult, even impossible, to believe that the happenings in the night were real.

Who are you? I was thinking, looking at his still face, so serene, so far away, obviously not in this world. Who are you? Who can do such a thing with the body of another human being?

He did not seem to take any notice of me. But I observed that each time he answered, before drifting back into the deep state, he gave a look in my direction with a kind of cruel half-smile, his eyes unseeing; or seeing perhaps, looking at something beyond the physical world. Every time he did it, a swift, piercing pain was felt in the lower part of my abdomen, like a stab of a dagger at the base of the spine. The vibration began, at first very gently, then quite noticeable . . . no other sensation except a low humming noise. It was so mysterious, so terrifying. This will be the end of me, I thought. I am not young; this body will not bear it and will go to pieces. Even the strongest constitution will not be able to bear this sort of thing for any length of time.

Felt very tired. Tried to rest in the afternoon, but the body was as taut as a string, and something deep inside kept burning, burning, and I could even HEAR the soft, hissing sound . . . it was dreadful. . . .

In the evening he told us the story from the *Mahabharata*: when Draupadi was going to be burned alive together with her dead husband, as it was the custom in ancient India, Bhima killed all those who wanted to do it. Arjuna lived in disguise as a eunuch at the King's court. He was teaching the ladies to sing and to play flute. "Oh Arjuna," said Draupadi, "what are you doing here? Why are you in disguise, doing nothing? Look at your brother, at his deeds, he is so strong and powerful!" "Oh Draupadi," said Arjuna, "Yes, I am in disguise. But soon the time will come, is coming now, when you will not recognize me any longer, and you shall see how strong I am again!"

At first, neither L. nor myself understood the meaning, and he said that it was meant for me. I gathered that, but still could not get it. But looking in between his eyebrows, and quickly down again, as he told me to do when I want to know his thought, I got the meaning: it flashed into my mind: **"You see me like this, unwell, weak; I am in disguise. Soon you will see the real me; soon you will see my power!"** He only nodded, and L. agreed that this must be the right interpretation.

22nd January

THE NIGHT WAS EVEN WORSE than the first—if such a thing is possible at all. It was unbearable. Beyond myself with desire, half unconscious, I suddenly noticed in the dark room around me, some kind of whirling, dark, grey mist. Trying to focus on it, I detected strange shapes moving about, and soon I could distinguish most hideous things, or beings, leering, obscene, all coupled in sexual intercourse, elemental creatures, animal-like, performing wild sexual orgies. I was sure that I was going mad. Cold terror gripped me: hallucinations, madness—no hope for me, insanity—this was the end. Buried my face into the pillow not to see—oh, not to see—perhaps it will go, will vanish. But the aroused desire in my body forced me to look. They did horrible things. I did not even know, not in this life at least, that such disgusting practices are possible—with dogs, humans, men and women, horses, the most ghastly spiderlike creatures obscenely exposing their private parts, a grotesque ritual all moving around, all leering at me, dancing, grey shadows. . . . Things I never knew could be done, could exist—the most lecherous filth, I had to witness—I had learned this night. Never knew? If I did not know it, how COULD I see it? It must have been somewhere in my depths, or else how, how could I see it? It must have been *in* me. I was sure I was going mad. I never suspected that anything like this darkest vice could be experienced by a human mind, for it was NOT WITHIN human experience. Such helplessness, such black depression came over me; I was a prey to some terrible cosmic forces unknown to me.

After a completely sleepless night, the body shaky, I was so weak in the morning . . . and full of shame.

Went early to his place, and sat in the chair in the garden, thinking nothing, just being so weak that I could hardly lift my head. He came out unusually early, shortly after 9 a.m. Without looking at me, he sat down and began his prayers. All was still. It was a lovely sunny morning. The sounds seemed muted to my ears—the click of the beads sliding through his fingers, the traffic outside the gate, a sudden chattering of a chipmunk. My heart was beating like mad, my head was spinning. I got up, my legs trembling. I stepped forward, fell at his feet, clasping them with both hands and pressing my forehead into the dusty soil.

"Why? Why? What is happening to you?" As if he didn't know . . . could not help feeling bitter.

Got up, went back to my chair, and sat down with bent head. My heart felt like jumping out of my chest. He did not seem to understand . . . or DID NOT WANT to understand. It was a silent cry for help; for how COULD I tell him? Could not even look at him, could not speak to him. What could I have said? What can be said in such circumstances?

At his place I saw nothing, no shadowy shapes grinning devilishly in derision; but I knew as soon as I went home, in the night, it would be quite another matter. . . . Oh, God, help me! I just sat there, half dead.

L. came. She said that she felt happy and slept well.

"Ask Mrs. Tweedie if she is happy!" he laughed. It DID hurt.

"I cannot," answered L. "Mrs. Tweedie is up in the air and down in the depths; I cannot follow her!"

I shook my head: "It is finished; no more ups and downs for me. It is the end." I had tears in my eyes. Will the torture NEVER end? She looked at me in surprise, and while the Guru was talking to the young man who just came in, I told her briefly in French my distress. Her astonishment was great.

23rd January

ONCE MORE THE NIGHT was a perfect hell. The creatures were nearer now, all around my bed—so near, that I was forced at times to dive under the sheet in sheer terror. The room seemed to be full of them in constant movement, in absolute silence—not the slightest sound, just the ghostly dance of obscene shapes and activities. Was this what is called the "Dweller on the Threshold?" All those evils must have been in *me*! Merciful God, help me! There is no escape for me but the mental asylum in India. A padded cell! That will be the end of the story of my quest for spirituality! I came to the dead end of my "spiritual" aspiration!

Body was trembling, head was empty, felt like vomiting, went to his place late. He was not well this morning. It was obvious. He came out late and sat with us in the sun. It was chilly this morning. Looking so frail, his face was full of inner light. He is not very dark. North Indians are much fairer than the Southerners. And some are very fair-skinned, like Pushpa's husband, for instance, or her father-in-law.

He sat cross-legged in his chair, dressed in his dark-brown overcoat. After a while he sent L. away to get some biscuits, for he couldn't digest anything else for the moment. Took advantage of her absence, and thought that it was better to tell him—it cannot go on like this. Perhaps he will know how bad it is; he will help me. Only one man was sitting with us, but I knew that he did not understand English. I told him.

"Yes, yes," he kept repeating, as if full of uneasiness. **"Is it very bad?"**

"Terrible!" I said. "Unbearable!"

"It will be better," he said. **"Be patient."** That was all . . . and he went inside.

24th January

IT WAS BETTER. The night was not too bad. Each time I woke up, I was conscious of some vague presences, but was too tired to bother.

He came out looking still very weak, but said that he felt a bit better. He is coughing much, but he said that the vomiting had stopped, and he could eat a little.

I asked if it is fair to him that I should sit not further than five feet away from him with this *Shakti* (power) in my body; will it not disturb him?

"You are still not quite there if you think that you can disturb me." He shook his head in disapproval. **"To stay away will be worse; the imagination will work".**

I was glad. To stay away would be hell. I am terrified to be alone by myself.

"Tell me your dreams, but do not tell them to L. Otherwise the Path will be taken away from you."

25th January

"BEAR IT," he said. **"Control it; if you cannot, you have to confess it to me."** I felt like sinking into the earth, chair and all on which I was sitting.

DREAM: I was in a hospital. A nurse came into the waiting room and said: "Your heart has to be examined before you leave this place." I saw the heart-specialist passing by in the corridor together with Bhai Sahib in conversation. He was tall, good looking, a pointed, black beard, Muslim fashion, and was elegantly dressed in a well-cut European suit, but he clearly was not European; he looked an Easterner. He wore a knee-long doctor's white coat over his European suit, had a handsome, fair complexion; he could be from the Middle East. I was already undressed, and had only a short garment reaching down to the knees. He put the stethoscope to my heart. I hope that he will not notice that my heart is missing beats, I thought. Bhai Sahib stood on the far end of the room.

Later, I went into a room with a large window on the opposite wall, through which a section of blue sky was visible, and a garden full of trees. Many people sat on the floor; the room was full; all were facing the window with their backs to the door where I was standing. All were in deep meditation.

"Interpretation is not needed. The symbology is quite clear; your heart is being examined." His face was hard and expressionless. I did not dare to ask further. He looked thin. He is not well, I thought, looking at him with concern. Cough was bothering him. Soon he went into a deep state. My heart went out to him in deep pity. L. did not come. I left after a while.

26th January

"NOT EVERY SHISHYA comes here for the highest state. Not every Shishya is supposed to get to the highest state. Shishyas are selected. How many disciples had my father and my revered Guru Maharaj? Perhaps not hundreds, but many. And how many have been selected? Only two. The Shishya has to follow the Guru step by step. Go on pleasing the Guru, and he will see to the rest. It is called 'Guru Krepa,' the Grace of the Guru."

L. said that there is a beautiful passage in the book of *Abinavagupta*, which says: "The Shishya reaches the highest state using the mala of the Guru as his ladder."

This morning, when he came out, the first thing he said was that his daughter, Durghesh, was delivered of a little girl. **"She is so beautiful,"** he said with a radiantly happy smile.

We all congratulated him. He must have been in a very deep state last night; the atmosphere in the room was beyond words. I told him so, and he confirmed—yes, he was in a very deep state, and he did not sleep at all.

"And how are you? Any trouble?"

"Plenty! I try to cope with it. I think that I will not go mad after all."

"No, no danger of that," he said, and his face was very still. **"No, I am here."**

My heart went out to him. I was in good hands. There is no need to fear.

"Is there any fire without smoke?" he asked in the afternoon. He sat in the big chair, the light of the sunset from the open door on his face.

"No," I said.

"And what is smoke?"

"The impurities which are expelled because they cannot be consumed by the fire."

"Correct," he nodded briefly.

27th January

HE WAS LATE this morning. Many people were sitting already, and he did not speak to us. Later L. was asking questions about Kundalini. I was sitting in the sun far away from them, not wishing to be indiscrete. L., after all, is his disciple for so many years, perhaps they would like to talk about things not intended for beginners.

The nights are a constant nightmare. I dread to go home every evening . . . lying still for hours, trying to control this body of mine, shaken by forces almost too powerful to be controlled. Am shaky in the morning; my knees give way, can hardly walk; a strong feeling of vomiting. I eat very little and often wonder, how is it that all the other functions of the body go on seemingly normal. A wonderful resilience and strength has the human frame. But how long can it last? How long will the body hold out without getting ill?

He looked so tired this morning, and as weak as a kitten . . . looking far away, his face dark, as if full of pain. **"Yes, yes,"** he said distractedly, in answer to my thoughts. **"You can ask!"**

"Is there a difference between the Souls of men and women? It seems to me that, on the spiritual level, there can be no difference."

"Yes, a Soul is a Soul, Atman is Atman; only on the physical plane there is a difference." He fell silent. I too was silent. Felt very weak, could hardly think, and had a sickly fainting feeling in the pit of the stomach when he happened to look at me. I think it is caused by fear. . . .

Everybody present was in deep Dhyana. The Indian disciples were seated cross-legged on a few tachats, standing around, or on chairs. L.'s face was so very peaceful. He began to speak quietly:

"If guests come to you, you will entertain them, even lavishly, if you can afford it; but do you give your property to them? Certainly not. Your property is for your sons and heirs. A Guru can have many Shishyas. Not all of the Shishyas are expected to reach the high level. Human beings are at different stages of evolution. Not every Shishya comes here for the highest state. The Guru is duty-bound, he gives what is demanded, according to the need. The Guru always makes a selection."

I sat very still. My heart was melting in gratitude.

"Something was done to you which I usually don't do so easily." He fell silent for a while. **"But you came from so far away, so I did it. The relationship with a Master is once and forever, and there is no divorce."** He was silent once more. All was so still, so peaceful. Even the garden seemed to listen. Some leaves were stirring in the light breeze high up in the mango tree . . . the poignant feeling of meaning, of some lost, long forgotten bliss.

Two men came in, and he spoke to them in Hindi, and then began to sing in Persian. But he did not translate. I was reflecting on what he was just saying to me . . . a warm feeling of deep gratitude in my heart. I MUST bear everything. I MUST. Even if it should break me. He knows what he is doing. I must not fear, must hold out . . . not to be a disappointment to him.

30th January

COMPLETELY STIFF, lying there, pulling in the muscles of the lower abdomen as much as possible; only so does it bring some relief to the unbearable tension in the lower region of the body. So I lie for hours, controlling the body, trying to control the mind not to run away with imaginings. Burning currents of fire inside; cold shivers running outside, wave after wave, over legs, arms, abdomen, and the back, along the spine, making all the hair rise over the body. It is as if the whole frame is full of electricity. Gradually, all the muscles of the thighs and the tummy begin to ache with tension. But this pain, gradually increasing by prolonged effort, somehow helps to relieve the desire. The ghastly shapes are here, sometimes clearly visible, sometimes indistinct. Strangely, I am getting used to them. Usually, out of sheer exhaustion, I manage to fall into a heavy sleep, at least for some hours, waking up with a dry mouth and a head as heavy as lead. Strong coffee and aspirins help after a bath.

31st January

I WOKE UP about 2 p.m. with a mental picture receding into the background: a clear picture of him seated cross-legged, the white blanket which I gave him some months ago wrapped around him, the brown, woolen cap on his head. It covered half of his forehead . . . only the shining eyes were seen. He was smiling at me.

Woke up with this picture vividly in my mind, and as soon as my thoughts became clear, I realized with surprise that my body seemed to be singing . . . literally so. Singing softly and resting in Him, in deepest pool of peace. It seemed to me that I never felt such a tranquil bliss in all my life! Stretched out comfortably with a sigh of relief; no torture, no tension, just stillness, and a kind of SOUND in all the tissues, as if the whole frame of the body was vibrating in gladness, to its own inner music . . . every cell, every particle happy in its own right. All my being seemed to be streaming forth in steady flow, but softly, gently, full of unearthly peace. It lasted for quite a while. Tried to think, tried to analyze, to grasp what was happening. Was that the feeling of Perfect Love, of Surrender? I could not know. And it did not mattter. Not really. All that mattered was that the dreadful tension was gone. But can I be sure that it will not come back?

As soon as I came, he asked me how I was. I said that I was much, oh much better! The trouble seemed to have gone away. He gave me a quick look and continued to walk up and down, mala in his hand. He looked very ill. L. told me later that he did not eat at all for days, and suffers from much vomiting. His skin seemed grey, and he looked old and worn out.

I was thinking of the reception at Professor Radesham's home the other day. I was invited together with L., Pushpa and her family— only grandfather had not come. The guests were mostly high government officials, their wives, one M.P. and his wife, university professors, lecturers, etc. It was all very elegant, a lovely home, and the food was superb. I felt so out of place. Here was the world with which I was familiar, the environment I was used to, the world I knew . . . my world until now. What a difference between this world, which was mine not so long ago, and the world of the Master! Looking at them, I was thinking how similar they were to us Westerners in their mentality; only they were dressed differently, the food was different and, though they were Indians, Orientals, deep down their humanity, their mentality, was so similar to the one I knew in the West. But the Master's world, obscure, disturbing, was still unknown to me, a dark *terra incognita*, full of enigmas, a disquieting mystery, and God knows what secret suffering. This was my world from now on. I myself have chosen it. More than ever before, the life of the world, as I knew it, seemed empty, devoid of all meaning . . . an empty shell. And I understood why, once on the spiritual path, one can never go back: not because there are such secrets which cannot be revealed, but simply because there remains nothing to go back to. A sentence from the Mahatma Letters to Mr. Sinnett came into my mind: "If you want to come to us, you must leave your world and come into ours."

16

Curriculum Vitae of Sins

1st February, 1962

"YOU MUST WRITE DOWN all the wrongs and evil deeds you have committed since your childhood. It will serve as a confession, a kind of *curriculum vitae* of your sins. Otherwise you may be called by God one day to account for it; but when the culprit confesses, he becomes free. Everybody has to do it. L. had to do it also. You must do it if you want to be taken into the Arena. There is no other way. Confession must be; there must be no secrets before your Teacher."

I went cold. That was an unexpected blow. How can I remember all the wrongs of my life!? What a dreadful task! But I understood the value of it.

He was sitting on the tachat, knees drawn up to his chin, the woolen cap he wore in the night covering nearly the whole of his face. He looked so stern; his voice was tired. Went home and cried for a long time without being able to stop.

It is a kind of traumatic state: crying, and sometimes even without apparent reason, forgetting things, being assailed by dark, terrible fears—all not normal reactions, obviously—magnifying certain happenings which are of no importance, and neglecting important duties, on the other hand. It does not look good; let's hope it will end without a permanent damage to my mental state.

In the afternoon we went for a walk. At my remark that I can make a mistake once but not a second time, L. laughed and gave me quite a sermon implying that one never should say such a thing. "One has to attach oneself to something. Rather say and think: with His Will, I'll be able to do it. Like this, no pride will remain in whatever you do or achieve."

2nd February

WE HAD A LOVELY brisk walk in the park. Again he was saying that only the Will of the Beloved mattered. The lover is a dead thing in the hands of the Beloved. Told him that I was crying yesterday because of my shaky state. I am subjected to an unusual strain, and not only that, but I was thinking that he was displeased with me.

To please L., we went into the rose garden which was a sea of color and fragrance. She was telling us that next month she would be going to Kashmir to her Sanskrit Guru.

In the evening many people came, and L. and I sat in silence. An Urdu conversation was going on. After a while he asked me why I was thinking that he was displeased, for he was not. I tried to explain.

"I am really never displeased; the disciple gets a chance again and again, hundreds of times; a good Teacher is never displeased, never."

But I could not quite believe that and was very depressed.

3rd February

IN SPITE OF MY WORRIES I slept well. Am not bothered much lately. He took it away, in His Mercy, to give me a breathing space, I presume. L. was saying that *Bandhara* (the opening of the gates of grace) is approaching, and he will be transfigured . . . he will be full of light. I see much light around him anyhow, but I said nothing to her. Tonight when walking in the park, he told me that he wanted me to buy some electric bulbs which will be needed for the *Bandhara*. I felt annoyed. Told him that he has so many young men and boys sitting around and doing nothing, his sons for instance. I am an elderly woman; to be sent on errands like that is not right. Not only that, but he knows well that I am always cheated; I have to pay more everywhere, being European. My Kashmiri friends never allowed me to buy anything by myself, for they knew that I was always swindled. He said curtly that he will do it himself. I understood that I made a blunder once again. Remembered too late that one of the rules of discipleship is that one must never refuse anything to the Teacher. And it was such a small, futile thing; it was petty of me . . . his face was sad. We were walking along; L. was ahead of us. I felt bad. He asked for a thing of little importance; he was clearly testing me to see how I react.

There was such sweetness in my heart in the night. Every time I woke up, especially about 4 a.m., such a deep sweetness was in the whole of the body, a languor, like a pull on the whole of the nervous system, so unbelievably gentle, like a caress.

5th February

WENT BY BUS to the bank this morning. Was painfully aware of the unreality of everything around me. The traffic, the glaring light of the sun, the crowds, the rikshaws, the noise of the bazaars. My head felt empty as if after a long illness, weak and languid. When coming out of the bank after completing the formalities—I had some money transferred from England—the feeling of unreality in the crude glare outside the building was very intense. Decided to walk to the shopping center nearby. Felt sharp pangs of pain in the stomach region—in the pit of the stomach, to be precise—and was very giddy. Had the impression there was not much connection between the objects of the outside world and myself. Kept looking at the shopping to do, all necessary things, but did nothing, could not face the crowds and the bustle of the bazaars. All I could think of was a small mirror (I broke mine a few days ago), and this only because I happened to notice some at a stand, while waiting for the bus. The bus took such a long time to arrive. Had a panic all of a sudden, was sure that I wouldn't be able to face the crowd in the bus, so took a rikshaw. Arrived giddy and completely worn out at Bhai Sahib's place. Told L. how I felt. He seemed not to listen, a slightly ironic expression was in his eyes. Went home. The feeling of unreality was still with me, very strong. All a crazy dream—nothing is real, I thought. Crazy and senseless. Completely purposeless the whole life.

In the afternoon he gave us a long and interesting explanation on the relationship between the Teacher and the disciple.

"Love cannot be more or less for the Teacher. For him the very beginning and the end are the same; it is a closed circle. His love for the disciple does not go on increasing; for the disciple, of course, it is very different; he has to complete the whole circle." He designed with the mala an imaginary circle on his blanket. **"As the disciple progresses, he feels the Master nearer and nearer, as the time goes on. But the Master is not nearer; he was always near, only the disciple did not know it."**

L. said that her love remained the same from the beginning, but I said that love must grow, become deeper.

"Yes, it is according to the temperament and the character of the people concerned. The Master must be strict, he has to be hard, because he wants the disciple to reach the high state. Absolute faith and obedience are essential; without that progress is impossible."

He demonstrated to L. the exercise which he had to do when he was young, in which one remains for one hour and twenty minutes without breathing.

"But you cannot do it now," he said to us. **"I would have had to have you here with me before you were eighteen and before being married. This exercise is a quick way to take up all the sex power to Brahmarandhra (Crown Chakra), by singing certain sentences in a**

certain way. My revered Guru Maharaj knew so many things which I don't know. But on the other hand, I know so many things nobody knows nowadays.

"There are people who come to me for the last sixty years, and they know nothing. This man who was here a few days ago and whom you thought to be so nice," he said turning to me, "he has been coming here for the last thirty-five years. Once he asked me, why don't I teach him anything, or accept him as a disciple. Why should I? I select my disciples. Absolute faith and obedience are required before one is taken into the Arena. If you have no faith and absolute obedience, you will not progress, that's all. Law is Law. One cannot cheat God.

"When we have reached a certain degree of progress, we acquire certain capacities and powers. Some come to us naturally, as we progress, and some are offered to us. My revered Guru Maharaj offered to teach me a Mantra (a word of power) to heal the bite of all the poisonous snakes: I refused."

I looked at him in amazement: "But why, Bhai Sahib? It is such a service to humanity!"

"Yes, and because it is Service, when I have this Power, I have no right to refuse. Never. So I will have here a procession of people day and night and will have neither peace nor time to do my own work. This is not very high 'Siddhi' (spiritual power); many Fakirs can do it. We are trained to do more important work, which they cannot do. I would be wasting my time. We are free; if I particularly would have wished it, I would have done it, but we do not wish anything. We are not after powers. We have no desires. Our Will becomes One with the Will of GOD. We are Instruments in His Hands. We are called: Slaves of the One and Servants of People. God has also a title, a Name; it is His favorite Name which He likes very much: 'The Servant of Servants.'

"The Goal of every Path of Yoga is to lead a Guided Life—guided by that in us which is Eternal. To be able to listen to this guidance is the whole purpose of the Spiritual Training. That's why we insist on surrender, and on absolute obedience; and this is the meaning of the sentence of Christ: 'I and my Father are one,' and: 'Thy Will be done on earth as it is in Heaven.'"

He fell silent. A cool breeze sprang up, and brought with it a whiff of a delicate fragrance; the lime tree behind the corner of the house was flowering. I took a deep breath . . . it was heaven. He suddenly threw his head back and laughed his young slightly metallic laughter:

"If I smell the fragrance of a rose," he translated from the Persian, "I say, how sweetly fragrant art Thou my Lord. If I taste a sweet thing, I say, how sweet art Thou my Lord!" And turning to me: "Thank, thank, go on thanking Him always, for everything, for good things, for difficulties, for everything! That's how you will progress!

"Now I will tell you a story," he continued. "I was very young at that time when it happened, but already for several years under the guidance of my Rev. Guru Maharaj. Somebody in our family was not well, so my father decided to take us to Musoorie, over the hot season. Perhaps some of you know Musoorie, how it is situated: on a high plateau over 7000 feet. Where the buses arrive from the plain of Dehra Dun on a winding serpentine road flanking the steep hill, they stop on a large parking space at the beginning of a street with shops and bazaars. All around are more or less high hills. Now, I was walking in the street one day, when I noticed a Yogi seated in meditation on top of one of the hills. The next moment I saw the same man entering a shop. I looked up; the hill was empty. I was amazed. And while I was still thinking about it, I looked again, and here was the Yogi seated in meditation on the top of the hill as before. I told you, I was young, and curious to know more.

"So, I went up the hill, and it took me more than half an hour of hard climbing. Having arrived there, I saluted respectfully: 'Maharaj,' I said, 'I saw you in deep meditation on this spot, and the next moment you were entering a shop down below in the bazaar, and a few brief moments later you were up this hill again.' He laughed. 'You noticed that, did you? All right, my boy, because you noticed it, I will teach you how it is done! Do you want to learn?' I wanted very much. And so he taught me how to do it. He gave me a thing—it was not at all large—made of leather, and I had to keep it in my mouth. And wherever I wanted to be, in a moment I was there! I was delighted. But I did not tell anybody, for this was the promise I made to the Teacher.

"Soon we all returned home, back to the plains. Now, it happened that my father had to go with his disciples, to a gathering in a locality, about 100 miles away. He asked me if I wanted to come. Usually I did, but this time I found an excuse not to go. I was looking forward to surprise them all by being there before them. And when the train with my father and his followers pulled into the station, I was sitting on the platform drinking tea.

"My father did not say anything. After the gathering was over, he said: 'Come with me!' And we walked down to the river. My father turned to me and said: 'Give it to me!' I pretended not to understand and said: 'To give what?' He stretched out his hand: 'Give it to me!' he ordered. I meekly took it out of my mouth and gave it to him, and he threw it into the river. 'Are you not ashamed of yourself?' he said to me. 'Are you after Truth or after childish play? I never should see such things again!' And he never did, for I was much ashamed. I understood . . . and never again was I tempted."

6th February

I NOTICED THAT MY MIND is only working insofar as my spiritual duties are concerned. For instance: I can write my diary. I remember fairly well all that he tells us, but I cannot do more than that; the brain is not good anymore for anything else. What he said or did, every word, every gesture, I can remember, and even days afterwards I can write it down, but for everything else the memory is hopeless. And what's more, nothing seems to matter any longer. Neither reading nor letter writing, nothing at all. All I want is to sit at his place, and even the silly, irritating chit-chat of the crowd around him seems to matter less and less. Everything seems to fall away from me, as in a crazy dream when all the objects are crooked, vacillating and empty of content.

This morning there was such a charged atmosphere at his place. It was like being in a power-house. It was wonderful, exhilarating! He was walking up and down. Then the barber came to cut his hair. A large marquee was being erected in the middle of the garden; servants were carrying carpets, long poles, cushions, *dharries*. He was directing it all like a stage manager. Light bulbs were hung around on the branches of the trees and on the sides of the marquee. I soon left for *Kirtan*. Such a waste of time this *Kirtan*. Better to be at his place.

Slept well. Could not reach him. He must be in a high state now. **"The doors of the *Bandhara* are opened since last night,"** he said to L. this afternoon. I did not sleep at all the night before. But all was peace. Only could not reach him, for he was in a very deep Samadhi.

7th February

THIS MORNING THE WORKMEN came to change the marquee and erected a much larger one. There was a lot of dust activity. The Guru was going to and fro; I was sitting alone outside. Saw him speaking to the half-blind man. Suddenly he came to me and, pushing a medical certificate into my hand, told me to copy it with one carbon copy. I objected because I could not read the diagnosis and told him that it is not of much use to copy it if the most important part cannot be even read correctly; besides, it is a confidential document for the doctor, and not for the patient to have it copied.

"This man wants a copy," Bhai Sahib said sharply. **"If the man wants it, he has the right to it!"**

I felt irritated. And what about my rights? Every peasant has the precedence, everybody has "rights." I seem to have only duties and am asked such obviously useless things to do, wasting my time. The fellow wants two copies just for the satisfaction of having them! What for: Such a waste of time! Lately he made me copy a certificate with six copies! My small typewriter can take only two copies, so I had to type it three times. I am not a good typist at any time, but now with the mind not working properly, I constantly make mistakes and have to re-write again and again.

Bhai Sahib turned to the man, and I heard the man say he wants the copy for himself because he has to give the original to the doctor. Well . . . I was really angry. This is a test again. I have to be very careful. He will keep asking me to do silly, irrational things just to see how I react.

I was annoyed with myself and resolved to be more careful than usual, just now, during the *Bandhara*. He was sure to test me, as he warned L. and myself some days ago. There could be false accusations, or something of the sort, and it will be done publicly. God help me with my character! I must not be resentful. One cannot cheat God, so he said. Obedience is so difficult. All day long I was sitting there alone, nobody taking the slightest notice of me. L. did not come; it was too much dust for her, so she said.

8th February

IN THE NIGHT something did happen. I am sure. But what? It is so subtle, impossible to describe, because it is impossible to be grasped by the mind. It is as if I was resting somewhere, body and all, in such happiness, such bliss, such intimate nearness, but to what? Impossible to know and to describe. . . .

A while ago I noticed something, but did not write it down because I wanted to be quite sure that I was not mistaken: every morning, about half an hour before coming to his place, something happens to my mind. It feels like a tight iron-circle closing tighter and tighter around the head; I get giddy and a bit unsteady on my feet, the brain slows down considerably, and for a few moments I see his face clearly before me. My only desire is to go to his place as quickly as possible. Everything else is forgotten. More than ever the world around becomes an empty dream, a *Maya*—unreal, silly, devoid of meaning, and the heart feels wounded. I can actually HEAR the Heart Chakra spin round and round at a terrific speed; the physical heart responds by beating madly, missing out beats, and behaving as if trying to jump out of the thorax.

A thunderstorm came in the night. I woke up about midnight. It interrupted a dream of a luminous quality, but I remember nothing, except an unusually wonderful light.

Woke up so happy and arrived there at 7:30. Everybody was waiting for the Guru. Under the marquee were pools of water; one corner was torn off, so we had to sit in the courtyard, but it was a good thing, because the children were not allowed in, and we were only disturbed by an occasional crying of babies. Very many people were present. The large courtyard and the verandas around it were full of people seated all on the ground. I found a place and a small mat nearly opposite him, next to a wall which I could lean against. I wanted to see his face, wanted to miss nothing. The feeling of great Power was such that it took my breath away. This kind of force, or energy, was gradually increasing for the last two days. It was difficult to bear. But today it was even worse. I was breathing with difficulty and had the feeling as though at any moment my head would fly off. Was glad to sit down; could hardly walk or even stand as soon as I entered his premises.

He came out and sat cross-legged in the middle of the courtyard on a carpet prepared for him. He was dressed with care and looked very elegant in white, woolen garments. Already when he came in, he was in deep Samadhi, looking like a statue of Buddha. I mean the expression, for Buddha is always represented without a beard. Nobody got up when he entered; nearly everybody was in deep Dhyana. No one stirred. The stillness was such that even the noises from the street and the nearby bazaar were non-existent. The peace was difficult to bear . . . felt light in my head and as if my neck was getting like the neck of a giraffe, longer and longer, my head somewhere in heaven.

9th February

I DON'T REMEMBER MUCH of the *Bandhara*. Very many people were there. Everybody was fed in the courtyard and in the verandas, seated on the floor. Somebody said that there were hundreds of people. L. told me that 3000 meals were distributed in three days. Calculating three meals per day, that would make more than 300 persons.

When people speak to me I answer, but do not remember what I say. We all went with rikshaws to the *Samadhi* of his father and mother. It was crowded, noisy, with too many children all running about and being restless and disturbing everybody. But nobody checked them; they were ignored. He was transfigured in those days. A different person. I could not take my eyes away from his face. The light about him, the stillness and infinite peace expressed in his features, were indescribable. He had a look of Divinity about him, merged in deepest peace. The Power seemed less today than in the last two days.

11th February

ALL DAY there was much coming and going. Many disciples from the provinces are still here. He did not even look once in my direction. Left earlier in the evening. Was tired and depressed; only Hindi was spoken.

17

Circulation of Light

12th February, 1962

ARRIVED THERE about 9 a.m. Sat alone around the corner near the lime tree, so fragrant, on a heap of folded tents. L. soon called me inside where everybody was having tea. Guru appeared after a while. We all got up, and he gave me a friendly look and a faint smile.

Had a bad, bad night. The power inside my body did not abate all night, and I could not sleep. If only the tormenting shapes would go. But I noticed something completely new; at first, it was indistinct; I had to concentrate on it. Then it became clearer. At first I thought that my blood was getting luminous, and I saw its circulation throughout the body. But soon I became aware that it was not the blood; the light, the bluish-white light, was running along another system which could not have been blood vessels. For I could see the blood vessels too; they were pulsating with every beat of the heart, doing their work of supplying blood to the tissues. But they were not the carriers of light. This strange unearthly light, clearly seen in a semi-transparent body, used other channels. . . . But of course! I suddenly understood; it was running along the nerves!

The whole nervous system was clearly visible, and the light was circulating in it just as the blood does in the blood-vessels. Only, and here was the substantial difference, the circulation of the blood stops at the skin, but this light did not stop at the skin level; it penetrated through it, radiating out, not very far, say about nine inches (I couldn't be quite sure, for it kept fluctuating, increasing and diminishing with some kind of flares). As I say, it came out of the body and re-entered the body again at another place. Observing closely I could see clearly that there were points, as though agglomerations of light in many parts of the body, and light came out of one of them and re-entered through another one. As those points seemed to be countless, it looked like a luminous web encircling the body, inside and outside. It was very lovely. The Web of the Universe, I thought, and was fascinated by the unusual and the very beautiful sight.

Soon, however, I became aware of something rather alarming. Because I was so absorbed and enchanted, or perhaps the heat at the beginning was not great, I became increasingly aware that the body seemed to be on fire. This liquid light was cold, but in spite of it being cold by itself (and for some inexplicable reason I was sure that it was cold), it was burning me . . . as if currents of hot lava were flowing through every nerve, every fiber, hotter and hotter, more and more unbearable, more and more luminous, faster and faster . . . shimmering. Increasing and decreasing. Fluctuating, expanding and contracting, all the time. And I could do nothing but lie there, watching helplessly, as the intense suffering increased with every second. Burned alive, flashed through my mind. This must be the end. Surely this time I will die. It became more and more unbearable . . . the whole body on fire. Hot light circulating everywhere, leaving not one particle of my body alone, everywhere it went. And when I concentrated on some part of my body, I noticed that the light and the heat increased to an unbearable degree, concentrating where my thought was concentrating. How long this intense and at times unbearable suffering lasted, I don't know. It is a kind of in-between state when it happens—neither sleeping nor fully awake. The body behaves as if in a high fever, full of perspiration . . . burning . . . a terrible pain, a kind of muddled consciousness not aware of time. It was all gone in the morning, leaving a great tiredness behind, but nothing else.

He was sitting with us; a few of his men-disciples were still here; he was supervising the taking down of the large marquee and the sweeping of the courtyard. Filibert and a woman, both L.'s friends, were expected from France and were coming in a few days. He did not ask me anything.

We went for a walk tonight in the park, and it was quite an experience. As soon as he came out dressed for a walk, I suddenly choked and could not speak or swallow. Kept in step with him which was not easy, for he is so much taller, and his legs are longer than mine, but it gave me a curious sensation of rhythm and elation. Was trembling, for such a force was sweeping through me that it was very hard to bear. Felt breathless, as if a strong wind was blowing through my heart, the same sensation when a gale blows against one's face making the breathing difficult. L. teased me because I did not see the roses when we were walking amongst beds and beds of them all in full flower. But there were no roses for me this time. I was fully occupied with holding this experience as long as possible . . . the feeling of elation, of a glorious storm blowing through my innermost being. . . .

All the time during *Kirtan* I tried to keep it, but lost it later while chatting and laughing during the dinner at Pushpa's. The whole night I tried to recapture it in vain. The body was still: no currents, no shapes. When we sat down on a bench in the park, I asked him (I could hardly speak, so breathless was I), if there was a danger that the heart could stop completely, or even burst, for there were moments when it felt like that. He shook his head.

"No, nothing will happen to you. On our Line the heart becomes very strong."

Could not help wondering if he had meant the physical heart?

14th February

SAT IN THE GARDEN. L. was late. I feel rather sad, for I notice that I am not invited to go inside lately. Everybody else is asked in, or just goes in as soon as they arrive. I have to wait. I can sneak in, only if somebody else comes; otherwise I sit alone outside for hours on end. He was in high fever last night, and I had a very bad night of restlessness. The body behaved as if it had high fever, but fever I had none.

I gave him the paper. I was in agony for days to compile it and try to remember all my failing and mistakes since my youth, my childhood even. Once when very young I stole a fountain pen from a colleague. I think she got it for her birthday—it was a shiny one, looking like gold. My desk was next to hers. She was heartbroken about the loss of it, and I promptly lost it and was also heartbroken about it. Silly. But it was something I hated to remember and tried to forget. It was like a dark spot I had pushed away somewhere, and now had to put it on paper. Many, many things I had to dig out, write down, and I hated doing it. It was most humiliating. I had an awful struggle to drag old skeletons out of the dusty corners of my memory, to dig out things I thought forgotten, of which I was ashamed. Felt dirty and small, and very miserable. Written down on paper, it was a crude, revolting, squalid document.

L. warned me not to give it to him before the *Bandhara*, for he is very busy and is capable of forgetting it in his kurta pocket, and his children could get hold of it. A chilling thought . . . I saw his children reading letters from his disciples.

He took the folded sheet of paper. **"Hm . . . rather a lot,"** he remarked. I felt like shrinking into a speck of dust. There were several foolscap sheets. . . .

"Will you give it back to me after you have read it?" I asked. He shook his head. "You will not forget it in your pocket; your children can get hold of them," I ventured with sinking heart.

"This is an impertinent remark." His face was somber.

I was so crushed and in my anxiety did not know what to say. After a while he said not unkindly: **"I don't need to read it; I take it in my hand and the meaning comes to me word by word."**

"And then? Then you destroy it?" I asked hopefully . . . felt like a drowning man clasping at a straw. He shook his head again.

"No, that would not be enough; it is made to go."

"Made to go?" I echoed, absolutely at a loss as to its meaning.

"Yes, it is taken away; the sins once confessed are taken away."

I did not press further. I knew, of course, that if one knows how to manipulate the laws of nature, the paper can easily be made to disintegrate. No great power is even needed for that.

His face is grey, and he looks very weak. I cried silently, much worried; my heart was aching, seeing him like that. Nobody saw me cry.

15th February

FILIBERT CAME in the morning, a typical French businessman, rather large with a soft face. He meditated with L. for the last few years and had a regular correspondence with the Guru. He was full of the deepest respect. I saw him going into Dhyana almost immediately. He sat there perfectly still, his eyes closed, oblivious to everything, and I was thinking that I am here for such a long time and still I don't know what this famous Dhyana is supposed to be. God knows if I will get it and if at all. . . .

In the afternoon, L. and Filibert were late . . . naturally so, with Pushpa having a new guest, how could it be otherwise?

I was alone sitting in the garden for a long time. He came out only when they arrived. He looked very weak; I felt worried to see him like this. But he was telling us that the Saint is usually ill all the time—his Guru Maharaj also was.

"When I am ill, I am really more healthy, for I am spiritually very powerful. When the body is weak, the Soul is very strong." The story of Arjuna which he told us some time ago came into my mind. Later he said to me: **"You were here shortly after 4 p.m."** I nodded. I already knew that he always knows when I come. Several times in the past he would say to me: **"You came at such or such a time,"** or, **"I saw you sitting there under the mango tree,"** etc. And I knew that he was resting in the courtyard and could not have seen me coming in— at least not with his physical eyes.

He also said once that the Guru is supposed to know what the Shishyas are doing all the time, but if he sees them doing something wrong, one never says so to them. So, it means that he can have a look at us at any time wherever we are and whatever we are doing. And if he sees us doing something private, I hope he will look away. I spoke to L. one day about it. She shrugged: "What does it matter? We are all human; we all have to do certain things; he will not be interested in that." Since I know that, somehow I never feel alone, and try to behave in such a way that I could be seen at any time of the day without being ashamed of anything.

He dismissed us very soon, for he wanted to rest. He was telling us about the relationship of the lover and the beloved. At the beginning, when the heart is not used to real love, there are many troubles and sufferings. But as time goes on, the Shishya gets more and more tuned into the wishes of the Guru—the same suffering becomes bliss, the pairs of opposites meet.

"So it means," said Filibert, "that the time must come when the Shishya has such a faith in the Guru that if he says, 'throw yourself from the third floor,' the Shishya will obey and, when he does, nothing will happen to him."

16th February

DREAM: I was in the water; he was standing on the shore telling me to swim to the distant shore; huge waves, like a tide, were carrying me there effortlessly, but I was arguing that this huge tide will dash me to pieces against the sheer rocks of the shore. High mountains were rising right from the water edge, rock-like walls—no hope to get a foothold anywhere. And I was telling him that I had better swim to the other side, to the right, where there was a flat sand beach. But the waves did not go there so swiftly, and I woke up without having reached it.

I think I know the interpretation: I am still not quite there. I still don't obey without arguing . . . still haven't got enough faith to throw myself from the third floor. . . .

In the morning sitting alone in the garden trying to read the *Gita*, I was swept all of a sudden by a terrific force, so that I had to sit quite stiff, and breathe heavily to be able to bear it. And I HAD TWO HEARTS. I had already noticed that in the night the first time. A strange feeling, to have two hearts. One must be large, going strong and rhythmic, and one smaller, which was quieter, more like my own. It was the strangest Maya imaginable!

Later L. came with Filibert and a friend from France, Mme. Vinod, who is an archaeologist and is in India on an archaeological tour. We were sitting outside all around him, and he was telling us about the qualities and attributes of a *Sat Guru*.

A Guru is not a Guru if he has desires left. The real Guru can be recognized because he is without desires. The Shishya must still have desires, but not the Guru—he has none . . . the same with a Saint. But a Saint need not be a Guru; that is a Teacher. The Guru will not do anything to damage the Shishya's reputation; he will never give a bad example or take advantage of a situation.

Women can reach a very high state. The desire for Truth is important; it is the greatest qualification for the Path.

A *Sannyasi* can have only a few real disciples, but a Saint—if he is also a Teacher and lives in the world and has his sexual vitality well transmuted—can have thousands of disciples; it matters not how many. The Vital Energy in human beings is the most precious thing. It makes a Saint fly; it takes him directly to God. The Vital Energy must be transmuted, so that it will function from the navel upwards and not below. Only then are high states possible. To expand, to flow out without any destination, this is our Path. "Those who have attained Pure Existence (*Sat*) become One. . . . Pure Existence (*Sat*) is the Truth beyond life and death" (*Rig Veda*).

We must live within the very turmoil of life, but not be influenced by it. We must get rid of likes and dislikes. We must return to the very core of our primitive being in order to become whole. This will naturally produce conflicts, for we have to accept ourselves as we are and not as we THINK WE ARE. If you suffer from fear or some sadness, it means there are still attachments to get rid of.

Every Guru has only a very few "Seed-ideas" which represent the fundamental note or chord of his teaching. Only those ideas which he has absorbed lead him to Realization. He cannot give more. He will constantly manipulate those ideas which took him to the Truth, through his personal effort, and which represent a living Truth for him. Consequently, no Teacher ever conveys the whole amount of his teaching, only what he himself has assimilated. Besides, no teaching can be transmitted until the disciple has reached the stage of comprehension; one cannot teach a small child the principles of higher mathematics. We have to grow to the Truth, and only then is it communicable.

The task of the Guru is to help the disciple to grow. How is it done? One has to merge into the Teacher. Only then the little self will go. It is like a voluntary death in the Guru's Essence. It is called *Fana*. A complete surrender to the teacher is the first step leading to complete surrender to the Will of God. Only little by little can we get used to this idea. It must be absorbed, become part and parcel of the blood, just as food is absorbed into the body and becomes part of it. It must be integrated as a Wholeness into the mind. This is the Goal of the Spiritual Training.

He was also saying that one does not need to ask questions; those of immediate urgency will be answered automatically, almost immediately, and the others which are at the back of the mind will be answered by and by as time goes on.

Last night when I came home, I still had two hearts going strong. What a sensation! Quite extraordinary! Lightning flashed on the horizon; a storm was approaching. Thunder and lightning about 1 a.m. woke me up. Noticed that I had only my own heart beating softly. Fell asleep. Woke up about 3 a.m.—two hearts beating strongly and not quite in unison. It went on, and I was listening. What a thing! Incredible! Have not even the slightest clue nor an explanation for this strange phenomenon. Fell asleep. When I woke up in the morning, the two hearts were beating fast and furious, the whole body reverberating with their rhythm. Since then it goes on.

17th February

It WAS RAINING this morning. I went at 9 a.m. The room was open. I hesitated, but went inside because it was cold and draughty to sit in the doorway leading into the inner courtyard. Through the open door I saw him having his breakfast in the next room. I timidly asked if I could sit here in the meantime because it was too cold to sit outside. He grunted something into his beard, and I understood that I was not welcome. So I went out and sat in the doorway. It was raining steadily, and a cold wind was blowing in gusts. I was cold. My feet were wet. I hoped that he would soon call me inside. But he did not. Sat there for many hours, and I must confess that I was resentful. Everybody else was always allowed to go in. As soon as they arrived, they went in. Everybody else had the precedence . . . always the last and the least and the shabbiest dog—that's me—I thought bitterly. If I wanted something of importance, there was never time for me. As soon as I opened my mouth, a procession of people would start—crying babies to be blessed, servants, people in and out, children fighting, or howling, or quarrelling, and so it went on. I was always the last. Felt like crying; my feet became colder and colder. When L. and Filibert came, I stood up and also went inside. He sang us a Persian song and translated it.

"Though it is a birthright for every human being to know how to love, we don't know how to do it, because there is the personality, the little self, which does not want to go.

"Until it goes, real love is impossible. For Love is the negation of the self. The Guru is well aware of the difficulties of the Path, and in his feet I take refuge. I have to cross the river, and the night is dark and stormy. I can see people on both banks of the river; they seem safe enough. Only I, in the midst of the stream, am tossed about helplessly."

Then he sang another one: **"The lover must be like a dead body in the Hands of the Beloved. How is the dead body? Helpless it is. If it is put in the rain, it gets wet; it if is put in the sun, it gets hot. It cannot rebel, it cannot protest. And it is by the Grace of the Guru that we are learning how to be always contented in the Hands of the Beloved."**

Though he translated it to Filibert, I knew the song was meant for me. I wondered if he knew about the dream of swimming in the ocean I had yesterday?

It is all very well, but could not help feeling bitter. Filibert comes here and gets all the attention, and nobody comes to disturb him when he is in Dhyana and when he asks questions.

Oh, Guru Maharaj! Bitter is your way! Much pain will be in store for me!

18th February

WHEN I CAME IN THE AFTERNOON somebody told me that the door was open and I could go in. He was with an old Hindu woman who was telling him her troubles. He nodded when I came in; his face was stern. L. and Filibert came and Mrs. Vinod, the archaeologist.

I was very depressed. Began to cry silently. Nobody saw it, for no one took any notice of me; they were all busy talking. Only Satendra asked me if I was not well. I lied that I had a cold. Saw the Guru glancing several times in my direction, when I was not looking. Then he sang a Persian song which he translated:

"Give me the pain of Love, the Pain of Love for Thee!
  Not the joy of Love, just the Pain of Love,
  And I will pay the price, any price you ask!
  All myself I offer for it, and the price you will ask on top of it!
  Keep the joy for others, give me the Pain,
  And gladly I will pay for the Pain of Love!"

This was the song his father had composed, and he used to sing it often, he told us. Again I was sure that it was meant for me. *He thinks that I am crying because of pain of love . . . and I am just resentful,* I thought. And when at home, I cried my eyes out. Just cried and cried. It brought a kind of relief.

19th February

THIS MORNING he was giving Filibert a special sitting. L. told me quite simply to wait in the doorway. I would have preferred if he would have told it to me himself. I confess I cried bitterly. Honestly, this is the limit! Everybody has the precedence! Every Tom, Dick, and Harry! Special sitting indeed! I never got a special sitting, and never anybody was asked to leave the room because of me! Everybody can speak to him, ask the most irrelevant questions, even those who come in from the street! And he is polite and full of consideration for everybody, but at me he snaps at the least provocation! I am left sitting in the rain, and if I have a question to ask, even a vital, an important one, I am interrupted constantly. Those things do hurt! Oh, how they hurt, Bhai Sahib!

After a long while, he came out into the doorway, just when I was thinking of going home, for I was stiff with cold, my feet were like icicles! He was dressed in his white Sufi dress and looked pale and severe. He spoke quickly, as if in an embarrassed way, that Filibert is here only for a short time, so I have to excuse them; they must not be disturbed. *And what about me?* I nearly burst out—how can I disturb by just sitting there quietly! Are some secret things going on? But I said nothing. . . . Had a feeling of suffocation in the Throat Chakra as soon as he appeared, and could not utter a sound. The light around him was blinding. I became quite helpless. He only nodded and went inside. It began to rain. Went to the bazaar to do some shopping and then home to cook myself a meal. Was frozen with cold. It was so draughty sitting in the doorway. . . .

In the evening Mme. Vinod was there. He was singing a song of being drowned in the Ocean of Love.

**"If you are going to love, if you can love forgetting yourself,
Only then you are drowned in the Ocean of Love!"**

Everybody was in Dhyana. I just sat there feeling awful. Two hearts were beating in my breast. Was hot, was deeply disturbed—a storm was blowing through me.

Later I told him that if he persists telling people that it is an effortless way, he is deceiving them! Love is the most peaceless state imaginable; and it takes the greatest effort of the whole being to be able to bear it, to go on. . . .

He seemed sincerely astounded: **"Deceiving?"** he repeated, **"but I would never deceive anyone! I never would so such a thing! IT IS an effortless way!"**

"I will invest in a drum, and if you persist in saying that it is effortless, I am going to proclaim by the beat of the drum outside your gate to keep away from this place! For I know how effortless it is!!"

"It will look nice, you standing in the street with a drum," he remarked coolly.

Later in the afternoon he was telling us that according to the System one does not need even to be acquainted with the Teacher or Spiritual Guide personally. One does get the same amount of grace.

"Many of my disciples never have seen me in their lives, and they never come here. They are treated just the same and get the same as everybody else."

"In this case," I said, "I need not be here at all. I can go away; it will be the same!" He shook his head. **"If one attends the Satsang, one has the chance to become the Master, because the body is included."**

I asked how it is to be understood, but he said it is not to be explained.

"All I can say is that at the later stages the teaching must be communicated from heart to heart; the physical presence of the Teacher helps very much; if you need to be the Master of the System, the body is taken into it. What it means is that the body is getting used to the vibrations gradually; it is 'quickened' as well. But it cannot be done rapidly. It takes time. The physical frame of the individual is dense. But not everybody needs to be the Master of the System, so all get the same; bliss, peace, everything the same."

Here could be the explanation for the treatment he is subjecting you to, old girl, I thought. . . .

I sat there suffering intensely. And from time to time, when I didn't look directly at him, I noticed that he was watching me.

"If there is love, there is great uneasiness," he was saying to Filibert. **"The greater the love, the more the uneasiness. Love is not the same all the time. It cannot be. Love at times is intense suffering."**

20th February

WAS IT BECAUSE I COMPLAINED yesterday, or because he was watching me and saw my depression? At any rate, I have deep peace today. And how good it feels after so much turmoil and torment. Just peace. It is like a rest. For how long? God knows . . . I am bound to get the lot; I have no illusions about that.

In the morning I was telling Filibert that Bhai Sahib is going to be massaged. If he should send us away, he should try to stay behind and see how Panditji does it, massaging Guru's feet with deep respect. "Great fun," I said, "such things one cannot see but in India." Filibert smiled feebly and looked doubtful.

Later when at home, I realized that once more I have committed a gaff; to say such things from the tourist's point of view would be no harm, but is it very respectful to say it in Guru's presence? Well, I will never learn, so it seems. When he puts me into trouble, I am respectful, because under pressure; but as soon as the pressure is removed, again I am laughing at him—a hopeless attitude from the point of view of training. Perhaps I should speak to him about it and ask for some help to get rid of this mental attitude. We will see. . . .

This afternoon, we four—L., Filibert, Bhai Sahib and I—went for a walk. Filibert was talking to L., and I was walking beside Bhai Sahib, falling into his step. The feeling of elation it gives me is due perhaps to the rhythm; our auras get into the same swing and gives a sensation of unity. They were talking about merging, and he was telling us about a woman in France who wrote to him how she was merging in him.

"Of course, I knew that she was in great trouble, so I thought that it was my duty to help her," he was saying.

I listened with interest. Would it mean that the Master must do his part for the disciple to succeed? If I only knew what it all meant . . . heard so much about it, since I am here. How is it done? So I asked him.

"Why do you want to know? IT IS DONE, that's all."

"It cannot be explained!" exclaimed L.

"If one wants to, surely it can be explained," I said. "I never get a question answered—that's the plain truth!"

"Why do you want to know?" he spoke sharply. **"Why do you want to understand how it is done? Try to grasp it; try to do it!"**

I felt a mounting exasperation. "But how? Is it not natural for me to want to know? I hear so much about it since I am here! Don't we all want to try to understand? Is it not the purpose of us being here, the purpose of the whole life, especially Spiritual Life? How can one merge into someone else?" I felt completely non-plussed.

"But it really cannot be explained," said L. again. He kept an irritated silence.

"Never mind, Bhai Sahib," I said; I was irritated too. Good heavens! Everybody else is free to ask as much as they like, anything and at any time, and he ALWAYS answers, but I cannot ask the most simple question! True, it is probably NOT the most simple question, but perhaps the most esoteric part of the whole System. Still, he could at least make some effort to help me understand, at least partially. Filibert was L.'s disciple for several years already and had states of Dhyana before he came here. We walked in the rose garden around the rose beds. I kept step with him, felt partly elated, partly bitter—a strange mixture. . . .

When I parted from them near Pushpa's house to go to the *Kirtan*, he hardly answered my greeting, in an irritated way. I feel that he does not like me to go to the *Kirtan*. It is just a feeling, but I may be right.

During *Kirtan*, kept thinking that I am a fool to be irritated. I know well that he will treat me badly, that he will wipe the floor with me. So, just as well; I had better try to get used to it.

When at home, went to bed immediately. The idea came into my mind that I may get an answer in a dream, but I dismissed it as wishful thinking.

21st February

DREAM: (of which I remember only the middle portion) He came surrounded by many people and said to me: **"I am going to show you how it is done; you stand by,"** he turned to Panditji, who came at once to stand near me. **"Stand by and leave her there,"** he said, while walking away with all the crowd, talking to them. I felt faint, and just dropped on the carpet. But the interesting part was the feeling quality: I was lying there, but felt one with him as he was moving away in a crowd of people. One with him, secure, peaceful. There was no difference between him and me, in the most intimate, complete, final sense . . . I WAS HIM, and that was all there was to it. When I woke up, I thought with slight amusement that now I seem to understand that it is impossible to explain . . . it is a state of being and feeling—how can the mind comprehend it?

Then, just between the dream and waking, I saw him walking to his gate. I knew he was going next door because there was some trouble; he was small in stature, not taller than Babu Ram Prasad (who must be scarcely five feet tall), and he had a white night-garment on. I thought, how can he go out like this?—he is not dressed . . . and he looked very old.

I remembered that L. told me that his Rev. Guru Maharaj was small. Does it mean that he, in his turn, is merged in him? Did I see it symbolically in this vision?

Told him about the dream and the vision. He listened with the usual faraway look, nodding from time to time. I wanted to know if merging was like this. "Of course it was presented to my mind in a symbolic way," I added.

"Yeees," he said slowly, "yees." From this reaction I gathered that there must be more to it than that.

"Why do you want to know the meaning? You told me about them; I have heard them; it is enough." His face was devoid of all expression.

"And what is this *Maya* about two hearts, both beating in my breast? One big and strong, the other weaker and slightly slower? No answer?"

He only shook his head. He was so full of light, and very still.

"Oh you are unkind," I said, but my heart was full of peace. His lips were moving silently, the mala slid slowly, bead by bead, through his slender fingers.

In the afternoon he came out late. It was already dark. I was sitting around the corner near the lime tree where I was sheltered to some extent from cricket balls. A cricket match was going on in the middle of the garden; Babu, his son, was the umpire. It will be my destiny in the future to sit in the dusty garden, unnoticed, pushed about, neglected and alone . . . and I was told that the temperature can reach 120° in the shade. I will be assailed by flies and hell will be better, as Filibert put it. What a destiny! Effortless indeed!

Filibert and L. came about six and sat waiting with me. When he came out, he proceeded to tell us how his Rev. Guru Maharaj never spoke to him in thirty-six years. It was difficult to believe that it was exactly like this. But he said that it was to cure him from his hardness because, being Hindu, he did not like Muslims. I wondered if he intends to do that with me too, to cure me of my hardness?

"When one is a victim of Love, one is taken into the System sooner or later . . . as a mango fruit is plucked when it is ripe. In our hearts can be only room for One."

I kept reflecting why he was smiling when I told him that in my vision he looked so small and so very old. I will probably never know the answer.

In the night the body was shaken with the electric currents, but the state of bliss made me bear it easily. The body seemed to dissolve in an ocean of light, a kind of state of non-being. There was nothing else . . . light, deepest bliss and then . . . nothing!

22nd February

HE CAME OUT LATE. We were alone, for everybody else went to see Dr. Aslam, a famous herbalist, and L. wanted to introduce Filibert to him. I did not say anything and saluted him only when he came out and sat down again. Was hardly able to bear the tremendous influx of power blowing like a storm through my very being. Could hardly breathe; the two hearts were still here as of late, both of them beating together. Noticed that once or twice he looked at me and smiled into his beard, but averted his eyes when I happened to look in his direction.

23rd February

DREAM: While waking up remembered the tail-end of a dream: he was talking to me. I think I was already awake, and I actually heard his voice: **"There is a special *Satsang* to help change (get rid of) the Sheaths. One of the Sheaths is called *Anandamayakosha.*"**

Waking up completely, I thought it must be important. Wondered what the meaning of it could be. Did not want to forget it so I got up and wrote it down. When I looked at the clock, it was twenty past one. Reflected for a while upon the meaning of his words. Did he mean the Sheaths (*koshas*) which cover the Soul or Atman? And what exactly is *Anandamayakosha*? I remembered dimly that, somewhere in our literature, I read about the *koshas*, but I don't remember what exactly. It was so long ago. In the morning I told him that I would like to speak to him; I had a strange dream. He said, **"Yes, later."** We were sitting in the garden under the trees. It was a lovely, clear day, as it is so often at this time of the year. It is getting warmer now, each day a little more. Such clear, sparkling sunshine. L. asked a few questions about Kundalini. Then he began to tell us how the Shishyas are trained.

A Saint has no desires; he never indulges in anything because he becomes universal, belonging to the people. It is a law that what can be done by simple means should be so done; no spiritual power should be wasted. One must never waste spiritual Energy. No two Shishyas are treated alike; human beings are unique, and the Guru, if he is a Sat Guru and knows his job, will treat them according to their possibilities, their character, and past conditioning.

The teaching is given according to the time, the place, and the state of evolution of the Shishya. A Saint will never give a bad example, but is free; he obeys only the Law of the Spirit, not the Human Law; but he will always conform to the law of the land; he will never go against any religion, for all religions for him are alike—they are only different roads to the One Truth.

"For the Roads to God are as many as human beings, as many as the breaths of the children of men, says a Sufi poet."

L. and Filibert left. I reminded him of my dream. He listened, his eyes far away as if covered with a bluish mist.

"There are five Sheaths which cover the Atman:
The Sheath of the physical body: Annamayakosha,
The Sheath of Etheric Energy: Pranamayakosha,
The Sheath of the Mind: Manamayakosha,
The Sheath of Buddhi, or Knowledge: Gñanamayakosha,
The Sheath of the Soul, or Bliss: Anandamayakosha.

"All those Sheaths still belong to the Illusion (Maya) which covers the Atman. They have to be gotten rid of, ultimately, when one merges into the Reality. In other words you have to renounce even the fruits which you have attained in the state of Samadhi; nothing must remain, if you want the Truth; nothing but the Ultimate Truth."

I told him how wonderful it is to be given teachings in a dream.

"It is done so in our System," he said thoughtfully.

Told him that I will try to refrain from asking too many questions in spite of my impatient eagerness to understand, for I begin to see that he will give explanations when necessary.

"Yes, do not run after explanations; some things will be told in words; some have been told already; some are infused; no speech is necessary. They are reflected from heart to heart; your mind knows nothing of it; but it will come up when you will need it."

Went home like in a dream. The bliss was such that I did not dare to fall asleep for fear of losing it, but finally fell asleep . . . and in the morning it was gone. Only the two hearts were laboring together heavily.

18

A Blank Check

FILIBERT IN CONVERSATION told me that Guruji said to him that I was progressing. I felt gladness, for my heart was trembling constantly; I did not know where I was . . . though I wasn't sure why he told me. Was it out of pity? Perhaps he wanted to give me a ray of hope, a little consolation—and should I believe it? He sees me sitting here, and I am sure they discussed with L. my case. Perhaps L. knows about my training much more than I suspect; he may have told her, or her knowledge of the scriptures gives her the clue.

In the evening we were in the room; he sat cross-legged on the tachat. He was telling us that if the devil comes we should make him our friend. If he is our enemy, how will we be able to fight him? We will never be able to get rid of our vices. But if he is our friend, he is harmless. I did not understand. Neither did L. So he said:

"If the devil will come, what will he do to you? Devil is evil, and he will do evils with you. He can take the shape of anything—of a man, or of a child, or of an old man with a beard; he will be clean and pleasant to look at; he will be nice; he can take the shape of a dog, an elephant, a tiger, a lion—anything."

He asked L. in which shape she would prefer the devil, and she said in the shape of a camel. He laughed.

"Good memory: camel, animal of the desert," he said.

I still did not understand and said so.

"If you want to steal, why not steal? Learn to steal well, to deceive well."

"If you order me to do it, I will obey," I said.

"Why should I ask you to be a thief or a deceiver?" he asked. **"The devil is the *Manas* in you; why say: I will not do such or such a thing because I have a strong character. Why not say: I am nothing!"**

I still did not know what he meant and he said: **"It will be for the next time!"** and changed the subject.

26th February, 1962

"YOU CANNOT SAY to your Beloved: I love you, but only so much and not further. If you love, you have to give a blank check. Even

143

BEFORE you know that you will get anything . . . a blank check of
everything you possess, but above all of yourself, in utter, complete
surrender. . . ."

We were standing under the trees out of the earshot of L. and
Filibert who were sitting in deep conversation near the fence under
the mango tree at the other end of the garden. He was in his dark
brown overcoat—for it was a chilly afternoon—standing with his
feet slightly apart, hands crossed behind his back.

"Of course," he continued, speaking very slowly, narrowing his
eyes to a slit, as if looking into distances of which the mind knows
nothing. "Of course, there will be a blank check from the Master's
part also. It is like a bond, and it is NEVER broken, CAN NEVER BE
broken."

He fell silent. I never saw such an expression on his face; it was
new, a personification of destiny itself, if such a thing is possible. . . . Again, I had this feeling of being on a crossroad; was it a
milestone, a turning point? I just looked and looked . . . this
expression . . . so infinitely mysterious. It evoked an echo in me
somewhere, and I was profoundly disturbed. As if answering a dimly
formulated question in my mind, he said softly in a low voice:

"There is only one Teacher, only one Spiritual Guide in the
whole world, for each of us. For only he alone is allowed to subject a
free human being to sufferings and conditions—only he and
nobody else. And now," he said aloud, rather abruptly turning away,
"I have to speak to Filibert, for he will be leaving soon."

He went and sat down on a chair beside them. I stood alone under
the trees. His face . . . my heart was heavy with premonition. . . .

The sky in the direction he was looking a moment before was of an
unbelievable azure—pure, greeny, the color of Infinity, I thought
. . . a window into Eternity. Oh, this blue, so clear, so transparent.
And his face. . . . To fly into all this blue, to be free forever. But
deep in me was fear; deep in me were conflicting emotions, half-
formulated, just on the edge of my consciousness. Verily, I said to
myself: from life to life—it is once and forever, and there is no
divorce.

I actually did ask him to come with me under the trees away from
the others. I wanted to tell him my troubles, wanted to ask for help.
My nights are dreadful on and off; last night I was watching the flow
of fire in my body and the dreadful shapes whirling their obscene
dance in close embrace. Once more the fear of going insane was
haunting me. But clearly he does not want me to speak about my

troubles. I have to cope with them as well as I can. But can I? And for how long? The body is burning, the pain is intense, the tension unbearable. Where to get help? Nowhere, seemingly. . . .

They were discussing important matters now, to judge by the attention they both paid to the words of the Guru. What a life, I thought; felt so lonely, forlorn, frightened and full of some dark, dreadful forebodings. Went to the bungalow and sat on a chair with my back to the wall. Two hearts were beating, and the vibration I dreaded so much was hissing at the base of the spine. . . .

1st March

FILIBERT LEFT YESTERDAY. He was quite dazed and had tears in his eyes. He said that the Guru was wringing all his insides out, as he put it. I knew what he meant. The vibrations he experienced in his presence were beyond imagination. Well, I believe him; I also know something about it.

He was telling us how one must trust God and never think of tomorrow. We are not allowed to make plans for the future. If we make plans, it means we lack faith. We obey orders. We lead guided lives. And this is the meaning to live in the ETERNAL NOW. We do not think of yesterday; we do not think of tomorrow; we listen within and act accordingly. The result is that we can only live in the present.

"I do not save money for the future; with one hand I get, with the other I spend."

There are four kinds of people:

1. PAMER: he is like an animal; he wanders here and there and he gets.
2. VISHAR: beggar, debauchee; with great difficulty he gets.
3. GIAGGIASA: whenever he demands, he gets.
4. MOKT-PURUSH: remains sitting, not engaged anywhere; he gets from people serving him.

Only the love of the Guru and Shishya is not *Moha* (attachment): every other love is *Moha*. The Shishya can never know if he is progressing; only the Teacher knows.

6th March

TREMENDOUS VIBRATIONS in the whole of the body. Very little sleep in the night. Watching the currents of light. Can still manage to control the body; but only just.

He does not speak to me at all. Speaks only in Hindi with others. I come and go unnoticed. He ignores my greeting.

L. is back from Delhi where she went with Filibert. He snubbed me because I plucked a small wildflower to show its beauty to L. Later he was kind again, talked to us, and explained that the group-soul theory is false. **"Animals can never become men, nor can the Devas. But it is true that the Soul passes through the Devic plane before it manifests on the physical.**

"There is nothing but ONE BEING experiencing through every-thing created. His Light is in everything. Why should animals become men? Has this tree an Atman? Surely not. But man has an Atman. Man is the King of Creation. But His light is not only in men but in every atom of His Universe."

We went for a walk in the evening, not in the park this time, but much further, to the water reservoirs. It was a beautiful evening. . . a sunset of fire and crimson and the most luminous gold. I said how I loved the deep, red sky, the dramatic sunsets of India, the graceful silhouette of the temple, the palm trees against the glowing sky.

"How many things do you love?" he asked. We sat down for a short while on a bench near the edge of the reservoir, the colors of the sky reflected in the water.

"Oh, so many," I replied. "The song of the birds at dawn, the flowers, mountains and sky, India, England, the forests burning with the colors of autumn, and people and. . . !"

"Your heart is like a hotel," he interrupted darkly. **"One can love only One. You cannot love two masters; either you love the world, or you love its Creator."**

"Oh, Bhai Sahib," I sighed. I did not know what to say to that.

How the red roses glowed in this light, as if the glow came out from the petals in an aura of red light. How they glowed. . . and the water so still. A complete, perfect reflection of the happenings in the sky. Like a hotel . . . YOUR hotel, I thought. And it was all so lovely, even if he says that the only lovely thing in the world is the human being. Roses in the dusk in the large beds near the bench on which we were sitting were so fragrant, the red and orange ones still seemingly burning with inner light in the dying red of the sky. Hotel? You too belong to my hotel . . . and we went home.

When I mentioned in conversation that pride is considered to be a great impurity, he said: **"Yes, but also a great thing; it is like the two opposite ends of the same stick: the pride of the personality and the pride of the Atman. The Garment of God is Pride, says a Persian poet. Sometimes somebody would say to my Rev. Guru Maharaj: 'It cannot be done!' And he would say: 'Oh? It cannot be done? It can! I** will do it!' And it was done. He had the right to speak like that. He worked from the Atmic level. Certain people, when they have reached a high state, cannot be measured by our measure, nor can they be judged. They are beyond it. The pride of the personality and the pride of the Atman are the two ends of the same stick."

8th March

DREAM: I was in a large building with many stories which belonged to an institution . . . could be a convent or a hospital. An unknown woman was telling me (it clearly gave her pleasure to give me the bad news), "In one hour's time, at six o'clock, the police will call with a van and take you to prison." "But why?" I asked. "It is for theft— you have stolen something." "For how long?" I asked. "For three months," I was told.

I was full of fear and sorrow, thinking what Indian prisons are; the food will be impossible, and I will be ill when I come out. "Who did send me to prison?" I asked. "The best person here did it, " was the answer, and I knew it was my superior, who was a woman—she did it. So, I began to pack hurriedly; there was no time to lose. First I will pack, then I will phone Guru Maharaj; he knows the law; he will help me, I was thinking, packing the necessary things in a small suitcase for the prison; and the rest I will pack away. "You don't need the winter things, leave them here; it will be hot in those three months," the woman was saying. I did not answer, but continued to pack everything, for I was not coming back to this place. Books, big and small, in a lovely red leather binding, came into my hands. I will throw them away. A friend asked me to keep them for her but they are too heavy. I will lie to her; she will never know. Plates, cups, glasses—they all went, were too heavy, dresses too . . . even things which I needed and was sorry to get rid of; and bundles of greasy paper, full of clarified butter used for cooking, dahl, and stale food together in a heap, which grew bigger and bigger. My heart was so full of fear and deep sorrow, so much so that when I woke up finally, I was glad that it was only a dream. Interpretation? None.

"It has a meaning, of course, but it is not necessary to give it just now."

I left him early, first because I thought that L. might want to be alone with him for a while, and second, it seemed that he wanted me to think over all he said to us yesterday. It is beautiful and touching that, when he speaks of his Rev. Guru Maharaj, his voice changes, and the expression of his face becomes tender, full of deep love.

9th March

"FIRST ONE LEARNS how to catch the hint of the Guru, and afterwards, when one is well merged, the Divine Hint, which is faster than lightning. The Guru will hint first; if the Hint is not understood, then he orders. An order is easy to understand, but the Guru trains the disciple to catch the Divine Hint rather. The Guru can give orders again and again if the disciple does not understand; but God does not do it, and the Hint is lost, and one may wait for a long time to get it again. To grasp it, one must be deeply merged, so merged that one even looks for a place to stand upon, for there seems to be none. . . .

"To grasp a Hint is to act accordingly, and not even to try to understand it. Acting accordingly is necessary, rather than understanding. The Grace of God cannot be seized: it descends. The actions of the Guru are nothing in themselves; they are to be seen in connection with the disciple. They are only for the good of the disciple. First one is loved by the Guru; afterwards the disciple loves the Guru, but this situation is rare. It does not happen often. Usually it happens that the disciple loves the Guru first and is loved afterwards by him. One must not even think: 'I love you,' because the 'I' remains, but: 'I want you to love me'—he wants only the Master and not what the Master possesses. Here lies the difference between the Bhakta (devotee) and the disciple. The disciple is after knowledge, but if you ask the devotee what he wants, he will answer: nothing!

"To say: 'I love you' is easy, but to realize it is difficult. Here is hidden the mystery of the Realization of God or Truth. Because you have to realize one fact: 'You are in my heart; you are everything; I am nothing.' If you begin to realize that, then you really love and your own self diminishes; the external things begin to lose all importance. The self, and everything else, remains with the Beloved from then on, and the Beloved remains with you permanently when there is no self anymore.

"The Guru will never put conditions, but the Shishya does; it is in the nature of things; it cannot be helped. When the whole life of the disciple is always according to the ideas or wishes of the Master, the training is terminated."

In answer to L.'s question: "To give a child to a childless woman by using a certain Mantra? No, I do nothing without a Hint. If a Hint is given, I do it; otherwise—nothing!

"Saints are like rivers; they flow where they are directed. A river never flows uphill. Small rivers join the large one, and they all flow to the ocean. Let's flow; we do not need to carry the burden when we let it flow.

"If a Hint is there, I have to do it, and if I don't, I am MADE to do it. Divine Hint is an Order. Sometimes the saints have to do things the people will misjudge, and which from the worldly point of view could be condemned, because the world judges by appearances. One important quality required on the Path is never to judge by appearances. More often than not things look different from what they really are. There is no good or evil for the Creator. Only human society makes it so. A Saint is beyond good and evil, but Saints are people of the highest morality and will never give a bad example."

In answer to L.'s question: "A man who is impotent can never be a Saint or a Yogi. Women too can be impotent. The Creative Energy of God which manifests itself in its lowest aspect as procreative instinct is the most powerful thing in human beings, men and women alike."

L. said that according to some scriptures women reach the state of wholeness through the "innate capacity" which is inborn in their essence, but men must make voluntary sacrifice and undergo definite discipline. "It is correct. The training in both cases is different."

10th March

POSSIBLE RELATIONSHIP between Guru and Shishyas:

1. Lover and Beloved (lovers in short). This is mostly practiced in Tantra Yoga; in our System such a relationship would be considered an obstacle.
2. Father and child.
3. Master and the obedient disciple.
4. Friends.

The relationship of Lover and the Beloved must be a very difficult one, commented L., and she was telling me that she thought that my relationship with the Guru is of a Teacher and of an obedient disciple, and she added that her own relationship is that of a father and daughter. "I never need to get up when he enters; I never touched his feet; I am treated like his children!"

"Only his children do touch his feet," I thought. But this is probably of no importance, for he said once that he does not want his Western disciples to touch his feet, as Indians do. "Your culture is different," he said.

DZIKR is the Constant Presence, the Constant Remembering . . . and the next step, love and faith in the Master.

According to L.'s explanation, the Divine Hint is a subtle desire or a prompting; to put it differently: the Will of God which flashes into a still mind, a peaceful Soul. The Saint has no desires of his own, but the Will of God which he executes. It becomes a Hint when the human will is not quite merged, not completely at-one with the Divine Will; otherwise the Hint would not be needed; it would be just and only the Will of God. Where there is a Hint, there some duality still remains.

The night was fairly peaceful; the two hearts are still there. Since the 22nd of February the nightmare situation persists every night, sometimes more, sometimes less. To control the body becomes more and more difficult. God help me . . . how long will it last? Where is it going to lead?

VISION: between dream and waking: saw him standing tall, dressed in white. He had a long rod in his hand at the end of which was a sparkling star. It was like a magicians's wand; he lightly touched my chest with it, and suddenly a tiny thing, like a spark, began to scintillate with a living light in my chest. It was an ignited star, sending out flashes of light.

12th March

WENT TO THE BANK to withdraw all the money from my account—over 700 rupees; it should be enough for two ceiling fans. Went to see the fans, a very lovely table-fan for him and a ceiling fan for me. Bought carbon paper, typewriter ribbon, and a calendar he wanted me to get for him with a picture of two Bengal tigers. Then I asked if I could speak to him alone. He nodded. L. had to go to the tax office, so we remained alone. Told him that I took out all the money from my account, for I understood that he wants me to give it away. Showed him the catalogue and the price list of the fans. He said that he will consult his wife as to which one to choose. Does he want me to go away in summer as L. does? He said that if I want to stay, of course I can do so.

"I know other Europeans who do stay; I don't know how they do it, because it is difficult even for us, though we are born here. If you are courageous enough, then you can do it; you would come early in the morning, go home before 11 a.m., and come here in the evening."

I laughed and said that here is no question of courage: I have no choice. . . . Later I said that it is frightening that all my money should go; what will become of me?

"If you are afraid, keep it," he shrugged. **"I don't want it for myself, at any rate."**

I wondered what he meant, and if after all I need not give it away. But something told me that this is not so. It is all so frightening, and my mind is confused.

19

A Flaming Row

13th March, 1962

"IF THE SHISHYA cannot love by himself and love has to be produced, can it be taken away?"

"What is given can be taken away at any time. But the Teacher does not take it away. The love ceases by itself if one has not got faith in the Master, or obedience. But the Teacher who has planted the love in the heart of the disciple will look after it, as the gardener looks after a plant; he does not want it to die. The disciple must surrender completely; only then the Teacher will judge if he is ready for more."

15th March

FOR THE LAST TWO NIGHTS it was absolutely unbearable. The body is breaking down. This state goes on for already two months with short intervals of peace from time to time. Fell down twice this morning. Did not go to him. Must have had fever. Mind did not work. The "creatures" were with me all the time—could not hide from them anywhere. Physical condition is deteriorating. Feel so weak. Burning. The spectacle of the flow of light is fantastic . . . and frightening. An old woman at the mercy of some cosmic force. . . .

Went at 4 p.m. He was walking up and down in the garden as if waiting for me, his grandchild in his arms. Went directly to him as soon as I came in and began to tell him that I cannot go on anymore, that I am going mad, that it is he, with his powers, who brings it on, and I went on and on accusing him, attacking him, desperate with frustration and anger. As soon as I opened my mouth, the kid took a look at me and began to wriggle and to howl—he could hardly hold it. Here I was in hysterics, practically breaking down; the child banging his face with his little fists, howling in a mad fury. It was slipping from his arms—he could not hear what I was saying, trying to control the furious child. I was nearly shouting in a vain attempt to be heard, but realized that it was useless to try to compete with a child screaming literally into his ears. I slumped down in helpless sobbing. He firmly got hold of the violently struggling child, and with quick steps went inside and closed the door. I realized afterwards what a blessing it was that nobody was present. Such a scene . . . and how was it that the noise did not attract the mother of the boy to see what was happening? But I know already that, when he wanted, the conditions were always suited to his requirements.

I kept sobbing . . . could not stop for a long time. Then the servant came and looked at me with curiosity. Realized that soon people will come, and I had better control myself . . . but nobody came. Sat alone in the darkening garden. L. came late. He came out after a while. She was telling him about her departure in a few days time. Then he said:

"Women . . . they have no perseverance. That's why a woman is not suitable for spiritual life."

I was boiling with anger. Nobody, not even his strongest men-disciples, are subjected to what I am—I was sure of that. Nobody. Not one of his disciples was left without a penny as I knew I would be. No perseverance indeed. . . . "I am of the stuff of which Saints and Martyrs are made; and you, you know it! And after all that is happening, you have the courage to talk of the lack of perseverance!" I glared at him. L. asked me if I was well.

"She is confused; take no notice," he said to her.

Went home early and slept in perfect peace.

17th March

L. IS LEAVING TOMORROW. He kept being difficult, telling me off for one thing or another. He will ask something, pull to pieces my answer . . . could not do one thing right. At last could not bear it any longer, burst out crying, took my chair and went to sit under the mango tree, near the fence, far away from them. And there I cried—it must have been for more than one hour. He kept talking and laughing with L.; perhaps they were laughing about me; God knows. Did not care, not really. My heart was aching so much, I had enough; but apart from that, there was such a longing. Please, a little, just a little peace, and kindness and compassion. A little encouragement . . . a little warmth. Was so lonely. Truth, oh Truth, cried out my heart: Hurry up! Or I won't be alive! It hurts so much! He hardly speaks with me for days, and when he does, it is only to increase my confusion, to hurt, or to create a doubt, a mental torture. Yesterday he accused me of something I have not done; it was an insignificant thing, but it was very hurtful, and he was so angry, oh, it did hurt!

L. again warned me not to stay here for the hot season. I will not be able to bear it, and she wanted to know why I was crying so much. I asked her for the sake of our friendship to abstain from questioning me. I cannot say anything, and if she mentions it to him he will seize the opportunity to torture me; and at any rate he will know even if she says nothing. So I left, and when at home, cried and cried, and could not eat anything; had some black coffee and aspirin and cried myself into a kind of a strange sleep, heavy, as in a muddy, hot bath. The heat increasing day by day does not help the situation. Strong coffee is a great help lately. Prayed to his Rev. Guru Maharaj . . . and cried some more.

When I went there in the afternoon, while he was talking to others, I often caught his unsmiling look resting on me, a quick questioning look. He was chatting away with the men in Hindi. L. was moaning terribly, in deep Dhyana . . . a small, dreadful moan as if she were on the verge of dying. She is getting worse, I thought. Her feet are swollen lately; the heat does that to her, and she is puffy around her eyes. The temperature is beginning to be too much for her, and it is already very hot.

18th March

IT WAS A CLEAR, luminous Sunday. Many people came in the morning and in the evening. L. left. I was glad. She was constantly giving me advice without the slightest idea what it was all about. I knew she meant well. She kept nagging me about money and not to spend too much because she was sure that I misunderstood his hints. She was here most of the time and heard what he was saying to me. People who lived as he did are at a high state already. She was sure that he did not mean me to be without money, because I am bound to be in great trouble. I kept quiet. What does she know as to what it is exactly that he wants me to be—in trouble! and the more the better! By the time he finishes with me, only he and God will know what will become of me!

To be in the hands of a man who will do anything, absolutely, for the sake of training, is a chilling thought. . . .

The money from the sale of my house, everything that my husband had left me, my own savings—all will have to go. I am so sure of it, as I am sure that I am sitting here, at this moment. What astonishes me is that, deep down, it is not worrying me much more than it actually does. I am resigned, really. I want Truth so much, so terribly, I will give everything and anything for it. I am worried, yes, but in reality I should worry more. For I will have nothing left. And my pension is far too small to be able to live on it, and at my age it is not easy to get a job. My lack of concern is amazing. A most strange state of mind. Confusing.

In the evening it happened (as always when he wants to speak to me) that everybody had left soon, and we were alone. He began by saying softly, with great kindness, that he did not understand why I was so upset the day before.

"The whole day my heart was with you, I felt it so much."

I tried to tell him that I was upset because he deliberately seemed to misunderstand everything I had said and was accusing me and was angry. He ignored this remark. After a while he said:

"If you knew what I have in mind for you, for your future, you never would cry, never would be upset. About the end of April a flat will be available for you, a more suitable one. And do not tell people that I told you to remain here. They will not understand, for they all think that you Europeans cannot stand the heat."

19th March

HE BEGAN TO SPEAK about Bogroff who died seven years ago of a brain tumor, and who, he said, was the best of all the European disciples he had until now.

"Where is he now?" I asked.

"In heaven," he said. I retorted that it is not a very high state— *Swarga Loka.* He shook his head.

"He will not come back. He will go to other Lokas where there is no death and where one goes from Loka to Loka without birth or death. Without coming into the womb," he said with emphasis. It made me smile. What an Oriental way of expressing it! He kept smiling too, half hidden under a towel which he had on his head because a strong, hot wind was blowing up the dust from the dry soil in the garden. A few drops of rain fell, and the horizon was full of distant lightning. But it cleared soon, and the stars came out on a deep velvet sky.

There are three Lokas:
1. MIRT LOKA—the Loka of the physical plane where we are born and we die.
2. KAMA LOKA—the Loka of the Desire of the physical body, or even desire by itself.
3. SWARGA LOKA—heaven, the world of effects where the good deeds done in the physical body reap their rewards.

From these three Lokas one comes back into incarnation again.

When we are in the MIRT LOKA, if we are attached to the Spiritual
Guide, or Master, and if the Master is powerful from the spiritual
point of view, he will leave no desire with the disciple at the time of
death; the desire would lead to another incarnation. The Master
serves as a focus of attention for the mind, for the mind needs
something to hold on to.

The Love for the Master is also *Vasana* (subtle desires arising from
samskaras, seeds of *karma*, which are impressions of actions in *chitta*,
universal mind), but it is this *Vasana* which will lead one beyond the
Lokas of change. It will carry one right through. There are four other
Lokas in which there is neither birth nor death. According to desire
or necessity, one goes from one to another in a glorious body made
of light.

"Could you tell me the names of those four Lokas?" I asked. He
shrugged.

**"I could, I suppose. But what for? The names are not to be told
because, if the names are told, an explanation is needed. Then it will
be the same as when an experience is described in a book; if one
comes to know the same experience as described, the value of the
experience is partly lost, for the simple reason that one knows about
it. Knowledge without experience is a hindrance. Those Lokas have
to be experienced by the disciple, so for the moment I only say that
there are four other Lokas, seven in all."**

He reminded me that I had better bring the fan tomorrow, because
the nights are getting hot.

20th March

HE GAVE ME AN ORDER to give some money to a fellow sitting there,
telling me that he was in need. Brought the table fan. It is a lovely one
and works well. I wonder if he will use it. I am prepared to bet that it
will be given to Durghesh or go into his children's room. He never
keeps anything for himself.

Too much talk was going on. Everybody seemed to talk all at once.
He was doing his mala and did not listen. It is surprising how he never
seems to be disturbed by anything. I left soon, this constant droning
made me tired.

The same retired police sub-inspector with the booming voice was
still there droning endlessly when I came in the afternoon. I
wondered if he kept sitting here since this morning. He was a
Brahmin and showed off his knowledge; but I think he is talking a lot
of nonsense.

When the Guru went out, he took the opportunity to ask me searching questions—why I did not marry again, and what is my opinion about the married life. He was such a bore; I took a book out of my bag and, to cut him short, pretended to read.

DREAM: I was looking at myself in a mirror and saw that I was very thin, very pale, my hair in disorder.

INTERPRETATION: **"It is a very good dream! Thin and thinner, until nothing will remain."**

"I am thin already, I can assure you," I laughed. I was hardly recognizable, lost so much weight, could not eat because of the heat; much perspiration and the tremendous vibrations did the rest, along with the lack of sleep, for the fire in the body was flowing, sometimes more, sometimes less. This fire causes intense pain in the body; it is a torture, lasting many hours in the night . . . I lived on black coffee and aspirins. Not much chance to get fat on such a diet. He only smiled gently.

The *Kirtan* was very dynamic tonight.

21st March

LAST NIGHT when returning from Pushpa's saw people still sitting in his garden, so I joined them. It was a lovely moonlit night. Everybody was very jolly, and he was telling stories in Hindi making everybody laugh. Sat there till after ten and then went home.

22nd March

"THERE COMES A TIME in every Saint's life, when Yama, the King of Death, becomes his friend. It is when the Saint reaches the point on the *Nirodika Path* where the *Devas* cannot go further, only humans can."

Tonight he came out at 6 p.m. I also came late, for it was the "Holy" which is a Festival in honor of Krishna when paint and colored water are thrown in the streets and it is not advisable to go out. But at 5 p.m. it is all finished.

The droning sub-inspector translated a Persian couplet: "When you have received the Wealth and want to drink the Wine of Love, do it silently, so that nobody should know about it."

Bhai Sahib explained the meaning: People can be an obstacle; they can shake your faith before you are firmly established in virtue; but once you are, everybody can know. He spoke of Mogul emperors; some of them were very cruel.

"Some Saints are cruel too," I said. He looked at me seriously.

"Yes, Saints are very cruel. It is because they want only the good of the disciple—that nothing should remain, no impurity, no obstacle, no defect to hinder him. Is the doctor not cruel when he takes the knife and cuts the abscess?" He had his searching, unsmiling look.

For the last ten days I seem to be completely alone. Cannot reach his Revered Guru Maharaj at all. Nothing . . . just a wall, an emptiness. I get lonelier and lonelier, and so great is the force of *Maya* that I do not even seem to feel the love and devotion in my heart. . . .

This love is a strange thing indeed. When I try to analyze it, I find that in reality I don't love him directly, as a person; what I mean is that I love something "beyond" him. How shall I put it? I love something, this Something for which he is a symbol. Is it so? This feeling is very definite and clear, and I had it from the very beginning. But yesterday he said that it is the attachment to the Master which will lead the disciple to the Ultimate Reality . . . and I am confused again. Will this kind of feeling I have for him be enough?

Still, I cannot help it. I look at him when I sit there. I see him even if I am not in his presence. I seem to see him all the time. I admire his divinity, which to me is so clearly visible and evident. In some human beings one has to dig very deeply to be able to perceive it at all. But with him one just KNOWS it. But is it *Love*, as we understand it? Probably it is, only it is not easy to recognize it as such, for it is the most difficult relationship.

I remember his saying that this is the most difficult relationship, because it belongs to the transcendent, the eternal part of the human being, and the personality is unable to reconcile the opposites, *i.e.*, of tremendous bliss experienced and the hard treatment one has to endure.

I am afraid of him. I could never think of him as the Beloved. When I think of the Beloved, it is always God. He is the only real Beloved of our Soul. The personality worship is never encouraged by a Sufi Master. The Teacher will attract your attention, and then will point away from him to the Eternal.

23rd March

THE TWO HEARTS are still here.

He was translating a Persian couplet:

**"When you die of surrender, only then you will live forever,
If you are put to death through surrender,**

There is no such thing as death for you,
For you have died already!"
And:
"The life of a man is a bubble on the surface of the water.
A bubble which comes and goes; the water remains the
same." . . .

The room was full of people. I sat in the big chair, and it was the best place. It was his father's chair; he sits in it and uses it for meditation. Later we were all sitting in the garden. It was filled with moonlight, and black were the shadows under the trees. Fragrant was the Queen of the Night, a shrub with small insignificant flowers, fragrant only in the night.

Went home late.

24th March

THIS MORNING THE POLICE INSPECTOR was already sitting when I came. He was very fat, and I think very ignorant. Again and again he was repeating that one should remember God all the time and how he wished to be like me, because he can see that I have renounced the world, etc. At first I was bored, but then his urgency struck me. Why this fear in him? Why the constant self-accusations? I looked at him with attention, and the truth dawned on me—he will not live very long, a few more years probably, and it is his Soul, his Atman, who tries to impress the personality with the urgency to think of God.

"If I go tomorrow, how can I stand in the Presence of my Creator, if I do nothing to merit His Grace?"

I felt sorry for him and began to watch the Guru. He began to talk to him as soon as he came out, with such love, such affection, explaining to him proverbs, telling stories. When he was looking at this man, his expression was so full of love—there was something in his face, this "something" I know from other planes, and which is like a haunting memory, beyond the comprehension of the mind . . . an impression only, a flaming face, of such infinite love, such powerful call. A bit of it was in his face during the *Bandhara*, I remember. Then I knew for sure that he was "fishing," the fisher of men . . . Fisher of Souls. . . .

"Show me your hand," I said, when the Guru went out. His life-line was short, and he was already sixty-four. Well, I may be right. . . .

"Deceive, do all sorts of evils, if you cannot help it; burn all the

sacred books; but never, never hurt anybody's feelings!" he was translating. So according to the Sufi doctrine, to hurt the feelings of others must be the greatest crime.

Truly it is said in *Light on the Path* (by Mabel Collins): "If you can speak in the presence of your Master, your tongue must have lost its power to wound."

I watched him when he was explaining, and the Compassion was shining from his eyes, and when a pause in conversation gave me the opportunity, I said: "Bhai Sahib, you are a great Teacher, a Fisherman of men, as Jesus said. You throw out your nets to catch a Soul. I am watching you for months now, and I see how you treat everybody individually, exactly as they must be treated; you give each and everyone what he wants; if he wants little, you give little; if he wants more, you give more."

He laughed heartily, his wonderfully young laughter, his eyes shining . . . and he nodded repeatedly, and his laughter deepened.

When the man had left, I said that I had a certainty that he will not live long. He gave me a quick look.

"Don't tell him that."

I said, of course not, it would be foolish, but I saw his hand; his life-line was short, and he is sixty-four already.

"Do not tell him," he repeated kindly.

"He told me that he wanted to live till he is 190; I only said that it was a good idea."

He only smiled, seemingly in approval.

25th March

FOR THE LAST FEW DAYS there is a special peace in my two hearts. Again the police officer was talking to him. I saw such a pity, such a compassion shining in Bhai Sahib's eyes, that I was quite moved. Afterwards, when alone with him, I told him that never, never have I seen such an expression of deep compassion in a living human face. One can see it on the face of the statues of Buddha, or in great paintings, but it must be rare to find it in a living human face.

"The man is frightened," he said thoughtfully; "I am giving him all the help I can."

"When you switch over and look at something else which is not physical, there is a misty veil over your eyes. While you were looking at him, you had it all the time; that's why this compassion—it has something unearthly about it . . . as gentle as a dove, we say. Do you know what a dove is?" He said he didn't. I explained that it is a white variety of pigeon, and it is supposed to be the gentlest of all the living creatures. He again smiled his very still smile. My heart was full of the deepest reverence.

26th March

WE WERE ALONE nearly all the time in the morning. He had his mala. It was very hot. I had a kind of restlessness in me like a foreboding. I saw him giving me a quick look, and I knew that he has seen that I am full of peace. Will you see, I said to myself, that he will take it away from me? We went inside, under the fan. When in the room, he was very kind and talked to me on all sorts of topics. Told him in conversation what I had wanted to tell him a while ago: Babu and Satendra, his sons, told me that they would like to come and see where I live. I don't mind that, but Babu is so curious that he constantly asks me where I am going and what I am doing. I find it annoying. I don't need to give an account of my life to a boy. It is not his business.

He took the opportunity to tell me off—how hard I am still, and that he is trying to change me, but without success. I was wincing under his harsh words.

"I am not going to waste my powers," he was saying. "I am not going to help you now! You must help yourself. I gave you such a big place in my heart, and you are still nowhere! You do not know what respect is! There are people who are so afraid of me that they do not dare to speak to me. And you? You are disrespectful to the family of the Guru!" And so he went on for a while.

He made me cry desperately; I could not stop crying and told him that he was right . . . what harm is there after all . . . what did it matter if the boy was curious? It is all pride again, because I thought that I am an elderly woman and it is undignified that a young boy should ask me what I am doing. So I cried, and he, murmuring something to the effect that his wife was going out and he had to see her off, went outside closing the door, but I knew that the real reason was that he felt embarrassed, was sorry for me, and could not bear to see me crying like that. A little later he came in and was very kind. He was telling me that the time has come to bring those things which you have learned into practice.

"You have been doing good work in the Theosophical Society. Now the time is coming when, if you have to love, you must love; if you want to serve, you must serve; if you want to surrender, you must surrender."

"But I am trying to do it, Bhai Sahib, I really am!"

"**I know that,**" he said emphatically, "**and I am realizing it. Sometimes I speak to you harshly, but forget about it. I am scraping off the mud; this time it is the finer mud.**" He smiled kindly. "**And I am pleased,**" he said, looking at me.

So, I knew that the telling off was a test. Have I passed it?

20

Our People are Tested
with Fire and Spirit

IN THE AFTERNOON he spoke to me a lot. I told him that there was a time when, somehow, he was for me like Surya, the Sun God. I had once a vision of a vast temple with white, red, and yellow columns, and long, dark, cool passages with stone floors. And there was someone who I knew was he, though he looked very different, and much younger. Then too, he was dressed in white, and I remembered clearly the sandals on his brown feet, how they looked, and I could describe them. His feet then looked exactly as they look now—long slender legs, like a statue of Mercury. Deep down in my mind, Surya-worship and him have something in common for me. He smiled, and asked me if I noted this in my diary. I said, not yet, but I am going to do it.

"Write all those things down," he said, **"they will be of help one day."**

He sent me to the post office to get some money orders which I had to fill out; he was dictating the names of the people to whom they had to go. **"They are all in need of help,"** he was saying; **"the wife of the one is in hospital with T.B. and he has four children. The other, in Jaipur, needed his roof to be repaired before the rains are due. The third is without work."**

And so on. I was filling out the money orders, one after another, the whole morning. He was dictating to me, seated cross-legged on his tachat, the address book on his knees. It was quite an experience.

27th March, 1962

HAD TO ASK HIM FOR HELP in the morning. The whole night, fire was flowing through my body . . . liquid fire in the veins instead of blood—it felt like that. All the chakras seemed in turmoil. Did not sleep at all; but all was peace, no "creatures" around me. Nevertheless, the physical body was suffering acutely, and the pain was unbearable.

The head is light this morning. Have an airy-fairy feeling of complete unreality all around me. Had black coffee and aspirins. Am better now. Brought some more money orders. He was dictating an endless list of names and addresses to me. We were alone . . . only the wife looked in for a moment but did not come in; then I went to the post office and posted them all.

Tonight he was talking to me from half-past-six to nearly half-past-eight. Of course I did not go to the *Kirtan*. He began by asking me what was the work of the Theosophical Society and its function in the world. So I told him the history of its foundation, about Mme. Blavatsky and Colonel Olcott, of their selfless dedication to the work of the Masters for the sake of humanity, gave him an outline of the Society's work in the world, and spoke in detail about the English section, the library, classes, lectures, etc. Told him the Society's main objectives, which are to form a nucleus of the universal brotherhood of humanity without distinction of race, creed, sex, caste or color. To encourage the study of comparative religion, philosophy and science, and to investigate unexplained laws of nature and the powers latent in man.

He listened carefully. Then he said: **"Each of us, we have a work to perform in the world. Some of us work on the inner planes, some are training people, some are in the midst of worldly events guiding human beings aright."**

"Also in politics?" I asked.

"Yes," he nodded; **"it was so in the past, it is so now, and it always will be. Humanity needs guidance. Where would the world be without Great Souls appointed to watch over the destinies of men?**

"The goal of men is to realize the Truth. This is the purpose of the whole of Creation. But what can you say after you have realized it? How can you describe things which cannot be described in human language? People run after the world and after worldly things—phenomena, sensations, illusions. They know not that they will remain in the cave forever" (allusion to the cave of Plato).

"First you realize who you are, then from where you came, and where you are going. After that no desire remains—everything is gone. One becomes silent; one has nothing more to say. You won't be able to lecture, but people will come to you, and you will take them one step nearer to the Truth. At the beginning and in the middle one has a great desire to work, but at the end even this desire goes; nothing will remain.

"You cannot realize God or your *Atman* through books or lectures. Never! How can we realize Truth through the intellect?

Where is intellect? Nowhere! In our System we never lecture, never write books. If one day you will see me go on a platform and lecture, then you will know that I came down!"

"I remember that you had said that you are training me according to your System, and still you want me to lecture in the future, and you also told me to keep a diary which will be a book one day?"

"This is quite another matter. Orders are orders. I have just told you that, each of us, we have a certain work to perform in the world. For a while this will be your work. Later, further orders will be given. We must all reach the stage where we are guided from within."

"If you are training me according to the Ancient Tradition, then the time must come when you will send me away to go and do some work. For as far as I know, this is the Tradition, is it correct?"

He nodded. **"I send my people away, as soon as the Training is finished. Now go and work, I say, and they go. My people are tested with Fire and Spirit, and then sent out into the world, and never, never do they go wrong!"**

And so it was, that from his own mouth I came to know for sure that one day I will have to go, broken-hearted I will go, leaving my Teacher behind. . . . May this day be far away, may it never come. . . . But after all, His Will ultimately will have to be done . . . only, please, may it still be in the far, far future!

It was a glorious night. The stars seemed so near, so large. Venus was low, and pale blue, huge, against the already dark sky. I was humming to myself . . . was singing softly all the songs I knew—they were not very many. Everybody was talking; nobody took the slightest notice of me. It gave me some kind of relief, to hear my own voice; there was a sort of trembling happiness which needed outward expression. I understood him so well when sometimes he was singing, marking the time by clapping his palms on his thigh. And sometimes he was talking so much and I wondered, why such a waste of energy? . . . because at times there is such a tremendous energy in the body that it must have some outlet. At home, for instance, when this happens, I begin to clean, to wash; the feverish activity brings a kind of relief.

Sitting near him, I was thinking that he told me last night to go home, to be in peace and to sleep well. It probably means that he is sure to prepare some other trouble for me because I have relative peace just now. A calm before a storm?

Looking at the stars shimmering above, in the clear Indian sky, during a pause in the general conversation, I asked him: "Bhai Sahib, can you go and have a look at one of the stars and see if it is inhabited?" He shook his head. "But why not?" I inquired, "there are no barriers for the *Atman*."

"But why should the *Atman* go there; this is the barrier!"

I had to laugh, so simple was the answer. *Atman* does not "GO ANYWHERE," it just IS. It is one with all. When one realizes one's own *Atman*, no desire remains; why should one come down and begin again to have desires?

Later I asked him about his ideas on God. He only laughed. Lately he does it often; he only laughs or gives me deliberately confusing answers, so that the mind has nothing to hold.

28th March

IN THE MORNING I was sitting in the passage which is the coolest place, for it is already pretty hot at seven; he came out only for a moment and sent me away saying that he is going to have a bath. He has his bath at least twice a day. We all sit in the garden and wait. Well, probably he just did not want me to be sitting there; he must have his reason. . . .

29th March

JUST SAT IN THE ROOM ALONE. He was resting in the other room. The ceiling fan was humming softly; the rhythm of the Indian household was all around me. The servants were quarrelling; the wife was cleaning the jars for the pickles at the fountain; water was filled into the earthenware jars, the crackling of firewood, the smell of food being cooked. A child cried somewhere, nearby. A woman's voice was singing softly a monotonous, sad, melody. It was hot. It was good. How I loved India—it was so much a part of me. Far back in London (it seems so long ago) a friend once said that England was temperamentally wrong for me. But India was right; I knew it as soon as I came here. I love every little bit of it; it is my home. Even the dust, even the smells are familiar, and they belong to the character of this land. Ancient *Samskaras* (impressions of actions in universal mind which lead to the wheel of rebirth)? Could be. Went first to the bazaar, then home. One must eat to keep body and soul together. . . .

In the evening we had a talk on the doctrine of *Karma*, which he said was a childish belief. I was more puzzled than ever. I retaliated with the arguments of its logic, how it explains so many things which otherwise would be incomprehensible, but point by point he kept defeating every argument, most brilliantly, with clear, sharp, logic. His ability for discussion is devastating; he leaves one mute, speechless. . . .

"It is difficult to become one with the Teacher," he was saying. His eyes were incredibly shining, looking right through me. In the light of the street-lamps his eyes were shining with brilliant, green light. A cat's eyes in the dark, as the eyes of all the animals when caught in the headlight of a car, shine brilliant-red; but his were emanating a cold, green light when he was talking, and the rays of the street-lamp moving through the foliage of the tree were catching his eyes. I never saw such a phenomenon in any other human being, or any creature, as a matter of fact . . . especially when he was gay and laughing; small sparks seemed to fly from his eyes.

"It is difficult to become one. *Manas* will fret and work on it and ask questions, until this happens. Then, of course you will know. But on the physical plane there will always be differences; this is quite natural."

30th March

ALL THE MORNING, sitting there alone, I kept worrying about the doctrine of Karma. If Karma does not exist, how can one account for the order of the Universe? One can see everywhere the Law of Action and Reaction, the cause producing its effects. He himself admits the existence of Karma by his statement that the attachment for the Master produces such a strong *Vasana* that it remains forever. And what is *Vasana*? Are not *Vasanas* subtle desires arising from *Samskaras*, which remain as impressions of actions in *Chitta* (universal consciousness)?

"This is part of the System," said Prof. Batnagar when we were discussing it: "to destroy all the preconceived ideas, all your beliefs, which come from learning and book knowledge. Perhaps some of the ideas will get confirmation later, but by then they will be a living experience, no book-knowledge any longer. As far as I understand, as soon as a Saint wishes to give you something, from the moment he sets his eyes on you, Karmas cannot reach you anymore. He does as he likes. He can give to anybody his property, just as he wishes. Karmas are for the ordinary people, still under the influence of the law of cause and effect . . . but no more for you if you are with a Saint. People do not surrender, they are MADE TO SURRENDER, said the Master. If I may give you an advice: put all your doubts and worries into cold storage. Leave them there. They will all be solved one day; then they will be in a new light for you. Do not ask questions anymore."

Wrote to Australia about my shares to be sold. It all has to go. The sooner the better, he said. I am quite resigned to it.

1st April

EVERY DAY it is hotter and hotter. A scorching wind springs up, pushing the temperature over 100. Nights, too, are very hot and windless. A few evenings ago, just when I was leaving, he said:

"Go home and sleep well, and have peace for a few days."

The few days seem to be over. Slept only from eleven to quarter to one, and the rest of the night I was lying awake, thinking and listening and watching the currents chasing each other in my body. The pain was bearable. It is a very well-known fact that when one cannot sleep, the mind begins to work feverishly; every problem becomes magnified. And if there is a pain in the heart, that can become unbearable. Lately, I noticed that the longing from which I am suffering so much since I am with Bhai Sahib becomes more and more difficult to bear. Something in me is full of sorrow, so deep that I cannot reach it, cannot analyze it . . . only the claws of pain are tearing my heart apart. . . .

Something in me is crying desperately. Cannot get a clear idea of this depression, why the sun is not shining for me, why all is bleak, and there seems no hope at all, anywhere. There are times when I think death would be better. . . . I cannot offer a rational explanation for this mood. I don't even know what causes it. It is just confusion, despair, sheer despair, quite simply . . . that's all I know . . . and endless longing. A terrible, tremendous desire, but for what? For that which is so evasive, so far away . . . a non-ending torment. . . .

He was telling me off: **"Sit properly; you have no respect; you don't know how to behave, how to sit properly in the presence of a Teacher. To sit in a chair crossing your legs is rude. To stretch your legs out is even more rude."**

I told him that I am so hot that I try to move my legs in different positions, to get some coolness, some relief. He shook his head in disapproval.

"You have to sit modestly, knees and feet together; never mind the heat." His face was as hard as stone, and he went on like this for a while, finding faults with my behavior.

I burst out crying and could not stop. Lately when I begin to cry (and I cry so easily—the least thing can cause it), I just cannot stop; such a helpless feeling of despair comes over me, my heart wounded by so much longing, I simply cannot bear it. Must be a kind of hysteria. My nervous system is shaken. Cannot bear seeing him angry or even to think that he is displeased.

"Keep walking," he said. So, I got up and began to walk up and down in front of the house. But it did not help.

"Keep walking," he repeated. He was sitting in his usual place in the big chair, mala in his hand.

"Sometimes I say to Miss L., keep walking! When my heart is melting, you feel it, and you cannot bear it."

Strange: how the telling off and the melting of the heart can go together? So I continued for a while. The trees smelled of greenery; the garden was dusty. He went inside. Like most men, I think, he cannot bear to see a woman cry, so he always disappears. . . .

When I was still crying and trying to cope with tears running down my cheeks, he came out silently and sat down near me on a chair. He began translating, in a low monotonous voice, a passage from the *Tulsi Ramayana:*

"A sweet smell has the dust at the feet of my Guru; never I cried before, but now there is no end of sorrow for me. . . ."

I tried to compose myself, coping unsuccessfully with a sloshy, slippery, hanky; it was quite embarrassing. . . .

"Do you remember that I came out to meet you when you came for the first time? When you came from the station and Mrs. Ghose brought you here? I never go and meet anybody! Filibert sat here for an hour before I came out to meet him."

I was still occupied with trying to dry, at least partly, my cheeks. My skin was burning and painful from salty tears mixed with perspiration. "It was an act of courtesy towards an elderly lady," I mumbled feebly.

"Yes, yes, maybe," he smiled. "Maybe it was, but perhaps there was another reason." His smile deepened . . . this expression again . . . this strange, luminous, expression. As if I always knew it so far, so deep in me, that the memory of it could not be pinned down clearly. This expression always profoundly disturbs me, haunts me like a dream of long ago. . . .

"The bird of Manas flies here and there until the hawk of love catches it. Where the King is, how can anything else remain?"

I think I mentioned before that all Yogis have good voices. His has a kind of metallic ring in it. Bell-like, I thought . . . awakening an echo somewhere.

"A Saint took a bath in the pool, and he felt a wonderful fragrance around him. 'Oh earth,' he said, 'I am a human being; I cannot have such a wonderful fragrance. From where have you got this lovely smell? Oh Saint,' said the earth, 'I am dust, a worthless dust only; but fragrant flowers grew all around here; they kept me company, and their fragrance remained with me.' "

"When I hear you sing and I close my eyes, I see endless expanses of sand, a scorching heat, the cold of the night under a dome studded with huge stars. Why do I see camp-fires going on all night, and your voice just like now, like a faraway dream? And why this feeling of breathless happiness which goes with it?"

He only smiled and resumed to sing: **"The Guru sees God, and the Shishya sees the Guru; the Guru is a transparent glass through which the Shishya can see God. The Guru gives to the disciple without conditions because he wants to give. With others he is polite, that's all. Always be polite. Never injure anybody's feelings. All right?"** he asked, when I was leaving. I shook my head.

"I am full of suffering."

"Suffering is good. Let it be. Go home and rest." It was terribly hot already.

3rd April

SO MUCH SORROW IS IN ME that there is no speech left to express it. Have no desire to speak to him. Go there in the morning and sit. About 10 a.m. he sends me home. I am sort of empty. Everything seems to be dead. No desires are left . . . only one—only this terrible, deadly longing. But there seems to be no hope. It is a sort of peace made of darkness.

4th April

HE DID NOT SPEAK TO ME all day, and I did not attempt to say anything. There is nothing to say, nothing to ask. All is dead inside me. Such hopeless feeling . . . and the most amazing thing is that something in me does not mind this sorrow. More and more of it . . . as if I were interested to see how far it can go. Where is the very depth, the end, the bottom of it? Or is it like a bottomless pit into which I will sink forever? The natural thing for a human being is to seek pleasure and to shrink from pain. But for reasons which are beyond my understanding, I want more and more of this sorrow, though I have no idea why I am in such a dreadful state. The reason for it is not clear at all. Pleasure and pain are the two poles on which the whole world of *Samsara* (the wheel of birth and death caused by illusion) is revolving. Pleasure and pain are the two opposites—the attraction and the repulsion. But I don't shrink from sorrow . . . why? It seems as if the whole of my desire would be to dissolve, to be submerged by it . . . what a strange state of mind . . . bless me, if I understand it.

Told him that my body is defeating me because of the vomiting condition, and I can hardly eat. I also have reason to think that my eyesight is deteriorating because I am weeping so much. I happen to know a case of someone who cried so much after the death of her husband that her eyesight became weak and the color of her eyes watery-blue.

"It was because she cried about worldly things. If one cries for love, it never happens. I cried for years for my Rev. Guru Maharaj, and my eyesight is all right. My father cried until the last moment before he died, and I myself . . . I really should not speak of it . . . well, I still cry. It will be not for a few weeks that you will be crying, but for months, for years. . . ."

I was grateful to him for alleviating my worry about my eyesight; but in reality I did not quite understand what he had meant.

All seems to be still inside me . . . as if something has died in me. Do not want to ask questions, do not want to speak, and if he does not talk to me, it does not matter either. Even the mind seems to be still.

"Keep being flooded with love for the next few years," he said. What did he mean by that? I was not sure. . . .

5th April

HE WAS CHANTING THE RAMAYANA. It was already dark, and I was watching his luminous eyes in the darkness.

6th April

SOMETHING HAPPENED LAST NIGHT. I cannot find myself. This morning I experienced the nearest state of non-being since I am alive. Mind does not work at all.

Tried to read a journal forwarded to me from Adyar and could not comprehend a thing.

He was praying silently. Every time I looked up, I saw his radiant face shining with a new light. Great was the pain inside me. The world around was a crazy, crazy, mad dream, and the brain refused to function.

He was talking to a very old man. When the latter left, we went to sit outside. But soon his wife called him and he did not come out for at least two hours. I was sitting alone. Lately, when there is nobody except myself, he does not come out. As soon as a man came, he too came out and sent me away to get a homeopathic medicine for the pain he has in his back. Went home early. Was tired.

7th April

THIS MORNING I was complaining publicly that I was unjustly treated; for hours they talked in Hindi. Bhai Sahib explains interesting things; I cannot follow; nothing is ever translated to me. I sit there like a cucumber and miss the benefit of his explanations.

The night was full of stars. So near. So large. Could not sleep at all. The fire in the body was terrible.

8th April

IN THE MORNING WE WERE DISCUSSING banking business. I will be transferring the greater part of my investments into his bank account which I opened for him. He is registered as a charity. I understand only too well that I have to give up everything, that I must be able to bow my head and learn how to accept.

9th April

STRONGER THAN BEFORE SEEMS MY LOVE . . . and the nearness to Him was great. When I use the word "Him" and write it with a capital H, I don't mean the Guru. I mean the Great Beloved Himself, God.

Sitting near Guruji this morning, my heart was beating so loudly that I thought that he would hear it too. For hours on end it was beating like that, stopping, missing out beats.

10th April

DURING THE KIRTAN I sat there and cried. Pushpa translated a verse from the *Ramayana* which they sang tonight:

"There are two ways how Thou canst love me;
    Either I should be so perfect that Thou hast to love me,
    Or I will surrender before Thee, and Thou who Lovest Thy
        Creation
    Thou willst love me for myself."

My heart was so full . . . full of tenderness and deep love. After the *Kirtan*, sitting with Pushpa in the hall upstairs, suddenly I felt as if the Love for Him is beginning to include all the living things, all His

Creation. Until now I felt love only for Him and Him alone . . . all I could do was not to hate and try to tolerate others . . . there was no room for anybody else. But now, it seemed to me as if all the Creation was contained in this Love through Him in the most wonderful way. And so Pushpa and I, we sat there quite still, and she had her eyes full of tears. I did not cry, but so wonderful, so deep was the Love. And the evening was still and warm. When I went home, such was the fragrance, every shrub seemed to flower in the gardens around.

11th April

HE WAS TALKING WITH ANIMATION seated as usual in his cross-legged position; plenty of people were sitting around him. I sat on his left. They were all talking Hindi. I had nothing else to do, so I began to examine the palms of my hands. He saw what I was doing and looked in my direction with a smile. I asked him what this strange line was, connecting my life-line and the fortune-line, forming like a large island in both hands; and it seems to be growing and changing in the last few years.

"**Do you really want to know what it means?**" he asked. I said, "Please, do tell me . . . even if it is something bad, I can bear it."

"**No, it is not bad, but difficult to explain; it is as if you would be put in prison. All the forces are scattered now, so to say, but then it will be all united.**" He took my left hand, and pointing to a small interruption in the fortune-line above the head-line:

"**This,**" he said, "**will join soon and will carry your fortune-line right to the middle finger.**" He smiled and pushed my hand jokingly away. "**Plenty of travels are there in your hands,**" he added.

In the evening, by questioning him, I was given to understand that the sex-urge was not awakened by him or his power as I assumed, but it was already there, latent, a sort of a powerful *Vasana*.

"**Ancient Karmas form part and parcel of the blood** (unconscious memories are stored in the blood-stream: C.G. Jung, *Memories, Dreams, Reflections*). **It was in you. It would have dragged you back again and again into the womb, but from now on it will burn itself out. From time to time this fire will burn in your body. This is a purifying fire, this suffering, and you will need a lot more.**"

Well, I thought, not a very bright prospect . . . and this is to put it mildly.

"**When you meet your Spiritual Guide, this is supposed to be your last Karma-bound life. After that, one is supposed to be free to** go where the Teacher directs you. There are many planes, besides the earth plane, where Service can be rendered. Disciples must be free. And if the Teacher is powerful, he will take them through all the three planes. But surrender and absolute obedience are needed."

When at home, could not help wondering how many evils I must have had in me to be burned to such an extent.

21

The Stages of Love

IT WAS LIKE A LOVELY DREAM. We all went with a truck to the *Samadhi* of his father, a lovely place, seven miles outside the town amongst the plains. The day was cloudy and not at all hot. How fragrant are the Indian plains, the wind coming from afar smelling of wood smoke, cow-dung and dust and sun-drenched distances. How I love this earthy smell . . . to me it represents the smell of freedom, if freedom could have a smell. Peace was in me. Such peace. The whole day it was like this. Told him that it was too good to be true, and I know that it will not last. And he nodded. Told him that I noticed that things first happen on the inner planes before they come to manifest on the physical plane. Many things are already happening somewhere; soon they will be here. He nodded again with a serious expression.

"The stages of Love: One can see women carrying jars of water on their heads, on their shoulders, in their hands. They do not spill the water, nor do they break the jars. But even if a jar is broken, there is but a small loss; another can be purchased and filled with water again. Those people are still far off from the Lane of Love.

"One can see acrobats performing on the rope and in the air. They can fall and have their bones fractured and even die, but they are still using tricks to safeguard themselves as much as possible. Those people just begin to come into the Lane of Love.

"Switch on a lamp, and you will see insects attracted to the light, and there is a great competition amongst them to come nearer and nearer . . . who comes first. They throw themselves into the light without reserve, without condition, and burn to death. Only this is the Great Love."

"Why am I in such a distressed state periodically? This fear of you? Such a fear of you that it is sometimes like panic."

"It is the mind again," he said softly. "And it will come again and again; it will come and go, until the mind merges somewhere."

"But no wonder that I am afraid of you, Bhai Sahib; I feel so helpless, and the feeling of utter helplessness is frightening. Human beings are afraid of the dark, afraid of sufferings. I am afraid of new sufferings you may give me; it seems I had enough of them until now. . . ."

"Sufferings?" he asked. "You did not begin yet!" I looked at him in amazement: "Are you joking, or do you mean it seriously? Do you mean to say that the horrors I suffered until now are nothing?"

"Nothing. Nothing at all. It has still to come. On our Line such suffering is given that there are no words for it. . . ."

"No wonder I am afraid of you," I said hardly audibly, looking at his serene face.

"But what's the use of repeating how much you suffered? What's the use of being sorry for oneself? Why not say courageously: It is nothing, I will bear more. The river has to be crossed, so let's go on. . . ."

"Thank you, it will be a help to think like this . . . you are right, it will help me in the future." He smiled. "Can I contribute consciously? Could I somehow direct the mind into the right channels, as soon as I know that it is the creator of all troubles?"

He shook his head. "No, you can do nothing; it has to be like this, otherwise you will not progress. Up and down it goes . . . full of love and empty again; in this Line in one second things are done, and in a moment the table is turned."

"Does it mean that I don't love enough?"

"No, it is BECAUSE you love deeply that it happens. Would the mind bother if there would not be the great disturbance of deep love? No, certainly it wouldn't. And the fact that the pain is sharper and deeper each time is a good sign. Pray that you should love more and more. . . ."

He got up and asked me to come into the room. There he took his *kurta* off, and Panditji began to massage him. I took a small carpet and sat down on the floor near the door. I am so much more comfortable seated cross-legged on the floor, and I was nearer and could hear what he was saying. The whole scene was so Indian: the devoted disciple massaging with reverence, with so much love, his Guru. The bearded Panditji looked most decorative; only his beard was black, and the Guru's white, or rather grey. And I thought with melancholy that when one day (let this day be very far away, oh Lord!) I will leave India, I will always remember this scene: him lying on the tachat and Panditji massaging him.

"This body is perishable, yes, but it is extremely important. Why? Because *Atman* is in the body; we evolve through this physical body. That's why we have to surrender the physical body as well. When the body is surrendered, the progress is quicker. The Master can do with the body what needs to be done to train it according to necessity."

"Even to kill it?" I asked.

"Yes, even to kill it," he repeated. "And sometimes it is done in a certain way. But not always is it necessary. At any rate it is much better to be in the Teacher's presence. Remember, the Atman pervades the physical body from head to foot, every atom of it."

I was sitting on the floor, near the open door; it was cool, and my heart was full of peace. All was well, once more. . . .

"If such thoughts are in your mind, if the suffering is here, why don't you ask yourself, what is in my heart?" He looked kindly at me. And Panditji's hands went on kneading his shoulders . . . like a bronze statue he was, shining with oil, and his face was all light.

"Why are cranks attracted to all spiritual organizations?"

"The question was put wrongly; try to put it right, then ask."

"How can I put it rightly? If it is wrong, I ask you as my Teacher to tell me how I should ask; please tell me."

"But you put it wrongly," he said impatiently, "are they not human beings? Those people whom you call 'cranks' are attracted to the places where they instinctively hope for help . . . but who is a crank and who is not? If you speak to the madman, he will say that you are mad and he is normal."

DREAM: (dimly remembered) There was a question of a long, white garment, completely covering my body to the feet, which I was supposed to wear instead of my usual kind of dresses. But he came in and said, no, not yet, I cannot wear it yet. Woke up with such a feeling of disappointment.

15th April, 1962

THIS MORNING THE OLD MAN who comes now every day was obviously in distress, and when the Guru came out I drew his attention to it. He looked at him with those eyes of his which see other things beside the physical ones, and went in Samadhi. The old man kept groaning softly, half unconscious. I sat there and suddenly felt him quite near, so I just rested in him and in the Love, and it was wonderful. He was somewhere, and I was with him, in him, together. Then the old man began to talk, and talked like a machine-gun for a solid hour, giving me an acute physical distress. I was so happy, resting in deepest bliss, and here was this voice, like a crow's, croaking on and on, talking perfect nonsense. It is this which causes such a pain when at his place:

people talking and talking with disagreeable, rasping or croaking voices for hours, when all I want is to be still, just resting at his feet in utter stillness. Luckily he left after this monologue, and we all, including the Teacher, were relieved. He asked us inside the room. There we all sat, and he was in the next room, Panditji massaging his body.

I sat there full of wonder. Where was the mind? For minutes—or was it much longer, for I had no sense of time—there was practically no mind left. There was, of course, the thought of the Master, the feeling of Love, the sense of being, but apart from that there was nothing . . . . Let's see where is this mind, I tried to think, but the thoughts were lazy; they came unwillingly. I had to make an effort to think. The question of good and evil, which worried me only a short while ago, did not arise at all; it was without importance, for somehow I saw both sides of the problem. My worries about the future and the finances were insignificant indeed. The only thing which mattered was His Will—this only was of utmost importance. I was sinking somewhere, but it was not a frightening experience. Not at all. It really amounted to resting in Him, in Infinite Love . . . a state of non-being, and this non-being was perfect freedom. I was astonished . . . never knew that not to be is to be free . . . but here I was: I was free, so wonderfully, so completely, because I WAS NOT: not as I, but as Him.

Before going to his Father's *Samadhi* last week, one evening I experienced a similar state sitting near him, and I remember thinking that it was the nearest state to non-being I had cognition of in all my life. This time it was even more marked, and I was wondering if that would mean the state of Dhyana after all. I noticed several times that he was watching me and looked quickly away as soon as I looked in his direction or opened my eyes. I was very much intrigued; in all the Yoga Systems one has to make an effort to still the mind, and what an effort it is! But here it represented an effortless state, and I had not only not to bother to try to still the mind, but had to search to find it! Well, well!!

When he came in from his bath, he walked silently into the room and went to the large mirror to comb his hair.

"Well, I had better be going," I said.

"Yes, yes," he answered, combing vigorously.

"Where is the mind?" I asked. "No answer, Guru Maharaj? Where is this *Shaitan* (Devil) of the mind? It is quite an effortless state, just no mind, and I am resting in Him in infinite Love. *Namaskar*" ("I greet you" in Bengali), I added, walking away.

"**Namaskar, namaskar,**" I heard him say, and from the tone of his voice I knew that he was laughing. God knows from how many human beings and how often he had heard this question: Where is the Mind, Guru Maharaj? Please do not cause a separation anymore—I cannot bear it! It becomes more and more difficult as the time goes on. . . .

DREAM: I was wearing a kind of petticoat like a sari petticoat, long, to my ankles, but from my waist the upper part of my body was bare. In a large room with low Indian beds many people were sitting around. He was explaining to me how the forces are taken to the *Brahmarandhra* in the case of *Brahmacharins* (those who practice control over the senses), in the case of non-*Brahmacharins*, and in the case of women.

"**Now I will demonstrate it to you,**" he was saying; he lifted his hand and I felt a sharp pain on the top of my head, such an acute pain, and asked him if the pain will remain.

"**No, I am only showing it to you,**" he said. I was thrilled, for I understood every word of his explanation. He was dressed in a white garment like a priest.

Woke up still feeling the pressure on the top of my head.

16th April

I ASKED Mr. Chowdrie, and he explained it to me: this stillness of the mind is the fifth state of the mind, as described in the Yogic treatises, and the outcome of it would be *Samadhi*.

"**You are in the higher state,**" he said.

So, he proceeds to take me to his God after all. It is not frightening at all; it is very peaceful. All the time sitting near him I was resting in Him, in God, and was so ideally happy. Told him that all the worries about the money matters and all else were useless, non-existent. The only thing which mattered was His Will and His Will only. He smiled: "**A very nice state, very nice indeed.**"

Then I told him that this state of separation becomes a problem; my eyes are red and sore from continuous crying for someone who is so far away. If it is His Will, nothing can be done about it, but if it is my fault, could it be corrected?

"**It is not your fault,**" he said softly, "**not at all.**" His face was full of tenderness. "**It will be like this for several years.**"

"For years? How will I survive if it is so bad already now?"

"You will," he smiled.

Told him that L. was never separated from Him, but he said that was not correct . . . for the first few years she was. This is the System, and nothing can be done about it.

But I think that it is so hard already, and the greater the love will be, the more the suffering . . . naturally so.

I was too happy; it was too good to be true, obviously, because it all was spoiled soon: a horrible man came and began a shouting conversation, lecturing for hours with the voice of a drunken *Rakshasa* (demon). I listened for half an hour or so, then could not bear it any longer and went into the street, to wait until he finished. Guruji joined me soon, and so we walked up and down together for a while. When we came in, the man was still there shouting as before, so I left in disgust.

17th April

"IF FOR INSTANCE I SAY: this is my chair, how do I know that I am not proud of possessing it? If I don't care about it, if I am not attached to it, then I am not proud of it. Can the pride hide itself? Certainly not, it always will put itself in evidence. If you don't care about possessions, then it does not matter even if you have them. Inwardly we are free from them. . . . You must forget everything."

"It will take time," I answered doubtfully.

"You are at a turning point; at any moment it can happen now, the Dhyana. The mind must take a dip before it can go to a higher state."

Had a night full of currents of love. Last evening, sitting near him, the body was full of an unusually peaceful feeling, a kind of indifference to the surroundings, and when he did send me home, I thought it was only half past seven, but when at home I saw that it was after nine. The time went so quickly. . . . So that is Dhyana . . . very peaceful . . . but not much consciousness. Some kind of state of being. Currents of love??

19th April

"IN THE WHOLE OF THE UNIVERSE there are only Two: the Lover and the Beloved. God loves his Creation, and the Soul loves God. In order to be able to create, the One Being had to become two, and logically there had to be a difference between the two. The creation was only possible because of the two opposites; everything in creation responds either to positive or to negative forces, or vibrations. There is the Sound and the Echo, the Call and the response to it, Light and Darkness; without the opposing forces, how could the world exist?

"Even in the Angelic Kingdom there are Angels of Power and Angels of Beauty. As soon as the Creative Ray of God touches the plane of Manifestation, those two forces come into play inevitably. On the physical plane those two forces will manifest either as masculine or feminine, as male or female.

"Both forces are inherent in everything, and either one or the other will predominate. Upon the predominance of the one or the other, sex is determined. Even some plants are either male or female. Every living thing had this procreative, or sexual energy, in its very make-up, for it is the Creative Energy of God manifesting on the dense, physical plane of creation."

Slept little. The currents in my body did not leave me in peace. I watch them for hours, their progress and circulation inside my body, and it seems to me that they have some kind of perception or understanding, some kind of purpose in them which is beyond my understanding. The physical suffering is great. The whole body is suffused with bluish light and is built around the most delicate web, or net, which seems to be its framework, its structure. Looking at it like that, it appears that the bones are not the framework upon which all the tissues, flesh, muscles, the vessels are built . . . but this fragile web, composed of the thinnest, hair-like threads, becoming more solid where they converge into thicker strands. The human body is built around a luminous web and not the other way round. At first I could not understand how that could be. Then it dawned on me that it is the nervous system, the millions of nerves, large and small, reaching from the end of the fingertips to the toes, which is upholding the body. It is they who channel the life-force (prana), and THE BODY IS BUILT UPON PRANA. I know it seems a strange statement, but it looks like that to me.

The currents of Prana are running along the nerves making them glow, like electric wires when the current passes through them. Only the electric wires glow red, but the light of the Prana is bluish-white. The web of the light of Prana in the body is like the web of the Universe, which is Prana too! Truly a confirmation of an age-old truism: a living experience of the fact that man is a microcosm within the macrocosm! As above, so below! It is really wonderful, and it looks lovely! The body feels full of fire even in the morning; no tiredness, though there is hardly any sleep at all. But I get thinner and thinner, and the vomiting condition does not help. Cannot eat much.

22

Casting out of a Spirit

THIS MORNING I WITNESSED something unusually interesting: Bhai
Sahib has driven an evil spirit out of a young man.

I arrived early. That means about 7 a.m., for it was very hot.
Everybody had already left, except for Happy Babu who was in deep
Dhyana. He asked us inside the room, where it was cooler under the
fan. It was very quiet. He was making entries into his diary. Both
doors, the one leading to the front of the garden and the side door,
were open, but the "chiks" were down. A "chik" is a kind of a
curtain, or a blind, made of thin bamboo sticks or thick stalks of
some kind of grass, loosely joined together with thick cotton twine;
they move constantly with the slightest current of air, preventing the
flies from coming in the room, and encouraging the circulation of air
at the same time being a protection from the glare outside.

It must have been around eleven when I saw two men coming
through the gate. One was old, the other very young; they were
dressed poorly . . . Muslim villagers, I thought. Satendra, who was
outside, went to meet them, then came into the room and gave a slip
of paper to his father. Bhai Sahib read it and said to tell them to
return on Tuesday and continued to write. A conversation followed
between Satendra and the men standing outside. Then the boy came
back and said that they came from a far-off village and could not
come back. Bhai Sahib put down his writing material, got up, went to
the door, and I was a bit surprised to see him standing inside the
room behind the chik talking to the men who were outside. It was
unusual, because he always asks everybody to come inside the room
when he was in. The young man sat down on the step before the
door, and the Guru, holding one corner of the chik slightly raised
with his left hand, just stood there looking at him. Nobody spoke.
The young man clad in a chequered cotton *dhotie* had a rather simple
and primitive look about him. Suddenly he uttered a loud cry and
then began to howl like an animal with his mouth wide open, his eyes
glassy and spent like the eyes of a dead man; the expression on his
face was terrible to see; it was like a contorted mask. "What goes
on?" I asked Happy Babu, for I couldn't see clearly what was going

on, Guru's back nearly filling the frame of the door and the chik
partly hiding the scene from me.

"I don't know," murmured Happy Babu. So I ran quickly into the
next room and through the inner courtyard into the front garden.
When I approached, the Guru gave me a quick warning glance. I
stopped. Bhai Sahib was still standing in the room behind the raised
chik, the young man was now lying on the ground having
convulsions, froth streaming from his mouth, his face contorted and
terrible. (Later I asked his eldest son why his father was standing
behind the chik, invisible from the street. It was because the father
did not want to create a sensation. Seeing a young man having a fit in
a garden, no passer-by would bother in India, but if a tall white-
robed figure pointing a finger at the boy was seen, a crowd of
onlookers was sure to assemble.)

"Don't touch me, don't touch me, I will destroy you!" he was
shouting; the voice had nothing human in it; it was like a desperate
wailing.

Bhai Sahib continued to look steadily at this unfortunate creature;
he was in deep Samadhi, his eyes like bottomless pits of still, dark
water, unseeing, veiled. . . .

The young man was shouting louder and louder; his convulsions
increased to a paroxysm. His father was squatting near the wall of the
bungalow, trembling like a leaf with fear.

Then with a pointed finger, very slowly, as if describing a circle
around this body torn by convulsions: **"Go away!"** He ordered
sternly, and repeated it twice. And the voice which came out of the
young man's throat and which had nothing human in it, shouted
three times: "I am going; leave me, leave me, leave me!"

"Go!" said the Guru, making a stabbing movement at him with his
raised forefinger.

All of a sudden there was silence. The tormented, frenzied body
became motionless, like emptied, devoid of any spark of life. He is
dead! I thought; how dreadful! But I knew it couldn't be. . . .

Bhai Sahib let the chik drop, still standing behind it. A few long
moments passed. A small bird whistled in the treetop somewhere; a
car passed by. Slowly, the young man sat up shakily. His nice, simple
face had a perfectly human expression again, and with a most lovely
smile, lifting one corner of the chik, he touched silently the feet of
the Guru. And so did his father, who until now was crouching in the
shade near the wall.

"Go, my son," said Bhai Sahib gently, "Go both of you in peace!" They went, dazed. Not a word was spoken anymore.

He let the chik fall, went into the room, and I followed him. He stood in the middle, motionless; he was still in Samadhi.

"Well," I said, "this was something! Never saw such a thing in the whole of my life! In the time of Jesus it must have been like this, driving the evil spirits away!" He fixed me with his eyes which see other worlds.

"IF HE COMES BACK, I will burn him," he said darkly. "Sometimes they are rogues, and then they come back. Then I will burn him and all his relations!"

So I went home most impressed, and I confess rather shaken. . . . When I came after 5 p.m., he was sitting outside in the garden, a few people were already there; he was laughing and obviously was telling them what had happened this morning.

"Mrs. Tweedie!" he called, as soon as I was entering the gate: "Tell them what had happened!"

I did. He was dangling his mala and was laughing. Then I asked him, what did he mean when he said: "If he comes back, I will burn him and all his relations?"

"Oh, this," he said, "it is quite simple: those kinds of spirits are rather powerful elementals. If they want an experience on the physical level, then they attach themselves to a human being. In other words they obsess him. They are really most horrible things, most ugly to look at. More often they attach themselves to women. In Rajastan I had to do some of this work," he added thoughtfully.

"Why women?" I asked.

"It is because a woman is weaker and easier to obsess. (The personality of woman, having been subdued for millenia, is more likely to be influenced than man's.) We all have good and evil spirits in us, i.e., the good and the evil in us, and who wins, is the master."

"I thought it is the mind," I said.

"Yes, the mind also, but spirits too. And is the mind not an elemental as well? Everything in Nature is the bitter enemy of the human being. Why? Because he is the King. Everybody hates those who command. The human being is the Master of the Creation, the Ruler. And also if I say: I will burn him . . . it is not so easily done; one does not destroy so easily. They also have the right to live; they are a parallel evolution to man. They have no notion of good or evil. If they have a desire, they fulfill it. But I have to protect my race, the human being, so I will help him and get the spirit out. If he should come back, I will drive him out again and give him a stiff warning. If he still comes back, I will destroy him then, and with him all his relations. *Shaitans* (devils) are many, the whole race of them, usually. But when the Saint is powerful, they are afraid to come back. With me, never, not one came back!" And he laughed his ringing laughter which made him look so young and so free.

Prof. Batnagar came and much talk was going on about Masters and the training. So very few people come for the sake of spiritual life; mostly they come for worldly matters; they waste the Teacher's time. They come for a bit of Dhyana or bliss, or they want children, or some other blessing. But few, very few, come because they want the Truth.

Then he asked all of us to come inside and was massaged by Panditji. I began to cry . . . was suddenly so full of sorrow, such dreadful loneliness. . . .

20th April

THIS MORNING WHEN I CAME, twice my eyes met his, and it was like a silent greeting. Of course, he knows that it is my birthday, and the loneliness is so deep, verging on despair. . . .

He translated a Persian song:

"Who is with me all the time, says the Guru,
Who is with me all the time day and night,
Who does nothing without me, nor eating, nor sleeping,
Whose thoughts are on me all the time;
I come and live in their hearts.
Who give up everything for my sake, I take them into my
    heart;
And even then, I think that it is not giving them enough
    credit. . . .
those who have nothing to pawn and go and pawn me in the
    market place,
I let myself be pawned by them, for never, never,
Can I refuse them anything anymore!"

21st April

I WAS HAPPY THIS MORNING. My heart was full of such peace. . . . Sat in his room under the fan. He did not speak but continued to write. Later, a few men came and sat there too in silence. After a while he began to talk to me and asked if I liked the discussion with Prof.

Batnagar. I said, yes, but most of all I liked the Persian couplet. Which part of it? he wanted to know. About being pawned in the market place, I said.

"**My Revered Guru Maharaj used to tell us this one,**" he said softly, dreamily, turning the pencil in his fingers. Then he sat up: "**According to the System, the Shishya is constantly kept between the opposites, ups and downs; it creates the friction necessary to cause suffering which will defeat the Mind. The greatest obstacle on the Spiritual Path is to make people understand that they have to give up everything. If I give an order, and they obey the order, there is no merit. They must understand it by themselves. Sometimes the Master will say: Bring your wife to me, or bring your child to me. Out of a thousand, out of a hundred thousand, only one will obey such an order. For he will think: why does he want my wife, or my child? The mind will give trouble; there will be doubt; they will lose faith.**

"**There is a secret behind it; if it is not obeyed, they will not survive. This is one of the supreme tests. Only a Sat Guru knows when to give such a test. That's why the Teacher will hesitate to give such an order. The Shishya is attached to them; he is after them; he has to give them up. And attachment is the greatest obstacle. WHAT IS DEAREST TO US MUST GO. This is the Law. One cannot serve two Masters. Either the world or the Guru. Everything has to be given up, absolutely; nothing should remain, nothing at all. Even the self-respect has to go. Only then, and then only, can I take them into my heart.**"

He was full of light, so full of dynamism, that even those few simple men who were sitting there were staring at him as if not believing their eyes.

Later, he said: "**Mental sufferings are Dwellers on the Threshold; bear them.**" He spoke very quietly. I suddenly was flooded with nameless sorrow and began to cry. "**Go home, may God help you.**"

I went out crying bitterly. Not so soon will I forget the expression on his face when he said: "**May God help you**" . . . he looked Christ-like, so deep seemed his compassion. . . .

25th April

PERSIAN COUPLET: "The love is from both sides: from the side of the Beloved all currents are absorbed and love is not shown. From the side of the lover, his love cannot be hidden. To be loved is an easy thing; but to love requires a supreme self-sacrifice."

Last night Pushpa had visitors, her friends who came from the United States. How elegant is the Indian dress, the sari. They all looked so graceful and colorful, even those who could not even be called good-looking. There was pleasant conversation as we sat on the lawn, sipping ice lemonade, then went for a drive. The whole afternoon after lunch, I stayed near the cooler which is installed near the bedroom. What a bliss it is for my body to feel cool air! Now the heat is such that even the fan does not help; it only moves boiling air about. Sitting on the lawn after sunset, cool drinks before us, and later when the car was speeding along on the near empty roads after dark, I felt so acutely, so sharply, the change taking place in my life. Pushpa's life was my life until now, the life to which I was used to. The security of a bank account was at my disposal, to be able to do what I wanted, to go where I wanted. Not riches, no, but comfort . . . essentially, an easy life.

From now on I will remain with nothing at all. I am a beggar. My pension is £150 per annum. It will be swallowed up by the monthly installments of my life insurance policy and the help which I am giving to my sister for my father. Not a penny in the bank or anywhere else will be left, and no income at all. Nothing for old age. All my own savings and those of my husband which he left me will soon be non-existent, when the money from my investments from Australia will arrive into his account. And it will rapidly flow through his slender fingers, as it already happened with a large sum recently.

"Bring me twenty, or thirty (or whatever it may be) **money orders."**

I don't know what the post office clerk must have thought seeing me buying money orders daily . . . but I go and post them mostly at the main post office, where nobody knows me. Those and similar thoughts were crossing my mind while there was much chatter about charming nothingnesses, like the flower exhibition to be held soon, or the latest issue of a controversial novel.

Dark streets. Lovely car. Security. Never, never more will life like this be for me. There was a regret, a finality about it . . . a finality similar to death? No, not quite so dramatic; rather, a finality of bridges being burned behind me. From now on my destiny will be to sit amongst smelly, shouting men, for hours on end, listening to stupid conversation which is no conversation at all to speak of, and at any rate it is mostly either in Hindi or in Urdu. Very often he won't be listening to me, when my heart will be heavy with some trouble, and my head full of problems. He will be doing his mala, or be in deep Samadhi, and I eternally sitting, occupied with important internal happenings, bothered by flies, by bad smells, and hoping in vain for a little, just a little peace.

A life without any security whatsoever. And it looks to me that it will be like that until the end of my days. . . .

26th April

ESPECIALLY THIS MORNING, there was such a crowd of horrid, smelly men, I was really in despair. Dust, heat, smells, yelling children . . . how am I going to stand it for years and years to come? Sitting here for hours and no hope, no change . . . being ground down to powder, every day the same, every day hotter, every day more disagreeable.

And so in a pause, I went after him when he went into the room and told him how difficult it is to sit for hours amongst a smelly, shouting crowd.

"I know, I know, my dear, I understand," he said quickly, **"I know. But the *Satsang* must be; it is essential; and what can I do if it is my life? These conditions are part of my life too."**

"But you can escape by going into deep Samadhi. L. could too; she did not suffer much from it—she told me herself. One simply goes away, but I cannot do it! I sit here fully conscious of the surroundings—it is an acute discomfort! I will go mad!" I added, and began to cry.

"No," he said softly, **"never will you go mad. There are things from heart to heart; this is the only real language . . . all else is nonsense."**

Began to tell him how my mind was giving me much trouble. Last night, thinking and thinking, because Pushpa's life was my life until now, and it is still so fresh and has much powerful appeal. I lost it forever, never will it be mine again. He nodded kindly . . . and looking at me with deep compassion, he said in a very low voice:

"Your mind is not likely to trouble you much more; ever. All this is in the past. The mind will not bother you for very much longer.

Could not help wondering how long the "not very much longer" could be?

27th April

SLEPT SOUNDLY till 6 a.m. Woke up crying, could not stop . . . such was the terrible longing. I can never make out, what am I longing for so much? It is just longing, just darkness, just despair . . . something so deep, so far down, that the mind does not know what it is longing for so much. . . .

Once I asked him about it; he only smiled. **"One day you will know"**—the usual answer.

28th April

WOKE UP SEVERAL TIMES covered with perspiration. It is getting difficult to bear the heat, especially in the night. One cannot sleep. The sheet under me is so wet it's as if I were lying in a pool of water. Only three nights more—then it will be better (I hope!) in the new flat where I will be able to sleep in the courtyard with a table fan beside, and not in a small, hot room, where I am now, with no ventilation at all.

Mrs. Ghose's flat became free. I will get it the 1st of May. Two small rooms, veranda, kitchen, shower closet, and a toilet, all around a small, brick-paved courtyard. A high stone wall around will make it private.

A feeling of non-existence . . . and it is perfect, absolute, bliss. Difficult to imagine, how non-being can be such a blissful state. I don't know how such a thing is possible, but it is so.

Not to exist at all, not to be able to think, to be merged into something which defies description is the greatest, the deepest, the most unbelievable bliss. Others perhaps would call it suffering. Still, it is a blissful state, and the more one sinks into nothingness, the deeper, the more intimate the feeling of bliss becomes.

His expression was so kind when, with slightly bent head, he was listening to what I was telling him, while others in the meantime were shouting at each other in banal conversation.

"I seem to cry now all the time," I was saying, "either because I feel so alone and full of longing, or because my heart is full of sorrow, or because . . . I just don't know why . . . a great loneliness, an emptiness, fills me with despair. It is not my mind giving me trouble this time; the mind is still, as still as a candle on a windless day. I will need much help; to sit here amongst evil smelling men is such an ordeal, and it will be my destiny for years to come. Please, help me to cross the bridge, to be able to reconcile it all within myself."

He nodded softly. **"This love should grow; try. Try to do it yourself. If you cannot, then the ladder will be there for you."**

"But do you mean to say that I am failing?" He shook his head. And just smiled.

But he is right. It is the lack of love for other people. I really cannot stand them. If I could have more compassion, I would not object so much to the smell and dirt and noise and ignorance. . . .

I had an auspicious dream, at least so it seems to me: I saw a magnificent rainbow from one end of the horizon to the other, and the colors so glorious, so vivid and alive, that I just stood there breathless with admiration. But the right side of the rainbow was hidden by a tall building, so the whole of it could not be seen. It seemed significant: a tall building to the right (Consciousness) hides the completeness, the whole, which is visible only from the left (Unconscious).

"Dreams are dreams," he said and gave no explanation . . . except the usual remark: **"You will know one day. . . ."**

30th April

WHEN I CAME, the doctor was just leaving; he was called because of a severe pain in the back.

1st May

THIS MORNING I LEARNED that he had left for Allahabad. It means that he will be away for at least three days, or perhaps even more. I am expected to be there as usual . . . his brother laughing and talking in Hindi all the time. Just now there seems to be an especially mad crowd, shouting all together, and laughing; such a din . . . Elaci Baba rubbing his shaved head with a *loki* (a variety of marrow) to refresh his brain, so he was saying. But the sticky juice dried on his head, giving out a sour smell. And I have to sit . . . and to sit . . . trying to bear it as well as I can. Yes . . . will need a lot more love, the kind of love which is called compassion. . . .

23

Mindless, yet One-pointed

9th May, 1962

HAVE BEEN IN THE NEW FLAT since the 1st of May. It is comfortable. Only—oh, so hot! The small courtyard paved with red bricks gets as hot as a baker's oven. Two communicating rooms nine by ten feet, both doors leading to a covered veranda. A shower closet, a lavatory, separated from it by a low wall, and on the other side a small kitchen, with the walls made of perforated bricks, no door, all open to the elements. All around a high brick wall making the whole unit very private, a heavy oak door opening into Mrs. Ghose's large compound, with open spaces and trees, and her own brick-red sprawling bungalow stands surrounded by flower beds. Chicken sheds are behind it, and the overall impression is of space and freedom.

It is a nice accommodation, but, oh, the heat! All day the sun is beating on it, but at least I can sleep in the open, covered by a mosquito net, the table fan beside me. But it is so hot that even the mosquitoes are dead, so it seems, for I don't see any.

On Tuesday I took the rikshaw and went at seven in the morning to the Pool Bagh, the large park near the railway station. I wanted to see the trees just now in flower, called the Flame of the Forest. A magnificent sight they are—rows and rows of them, feathery foliage of deep green and covered with large clusters of blossoms ranging from the deep orange-gold to flame and even crimson. Have spent three serene hours wandering and thinking many things over. The longing is such that I have absolutely no words to describe it. And it seemed that the glory of the scarlet, crimson and orange flowers, as though painted on the deep blue of the sky, and the strange terrible longing, for some inexplicable reason, are one and the same thing.

I remembered that once in Kashmir (how long ago it seems!), we were talking with L. about the training. She was telling me that the disciple is subjected to such states of loneliness and longing that it could be almost suicidal. A great Master is needed to get the disciple through this state of separation. St. John of the Cross has a good description of those states of darkness; he calls it: The Dark Night of the Soul.

Guruji came back on Thursday looking very tired. Told him about the complete separation and darkness. He only nodded. For the last few days he just answers in monosyllables or nods without answering. I have the feeling that he does not even listen. With others he will talk for hours on various topics, has an infinite patience to listen to everything they say. To me he hardly listens and I am interrupted constantly, as soon as I open my mouth, either by him or by others.

For the last few days the mind is not working at all.

"Love is a gift," he was saying to a man who came for the first time. **"Love is a gift and it remains forever, once it is given; only sometimes like embers, it is covered by ashes and it is not evident."**

I wondered what those ashes were . . . our little self, the "I"? Or is it the world closing tightly around us?

Have no money at all. A few rupees are my only possession. It is surprising how little it matters. No money at all . . . a strange feeling. Whatever will arrive from my investments from now on is not mine anymore; it is already his. It will go into his account, to be distributed to all those who are in need. To be a mindless creature . . . how strange! It is quite painless, just strange. I can still do my daily chores, things necessary for life, like washing, cleaning the flat, having a bath, keeping my personal things more or less in order. But for anything else beside these elementary things my brain is not good anymore.

"I am nowhere; I cannot think," I said to him, and he nodded gravely. To be nowhere is also a strange feeling; I sit here; so clearly, I must be somewhere in space, but I am certainly not in this world . . . everything seems to be just a funny, crazy, dream, a *Maya* of some kind. The heat and the glare, and the vomiting condition, and people, and feelings of fear and loneliness and the simple necessities of life . . . just crazy . . . difficult to reconcile all this . . . impossible to understand.

The silly talk of the noisy crowd did not seem to matter at all today. It simply did not exist. I was in a kind of half-state . . . cannot think. The mind is of such stillness; it seems permanently fixed on him, in fear and apprehension; what will he do next? Only this concentration on him is effortless, easy and natural; all else is an effort. It appears that the only effortless state is thinking about him, for it is quite automatic. It appears to be an automatic function of the mind at this stage, to think of nothing else.

I suppose this is the reason why in this System of Yoga a Teacher is essential and is considered absolutely necessary: he becomes the focus of attention for the mind. I could see how, by this method, one-pointed concentration is achieved, a thing so difficult to achieve in all other schools of Yoga. Here with this system it becomes effortless. The effort lies somewhere else—in the power of endurance, the capacity for sacrifice, the will to go on, to hold out at any cost. And also the eagerness, the perseverance—this is the Shishya's part to play. And it is here where the greatest effort is needed. A very great effort indeed. . . .

I discovered something else. If by an effort of will, I somehow manage to concentrate on something else beside him, then the thought is so sharp, so clear . . . the power of concentration is greater than usual. Is it because one has made an effort that it happens like that?

The stillness of the mind during the day is wonderful, a complete or partial suspension of the thinking process is taking place.

11th May

THERE IS INSIDE ME such a sorrowful stillness, I don't seem to have even the strength to breathe. The heart is broken and sore; it is like a deep wound, bleeding slowly. Such a loneliness. Such darkness. There is nothing left, nothing at all. . . . Had a vision of myself being suspended naked on a thin thread, over a bottomless, completely black chasm . . . ready at any moment to crash into it . . . very disturbing . . . am afraid. . . .

The money arrived from London, at last. It is already not mine; it is all in his name in the bank. Have never been so poor in all my life. An extraordinary feeling: have to depend on what he will give me . . . am a beggar in the very sense of the word . . . I have to learn how to be a beggar . . . how hard it is going to be. I have to trust Him and Him only. This is the purpose of it all.

A VOICE IN MY DREAM: "Only the one who is loved is tortured."

When I woke up, was lying for a long time awake, thinking: it must be difficult for him—for he is a naturally kind man—to be so hard with me. He is always so kind to others. There must be a reason why he is like this towards me. Though I know that the training according to the Ancient Tradition must be hard, and he is in his right to be like that, still, I am hurt; I still complain and rebel. Am foolish. I know I am.

Could not speak to him at all. Too many people, all wanting his attention. A Frenchman came, sent by L.; he is one of her friends. He is a nice, quiet, youngish man, and we had a long talk in French. While the Guru was occupied with others, he asked a few questions about him and his Yoga system. Could not tell him much about that, but told him how he exorcised a spirit. When I remarked about the silliness of the crowd which assembles here, he said, yes, such people like the Guru have no center of the "I," for them all human beings are alike; he himself had such moments, and he knows how it feels. I liked his way of putting it, told the Guru about it and reflected upon it for a long time. No center of the "I". . . . That's why he never seems to be disturbed and tolerates all this crowd around him. . . .

"I am never disturbed," he told me once. Only then I did not understand the meaning of it. I think it is never possible to understand for anyone until one reaches this stage.

Am completely without money. Had practically nothing to eat. Tomorrow must have a day of fasting. Hope he will go to the bank tomorrow.

14th May

FASTED FOR TWO DAYS. No food at all. When I went to him, had a palpitation and pain in the heart. Probably brought on by the emptiness in the bowels due to the empty stomach.

He did not go to the bank and said that an employee of the bank will bring some money. I doubted it; could not understand why he did not go to the bank himself. His expression was severe, hardly looking at me, speaking abruptly; he looked remote and ruthless, his face like a stone. In my heart there is much fear when he is in this mood. He stood at the gate waiting for the bank employee to arrive, and I went home to take some medicine to stop palpitations. When I came back, he was talking to two young men at the gate. They were from the bank, as he later told me. The money arrived; I was relieved.

"You were perplexed," he said to me. I explained it was because there was something wrong with my heart; my body seems to be well in spite of the heat; I did not expect to get such a reaction after only a short fast. He said that he will give me some money tomorrow.

15th May

HIS FACE WAS STONY. He was talking to two men already sitting there when I came. He did not acknowledge my greeting. How much fear there is in me when he is like this . . . I am terrified of him and speaking becomes difficult. I asked him timidly if I could have some money.

"Wait," he said.

When the two men had left, he got up, went inside, and then gave me some money. That will see me through till the end of the month, I thought.

"How is the new flat?"

I said that it is very private, very pleasant. It looks like an Arab home . . . my little white home in the East.

He did not come out in the evening last night. After having given Babu, his son, his English lesson, I sat alone. Lately he takes every opportunity to make my life as uncomfortable as possible. He decided that Babu needs his English improved. The boy hates it and does not hide his feelings. I have to come at 4 p.m., when the heat is simply suffocating. After he has his lesson, I sit alone. It is all so difficult, for the mind is not working and the heat does the rest. Furthermore, I have to type endlessly, with several copies, job applications for his son, or medical certificates for the half-blind man who is coming daily. Needless to say, the certificates have to have several copies as well. Much later the usual crowd arrives; his brother lately is always present, talking and talking.

In such cases I go home very early, before eight. It is a pity to leave so early, for the evenings are very pleasant, and it is relatively cool in the garden. But I have to go; all of a sudden I seem to flop . . . feel so deeply tired, like a bag which suddenly has been emptied. Cannot stand it for one moment longer, so I go.

Now the temperature is 108-110° in the shade, and every day the *Loo* is blowing from 9 a.m. until 6 p.m. The *Loo* is a hot wind coming from the deserts of West Pakistan, pushing the temperature up to 120° in the shade sometimes, so I was told.

16th May

HE DID NOT COME OUT last evening either. He was feverish and rested after having had his lunch. A few people sat talking Hindi. Went home early.

17th May

IN THE EVENING a few people were sitting and talking to his brother. He came out and began by telling me that one should not sit on the same level as the Guru. I said that I never thought that I did, but he ignored my remark. He continued by saying that many people object to many things, and I asked if they objected to me. Yes, he said, and they object to Filibert. People are free to object, and he satisfies them.

"Look at my devotees, how they behave when they come here; I personally don't mind; it is not for me, but for the people who come here and object."

I said that I respected him so much I never thought that I at any time behaved badly.

"You must become part of our culture; I took on the culture of my Revered Guru Maharaj; you must take on mine. You will be changed."

I was perplexed. "But Bhai Sahib, I have been in your hands for only such a short time; how can you expect me to change so quickly! I know I have to change, and I am prepared to do it as quickly as possible; I will cooperate in every way, but give me time!"

"You see," he laughed, "it took you more than ten minutes to understand what I want. Look how dense you are!"

"Yes, when you speak to me, my mind goes blank; you speak in a manner difficult to grasp for the Western mind. Your mind works in a different way from ours! Your way of expressing your thought is different."

"First one must learn how to obey, then how to understand the Hint."

"I will try, Bhai Sahib." He nodded with a smile and went inside. I sat for a while thinking over what he was telling me and then went home.

18th May

I FORGOT TO MENTION that when the Frenchman was here, he asked a question on *Ahimsa*. What is *Ahimsa?*

"The non-killing is only a crude conception of *Ahimsa*; for it is much more than that. The real *Ahimsa* is not to injure the feelings of others, not to injure oneself. That is, not to harm others and not to harm oneself."

"How can we injure our own feelings, or harm ourselves?" the Frenchman wanted to know.

"You injure your own feelings by creating habits. If for instance you are addicted to drinking tea, and you cannot get it, you suffer, don't you? So your feelings are injured by the created habit. Never, never, to injure the feelings of anybody and never to create habits, is real *Ahimsa*. By creating habits we imprison ourselves; imprisonment is limitation. And limitation is suffering."

I think that it is a very interesting answer; and here would lie the explanation why the Guru has no fixed habits at all. I keep coming here every day, and every day it is different. One never knows how it is going to be. Sometimes he is here; sometimes one learns that he is away; and never the day or the time of return is known. Or he would be gone for a walk, or resting, or having a bath. He will sit outside or inside, or he will not come out at all. He has no fixed hours for anything. He might sit in meditation the whole night, or sleeping till 9 a.m., his first bath at 4 a.m., or at midday. At any time of the day he may announce: **"I am going to have my bath."** I think he has two or three baths every day. One never knows what he will do or not do. One day he told us: **"Even my wife never knows what I am doing or how much money I have. Sometimes I go out without money and come back with a large sum. Sometimes I go out, my pockets full of money, and I come back without. The only thing I can say for sure is that I don't go out of my premises without an order."**

At that time, it was quite at the beginning, I did not understand what he had meant; now it seems to me that I understand, at least partly. L. said that all Sufis are like that. They do not try deliberately to be—they become like that by following the System.

20th May

THE WARDROBE is not very well finished; it does not close properly, but it will be all right. I needed it badly with the dust storms blowing, and the dust getting everywhere into everything.

Only now the ceiling fan has been installed. He made me wait for it until now. I waited and waited that he should give me the money to buy it. The table fan was not mine; I had to give it back to Pushpa more than two weeks ago for she needed it. Was without a fan, and my courtyard and the whole bungalow were a furnace. I kept walking up and down in the afternoon, up and down in the veranda, wetting myself under the shower, the brain aflame, stark naked, hoping for a little freshness, like in a mad dream, blood boiling, drinking and drinking water from the earthenware jar . . . it was indescribable suffering.

And the still, windless nights were sleepless because of the heat within . . . burned alive within and without . . . a sacrifice to *Agni* in the real sense of the word.

Each time I mentioned the fan, he would say, tomorrow. But each day there was something else; either he was not well and could not go to the bank, or he had visitors, or people came for healing, or blessing, or he just forgot . . . so, I waited. My only relief was to sit under the fan in his room, but even that was often denied to me for his room was closed, or we all sat in the garden. I just waited. I confess that I was resentful. I cannot deny it . . . for my body suffered very much, could not eat at all due to the heat, and the perspiration streaming from me day and night made me feel very weak.

At last he gave me the money for the fan. The electrician took two days to install it, and now with the ceiling fan in working order and my dresses protected and safe in the wardrobe, I felt more secure, not to speak of increased comfort. It seemed to me that I have settled down for years to come. . . .

24

"The Sun Cannot Harm Me Either"

IN THE EVENING when I arrived, he was sitting alone in the garden, and when I sat down I thought that he would get up and go inside as he has been doing lately. He avoids sitting with me alone and never comes out when I am the only one there. As soon as somebody else arrives, then he will come out.

But this time, to my surprise, he began a kindly talk with me. At first he told me about himself, how he became his Rev. Guru Maharaj's disciple when he was only fourteen years old, and how he loved him. Then he talked about his journeys and how he intends to spend the money which will come in July. This was the largest amount, in fact all that was left of it. Told him how much I wished that I had more to give him. It was the last large sum from my investments in Australia. It will flow through his fingers like water in a few weeks, perhaps even in a few days. There was still something left in London, but it was less than the one which was due to arrive in summer. I was surprised at myself that it did not even hurt to see it go. I think I am too fascinated to see how he deals with it to have time to be really afraid. I woke up from my reverie as he was saying:

"You come naked into the world and you go naked. When you come to the Spiritual Teacher, you have to be naked!"

Suddenly it dawned on me: of course! It was the second birth according to the Tradition! And silently I thanked my good star that I was able to offer him all I had, sensing somehow, however dimly, that I had to do it. . . . It was not a knowledge: rather a FEELING, an intuition that it HAS to be, that it was EXPECTED of me, that there was no other way to go. And I remembered that not long ago, he said, that the Shishya has to give away everything, but he must do it by himself; the Master cannot order it, the Teacher cannot say: do it! For then it will be an order and then there is no merit attached to it. Besides, even if the disciple gives everything up out of love or regard for the Teacher, who can say that deep in him no attachment has remained? One does not get rid of desires and attachments by ordering them to disappear. It will never work this way. One has to reach the stage that everything begins to fall away from one. Possessions are attachments

200

and are, or can become an obstacle to Spiritual Life. If one understands it and acts accordingly, the way is free.

I confess I did not grasp it as clearly as that; I just felt I had to do it. That's all. To leave all security behind, to be in the Hands of God from now on; heaven only knows how much help I received unknowingly; only He knows and the Guru; I probably never will. . . .

He went inside. I remained. A few people began to arrive and Satendra told me that his father is going to Lucknow tomorrow. He came out again. It was a lovely hot evening; I was at peace. The longing was gone. A deep happiness, like a sound, a happiness not of this world filled my heart. It reverberated in the whole body, like a distant, dimly audible vibration. It would be mine—for how long? At present it seemed to be eternal; it seemed that it would last forever . . . though I knew very well that tomorrow, perhaps even tonight, I can be desperately lonely again, crying before a closed door.

24th May, 1962

COULD NOT SLEEP, so hot it was. The ceiling fan did nothing else but move boiling air around. As I had no table fan anymore, I had to sleep in the room, could not do so outside; it was too hot without a fan.

When I was coming through the gate, his door was open; he was sitting in the big chair, his wife standing beside, talking to him. As soon as she saw me, she smiled and obviously made some remark about me, because he looked up with a smile as I came towards them.

"My wife is just saying how is it that you never wear a hat or a headcovering, not even an umbrella as many Europeans and even Indians do . . . why?"

I laughed. "I never cover my head; I love the sun; my body is only happy where the sun sees me! I have a pact with it: I worship it; and it does not harm me!" I added jokingly.

"Hm," he said, looking at me attentively; and then: **"How can you worship a God who sets?"**

What an answer, I thought, and did not know what to say. He translated what I said to his wife. She laughed and went out. I sat down under the fan, grateful for a little coolness. And then, after a while he said:

"I also never cover my head; the sun cannot harm me either."

I caught my breath . . . the sun cannot harm him either. . . . That can only mean that he and I are bound together somewhere, or belong to something which had to do with the sun. Suddenly I felt a deep happiness . . . like a wonderful, secret, complicity . . . cannot harm me either. We did not speak anymore. There was no need. His lips were moving in silent prayer; the beads kept sliding rhythmically through his fingers. I just sat there experiencing the pleasure of the whiff of cool air periodically refreshing my burning cheeks and moving my hair. And I was deeply, completely, happy.

In the evening I told him that I needed some money. The one he gave me was finished. He wanted to know details. I explained that I had unexpected expenses, for I had to buy a few necessities for the new flat—for instance, a curtain to cover the entrance door leading into the courtyard; it is full of large cracks; I had no privacy . . . little boys peeping through the cracks.

"Don't buy me fruit, if you are short of money."

I protested; he eats so little; fruit juice is good for him. I feel at least I do something for him personally; all the money goes for others, elsewhere. But he shook his head with a severe expression, and I knew that it was an order. He looks tired. He suffers from dysentery with blood discharge; his face is grey. My heart was heavy . . . dear Guruji. . . . And then a thought came into my mind: and what if he dies? I have nothing more left in this world . . . hoping to remain here for many years. What will I do? But I chased this thought away as quickly as it came. He will not die. People live with this kind of illness for many years. In India most people have it. I felt miserable.

"You make it difficult for me; you say one must never disobey the Teacher. Cannot one make an exception sometimes? I want so much to buy a few oranges for you." He remained silent, his face severe. "Oh dear! One cannot remain happy even for a short while—you plunge me into difficulties again!" He nodded gravely. Went home feeling sad.

As so often, in the night, when I needed help, I speak to his Rev. Guru Maharaj with surprising results. This time too, I asked Him: what shall I do? It goes against love. I know he needs fruit juice now. I see that he eats the same food as the rest of the family. He never wants an exception to be made for him. But they are healthy people, and he is ill and weak, and he vomits nearly every day. It was a service of love which I did for him, and did it with such a pleasure. Deprived myself of things lately, because money was scarce, but I never failed to buy fruit for him. What shall I do? My heart tells me to disobey. So, what shall I do? I asked. No answer came. I waited. Waited for a long time. And all of a sudden I knew that I had to obey. Obedience has the precedence over all other considerations. Always. And especially just now I had to obey more than ever, because he waited for every opportunity to catch me out, to hurt me. I knew by experience that he can burn me if I dare to disobey; he will put fire into my blood again and burn me. . . .

"Yes," was the answer, "and in the future you will get many more tests on obedience, because obedience is difficult for you. And they will be no simple tests, but complicated ones, where you will have to use discrimination."

25th May

I WAS BUYING A SMALL MELON for myself at a stall . . . I saw that they were going cheaply. Have to be careful about my expenditure and also have not much desire to eat in this heat; a slice of melon would be just the right thing.

"What are you purchasing?" I heard his voice behind me. Surprised, I turned round. He stood behind me clad in white *kurta* and *longhi*, surrounded by his disciples. He inquired about the price of the melon, checked with the vendor the weight and examined the quality. While walking along he explained that somebody had died of an accident and he was going there, for help was needed. I asked if I could come too. So we went to the house where a lot of kids were standing in the street outside, as well as a crowd of passers-by. We went inside, and he talked to the relatives of the dead man for a while. It was a rikshaw accident; the lorry killed the man instantly and severely injured the child who was with him, but the child was out of danger by now.

We went back and much was talked in Hindi about the accident. I was walking beside him carrying my melon, and he said that as soon as I had left last evening, he came out and sat outside till half past ten. I remarked that I was sorry that I had left; I was thinking that he was not well. He said that it was his intention not to come out, but people came.

"Actually I went inside because I didn't want to give you an answer," he kicked a small stone out of his way.

"I don't need an answer anymore; I know what to do." He nodded.

"That's right; but you said that you are short of money. It will be done, it will be done. . . . Sometimes I speak, sometimes I don't; sometimes I am short-tempered. There is always a reason for it. Those who know, do not take it ill."

"But how can I take it ill?" I exclaimed. "You do your duty, Bhai Sahib, and I try to do mine!"

"I am glad you think like this," he said with a smile. The whole crowd filed into the garden, sitting or standing around him, still discussing the accident.

Later, in the room, he repeated that yesterday he did not want to discuss the money question, but he will do it now, and how much would I want. I said that I was thinking over what I would need. My monthly rent was forty rupees. If he could give me another hundred rupees, that would work out roughly at three rupees per day for food and any little extras. One hundred forty, per month; I think I could manage on that. He nodded.

"Three rupees per day for one person is ample; very many people live on much less. At any rate it is all your own money," he smiled.

"No, it is not mine anymore," I said, and I told him that, at first, I wanted to ask him to leave an amount for me in the bank, to draw for my needs, say, 2000 rupees, to last for one year. But then I dismissed this idea. It will be better if he just gives me each month for my needs. Then I will be completely dependent on him. I feel that it is what he wishes me to be. "From now on I will be even financially completely in your hands." I looked up. The expression on his face was most strange: so transparent, so still (old Tibetan, flashed through my mind), a smile, so mysterious, impossible to describe. . . .

"Yes, this is my wish too," he said very, very softly, and I was amazed, for his voice did not seem to be his usual voice at all—a pleasant baritone with a bell-like ring in it—no, it was so still, rather high-pitched, as if coming from far away, as if he spoke in a sing-song of a different language. A kind . . . a kind . . . no, could not think; the mind suddenly, abruptly stopped, as if knocked out of action. I just stared speechless. His face was so tender. I never saw it like this. How tender he can look. His strong, masculine face was capable of such a tender expression. I was moved by it when for the first time I saw him holding his grandchild in his arms, or was "fishing" for a Soul. But this time it was for me. It was never for me until now. For me was severity, a hard, stony face, or indifference altogether sometimes, but more rarely a kindly smile—that was all I could expect. Now, for the first time there was a quality in it which was . . . how difficult the thinking is. . . . Yes, I suddenly knew: dim memories were like this, memories of visions and dreams in the night . . . glimpses of places not from this world, as if of times so long ago. I sat there full of speechless stillness and deeply moved. *Pralaya* (cosmic dissolution before *manvantara*, which is coming into manifestation) must be like that, I thought, and a deeply ringing gladness, like a Great Sound, permeated my whole physical frame.

In the evening I saw that he did not go to the bank. He looked grey and very weak. The night was restless. The body behaved as if in fever. The heat was great; I was not under fever . . . but he was.

26th May

IN THE MORNING everybody had left early, and he went to the bank. Afterwards he gave me one hundred rupees and said that it should last until the end of June; the rent was already paid by me until the end of June, when I took the flat in May.

In the afternoon, I came at half past five, rather early, for it was very hot. Lately, Babu was never at home when I came at 4 p.m. to give him his lesson, so I stopped coming as early as that.

Guruji was sitting in the courtyard, and I asked if I could go into the room to sit under the fan. At first I sat alone in the dark room, listening to the peaceful sound of the softly revolving fan; then Satendra and Virendra joined me. Satendra was telling me that his father will never pray for the members of his family; according to the System it is not done. "He will pray for you being his Shishya."

I said that once I was in big trouble, but his father refused to pray for me.

"That's what he would say," he replied; "but after midnight he prays every day; you could see him doing it if you were here. When everybody is asleep, he prays."

I heard his voice in the garden and saw through the chik that he was standing outside directing Panditji who was sprinkling the place, splashing the water out of a bucket with his hand. Then he put the chairs out. I came out and he told me to take away the bottle with the methylated spirit because it smelled, which I did. I bought some methylated spirit for my cooker and had left it standing outside the door. When back, I saw him still standing in the middle of the garden. He looked up and smiled at me kindly. Then he sat down on the tachat. Nobody was about, a rare thing. He began by speaking about his Guru Maharaj . . . how he and his father were both his disciples.

"We are Hindus; he was a Muslim. Hindus are supposed to be proud. He made us stand, my father and myself, outside his door. There we stood, for hours, with folded hands, in blazing sunshine, and he did not open. Everybody could see that we Hindus were

standing in front of a closed door of a Muslim. He was a hard
Teacher. Very strict. I was a wild boy and I did not like him at first. I
suppose I had some narrow-minded ideas. I was very young, then.
One day I saw him coming through the gate with my father and
other disciples. He stopped in front of me and looked at me and my
heart melted. He said: 'You will massage my feet tonight.' So I did.
And from that moment I never looked back. My love for him grew
all the time. He was a great man. Miss L. knew him." He concluded.
How his voice changed . . . became so moved and tender when he
spoke of his Rev. Guru Maharaj. I felt moved too, just by listening to
him.

It was hot. The soil smelled fresh of moist earth where Panditji had
sprinkled it. The garden was dry. Nature was waiting for the
monsoon. I asked him how long will I have this fire in my body.

"Let's see," he said reflectively, "you have completed your 54th
year; well, you can have it till you are 65; it depends. . . ."

I was horrified: "I will not survive this torture for so many years!"

"It will be on and off; you won't have it all the time. One day you
will understand; just now, understanding is impossible for you."

He said it with infinite softness, closed his eyes, muttered
something, arranged his legs in a different *Asana*, and went into deep
Samadhi.

27th May

A MAN CAME TO SEE HIM from Delhi. He was from the radio and a
journalist. He asked if Bhai Sahib would be interested in principle to
give a talk on the radio, or if an article in the paper would be more
suitable. He said that he was not interested at all.

"It does not belong to my work; we never advertise. It is not found
in the public places; it is not sold in the market. . . ."

"May I ask a question?" the young man asked. He behaved very
respectfully and clearly was impressed. No wonder, Guruji made an
impressive figure, all in white, full of dignity, and we his disciples, all
seated around.

"Ask as many questions as you like, even the most difficult ones;
and if I cannot answer them for you in ten minutes, to your full
satisfaction, it is my lack of knowledge and not your lack of
understanding. My knowledge is not in the books. It never was.
Only fools and idiots write books for money. What knowledge is in
books? Did books ever make somebody realize God? It is all
nonsense!"

What an answer . . . only the Great Ones can be so humble. That should be written on my banner as an inspiration for the rest of my days: **"If I cannot explain it to you to your full satisfaction, it is my lack of knowledge and not your lack of understanding."** Here is a guideline for the future . . . a clear pointer for me. . . .

At home there was such loud music from a loudspeaker nearby, a wedding, or a festivity of some kind. Could not sleep. And had a bad head cold into the bargain; the body felt miserable, full of perspiration, could not breathe freely and was feverish.

28th May

HE IGNORED ME COMPLETELY. I greeted him as usual when I came in. He was walking up and down on the brick elevation in front of the house, mala in his hand. Had a premonition of some trouble brewing, but chased this thought away. He gave me a quick look and continued to walk up and down. Then I noticed: the Great Separation was here . . . it is useless to try to describe it to someone who never experienced it.

"Nur wer die Sehnsucht kennt weisst was ich leide" ("Only those who know the longing know how much I suffer"). Was it Schiller or Goethe who wrote it? It is a peculiar special feeling of utter loneliness. I use the word "special" intentionally, because it cannot be compared to any kind of feeling of loneliness we all experience sometimes in our lives.

All seems dark and lifeless. There is no purpose anywhere or in anything. No God to pray to. No hope. Nothing at all. A deep-seated rebellion fills the mind . . . only this time it mattered less than usual. The mind was in such a state . . . there was so little left of it. No trouble at all to keep it still; it was automatically blank. I just sat there; the thoughts, if any, happened to float in, were drifting slowly, lazily, passing by as if on a screen, and then all was blankness once more. This state was not new to me; it had begun to come on periodically for the last few months, increasing gradually in intensity, each time it happened.

There is a wind coming from the deserts of West Pakistan which is blowing in this part of north India, from the end of March till the rains of the monsoon begin. It is called *Loo*. It usually starts at 6 a.m. and lasts till sunset; it can push up the temperature to something around 120° in the shade. The nights are still, full of stars and oven-hot. A sheer agony. My eyes were constantly red and inflamed from the perspiration running into them. Men went around with twisted handkerchiefs around their foreheads to prevent the perspiration from running into their eyes, and some wore permanently twisted towels round their necks. I had showers three or four times per day. But there was no relief . . . the water tank is on the roof, and the water is boiling hot.

Today the *Loo* was terrible; the temperature was 117° yesterday in the shade, so the papers said. Today it felt even hotter. My kitchen was so full of the wind that from time to time I had to escape into the room under the fan while in the midst of cooking. It did not help much, though. It felt like the entrance hall of hell. . . .

29th May

THIS MORNING the *Loo* storm began at half past five in the morning. It increased during the day to a violent dust storm, and was blowing all day till seven in the evening. The air is dark with evil smelling dust which the wind sweeps up from the unpaved streets. To think what we are breathing in makes me shudder. For two days the head cold has not improved. To get at least a little relief from the heat, I kept wetting myself under the shower and sat wet under the fan. I was warned against doing it, but as usual did not heed the warning. Thought that nothing could happen to me; how can one catch cold in this heat? The result was a bad cold; I was feverish, and last night the breathing was difficult. When I mentioned it to Bhai Sahib, his only remark was that he too could not sleep because of the heat, and he kept twisting and turning all night.

"You take too much upon you," I said, but he jerked his shoulders nonchalantly. "You strain your body too much: meditation during the night, you don't digest your food, and all day long people are sitting here, all wanting to talk." He looked at me ironically, as if to say: and you? You, too, sit here and want to talk to me . . . but all that he said was:

"When I cannot sleep, he, my Rev. Guru Maharaj, is with me. When I am asleep, I am with my superiors and with him too. It is of little importance if I sleep or not."

I could not sit in the garden because of the dust. In the street when going to his place, I could hardly fight against the wind, and was pressing my handkerchief to my nose and mouth in vain protection against the fine powdery dust. The swirling gust of the strong wind filled the air with so much dust that one could not even see the ground under one's feet. My eyes watering, I kept sneezing and coughing—it was very tiresome . . . had a severe headache.

A young Indian woman with a small child was sitting with him. One could see that she was in trouble; he spoke to her kindly and was giving advice in some complicated family matters.

When I went there at 6 a.m., the *Loo* storm was beginning to die down, but it was still unbearably hot. I sat in the room in complete darkness under the fan; the doors and the wooden shutters on the windows were closed. In spite of that, fine dust, like powder, was accumulating on the window sills and under the doors. He was in the next room praying silently. Panditji was wetting the ground outside, as he does every day before putting the chairs out.

Then we went out. It was already bearable. The wind nearly stopped. People began to arrive. As soon as he appeared, my mind stopped abruptly. I just sat there, felt giddy, completely lost, in a void. What a nice state it is to be mindless.

Pushpa sent me a message that she was back and wanted to see me. Went to the *Kirtan*. When returning, saw everybody in the garden and sat there with others till 9:30. There was much longing.

25

Who Will Remember?

30th May, 1962

WILL I EVER REMEMBER those days, without peace, days with no mind, and of the most exhausting heat? Of the most terrible longing? When the call of the Indian woodpecker is in the air—I call him the sugar-mill bird—his voice sounds just like a sugar press working at full speed. One's head is like a leaden weight sitting on the neck, the bones of the skull like an iron ring pressing tighter and tighter around the brain. All the objects in the room are so hot that sometimes it burns the fingers when touching them. And it is hot . . . it is hot . . . oh, is it hot!! And the mind does not work. I fail to understand the simplest things and forget what I did only one moment ago. . . .

The longing . . . seems part of my blood. . . . When it is throbbing in the background softly, it is a wonderful feeling, mindless as I am. But . . . when it begins to be a torment—which it is more often than not—then it is the darkest thing in the world. There is nothing darker, nothing emptier, nothing so full of indistinct terror. And there is a moment when the longing, the mindlessness, the stillness, and the terror form a complete circle, in which the disciple is made to revolve endlessly; nothing is left out, and the body is included in it too. Yes, I am bound to forget those restless days, the longing, the fragrance of some exotic blossoms flowering nearby, the blinding light, and the bliss occasionally coming from . . . where? I don't know. . . .

How can I remember if there is hardly any mind left to think? With WHAT will I remember? Those priceless days? I know they are priceless, because they are leading me somewhere, in a definite direction; but where? I don't know. . . .

"Have you ever been drunk?" I asked him jokingly, as soon as I arrived. He was already sitting outside; only one man was with him, but he did not understand English.

"No, never," he answered.

"Well, I have been sometimes, long ago when I was young. My husband was very fond of drink, and I too had sometimes a bit too much. I know how it feels, and now it feels just the same as if I were drunk. I cannot even walk properly." He did not answer. Proceeded to tell him about my experience of trying to live practically without mind. . . . What a pity it is that I won't remember these states in the future, the states which are leading me into a dimension not known to me. No one will be there to remember, for there is no mind. I talked for a while; he listened quietly. We were not interrupted, not even once.

"Where is intellect, there is no love. Love begins where the mind stops."

Pushpa brought me from Delhi a very nice flower pot, a red one on a white tripod in which she put cactuses—two small ones, one yellow and one green, like round, hairy balls. I had pleasure with them and put the pot in my veranda. I went for lunch at Pushpa's and learned that K. Junior was going to London and wanted £100 to be put at his disposal there.

He was standing in the garden when I came, looking at the sky. A dust storm had been gathering on the horizon for the last half hour. As soon as he saw me, he went in and closed the door. I went into the doorway, not daring to go into the room, and sat there in the passage in the whirling dust. He was inside the courtyard, where Panditji was wetting the pavement stones with a hose. He did not take the slightest notice of me; his back was turned; he was talking to his wife and to his brother, and I sat there crying bitterly. How hopelessly inadequate I felt: mind not working, only half-understanding, and feeling deeply the humiliation of not being asked into the room in these appalling weather conditions.

The dust storm soon subsided, and Panditji began to wet the ground in the garden. Guruji came out and began to walk up and down, while Panditji splashed water about, with a serene smile on his face.

Panditji always looks so serene, existing in a world of his own, distant, tranquil, living very much his own inward life, mostly sitting in Dhyana, or massaging Guruji's feet. Sometimes, one could see him standing and staring with wide open eyes . . . and such an expression of bliss, such a tender quality in his face, a happiness unknown to me and probably to others. He was a silent man; very often he walked about, smiling to himself as though he were observing things so strange and wonderful . . . which all others knew nothing about. He was a bit of a mystery to me.

Prof. Batnagar came and we had a talk. He said that I do such a *Tapas* (penance) by staying here in circumstances to which I am not at all accustomed: I probably get so much bliss and happiness, otherwise I would not do it.

"Oh, no, no bliss, such things are for other people; I have trouble only." Bhai Sahib, who was talking to a group of villagers turned and looked straight at me. His eyes were shining like diamonds in the half-darkness, illumined only by the light of the street lamp filtering through the foliage of the tree. Prof. Batnagar left soon.

"He has a very interesting conversation," Bhai Sahib turned to me—**"highly intelligent man. He comes here often, but he is not my disciple; neither was he my father's. You see, he is my neighbor; sees too much of what is happening here—how many people are living here and all of what is going on. He does not understand why I give hospitality to so many people of low caste who have such a low standard of living. He is a Hindu, a Brahmin, and a man of property; no wonder he does not understand, though he knows in theory our attitude and our System very well. But to know the theory and to be it . . . is a great, very great difference."**

He looked into the distance, and after a short silence: **"Believe me, not even my family understands me. For one moment you thought this morning that it is your money which is being used to repair Tulsi Ram's dwelling, and you felt annoyance. You were right; a little of your money will be in it too: but what business is it of yours? This is ignorance. Once it is given, it is mine, and I do what I like with it. I cannot be limited. No more. Once one has surrendered somewhere, no limitation is possible, nor is it tolerated."**

Then he proceeded to tell me how he does not like to hurt people's feelings, but he had to tell me what was necessary this morning, otherwise he would not have done his duty. Actually he was telling me off this morning about something which I don't remember, because of my mind being in such a state.

"My revered Father and my uncle were surrendered before my Rev. Guru Maharaj in every possible way, and still he often told them: 'You understand nothing; you don't know how to pay regard to me!! Prof. Batnagar can tell you how my Father payed the greatest regard to him always. Of all his disciples, he had only two who did completely surrender: My Rev. Father and my uncle."

"How great is the capacity of a human heart?" I asked.

"No limit. . . there is no limit!" He smiled his radiant smile. **"The human heart is limitless, for it forms part of the Great Heart."**

Went home full of stillness. . . .

31st May

MIND NOT WORKING, feeling giddy—all around is *Maya*.

Only one man was sitting with him this morning. Told him that I cannot be a good advertisement for him, for I cannot even walk. This morning I was walking zig-zag, like a drunkard. My feet did not obey. People in the bazaar must have been thinking: look at this old European woman!—she is drunk already at seven in the morning!

He gave me a kindly smile fingering his mala.

"Yes," he said thoughtfully, **"the poets call us drunkards; we are drunk with the Wine from the Eyes of the Beloved. . . ."**

Then I began to talk. It must have been for a long time, over an hour, non-stop; it was like an urge, an inner necessity. One moment afterwards I did not remember what I was telling him. It was like a half-unconscious state. I remember, though, that I said that I was talking too much. If he thinks so, he should stop me; I have no possibile understanding of what I am doing. But he only smiled gently and said nothing. Plenty of people came in a crowd, and until midday they were discussing all kinds of topics: the price of butter, the Chinese trouble on the frontier of Tibet, the pruning of trees, and the immortality of the Soul. I was sitting cross-legged on the tachat next to his; all others were sitting on the chairs facing him. When everybody had left he said:

"This morning you were telling me that you were talking too much. Sometimes one is made to talk. The Divine Power wishes it so. One HAS to talk. I am supposed to hear everything, to listen to everything. If the disciple is asleep, the Master is behind; if the disciple is in trouble, the Master is with him. It is a troublesome job to be a Guru and a Wali," he concluded.

I asked him if he would know if I was in danger, and he nodded. His face was very still. I asked what he meant when he said: **"One is made to speak."** I felt an inner urge, an irresistible desire to say all that was in my mind. Is it done to let him know things which he perhaps may have overlooked? He nodded absent-mindedly. I was not sure he was listening.

Went home. It was very hot. Yesterday it was 114° in the shade, but I hardly felt the heat . . . perhaps because the mind is not working, and when it does not work, there is hardly any suffering.

Wanted to do some typing—entries in my diary, but could not do that either. Could not concentrate at all. So I slept for a while, then got up, had some fresh lime juice with bicarbonate of soda . . . it was refreshing. The heat was deadening; the fan was useless.

I am baked alive, I thought, and fell asleep, or was in an unconscious state—I really don't know. Suddenly, I saw his face in profile, very clearly, just one foot from my face . . . was not even surprised. He was probably having a look at me. Well, Bhai Sahib, I am grilled. Now I know a little how St. Lawrence must have felt when he was grilled alive, I thought, full of tiredness. Had a bath, tried to think, saw his face so clearly again.

Then I went to his place. A dust storm was gathering and had just started to blow fiercely when I was entering his gate. It became quite dark. They all sat in the small room playing a game of cards. I waited for Babu to give him his lesson, but he did not turn up. I didn't care. I feel so humble now that I don't even mind waiting for a boy who does not turn up. Later I saw that he was playing cards with his father, and I suppose that it was more important. . . .

The dust storm resolved itself into a brief shower. The air became lovely. Went into the garden, sniffed the fragrance of the moist earth and damp foliage. The atmosphere cooled down considerably. Talked to his brother for a while; later he came out while Panditji was still wetting the place for the chairs. The short rain was not enough to wet the soil properly. The hot, thirsty earth sucked up the moisture in no time.

He sat down, and as if it was the signal to begin, I started to talk . . . and talked . . . and talked. Do not remember a thing. It poured out of me—disjointed ideas, memories . . . heaven knows what!

He seemed to listen quietly, doing his mala. There were not even the slightest interruptions. Nobody came. We were sitting alone. "Unusual," flashed through my mind, but had no time to reflect upon it; such was the urge to speak. Then I noticed that it was already dark. I halted, looked around me in surprise; hours must have gone by! He sat there, in silence, composed, looking indifferent, mala in his hand.

"Now you can go home," he said quietly. I went, profoundly puzzled.

In the night at 11:30, it began to rain. Took my bed from the courtyard into the veranda. Rain woke me up. Had the feeling that something was taken away from me about which I was sorry. Fell asleep again about 1 a.m.

DREAM (towards the morning): He was standing beside me dressed all in white in a pool of clear water and, bending down, I was washing his feet and my own in it. The more I washed, the clearer, the purer, the water became. "Look!" I exclaimed, and woke up. The feeling quality of the dream was that I was performing a very important work, and I did it with utmost care. I also remember dimly a feeling of awe or reverence of some kind.

1st June

WROTE TO THE BANK in London to have the last large amount transferred into his account. Remembered to leave in my a/c £100 for K. junior.

2nd June

WHEN I ARRIVED, I found many people already sitting, and I thought that it will be difficult to speak to him. So I just reminded him that I had to show him some letters and discuss business matters.

"All right, later."

But more people kept arriving—the horrible Elaci Baba amongst them. I got more and more irritated; it is enough to have something of importance to discuss, and immediately it becomes impossible! Crowds would want to speak to him for hours; he will give unending explanations in Hindi, how to get a male child, or how to meditate— there is no end to it. . . . At last, he told me to go into the room and wait for him. I was afraid that Elaci Baba will come too, so I closed the door. Sat in the chair waiting . . . was in a kind of unconscious state. He came in. He was surrounded by a blinding white light . . . closed my eyes—it was like looking at the sun. He sat down on the tachat. I lifted my head and all I could say was: "You shine like an electric bulb."

"What did you say?" he asked, adjusting his legs in a comfortable position. I repeated. He ignored it.

"Where are the documents?"

In this very moment the wife stormed in talking rapidly in a loud voice. Somebody had upset a jar of pickles in the courtyard, and there was a commotion. Oh, dear, never alone, not even for an important matter like this one. He looked through the letters and wanted me to type them all over because his address, according to him, should be worded in a different way. I did not like it at all in my present state . . . the mind not working . . . I knew that I would be making many typing mistakes and will have to write the letters

several times to get it right—it will take up much time and effort. But
I said nothing . . . only remarked that in the state I am now, worldly
things seem so hopelessly difficult and even silly.

"Just go home and do as I say." He dismissed me.

Posted the letters which I wrote with the greatest difficulty. And
when already posted, I remembered that I did not begin each letter
with: Dear Sir, but simply began with the text. Hopeless. . . .

In the afternoon when I came, he was in the room under the fan.
His wife was there too, talking. Some workmen came and were busy
with the electric cables in the garden. When they had left, I closed my
eyes to merge into stillness, for I thought that he will go inside. But he
began to ask about the letters and some information about the bank
through which the amount from the Australian investments will
come. Then he began to talk to me kindly; he must have talked for
over an hour, and there was no interruption. . . . But who will
remember what he said? Where was my mind??

4th June

THE BODY ON FIRE. Mind is not here.

6th June

THIS MORNING AT SUNRISE, about 5 a.m., the sky was covered with the
most exquisite pink clouds. I was lying on my charpoy in the middle
of my small courtyard, looking at their delicate formation . . .
feathery, magenta-pink. Deep in me, there was a strange, never
experienced happiness—it was different, different from the glimpses
I had of it before. It is so ethereal, so elusive, one cannot pin it down.
It seems to have nothing to do with me as a person, nor with my
environment, nothing with my state of mind. It just comes. It is just
here. Appears like a state of Grace, and I cannot create it at will. It
comes when it wants to come, and it goes so silently that I don't even
notice that it has gone. I only realize, suddenly, that it is no more. In a
strange way, it does not belong to me as an individual; I have nothing
to do with it.

Last night, while I was looking at the sky, I noticed an object lit
brightly. It seemed to be triangular against the dark, cloudy sky, but I
could not be sure because only the rear part of it was brightly lit, so it
was difficult to judge the exact shape. It was passing at a terrific speed
in complete silence; no engines could be heard, nor a motor noise,
and the speed was far greater than that of any airplane. It passed right
across the sky, coming from the west, and disappeared behind the

roof-tops to the east. I was wondering if it was one of those things people call a flying saucer? But I was not really much interested, nor excited by it. At that moment I was doing something more important: I was listening to the currents inside my body. For my body was full of Sound . . . a Sound connected with the light circulating in it, with this mysterious Web burning my tissues. The outlines of the heart were clearly visible—it was surrounded with a faint bluish light, beating regularly . . . a beautiful sight. . . .

It was a windless, very dark night. Later, I saw another object passing, also very swiftly, but slower than the first. This one was dimly lit with a sort of hazy light and could not be discerned clearly. It seemed to be round, or of a roundish shape, and it was flying lower than the first, and it disappeared to the right, to the South. But I was listening to my heartbeat, to the increasing and decreasing rate of it— that seemed to be much more important at the moment.

No, as I already said, I will probably remember nothing of these days full of dust, heat, hot wind and wonderful fragrance drifting from the gardens behind high brick walls where white bungalows stand in sheltered seclusion . . . mindless days . . . of the longing so strong that I cried aloud sometimes in sheer physical torment—such was the pain in the heart. . . .

There will be no one to remember. Without the mind? And it is a great pity, because those are water-shed days, milestones, on the way, leading me somewhere . . . they are a transition to something else.

Strong vibration was at the base of the Spine Chakra this morning. Wondered if there will be trouble again, but there was none. The sky was a livid mother of pearl and turquoise, and delicate feathers of such tender pink were painted on it by the Great Painter of the World.

"Drunk," I said, this morning when I came. "Drunk I am." He did not answer, but continued to pray, giving a slight shake of his mala from time to time. His lips formed a long succession of soundless words.

Talked to him for a while. Don't remember one word . . . only remember saying that I saw one object in the sky.

"There were two of them," he said quietly, interrupting his prayers for a moment to change the position of his legs.

"Yes," I said, "two," and I described them. "Do you know what they were?" He nodded. "Will you tell me what they are?" He shook his head. He and his family sleep on the flat roof, like most of the

Indian families at this time of the year, for it is much cooler there. He must have seen them too. When later, I asked him again, as politely as possible, to tell me what they were, he said sternly that one should avoid useless talk. And that was all.

7th June

THIS MORNING WE SAT in the garden and were quite alone. I spoke a little, trying to merge into the stillness of non-being, but he began to speak, and remained with me for over three hours . . . something which I think never happened before in all those past months. Not only that, but there were hardly any interruptions to speak of. He touched upon all the possible topics, but he began by saying that today, on the seventh of June, his Rev. Father had expired. It was the anniversary of his death.

"He knew that he was going, and he kept hinting to us for months, but somehow we did not understand. He remained alone in the room, went into deep Samadhi and did not return."

He was playing with his mala while speaking, winding and unwinding it around his fingers; his face looked transparent, the eyes half-closed, looking into the distance . . . Asiatic, oblique eyes, like an Oriental mask. Could not avert my eyes from it—it was not his usual face. One could sense how he loved his father by the special tenderness in his voice.

I will try to remember, try to write it down, must remember . . . remember . . . it will be fragmentary. Still, I MUST remember, somehow . . . how hopeless it seems. The mind . . . Hmm . . . where are you?

Told him that the vibration was at the base of the spine again this morning, and I was afraid that the horrible visions would come back. He shook his head.

"Forget it. This is in the past. It has been taken away." I suddenly realized that from the moment, in March, when I was breaking down almost in hysterics in his garden, I never saw them again.

"I told you, if I remember rightly, that past Karmas form part and parcel of the blood."

"But what I saw was so horrible! I did not even know that such things could exist!" I protested. He slowly shook his head.

"Souls are old. How can the Soul remember everything . . . all the past? It was all there, in your blood. It was the worst situation possible. If this room is full of water, all the doors and windows are closed, and the water cannot flow out—what will happen? It will get

foul. If the patient has to be operated, and the doctor operates on him, for a while the patient may even curse the doctor, but the doctor will do his duty just the same. It is not, as you have accused me, that I have caused this trouble by using my Yogic powers; why use the powers to do such a thing? If a horse is going slow, and another, a quicker one, overtakes it, the first horse, quite simply, gets wakened up. That is all there is to it. Why can't you understand it? Why should it be so difficult to grasp? Why do we insist on *Satsang?* Because it is a quickening. We do not teach—we quicken. I am stronger than you. So your currents adjust themselves to mine. This is a simple law of nature. The stronger magnetic current will affect, quicken the weaker. If you let flow an electric current through two wires, side by side, one a strong one and the other a weak one, the stronger will affect the weaker; it will increase its potency. It is so simple."

DREAM: "You were the owner of a six-story building, and you said to me: 'If you want to go to the three lower stories, you have to go up higher than that and then come down, because I have nailed up the doors of the three lower stories.'

"But how will the tenants of the lower flats reach their homes if the doors are nailed up?" I asked.

"Oh, they have front doors, which are open, but from the back where you have to go, you have to go higher and then come down. The doors were old, worm-eaten and useless. That's why I have nailed them up."

Tried to get an interpretation of this dream.

He did not listen. As soon as I began to speak, he commenced to shout instructions to Babu who was buying mangoes from a barrel in the street. So, I don't even know if he heard me at all and cannot ask him for explanation again. . . .

26

Drunk

"COMPLETELY MAD!" I laughed. "Gloriously mad, irresponsible and drunk with joy!"—he was standing inside the fountain, his torso bare, clad only in a pale blue *longhi*. He only glanced briefly at me, occupied as he was in pouring buckets of cold water over his head and blowing like a walrus.

I felt fine, so free, so mad. Where was the mind? One is better without it, really. . . .

"Today my Rev. Father was taken to *Samadhi*," he said, rubbing his shoulders vigorously with a towel. Some *prasad* (blessed food) was distributed later to a few people who came. Then we remained alone. It seems to me that I accused him of some contradiction.

"No contradictions here, only your mind makes it so. In the morning one says something which belongs to the morning; at midday one says things which belong to this time; in the afternoon and in the evening one will say what is suitable to that particular time. There is no contradiction. We speak according to the time, the place, and the state of the progress of the disciple. . . . I never will say anything praiseworthy about you to yourself, but to others I may."

While he was talking, I kept looking at him. How is it that he has changed so much lately? He IS different—there can be little doubt about it. He seems to acquire a different quality, a non-human aspect, a kind of transparency, something unearthly about him . . . a being from another world, so strangely beautiful . . . a quality of inner beauty coming more and more to the surface, becoming more and more visible to me.

Cannot explain what is happening. Can only look and wonder. When I told him, he had only a boyish and happy laughter in response.

"Only things which you cannot explain are lasting. What can be comprehended with the mind is not a high state. If you cannot

express it, cannot put it into words, those are things not of the mind, and they will go on forever!"

"Oh, please, help me! I am so confused!"

"Why should I?" He looked straight at me. "If I begin to help you, you will ask again and again for help: how will you cross the stream? You must do it yourself; I will not help. We all had to cross the stream alone.

"Don't you realize that this is the way? I am telling you, showing you the way. THE ONLY WAY. Why don't you realize that you are nothing? Complete surrender it means! It takes time. It is not done in one day. To pass an M.A. examination takes years. It takes time to surrender. . . ."

"How long?"

"The whole life, twenty, thirty years. If you live 1000 years, 1000 years won't be enough. Sometimes you are near, sometimes very far away. I am helping you, as a matter of fact, but you cannot be aware of it, and I will never say so. My harsh words help you; my sweetness never will. Now, let's take your case: you have renounced the world; all the material things you have renounced, apparently. But the invisible things, have you renounced them too? Renounced your character, your will, everything? The character one gets inherited from the parents, and together with the will it molds the life of a person. If you have not renounced your will, your character, in your case the surrender has not yet begun. Only the surrender on the physical level has been achieved, but this is the easiest one to achieve!"

Could not conceal my disappointment . . . how disheartened it made me feel—I doubt that I ever will reach the goal!

"Never, never think like this! Those are negative thoughts! Failure should never be contemplated! But you should not lean on me; you must be able to rely on yourself alone. I am helping you and will do so in the future, but never will I say so. You will not know when and how you are helped. You will have to cross the stream— not I. I can only create the conditions that you should be able to do it. And whatever you do, I will always tell you that IT IS NOTHING, and you should do more! Otherwise, how will you get rid of the *shaitan* (the devil) of pride?? However high you may think of me, believe me, I think ten times so much more of you!"

"Oh, Bhai Sahib!" I said, and felt quite awed at this statement.

"But I will never praise you; I may do so to other people when

speaking of you. . . . Surrender is the most difficult thing in the
world while you are doing it, and the easiest when it is done. I was on
the line of surrender; my father, my uncle surrendered. I only
followed them; it was not my merit at all. I just followed them. . . .
And it is not a question of a day or two; it takes time. Those people
whom you see here, most of the time, they don't know how to sit
before the Master, how to speak to the Master. All sorts of silly talk is
going on!"

"But those are only outward, exterior attitudes—they cannot
mean much," I said.

"What is in the heart becomes expressed outwardly. The exterior
reflects the inner attitude; it cannot be helped. If one feels
reverence, it is bound to show itself. It is like love; it cannot be
hidden. If I don't speak to you for days, you just sit; if I speak, you
speak, and never, never, must you complain.

"And this is the door; the ONLY DOOR to the KING OF THE HEART.
What is surrender of the Heart, you people do not even imagine . . .
not only you Western people . . . I mean Indians too. . . . Learn to
be nothing, this is the only way."

He looked so gentle. He IS changing . . . or is it I who am going
around the bend? Could not take my eyes away from him. Elegant.
All in white. How the bones of the cheeks shone through the bronze-
colored skin. A kind of transparent impression it gave . . . the half-
closed eyes, an Oriental face all right. . . .

"If you understand it, if you can express it, it will not remain, so
you have said just now. So what kind of experience is that of which I
can know nothing, and cannot understand? It is not mine, if I know
nothing about it!"

"I told you so often: try to know my thoughts and wishes. Why,
for instance, have you always adverse ideas? So many doubts? It is
your character! It is rare that anybody surrenders at the first go—
very few do it. Sometimes one is very near, sometimes very far away.
If the mind goes, where does the character remain? When nothing
remains, what will remain?"

"Only love," I said.

"Exactly," he answered, and his eyes shone like stars. "Look what
you were seven months before, and look where you stand now."

"But there is such a long way to go," I said, and felt very
discouraged.

"This is the wrong attitude!" he exclaimed with emphasis; "never
be discouraged; never think like that!"

"I do want to surrender completely, believe me; but how to manage it, how to achieve it? I feel an urgency; something is telling me that there is not much time left," I said, and felt quite desperate.

"You will," he said, shifting into a different position. He sat now in Guru *Asana*; he often sat like that when he was talking to me. No one has the right to sit in this *Asana* in the presence of the Teacher, so the tradition goes.

"You will," he repeated; **"you are put on the line and you will."**

"Oh, I wish you had told me all that before; so clearly and in detail, I mean. It is such a great help. But you never seem to have time to speak to me, even if I sit here for hours every day! Only lately it is different—you speak to me sometimes. . . !"

"Again: why such adverse thoughts come into your mind? I speak to you as I never spoke to anyone before! You must understand that you have to change completely. Everyone says: my character, my intelligence; everybody desires self-expression, to assert his individuality. You, for instance, have been successful with it in the world. Your will, your character still runs after the worldly concepts, as they were used to do for so many years. You see, now it must be completely changed."

He fell silent. . . a silence, almost physically felt, descended in the room. It was deep, so solid, one could hear the ringing sound of absolute silence. He glanced at the clock standing behind him in the recess.

"Are you satisfied? You can go home now," he added casually, and I went. But I touched his feet before I left.

"May I do so? You don't mind?" I asked. My heart was so full of gratitude.

"Yes, yes; it is a sign of true love, when the heart is full," he smiled.

In the evening he was mostly speaking in English and translated some couplets: **"The Beloved loves first, and the son is known by his father."** I did not understand but did not ask.

"Those who have no bondage, they keep no money, no worldly things remain with them. If you say to your lover: I will give you all the world—will he abandon his Beloved to get it? If you pour water through the sieve, those without bondage are the same. . . ."

9th June

I WAS SILENT THIS MORNING . . . had nothing to say. Neither had he, for he prayed. Was still thinking over what he told me yesterday. All things of importance in my life usually happen on Friday. Felt that yesterday's discussion foretells a change. It was an important day, and it was Friday. Some turning point is imminent. But what? I could not know, of course.

Slept little in the night. Thinking of the line of conduct to take, the difficulties ahead, and the thoughts were slow—the mind was revolving in a kind of slow-motion. Was very tired in the morning; the sheets under me were completely wet with perspiration; felt weak. The head was aching as if an iron band was screwed slowly tighter and tighter around it. A strong *Loo* was blowing. Left early for the Guru's place. He did not come out. The headache became unbearable. Made myself a mango drink—it helps apparently against the effects of the *Loo*. Took a strong dose of aspirin. The headache went. Could not do a thing, it was so hot. Was lying half-dead on the tachat. The ceiling fan was moving boiling air around, with no refreshing result. The kitchen was full of hot air, and every object was covered with a fine sand.

In the evening he was recounting stories from his Rev. Guru's life. "There are things which are true and real but which cannot be explained. You speak often enough of him, and I know about your Rev. Father, and though I feel the greatest respect for him, because he is your father, still it does not mean to me more than that. But your Rev. Guru Maharaj was so real to me . . . from the moment when, in this room, for the first time you told me about him—just as real as yourself. So real, it seems to me that I even could describe what he looked like." He listened, dancing sparks in his eyes, luminous in the fading light of the sky. Those eyes are stars to guide me . . . my guiding stars. . . .

The prayer in the night went so well. It was a wordless pouring out of the whole of my heart. Such sweetness was in it; I was alone with his Rev. Guru Maharaj. . . . There was a moment when I had to stop, turned over, and went to sleep. Had to stop, the physical heart was aching so much, and I could hardly bear it.

10th June

WHEN I WAS ENTERING HIS GATE in the morning, he was sitting already, and quite a few people were present; he was talking to a man standing in front of him. Like a physical blow into my heart it was . . . to see him so full of light. Had a moment of deepest joy for being able to see it; it was as if his physical body was not a reality; it was submerged in the light surrounding it . . . only the light was real, but not the physical being.

I sat down. He did not seem to have noticed me and did not acknowledge my greeting. Later, in the room—we could not sit in the garden because of the dust—the same man was there who wanted a male child, and the baby of Durghesh was brought in, the little boy. Guruji took the child from the mother . . . such tenderness was in this gesture as he was gently rocking it. I was deeply moved. When he looked down at the child in his arms, he seemed like one of those timeless statues of the Buddha of Compassion. And then I knew what was the transformation in him—the change which was the cause of constant perplexity lately—it was this: this quality of the super-human in him. Whenever there was an opportunity, I kept asking people if they found any change in Guru's appearance . . . in the last ten days or so. But everybody said, no, he was the same as usual. So, it made me think that it was only I who noticed it, and could not explain it. That is all I could say, but knew for certain that it was not due to imagination. I asked even Virendra, his youngest son; no, father is just as he always was, spending much time in Samadhi when he was alone, talking to people when they arrived. But to me he appeared so much more beautiful, more transparent, more full of light as the days went by. Clearly, I must be the only one who saw it.

When asked, he never gave an explanation; he only laughed or remained impenetrably silent. Watching him, I began to realize that he looked more and more as he did during the *Bandhara*—inhumanly strange, godlike, glorious. Yes, that was it . . . and I was full of wonder and very puzzled.

"Look at the child," he was saying, **"how beautiful he is."**

"What is that?" I asked, pointing to an object in a piece of cloth which the child had around his neck.

"It is a *Yantra* which I gave to his mother before he was born. After years of married life, my daughter had no children, only miscarriages. My wife said to me: you give so many things to others, but you do nothing to help Durghesh whom you love so much. I refused then, at that time. But the Hint came from my Rev. Guru Maharaj, and I gave her a *Yantra*. And when we were at the *Bandhara* of my Rev. Guru Maharaj, he told me to go home, for I will have good news. When we went home, Munshiji came running and said that Durghesh had a male child and all was well. But he was

so ugly when he was born. So ugly for the first few months. Black
and ugly. My wife said to me: it is a male child but . . . it is as it is . . .
not too beautiful . . . nobody will love him. . . . Wait, I said, he
will be. And now: look at him, how beautiful he is and how fair!" He
was right; the child was very lovely. "How I love him; of all the
children, I love Durghesh best, and he is my most loved."

"But Bhai Sahib, is it not *Moha* (attachment)?" I asked. He shook
his head.

"If you go and have a bath in the Ganga, and you go out, does it
remain with you?—of course not!"

"Oh, Bhai Sahib, every time I see you with this child, I have such a
pity for you; poor Guru Maharaj, surrounded by so much *Moha*! It is
bound to drag you into the womb again and again!" He shook his
head ever so gently.

"So, the Shishyas want to teach the Guru and have pity for him. Is
it so?"

"No, no," I exclaimed, "not to teach you, surely!"

"But you pity me, is it so?"

I confessed that I did.

"Those who are always with their Guru do not possess worldly
things. They rest in their Guru, and everything else does not touch
them. I am merged in my Rev. Guru Maharaj. All else is here; I
partake of it; I live my life according to my lights, however dim they
may seem to you."

He closed his eyes, rocking the baby gently; it was fast asleep in his
arms. Durghesh appeared at the door from the next room. He gave
her the child; she smiled and went out, the green curtain closing
behind her.

"Let it go, let all things go, and see what will happen. This is the
Way. Let it go; this is the answer, the Royal Road to everything."

Complete silence fell. People who came in the meantime, sitting
around, were all in Dhyana. Once more, I had the feeling that there
was a meaning, a special meaning, intended for me alone. Mind was
still. Truly, only Stillness is Reality. . . .

11th June

IN THE NIGHT COULD NOT SLEEP. All the *Chakras* were humming . . .
fire was burning inside my belly . . . blood was liquid fire. . . .

"You are the King of Contradictions; just to give an example: once
you said, when L. was here, that there is no love in your heart, for
anything or anybody except for your Rev. Guru Maharaj. A few

weeks back when Prof. Batnagar was here, you said that your heart is so barren that you cannot love anybody at all. But one needs only to see you together with your grandchild, or to notice the look in your eyes when you were talking to the old Gupta yesterday afternoon, to see how much love is in your heart. How can I reconcile all that?''

He suddenly smiled, gaily and boyishly—the smile when he is much amused—but he said nothing. And so I sat there, talking all sorts of things, how to reconcile this and that, things so difficult to understand, and how untruthful he is, how he keeps denying what he said only a short while ago, and so forth.

Do not remember much, only his very still face, mask-like, devoid of all expression, as if separated from all else in space, and the mala slowly revolving in his brown and slender fingers.

14th June

JAGAN NATHJI TOLD ME in the evening, when Bhai Sahib was inside, that I should offer myself as a disciple; in his case it made all the difference, so he said. *Prasad* will be distributed, and he will accept you as his disciple. I said that I never thought of that. I feel that I am his disciple, and I am certainly treated as one; one need only look at the treatment he subjects me to, a treatment which, as far as I understand, is quite in keeping with the ancient Tradition.

Kept thinking of it though, during *Kirtan*; it didn't seem to be a good thing to do somehow . . . will it not be wiser to leave it to him?

15th June

TOLD HIM THIS MORNING about it; he shook his head and agreed that I should not ask for such a thing.

"It is not for you," was all he said.

So, in the evening, when Bhai Sahib went for a moment inside, Jagan Nathji asked me if I did as he suggested. I said nothing to him that I had consulted the Guru, but told him only that I thought it over and decided against it because it would be in contradiction with what I am trying to do, namely, grappling with the gigantic task of learning how to become nothing. If I ask him to become something, his disciple, that would be a limitation. It would be a contradiction in terms, an impossibility. In my relationship with him there are ancient rights and ancient duties. What he did to me since I have come here could not have been done to a greater degree even for a disciple, and I think I had better leave it entirely to him.

Related to him this conversation later, and when I mentioned the sentence about the ancient rights and ancient duties, he closed his eyes with the expression I know so well by now. . . . And when he prayed, he looked so pure, so serene, not of this world at all. Mentioned how much I doubted yesterday and that the mind did not give me peace.

"It is not doubt," he said, "it is so done . . . pressure is applied— otherwise how will you be purified? Little by little you learn to be on the road without doubts, even without a shadow of a doubt. And even if you tell me about it or not: He who knows everything will tell me, and I will know."

16th June

"TRUTH IS ONE; learned men call it by different names" (*Rig Veda*). Prof. Batnagar quoted it. It was during a conversation in which he also was saying: "If you want God, you have to sell yourself first. This is the essence, the core of every religion, of every philosophy as far as I read and understand. Reduce yourself to nil, to nothing, and you will realize the Truth." I asked him if he can notice any difference in the outward appearance of Bhai Sahib. "The Transformation of the Guru is one of the Mystical Experiences. It is mentioned in the Yogic Treatises. It is the developing capacity of the Disciple to recognize the Divinity of the Guru."

I glanced at Bhai Sahib. His face was quite expressionless; he did not seem to listen . . . his eyes were closed.

Speaking of the Path, I said it was depressing that all the odds were against me; I have to fight against my character as an elderly woman already crystallized in a certain pattern of behavior. . . . "And," he interrupted me, "the 3000 years of European civilization as your heredity, your education with the emphasis on competition, on assertion of the individual with all its ramifications, i.e.: freedom of expression, emphasis on self-respect, etc."

"Yes," I said, "and also the fact that we are conditioned to consider your civilization somewhat inferior to ours; and also the Guru's ideas are sometimes old-fashioned and out-of-date; further-more, he deliberately puts all the appearances against himself; sum it up together, and you will see that I am at a disadvantage: have to overcome many more obstacles than anybody else in this circle; all seems to conspire against me!"

Prof. Batnagar was of the opinion that Sufism was Islamic Buddhism, but there are no historic evidences of such a thing, as far as it is known.

Bhai Sahib was very much against this idea; he said that Sufism is very much older than Islam and even Buddhism. True, it took on the terminology of Islam, but this was due to the customs and religion of the country where it was allowed to flourish, that is in Arabia and later in Persia.

Lord Mohammed was asked once to which religion did he belong, and it is said that Christ was asked the same question. The fact is that all Saints, all Prophets, belong to the same Religion: the Religion of the Lovers of God.

18th June

USUALLY THE MIND is out of order in the morning, so I assume that either in the night or in the morning before I go to him, something is done to it. But in the evenings it works fairly well. Yesterday he was singing and Jaga Nathji translated: "Every night is wedding night." Of course it is a well-known fact that every night the Guru unites the Souls of his followers with his, and as he is one with God, every night is a wedding night: the Union with God.

The loneliness and depression are terrible. The heat is slowly grinding my body down. All is dry. The rains are late this year, and every evening when I go home I smell this sweet and tired fragrance of flowering shrubs, too thirsty and longing for moisture. Even so, the earth is sweet, but the nights are a nightmare—the body seems to shrink with perspiration. I drink over a gallon of water per day. Two large gallon jars of water stand always full in the shade of my veranda. Still, all the water goes through the skin, and the kidneys hardly work at all . . . have to change my dresses at least three times per day, so wet they become, smelling sour and stale only after a few hours.

The day before he was sitting on his tachat; the nuisance of a woman who wants a male child was there again, trying to talk to him. He was sitting cross-legged with an absent expression, not listening. Suddenly, he assumed a wonderful expression; I just looked and looked . . . it was glorious. The dynamism, the smile, the expression of the eyes—it could be called *Devic*. The woman fell silent and looked in wonderment.

"I know of whom you were thinking just now," I said, with a smile as soon as he seemed to be back on this earth.

"Of whom?"

"Of your Rev. Guru Maharaj!"

He shook his head slowly. **"I was in Absolute Truth,"** he said. I was astonished, and asked him the next day about it, but people came, and I got no answer.

I thought that the Saint has to be in deep Samadhi to be able to be with God, but he was in full waking consciousness, very obviously, and not even in Dhyana; it must be a very high state to be able to do so. He smiled kindly.

"At the beginning one has to be in deep Samadhi, but later one gets used to it, and one can do it at any moment."

I was very impressed.

Last night, just as I was waking up, I felt such a wave of love, it shook me like a sharp unbearable pain, and the first conscious thought which flashed into my mind was: Good heavens, one moment more of it and I will die! It is impossible to bear! Then I woke up completely and was lying there thinking. So this is the feeling of love somewhere; on a plane where the mind cannot reach. Perhaps a glimpse of the Atmic plane? Such a condensed feeling of love—no wonder one is not allowed to remember it . . . the mind, the heart, would burst. . . .

There was only one star in the sky, and I was thinking: as fair as a star, when there is only one in the sky, He is—and such was love that it did hurt. . . .

27

Those who are Dead do not Remember

21st June, 1962

"YOU USED HARSH WORDS last time when I said to you that for me the Guru and God are one and the same thing."

"I use words which seem hard to you because this is sometimes the only way to make the Shishya think. We teach according to the stages. There is nothing wrong, nothing right. When the child is in the cradle, he will think that the cradle is the whole world. Later, he will think the room is the whole world. Later still, the veranda, the garden, and so on. To think that the Guru is God is a very preliminary stage."

Kabir said: "When two stand in front of me, the Guru and God: who is the greater? Surely the Guru, because he will take me to God." I quoted. "And if it is good enough for Kabir, should it not be good enough for me?"

"Who is going to listen to Kabir? Kabir was only a poet! If somebody is saying that stealing is a good thing and should be done, am I going to listen to him, only because he said so?"

From this morning's conversation, Jagan Nathji told me that Bhai Sahib could make me see my dead husband in a moment if I wanted to and would ask him. Then he left. We remained alone. I said that I would not be at all interested to see Charles, as much as I used to love him. What for? What is the good of it? He nodded.

"He will not recognize you," he said. "Saints do recognize, ordinary people do not. But they are made to recognize: of course, it can be done. But by themselves they will not recognize. How could they? The mind is not there; everything is changed; you are a thing of long ago for him. If he sees you and will be made to remember, he would say: 'Oh, yes, she was my wife; oh, yes, I remember,' and that would be all. In your Christian faith there is no belief in Reincarnation?"

I said, no, it does not form part of Christian belief.

"In this case there are no *Samskaras* of this kind and people do not come back to this earth because there is no desire of this kind."

"But where do they go?" I inquired. "I thought until now that whether one believes in Reincarnation or not is of no importance: one will reincarnate anyhow."

"They go to other Lokas," he said. **"Drunkards and gamblers go to a Loka where they drink and gamble. This world is not the worst one. Here you can make Karma. There you are helpless."**

"But how can one get out of those places?"

He shook his head. **"Very difficult to get out of them. People do not get out; they are taken out."**

"Do you mean to say that there are souls appointed to do this work, to take out and help those who are in such places?"

"Yes," he said.

25th June

GREAT STILLNESS. A kind of inner security. Until now the mind was in the most restless, insecure state. I wonder how long this Stillness will last. . . .

30th June

THE MONSOON IS STILL NOT HERE. Long, hot days . . . very often with no ventilation, not even in the mornings or evenings, and the nights are as wind-still and as hot as in Madras. I am steaming with perspiration. The body begins to give way and gives me trouble . . . giddiness, headache, general weakness in the morning, so that I can hardly get up . . . an unusual thing with me; in the morning I am always on top of the world. Writing this entry into my diary, for instance, I stream with perspiration; to keep still is painful. One is inclined to fidget constantly in the vain hope of a little relief . . . some coolness reaching the skin. Cannot even see properly . . . the sweat running into my eyes from the forehead keeps blinding me.

My eyes are red and inflamed all the time . . . must look like a St. Bernard. Most uncomfortable, and the mind works badly. Cannot see the whole aspect or idea—only a small part of it—and if I try to grasp the other side of it, I have already forgotten the first part of it. Keep forgetting the most simple elementary things, or do them twice, for I don't remember that they were done already. And my life is very dull. The other evening Jagan Nathji translated a couplet:

"The pangs of separation were too much for her, she could not bear them.

She decided to take her life. And in her anxiety to kill herself

She was running after the moon, the lotus flower, and the
    fragrant air."
Interpretation: A Lover loves the moon, the lotus and the fragrant
air, and so the same things which gave her joy will give her death. He
told me it is the same idea as in homeopathy: if the disease gives you
the same symptoms, as for instance poisoning with arsenic, only
arsenic can cure it.

An anecdote from the life of the Father of Bhai Sahib: he was a
great Saint and had many disciples. One day a drunkard came to him
and sat near him on the *dharry* (a heavy cotton carpet). He asked:
"Should a man fear sin?" The Saint replied: "If the man fears sin, he
will be drowned in an ocean of sin." The man left, and soon
everybody had left too. "But I remained," said the doctor who was
relating the anecdote, and asked: "How is it to be understood?
Should we sin?"

Then the Saint told him a story: There was a Saint, and a man used
to come to him, and he was pestering him with the request to give
him a *Mantra* to become very rich. But the Saint kept delaying it and
was telling the man each time, he will give it to him some day . . .
later . . . not just now. After a few years, the man was still there, still
pestering him, and one day the Saint said: "Get up very early in the
morning before sunrise. Recite the Mantra of Ram 12,000 times
every day, and after three months you will be the richest man in the
province. There is only one condition attached to it: Never, not even
once, must you think of Hanuman" (the Monkey God who helped
Rama to recover his wife abducted by the demon of Ravana).

"You see," said the Father of Bhai Sahib, "with sins it is just like
that; if you fear them, and try to suppress them, they will drown you.
Try to do good, forget the sins, live righteously, and you will reach
the Truth."

A Persian couplet:
    "Go to the door of the Tavern where the Wine of Love is
        distributed.
    Go and sit there as a beggar would. Even if nothing remains
    For you, but just the film on the bottom of the bottle, even
        then
    It will be enough to take you right to God."

1st July

"THERE WERE TWO LOVERS and two beloved. Both got letters from their lovers. The first one worshipped the letter. She pressed it against her forehead and her heart; she took it out and read it, put it back, took it out again, and finally put it under her pillow to sleep on it.

"The second one took the letter, looked at it and said: the pangs of separation are so terrible, what can this letter do to me? And she burned it.

"Now this would seem to you a complete contradiction, is it not? But it is all depending on the stages. The second one was on a far higher stage than the first, though from the worldly point of view it would not seem so. So, the Guru explains everything according to the stages. Keep it in mind." And Jagan Nathji laughed, saluted the Guru, and left.

Lord Buddha was talking to his disciples; suddenly he stopped; the sun was setting and he said: Let's disperse and do what we ought to do. He got up and went inside the house. The disciples of his, who were thieves, thought: Guru Maharaj said we should go and do what we ought to, so let's go and do some stealing. Those who were weak and had desire for women went to prostitutes, thinking that they are justified to do so; those who were religious went to do the *Pooja* (worship), and so on. Everyone interpreted his words according to the working of their minds. And the Buddha did not mean anything of the sort; he simply said that it was late, and everybody should disperse.

"I was so proud of my learning, but when I stand in front of Thee

Oh my Guru, my mind is blank; I have forgotten everything," goes the text of one of the Persian couplets. Well, it could be my case. I was thinking only this morning that I seldom remember anything of my past—never think of it. Thinking has become a laborious job, at any rate.

Where are my qualifications? Travels I have done, knowledge which I have accumulated during so many years? Gone! Seems to never have existed! Thinking is an effort.

Only, I find that there is still much resentment in me. He treats me so badly. Idiot, stupid, he calls me in front of everybody, at the slightest provocation. I complained. I protested. He hissed at me because I said that his wife asks sometimes pretty unintelligent questions; what about that? If you say that people are at liberty to criticize me, am I not at liberty to criticize others? Wife or no wife, if she asks a silly question, I will say so. He himself said that he is not a

God; if so, then he is not infallible. It follows that I am at liberty to find faults with him too. You can make mistakes, and if I notice it, why can't I say so? Why is this distinction? One law for others and another one for me? Is it not a free country? Are we not free citizens? But he glared at me, called me ignorant and impertinent, and I don't know how to respect a Teacher and his family, and so forth. . . . Well, Teacher: o.k.—but why should I respect his family? What have they to do with me, or I with them?

Once, some time ago, he asked me if I think sometimes of my father or my sisters. With surprise I realized that I never do lately, but no wonder, for I hardly remember anything nowadays. I also told him that if I have to work out a problem, I am unable to see it as a whole as everyone else is able to do; in other words I cannot synthesize at all. I can only see one side of it, and when I try to grasp the other side, or aspect of it, I can do it, but in the meantime I have already forgotten the first part of it. Life becomes difficult and rather confusing in these circumstances. . . . Asked him the meaning of what was really happening.

"Sometimes your mind is made to work only at 50% capacity, sometimes at 25%, and sometimes it stops working altogether."

I wondered what happens if it does not work at all? Must be an unconscious state . . . perhaps a sort of sleep? But I have the feeling that it cannot be sleep, though the hours slide by unnoticed. Heaven knows where the mind goes . . . it just vanishes . . . emptiness. Suddenly I notice that it is already afternoon, and I have to go to his place. Or I think that I went to bed in the evening, and I am still sitting on my tachat and it is late . . . strange. How relative time is.

2nd July

"THE THINKING FACULTY OF THE MIND which is called in the Yoga Sutras 'the modifications of the mind,' with its constant movement, prevents us from perceiving Reality. In order to help the disciple, the Teacher will 'switch off' the current of the Mind . . . will paralyze it temporarily so that the Buddhic quality can come through.

"The mind cannot transcend itself. Some help is needed. We live within our own mind. How can the mind get out of itself?"

"Do you mean to say that it is the Teacher who, by his Yogic Powers, puts the mind out of action?"

"It is done," he said, ignoring the first part of my question. **"And it is done very simply by activating the Heart Chakra. The more the**

Chakra is activated, the less the mind is able to work. It is quite a painless process.''

Oh, I know that all right; it does not hurt at all to be mindless: one cannot think—that's all.

"Even on the worldly platform it works in a similar way. If one is much in love, the lover is forgetful of everything else except the object of his love. He is distraught; people call him mad. The law is the same on all levels of being. Only on the spiritual level the law is more powerful because there are no obstructions caused by the density of matter." After a moment's silence, he added with one of his flashing smiles: **"We are called the fools, the idiots of God, by the Sufi poets."**

Tonight he left with Babu for Allahabad. I was there at 7 p.m. He came out looking very smart in his long *Kurta* and white trousers, white *topi* on his head, all freshly laundered. His skin was golden, full of light . . . sparkling eyes—he looked so young.

I know for sure now how old he is; the other day he was telling us that between him and his elder brother there was only two years difference, and his brother retired in 1951 at the age of 60. It does not need a great knowledge of mathematics to work out how old he is now.

He told me to do my duty and come as usual. I said that I always come when he is away, only I don't stay so long. I will take advantage of Pushpa's cooler.

"Do by all means," he said. Could not avert my eyes from him. So full of inner light, looking so young, and nobody seems to see him as I do. If they would, they would be full of wonder just as I am. His wife, his brother, his children—they do not notice anything unusual. But he certainly is quite different . . . the knowledge of it is like a sweet secret, my very own. It must be his grace that I am able to see it.

4th July

WAS AT PUSHPA'S PLACE nearly all the time. Today I am writing letters. The heat is unbelievable. I never imagined that one can suffer so much. The monsoon which promised to break out in the middle of June produced only a few very light rains and passed us by, went south, Agra way. This part of Uttar Pradesh is still without a drop of rain. The hot wind, the *Loo*, stopped. The humidity content of the atmosphere increased considerably because it is already raining heavily all around in the plains. The temperature is much lower than before, but it is sticky, as in Madras, and the perspiration does not dry off. Never thought it possible that the skin is capable of emitting so much fluid . . . the suffering is intense. While writing, I am sitting in the nude under the fan; the chair is wet under me; sweat keeps running into my eyes, making them smart, which is a great nuisance. While he is away, I thought much and took stock of my situation. On the 2nd of July I have been here nine months, and it seems to me that I am further away from him than ever . . . nine months . . . the time to produce a child. What kind of a child did I produce? None at all, so it seems. . . .

Two days before he left he was explaining a bit about his seeming rudeness. **"If one chooses the Way of the System, if it is done according to the System, then it takes a long time. If one chooses the Way of Love, it does not take long, relatively. But it is difficult. Life becomes very sad. No joy. Thorns everywhere. This has to be crossed. Then all of a sudden there will be flowers and sunshine. But the road has to be crossed first. There is nothing which can be done about it. People will hear one day that you have been turned out; and not only that, but other things too. And it is not the disciple who chooses which road to take; it is the Teacher who decides.**

"There are two Roads: the Road of *Dhyana,* **the slow one, and the Road of** *Tyaga,* **of complete Renunciation, of Surrender: this is the Direct Road, the Path of Fire, the Path of Love."**

"But will you not treat a woman differently from a man? A woman is more tender; the psychology of a woman and of a man is different!"

He shook his head. **"The training is somewhat different. But it does not mean that because you are a woman, you will get a preferential treatment."**

"But don't you see that I have more odds against me than your Indian disciples?" I exclaimed.

Again he shook his head. **"No, it is always difficult. For everybody. If it is not one thing, then it is another . . . human beings are covered with so much conditioning. . . ."**

6th July

HE WAS BACK THIS MORNING looking weak and having an eye swollen with a painful stye. I left soon; nobody was there, so he went to have a rest.

Fire is back in my body. The old body is weakened by heat, and I discovered that the symptoms from which I suffer, i.e., extreme tiredness, fatigue, giddiness, vomiting condition, great and constant depression, are an effect of emotional fatigue. I am under a severe psychological pressure, and the heat does the rest. In this temperature the body reaches a state of a kind of ring-pass-not; it just cannot go on . . . I remembered what he once said to us:

"My Rev. Guru Maharaj did not give to me because I was the best, but because I was the strongest. A strong constitution is needed if you want to progress on the Path of Spiritual Perfection."

May God give me this strength . . . to be able to bear those extreme conditions. "To fight the fatigue one needs a strong stimulus; keep the Ideal before your eyes: the Goal. It will help to fight exhaustion. Stick to your purpose. Refuse to accept frustration. Will-power will see you through." I repeated that to myself aloud to give me courage, many a time. . . .

8th July

LAST NIGHT he was sitting outside the door of his room when I came. His wife came and did some fomentation to his eye. His stye is a bit better but still very painful, and quite a lot of pus is coming out. It gives him much suffering. The wife went back to the kitchen, and he began to tell me how all Muslims, even the least educated ones, are polite, and have a very polite way of speaking. There are many regards to be payed to the Master; in the olden times there was quite a ritual in this respect. I asked him to tell me at least some of the rules; I would like to follow them. He shook his head in his habitual way.

"At your age you cannot do it; it will make your life even more miserable; the times have changed; now humanity is different. Who is disposed to make so many sacrifices? And who is disposed to accept the complete surrender, all the difficulties of the Path? There are people who sit here for the last sixty years; they have been already my Rev. Father's disciples. But are they eager? Nothing of the sort! There is no eagerness, no power of sacrifice. But if somebody is found to accept the difficulties, then the Master acts accordingly. I have the intention to ask permission of my superiors to change some things in the training, to adapt it to modern times. My father and my uncle changed something too. I will do the same. Something ought to be changed to make it acceptable to the mentality of the people not born in this country. Not the fundamentals, no, those cannot be changed. They have to remain. How can one change the Law of God?"

"But the presentation of it—that can be changed, because, believe me, some things do put the modern, especially the Western mind, against some aspects of the Tradition."

"Yes," he said, "I understand that."

Then he went inside, to do some more fomentations, and told me to come in too. I sat in the courtyard and was surprised to what extent the atmosphere was peaceful there. I never had the opportunity to notice it before; though I passed through the inner veranda sometimes, I never sat there for any length of time. When I told him so, he smiled. While he was talking to his wife who was applying hot pads to his eye, I looked at the reflection of the fire in the kitchen dancing on the wall, and was thinking that it seems to be like my home now . . . and to think that I even hated the look of it, when I arrived here first. Like home . . . it was strange, how I felt like coming home when driving to this place from the station nine months ago. It must have been a premonition, of things to come, perhaps of my long stay here. Who knows . . . I left soon. He went to bed and did not come outside to sit with the people who began to assemble—he was not well enough.

It was hardly 8 p.m. when I went to bed and prayed, felt serene and nearly happy. Somewhere in the north an enormous thunderstorm was raging, three lightnings per second I counted . . . then fell asleep. Still not a drop of rain.

"You don't need anything, no *Sadhana*, no discipline," he said last night. "My father and my uncle emphasized love, and love only. Just love, whatever happens, and in a few years you will be . . ."— he made a jesture of a bird soaring into the sky. . . .

Love whatever happens. . . . What will happen? Sounds ominous. . . .

9th July

IN THE EVENING when I came, he was in the inner room sitting with an Indian lady under the fan. He asked me if I remembered her, and it seemed to me that I had seen her during the *Bandhara*. I asked if she spoke English, but he turned quickly to me before she could answer:

"She will not speak before me; Durghesh will not speak before me; my son-in-law will not speak before me. This is the way to show respect to the Elders." I pricked up my ears. This is a clear hint. Hm . . . something is preparing . . . be careful, old girl. Later in the garden during the conversation he said:

"And of course, neither my father nor my uncle were ever

allowed to speak before my Rev. Guru Maharaj." Now I know for
sure that it is a hint. So, later in the evening, after some opening
sentences from his side, I said to him:

"Bhai Sahib, you gave me a hint tonight."

"What sort of a hint did I give you?" I told him. "It is not for you,"
he said.

"But I intend to follow it," I answered.

"If you can do, do it. If you cannot, leave it. Do what is easier and
execute it."

It will not be easy, I was thinking, but I will try, for it seems to be
his wish. . . .

28

The Terror of Love

I AM DEFINITELY SURE that I am in a much happier place when asleep than in my waking state, such a life of misery I am leading. Just in that moment when I was waking up, there was such a pain as if the whole body was crying out in agony, in supreme pain, a kind of panic, as if the whole of my being was screaming: No! No! and whoop! . . . the physical consciousness takes over. It is all as before—the white walls of my room, the veranda, the sky above, the pain in the joints, and the mental and the emotional misery. . . .

13th July

FOR THE LAST FEW DAYS a kind of re-orientation has been taking place. At first I had a kind of peace—not a peace in the real sense of the word: for that there was too much pain in my heart, but a kind of stillness. Is it a hush before the storm? Or simply a kind of numbness due to too great a stress on my physique? This morning I woke up deadly tired and weary. The whole body was aching. Dragged myself to the kitchen . . . aspirin and black coffee helped a little. The sky was serene as ever, and still no sign of rain. Dragging myself painfully along, trying to do the few necessary jobs before going to his place, a bit of washing, tidying up my room—another large cup of very strong coffee . . . kept thinking and thinking.

When going to Pushpa's for lunch today, was so acutely aware of the suffering of Nature, of so many little things dying in the drought . . . the air boiling, the soil powdered, Guruji's garden withered, leaves hanging from the branches getting brittle and yellow . . . and in the country it must be even far worse. . . .

Still, I was aware of a kind of peace. A heavy, leaden peace, joyless, dark, and nonetheless it was peace. There was much heartache . . . much pain. And still there was peace too, in spite of the most severe separation for the last few weeks. Even the feeling of love is no more. Such is the *Maya*. Nothing remained. Only the pain in the heart is here; but this is a permanent feature nowadays. Still, in spite of all

241

this, the feeling of peace is endless, eternal and, it seems, will last forever.

At Pushpa's place got feverish once more. Went to Guru's place, but could not sit there, felt awful. Asked Satendra to tell his father that I went home because I was not too well. At home felt even worse. Measured my temperature—it was 40.1C. Took aspirin, turned the fan off, and slept very badly.

14th July

HE ASKED HOW I FELT, and I said that I was better. Told him about the feeling of peace, so deep and seemingly lasting, an unusual peace, heavy but great, a kind of sorrowful *Pralaya*.

"Love assumes many forms; sometimes it is peace, sometimes it is happiness, sometimes bliss or joy. Restlessness or sorrow. Love is the Root, and like a tree it has many branches spreading around. . . ." He made a wide gesture with both hands to illustrate spreading.

Later he said: **"When we are ill, then we know that our body is not us. When we have a headache, who is going to help us? If we are amongst the crowd, or alone in the forest, who can help us? Nobody! If the mind is not there, if the body is not ours, what remains? Only the Soul. Only the experiences are ours. Only those are true.**

" 'Like the wind, who carries the perfume of blossoms from bough to bough,' says the Persian poet. This only will remain."

He also is not well. I wonder if he took my feverish condition, but I knew I couldn't very well ask him. I already know him sufficiently well to abstain from certain questions. . . .

15th July

THIS MORNING AT SUNRISE, when I opened my eyes and looked up into the sky—the first thing I always do on awakening, for my charpoy is standing in the middle of the courtyard—I saw a large, pink cloud, striped with delicate mackerels. A mackerel-sky means water, at least in England. Told Bhai Sahib this morning: we might have rain.

The mind is not working at all. It feels as if I was given an anesthetic . . . sort of funny feeling in my head, similar to giddiness. If I turn my eyes either to the right or to the left, then there is definite, strong giddiness. Understood hardly anything. Cannot remember either.

"How are you?" he asked, when I came in. He was standing in the middle of the garden, clad only in the pale blue *longhi* I gave him this winter. His torso was bare. He looked like Surya (the sun) himself, his skin emitting golden light.

"Physically I am O.K., but something is happening to me; there is a change somehow, but I only feel it—I cannot describe it." He smiled. Of course he knew what was the matter.

"I would be a fool not to know: for I am giving it to you," he said once on a similar occasion.

He did not speak to me. Looked so magnificent . . . a Deva, I thought, and could not take my eyes off him. He soon went in and fell asleep. I was sitting all the time outside.

The rain came in the afternoon . . . and it became cooler. So, mackerel-sky means rain, also in India. . . .

18th July

WHEN I TOLD HIM that I could not pray for the last few days because it is like a dark curtain between myself and his Rev. Guru Maharaj, he answered:

"Yes, sometimes it happens like that. It can be like a dark curtain or sometimes like a curtain of light. One can pray and then one cannot. It is good that it should be so. Otherwise how could one progress? Doubts, and fears and anxieties . . . I myself have them. Now, for instance, I don't pray for over two months; to whom should I pray, I ask myself."

It took my breath away: "Bhai Sahib, what a glorious state!"

"Oh, no, this is my pride," he said with emphasis.

"But you have no pride! You, for sure, are beyond that!!" I exclaimed. He smiled his still smile.

"That is what you say because you are so devoted. But on the physical level, some imperfection will remain always."

It made me think. I still believe how wonderful it must be not to be able to pray, for such is at-onement—that no difference remains, and one has to ask oneself to whom one should pray. . . .

Fell asleep full of such longing. When it is so strong, it is terrible. Woke up in the middle of the night with such a tremendous feeling of love, so full, so rich, so deep, that it was like a sharp pain, unbearable. My first thought was: if I have it for a few moments longer, my heart will burst! I woke up completely trembling, the heart beating wildly. Good heavens! That's how love is experienced on some other plane. If I had it to such a degree, even for a short time, surely the body would not be able to bear it and would go to pieces! I only had time to think that, then had a definite feeling that I was like a candle snuffed out with a bang, and fell asleep immediately.

In the morning on awakening, there was the usual aridity of late, hardly any feeling of love at all. I remembered that I had the same experience before, though less intense, which shows that somewhere there is love to such an unimaginable degree . . . only the brain knows nothing about it. I have the sneaky feeling that I was deliberately cut off, abruptly; perhaps I tuned into an experience I was not allowed to remember . . . quite possible. So, better not to speak about it, nor ask anything. It must be the state of love on the *Atmic* level. It was a split-second memory slipping somehow through the density of the mind, and a complete memory of it could kill. That's why it is better not to remember; one cannot bear it. I am sure it will take a long time, many years perhaps, to train the mind to be able to bear it without damage. . . .

Yesterday was *Guru Purnama* (the day when the Guru receives presents, according to tradition). I did what he told me to do: brought some sweets, some fruit, and a few rupees in an envelope and, offering it to him, touched his feet for the first time in public. I found it easy to do. Don't mind at all. It comes natural, and I never cared for the opinion of others at any rate.

20th July

WHAT IS THIS STILLNESS? Could it really be peace? Isn't love the most peaceless state? I don't remember having ever experienced such deep, uniform state of stillness and lasting so long.

"I call it the natural state," he answered. "Why should I say that I am giving it to you? It is given; that's all. And it is the natural state, but one does not always realize it. The Soul is covered with so many sheaths, veiled by many curtains."

"One curtain has been withdrawn?" I suggested. He nodded. "But there is so little understanding left . . . I am puzzled. . . ." But he was in Samadhi.

The money arrived from Australia. It hardly hurts that it vanishes so quickly . . . only a little. . . .

21st July

WHILE HAVING MY CUP OF COFFEE in the morning, I suddenly realized in a flash that love cannot increase in quantity, cannot grow bigger. It is given from the beginning in the exact quantity the Master wants to give, according to the size of the cup the Shishya brings with him. If the cup is large, more love can be poured into it; some containers are larger, some smaller. The quantity—let's call it quantity X— is always the same: only the Shishya learns to respond to it better and better, so it seems to him as if it would grow. The love at the beginning and at the end is the same. I was astonished at this piece of knowledge, for the mind cannot even think properly. Philosophically it must be correct—I know it. The beginning and the end from the point of view of God is the same always; it is a complete circle. I know it from books. But now I experienced it as my very own flash of knowledge into a mind which is sterile. . . . Strange . . . and wonderful. My work will be the same as before: I had to work with people trying to help them to come one step nearer to the Truth. When I leave this place (may this day never come!), I will continue on the same lines as before, though the conditions will necessarily be different (or perhaps not?), but the work itself will remain the same. We are given work according to our capacities. I will never be asked to work in leper colonies, for instance, for I am not trained for this kind of work. Neither will I be asked to work with children, because I never had anything to do with education. But I could give lectures in philosophy, help with meditation, work for the Theosophical Society in London.

He smiled when I was relating all this to him, and when I asked how is it possible that any glimpse of knowledge can come to the brain which can hardly function, and with the greatest difficulty can put thoughts together, he said:

"If the cup is empty, it can be filled. It is the Knowledge of the Soul which comes through. It comes to the physical mind and then it becomes the Real Knowledge, the integral part of you. If I would tell you, and you would have faith enough and believe me, then the faith and the knowledge would be two things, is it not so? But like this, nothing is told. You will realize it yourself; it becomes part of you; there is no duality. . . . You see how it is done, how easy?"

Then he began to tell me how men and women are trained—the differences in the practices; the approach to the psychological make-up of the trainee; how the forces from the depth of the unconscious are gathered and channelled. This is the work of the Teacher, and each individual is treated differently. I listened fascinated, hoping fervently to remember it all.

"From what you have told me just now I have to conclude that you wish me to guide people," I asked. I felt disturbed . . . did not like the responsibility . . . it frightened me. . . .

"Without being a guide, nothing can be done; there is no Power."

I remained silent. This was something . . . the responsibility . . . I confess I was shaken. Did not expect it to be quite like that. . . . "It is a great responsibility! Do you realize to what kind of life you are sending me out?"

He did not answer, but gently looked down at his feet as if examining his sandals.

"I hope, I hope that I will not go wrong . . . to have power is a terrible thing," I said, fear creeping from the very depth of my being into my heart.

"**I know,**" he said, half audible with a still and serious expression.

"Is it not too heavy a burden for the shoulders of an elderly woman? I will be accused of contradictions. If I have to live like you, I will have no habits; I am bound to do and say things which people cannot or will not understand. My words will be twisted, misinterpreted. There might be lawyers in the audience who will twist my words, accuse me of contradictions!"

He suddenly laughed. "**Lawyers know of one thing: the transfer of property! The property, the power, the knowledge will be transferred; there is no question of being a woman or not. It makes no difference.**"

I was disturbed. You are sending me to Calvary, Master, that's what you are doing, I thought. . . .

22nd July

"BHAI SAHIB, THIS VIBRATION which I had in January-February, do you remember?" He nodded. "I have had it very strong for the last few days, as soon as I open my eyes in the morning. It usually goes away after I have a cup of tea or coffee, but every day it returns stronger and stronger. It leaves me uncomfortable during the day."

"**Does it?**" I saw an amused smile, half-hidden in his beard.

"Could it be transmuted somehow in some way? This body is much tried by the heat and vomiting condition. Wherever this vibration goes, it creates a disturbance; if it is in the throat, there is a choking condition; if in the heart, the heart goes wild; or there is vomiting when in the solar plexus. It kept playing like that during the whole of winter, but it seems to be increasing."

He was writing something into his housekeeping account book and continued to smile. All of a sudden my heart made a violent jerk as if trying to jump out of my chest, then became positively mad, beating and stopping and racing again. Well, I thought . . . this is really amazing. . . .

"*Shaitan*, Guru Maharaj," I said. "Not one *Shaitan* (devil), but ten *Shaitans* in one!"

His smile became a broad grin inside his beard. He left the room and went into the inner courtyard. I sat there listening to the acrobatics of the heart, and wondering. . . .

"Like a monkey in the hands of a monkey-trainer, am I in your hands," I said, when he came back to fetch his towel. He kept grinning all the time, went out again, still smiling. I was alone for quite a while. Then he came in and said that I can go home. Left dazed . . . like drunk.

It has been very hot for the last two nights. Too much perspiration makes one feel quite weak in the morning. The rain does not come; it should rain heavily to change the atmosphere and make it bearable.

23rd July

PLENTY OF PEOPLE WERE SITTING this morning, talking, and he too talked a lot. For hours I just sat looking at him. He seemed to be a Being of Light. It surrounded him. He was beautiful.

"Thank you for being you," I said when everybody had left. "If you remain like this for me, the most difficult thing in the world will become easy." His smile was lovely and tender when he slipped his feet into the sandals and went out, the towel over his shoulder.

24th July

IT IS RAINING . . . a soft drizzle, and it is hot. I asked if I should remain vegetarian. I know some of his disciples are, and some are not. He said he leaves it to me. Vegetarianism can become a creed, an obstacle, a religion.

"You cannot eat yourself into Heaven; do what is the best for you."

29th July

"WHY DID GOD CREATE FLIES?" I asked, disgusted with so many of them.

"Who are you to ask such questions?" he turned to me. **"Do you know why YOU have been created? And supposing you do know; do you fulfill the purpose for which you have been created? You commented on the fact that I am so free, that one day I do one thing, the other day something else; I am outside or inside, I speak or I do not, am in or out. Now, if even I, in my limited way, am so free, what about Him who is the Lord of Freedom? He knows what He is doing."**

This did sound very much like Christian terminology, but I said nothing, or course. . . .

Later: **"He is no father; He has no son or any relations; He is definitely and most emphatically alone."** That didn't sound Christian at all. . . .

Still later, he was telling me that I don't follow him as I should, because I still love to go to Pushpa's *Kirtan*. I told him that lately, more and more I feel like that too, that it is a waste of time, but have not the courage to stop going, for fear of hurting her feelings.

"*Tabla,* harmonium, the singing, it pleases you—you like it—you do not realize that it is useless from my point of view."

So, I had better tell her sincerely why I have to stay away and just hope that she will understand. . . .

"Human beings are full of errors, and if it wouldn't be for errors, how could they progress? We are the result of our failings and errors—they are a great lesson. I never act myself: I do as I am directed." And he made a graceful gesture with both hands to illustrate the channelling from above.

"Saints are like rivers; they flow as they are directed. Those criticisms they will go; never complain, never. If you don't complain, they gradually will go completely. Pray for it. Pray to the Higher Ones or to God, or to whom you will. Pray that such feelings could stay away, and if they remain, the love should be greater. In your case they are not so many as with some other people. You are only six months in training. Look where you are—are you not much further . . . is there not a great difference in you?" I had to admit that there was.

"Nearly everybody has these doubts and criticisms. I had not. Never. But I have seen how my father and my Rev. Guru Maharaj were training people. This is the way of training, to make you speak as you did: I make you angry, and then you speak, and I know what is in your mind."

29

The Turning of the Heart

3rd August, 1962

IT WAS STIFLING, unbearably hot. The rain downpours are few and scarce, the heat humid and sticky. Only Bandhari Sahib was there in the morning at first, and because of the heat we soon went into the room to sit under the fan. Then came the smelly madman who belches so much. He never came into the room before. He seated himself next to me . . . and here he sat belching, speaking loudly, making silly remarks and grunting noises. The smell from his mouth was abominable and sickening. He is about seventy, and his black and yellow teeth must be full of pyorrhea. Some weeks ago he said to the brother of Bhai Sahib that washing is not necessary for him because he does not perspire. One can imagine what that means in the tropics! I was thinking, not without bitterness, why all the most disagreeable people are attracted here, and why on earth will they always sit near me, or be shown to sit next to me; why must I suffer such additional difficulties, when the physical conditions are already difficult enough and hard to bear . . . and suddenly the Cognition came: it came like a flash of light into the mind—he is training me to be able to detach my mind at will from all that I do not wish to notice . . . to conquer the small irritations. Immediately the full significance of it became clear: here is partly the answer to the fact that he can live with his family without ever being disturbed; he does not need to go into Samadhi to escape the physical conditions, and he is teaching me to do the same.

"Help me to build the bridge, to reconcile," I said to him some months ago, when I was practically in despair because of the smelly crowd of dirty men. "You can escape to a different level; you need not listen to them, or even see them, but I cannot—I have to endure it here and now, the lot!"

He only smiled then; he did not tell me: I am showing you the way; I am showing you how to do it, if only you are able to see it. He did not say so, because at that time I would not have understood, nor accepted it. He was training me all the time; this is the answer: to understand how it must be done. It meant, in practice, that whatever happened around me, if I wanted it, I need not notice it. I could remain at his feet in stillness, always in peace, somewhere. . . .

"I don't look at many things; I don't want to burden my mind; and if I do look, I don't keep or hold it in my mind. I don't want to burden my brain, so, I simply don't see it, and don't remember it either," he said one day when I laughingly told him that he does not look at the ladies.

Once he was telling me in L.'s presence how he made her suffer by not speaking to her for weeks.

"You know," said L., and she laughed, "he thinks that he made me suffer so much . . . let him think so; he will give me better and more bliss for that, if he thinks so. But I didn't suffer even 10% of what I would have suffered if I were completely conscious. I was in Dhyana all the time, lying under the fan all day long, with the currents of love inside me. What did I care if he did not speak to me? Often I did not notice it at all!"

Clearly my case was different. I had to learn how to exclude it all in full consciousness. Obviously this will be the basis of my training for my life in the future. True, my mind does not work at the moment to its full capacity; still, there is enough of it left to feel suffering and the discomfort.

All this was going through my mind, and then I noticed that he was looking intently at me. Then I knew that he was aware of what I was thinking. Bandhari Sahib was writing down some Persian couplets:

"I am immersed in the mud of the world (Maya),
    And my boat is in the whirling river;
    Even if I suffer death, I don't care,
    Provided I hear always your Voice!"

The other one went like this:

"Those who are surrendered, live in the Will of the Beloved,
    They bear everything without complaint;
    Because they get new life every moment from the Real
    Bandhara."

Bandhara is the Reservoir of all Grace.

He was feverish in the evening, and everybody left soon. But before I left, I had the opportunity to tell him that I understood the lesson: it would mean that, later in life, nothing can harass me if I don't allow it. It would mean acceptance, and the ability to remain in contentment at His Feet always. I got up and knelt down, touching his foot with the crown of my head. "Thank you, and God bless you, and get well soon," I said. His head lowered. I could not see his expression, but I knew his heart was too full to show it.

At Pushpa's place I thought about it all the time, and the more I did, the more important it seemed to me. . . .

4th August

IT BEGAN TO RAIN in the night, not much, just enough to drive me inside the room . . . then it stopped.

When I was sitting in his garden about eight in the morning, it began to rain in earnest. All the chairs were taken into the doorway, and everybody went home. I sat alone. Bandhari Sahib came shortly afterwards, and he began a discussion whether it is more difficult to do as I am doing—to be with the Teacher without any worldly responsibilities and worries, in a word, renouncing the world—or to do it while remaining with the family and accepting all the responsibilities it implies. I was of the opinion that my case was the easier one; those who remain in the world have it much harder, subjected as they are to all the pressures of life.

Guruji joined us about eleven, looking frail and tired. He was obviously still not well.

"What talk was going on?" He wanted to know. I told him. **"Only when the Manas is dead, the real Sannyasi-life begins. Sannyasis do not necessarily renounce the world and are without desire because they happen to wear the orange robe. The middle way is the best. On our line, we remain in the world and reach Reality in spite of that, or if you like, because of that."**

8th August

HE ASKED ME last night why I didn't go the *Kirtan*. Told him that I never will go again, and I have talked it over with Pushpa. In this moment we were interrupted—several people came. So, I knew that he is bound to ask me this morning about the details, which of course he did. Told him that I felt that sincerity is the best policy; I simply told her the truth, that it was his wish that I should not go.

"Please tell her," he said after I had finished, **"that I will never ask you not to see her. Friendship is something very different from religious services or *Kirtans* or the like."**

I told her this afternoon, and she seemed pleased about it.

Told him about the strange irritation I feel against everything and everybody, and he is included in it.

"It is good and bad," he smiled.

"Good?" I wondered.

"Yes, not bad. But the best would be if you never doubt. This is the ideal condition, but it is very rare. I personally don't understand it because I never doubted or criticized my superiors. Never. But I have seen how my Rev. Guru Maharaj and my father did train people, and I do it too. This is the way. Little by little the mind will give in. Then there will be no trouble."

Told him that Bandhari Sahib was telling me how his brother could turn the heart of anybody in a moment. He began to tell me about his brother and his uncle . . . how handsome they were, and how generous. And I was thinking, while listening, that never could anybody be more beautiful than himself. Like a golden God, sparkling eyes, this special dynamism of a non-human quality, and he is not even well, feverish, and looks tired this morning. . . .

There must be a way that can help when the mind plays up . . . there must be a way to reason with it.

"By reason, you will achieve nothing. It then remains on the level of the mind, and the mind is very clever. The Mind is the Shadow of Shaitan, as the Persian proverb goes. If the Shaitan has yielded, the whole barrier is gone. But for the complete surrender one needs more than that; I said, there is not only the Mind, but the Will and the Character to be surrendered too. But already a great step is done if the Mind has yielded . . . a very great one. It is the Victory. Little by little it will be done. It takes time."

How wonderful he looked today, and I said so. It is not so much the features—it is the expression. "But this special expression you do not always have. Last winter when I had those big troubles, very often I was so bitter because I was convinced that you had created those conditions with your power. And I used to come to you full of resentment, and you just sat there and looked like Buddha himself. And the whole resentment used to vanish, was gone—I just took it; what could I do, thinking that you could not have known how much I suffered, otherwise how could you have such a wonderful expression, this gentleness, and compassion?"

He smiled . . . then he went into Samadhi . . . and see! He looked once more like those famous statues of Buddha of the Khmer period—so tender, so still, so remote, just a suspicion of a smile on his lips, the bliss of another world . . . and the tenderness. I looked and looked, entranced. . . .

People came. Acharya was talking a lot. I sat there absorbed, trying hard to be with him alone, undisturbed, and it worked; but will it work in the period of dryness? I wonder. . . .

The people went. Silence fell. Deep hum of the fan. A large fly kept buzzing around in the room . . . a sound of summer. It awakened memories. The buzzing of a large insect caught in the room, the noise of a lawn mower, curtains agitated by the wind in constant movement in front of the open windows, the breath of summer composed of the smell of cut grass, the fragrance of flowers, and hot earth. Since I was a child, this represented summer to me—with the freedom of cotton dresses, and open air, and other things so precious to a child's mind.

He was lying on his tachat, on his back, the legs crossed one knee over the other. Suddenly, I had a sensation similar to an electric shock in my breast, and for a few seconds the whole room was spinning. . . .

Bhai Sahib, oh, what are you doing? I tried to speak, to formulate the words, was breathless—the room was spinning more and more, the mind stopped working in a second, and there was a flood of love, like a wave submerging everything.

"You did it rather sudden," I laughed . . . it seemed funny.

He got up and closed the door leading to the garden.

"I will be coming back," he said, taking the towel.

"I also will go," I said, getting up. Well, well . . . what you do to human beings, I thought. Like a monkey in the hands of a monkey trainer are we in your hands. . . .

In the evening he did not speak to me at all. Went home early.

9th August

"THIS IS HOW it is done in our System," he said. **"For the one to whom it happens, it is very wonderful because one cannot do it by himself alone. But for the Guru it is a very ordinary thing to do. And this is what Bandhari Sahib meant when he was telling you that his brother used to turn the heart of people."**

"Oh this is it!" I exclaimed, very much interested. "And it is done through the Heart *Chakra?*"

"Yes, and there is the place which is called the Heart of Hearts, but to the public we just say: it is the Heart; it is good enough."

I was interested and very impressed.

"But this you do every morning," I said, and he smiled. "You turn my mind off, and only for the sake of demonstration you did it rather suddenly this time. In the mornings it is done in a more gentle way; it happens gradually. At any rate, I never know the exact moment when it happens; it is just there; then I know."

"When you will tell people about those things, they will be impressed. Write down everything. It is such a subject that you can speak of it for months, for years. For instance . . . what happened yesterday, and how it happened. Our System is the best. After two or three years you will say: In what a wonderful System have I been trained . . . how human beings are trained in the simplest, the easiest way . . . how they are put to work according to their abilities and desires. Then, the desire is taken away and the Shishya must do the Will of the Guru. But the Guru puts him to do exactly what he originally wanted to do, and can do best, of course. But there can be no self, or ego anymore now, because the Shishya does not do his will any longer, but that of the Guru."

"How clever! What a wonderful training indeed!"I exclaimed.

And so I was right when I was thinking that I will never be asked to work in leper colonies or hospitals, for I have not the necessary qualifications, nor am I interested in nursing, nor will I have to deal with children, because I know nothing of education; but having metaphysical inclination and being interested in metaphysical matters, I always felt that I will be asked to help people one step nearer the Truth.

Speaking of himself he said: **"When I am told, or made to understand, or it is hinted, I do my duty to my best knowledge, and there is nothing but duty for me."**

Here again, our characters are similar, my dear, Revered Guru Maharaj; duty for me, too, is the most important thing. . . .

10th August

TOLD HIM ABOUT the dancer-like quality of his movements—so Oriental, so smooth; no one of his family has it, neither his brother nor his children. I saw it in India in the professional dancers . . . such cat-like grace, and only in Hatha Yogis, but only the best ones. They walked like gods and moved with the same feline grace. But they were very much body-conscious, very much aware of their movements. But he was not. It was completely unconscious with him. He smiled quietly.

"It is because at the stage I am, I can leave my body at a second's notice, a split-second's notice I should say; and the body expresses

the state as well as it can." I understood. Here lies the explanation of his Christ-like or Buddha-like quality: the body mirrors, reflects, the higher states of consciousness. That's all.

DREAM: He and I sat side by side in a room, the door of which opened into a large courtyard. In the courtyard, leaning against the wall, sat a man. "Tell him!" he said. I turned towards the man: "Don't be discouraged—Guru Maharaj is pleased with you!"

"What sort of person are you?" he interrupted me briskly: "You don't know how to respect a man like me! How dare you say that I am pleased! It is not your business to say so!"

"But I thought that you wanted me to tell him!" I said very much puzzled. He quickly got up and went to the man who fainted as soon as he reached him. Other people came running. The man seemed to be dying; there was some kind of big trouble. He knew that the man was going to faint, I thought; he got up BEFORE the man even began to faint and went there. Suddenly I felt awful. I was gasping for breath, suffering greatly. I was dying too. Was it a mistake to die? Or is it his intention that it should be so? I thought—while waking up—so great was the suffering.

He did not interpret it for me. He just went to sleep. It seems to me there are three important points: 1. I did something according to my own and not his will, and was reprimanded severely; 2. that I was dying under great suffering; dying, NOT dead; 3. the process was going on; it is not finished.

He looked at me with an undefinable expression when I told him how glad I was just to sit here and look at him, for he is so transformed for me now. As soon as I said it, I wondered if he will take it away from me. I seem to be deprived lately of everything which gives me pleasure or consolation.

11th August

THIS MORNING I FELT VERY BAD . . . vomiting condition, and severe headache. Took some sodium sulfate, Glaubers salt. But it did not help and upset me very much. Took two aspirins. Dragged my body along all morning, trying to do some housework.

Went there about nine. He was not outside; Babu sat in the room under the fan. I asked him if I could sit in the room too; I felt so hot; the night was stifling hot. Felt miserable. Not a leaf was stirring in the trees, and it was very sticky. Exchanged a few words with Babu.

He came in after his bath; I asked if I should go out because he may want to dress, but he said that I can stay. He was talking and laughing with his wife. When the wife had left, I told him how I suffered last night. I must confess, I was sorry for myself, could not sleep, so much was the perspiration and headache.

"You should not sit here for hours," he interrupted me sharply. **"It won't help you. The mind is not working; you are apt to criticize; unnecessary questions arise in your mind which you may think helpful, but they are not; they are of the worst kind! You come here from nine to ten, for one hour in the morning, and then in the evening for a short time."**

I began to weep. "You are sending me away into the heat! How cruel! You know that my flat is as hot as a baker's oven—the coolest place is this room of yours under the fan!"

"You just come here for one hour in the morning," he repeated; **"what are you doing here?"**

"What am I doing?" I said blankly, the mind not working. "I suppose I am here to be with you . . . you insisted that *Satsang* is essential—ten hours per day I spend sitting here . . . I understood that is how it should be."

"To be with me," he repeated scornfully . . . **"others are with me too. My wife, my children are with me too; my wife massages my body for several hours daily; my children serve me! But you, what are you doing?"**

By now I was weeping bitterly. No use asking me what I was doing, because the mind refuses to function, and I cannot think at all. All I knew was that I was being deprived of his presence. He seemed angry. So, I went about ten, still weeping all the way home. It is going to be very hard to stay in the boiling hot flat nearly all day long.

"Go for a walk at eight in the morning," he said.

But if it is already so hot at five, how will I be able to? And the housework? When shall I do that? I do it early, for later in the day I am unable to do it. How difficult my life is with him! If there is not the one thing, then there is something else; I never know where I am. Bitterly I was crying at home for hours. . . .

To drive me out of the only cool place, a little ventilation in his room . . . one would not do it even to one's enemy; I cannot stay with Pushpa in her bedroom with the cooler every day. It is a shameful thing to do—to refuse hospitality to somebody who is already suffering so much. No, it is not him; it is not in his character; it is done for a purpose; it must be a test. The mind went still when I thought it over, and did not give me trouble. It seems so clearly to be a matter of training . . . the mind will not give me trouble, because it will understand the reason for this incident. But will it? Can I trust it?

Was sewing the new dress I was making. I cut it the other day and passed it on Pushpa's sewing machine. Bought cheap cotton material in the bazaar with the money saved from my food. Must have another cotton dress; nylon is not at all suitable—encourages prickly heat rash. Have only one cotton dress . . . felt guilty to spend some money on myself. Went there in the evening as usual. He was sitting outside and asked me how I was. Now I am sure that he is testing me, for he expected an act of rebellion and complaint. But I only said that I was all right. He looked very weak and told me that he did not feel well at all. Told him that if I have to spend so many hours at home from now on, I had better look for another flat for the next hot season in May.

"Who will think of the next year? Who knows what is going to be? . . . never think of tomorrow. . . ."

12th August

W HEN I ARRIVED, he was playing chess with a friend whom I never saw here before; I think he lives somewhere in the South.

"You are very late," he remarked.

"I do what you have told me—you ordered me to come from nine to ten." He nodded, continuing to play. His torso was bare; he was clad only in his *longhi*, and looking at him I was reflecting how much light a human skin can contain. In his case it did not look like skin at all, just a radiation, a golden glow. His opponent was a thin man with a serious face. Both were engrossed in what they were doing. I watched fascinated. Last night I was crying silently, thinking to what lonely long hours he is condemning me, but there was like a secret communication with him, like a subtle thread. And I knew that he was aware of lying there crying.

Listened to the clock ticking away, thinking that soon I will have to go. But when I got up at ten, he asked without looking up:

"You want to go?"

"It is ten already—you wanted me to stay only for one hour."

"No, you can stay here," and I sat down again.

He played with concentration; his opponent seemed to be a good player. I tried to tune in to his thought, as he wants me to do. But I saw soon that it wasn't the right way to proceed. The mind creates a barrier, and one does not get anywhere. Those flashes must come from beyond the mind; I cannot force them; they must come by themselves. Finally I decided that he wanted me to go at half past eleven, and so I did.

In the afternoon I was lying on my bed; I just finished my midday meal of some rice and vegetables; it was quarter past one. Was thinking how maddening it is that I can never capture his thought, even if I have such a keen desire to be able to do it. There was a time when I was quite good at getting other people's thoughts, but with him it does not work. Probably he was just occupied with the chess game, not thinking about me at all, when I should go home. This is also possible. Then of course, I would capture nothing.

Suddenly I became aware of a strange behavior of my heart: it was beating strongly and very rapidly, as in a high fever, on and on regularly. I remembered that I had such an experience before, so I just relaxed and decided to rest for one hour. But I fell asleep until 4 p.m. When I woke up, the heartbeat was normal again. Only there is this strange feeling that it was not sleep; there was a kind of awareness, but who can say? What was it?

In the night slept fairly well, but every time I woke up, and I did it often, I felt the unusual heartbeat which subsided each time the waking consciousness took completely over.

30

We have Two Hearts

"YOU WANTED TO TELL ME SOMETHING?" he asked, because I mentioned last night that I had an unusual experience which I will tell him tomorrow. He hardly ever asks me if I want to speak to him. On the contrary, when I have to tell him something, he usually avoids me, and interruptions would begin. Told him about the heartbeat and the sleep which did not seem to be a sleep. His smile was tender and strange.

"Do you remember, in spring, I had two hearts beating in my breast . . . such a strange *Maya* it was."

"**You are right,**" he interrupted, "WE HAVE TWO HEARTS."

"One beating rapidly and strongly, and the other my own?" I asked, and he nodded. Did not ask further . . . had the feeling he will not say more. The one must be the Heart of Hearts, which he mentioned sometimes. Is it etheric? Or even more subtle? Heaven knows. I dimly remember. I think it was L. who told me that the Heart of Hearts is the Atmic Heart. I will know one day, of course. At least he always says so . . . must not be impatient . . . must train myself to wait in stillness.

I was there at nine because I went to buy some bread for him, and stayed until half past eleven . . . then went to the bazaar. In the afternoon went to Pushpa. He did not come out in the evening. I gave Babu his lesson and saw him playing cards in the courtyard, sitting on the tachat with his wife and Durgashankar. He is not well, very weak, coughing—he has bronchitis—it is evident to everyone. It was drizzling. Went home and slept inside the room. It was hot and sticky, and I woke up with a headache.

14th August

HE DID NOT SPEAK TO ME all day . . . stayed for two and a half hours in the morning. In the evening he did not come out, so I went home at seven.

15th August

HINDU HOLIDAY. Babu asked to be free, so we had no lesson.

16th *August*

HE DID NOT COME OUT last evening. After sitting alone in the damp
garden, went home early. Since this morning I am suffering from
irritation. This irritation seems to be something new. It is so
unreasonable, against everything and everybody . . . though he
seems to be excluded from it. Sometimes, however, the irritation is
directed against him.

He, too, seemed to be in a bad mood; he ordered me to plant some
vegetable seedlings which one of his disciples brought; but I argued,
what's the use of planting such tender things if they haven't got the
least chance of survival. First get rid of the goat, I said, which those
dirty people living in the shed let loose all the time to roam freely in
the garden. And what about so many children and stray dogs coming
in from the street? . . . and the cows wandering in . . . Munshiji
running after them, chasing them out?

But it was no use. He became annoyed. I planted the seeds. Later
he gave me a letter to type. Was very irritated, and the mind gave me
trouble. We had an unpleasant discussion, and he told me that I have
no brain and no understanding and am stupid, and he kept abusing
me, and I fought back. Then he said: **"Come inside, why should you
sit here alone."**

"You mean inside the courtyard?" I asked in astonishment, and he
said, yes. Well, I thought, full of amazement, he was never concerned
if I was sitting alone . . . I do it for months on end, in the cold, in the
dust, unnoticed, forgotten, neglected, resented even, by some
people.

So, I went inside . . . they all played cards for hours. I just sat
there and watched. I always thought, and still think, that the card
game is a waste of time. But for him it is not. For him, no matter what
he does on the physical plane, it is all the same. His consciousness is
partly somewhere else anyhow. This state is called *Sahaj Samadhi*,
effortless Samadhi, and to this state his Superiors brought their
Shishyas effortlessly—so he said once when I commented on this
capacity of his to be in two different states at one and the same time.
When he was playing cards, it was very evident that, though he did
pay attention to the game, he was somewhere else too. One could see
it by the expression of his eyes.

Went home early, about eight.

17th August

IN THE MORNING there was a new young man whom I never saw before, and Bhai Sahib spoke to him in Hindi explaining the System. He used several times the word "Self Realization," in English, in course of conversation. An idea arose in my mind: "Please Master, could you tell us, because it is something which very much puzzles me . . . how does one know that one has realized God? How does one know that it is not an illusion, a *Maya* of some sort? I met so many *Sadhus* and *Sannyasis* in Rishikesh and elsewhere . . . they all called themselves 'Realized Souls.'"

"If one says that one is a realized Soul, one never is. It is NEVER said. A Wali (saint) is a balanced person; he knows that this world is not a bad one, and he has to live in both worlds, the spiritual and the physical, the life on this earth. There is nothing good or bad for him; good or bad are relative concepts."

"But I have so often heard you condemn worldly things!"

"Because to the ordinary people one has to speak like this," he laughed. **"How will they know that gambling or chasing after worldly possessions is wrong? But why bother to understand? To realize it is important. Only the things we understand through Realization are really ours."**

Later: "I gathered that before one comes to the Master or a Saint, the Karmas are valid, but as soon as the Saint takes you in his hand, no Karmas remain."

"Not immediately; but little by little, as the desire goes, no Karmas remain, and another set of Karmas takes over. One makes other Karmas which bind you to the Master and which take you to Realization."

In the evening was the same story: they were playing cards, and I was watching them for a while. Went home early. It was raining heavily.

18th August

HE WAS SWEEPING HIS ROOM when I arrived. I was full of laughter and joy because of the heavy, tropical rain. Have never seen such a downpour—it was like sheets of water . . . there was no question of "drops." It made the air so gay, so pure and fragrant afterwards.

Then we both sat down, and I told him about the depression I had last night; it really lasted for the last three days, but yesterday it was very bad. I was at home early, sat on the tachat, and was knitting—

such was the depression because of the miserable life I was leading
. . . life without joy or peace.

I have had periods of misery in my life—who has not? But I don't
think I have ever been so miserable in all my life. . . . Does he know
about it? He nodded.

**"There was some depression, and something was done that it
should not last long."**

Then I proceeded to tell him that I was irritated because of the
shed in which Tulsi Ram's family lives. It is painful to see that he uses
some of my money to repair the shed of dirty people who give him
trouble and annoyance in every way. After all, it was the money from
selling my house, and the money my husband had left me; it would
have served me for my old age. I gladly give it to him for a worthwhile
cause, but it is hard to understand why he does certain things. After
all, they ruin his garden, quarrel, and make a mess; he, Tulsi Ram,
does not want to work, and a shed like this one, they can erect
anywhere in the Indian plains—why should it be in his garden?

He listened silently. Then he told me how L. gave a blanket to his
Rev. Guru, and he was so pleased with it . . . but a few days later he
gave it to somebody else.

**"I must admit, I hoped he would give it to me, but he gave it to
someone who did not matter to him at all . . . it is done like that. We
give things away; our family, our property, matters little. I never
came with empty hands to him, but the things which I was bringing,
he distributed immediately amongst the people present, and they
did not mean anything, either to him or to us. It is done like that."**

Told him during the conversation that I was looking forward very
much to the *Bandhara* this winter. I felt it will be important to me, in
what way I couldn't say, but it will be important. He nodded. About
twelve, I went home. We are without electricity in our bungalow; the
thunderstorms disrupted the electricity supply. Very difficult
without a fan.

20th August

WHEN I WENT TO HIM THIS MORNING, the irritation was still with me,
more than ever. Like a storm, it was blowing inside my soul; my very
insides seemed to turn.

We are still without electricity; it is the third day. Some relatives
of his arrived from somewhere in the province; the house was full of
bustle and noise, the comings and goings; he looked so weak . . . and
I heard him coughing so much. . . .

In the evening he came out, and they played cards again in the courtyard. Had moments of fleeting happiness—wonderful, light, airy, not of this world, like a golden cloud inside my heart. . . .

21st August

YES . . . THE LONGING . . . the Great . . . the Endless. . . . Let us remember how it was exactly: I was just waking up at the usual hour about six, or perhaps it was earlier. And there it was, between the waking and sleeping state—the Longing. . . . So great, so endless, and oh, so sharply painful, and so deep. . . . Longing for what? was the first thought, as soon as the waking consciousness took completely over. I really did not know. I never do. Since I am here with Bhai Sahib, it is just Longing. From the very beginning it was in me—sometimes appearing, suddenly taking me unaware . . . sometimes like a deep sigh from the bottom of my heart, it seemed to relieve tension . . . or I had to cry out loudly . . . it was so sharp, so cruel. From the very beginning I never knew for what I was longing. Confused, tortured, the mind not working, I did not, could not analyze it. It was just "longing" from the very depth of the heart, the poignant feeling of some vanished bliss. . . .

At first, at the very beginning, it seemed just a longing for its own sake, for nothing in particular. At times it was more, at times it was less, but it always remained in the background, throbbing softly. I was never without it, and it could grow so terrible at times that I would lose the will to live. . . .

There must be a reason for it; didn't he say that there is a reason for everything?

I looked deeper into myself . . . deeper and deeper still . . . and it took me quite some time this morning to discover that it was in reality the same yearning I had all my life, since childhood. Only now, it was augmented, increased to the utmost degree . . . and it must be very deep, in the deepest recesses of consciousness, and it was always with me. Even when I was quite small, every time I saw golden clouds at sunset, or the sky so blue, or heard lovely music, or saw dancing sparks of sunlight on the trembling surface of the water—each time it came, an endless sadness . . . something was crying to me. . . .

The blaze of gold before dusk, or the pinks painted on the mother of pearl sky at sunrise—I had this strange, powerful feeling, a nonending wave of yearning which was tearing my soul apart . . . the overwhelming desire to fly up there, to disappear, to melt, to vanish, to dissolve in the windows of deep blue between the clouds, or in the blaze of golds and crimsons . . . to be spent in the last supreme firework of joy. . . .

Often I wondered what this yearning could be . . . never understood it . . . not really. Was it my Slav heredity, the innate sadness of Russian temperament? Or just a fantastic idea? This morning I knew: it was the cry of the imprisoned Soul for the One, the Lover crying for the Beloved, the prisoner yearning for freedom . . . for the Longing this morning was not different; it was the same I always knew, only stronger, more positive, more definite. For a few seconds it seemed to be breaking my body apart, so strong it was, causing even bodily pain. Then it ebbed away, leaving the understanding of its very nature behind. So simple: all the time it was never anything else but THE CRY FOR THE REAL HOME!

We bring it with us into physical life. We bring it from the other planes of being; it forms part of the very texture of our Soul; and it is intended to take us home again where we belong. Without this Longing, which is a gift not from this world, we, deluded as we are, would never find the way home. . . .

If you love, and you were asked: why do you love? . . . and you are able to answer: I love because of his or her beauty, or position in life, or charm, or good character—in other words, if you can give the reason for your love, then it is NOT love. But if this question is put to you, and as if in a sudden wonder, you must admit that you don't know, that THE WHY never occurred to you—you just love, that's all, so simple. Then only, and only then, it is a REAL LOVE.

He looked weak and slept nearly all the morning. I tried to keep the flies away by closing the shutters and the doors and fanning him while he was turned against the wall. Went home early. In the evening he did not come out. I was glad that he was resting. Dark was the night and fragrant. Frogs made an awful noise somewhere nearby. The wind smelled of moisture. Dimly I remembered that he told me once, alluding to Longing: **"You will always have it."** I always had it, Bhai Sahib. Only now . . . it is . . . terrible!!

22nd August

IT IS HERE AGAIN in the morning. Very bad. Last night for about half an hour before I went to bed, it was like a slow torture . . . so strong that I had to walk up and down pressing my heart with both hands. For I felt physical pain. Had to stop walking, for I became tired all of a sudden and had a cup of tea. Then made my bed in the courtyard as usual. As soon as I was in bed, here it came on again. Terrible. Calling, calling. . . . Though it was extremely painful, I could not help thinking what a beautiful feeling it is—so tender, so powerful, and so strong. Really a pull . . . it had a richness in it, great poetical quality. Magnificent! The most tender feeling of deepest sorrow, an offering of the whole of one's being, a negation of everything, except the desire to be with IT . . . no matter what sacrifice, no matter what suffering!

But, oh, how painful it is!! It lasted again for about half an hour. Then I tried to pray, but could not . . . and fell asleep at last. . . .

The vibration is going strong again. Told him about it. A quick glance with half-closed eyes, then went into Samadhi. I knew what will happen: he will raise the Energy from the *Muladhara Chakra* into the heart. Sure enough, after a few seconds, the heart began to play havoc; the pressure and the sensation of heat at the base of the spine at first diminished, and then after a few minutes went completely. I had to laugh aloud; it seemed so funny, and at the same time it was like a miracle.

"What is vibration?" he said some time ago. **"It is the impact of Power; the resistance to it causes vibration."**

So it means that if there is no resistance to the power, no vibration would be felt. If one is purer and finer, one would not feel the vibration? But when I asked, he did not answer, but began a long conversation in Hindi with Sitla Prasad who was sitting next to me. Then he fell asleep. Flies bothered him, so I got up and fanned him with a towel . . . managed to chase out all the flies. Acharya came and talked much. Guruji looks tired, I thought, and he became thinner lately, and his face is drawn. But the light in him and around him is startling. Then he went to have his bath, but told me not to leave.

"You sit here," he said, so I knew that he wanted to speak to me. He came back clad in white *longhi* and made himself comfortable in the big chair.

Told him about the vibration which disappeared so quickly, and he smiled. **"Now is the time,"** he began, and suddenly I felt that he is about to tell me something VERY IMPORTANT, and I listened carefully to what he had to say.

"Now is the time that you should note down all the experiences."

"I do; everything I write down, what you tell me, and my own experiences, and all my doubts and comments—everything."

"Doubts should be noted down," he nodded; **"otherwise how will**

the solution be understood? It will serve for the book you will write. The experiences you have, and will have in the future, you can find only in the Persian language, mostly in the form of poetry, and very little of it has been translated until now."

I listened, partly with astonishment, partly greatly interested. The importance of this statement was evident.

"I abandoned the idea of writing a book long ago, because you had said that those who write books are idiots, and so are those who read them. But nevertheless I kept a diary; I remember you told me once that the diary will help me." He nodded.

"Those who write from reading other books and not from proper experiences are idiots, and idiots are those who read them. But you will write from your own proper experiences, living experiences— your own. We live in the age of knowledge; some knowledge has to be given out to the world. I want you to do it. You will have to take my message to the world. All the doubts, the trouble the mind gives you, do not really interfere with love. Not really. The mind tries, but the love is not really affected. Had it not been so, I would never have diverted my attention towards you." And he smiled kindly.

His wife brought a letter from a French woman which he wanted to be translated. Then he sang a Persian couplet:

"The lane of love is not a thoroughfare; once entered, you
    cannot pass through. . . .
Now what can I do? I am helpless. . . ."

Yes, the chief feature is complete helplessness; one is completely helpless! I remember how I wanted to run away; it was in April, I think, but always I knew that I will never be able to do it. The same couplet he told L. and me in December, if I remember rightly, and I am sure now, was a hint and a warning for me. The Master warns, but the Shishya is made to forget, so he said once. Even then, I knew intuitively what to expect, and still I stayed. . . .

A man came with a worldly request, some help in a court case, or the like. When he had gone, I asked: "How many people come for the sake of spiritual instruction?"

"Very few," he screwed up his eyes looking at me, "very, very few. And those who come here are not very keen. If you write the book, do not forget to emphasize how love is created. We are the only Yoga System where love is created in this way. My Rev. Guru Maharaj was always saying: If you can find a better, a quicker way, do go away, by all means . . . so broad-minded he was. But where will you find a better one? My disciples, if they live as I expect them to live, and they follow me in everything, they realize God IN THIS LIFE. Absolutely. And if they are too old, or the progress is too slow, I make them realize on the deathbed. God MUST be realized in one life, in this life—this is the only System which does it. After a few years you will say: to what a wonderful system you have been attracted."

"Yes, it is a simple and a clever way to get the human being exactly where one wants."

"True; and I am scolding you because I know that love is greater than everything. My Rev. Guru Maharaj kept scolding me, and I just sat there with my head bent. I kept thinking that he is right, and I am a fool to rebel all the time. He never scolded anybody else as much as he did me."

31

Dhyana is the First Step

23rd August, 1962

WHEN I ARRIVED, his wife was massaging him; he was turned against the wall; I sat down. When the wife went out, he seemed asleep; flies were bothering him; I began to chase them with a towel. He does not want the fan because coughing and perspiring. . . currents of air are disagreeable in this condition. The fan as a rule keeps the flies away, and there are plenty of them because of the buffaloes at the back of the building.

Sitla Prasad came and Happy Babu. He talked to them for a while.

"When this book is going to be written, and it will be written, there is no question about it because I see that it is your wish; it will be for your glory."

"The books are mostly written when the person in question is deceased. . . ." He spoke slowly with closed eyes.

"But can I write it before I have achieved at least something? I will have to wait though. And it is not going to be easy. Many things cannot be expressed. I hope it will prove of interest. It probably will be long. You had said to me that I am the first woman to get the Training according to the Ancient Tradition."

"I told you already that the experiences are not recorded anywhere except in Persian writings. I did the easiest thing: I am giving you experiences, and you do with it what you like."

It will be dedicated to you, my Rev. Teacher, I thought with gratitude. . . .

He looked very tired today. Tired and old. So ethereal, so thin.

"I ask you to pray for me; you will not refuse now?"

"For what purpose?" he asked slowly. Told him about the forces sweeping through my body—I only hope this old horse of a body will be able to stand it. He kept nodding slowly. My fingers kept twitching, and I had twitchings in my inside too. He talked to others for a while; I went home.

When arrived home, I noticed that all vibrations were gone. All was quiet in the body.

"It is not given to children or to sons; it is not automatically inherited like worldly possessions; it is given to whomsoever can take it: it is a Gift," he said a few days ago.

"There is a prophecy that I will be the last man of my Line."

Later he was saying to Tasseldar: "She does not know Persian, so what I did, I ordered her to write all the experiences down; she will have a full account of our System, not from the books, but from her own experiences."

"A few questions you may ask sometimes to complete and enlarge the knowledge," he said, turning to me.

What's the use, I thought, if every time I ask, either you don't answer, or tell me off, because I asked a "vague" or an "irrelevant" question.

Even in his tiredness he looks like a God.

"When at the end of June you told me that only the physical surrender has been achieved, I wondered how long it will take to complete the great, the real surrender."

"At the rate it is going, it will not take you long . . . not long at all. . . . Many surrenders have to be achieved; one surrenders gradually, then a relapse is possible, and one has to begin all over again. Look where the mind is! Nowhere!"

"It still gives me trouble," I said. He shrugged distractedly, but clearly he did not listen to what I had said. A strange, gentle smile was on his lips; he seems to listen to something within, to something secret and wonderful, when this strange, tender smile plays on his lips.

This morning when I arrived, the young man was already there listening intently, for again, as he did last evening, he was exceptionally kind, explaining so many things that it made me think: here is Peter the Fisherman fishing a Soul. . . .

Then he sent Satendra out of the room and ordered the door to be closed. The young man arranged his legs in *Siddhasana* (one of the yogic postures), and it was clear that he was giving a "sitting," as they call it here. I got very interested and watched carefully. Bhai Sahib seated himself in Guru *Asana* (a traditional teaching posture), his hands clasping his toes. I wondered if it was done to close the circuit of the auric forces. The young man sat still, his eyes closed. The guru did the same; his countenance expressed infinite love; his lips had a tender smile. He looked so wonderfully young and full of love. I did not notice the precise moment when the young man went into Dhyana. As I happened to glance at him, he was unconscious. The guru sat motionless for about fifteen minutes, the same tender smile on his lips. Then he opened his eyes and looked at the young man. I saw clearly that he did not look at the physical body. I knew this expression by now, when he is observing something non-physical. The young man did not stir; his eyes were closed; he did not even seem to breathe. The Guru closed his eyes again for a while. Then he opened them again, looked at the young man in the same way as before, and relaxed. He crossed his arms and looked outside the door through the chik. A fly was crawling on the young man's cheek; he did not feel it; only when it came too near his mouth, he twitched his lips, but did not wake up. For another ten minutes or so, the Guru sat thinking, looking sometimes through the door or the window. Once he glanced at me, a passing, indifferent glance.

Then: **"BASS BETA"** (enough, my child), he said softly in Hindi, and the young man came to his senses immediately. The Guru began to talk to him in such a kind way that I could see that the young man's heart was melting. After a while he sent him away, because the servant came to tell him that the tea was ready. He went out, and I remained alone for a while. I began to cry silently. Felt so hurt, so lonely. No interruptions at all. And when I have to say something, how many interruptions there would be. . . . And my questions are dismissed as "vague" or "irrelevant," and as for a sitting, I never had one. Stopped crying after a while; what could I do? . . . When he came in, his face was stern, hard, without expression, as though carved of stone. He sat down in the big chair.

"How are you feeling today?" I asked.

"Better than yesterday," he answered in a harsh way.

"May I ask a few questions?"

"Yes," he said briefly, his face was stony.

"Was this a 'sitting'?"

"Yes, it was."

"You met him for the first time yesterday; Gandhiji brought him to you?"

"Yes."

"You put him in Dhyana; I saw that his face was twitching, so I knew that something was done, and he listened so attentively to what you had to say. You sat in cross-legged position, and with the fingers of both hands you were clasping your toes. From the books I have read in the past, I learned that this is done to close the circuit of the auric forces—is it so?"

"Why should I tell you what I was doing?" he replied. "If I would, you will misunderstand and misinterpret it. It is beyond your understanding just now. What I do with others is not your concern."

"I thought it would make an interesting entry in my diary," I said.

"Write in your diary your own experiences only; other people are not your concern, nor what I do with them."

"You told me in the past that you had said to Mr. Chowdrie that he could sit in any position he liked, when for the first time he was put in Dhyana. It is many years ago now; but this young man was sitting in *Siddhasana*; why so?"

"I did not tell him to sit in any particular *asana*, he did it himself." He spoke, got up, and went to lie on the tachat. I felt deeply frustrated. Here we are, I thought with bitterness. There seems to be two laws; one for me and one for others. . . .

Others can ask the most stupid questions, anything at all, but mine are not answered; and I have questions sometimes which torture me for months. But they are considered "vague," and he can even get quite rough and annoyed when I ask.

"Please," I said, I was so upset. "Tell me one thing: is he completely surrendered?"

"How do I know if he will surrender completely?" mumbled the Guru, visibly irritated. I was surprised.

"But I understood that one gets Dhyana only when one is completely surrendered! I thought that Dhyana is the last stage!"

"Dhyana is the FIRST stage, the first thing according to our System . . . the first step. Before you have reached this stage, you haven't even begun." Now he was really vexed. "I told you so often, why don't you listen properly! One begins with Dhyana, and then goes on from there!"

"But why in my case is it not like this?" I was even more puzzled now. "Does it mean that I cannot go on?"

"You said and repeated so often that you don't want Dhyana! You will get an experience of Dhyana, but it is not your Path. You are trained in a different way; your way is the other way . . . in full consciousness."

"But according to your System, Dhyana comes first . . . you told me . . . you never answer my questions clearly, or they are dismissed as vague and stupid; how can they be if they torture my mind for so long? They are important!"

"They are vague, and you don't know how to ask the right kind of questions and how to listen properly. Don't you see how confused you are? Look at yourself! Your mind turns round and round!" He turned to the wall.

I sat there profoundly puzzled. What on earth does he mean by the right kind of questions? When he turned in my direction after a while I said: "As far as I understood, I am supposed to be on the Path of Love . . . which apparently is not your System then? In this case, which System is it? It is all so confusing! L. got the Dhyana in the first fortnight, so she is trained according to the System, is she not?" He was lying there on his back, hands crossed behind his head, looking more forbidding than ever. "Please, say if I understood well!" His face hardened. I began to cry . . . and couldn't stop. His wife came in. The servant. The children. Could not care less. It was all no use. I have to take everything. He is burning me. And when somebody is jealous of me, as I have learned that some of his disciples are, just tell them what you do to me, how you burn me; and if they want it, they are welcome to it too . . . I thought bitterly, and went home. At home I did not cry. Was like numb. And the heart was aching and aching . . . endlessly. . . .

27th August

LITTLE BY LITTLE. Painfully. Laboriously. Bits and pieces of knowledge are fitted together. Not even this is effortless on his "effortless" Path . . . with the mind not working properly, with thousands of interruptions, with the heart playing havoc with my circulation, fire burning my inside. The sun is not shining, and the grass is not green for me; and wherever I look, I see confusion. . . .

Had a bad vomiting condition this morning . . . and the mind was very troublesome. Lately, each time I am going to him, I feel like someone condemned to death going to my execution. What will he do today? What pain is awaiting me, what torture? I walked along resigned . . . expecting anything. . . .

This morning the mind was so well switched off that I could hardly walk in the street. Remembered that he said the day before: "The physical surrender is not asked from everyone. The surrender is absolute. Final. And not for this life only."

Speaking of the young man whom he put in Dhyana, he said that he did not feel much. In the beginning one does not understand; one does not feel. Too many are the sheaths covering the Soul.

28th August

IT SEEMS TO ME that the love will go away soon; there are small signs pointing to it. Only the Longing will remain. The dryness. And the Pain. Oh, God, what a life I have! Oh, Bhai Sahib, my revered Guru Maharaj, make it that such feelings of criticism should not remain; and if they have to remain for some reason: Love should be greater!!

In the evening a new lady was sitting with him.

"She said to me that for the last twenty years she did an *Abhyasa* (practice), and I explained to her that she should not take a Guru until she is quite sure. And I told her what the signs of a good Guru are."

"And what are the signs?" I asked, hoping to hear more.

"I told it to you often before."

"No, Bhai Sahib, perhaps you said it in Hindi, to somebody else, surely not to me."

"I did; I remember well," he answered with irritation. **"You never know what I say to you."**

"I will not contradict you, but really you didn't tell me," I said, getting confused.

"This is your attitude . . . always like that," he said annoyed. **"A very wrong attitude it is!"** Tears came into my eyes. The way he said it was hurting deeply. Strange, how I overreact to what he says to me; the slightest thing hurts so deeply. I was annoyed with myself for this lack of control. If the feelings are hurt, then the feelings are stronger than love. If Love is the strongest, nothing should hurt. He continued to talk in Hindi. I just sat there.

Later he was singing: **"If I knew how troublesome it is, I would have proclaimed by the beat of drums: don't come near to the Lane of Love! It is not a thoroughfare! You cannot sleep; you cannot eat; you don't enjoy the world anymore! Don't even look into the direction of the Lane of Love! What can I do? Helpless I am."**

Here he goes again, I thought. I had better prepare myself. I understand; look out, old girl; something is brewing. . . .

29th August

YES, THE WAVE OF LOVE is slowly ebbing away. He will be friendlier today . . . he always is, when I am in trouble.

As soon as I came in, he told me that he is feeling better. We were talking about the Gurus and the Ashrams, and that there is not much spirituality to be found in most of them. Told him that I did not really believe in Gurus, but went to see some for the sake of curiosity. As soon as I saw those *Swamis*, each time I thought: this is not much of a Yogi or a Saint. About you, I could not think like this . . . it was something very different. He smiled slowly.

"It must be said," he began, and suddenly I knew that he is about to make an important statement.

"It must be said, that we human beings . . . we sometimes have links with each other from the past . . . from other Lokas, from where we came. My Rev. Guru Maharaj told my uncle and my Rev. Father that we have connections with each other from another Loka where we were together. And the connection is improved this time. My uncle said in the presence of my Rev. Guru Maharaj that his duty was fulfilled because he brought us, my brother and myself, to the System. But my Rev. Guru did not train us for the first years."

"Perhaps he did," I said, "but you knew nothing about it."

He gave me a quick look with a hidden smile in his beard. **"And he treated my Rev. Father and my uncle until his last years in the same way, roughly, as he treated us, my brother and myself."**

I understood. It was a "Hint" for me.

"Trainings are different," he said after a while. **"Some are trained according to the System, and it is a long way. Some are trained according to their liking. Some are trained according to the will of the Guru."** He fell silent. Then he got up from the big chair and sat himself cross-legged on the tachat and began his correspondence.

"You really feel better," I laughed, "when you begin to answer your letters; this is a good sign!" He just smiled broadly without answering. "I would like to ask you something. I am not expecting an answer, for I suspect that you will not answer this one. I'll just take a chance. When I cannot sleep in the night, do you put me to sleep on some occasions? There are many nights when I hardly sleep at all . . . just watch the stars and think and think. . . . But very often—and it always happens between two and four a.m.—all of a sudden there is like an inner call, a great peace, a sweetness, and a deep longing. The body relaxes . . . it is a lovely feeling of surrender to this peace, and I go off like a candle which has been blown out. I keep wondering: is it you, or is it something else perhaps in me, which puts me to sleep? Who knows? . . . As I said, I don't expect an answer: I put it before you and leave it with you."

His smile was delightful to watch. His head was lowered, and he obviously did his best that I should not see it. For a while he continued to write. Some sparrows were quarrelling on the windowsill outside. With a great rattle, a lorry passed by. All was still in the room. Then:

"Tell me everything," he said, slowly raising his head. **"I am not supposed to give an answer to everything. Tell me your troubles, everyone of them."**

"I try. Only I wish my mind would remember more of the help you are giving me," I said regretfully. His face was expressionless once more. I sat in silence and left at 11:30.

"Even on the worldly platform, love is a painful thing. But sometimes there are spells of great happiness. But it does not seem to be the case with spiritual love. My love is one-sided. There is no happiness in it. And by now I am quite sure that it is not love for you . . . not directly, at least. Difficult, practically impossible, to define. It is AS IF I WOULD LOVE YOU; but when I look at it closer, I see that I love something BEYOND you. Strange, isn't it?"

"Love in the world is not love. It is *Moha* **(attachment) and** *Moha* **only. The only real love in this world is between Guru and Shishya, and it is once and forever, and there is no divorce. . . .**

"The love for the Guru takes time to stick firmly. When it does, then the greatest happiness will be felt. People in this world love this and that. There is the deepest purpose that it should be so. But when the Real Love comes along, everything else loses its value; one cannot love or be interested in anything else. . . ."

Speaking of Andrée: **"God is so kind to people; if they decide to take the short-cut, incredible things are done for them . . . for He is so kind to them. . . ."**

I was complaining about the strong vibrations. It is wearing my body out. "Just see how thin and dried up I am. It causes vomiting condition; I cannot eat; fire flows through my veins, as if the outer temperature would not be enough by itself." So I was talking for a while, telling him that he will ruin my body permanently; the conditions here in the Indian plains are difficult enough, even without this additional suffering.

He sat up slowly from the lying position; he bore a hard, cutting expression. **"You have no brain to understand,"** he began ominously. **"Why do you say that I am putting you into this condition? You are a believer in Karma; why not say: it is your Karma which makes you suffer? If you believe in Karma, you will suffer from it. Don't you think that all the wrong done in the past must be payed** up to the last farthing with suffering? And on the other hand, if you don't believe in Karmas, where are the Karmas? But you believe in them, so you must suffer. . . ."

"But didn't you yourself say once that this earthly plane is not the worst Loka, because here we can make Karmas? So, is there such a thing as Karma, or is there not?" I asked, very much puzzled.

"Do not repeat what I have said," he remarked severely. "I say that I myself don't have faith in such a thing as Karma; it is all nonsense. You don't follow me, if you have beliefs contrary to mine!" He continued in this tone for a while, breaking down one by one my remonstrations and objections. Like a public prosecutor with clever advocate tactics, he began to corner me, to twist and turn my answers; he proceeded to break down all the barriers of my logic, all the beliefs to which I clung, for they seemed to me so necessary, so reasonable, and they explained all the injustices of this world. . . . His angry, hard, ironic way made me cry. So, I sat there and cried. His wife came, and they talked in Hindi endlessly, and I cried silently for two hours.

When at home I was thinking and thinking. . . . I saw that he was right: until I give up all beliefs, there can be no humility. If I believed in Karmas, I was making *Samskaras*; any belief will make *Samskaras* as a corresponding result. Of course, I AM CREATING them and nobody else for me. But if I could switch over somehow, believe in his God (if he has one), that would be an act of humility. Then I will be nothing . . . have no beliefs of my own . . . accepting Grace or suffering as it comes, in humility . . . like Job, sitting on the heap of his lost possessions. . . .

32

The Last Belief Must Go

IN ESSENCE IT BOILS DOWN TO: "Thy Will be done and not mine."
Where are Karmas then? If one is not the doer anymore? . . .

To give up the belief of Karma . . . I realized that it was the last
belief I was still clinging to. It seemed so logical; it seemed to explain
so well the order and the justice in the Universe. And supposing the
created Universe is beyond justice, beyond order, as we know it?
What then? This thought filled me with such terror that I began to
cry. Became completely confused. All my beliefs he takes away from
me! I seem to have nothing left! This was the best, the last, the most
logical belief; all the others I have lost somewhere on the way. Did
not even know in what kind of God he does believe . . . and if at all.
Nonsense: he speaks like that because of the training. Every Hindu
believes in Karma . . . MUST believe in Karma. But here apparently
lies my mistake; he said that he does not believe in Karma, even if he
is Hindu by birth. I also know that if you ask a *Sadhu* about the
working of Karma, he will answer you: "Karma will be for you, but it
is not for me."

A great fear seized me: what will remain when all beliefs are gone?
Love alone will remain. This Love which is drying up my body and
my brain . . . the Terrible Thing in my heart—in which direction is
it leading me, I know not. Whom or what do I love? The Guru? Yes,
in a way, but not quite! Him, or rather IT, the ONE? But who is the One
to be loved? And didn't he say, some time ago, that even Love will
have to go one day? What then? But I knew that one thing will
remain: this terrible Longing. So full of terror did this thought fill me
that I wept and wept helplessly . . . sobbing like a child . . . and
could not stop. . . .

When I arrived at five (for Virendra now had to have his lesson,
but the boy disappeared), he, the Guru, sat in the courtyard on the
tachat. He did not play cards as usual, but he seemed to be waiting for
me. I went straight to him: could not wait to tell him as quickly as
possible, for I was desperate.

"**Why?**" he smiled, as if nothing had happened.

"The human being MUST believe in something! I burst out, crying to my great annoyance, for I firmly resolved not to do so. Could not control it . . . so deeply was it burning inside me.

"You take all my beliefs away from me!"

"I try!" He laughed gaily, **"I am trying, but until now I was not successful. So strong is this belief that you stuck to it until now, in spite of everything. It will take time. By and by this too will go."**

"But you take a belief away, and you don't give another one?" I exclaimed exasperated. "You don't take even the trouble to explain anything!" He got up from the tachat and stood leaning leisurely against the column.

"If you let the belief go, then after a while you will discover something very different," he said quietly, looking afar with half-closed eyes; he stood very still, and again this feeling of MEANING came over me, so strong, so powerful, like a touch of the finger of destiny.

I cried openly . . . his family sitting all around us on tachats, discussing and looking at me with curiosity, and the rascal Virendra was also there, standing near the door, to disappear conveniently in case the situation should arise that he must have his lesson after all.

Then I went out and sat on the tachat in the garden—I was alone. They all played cards now, the whole family.

A yellow sunset dramatically lit the sky; everything around was glowing with gold. Sunsets in the tropics . . . they must be seen to be believed. . . . The daily drama of darkness conquering the light, and the latter, in the last supreme effort displaying itself in all its glory, the splendid colors like a message of hope: tomorrow . . . tomorrow again I will be back. Always they are different; I have never seen two sunsets alike. Never. And nowhere in the world. Tonight it was an orgy of purest gold.

I lifted my face into it; oh, to merge in all this wonderful gold, the color of joy! Disappear in it forever, to forget, not to think, not to doubt, not to suffer anymore! In the west . . . the liquid azure and aquamarine between the delicate feathers of shining gold, deepening golden light all around me, shimmering through the foliage, a feeling of magic as in dimly remembered, half-forgotten dreams of long ago.

Why should I believe in his God? I thought, full of resentment. The theory of Karma is so philosophically right, so logical, so satisfying. Why should I give it up?

The air was so pure, the earth so fragrant. All the objects around— the trees, the leaves, the stones, the whole town—seemed to breathe, to radiate the golden glow from within. I took a deep breath and lifted my face into the radiance, felt the glow permeate my skin, shine into the depth of my being. . . .

Oh, you, whoever you are, give me a sign!!

Everything in me cried out in despair, confusion and loneliness, while my face seemed to become part of the light in the sky . . . melting into it. ... .

And then something happened. It felt like a click, a snap, and then stillness. Quite abruptly. Just stillness, where a second ago was such a storm of contrasting emotions. I listened; it was like a call . . . a call from very far away, coming from a long distance, a stillness, a peace. Like a foreboding of something, but so elusive, a stir inside my heart like the touch of a swiftly passing wing, already gone before you could even grasp what had happened. And crystal-clear, ringing, a bell-like thought floated into my mind: a belief which is taken up, can be given up; after all, you were not born with this idea of Karma. You accepted it; what is accepted can be rejected. The mind can accept any idea, any concept, and likewise can give it up, can change it. This is the way the mind is made. . . .

Well, I thought, that's that. And went home. Did not want to see anybody, the Guru least of all. Needed to be alone. And the stillness remained with me.

The streets were full of puddles, the orange of the sky reflecting in them—rikshaws, children, roaming dogs, the voices of street-vendors. Mrs. Ghose's garden had a fragrance, so sweet, so fresh. The stillness . . . like a secret message in my heart. . . .

31st August

HE SPOKE TO ME for a long time this morning, telling me how much his father suffered, how he was warned that he will get the most terrible suffering. Human beings are made like this; they have to suffer. Suffering has a great redeeming quality. It has to be.

"If I say you have no brain, it must be understood that it is from my point of view. Do you think that I am your enemy?" he asked kindly.

"No," I said, "but you behave sometimes like one."

"Everything is done as it should be done. Love like this cannot be destroyed; it will grow—this is the Law. Nothing can interfere with such a Love, ever! Your mind is still just now, but after a few days the mind will begin again . . . it will say this and that against me."

Later during conversation: **"The human being is the greatest. He** is the King of Creation. Sometimes he says in his arrogance: I am God! Then he repents and falls upon his face and asks to be forgiven. And God says to the *Devas*: Look at him! And the *Devas* will answer: Yes, you are right; he is the greatest in spite of everything!

"Jinns always put on a white dress, always white," he was saying. "It is not so simple to train a Jinn. Very powerful, very intelligent. Harmful, yes, weaker wills are subjected to them."

It was nearly one o'clock when I went to Pushpa for lunch. I MUST give up everything. I MUST. This going backward and forward has to stop! Amen!!

In the afternoon: "From my point of view, what you did and do is nothing. From your point of view and from the point of view of others, what you did is very meritorious because you did it in a very short time."

I wish I knew what it was I was supposed to have done! It seems to me that I am the same as before!

"From the moment you are united with the Master, it becomes completely effortless."

"You see!" I exclaimed, "your statements until now are either incorrect or incomplete! I always contradicted you when you were affirming that it is quite effortless! I told L. that it is impossible! It is the law of the physical world that one ALWAYS has to make SOME KIND of effort. And the greater the thing one desires, the greater the effort will be! And if you desire the WHOLE THING, the whole of yourself must be put to stake!"

"Yes, before the Union with the Master, effort is necessary." He smiled kindly. "But I speak always like this in front of people; always, because everybody can take from it what he wants. I have to get them interested." He smiled again.

"You Fisherman of Souls!" I laughed. "At any rate, I was telling L. that if it is effortless for others, it won't be for me; in all my life I had to have it the hard way!"

"A keen desire is necessary," he said; "without it your own effort is of not much avail."

"But a keen desire in itself IS AN EFFORT, and how!"

He nodded softly, imperceptibly, with this faraway look of his which seems to penetrate beyond the visible strata of our world.

1st September

HAD A GOOD NIGHT. A bit headachy this morning; every time I go to Pushpa and have my food there, I have trouble with my digestion and have a sickly headache; she puts ginger in nearly everything, even into dahl, and this does not agree with me.

This morning the mind began again; it was purring with pleasure. You are such a lover, said the mind; look what you are doing, how you love, how you try to increase your love. True, you have been given it; it did not arise by itself; still it was not given to others but to you, because not everybody is capable of holding it. You are a born lover; you can hold, can improve it . . . and so it went on . . . special *Samskaras*, concluded the mind. No, I said to myself; if I go on like this, the little self will never go. Surrender is still far away. . . . The smallest praise, or even a hint of a praise, produces this sort of pride? I was getting myself into a dangerous impasse . . . all done by myself: "I" and "me," and no end of it. . . .

"Throw the mind behind you," he said once. I really tried to do it; whatever came before me in the last few months, or rose within myself like a wave—I looked at it and endeavored to throw it away. Not worth having—let it go! And the stream of love carried it away.

Beliefs are things one takes up and collects on the way. Let them go! This belief in Karma has to go. I have to switch over, somehow. To what? A God? Which one? A Nothingness? The mind turned round and round like a squirrel in a cage.

When I arrived he took a look at me and said: **"Remember, beliefs and conceptions are not renounced just by willing to give them up; it has to become part of your mind; the attitude must change, and that takes time."**

He knows my mind, I thought. Tried to explain. He listened in silence.

"Why don't you pray?" He startled me, for he threw this sentence like a stone at me.

"Well, I sort of pray to your Rev. Guru Maharaj," I said hesitantly.

"To pray to someone is not a prayer." His face was as if carved out of stone. So how should I pray? I was profoundly puzzled; what on earth does he mean?

"The only real prayer is merging," he said darkly; **"you are dull; you still don't understand it."**

Somebody came, and they talked in Hindi for a while.

"I am going to have my bath," he declared getting up; **"some blankets and sheets are in the garden, in the sun, keep an eye on them."** And went out. I put the chair near the door, to keep an eye on the sheets and blankets, all spread out on tachats and chairs to dry in the sun.

While he was talking to me, I noticed with alarm that a tremendous vibration began in the *Muladhara Chakra*. I listened to it, and it was interesting to observe how, by and by, it was pulled up into the Heart *Chakra*. The heart went wild, beating, missing beats . . . the pulse-rate increased to an alarming degree. My head was spinning, and after a short while no noticeable vibration remained at the base of the spine except a feeling of pleasant warmth.

"You are still here?" he asked, returning after more than an hour.

"You told me to keep an eye on your things, so I did; how can I go without your permission?" He nodded. Told him how the vibration was raised into the heart. "You did it most expertly," and he laughed his happy, boyish laughter, rubbing his hair vigorously.

"Do you remember? What is Vibration? It is Power and the resistance to it. When there is no resistance, nothing is felt." I saw his smiling eyes in the large mirror on the wall; he was combing his hair and his beard.

Had a good afternoon. Noticed that Love had a different quality . . . soft, even, smooth.

In the evening when he came out, it was nearly dark; we were alone for a while.

"This afternoon Love has changed," I said.

"What do you mean?" He turned a stern face in my direction.

"It seems to be richer, fuller—it is all I can say."

"You explained nothing by that."

"You are right," I admitted. "It does not convey much to you, I know; all I can say is that it became like a melody, like a song, full and strong." He did not answer. His eyes in the darkness were looking at me. Could not see their expression, but, oh, how luminous they were! He closed his eyes. The light went out.

Went home early. Pray. Hm . . . merging. Hm . . . here we are at square one. Had a slice of papaya. Put up my *charpoy* (a rope bed) in the middle of the small courtyard and draped the mosquito net carefully around it . . . inspected carefully that not even one mosquito was hidden in the folds of it . . . and went to bed lying on my back looking at the sky . . . the lovely southern sky I knew so well by now. Every two hours a sign of the zodiac followed another, just above my head. How many, oh, how many sleepless nights, full of longing, counting the stars as all lovers do. . . . It was still early, perhaps not later than 8:45. The streets were alive with evening noises. Some music came from a loudspeaker in the distance. Was looking into the dark infinite shimmering through the mosquito net with millions of worlds. The mind worked feverishly, anxiously; what to do? How to pray? The first thing would be to relax, obviously, to let go. I tried. Could not, somehow. . . . The whole of my being was one question mark. Relaxed even more. Was waiting. Listening within. Then a feeling of deep despair seized me . . . oh, you whoever you are, help me! Hear me! I want it! I want it so much!! I think I cried out loudly. It was a sort of despair.

Then it happened. It was as if something snapped inside my head, and the whole of me was streaming out ceaselessly, endlessly, forever, without diminishing, without becoming less. . . . It went on and on. And it was absolute glory. There was no "me." Was just flowing. Just being. A feeling of non-ending expansion, just stream- ing forth. But all this I knew only later, when I tried to analyze it, to remember it. When I came round, the first clear, physical sensation was of intense cold. I got up. With trembling knees went into the room to see what time it was . . . wanted something hot to drink . . . will make a cup of tea . . . it was midnight. Where did the hours go? Only a moment ago, so it seemed, I went to bed. Was still trembling while I was drinking my tea . . . and it was not the cold which had caused it, for it was not cold at all. It was a warm, starry night.

It was shattering. It was wonderful. But what was it? WHAT WAS IT? It could not have been a prayer in the ordinary sense, at least. Was it a prayer at all? For a Prayer there must be somebody to pray. But I was not. I didn't exist. So, it couldn't have been a prayer. For a long, long time I was lying awake. Orion was right above my head in zenith. Slept well till 6 a.m.

2nd September

"WAS IT GOD?" I asked, starry-eyed and still shaken. "But are you listening to me?" He had his eyes closed and seemed to be in Samadhi. He did not hear. Will tell him later. . . .

In the afternoon I waited, but he did not come out. Several people were sitting. Idle talk was going on. Went home early.

Went to bed . . . tried again. The first step was done: I knew the way now. . . . Sinking into Something, a tremendous pull, a wave of love . . . endless . . . a flowing, a state of being and of dissolution at the same time—that is all one could say . . . terrible, difficult to define. If I would say that the whole of me became a great chord, a sound, as if of an organ, filling the entire space, this definition would also be more or less correct. And if I would say that it is an explosion, a hurricane, that too would be true. But at the same time it was the most glorious stillness, the bliss of perfect nothingness. And it was very wonderful.

3rd September

HOPED TO BE ABLE TO TELL HIM all this in the morning. But when I came, he was lying on the tachat in deep Samadhi. When he opened his eyes, I stood up and said, "*Namaste*," the usual greeting. He hardly answered. Had the impression that he did not register it. Later, I noticed that my mind began to be "switched off."

"I would like to say something to you," I said when he stirred, fearing that when the mind goes I won't be able to explain anything.

"**Mmmm**" was all he said—his eyes were closed. I repeated the request. "**Mmmm**" he said again, sat-up cross-legged and went into deep Samadhi.

In the evening I was able to tell him that Love was definitely rounder, fuller, more complete. "Now you will torture me," I laughed. "Each time the love becomes stronger, I am being frustrated in every possible way; and each time there is separation, you are kind to me!" He did not answer but began to talk in Hindi.

"What was it? Is it God?" I asked, when he happened to look in my direction. He gave me a hard, penetrating look and continued to talk to others. I left after a while.

"**Yes, yes**," he drawled in a rather irritated way when I saluted him when leaving.

To get to bed now—it is a secret joy, an appointment with THAT. The door was open: door to what? But whatever it was, it was wonderful! There must be an infinite sea of it—it is endless, it is lovely . . . like a terrific pull of the whole of one's being. Is this the prayer of the heart, is this "merging?" I don't know, because when I am in it, there is no mind; I seem not to exist at all; and when the mind begins to know something about it, it is already past. Even the idea of praying to somebody or something seems ridiculous and pointless now. Was lying awake for a long time. Wondering. A girl was singing a monotonous lullaby, her soft voice coming from far away in the warm moonless night, and the breeze and the stars and the sky, and myself, it all merged in one wonderful feeling of completeness, of deep purpose. . . .

This is ABSOLUTE security, I said to myself, but to reach it one has to traverse the no-man's land; one has to wade through the morass of insecurity, where there is no firm foothold of any kind, a sort of mental fog, and one cannot see even the ground under one's feet. And with a sigh of relief I fell asleep, blown out suddenly like a candle by a gust of wind.

4th September

HE WAS STILL ASLEEP when I came, and when I noticed how much medicine he still had left, I knew that he did not take it anymore. I became worried; something was very wrong. When he woke up, he told me that Ramji said that this medicine has after-effects and is of no value. He has been having severe stomach pain since Sunday. I became very worried. He changes his medicine every few days. I think it is the worst possible thing to do . . . it is like changing Gurus, I told him once . . . one does not get anywhere. Hopeless situation, and he gets weaker and weaker. Recently he said: soon I will leave all worries behind, meaning me; and here I am not only having my own, but also worries about his health.

A storm blows through the whole of my being, and it feels as if my head will be blown away at any moment. The currents in the body are strong, flowing fiery and fluctuating . . . sensation of heat . . . sensation of taking off at any moment—a kind of pointless irritation against everything and everybody except him. I think it is because the mind is so puzzled; it cannot think of anything else except being just irritated.

5th September

LAST NIGHT he did not come out into the garden. He is very weak. His face looks transparent and thin. How my heart was heavy; how I prayed seeing him like this . . . wept silently. He is very ill, no doubt about that. He suffers from amoebic hepatitis. He has suffered from it for many years already. And in the rainy season, this condition gets worse apparently. When at home I made a firm resolution not to sleep, but to try to analyze the new state. Well, it is really impossible to describe . . . this one thing is evident.

33

Is It God??

THOUGH I AM *QUITE SURE* that I was not for one moment unconscious—and I went to bed at nine—after seemingly five minutes past ten o'clock . . . and then eleven, how was it, I wondered, that the sense of time is completely lost? Time does not seem to exist. I could put my hand in fire, so sure am I that I was completely conscious all the time . . . only it was a different kind of consciousness. There was no interruption of conscious feeling, like in sleep, or even in Dhyana. Tried to get hold, to analyze, to fix the impression in my mind . . . and could not. It is a state of incredible dynamism, not even of bliss as such, for even bliss seems a passive state in comparison. I think it is the most dynamic state imaginable, though I am perfectly aware that I don't even touch the outermost edge, the narrowest brim of endless possibilities. I KNOW that there is such happiness . . . unimaginable, no end of it, no limits whatsoever. Even as it is at present, it proves to be too much for me. I can hardly bear it. After a while a certain indifference sets in; the mind begins to work, at first slowly, hesitantly, then more and more, thinking this and that, and the state is lost. I think that is the self-defense instinct of the body itself which intervenes when it gets too much. The natural defenses of the body cut it off, sometimes abruptly, sometimes gradually. Then I usually fall asleep immediately.

This afternoon he went for a short walk in the park. He seems a bit better. In the evening he was on the roof, and a man went to see him. I sat alone for hours in the darkening garden. Felt so disappointed. It was dreadfully hot and close, not a breath of air. It is much cooler on the roof. He did not ask me, I thought with bitterness. Other people can go . . . I can't. In all those months how many times was I sitting alone in the dust and heat, unnoticed and forgotten. He is bound to treat me even worse now. For when the human being is in despair, he turns to God. When he is happy, God is forgotten. He will drive me towards his God now . . . I feel something is coming. I began to cry, so lonely I felt. When it was dark completely, I saw the man coming down and leaving, and a few moments later he appeared. We were alone.

"Is it God?" I asked again, trying to describe the nightly experiences. Could not see his face in the dark. He silently listened to me . . . or perhaps he did not. Who can tell? He was silent.

Then he began by saying that some people will come from France. **"I never care; if they are destined to meet me, they will be guided to me by Him; it never depends on my will. I never even think of it,"** he repeated thoughtfully, and getting up told me to go home.

6th September, 1962

THIS MORNING THE VIBRATION was strong in all the *Chakras.* The body was literally on fire. Again as before, I saw light circulating in the body, going here and there, seemingly purposefully. When I told him, he was writing; he did not even look at me. I sat there, such was the power surging from below—the base of the spine—that at one moment I nearly blacked out. The head began to spin—all the objects in the room began to vascillate, to turn around—the mind became empty. I experienced a feeling of great fear, of falling . . . falling . . . and clutched to the side supports of my arm chair. Then as quickly as it began, it stopped all of a sudden.

Went home afterwards. No trouble with the vibration anymore, only walking was a bit difficult—was like drunk. But the strong sense of irritation remained. This irritation is something new because it has constantly been increasing slowly for the last few weeks.

8th September

WHAT I AM DOING IN THE NIGHT frightens the mind now—a state of being as if thrown Somewhere or into Something, and what it is the mind knows not. God, it cannot be; one cannot reach God after only nine months of training. I am satisfied to know, or to think, that I very probably tuned into the Sheath of the Soul, for there is love, unimaginable happiness, and time is not there. But the mind is experiencing a feeling of great fear. First, it wants to know and understand what these states are—for they are a nothing, a complete insecurity, from the point of view of the mind. Secondly, I firmly decided that the belief in Karma has to go, and this represents an additional insecurity. Every belief to which we cling gives us a bit of firm ground to stand upon, a security. We give up Religion, and become Vegetarians, or Theosophists, or Agnostics; and each of these new beliefs is a substitute for the old, a new ground to stand on where we feel safe. How little we know that we build our castles on sand. . . .

Spiritual life is the tearing down of all the castles, of all securities. For only then, and then only, we can reach the Ultimate Security. It seems to me that, if I don't give up all beliefs absolutely, the little self, the pride, will never go. It is of no consequence if the belief is a correct and valid one or not; it has to go. It has to be an act of faith, the act of faith in the Guru, in his Wisdom, and it is the only weapon I have to defeat the self. But what is rather disconcerting is the fact that the whole of my personality is standing up in front of me, fighting me; everything in me is united against me, so to speak. I have the feeling that the last, the supreme fight has begun. It may last for years, of course—one can never know how long it is going to be.

"And you will drive me into the arms of your God by giving me sorrows and despair much more than I had until now." Then I told him that my mind was giving me trouble because of an ungenerous remark he made about Mrs. Bogroff, who wrote to him about her troubles. What he had said was expressed in ungentlemanly terms— one should not speak about a woman in this way. Nobody is free from faults.

"You have a way of bringing people's faults to light, to bring out the worst in them; you do it to me constantly, for instance. It is a kind of vibration, something in you which makes people react in this way."

"But why should I do such a thing?" he asked angrily. **"It is the evils in everyone which come out!"**

"But if you know that, then you should be even more generous; if by simple contact with you, people's faults come to light, then to talk as you did, in front of everybody, was most ungenerous! You yourself are not free from faults; no human being can be. A great Master said somewhere that he is infallible only when he is not functioning in his physical body, using his brain. As a human being he is fallible and liable to make errors. Surely that would be valid for you too? There are many things in your environment, your family, and your way of life which I could point out as being far from perfect!"

"I don't want to listen to you!" He hissed at me. **"You don't know how to respect people like me; you never learned what respect and reverence means! You don't know how to behave in company of**

such people! You are nothing but a stupid, dense and ignorant woman, and you try to preach to me?"

"I am nothing of the sort!" my anger was roused. "I have eyes to see. I have been sitting here for months, plenty of time to be able to judge you and your way of life. I have enough of this treatment. You are an arrogant autocrat, that's what you are. All I was asking this morning was to be helped to cope with this vibration which is getting beyond my physical endurance. For nine months I am pleading with you, but it is of no avail!"

"Did I give it to you?" he hissed furiously. "It is your own sins which are coming back on you! The evils in your blood!"

"But it is YOU who put me into this state!" I nearly shouted, beyond myself with fury. "All I ask: do it gently! I understand why it is done, that it is necessary—but have a heart, I am at the end of my strength!"

"Nonsense!" he shouted back, leaning forward and glaring at me; "You idiot! You . . . you . . . so disgusting you are! So revolting! I hate all the evils in you! I hate them! I hate them!"

"But all the people with whom you are coming into contact cannot be evil! If you see all these evils in them, they must be in you! Look how full of hatred you yourself are!" I was blazing with anger. "You are full of evils too! Look into the mirror just now! Is it the face of a good man? It is time you should look at yourself and not seek out evils in others!"

And all the time there were hundreds of interruptions—his children, the wife, the servant—all kept popping in and out for one reason or another, bringing with them loud bits of conversation carried on from one room to another. It made speaking difficult and increased my irritation to a paroxysm. At one moment he pretended not to listen anymore but went into Samadhi. I began to cry. It was too much; I had enough, absolutely. . . .

"Women can only cry; this they can do very well," he said disdainfully, opening his eyes.

Once more I burst out, telling him all the miseries I had to go through since I am with him—the loneliness, the hopelessness of the whole situation, the lack of money and of the most elementary physical comforts, and the dust, and the flies, hours alone in the dusty garden, treated worse than anybody else. When others do a thing, it is considered all right and legitimate. When I do the same thing, I am wrong and am shouted down in front of everybody. It is

time it should stop; enough is enough. You act as my enemy. . . .
Why? What harm did I do to you?" I talked for a while on those
lines, pouring out all my bitterness, the accumulated frustration. He
listened, apparently, sitting in his big chair.

Then I looked up, for in my fury and anxiety to tell everything
quickly, I hardly had time to look at him. I saw that his eyes were full
of tears: a large tear was rolling down slowly into his beard. I knew
what was happening: his heart was melting—he was full of pity for
me. I began to cry and could not stop. "I am going," I said, trying to
control my sobs, and I nearly fell down getting up from my chair . . .
my knees were shaking. "Drunk again" I murmured, full of
embarrassment, trying to smile. "NAMASKAR" . . . "and may God
bless you always!"

I nearly ran out of the room, and when at home tried to eat
something, but could not. Fire was circulating in my veins. The body
was trembling . . . a small, nervous trembling impossible to control.

Felt I couldn't go on anymore. Shouted at, pushed about,
subjected to all sorts of pressures and humiliations—if I don't put
my foot down, where will it end? I had nothing left anymore,
nowhere to go . . . a hopeless, distressing situation to the utmost
degree. Began to cry again.

When he is talking to me, my mind stops, and very often I miss the
meaning of what he is saying; it is like being before the sun—one is
blinded. If I try to speak to him, the opportunity is lacking, or again, I
am as dumb as a cow. Decided to talk to him tonight—there is such a
thing as human dignity: enough is enough.

When I came at six, they were all playing cards in the courtyard,
Munshiji included. I advanced towards him; he looked dark.

"Please," I said, "I would like to speak to you before somebody
arrives; it is important."

"Not now," he said shortly, "leave me free."

"I don't mean this very moment of course, but later, please, it is
important." So I sat outside full of torture, thinking it out in my
mind how and what to tell him. I was very hurt. The sunset was
lovely. Gold and streaks of orange, crimson feathery clouds changing
gradually to ominous dark reds, as if painted on with a brush on soft,
grey clouds.

He came out when it was darkening already and immediately I
began, afraid that I wouldn't have time to say everything I wanted.

"Do not talk to me at all; I don't want to hear anything!" he said
furiously. I never saw him so angry. But I was angry too. So, I told

him that he dares to speak to me like this because I have no brother,
or any male family member to protect me; he takes advantage of me
being alone and helpless; he would not dare to talk in this way to an
Indian woman, for her brother would soon give him a good
thrashing. Does he realize the enormity of all this insulting
treatment?

"Don't speak anymore—I hate to hear your voice!" He shouted
loudly.

"I will ask one of your more intelligent pupils, say Prof. Batnagar,
to act as my brother and intervene on my behalf and protect me
against you! You ought to apologize! I expect an apology from you
for your rudeness!"

"Apologize?" he shouted. **"All what you people from the West
know how to do is to defame!"** He was roaring now. **"Defame, yes!
You are not better than the least street woman—they are known to
be expert in this business of defamation!"**

"Master," I began, and then stopped—I went very quiet and very
cold. I was really too astounded at this incredible accusation. . . .

"You are lying shamelessly!" He suddenly came quite near, his
voice sounded like a roar in my ears.

"Professor Batnagar!" I shouted. "I am calling him now; he lives
next door; he will hear me! Let him come and see for himself, and
you will see what will happen!"

**"If you dare to come once more to my premises, you will be turned
out—you will not set foot into my premises; I can guarantee that!"**

"But why do you go on offending me like this?" I was really
astonished; he looked terrible in his anger, and my heart was
stopping, kept stopping more; it was quite alarming. . . .

I think I must have lost consciousness for a while, for when I
looked around, I saw several people sitting, somewhere in Dhyana,
and he was talking in his usual way explaining something. I looked at
him. Nothing gave away his fury only a short while ago . . . only his
pallor, the greenish tint of his skin. His voice was even and
melodious as usual.

I cried . . . I cried . . . and I cried. It must have been for hours;
people came and went until 10:30. I was still crying . . . could not
stop.

"You can go home now," he said coldly, after the last old man was
hobbling away.

"I will stay here all night, sitting . . . as a protest against the bad
treatment I constantly get from you! I will not go!" I sobbed. He went
inside.

After a while he came out. I saw his wife and his sons standing in the doorway. He stood tall in front of me, slender, all in white, full of light—a great Master, every inch of him.

"It will be better for you to go," he said quietly. The authority of a Teacher was in his voice and . . . a threat? Something in his voice sounded like a warning . . . but I had no time to reflect:

"No!" I exploded, beside myself with despair—"No! I am NOT GOING! The whole town should know—everybody should see what you are doing, how you are treating me! Kill me! Drag me away! I disobey! I am desperate! Kill me! Death is better than this life of misery!" He turned abruptly and went inside followed by his family.

A little later his wife came out with his sons, asking me to leave. I refused point blank. If this is the way to treat a guest from another country, if this is the famous hospitality of his culture, let the whole town see it. . . .

"Father will not come out," said Satendra with a wicked grin.

"He'd better not; I don't expect him," I said darkly, adjusting myself in the most comfortable chair. Just as well . . . I can be as comfortable as possible. . . . So, all doors and the large gate in the passage leading to the courtyard were locked. I remained alone in the garden. The hours were passing quickly. After a while I stopped crying. Was thinking it all over. Mind did not work much. I hoped it will serve as a lesson to him.

True, I was very rude, but my patience was exhausted—I could not go on like that anymore. Inside, somewhere, very deep in me, was a small trembling, like a swift throb of an engine. The sky was full of stars. It was a warm, still, September night. A light breeze rustled high up in the trees from time to time. Listened to my heart pounding like a gong. The yapping and the howling of dogs roaming the streets came from the direction of the bazaar. Otherwise the streets were empty. About 4 a.m. Gandiji came—he does it apparently every day before his meditation and his bath in the Ganga—saw me sitting there, gave me a surprised glance, then stood facing the door of his room praying with folded palms; then as silent as he came, he left. I listened to the sound of his soft sandals growing more and more distant till I could not hear it anymore.

Went home at 5:30. Had a bath and strong, black coffee. Had a rest and at nine, as usual, was at his place. If one can swallow all that had happened, and still wants to come back, then one can swallow anything, I thought. But I knew that I had no alternative; there was nothing else left for me. Only this forlorn hope, to reach the Truth, somehow, at any cost. But the heart was aching too much; why, I didn't know . . . it was a strange pain. Surprising, how he can hurt me; the least thing he says carries such weight with me. And now this flaming row . . . if I stood that without dying of pain, nothing will be able to hurt me anymore in life—this hurt was the worst. . . .

"When neither foes nor loving friends can hurt you, if all men count with you but none too much. . . ." Perhaps it will be like this one day. . . .

9th September

HE WAS LYING ON THE TACHAT . . . and his entire family was in the room: wife, children, grandchild, all of them laughing, talking, the child screaming; nobody took the slightest notice of me. I understood that it was done deliberately. He did not want to be alone with me in the room. He laughed and joked with them, played with the child—they all made such a noise. I was sitting near the door, apart from it all, was very tired, with a sort of indifference, a kind of dull peace, which one experiences after a psychological shock, or a great sorrow. Went home at eleven. Had something to eat. Was there again at six. He did not come out. Nobody came. The garden was silent. Went home soon and fell asleep immediately.

10th September

HE IS VERY ILL. I learned that as soon as I came in. Terrible heart-pain across the chest. Fever. When I came and saw the chairs outside, but the door closed, I knew that he must be unwell. Babu told me that he was very ill.

Did not want to disturb; so I went home and came back at noon to inquire how he was. Was allowed to enter the room. Babu was massaging his feet. He was lying motionless and very pale. I left soon. Went to Pushpa. Came back at 4 p.m. The situation was the same, but I was told that the doctor was there in the morning, and he is getting the homeopathic treatment.

13th September

I AM WEARING MYSELF OUT with worry for him. He seems to be very ill. I think it could be a liver attack . . . it looks like it. His face is yellow and drawn, which is one of the symptoms, so I was told. The pain in the region of the liver and the stomach is acute—he lies there, moaning with pain. I don't stay long; it could be embarrassing for him, for he is not free. Cannot bear to see him suffer like this. It is so miserable to sit there and not be able to do anything. His family takes turns to massage his body day and night, all twenty-four hours. His wife is with him all the time; I feel so useless sitting there not being able to help in any way. And when at home, I worry and worry. When I go back, he is always the same. Go home. Worry. And so the hours, the days pass, full of misery.

Had plenty of time to think in those days. From the way he treated me, and to judge from the acute pain in my heart, as well as from the state of complete separation, I am sure that the last act has begun. The last act of the drama . . . the final breaking down. How long it will go on, I don't know. He will know it, of course, but for me it is impossible to know. Perhaps after many years I will understand. He mentioned one day, it was in the courtyard when I was crying because of the Karmas, and Babu said: "You will be all right by this *Bandhara.*" "No, no," he said, "not this *Bandhara,* but the next one . . . yes."

So, let's hope that it will last only for sixteen months. But it may be much, much longer. . . . Resolved not to speak to him anymore unless spoken to. I will need all my energy to be able to bear it. Cannot afford emotional outbursts.

"Suffering? Under pressure?" he yelled at me on Saturday. "It is nothing! It is only the beginning! Soon much more will come!"

Remembered, when writing to Maritje some months ago, I said: he is taking me along my Calvary. I used it only as an illustration. But thinking it over now, I realize that it is literally so. Because what is done is in reality a crucifixion—the burning away of the self, the supreme final sacrifice, mentioned in all the Myths, in all the Sagas. . . . It is the story of the final giving up of the personality, the great drama of all the ages. In the Sufi System the final surrender is done to the Master.

"The most difficult thing in the world while you are doing it, and the easiest one when it is done," he said once, I remember. . . . So, I have to brace myself. Pull the belt tighter, old girl, as the wrestler does, before the fight. Keep still my heart, and face it. . . .

Was very depressed when at Pushpa's place. I suppose because my heart was so full of anxiety I spoke about my worries and my daily travail, and I think I even cried. Mrs. Ahuja, Pushpa's friend who was there too, told me a story from the *Upanishads*:

Once upon a time sons of Kings and even of *Devatas*, who come to earth for this purpose, were sent to stay with a great Master, to serve him and get teachings from him. One of them, a son of a King, was serving a great *Rishi* who had his *Ashram* in the forest on the bank of the river Ganga. He served him for nine-and-a-half years, but the yogi did not teach him anything. One day the boy received a letter from his father telling him that it would be time to go home, for he, the King, was ill and soon he will depart from this life. He should come back to take his rightful place as a crown prince and serve his people wisely, for he must have learned Wisdom from his Teacher. So the boy went to his Teacher and said: "Guru Maharaj, I am serving you faithfully for over nine years, but you did not teach me anything. Now it is time to go back home. Will you teach me at least something now, so that I may be a good King to my people?"

"Yes," said the Master, "but you must not take any food at all. Take your begging bowl and go and beg some food for the *Ashram*. But everything you get, bring back to me—you must not eat it yourself." The boy went and did as he was told, but after a fortnight the Teacher called him and said to him:

"What are you doing? You are not very much thinner? You are eating my food—you are stealing from the *Ashram!*"

"Master," said the boy, "I did as you had told me. But when the housewife had given me for the *Ashram*, I asked for one more *chappathi*, and this I ate."

"What?" said the Master, "you are taxing the housewife! This is wrong! You have no right to do that! You disobeyed me! As a punishment, go and look after my cows: but mind you, every drop of milk you have to bring to the *Ashram* is for my own use!"

And the boy went to the pastures and looked after the cows. But hunger is a thing very difficult to bear, and he got very weak. So, after milking the cows, the little milk which remained in the udder, he took that. Again after a while the Master asked him what he was doing and, when told, said again that it was very wrong. He disobeyed him once more. "You are taxing the cow; this milk is intended for the calf!" So the Shishya stopped this practice too. But soon he could not bear the pangs of hunger. Some milky foam remained around the muzzle of the calf after it had drunk, so he took that. But the Master asked him once more, and when told he said: "The cow knows what you are doing, and she gives more milk because of that—you are taxing her even more! You dared to do the wrong thing; as a punishment go into the forest . . . I don't want to see you anymore!

And he gave an order to the Shishyas to drive him out into the forest. It was the dry season, and there was hardly any vegetation left.

Only one kind of plant grew which, when broken, gives out a sort of milky juice which is poisonous. One gets blind from it. In his distress he began to eat it and became completely blind. Wandering about, he fell into a half-dry well. There was a bit of water but not enough to drown him. So he sat in the water up to his belly, crying and praying to God to let him die and to deliver him from his suffering. The Master got worried in the meantime and sent out people to search for him. They found him inside the well, half dead, pulled him out and brought him before the Master. And only then, the Master gave him the final initiation and all the teaching which went with it. His blindness was cured.

It was a lovely story . . . told to me at the right time. And thinking it over, I feel my lot is not quite as bad as the poor blind Shishya.

But one does not know what is in store for me, of course. I am being trained according to the Ancient Tradition. One never knows what flowers will fall to my lot . . . or thorns? Rather!!

34

Serious Illness

WHEN I ARRIVED AT HIS PLACE, he sat in the big chair looking completely pale and rather yellow. A *Sannyasi* was sitting in front of him talking and talking, and the Guru was delivering what seemed to be a religious lecture in Hindi . . . his eyes popping out with effort, so difficult was speaking for him; breathlessly, he went on. I nearly cried with frustration.

When I could not keep it any longer, in a pause, when he stopped for a moment, I reminded him that the doctor ordered him not to talk: it is bad for him to make any kind of effort. But he did not like my interference; I could see it and the wife definitely resented it.

But the *Sannyasi* left shortly afterwards, thank heaven, and he went to bed. I sat alone outside full of most terrible worry. Later, at home, I posted a letter to L. in which I told her that I have the greatest apprehension for his health. To massage the feet of the patient, as his family does in turn all round the clock, does not seem to be quite enough. Does the homeopathic doctor do his duty? I was told that amoebic dysentery cannot be cured homeopathically. Nobody takes the doctor's order seriously that he must be quiet and left in peace; everybody speaks to him and expects him to react; he is constantly consulted about family affairs. I know L. will be very worried, but I cannot help it; it is better that she should be put in the picture. In the evening he had high fever, and I sat there in sheer despair. . . . Went home and cried and cried . . . could not even pray.

14th September, 1962

HE SEEMED WORSE THAN EVER THIS MORNING. Half unconscious, his eyes wide open with effort, he talked incessantly, murmuring feverishly, his hands like restless birds wandering about on the blanket. Toxic phenomena, I thought. Told Babu that perhaps hospital treatment would be advisable, but got the resentful answer. Only much later I knew why: Indian hospitals are not like ours— they are horrible places. "Most certainly not," he said, "at home he gets the best treatment," etc. And when I mentioned that one should tell his wife—maybe she does not know about the doctor's orders that he should not speak—there Babu was positively rude, and sharply said that his mother must speak to his father. And I am sure he reported this conversation to her, because she came out into the garden, saw me sitting there and stood glaring at me.

Cried at home. Guru Maharaj . . . such is despair in my heart . . . it is eating me alive. . . . In the evening when I came, I became deeply alarmed. He seemed to be more there than here. Two of his sons were massaging him. **"Who are you?"** He was asking Satendra. **"I don't know you."** "I am your son," he laughed, massaging vigorously. The boy was streaming with perspiration; it was very hot, but he did not want the fan owing to the fever; he felt too much the air current.

"I don't know the name of my mother, of my father," he continued. **"I don't know who they were. My father, my uncle, my grandfather, my brother, all died from liver trouble. I will die of it. Why not now? My time is up. I am going."** And so he went on for a while.

When later Satendra told me what he was saying, because he was speaking in Hindi, I became terribly worried. I feared that he will go into deep Samadhi and not come back . . . and that will be all. So I asked if the doctor was coming tonight. Satendra knew nothing. Went out into the garden; Babu was talking to his mother. He said that the doctor told him that one should not wait for him; it was not sure. So, I suggested that I and Satendra go by rikshaw and fetch him. "If you like," said Babu doubtfully, and the wife said nothing. So, we went. I was crying. Oh, God, I thought, if you go, I go with you!

The doctor lived very far beyond the slaughterhouse, in a little street behind a big temple. Crowded with children, the street was narrow—cows, goats, chickens, noise, dust, temple bells. The doctor was sitting on a sofa, half-naked in his consulting room which was opened into the street; he was conversing with a man. I told him how worried we were and that I saw several times Bhai Sahib twitching his face, a toxic phenomena, presumably, which is a bad sign. He came with us. My heart was in complete despair. It was dark when we arrived, and the doctor went inside. I waited, seated outside in the garden. Babu called me in. The doctor said that he was really better; the fever was not too high, and the homeopathic medicines take time to act. He was talking too much, and so it was obvious that the fever would go up in the evening. We sat there; the poor Guru was talking to him; the doctor was restraining him, trying to impress upon him the necessity to rest. His face was strange with the effort of coughing, the eyes dilated; he did not seem to understand half of what was going on. The pain was severe, for the last few days without stoppage.

Later, when I was seated in the garden, it was distressing to hear him vomit every few minutes. A painful, loud vomit, clearly causing much suffering . . . and the cough tormenting him all the time. Went home, not at all reassured, and could not fall asleep. How desperately I cried. For hours. If you go, what will become of me? You MUST take me with you! I have nothing left! How can I live an empty life as I did before? Without you? My work in the Library in London . . . the dreariness of existence . . . and the years will go by . . . and I will forget this love maybe, and become immersed into the world of *Maya* once more. Will read. Will fill my brain with book knowledge. Just now, I seem to have forgotten everything. I don't remember any knowledge at all. Hardly remember anything of my life in the West. The world is falling away from me, and now I will be pushed into it once more . . . lonely, separated, forever. Take me with you! Unite me with you! Take me into the Loka you are going, to the Glory of your life! I don't want this world anymore! It is dead for me! So I wept, and prayed to him, but to God I could not pray. Had a kind of rebellion in me, and I didn't even attempt to pray. In the night kept waking up with the bleakest despair in my heart. No hope . . . life was worthless . . . oh, take me with you, if you should go!!

If You let him survive, I prayed, if You let him live, I swear by the salvation of my soul that I will be a dead body in his hands! Will do my best to accept everything! It is the only thing which is left for me: my desire for Truth . . . only he can give it to me, help me to it: my life is worthless without him. He is my anchor of salvation . . . the only thing to live for. I have nowhere to go; only he can take me to the Truth. . . .

15th September

IN THE MORNING WHEN I CAME and asked Satendra how his father was, he answered: "Father is well!"

He was lying in the veranda of the courtyard, quite motionless, on his back. His wife was fanning him. He was unrecognizable, so thin, hollow under his cheekbones. I just sat down outside and wept. I knew that nobody was about; nobody saw me. A great hubbub was going on in the next room to his; a telegram was being composed to Ragunath Prasad, his best disciple, who was living not far away, in the next town, to his son-in-law, and to his eldest son in Allahabad.

His wife was called into the room for consultation. I picked up the fan she had put down and began to fan him gently. How he managed to look so beautiful even when half dead, I could not understand. Thin, tired, ethereal, the face of a transparent pale yellow. He opened his eyes and saw me.

"You said, yesterday, that you are going and your time is up. If you mean it, if you are serious about it, take me with you!" He closed his eyes for a second. "Please," I pleaded urgently, weeping, "take me with you! I mean every word of it! You cannot leave me behind!"

He nodded imperceptibly, gave me a quick glance and turned his head away as if in pain. His wife came, talking rapidly about the telegram and the text, and took the fan out of my hands. Crying bitterly, I sat down; he could not see me, so I didn't try to conceal it.

Later in the room, he was sitting in the big chair; I came in and sat there in silence. From time to time I looked at him; his eyes were closed. So thin. So beautiful. So dear to me. . . .

Told Pushpa, when I went there for lunch, how bad he seemed to me. Came early and sat in his garden under a tree. It was too hot. Went home, had a bath, came back. Sat in the darkening garden. People arrived, Tasseldar, lots of talk was going on. . . . Bleak was the world. He is going. . . . I will go with him. How can I live? Nothing remained . . . only the hope to reach the Truth . . . and without him it won't be possible. . . .

16th September

LAST NIGHT RAMJI, the son of Ragunath Prasad, arrived, and this morning Durghesh and her husband, and in the afternoon his eldest son, who works in a bank in Allahabad. The relief I felt cannot be described. The fever was 103.5° in the afternoon. Every time someone of the family arrived, he cried and got very emotional. He very easily has tears in his eyes; his father was the same and, I was told, even more so. The doctor said he must not talk at all; otherwise he will have high fever. But how can it be avoided with the houseful of people milling about? He seems to be in the same condition . . . only somewhat clearer in his mind. He does not speak to me which is good. God give him health . . . it's all I want.

17th September

DAYS OF NIGHTMARE THEY ARE . . . coming and going, from and to his place, like a restless soul. Such is the longing that the body seems to break under it. . . .

This morning when I arrived, he was in the big chair; one of his disciples who arrived last night was fanning him. He looked even thinner, yellow; his cheeks were hollow. He just nodded ever so little, in acknowledgement of my greeting, and the disciple told me that he was feeling a bit better. Went into the big room where his family was having breakfast. It was packed with family members . . . children yelled, his wife came and went, Durghesh was serving fritters. His eldest son told me that nobody slept all night, but the father slept a little.

And this morning he was definitley better; so he said, and I hope that it is true. So often I heard this tale, but the contrary seemed to be the reality. The son told me that the medicine had been changed yesterday, and he responded to it well. This story I also know well. The medicine is changed constantly . . . he seems to respond, then he relapses worse than ever. I can only hope and pray that this time it should be permanent. I just looked at him through the door; he was in Samadhi, and I went away; too many people were sitting and standing around already.

Yesterday waiting for Pushpa I was reading an article in the monthly magazine, and there was a quotation from the Sind poet, Darya Khan: "When I perceive the Beloved in my heart, there is no form; it is only the fullness of love. . . ."

I remembered that I had it written somewhere—I made a copy of it in Adyar; but have completely forgotten it. I was filled with wonder and amazement; it made me think: what I perceive in my heart when I have these wonderful states which puzzled me so much was exactly that: the fullness of love. . . . So simple, the fullness of love. . . . So it was . . . perhaps God after all? . . . To call it God for lack of a better definition? A Union with Something? Sometimes there is such a happiness, sometimes only a Longing, but love is always there, but no shape . . . and the same love I feel for his Guru Maharaj—it is the same quality, the same tenderness. Could it be those wonderful states? Could it be that I merge in the Presence of God, or whatever it may be called . . . only after nine months of training? How can it be possible? Or it is quite simple: God is in the heart of everyone, men and women, and we have only to learn how to recognize Him. My mind is more puzzled than ever.

In the meantime, last night it was simply wonderful . . . the love I felt, so deep, ringing, eternal. All the tenderness, all the poetry, all the power was there, still, infinite, endless. I prayed without words and I believed in His Greatness . . . My Revered Teacher is His

Instrument, His servant. What do I care who He is? If He is good or
evil, limited or not? He is my Love, and my Rev. Teacher is His
ambassador . . . I surrender to You, oh Lord of Infinite Love. If I
surrender to my Teacher, I will be a dead body from now on in his
hands, if You let him live. And if it is not Your Will, then take me to
You, because this world has lost all attraction for me long ago.

This morning there is such sweetness inside my heart. For He,
Lord of the Universe, is in my heart . . . and I am loved by Him. He
loves all His Creation, so He must love me too. Deep was the
tenderness. Gratitude. The wonder of it . . . all the time it was He
and nobody else, and I did not know. . . .

18th September

HE HAS HIGH FEVER ALL THE TIME. And I keep coming and going. But
now at least the whole family is here, responsible people, like
Durghesh and his eldest son, and Durghesh looks after him well. I
hope he will live. Am full of such nameless misery. I gave up all I had
for the sake of Thee. Will you let him die now? No, that CANNOT BE!
God DOES NOT CHEAT! I kept my bargain, oh Lord! You will keep
yours!

19th September

HARDLY SAW HIM. Avoided to go inside, so many people were in the
room and such a din. And the doctor said that he must have quiet. In
the afternoon he was sitting in the big chair. He is ever so slightly
better. I sat there for a few minutes. His wife and Durghesh were
exchanging remarks and laughing about me. I don't care. It is healthy
for my ego. He does not look at me at all, and I get used to it
gradually. The main thing is that he should get better. . . .

20th September

HIS ELDEST SON RAVINDRA told me that he asked him about me when
he was massaging him and they were alone.

"How is Mem Sahib? What is she doing? Is she well?" He answered,
"Yes, she is well," and he closed his eyes and went to sleep.

He had a better night, slept peacefully, at least for a few hours. I
was afraid to disturb, so I stayed only for a few minutes and just
looked and looked at him. Everybody when ill looks it, but he was
unearthly beautiful: thin, transparent is the skin and very fair
because so pale. The wife came in and sat in front of him so that I

should not see his face. She is resentful because I mentioned hospital treatment a while ago.

21st September

KEEP WORRYING: MY FUTURE IS VERY DARK. If something happens to him, what will I do? No money at all; how will I live? How will I find a job at my age? Will have to borrow money to go back to England. Heaven knows, it is all very worrying. I arranged all my affairs to stay with him in India for many years, so I hoped, till the end of my training. I think he does not want to live. His son told me this morning that he said to him: **"There is no fixed time how long one must remain in this world; some remain for twenty, some for thirty, some for sixty or more. You should not worry."**

"But," said his son, "what talk is that? How can we not worry? It is our duty to do our best!" And he is right. Doctors . . . some more doctors will arrive from Lucknow today. His brother asked me for money. I did not give. L. warned me that one should not give him. I told him that by Bhai Sahib's orders I must neither borrow nor lend money to anyone.

23rd September

THIS MORNING DID NOT SEE HIM; he was asleep, his face turned to the wall. Was told that he was a little better. Since this afternoon He came and rested in my heart. It announced itself by a few rapid heartbeats, and I knew that it must be the message from the Master. Until now I was under most severe separation, and, with the worry about his health, truly, I was pretty desperate. When exactly He came into my heart, I cannot say . . . noticed it only when He was already there. How relaxing it was, after such a long separation. Beloved, oh Beloved, why, oh why do You hide Your Face? Must we always suffer from that?

When I came to his place, I was told that he was definitely better. Did not stay. Had a few *chappathies* and a tomato salad which needed no cooking.

One of his disciples from Allahabad is here. I saw him for the first time this morning. He was massaging Guru's feet. In the evening he told me that he asked in the morning: **"Was she here?"** "Yes," the disciple answered, "she has just gone." He told me that he has been Bhai Sahib's disciple since 1948.

"I am quite new," I said.

"There is no question of new or old," he answered; "it is a question of Nearness . . . it is a question of love. You have seen me for the first time, for instance; if you love me, I will be near to you. On the other hand, one can live near a neighbor for many years, and he is as far away as anything, and one hardly knows him. It is all a question of love." What an answer, I thought.

Expected to be able to pray well tonight, with Him in my heart. But no. Could not. Felt full of stillness; the body was relaxed, was so tired after so many days of tension. Could not pray; just slept. And in the night the suffering was there every time I happened to wake up; just for a few seconds in between the wake and sleep . . . was such an acute sorrow, such an acute pain to break the heart. Oh God, I thought, what suffering is love! No suffering could be greater!

24th September

THEY SAY THAT HE IS BETTER. But I saw him this morning for a moment—he was looking so weak. Did not stay long. People were massaging him. I went. Outside his premises a cow was lying in the street. I came nearer; they usually don't lie down like that. It was dead. A strange sight: a big, dead animal on the pavement. Sticky flies were covering her eyes completely. India . . . how many sights have you, so strange for us from the West. But the air was fragrant; grey clouds were chasing each other; some dogs were fighting, and they looked funny. A large shrub in Prof. Batnagar's garden was full of flowers. I sniffed the air; my heart was full . . . perhaps life can be good after all?

Last night did not see him at all. Did not go inside; he had fever, 102°. But He, the Infinite One was in my heart. Merciful, merciful God . . . keep him alive. . . .

In the afternoon when I arrived, he was sitting in the big chair surrounded by many pillows. He was breathing with difficulty. I touched his feet when leaving—they were hot; clearly he has fever. Please God, keep him alive. . . .

25th September

WOKE UP ABOUT 1 A.M. The longing was dreadful, a real physical pain. What suffering such a longing is! I don't think that I suffered so acutely, so terribly, in all my life! How could I live now, if he should go? If I don't reach the Truth, what will I do? He is my only means to achieve it; if he goes, what then? For hours I was lying awake, thinking . . . worrying . . . and suffering much. Death is better than an empty life for perhaps twenty or thirty years, deprived of any hope of achievement. Darkness, loneliness, longing. You took my mind away; I forgot everything. You took my heart away; how can I live? Don't remember anything anymore, can hardly write English properly. Have nothing left, no money, no mind, no memory, nothing. Have no choice but to go with you, if you choose to go, my dear. Every penny I possess will go to you; I will not need it. If you live, I will be with you and will not need it. If you go, I will go with you, and then again, I will not need it. And with that thought implanted clearly in my mind I felt a sudden, great peace. There were no worries anymore. Not even a little. And I was worrying and fretting for weeks . . . terribly so. At once there was stillness, no worry at all. The decision was taken. No beating of drums, no drama. Just a quiet decision to go wherever you go, because life without you is impossible for me any longer. Just that. As simple as that. Important decisions are simple. They are the outcome of sufferings, the final result of mature reflections, the last act of a situation. . . . So, you see, my Rev. Guru Maharaj, you got me where you wanted me: nothing remains but love . . . and even life does not count anymore. . . .

Discussed the financial situation with his eldest son. He said he will give me some money today or tomorrow. It has been raining since early morning; it is cool, and the world is more *Maya* than ever as I cook my meal and do some shopping.

35

The Most Difficult Year of my Life

HE IS BETTER, and I know it by the churning of my inside. The Vibration is very strong this morning.

"Let me look at you," I said to him yesterday, sitting myself in a chair next to his. "I didn't dare to look at you all those days!"

He turned his head slowly in my direction and regarded me seriously.

"I hope you are not angry with me," I said softly; my heart was so full that I could hardly speak, so glad I was that he was better. . . . "You could be angry, I know, because I said and did things which I should not have done, but I ask your forgiveness," I added in a very low voice, so that his brother should not hear it; he was standing nearby, listening to every word. He did not answer, but looked away while I was speaking.

We went to an anti-malaria station to get a blood examination; the young doctor came with us and said that it was not a case of malaria; he can accept any challenge on that; it is a case of amoebic hepatitis. As Bhai Sahib refuses anything else, he is treated homeopathically.

28th September, 1962

THIS MORNING I SAT for about one quarter of an hour in the room while he was being massaged. Then he sat in the big chair; Ragunath Prasad was reading a letter to him. Last night I went to Pushpa only to tell her that he was better. Stayed there for supper; we had a long chat on many subjects. My heart full of such stillness and peace. The prayer went well; the mind is empty, and great is the nearness.

1st October

LAST NIGHT FROM SEVEN TO EIGHT in the evening I had such a heart condition that it was alarming, and until 4 a.m. the heart was missing beats. Sleep was out of the question, and I am short of breath this morning, but the heart is normal again, that is, until I sat down in his garden, and then it began beating rather strongly once more . . . and even while I am writing this.

He looks angry. Did not speak a word to me since he became ill. Neither does he acknowledge my greeting when I come or go. He just sits there looking severe. I see him for a few moments in the morning and a few moments in the evening. Usually, as soon as I arrive, he asks for hot water to be brought in for washing, and the wife sends me out by just pointing to the door. I am sure he does it on purpose, so that I should hardly see him at all.

The days are lonely, dragging endlessly, and full of most acute longing . . . non-ending days full of misery . . . and it seems that the sun does not shine for me, the grass is not green for me, and there is nothing left but this terrible, all-consuming, torturing, yearning. It is so difficult to bear . . . and the mind is in the most hopeless state. In the night, for hours, I am listening to the breathless rhythm of the heart. Where are you running? I keep asking, but there is no answer.

And so the days slide by. The rainy period has ended, so I have been told. Every night, and all nights, I sleep in the courtyard, with a blanket this time, because it gets cool towards the morning. And the nights have very little sleep in store for me, but much longing, much heartache. "Give me only the pain of love," sang a Persian poet. Yes. And WHAT PAIN it is!

5th October

ON THE SECOND OF OCTOBER in the morning I went to the shop in the bazaar and bought some Indian sweets, a whole box of them, the best ones, and enclosed a note: "Today is exactly one year since I have been with you. It was the most difficult year of my whole life. May God bless you and give you many years of good health."

As I could not find his brother anywhere, I asked Durghesh to take it to her father. But after quite a while, I saw that they were all crowded in the next room including the wife. Durghesh was reading my note, translating and commenting on it. "Take it to your father, dear," I said, and she went inside. I left. Intended to come later, which I did. He was sitting in the big chair and did not even look at me. I did not expect any reaction from him . . . not particularly. Had peace and stillness in the evening and prayed well.

Yesterday I saw him dusting the shelves in his room. I first looked in at the open door, and it seemed to me that he wouldn't mind me going in, but soon I saw that I was not welcome. So I sat outside, then came to the door later. He was still dusting busily with his back to the door.

"May I come in?" He very slowly and deliberately turned around and gave me an ironic look without answering. I came in and sat for about fifteen minutes. By then he finished dusting, and the hot water was brought in for him to wash. I went. This is done on purpose; it is quite clear. As soon as I come in, he will call for hot water or something else, and the wife sends me out. Just points to the door: out! And I go. So, I see him only for a few moments each time. That's all.

8th October

WHEN I WAS COMING, I saw that he was sitting alone in the garden, but as I came in through the gate, he got up, went inside, and closed the door. He will avoid me now, to increase the loneliness. The mind gave me some trouble last night. In the last days the mind does not work well at all. Blankness, complete emptiness periodically, difficulties of thinking and of understanding the most simple, elementary things. Events from the past kept coming into my mind: stupidities, blunders made in the past, things so far away, when I was still a school girl—humiliating situations when I was hurt, and had no sense of proportion and suffered from it. Injustices real or imaginary crept up, crowded in. I regretted all those faults and blunders. Felt dirty and small. "To regret well is to live afresh," said Thoreau. Is it? So much pride in me. Pride of what? Of all my life which has been wasted? Stupidly wasted? Pride of learning? Which learning? Where is it now? What is the learning; where is the mind? Is it all worth it? No, I have to change, to quicken the process. I am tired of myself.

9th October

I CHANGED THE HOURS in the morning; I go there about eight, but don't go in. He is being washed; he has his breakfast; I would be only disturbing. So, I go in about eleven. But it is of no use—he repeats the same story: after a few moments he shouts for water. The wife brings the water to be able to send me out, and the water is put there for later use. Today I came at half past eleven, sat there looking at him being so pitifully weak, so pale—there is no flesh left on him. A few minutes later he said to the wife in Hindi: **"Bring the children!"**

"They won't come—they are afraid of her," said the wife. (By that time I already understood enough Hindi to grasp what she said.)

"Send her out!" said the Guru, and the wife turned to me and pointed the finger at the door. I went. Walking down the street, I was thinking that it did not hurt so much anymore. I was only sad because I was not allowed to see him for more than a few moments at a time. The children are there all day long; can't he spare at least a little time for me? But obviously it had to be like this. . . .

In the evening after a few moments I was sent out because his tea was brought in. Even to drink tea is now an excuse to send me out. Sat outside on the tachat; no chairs were put out. For me alone nobody bothers to do anything. Even the servant seeing the treatment I am getting is treating me with contempt, grins impertinently each time he has the chance, passing by and seeing me seated alone. He does not do it though when somebody else is present.

Looking up to the evening sky, softly colored with dying light of the sunset, was aware suddenly of deepest peace. It was not just the usual stillness; this time it was really deep, so lasting, so wonderfully even. Endless. When it is like this, it represents a sort of strange happiness and is really lovely. I keep forgetting what happiness is, for my memory is so weak lately, but here it was. When it is like this, it seems it will last forever. But deep down I knew that at any moment I can be plunged into the darkness once more. Again and again. Endlessly. . . .

Went home as in a dream. My prayer, if I can call it so, was impossible to describe. No words exist to define it, for it is dissolution, and the most COMPLETE existence in SOMETHING; it is mute, so much so that it transcends the deepest stillness. It is so intimate that it was like a physical pain. I prayed that if he should go, I may go with him. This world has been taken away from me for good with nothing left—how can I be left behind? Every time I happened to wake up in the night, the longing seemed to tear not only my heart but the whole body to pieces. It really WAS a physical pain. . . . That's how it is done, I thought—you put such a longing into my heart, nearly to breaking point, and then when it will become so unbearable as the desire for air when one is drowning, then and only then, I will be able to know the Truth. Verily, the keenest desire is necessary; the Master cannot give us more than what we ourselves desire.

"Your own effort is of not much use," he said sometime ago. **"The keen desire is essential, only this you must have. . . ." "And it is a gift to those who can take it,"** he said at another time. Let's hope that I will be able to hold it, not let it go. And if I die of it, so much the better. . . .

Great was the nearness yesterday. The heart becomes so full that I have no words, not even a clear thought to formulate a clear idea of it. This morning when I woke up, the sheer physical pain caused by longing was unbearable.

He was coming out just as I came in, took a few brisk steps in the shade, and then sat down. So frail he looked, thirty years older, and I wondered if he will ever be the same again. Something told me that he never will be; he will remain very frail. Then he went in. Guru Grant Sahib was sung in Punjabi for the *Dussera Pooja* (a festival of the Sikh religion) in the house next to Deva Singh Park. The house was decorated with festoons and lanterns, and a big crowd was there in the street. My heart was so full of this tremendous peace which is all power that I thought it may disturb him; he is bound to feel this flood of feeling. When he went in, I first sat outside with others, then the desire to see him once more prevailed. I timidly lifted the chik to see if I could go in. He was sitting in the big chair listening to the chanting in Punjabi. As he did not seem to mind—he actually took no notice of me—I sat down and immediately the heart began the rapid beat.

The wife came in with a soup. **"Send her out!"** he said, and she pointed to the door. I went. Sat outside listening to the chanting. I liked it. The sky was clear; it was not hot; it was lovely in the garden. And the worry for his health, the longing, the deep peace, and the concern for my future, were all there as one in my heart. . . .

DREAM: "If something should happen to you, I have been told to go to the forest," I said to him, sitting next to me looking very frail and ill. He shook his head slowly: **"This is no life for you to go to the forest; there will be years of interesting training for you."** Interesting? I found myself thinking. And the sufferings? What about those? But his words give me good hope; it means he will not die, I thought, at least in my dream. Drinking my tea, was reflecting that it must mean he will live. How can the training continue if he is dead?

I accompanied Ravindra, his eldest son, who is treating him. He seems to be optimistic and said there is no danger anymore. The liver abcess will heal up now; he will recover slowly as time goes by. But I see him so weak, so bloodless. Never will he be the same again. . . I feel it. . . .

Awakening in the night I had a thought in my mind that I will NEVER GO MAD. I can dismiss it for certain now; it was lurking like a half-admitted fear at the back of my mind—now it is gone; for some reason I knew it for sure.

I don't even want to speak to him anymore. The worse he treats me, the nearer I am to him.

"The day will come when you won't want to speak to me anymore," he said many months before. This seemed to me very improbable at that time. He also said that this will be the beginning of surrender.

10th October

I WENT IN LATER thinking that because his son-in-law was sitting with him, he won't mind. But he told him to send me out. But I saw that he became very embarrassed, obviously reluctant to do it, and he went out. Immediately the wife came in and pointed to the door as usual. I went. Later the old Takur went in and stayed for a long time. Nobody else came.

11th October

HIS REVERED GURU DID IT TO HIM and he does it to me . . . nobody is treated as I am. This is a fact. And it should give me good hope. **"My Revered Guru Maharaj was scolding me all the time, never spoke to me for many years unless to give an order. The people thought that he hated me. I also thought it at one time. Only later, just five years before his death, I came to know how much he loved me. And he never scolded anybody like that; only to me he was like this."** Well, now, it seems to be my turn . . . now you do it to me: the burning down. . . .

Did not even try to go inside; he clearly does not want to see me. Sat in the garden, and through the open gate saw him walking in the courtyard with the help of a stick. He looked frail and fascinating in a slightly frightening way. This fear of him, deep, deep somewhere in me . . . no wonder. . . .

Later, sitting quite alone under the darkening sky after sunset, I reflected that in spite of the difficulties I have great peace sometimes, as today, for instance. But I forsee that in the months ahead, more than ever this dusty garden will be my only domain. Probably I will see very little of him. Went home when it was nearly dark. Venus, bright, very large, shimmering blue, was the only star in the fading light of the sky. Passing the open door with the chik drawn up, I saluted him, seated in the big chair by pressing my palms together. He acknowledged it with a slight movement of his hand. When in bed could not fall asleep, such was the longing. Oh, good God, God of Infinite Love, help me to bear it! This is the ONLY WAY to bear it all

. . . to pray. . . . Was waking up in the night full of peace and deep love. God was in the most intimate hidden corners of my Soul, in the very core of every cell of the body. My heart was trembling . . . and at the same time I was lonely and frightened and asked for help to be able to bear it, to bear what was bound to come. . . .

12th October

NOBODY ELSE WAS THERE; he walked up and down; there was a ghost of a smile hidden in his beard. Looked at him fascinated; he did not look human . . . this light . . . becoming more and more like a being not of this world. . . . Workmen arrived to whitewash and redecorate his bungalow.

In the evening he sat outside on the tachat surrounded by his family—wife, sons, the grandchildren and Durghesh with the baby in her arms. I was sitting far away from them, under the trees.

15th October

THE LOVE WAS LIKE A PAINFUL FLAME . . . burning, eating deeper and deeper. . . . The mind does not give me trouble. Not even a little. The Grace of God is with me all the time. I think I AM IN THE LANE OF LOVE.

18th October

HARDLY SEE HIM. Workmen make a lot of dust. The outside of the house is being repaired and cemented and whitewashed.

Sleep so badly. Have nightmares . . . a rare thing for me. Usually I never, or very seldom, have bad dreams. Was awakened many a time because of one or another horrible thing happening in my dream. Saw the Master, in between sleep and waking, coming out of his doorway with a disfigured face, no chin or mouth, as if eaten away by birds. Only the eyes were like burning coals. Was very frightened. The mind hardly works. The storm I know so well by now was blowing through my inside. Now, in nearly all my dreams, I search for something without finding it, and the feeling of frustration is intense. Yesterday, for instance, dreamt that I had the keys of L.'s room and searched in all her drawers and cupboards amongst her nylon lingerie and dresses (such frilly things they were), searched for my black bloomers, so it seems, or some other garment which belonged to me. Woke up most unhappy. Am under great suffering, but what it is cannot say—a sort of depression and giddiness, a sort

of fear, a panic rather, and immense loneliness and such sadness . . .
a sorrow as large as the universe. . . .

Mind does not give trouble. It is hardly existent at all today.

19th October

THE FAMOUS VIBRATION is inside the *Muladhara Chakra* . . . going
strong already for many days, especially today, very, very strong. But
strangely enough, no suffering is attached to it. It just buzzes and
buzzes with the sensation of heat, so strong that when I press the ear,
especially the left one, against the pillow, I almost can hear it: SSSS, it
goes . . . a kind of hissing sound. In the evening saw him for a
moment standing at the door. He looked irritated and angry.

22nd October

IT IS IN SILENCE and in darkness that the seed grows. . . . These are
days of great stillness and peace. At least, every evening it descends
upon me like a blessing. To rest in peace . . . how good it is.

He looks a bit better, though I saw him only from afar. He is still
on fruit and vegetable juice, no solid food, so his daughter told me.
One cannot gain much strength on such a diet. He looks bad-
tempered, and I heard him speaking severely to the servant and his
sons who were coming and going intent on their affairs. But to me he
seems to be magnificent. A kind of hardness about him, a sharpness
of features. What a glorious human being. . . .

Looked at the calendar of 1963 in my notebook. Could not help
thinking what a difficult year it is bound to be. How far will I be at
this time next year? What is going to happen to me until then?
Anything can happen . . . anything absolutely.

23rd October

LAST NIGHT, IT WAS DARK ALREADY; he came out and sat with us for a
while. A few people, not many, were sitting around. Could not see
his face distinctly. The night was windless, peaceful, full of fragrance;
something is flowering nearby, smelling sweet and fresh. The sky was
magnificent . . . Orion right in the zenith. Happiness suddenly
pervaded me . . . deep, deep happiness. It seemed to belong to all
the world, and for some mysterious reason which eluded me
completely was mine alone. It seemed to grow out of the fragrant air,
out of the serenity of the brilliant stars, the velvet of the sky . . .
coming from space, it seemed.

36

The Dream

AM DEEPLY CONCERNED about the Chinese situation on the frontier. What will the future bring? How will it be if there is a war?

Every day since his illness I have been reading Rudyard Kipling's "If" aloud. It helps me.

"If you can force your heart and nerve and sinew,
   To serve your turn long after they are gone,
   And so hold on when there is nothing in you
   Except the Will which say to them: Hold on!"

Yes . . . just to hold on . . . in spite of everything. It is a consolation to read it aloud. It gives a kind of sorrowful pleasure. . . .

27th October, 1962

"YES" HE SAID, looking up from a deep Samadhi, **"I was ill, very ill, the illness was about to be fatal. But I was so hinted by my Rev. Guru Maharaj and by my father that I still have to live. I will live for a while more . . . until . . . until you can do your work,"** he said it half-audibly, and closed his eyes.

Later he said softly, shaking his head in answer to my remark: **"No, I was not angry, never angry, never. No such feelings are there for you in my heart. Now I will stay here for a while."** He smiled kindly. **"If you will be ordered to stay behind and finish the work: you will do; if not . . ."** and he made a gesture, his hand pointing skywards as to indicate that I will go with him. His smile was something to be seen. Yes, Bhai Sahib, I KNOW: you will be with me always (and I will be with you), until the end of time. . . .

28th October

IN THE MORNING THE MIND was worse than ever. Such power was rushing through the whole of the body, could not sit quietly, was fidgeting—it was a suffering. He came out and walked up and down. I noticed that he gave me a quick look, then went inside. Something has been done while he was walking, because the flow of *Shakti* was increased. It was like being tortured, the storm blowing through me. Went home full of peace, in spite of the raging storm inside. Did not write the letter to the bank as intended. Tomorrow is a holiday, *Divali*, so there is no hurry. Wrote a bit in my diary. Hosla, the servant, came at quarter past four telling me to come; apparently all were going to *Samadhi*. Was not yet ready. Hurried, though I knew that nobody will be ready, anyhow, in time. Nobody was, of course. I waited at his place for more than half an hour. He came out walking with a stick very slowly with difficulty, and he looked very weak. We all crowded into the lorry. He stood there watching us embark.

During the journey everybody was very jolly, much talk and laughter, especially when the driver had to brake suddenly at the traffic lights, and everybody fell on the floor including his wife and all the children. I was as in a dream. When we arrived, the sun was just setting in the transparent, greeny sky, not a cloud in the air. It looked like a large Chinese lantern suspended low in the orange haze. The plain was still, serenely waiting for the darkness . . . and so much fragrance of some herbs smelling bitter-sweet. While we were walking down to the mausoleum, the sun disappeared behind the groups of mango trees in the distance. He was walking in front, so infinitely weak he was; I think he looks so frail and so old . . . thirty years older, so it seemed. When seated down, he fell immediately into a deep state, but not for very long. Children were screaming and making much noise as usual, but somehow it did not disturb me as in the past.

I felt the power of the place, the atmosphere, the lovely evening. How exquisite can be the evenings in India! Something special about them. Nothing really could disturb the peace of such an evening, ever. Spiritual life for me, always, and nothing else for the rest of my life, I thought. We walked back to the truck, the plain was in the dust already, the sky of the palest orange, so delicate. It was so peaceful. On the way back, while the lorry was bumping along through the brightly lit bazaars full of children, *Divali* crackers, fireworks and much noise, I thought that really my troubles are now over. In peace or in war, if you go or remain, no matter what you or I be doing, I will be in infinite peace. Will be with you somewhere in stillness. You will be with me until the end of the days, to paraphrase the words of Jesus.

This is the end, Guru Maharaj; when you were so ill, all was dying in me. The mind crashed before me and will not give me trouble anymore. It is the end. The end of a period. A milestone. While we were sitting inside the mausoleum, the vibration was so strong that it bothered me with the sensation of intense heat. And even now it is

going on while I am writing. Have a nervous stomach condition, and
the body feels weak. Went to bed with the feeling that my troubles
are over. . . .

29th October

HE SAW ME COMING but did not acknowledge my greeting and looked
away, talking to his wife. I don't mind. No more. There is a certain
understanding now—that it has to be like this, and it is for the good.
Went home soon. There is less power bothering me today. Had great
peace sitting in the garden, thinking that it will be always like this
now . . . at least some kind of peace. Everybody says how peaceful
his place is. It never was for me, or very seldom. Perhaps it will
change now? Did not see him in the evening.

31st October

HE CAME OUT SOON AFTER I sat down. Talked to Sageji and the one-
eyed Takur.

"Posted the letter?" he began as an opening. I said that I did it long
ago. But I was not sure which letter he meant. He was telling me that
he got some news from Mme. Bruno and Gretie and that they were
coming in '63. I managed to tell him in between that the vibration
was in the soles of the feet.

"It has a reason," he said quickly, **"everything has a reason.
Sometimes there is an increase of sex feeling, sometimes the mind is
affected, sometimes something else."** He looked at me thoughtfully.

I pondered. I knew that all those vibrations have to do with *Ida*,
Pingala and the *Shushumna*, only he uses different expressions to
describe them. (*Ida, Pingala,* and *Shushumna* are the principal *nadis*
or conduits of pranic force in the human body to which all others are
subordinate. Of these three, *Shushumna* is the most important,
situated in the interior of the cerebro-spinal column. *Pingala* is on
the right side of it and is the conduit for the positive, solar current of
prana, whilst *Ida* on the left side is that of the negative, lunar
current.) But what is the vibration supposed to do in the soles of the
feet?

I said that the vibration is a kind of handmaiden who does the
cleaning work, a kind of purifying process. If it is in the heart, the
heart goes wild; if it is in the throat, there is a sense of choking or
suffocation, and at the base of the spine a sensation of heat; and I told
him that I can't understand why it is in the feet. "I just stick my feet
out and go to sleep," I said.

He smiled with half-closed eyes. **"I never cover my feet,"** he said with a smile, closing his eyes completely. Was it a hint? Meaning that he too has the vibration in his feet? I wondered. . . .

This afternoon I experienced what must be pure bliss. I always thought that bliss must be a kind of passive joy. It is. It is made up of non-being and stillness. A nearness immersed in infinite stillness. It is not so dynamic as the state I call "prayer," which is a kind of pouring out without ever being diminished, and at the same time a flowing within, in absolute glory. Bliss is different—a state of being composed of peace, and it is so tender.

He came in with his wife from the street armed with a walking stick; he was probably out for a walk or to see a neighbor. Babu brought him a chair; he sat down and his wife went inside.

"There is no enjoyment in this world," he said with a smile. **"None at all. They say that to have a wife, to have children, is a great pleasure: it is not."**

I said how right he was. Later, when he came back after having had his milk, he was silent for a long while.

"My Rev. Guru Maharaj was so beautiful, so radiant, when he was about to leave this world," he said dreamily. **"He was telling me this and that, giving me the last instructions, and I kept thinking how wonderful he looked and what joy it must be for him to be able to go."** He fell silent.

"I will finish the work somehow or other, and I will go too." Again he fell silent. For half an hour or more, we sat in silence. There was the most perfect peace. I was thinking how the situation had changed for me; before, I would have thought to say this or that to him, or perhaps wondered why he does not speak. You gave me this gift of God, this Love, I thought. Why me? There must have been orders behind it, or course. Perhaps I will know, one day. Or perhaps never. . . .

1st November

YES, I AM NOT MISTAKEN; the vibration is no more at the base of the spine where it was going strong for many weeks with a sensation of heat; it is now in the soles of my feet . . . and somewhat stronger in the left foot. For the first time I felt it a few weeks ago, but thought that I was mistaken. Now there is no mistake. It is going on softly, and I had to sleep again with my feet uncovered, so hot they were, though the night was very cool. What could it be? There are small *Chakras* at the soles of the feet, as there are in the middle of the palm of the hands. But why should the vibration go there? What is the purpose?

In the morning he came out and sat in the sun for quite a while. But he did not say anything to me, and I don't speak to him lately when he does not address me. The whole family including the wife were crowding around him discussing all sorts of matters. I just sat looking at the garden, the chipmunks running up and down the trunks of the trees and making funny chirping noises.

In the evening he came out for a moment, gave me a quick glance, and went inside. He must have seen that I had peace. This is the System: when the Shishya is in the state of nearness, the Guru will avoid him, and be kind when the trouble begins.

2nd November

HE SAT OUTSIDE but did not talk to me. A young disciple was there who came to see him after a long absence, so he was talking to him all the time. The whole family was there too, standing and sitting around, and once he looked at me and asked: **"Is there any news?"**

I did not answer, could not, so much power was rushing through me like a noisy cataract—only made a gesture with both hands to denote that there was nothing new. There was of course; but how could I tell him in front of all the others?

Then he went into the room and asked me if I wished to remain or wanted to go home. I said that, if he does not mind, I would like to stay. So, I went inside with all the others; he was talking to the young disciple all the while. I sat there and was thinking that I haven't been in this room for many weeks . . . since his illness, actually. The room was badly distempered in green, as it was before, and the person who did it had no idea how to do it properly. Was reflecting how I redecorated my own house myself, in Harrow—it was a very different matter, even got a compliment from a professional decorator; he never suspected that I did it myself, and told me that I had a good workman do my decorating. I thought it was a compliment.

3rd November

LAST NIGHT HE DID NOT come out at all. Am full of peace. Fell asleep praying. There was no vibration at all save for about ten minutes when I was waking up. It was at the base of the spine, but it stopped soon.

The young disciple came and they were talking. I asked if I could ask a question. He looked at me kindly: **"Yes,"** he said. Told him that, as he already knows, for the last four days the vibration was in my feet, but yesterday it stopped. It was much stronger in the left foot, and the left foot was hotter . . . has it to do with me being a woman?

"Things come and go. And that it was felt stronger on the left has to do with the circulation of the blood. It has nothing to do with you being a woman. Some forces are different with men and women, some vibrations too, but not this one. If there is no circulation, there would be no vibration. If one is healthy, one feels these things much quicker. If there is no cavity in the heart, the heart is healthy; but if there is one, how can the Guide find the way to the Heart of Hearts? A healthy body does not mean a fat one; one can be thin but healthy. I was the youngest disciple of my Rev. Guru Maharaj—youngest in years, but I was the healthiest one. The heart must be good. There must be nothing wrong with the heart; this is important."

I knew what he meant of course; the Heart of Hearts is the "Inner Heart"; he mentioned in the past that we have two hearts. Then he proceeded to tell us how many astrologers predicted his death especially in the year when he got his *Adhikara* from his Rev. Guru Maharaj, and were astonished that he was still alive. I told him that according to some books, when one is on the Path, all predictions are wrong because the human being takes the destiny in his own hands.

"Maybe, maybe," he said thoughtfully, **"but it also could be that the question of death was wrongly interpreted."** I understood. *Adhikara* would be the death of the self . . . not the *real* death of the body. Told him I think that in his illness he himself crossed another barrier, passed a frontier, so to say.

"You are right; it is so." And he looked far with a distant expression in his wonderful eyes.

If I remember well, it was the French archaeologist woman who had said that from the mystical point of view his eyes are exceptionally beautiful.

He went inside soon afterwards, leaving the young disciple sitting there. His brother came and began to talk and talk; so I knew that he wouldn't come out anymore.

When I came in the afternoon, the servant boys were sweeping the garden with such a display of dust that I had to shift my chair several times to escape the worst clouds of dust. I saw him sweeping his own room—he does it for the sake of exercise. He came out looking absolutely godlike, and was directing and organizing the boys, standing at a distance at the other end of the garden. What a splendid human being, so tall, emaciated, looking so thin, the beard flying . . . sparkling eyes. Magnificent. He came nearer.

"They need supervision," he said bending down and picking up a dry leaf.

"They certainly do," I said, "they are children after all."

He walked further away and sat on the tachat. The boys with their brooms moved too near, so I went to sit near the tachat as well. He was sitting with his back towards me; he turned and said: **"I cannot write; my hand shakes; I had to write a few letters but had to stop."**

"I will write any letters you wish."

"They are in Urdu; many people don't speak English." He kicked a small stone with the tip of his sandal.

"Bhai Sahib, may I say something if you allow me?"

"Do," he said looking at his feet.

"Since you have been ill, I am acutely aware of the fact that you are not here, if I may put it so."

"I am never here," he smiled faintly.

"No, it is not quite what I mean. What I mean to say is that what is here, what we see, is a sort of *Mayavirupa* (a body of illusion), only one part of you is functioning here on this plane."

"You are right," he nodded emphatically, giving me one of his strange looks and a radiant smile; **"you are quite, quite right!"** he repeated.

"You see," I continued, encouraged by his friendly attitude, "it is as if you would need to keep this body for a certain time, to serve as a necessary link, but you, yourself, you are no more here."

"You are absolutely right," he repeated, and how young he looked, how golden was his skin in the fading light of the sunset.

"And the main work is done in the night, mind you; I have no memories anymore—you took them all away—but I know, for sure, that it is so. Something comes through sometimes." He had a pleased expression and a tender smile, but he looked away from me at something very far in the distance. . . .

Sitla Prasad came and began a non-ending talk. This feeling of non-existence . . . IT MUST BE the bliss they talk about. . . .

4th November

THIS MORNING HE WAS TALKING to Tulsi Ram, the man with the large family in the *kaprail* shed (a shed for goats). It was so unpleasant to listen to this croaking, excited voice jarring on my nerves. He is fat;

his mind is unbalanced; he cannot keep a job and has a child every year. Oh, Bhai Sahib, I am by far not surrendered as yet! I should not suffer so much because of such futile things. Am full of terrible longing and restlessness and pain in the heart. Heaven knows why I am doing the most difficult thing in the world. And it is heavy and painful, and sometimes I feel that I go along with dragging feet. And there is a worry deep down somewhere, a worry, and I don't know why. . . .

5th November

HAD A RATHER BAD DAY YESTERDAY. When he got up to go inside and I was just about to leave, I realized suddenly that he had created a complete separation. When I joined my palms in greeting, **"Yes, yes,"** he said with a smile and . . . I was alone! Completely alone . . . in utter misery I went home. Was miserable all day long fearing that the mind will give me much trouble; in fact it began a little, but I could reduce it to reason in a few minutes. I knew all the time this nearness was too good to be true; a separation was bound to follow.

When in bed could not pray properly; the mind and the worries interfered. At last must have fallen asleep while praying, for I don't remember anything else.

DREAM: a beautiful one, because of the rich feeling of love. With many people we were going by train to a beautiful town. The train was running through a lovely landscape, hills, meadows, high mountains. Look at those mountains, somebody was saying. I looked outside the window and at first could not see the mountains. Then the train went into a wide bend and suddenly a magnificent range came into view. Peak after peak, white with snow, and quite near. How very lovely, I thought, and how near! In the town we have been given a theater for the great performance tonight. I was busily cleaning the floor, carefully, with utmost concentration. The floor was shining; it was a highly polished, waxed floor as we used to have in Europe and also in England. I was cleaning the stage, carefully and gladly, because Guru Maharaj, who was the main actor, was expected tonight for a great performance. He was the principal actor of the play. Then I saw myself cleaning the theater outside, creeping on ladders and stairs and washing it. The building was white, perhaps white marble, with balustrades and small columns. Dimly, I saw the street below. It was near the stage door, when I was leaning so much forward that somebody cried out: she is falling down! But I knew I wouldn't fall down, so I leaned even more outwards, supporting myself with the right hand on the stairs leading to the small stage door, and with the left pulled myself up with great difficulty. Only then, I noticed that I was naked, but everyone else was dressed. But there was no time to bother about such matters—was too busy cleaning. The people, some ladies as well, came out, and the door was closed and locked for it was all clean and ready for tonight. But Bhai Sahib's brother took a bunch of keys, opened the door again and went inside; I was thinking that something has been forgotten, but I heard him say that he will make some hot water—Bhai Sahib would want a hot bath tonight . . . he will be tired. This brother was not the one I knew: he was slender and much more handsome; he looked more like Bhai Sahib, but not quite so, and his skin was darker. I woke up and was thinking of the dream, that I should not forget it and write it down in the morning as it seemed to be important. Then I must have fallen asleep for a short while, because I suddenly saw him seated opposite me at a large highly polished table, dressed all in white, as usual in my dreams. He looked so young and wonderfully fit. He stretched his hand affectionately across the table and said to me: **"You must also perform tonight!"** But I had no ambition, no desire, to show myself on the stage; so I said: "How can I show myself? I have nothing to wear, but I will perform hiddenly—I will be behind the scenes!" All I wanted was to be near him, and that was all.

I think this dream has a deep meaning and it is clever; if I would have invented it I could not have done better. The first Actor, the Principal Character in every play, is the Great Lover. I was cleaning the stage and the building for his appearance, and was invited to participate in the play, but refused for: "I had nothing to wear," i.e., was naked . . . very significant. . . .

37

"You Have to Go"

HIS CHAIR WAS NOT OUTSIDE this morning, so I imagined he would probably not come out. He came out only for a moment and stood in the door of his room. He was tuning into my mind to see how it was going; I knew that. I stood there waiting.

"You can sit down," he said walking away. He saw everything was O.K. I was full of such deep love this morning. So naturally, he did not come out. Ramji was with him in the room; I was sitting outside, alone; nobody else came.

"YOU HAVE BEEN GIVEN A HINT IN YOUR DREAM. Soon you will come to know."

I did not press for further explanation. Its loveliness, the warmth, the feeling of love are still with me. I don't think it needs an interpretation . . . not really.

Bits of conversation remembered: **"It does not matter if you are against me; it is not bad really. Only nobody should know about it. People are bound to misinterpret it and think badly of you."**

"Karmas are for those who are with them." I looked at him trying to understand what he meant. **"Only those who are already beyond Karma have the right to investigate the laws of Karma. Only when you reach a certain stage, have you the right to inquire into the Laws of Nature."**

"While we are inside the Karmic Laws, we had better leave them alone, because otherwise we may do things in order to produce good Karmic results, and it would mean that the self would reappear on the higher level. We may plant a huge weed, and to eradicate it would be practically impossible for us. We should do good for the sake of doing it and not to produce good Karmas."

"Since I have been with you, I don't seem to be normal. You don't know me as I used to be in the West. I was never as I am now. It seems that you brought out the worst in me; I am constantly doubting, or attacking you; I am discourteous, even rude. Cannot even speak to

you, and never could in the normal way. As soon as I begin to speak
to you, something happens to the mind—I become over-emotional,
breathing heavily; the mind stops working; there are interruptions,
frustrations; I get quite worked up . . . it is very difficult."

"It will change some day," he smiled quietly with a distant
expression.

8th November

HAD MUCH SHOPPING TO DO in the bazaar. When returning with a
heavy shopping bag, just before putting the key into the lock, I
suddenly had a memory, but it was too subtle, too fleeting to be even
called a memory . . . of a happiness experienced last night: such a
tremendous, wonderful happiness, that no words could possibly
describe it. Endless horizons full of transparent light, of bliss non-
ending. But above all, a feeling of freedom, the absoluteness of which
is unknown to the mind. . . . The whole day I was under the
impression of it, like an echo lingering somewhere in the hidden
recesses of memory.

Last night saw him from afar standing in the courtyard talking to
Virendra. Today he did not appear. Satendra was sitting with me,
telling me how his father knows everything, the thoughts of all the
people around him. Told him we all know that; we all experienced it
to various degrees. Went home at seven. Still have a bad cold.
Cannot get rid of it this time.

9th November

BITS OF CONVERSATION (all I remember): "There is a fact which
worries me a lot: I seem to hate everything and everybody—hating
them thoroughly and completely. Everyone seems to be disagreeable, ugly, even horrible. A constant irritation about practically
everything surrounding me. I seem to have become barren and arid.
Surely this is not an improvement?" He smiled.

**"It is a stage one is passing. There was a time when I too hated
everybody, when I was with my Rev. Guru Maharaj."**

"But L. told me that she feels universal love," I said.

**"This is something else; once you love God, you love His Creation,
and then you do not hate anybody anymore."**

"But for the moment when the heart is occupied with the One,
how can it love anything else? Everything is felt as an intrusion;
everything is rejected."

"Yes, it is so at the beginning. It is a passing stage, as I just told you."

A jolly uncomfortable stage, I thought. . . .

10th November

I SEEM TO SLEEP WELL NOWADAYS. He began to switch off my mind at quarter to seven, instead of seven as usual. I suddenly felt a great dizziness which I know so well; the heart began to beat wildly, missing the beats. He is doing something out of the usual, I thought. Sat in the sun in his garden thinking very little. He came out for a moment and went out with the pandit next door. Came back and sat near the trees far from me. My mind was paralyzed. Shreds of thoughts were drifting lazily, fragmented and incomplete. He got up and came to sit in his usual chair. Got up mechanically at his approach and sat down again.

"I want to quicken you after this dream; it was a beautiful dream and a good dream," he began. I sat quite still. I suddenly felt something . . . something is going to happen. A quick feeling of panic seized me for a second and vanished . . . the heart gave a thump of joy . . . to quicken . . . a hot feeling, a crazy feeling of hope . . . to quicken . . . it passed. . . . I stared at him blankly. A dull fear, like a thick fog, rose from somewhere . . . tried to collect my thoughts. Tried . . . it was too late. He spoke again: **"I am trying to speed you up very much in order that you should go for two or three years and work while I am alive. Then you will come back."**

"But how?" I stammered, frightened at the perspective of leaving him just like that. "How will I come back? I am a beggar now. The journey to India is expensive!"

"Oh, I will arrange for you there," he smiled. **"It will be done. But I have been hinted that you should go and work for a while. Otherwise how will I know if you are successful or not? I also have been sent away by my Rev. Guru Maharaj, and I have met many people, Mahatmas, Sages, all sorts of people; but I never wanted to be with anybody but him. People will come to you,"** he looked straight at me with a smile; **"some will try to get you on the wrong Path; when one is on the Path, reaching a certain stage, temptations will come his way, and one has difficulties which have to be overcome."**

I was so thunderstruck that I could hardly speak. Cartwheels were spinning in my brain. I swallowed hard.

"But if I have to go, I never will see you again; you know that your health is not too good, and you recover most painfully and with difficulty."

"**You will,**" he said smiling with his eyes, "**you surely will. But now you must go. Here you cannot work; and you must work. Remember, we are not given for ourselves, never; we are given for others. And the more you will give, the more you will receive; this is how the Essence works.**"

"What work do you want me to do?" I asked blankly, terrified at the prospect that I will have to find a job, and at my age it will be practically impossible.

"**What work?**" he lifted his eyebrows, "**You have been working for the Theosophical Society. You will do it again.**" I just stared. "**Anything,**" he said, as if answering my non-formulated question. "**Any work which is offered to you, you will do—lecturing, other work, whatever comes your way.**"

"But it will be difficult; I will be helpless without you; I could go 'wrong,'" I stammered. My head was spinning; the chair seemed to rock under me.

"**Yes, it would happen, if you forget me,**" he said slowly, his eyes veiled as if in Samadhi. "**It can only happen when you forget me; only then you can go wrong. Keep writing to me always and you will be with me. How far are you in your diary?**"

"Well, I write down everything you tell me, and my experiences as well as I can; some are difficult to express." He nodded. Went home crying. Cried in bed for a long time.

11th November

HAD A RESTLESS NIGHT. In the morning the mind was working very little. I began to realize that what he said to me yesterday did not sink in. Somehow, I did not get the full significance and all the implications it will bring. To go away . . . but the mind was half paralyzed . . . could not think . . . was like drunk.

He came out soon. First he talked to a man seated there, one of his old disciples, then turned to me: "**You wanted to tell me something, so you said, before you went home.**"

I made a helpless gesture as if to say: what's the use? He went in Samadhi last night when I tried to speak. . . .

"**Get me a revenue stamp of 10 n.p. if you are going to the Post Office. Otherwise I will send Satendra.**"

I said that I would do it. "But what is the use of telling you anything if you don't care to listen?" He shook his head in utter disapproval.

"You still have the same attitude: I take so much trouble, and you are still the same; you don't change your attitude! I am at liberty to listen or not to listen, as I like! Do you mean to order me about? You don't control your mind—this is your trouble!"

I bowed my head thinking that he was right; here I was criticizing again. . . . "I apologize," I murmured.

"You always say so, but you don't improve! Sometimes you are very good, but if you are good for one year and a for a few times you don't control your mind, you upset everything! You come twice daily; you sit here alone; this is the training, this is done so, this is the System! Obedience, faithfulness, respect to the Master! If you don't do it according to the line, and THIS IS THE LINE, how will you progress? And I take so much trouble with you . . . and you don't obey. I told you many times before: this is the Line; if you obey implicitly, respect absolutely, are faithful, you are bound to succeed. That's why you will have to go. Who remains with me all the time does not progress. Not those who are put on the Path you have to take. When you are away, you are alone; you will have to control yourself. Later you will come back and progress again. When I am inside, you think that I am doing nothing? I do something to you who are sitting outside, to those who are here, to those who are far away. It is so done . . . this is my work."

"When do you want me to go?" I asked like in a dream.

"In the spring; perhaps March or April, we will see."

"It seems so cruel; March is so near, only four and a half months away . . . we are nearly there. I will not be able to see you. . . ."

"What do you want to see me for?" he asked. "We are not on the worldly platform; bodies don't matter."

"But is it not a pity to interrupt the training, just now, when I seem to get some new experiences," I said, not knowing what else to say, for I was lost completely.

"Do you really think that time and space matter to me?" he asked looking me straight in the eyes. I lowered mine. Blinding light is difficult to bear. . . .

"Hundreds of thousands of people do every year the pilgrimage to the Kaaba. Says the poet: None of them cares to win even one heart. . . . Because to win somebody's heart is more than all the Hajas (pilgrimages) in the world!"

By announcing that I will have to go away soon, he took away the ground from under my feet . . . all is so insecure now. . . .

13th November

SAT IN THE DARK GARDEN weeping bitterly. I made up my mind to stay here for many years, and now. . . . Dangerous living it is indeed—no money, alone, no security: that's how my life will be from now on—just trusting in God; my goodness, it makes me feel giddy!!

14th November

THE WHOLE HORROR OF BEING SENT BACK to England, penniless, was dawning on me clearer and clearer, slowly, making me cry intermittently. "You are subjecting me to a very severe test," I said quietly, but I was trembling inside. He became very still, tilted his head slightly backwards, then nodded slowly with the grave expression I know so well by now. "For you are sending me away just shortly after the large check from Australia will arrive; you don't just take all the money away from me and then throw me out. Oh no; you do it much more subtly than that. You want to see what difference it will make to my attitude, what will I do now, because the situation is completely changed. But I can tell you already that it will make no difference: a promise is a promise—it is all yours. I will go, trusting God and you, my dear. Once I challenged you in unbelief and arrogance. This is also a challenge, but of a different sort. I am challenging destiny and you, by complete trust, this time. I know there will be even greater tests to come in the future, but I am prepared."

He kept nodding, slowly, gravely; I could not see if his eyes were closed or open, his hands were lying in his lap; but for his head, he was absolutely motionless, like a statue.

"From the very first days since I have known you, I noticed that you are beating the same chord again and again: you put all the appearances against you, and one has to have faith in spite of everything. The ways of the Masters are seemingly the same as the ways of the world: you made me penniless and then you throw me out . . . and this is the test."

All the while I was speaking I kept crying; my heart was aching, it seemed so cruel. . . . No sound, no movement came from him, not the slightest, the tiniest sound or movement; only this time I knew that he listened not only to every word, but to the very inflection of my voice. And for reasons I am unable to explain, this very silence seemed to confirm me in my faith, and kept the doubts away from my mind.

15th November

FOR THE WHOLE MORNING had a vomiting condition; had hardly anything to eat. The body feels very weak, and the head is like a ballon. For the first time I felt a distinct vibration in my head, somewhere in the forehead. Must be the brow *Chakra;* until now the vibration never went higher than the throat *Chakra.*

He was talking to his brother about a frontier incident. "Yes," he turned to me; **"why should I listen to you? What you have to say is not at all important to me."**

"But to me it is so important, and how! I don't even know what sort of work you want me to do and if I will be useful at all."

"Why should I tell you in detail what kind of work? You will be told in time." He grumbled, combing his beard with his fingers. **"I hint to you; this is enough. Who has the time to explain all the details to everybody."**

To everybody, no, I thought sadly, but to me, yes; you are training me; with others you speak about politics.

"Who would have dared to speak to my Rev. Guru Maharaj, as you spoke to me just now—not even my father or my uncle; not to speak of my brother and myself."

I looked at him; for I did not say anything; I have been only thinking. . . . **"You don't know the respect."** And I sat there with lowered head thinking that he was right. But on the other hand how COULD I know the respect due to an Oriental Master? . . .

16th November

WAS FULL OF STRONG VIBRATIONS last night . . . and could not sleep because of many worries. What will the future bring? Seems too dreadful for words. . . .

Early before seven, Pushpa came with the car to take me to the *Satsang* of a supposed great Saint, who is here from Delhi. We went there by rikshaw. In a large *marquee,* as they use it here for wedding ceremonies, *dharries* were laid out on the floor, and hundreds of people were sitting on them. The Saint, an old man of dignified appearance, sat near a platform with microphones. He is of the Sikh religion and was considered to be a great Saint. To me he was just a very ordinary looking old man and very repulsive. He kept spitting on the carpet in front of him, then rubbing it in with the fingers. I thought it was a disgusting thing to do in front of all the public. But in India such things seem to matter little if at all. Then he periodically kept rubbing his teeth with the forefinger as if to clean them from the remainders of food. This too I found most unappetizing. He gave a talk in Hindi, and then he sat in meditation. But the audience was restless, much coughing was going on.

Sat in the garden afterwards. Alone. Guruji did not come out at all. I heard him sweep out his room; the door was closed, a sign that he won't come out and wishes to rest. The vibrations were terrific; fire was burning inside me, the whole world was a *Maya* devoid of meaning, a crazy dream . . . as in reality it is. The mind works little and the worry is terrible, slowly nagging and nagging, biting deeper and deeper.

17th November

THE WORLD WAS SINGING around me when I was going home. I was happy, so happy, after a long time. He was so kind to me, and we had a long talk. And the future did not seem to be so dark after all. . . .

Woke up about three. The courtyard, the mosquito net, my bed, myself, all was suffused with the soft light of the waning moon. The walls of my little white home looked as though covered with snow. The stars were pale. In my heart was stillness. Perfect peace. Was thinking much. Crying from time to time, because of so much longing. How will I go? I will go anywhere with your blessing. Heartbroken . . . but I will go. I will think only of coming back, live only in the hope of return. A nightbird was calling. India. Beautiful India . . . how much I love you.

When at his place heard him again sweeping his room. Thought that he might not come out after the important talk last night. But he came . . . looking very weak; his skin was grey. The *Sannyasi* was sitting too. He asked if the money from K. junior would be here by the 15th December. I said, yes, surely, it will be. He asked if I wrote to the Insurance Co. in London and if the money will be here for the 15th of January. I said I hoped that it would be, but it depended entirely on the Reserve Bank of India.

"Money," he said with a sigh. "I get hundreds of rupees every month, and I am always broke, it all goes. . . . It is like this on our Line. Money comes like water and flows away like water. Money is less than dust. What I do with the money nobody knows, not even my wife; she knows that I may have hundreds of rupees; what I do with them she does not know. It is not known but to those who have

to do it, the work, I mean." Those are instructions, I thought, I had better remember.

"I am not at all clear in my mind what sort of work you would want me to do, Bhai Sahib," I began.

"What work?" he quickly turned to me. **"What work would I want from you but that you should lecture and write a book? People will come and sit with you."** He looked at me fixedly, then closed his eyes and fell silent. I held my breath. That can only mean according to the Eastern Tradition that I am supposed to help people with Meditation, help them to take a step nearer to the Truth. That would mean a certain responsibility, naturally, and I wasn't very keen on this idea. To guide people is a great responsibility; it is a commitment not easy to bear. . . .

"Was something done last night when you spoke to me?"

"Done what?" His eyes where smiling.

"Because something had happened."

"Happened what?" he wanted to know.

"I woke up about three, and there was peace and little worry, so much stillness, and I wept and wept and the vibration is now in the head, permanently. And this morning all the vibrations are going strong, but in spite of them I have peace."

"You will have all sorts of experiences," he said nodding with assent, **"all sorts of experiences. But I may not speak to you at all, for this is the Line. Things are done in silence—somewhere. Note it all down; it is important."**

I showed him the pamphlet of the Saint I saw with Pushpa. He read it through. Shook his head in disapproval.

"Propaganda, advertisement, this is not good. We don't work this way. Articles, propaganda: no, this is not done."

"I have the horrible suspicion that I won't see you again."

"Why have such thoughts?" His eyes were smiling into mine.

"It is like an agony, a terror, never to be able to see you again, and I am deeply unhappy about it."

"Well," he said looking afar, **"I can give you only a hint, but it is a very clear one."** He spoke slowly, measuring every word. **"About November in '65, not before, there is a holiday** (it must be *Devali*, I thought very quickly listening to every word), **then I would want you to come back."** Suddenly it was like a flood of love in my heart; full of gratitude I bent down and pressed my forehead lightly for a few seconds against his right foot, for he was sitting in Guru *Asana*. His skin was cool; he is so weak flashed through my mind, and a current of tenderness, of pity ran through my mind. His eyes were closed; he sat perfectly still. **"I am glad that you have got what you wanted," said the _Sannyasi_,"** Bhai Sahib translated. **"No, I got much more than I dared to expect, due to the Lotus Feet of my Revered Guru Maharaj."** He laughed and translated it to the Sannyasi.

"I only ask for your blessing!"

"You will have it," he nodded gravely.

"Give me your blessing and humility, and I will go anywhere at any time, to do any work for you."

"Why ask for humility?" he smiled. **"Why do you want to limit yourself? It is a veil between us! If the Beloved would ask you: become naked before me—and you say, yes, but only for one hour, then it is a limitation, is it not? You put conditions! No such ideas should remain in your mind!"**

"But with my character I may finish on the wrong path if I have no humility!"

"No," he shook his head, **"no, it is not so; when we send to work our people, they need not fear; gold can be put before them, anything in the world, they don't budge. . . . Our people are tested with fire and spirit and never, never do they go wrong! By the time you leave,"** he said softly and very slowly, **"by the time you leave, I think there will be no veil of separation left between us."**

"Amen, amen!" I said, putting all my yearning into the words. What a System . . . even to put conditions is a limitation, is a veil. Even to ask for anything at all represents a separation. . . .

Later he said that the Lord Buddha was the first to preach how important it is not to injure anybody's feelings; one must never hurt. I knew it was a hint, a clear reminder for me on my future behavior. Now, I have to listen with a special attention and note it down, not to forget it, for he is bound to give me more hints and instructions as time goes on.

Told him this morning that there is such a contrast between the happenings on the physical plane, where he does not speak to me, where he threatens me sometimes, where there is so much suffering and life is a constant, deep misery; and the other side of it where I only get occasional and rare glimpses—where there is stillness and peace, and time is not. I tried to define those states in my diary, to formulate them clearly into words: it is bliss composed of non-being, non-existence and perfect stillness, and when magnified a thousand times it must be Nirvana; so this state would represent the nearest condition to Nirvana on earth. He nodded gravely and emphatically with a pleased expression.

"Yes, it is quite correct: non-being. In the *Ramayana* it is said:" he quoted it in Hindi and translated: **"You must become less than the dust on the Lotus Feet of your Guru. Less than the dust,"** he repeated, **"Nirvana."**

The mind is working so badly that it is hard work to write it all down. Have to stop from time to time and think again and again, and it takes time, sometimes a long time to remember.

The feeling of blissful dissolution is the nearest to Nirvana, then . . . where are you leading me Bhai Sahib? It seems it is the road which leads beyond the stars.

38

"Time and Space are Nothing to Us"

WHEN I ARRIVED AT FIVE as usual, people were sitting inside. I took a chair and seated myself under the mango tree and listened to the voices inside, to his laughter and his voice, with a ring of metal in it.

It was the softest evening; the sun was setting gently beyond the houses on the other side of Deva Singh Park. The sky was of tender transparent gold. Kept thinking and thinking, full of apprehension for the future. . . . India . . . for how long? Then I cried a little. What does it cost you, I thought, not without bitterness, to let me sit inside with others? If you are alone and resting, I understand . . . but if others are here? Could I not sit in the room too? I don't speak to you . . . you don't speak to me . . . just to be able to look at you, for I will have to go soon. . . . So I cried. I heard him laughing, his lovely young laughter. You know how it feels, I was telling myself: you were sitting outside too, and your Rev. Guru Maharaj was inside with others. His voice must have sounded just as lovely to you, as your voice sounds to me. . . . Darkness fell. Mango leaves were rustling gently in the light breeze. They were drinking tea inside now; he was laughing, and others were laughing with him. It was obvious that funny stories were told. Sitla Prasad came, then some more people. I took my chair and went to sit on the brick elevation outside his door. Doctor Krishna Bahadur came out; he approached and said that he stayed away because of a slight attack of angina pectoris. He did not look too good, got fatter . . . and I had the impression I sometimes get about people, that he will not live long. . . . He talked about Bhai Sahib and said that now he will come often because Guruji is well again. They all began to leave. The garden was still; something happened to the street lamps—they were not lit. Soon he came out; I fetched a chair for him; he sat down; a few more people came, and they were discussing some frontier incidents on the Tibetan border. I sat, happy to be there, even in the darkness, just to be in his presence . . . it was such a blessing.

"Have you seen Dr. Krishna Bahadur?" he asked turning to me. I said I did, and I did not like the look of him. He looked inquiringly at me; I explained that it seemed to me that he is very ill; he did not look too good to me. . . .

"Yees," he mused, "Angina pectoris, a nasty thing it is, is it not? What did he say about me?"

"Nothing of importance, only that you did not believe in orthodox medicine, and he will come often now to give you homeopathic treatment."

"He was very impressed that you came to him that day." I looked at him. "The day I was so ill—you went with Satendra . . . have you forgotten?"

"Oh, no, how can I ever forget it! We thought that you were dying; we were all terribly worried!"

"From the Doctor's point of view I am going," he smiled.

"Oh, it was only too clear to me too; it was a very near thing," I said.

"It will not be long." He smiled dreamily. I looked at him; how his eyes were shining in practically complete darkness. Like two mysterious moons when reflected in the still, dark mountain lake . . . those eyes—like stars they led me. . . .

"And how are you?" he asked suddenly after a prolonged silence.

"I am deeply worried . . . cannot sleep because of worries."

"It will go," he nodded slowly, "it will soon go. Where is much vibration and longing, worries will be. I am trying to do something to your mind—that all the resistance should go; not the mind, not that, but all the trouble the mind causes, will go. It does not depend on the Shishya, the Guru has to do it; it cannot be done so very quickly, and this is the only delay. But it will be done. So, the ego will go. But who wants such a thing? People love their selves—nobody wants it to go!"

"But I do!" I exclaimed. "Did I not ask you yesterday, that I want it—otherwise I may go on the wrong path! But does not the ego automatically go when one merges into the Master?"

"No, it does not work like that; the Teacher does it—it is not an automatic process."

He began to talk in Hindi to others. "I must talk to them for five minutes," he said, and I wondered why such a politeness towards me, even to trouble to tell me. Chinese frontier incidents were discussed. It was on everybody's mind, a non-ending topic. In a pause of the conversation I said:

"So dreadful is the test you are subjecting me to, that I feel I have to put a condition: you must not die until I come back! I must see you for a while, stay with you for a few years!"

"**This, I will tell you when you go—there will be a hint—I cannot do it now! Some experiences have to take place when there is no physical presence. You will not have those experiences if you stay with me . . . it takes a long time to prepare somebody . . . it is not done in a few days. It took my Rev. Guru Maharaj thirty-six years to prepare me.**"

I looked at him in amazement. "So, why do you send me away? Is it not a great pity to interrupt a training?"

"**No, not at all . . . I told you that before. The training will not be interrupted.**"

"Even if I am so far away?"

He nodded. **Even then. Time and space are nothing to us.**"

"I am not at all sure of myself; I have a strong suspicion that once I was on the Path of Power, and I may choose again the Path of Power instead of the Path of Love."

"**Why such adverse ideas in your head again?**" he asked. "**Why think of it? When you think like that** Shaitan **is there. It will be thrown away; whatever was, will go. Nothing will remain!**"

"And if pride will pop up on the higher level?"

"**Stop thinking!**" he smiled.

I told him that since I know that he treats me as his Rev. Guru treated him, I feel pride sometimes.

"**It is good in a way,**" he said thoughtfully, "**don't worry, it will go!**"

"When I am sitting outside and hear your voice, just as you did when you were sitting ouside, I know how you must have felt. . . ."

"**Yes,**" he said musingly, "**I sat there under the mango tree; there was a thick shrub then—you don't know how thick it was—and he was resting alone in the room. When the idea came into my head, I went to the door and looked inside; 'Come in!' he used to say. I never went inside without being asked.**"

"I think that I told you before that between two and four in the morning, when I cannot sleep, there is something which I call: THE CALL FROM YOU. It actually is like a call—everything in me seems to relax, and I fall asleep immediately."

"**Yes,**" he interrupted, "**I am never careless with you. I do what I ought to do. I sleep only until eleven, only while Satendra massages me I sleep, otherwise I don't. I do my duties whatever they may be.**"

Told him about the vibration in the brow *Chakra*; it was going softly.

"**Yes, it was going softly,**" he repeated, nodding with a smile. There was an interruption. . . but I was determined to know more. "Is this the *Chakra* which, when developed, causes us to become clairvoyant?"

"**Yes, yes; but what do you mean by 'clairvoyant'? It is not a very high state!**"

"You told me it is still on the level of the mind."

"**Yes.**" And after a moment of silence he added: "**It is the *Chakra* of order.**"

"Why order?" I wasn't quite clear what he meant.

"**Orders are issued from there!**" he laughed, and turned to others to plunge into a vivacious discussion. I knew the interview was finished for tonight. Soon he got up and sent us all home. Walking away, I knew that orders are not only issued but also received in the same way. That's how it is going to work, when I am away from him, I thought: he needs to give only a half explanation, and full understanding comes . . . it is great really. . . .

18th November, 1962

I WOKE UP ABOUT 4 A.M. Got up, and there was no vibration at all. I was full of stillness. Bhai Sahib has forgotten me—he is probably full of pain, suffering . . . perhaps he does not sleep. Is it possible that I should be without any kind of sensation—even if it means trouble—after I had them for so many months?

The mind seemed to work well when I went to his place. Satendra told me that father was full of pain all night. He came out after a while and sat in the sun.

"**Too much weakness is there,**" he said shaking his head. "**And severe, constant pain. It is a bit better just now.**"

How weak he looked . . . it was painful to look at him. I asked him if my answer to Prof. Batnagar was correct. . . that love in itself had nothing to do whatsoever with sex feelings. Sex feelings are something quite different . . . they belong to a different level of being; and if one has them, they interfere with spiritual love.

"**Quite to the point,**" he said, "**absolutely; and after you had explained it to him, he understood, and what is more, he accepted it.**" He laughed his young laughter. He was sitting on his chair, knees under his chin, laughing gaily and translated it to the *Sannyasi*.

Later, in conversation, I said that it was interesting to observe how, at the beginning, the Guru IS God; it is as if the human being embraces tightly the idea of the Guru as being everything, but little by little the Guru disentangles himself from the embrace, so to say, and points to God. He smiled happily.

"Yes, at first the Guru IS GOD for the Shishya. But when you begin to merge into the Guru, you begin to understand that there is Guru AND God. Later only One will remain. When you are not merged into the Guru, how will you realize God?"

He told us a Persian story in which the disciple is asked by his Guru to believe in God . . . just to believe blindly, without asking why. **"If you don't believe in God, you cannot realize Him. How can one realize something if one does not believe in it?"** Only too true. . . .

And later: **"It is the Law of our Line: you get as much money as you spend. At first the human being relies on himself, on his own cleverness, but later, he is taught to trust God, and God provides for him. . . ."**

Frightening, I thought . . . very much so. . . .

Evening

A FEW TIMES DURING THE DAY I was thinking: Guru Maharaj has forgotten me . . . no vibration, no longing, no despair—nothing— just stillness. Fancy that . . . my body is so used to violent pressure of all kinds, my emotions are so used to turmoil by now, that anything, even trouble seems better than nothing.

When sitting in my kitchen and drinking tea, I happened to look inside my heart; then I knew that I was not forgotten . . . I was resting in Him, the whole of my being, body and all. On the level of emotions there was a glittering, limitless Ocean of Love . . . no end of it, wherever I looked . . . I could see no shore . . . it stretched beyond the horizon, and I was drowned in it . . . but peacefully, gently. The mind was still, a silent pool, where only His Image was reflected . . . an Image which was no Image at all, for it had no shape, only KNOWING. The thoughts were slowly circling around this non-Image, like gliding birds on the wing, and there was the softest longing. . . .

Somehow I WAS NOT, and I WAS, so deeply, intensely alive, like never before . . . NON-BEING, in the deepest, fullest meaning of existence. Nirvana. The nearest to Nirvana on earth. The words— Nearer to you than breathing, closer than hands and feet—came into my mind, and the sentence from the *Koran:* "I am closer to you than your very neck-vein." And I knew that even when separation is created in the future—as alas, it often will be—the feeling of this sweetness, of absolute belonging, will haunt my memory forever. It cannot be described adequately, fleeting as it is, so intimate, so subtle.

Will try to speak to Bhai Sahib if I have the chance. To talk to him becomes more and more difficult as the days slide by. I sort of dissolve, or go down-under, when I am before him. Such evanescent, subtle things, how can they be expressed when one feels like falling at his feet? Is it surrender? Is it that? Since September the nearness, each time it returns, increases day by day.

Sat outside as usual tonight. There was much coming and going—the brother was giving a tea party. It was dark in the garden; the street lamps were not lit. Could not go away . . . heard his voice, so sweet in my ears . . . heard his wife's laughter . . . then he was speaking and again this laughter. Remember, sang my heart . . . remember . . . soon it will be a memory. . . . Few clouds were floating in the serene void; big stars shone in the southern sky.

19th November

VISION: In the morning just as I was waking up, I saw him clearly: he came out of his door and looked at me—he had no mouth, no nose, and the whole lower part of his face was missing . . . only large, luminous, enormous eyes, blazing with green-golden light. It was a strange face indeed, and I was most astonished. He looked at me fixedly and went inside. Kept wondering, when awake. . . .

"This is the second time that I see you coming out of your door with the lower part of your face missing . . . and enormous eyes of green-golden light. It must have a meaning—you looking at me so fixedly."

"It is not to be explained just now. You will know it one day." The usual evasion . . . tiresome. . . .

"It has a very deep meaning," he added and went into Samadhi.

"Do we surrender to our Master or to God?" I asked.

"You should not ask this question now," he said. Perhaps because the man with whom he was talking at the moment knew English very well. The man stayed for a while talking and left when he began to sing. I waited. He sang, and each time it does something to me when I hear it; it reaches right beyond the mind. He was singing for a while, and I knew that it was done on purpose, because I have to learn to wait before I may speak. Tears were running down my cheeks. I remembered that, when he was so ill, I thought I would never hear him sing again. When he stopped and remained silent, I waited for him to begin once more, and when he did not, I said:

"Do you know, this is the first time that I have heard you sing since you were ill? If you only knew how often I was thinking that I will never hear you sing again." He made a movement with his head which could be interpreted in any way, but his eyes were tender.

21st November

WE WERE SPEAKING OF MY FUTURE WORK and how to present it to people. He said one should always say something for the good minds, something for the few, and the rest for the general run. His teaching is full of contradictory statements.

"Contradictions they are not," he said with a smile, **"because from the level you look at them they will prove to be correct . . . according to the state you are in. You will understand it one day, what I mean, and you will speak automatically . . . the right thing according to the necessity of understanding of those to whom you speak.**

"Avoid speaking about Karma. The time will come when you will understand yourself, but avoid explanations. It is not helpful. It can only be comprehended when one has reached a certain level of understanding. And this level is not of the mind."

22nd November

WHEN I CAME, HE WAS SITTING OUTSIDE ALONE. Unusual. As soon as I sat down, immediately a terrific storm began to sweep through me, turning me inside out. Could not move . . . was fighting for breath—it was like being beaten down. He stood up, walked up and down for a while, then went inside. Just when I began to think that he will not come out anymore, he came out and sat down again. He translated a Persian couplet which he sang to the *Sannyasi* in Hindi:

"If somebody speaks ill of you, give him the place of honor in your courtyard; for he will be the cause of you being able to better yourself. A friend will not tell you the truth, but an enemy will; and it is a Grace and a Good Fortune to have a Sat Guru, for it is due to him that you will be able to bear cutting remarks and become better."

"I wonder if, for instance, the disciple is united with the Master and the little self is no more, can he still be affected when people speak ill of him or cover him with calumnies?"

"Such people are always offended by others," he said.

"Yes, but do they FEEL offended? If they have surrendered and have no self?"

"Why not? Even God can be offended!"

"How amazing!" I exclaimed, "I did not know that! They say in the Christian religion that one can offend God, but I did not believe that. I thought that God can never be offended; how can our offense reach such a Great Being?" He shook his head.

"This is another matter—that He cannot be offended; but if you don't believe in Him, you offend Him, is it not?" I could see what he meant.

Later when we were alone for a short while, I told him I felt it a great and incredible experience: the nearer I am to him, the nearer I seem to God; the more I pray to God, the nearer I am to him. It is a closed circle. He nodded very slowly.

"I complained some time ago that this love is one-sided—it has no happiness, no peace in it . . . at that time it was like that. But now it is utter bliss and just carries me along, seemingly effortlessly. Only it is not in my character to sit back and do nothing, so I still make an effort: I pray like mad. . . . Last night I prayed and prayed and got myself into big trouble: the vibrations became so strong that I could not sleep. He nodded repeatedly his assent as if he already knew all about it. "What is the meaning of green-golden color?' And I told him about my vision: a face with no nose or mouth, or beard—just huge blazing greeny-golden eyes, staring at me for a moment . . . and then he went inside.

He nodded softly and said, "The fact that the Vision came twice is of deep philosophical meaning; just go on noting down everything, every experience. Through experience, understanding will come. I cannot explain it now; it would be beyond your understanding. Colors have a great significance; nowhere is it explained so well as in our Yoga System. Green is the best possible color: it means that you will soon realize the Absolute Truth."

I held my breath. Good God, I thought. . . . "And the golden color?" I asked, looking at him as if hypnotized, not daring to think, not daring to hope. . . . "All I know is that the golden color is of great spiritual significance."

He nodded. **"Our Line, the Nakshmandia Dynasty, is called 'the Golden Sufis.'"**

"What a significant vision!" I gasped, "but the meaning of no nose or mouth?" He did not answer, but went into Samadhi. Can it really be true, that soon . . . did not dare to believe it.

He opened his eyes: **"Many and wonderful things can be given,"** he said gently, **"but who wants them?"** His expression was remote and infinitely sad.

I want it, I thought ardently, and you know it! Oh, I want it and how!

"Sometimes one takes somebody to a high state and they do not progress—there is no desire." He fell silent suddenly and looked so sad, as old as the hills. Nobody wants Him, he seemed to think tenderly; Him who is Infinite, Endless, the Fount of Inexpressible Bliss . . . nobody wants Him. . . . "There is only one way," I said and felt like crying, "to pray and to pray with the whole heart!" He made a movement with his head sideways which could be interpreted in any way one wished.

When I left, my heart was singing, and I was walking on clouds. Is it true? Could it be? I dared not believe it . . . I will progress, I thought, I will!! Because I want You so badly, so infinitely, so endlessly! I want the Rootless Root, the Causeless Cause, and I will not rest till I have reached the Goal!

The Union with the Master is the first step, that much I know; later comes the rest. And the rest has no limit. . . .

Bits of conversation belonging to this period: What is a vision? Something invisible which becomes visible. Clairvoyance is not a high state; great importance is attached to it in the West, but it is nothing; it still belongs to the realm of the mind. What is of the mind can never be of a high state. High states can never be registered by the senses.

"In order that the self should go, I switch the mind off and put the vibration on. Of course there is trouble: there will be trouble. Who wants the self to go? Who wants those things?"

"Oh, I do," I said. "And I prayed so much for help, and you know it."

"Yes, I did know it," he laughed merrily. **"You should pray . . . it is very helpful. The process is very simple: the heart *Chakra* is activated, and when this happens the mind automatically slows down. The *Buddhic* quality has the chance to break through, and**

ultimately the self will go." (Discussing future work) **"You will stand up and speak: but somebody else will speak for you."**

I quoted a verse from a poem of Jalal-uddin Rumi: "Who cries for the place of pain in the receptacle of Love?" He softly closed his eyes and made me repeat it slowly, then he nodded.

"Do you remember what you said this summer? 'Only idiots follow me.' I would consider it an honor to be called an idiot by you. We are called the Idiots of God."

"I only remember the essence. I avoid to burden my mind. Things are said as they are needed at the moment . . . in order that they should help for the moment when needed . . . for a while. Then one can forget them. And it is never a contradiction; one speaks according to the stage on which the disciple is at that moment.

"In the Indian Scriptures they believe in *Devas*; **they say** *Devas* **are higher than men. We, Sufis, we don't think like that; we say man is much higher, can go higher than the** *Devas*. **There is a point, a barrier on the Path of** *Devayan*, **where** *Devas* **must stop; they cannot go further. But man can—right to the Union with God.**

"Book knowledge . . . people are obsessed with it. The real Knowledge, the Wisdom, is in the Soul, in the Heart of Hearts. They should try to realize the Self—for that no books are needed. . . .

"My father also gave me something. But he gave it to me AFTER my Rev. Guru Maharaj gave me what he wanted to give. He couldn't do it before, because nobody can give before the Guru gives; it would be useless. . . . My Rev. Guru Maharaj was of the Nakshmandia Dynasty, or Line, and my Rev. Father of another Sufi School. I represent both Dynasties through their Grace.

"You must want the Truth as badly as a drowning man wants air; and the roads to God are as many as human beings."

39

"And the Grace of God Will Be with You"

23rd November, 1962
LAST NIGHT HE WAS NOT THERE at all, and I have not seen him. I sat outside as usual; a golden sunset was declining gently; the sky was full of small luminous clouds. A large star floated inside all this gold . . . it must be Venus. Peace was with me, perfect bliss and nearness. Satendra was talking to me, but it did not disturb the peace; the utter serenity of the darkening garden and the fading light of the sky all seemed to deepen the peace within. Such unbelievable bliss; it can only be expressed in cliches such as, bliss which passeth understanding, and similar dramatic similes . . . but they don't convey the real glory of it. After all those months, more than one year of trouble, it felt double wonderful, like a blessing.

People came and I went home. There was very little vibration: I am sure this was so because I told him yesterday that by praying intensely I put myself in trouble and could not sleep. It is enough to mention the trouble and it is gone. . . .

DREAM: I was just about to open a door, when it opened and a group of men came in, and I and Bhai Sahib, who was standing beside me, stepped respectfully back to let them pass. A man was in the middle of the crowd of others who seemed to be his disciples. He was magnificent, not too tall, slender, a regular face, rather dark complexion, a jet-black, well-trimmed beard. He wore a sort of light brown *kurta* and white *longhi*. Immediately it was apparent to me that he was a great man, and how handsome he was! In passing he said to us with a smile: "Was it you two who bothered me last evening?" He passed by laughing, followed by others, and I wondered who he might be. His remark was clear: "you two" meant Bhai Sahib and myself, and I dimly remembered that Bhai Sahib spoke to me about this man, and this man seemed to know about it. Then they all went into a large room, like a glass-covered veranda, with a glass partition through which I saw that very delicious tea was served to them, but only men were present. What a pity, I thought, that in the Muslim countries at such gatherings only men are present; ladies are not allowed. I was in the adjoining room seated at a large table with women and children; we were having tea too, but I was watching servants carrying cakes and sandwiches through the veranda. As soon as the guests began to come out, I went to them, for I wanted to know who the great man was.

"He is a high ecclesiastical authority," one of his disciples told me.

"Is he a Bishop?" I asked.

"No, no," he said, "he is on the same Line as Bhai Sahib, and he is very fond of joking; speaking of himself and those like him, he will say: 'Nous autres balayeurs' " (which means in French: "we sweepers").

"Oh, I see!" I exclaimed, "it is because they clean the hearts of the people!"

"Precisely!" the disciple said.

Well, it would seem that I have dreamt of one of our Superiors, one of the Great Sufis. I hope that I will be able to ask which one it is and to tell my dream. But it was not possible . . . too many comings and goings, as so often when I want to speak to him.

24th November

IT IS VERY COLD THIS MORNING. Two men from Ferruchabad were staying with his family, his disciples; they were washing themselves at the water pipe in the garden. Apparently they slept in his room. I suppose it must have been very late by the time they finished talking, for he looked very tired. He came out only late in the morning, when the sun was already high in the sky and it was warm. He showed us the photos of his father. I was surprised, for somehow I did not expect to see how very like his father he was. The same face! But when he was young, he looked quite different, had a short mustache, and I told him that I would not have recognized him at all. He said that even old people don't recognize him, as he is now.

"This is my Rev. Father's album; by and by I will show you all the photos." I enjoyed looking at them, especially the one where his father is in deep Samadhi. The expression, the serenity of his countenance was remarkable. Later I had the opportunity to tell him my dream. He did not comment on it . . . only asked if I dreamt it last night, but I said that it was the night before.

"Many Great Beings come in the dreams; there are many Superiors on our Line." His eyes were veiled, and soon he was in deep Samadhi.

Went a bit earlier in the afternoon, and he was outside sitting with his wife and Virendra. He nodded cooly in answer to my greeting. I knew that he wanted to be left alone. Virendra offered me his chair, and I asked it to be put under the mango tree . . . did not want to disturb. There I sat thinking how strikingly different his private life was and his life as a Guru. He is so deeply involved in his family affairs—how can he bear it for so many years, I thought. It must be very trying. Maybe he is so used to it that he does it automatically and does not even need to listen. But not to listen to the wife must be difficult—she insists, waits for an answer . . . but perhaps he answers also automatically, for only one part of him is functioning here in this world. . . .

For over an hour they were sitting there in the sun, he with his back towards me . . . then he went in and not a glance in my direction . . . I did not exist at all. . . . Went home early—it was only six. I had my light suit on, and it was too chilly to sit outside. I began to putter about, got my winter dresses out, prepared this and that to be ironed for tomorrow. Was thinking that I would need a dress for lecturing, a black one, and for the next winter a warm coat—the one I have here in India is not heavy enough for England. Looked in the mirror . . . was surprised how really old I looked. I don't seem to look at myself properly when combing my hair in the morning. But now in the evening light, I saw what an old woman I was already. What will my friends say when they see me looking so old? They will say India did it to me. No, my friends, not India . . . worries and sufferings don't make a woman either beautiful or young looking. I began to think of my finances and my frightening, disastrous situation . . . thrown out into the street, without a roof over my head, no money, no mind, the worst possible condition. And one cannot even tell it to anybody; the world will say: it serves her right. . . . And I wanted so little. . . . To sit in his dusty garden—I was resigned to do it gladly for years, such was the love, the desire to KNOW the Truth. . . . But he kicks me out when the money is finished. . . . Went to bed. Kept thinking on those lines . . . and then started to weep, and the mind gave me plenty of trouble.

I am afraid, oh so much afraid, Guru Maharaj, I was saying mentally—do let me remain with you! Not to be able to see you for years! This is the worst part of it . . . I wept for a long time. It was twelve when I got up to fetch a dry hanky. Went to bed again. Cried a bit more. Then happened to look up to the star-lit sky. It was ablaze with enormous stars. And I won't be able to see—heaven knows for how long—the lovely Indian sky I love so much. Cried a bit more for that reason. And then quite suddenly I noticed that I was not really worried. I HAD FAITH IN GOD. Yes, just like that, as simple as that. I was so surprised that I stopped crying.

"I have faith, deep faith in You," I said to Him who was in my heart. "I know there is nothing to worry about; I know You are with me. . . ." Pooh, said the mind, He will create a separation; it would not be the first time you have experienced it by now. He will disappear as if He never existed; you have faith now, because He is with you, but what will you do if He is not?

"He will not go," I said to the mind, "and if He does, He will come back." You believe it, you fool, said the mind; what proof have you that it will be like this? What proof have you that He will help you? He never helped you until now!

"But why should He?" I asked; "I hardly believed in Him!" But how many people believe in Him? Don't you know how many deeply believe in Him, and He never, never helps them? You know it, so why should He make an exception for you? The mind went on, clever like an advocate, and it was right from the worldly point of view. All arguments were valid, logical, correct. I knew it was right for things as they were before, but wrong because now the situation was entirely different. I have this Love . . . and it will make all the difference. Even if I should remain with empty hands, I still have this Love. The situation was not the same, for I have faith . . . and I was glad, full of wonder. But the mind was laughing at me—such a fool, at her age, look at her. I was ashamed because the mind seemed so logical, so right, and it did look as if I were a hopeless fool. But here it was: I HAD FAITH, absolutely, and there was a strange duality: half of me was terribly afraid of the abysmal future, and the other half was serene, trustful, full of strong faith. It was so incredible that I could not help wondering . . . and then I realized that for the first time I had solved my troubles by myself, alone, without any help from Bhai Sahib. I will tell him if I have the chance, because I tell him everything, and I feel he ought to know; but if I have no chance, because he perhaps won't want to speak to me, it does not matter. I have solved it by myself for the first time—it makes all the difference. Full of wonder, I fell asleep. Had no dreams.

25th November

THE MIND SEEMED TO WORK FAIRLY WELL. Wondered if I will be able to speak to him, but it was not essential. Perhaps I will get a Hint. It was bitterly cold. Put on stockings and a warm woolly. The climate here in the northern plains can reach freezing point in winter, or 120° in May-June. He came out after ten, followed by two men staying with him. He was dressed in a flimsy cotton *longhi* and a thin cotton shirt. I was horrified. But the wife called him and, like an obedient child, he went inside . . . came out soon afterwards, dressed more reasonably in warm *kurta* and wrapped in a thick blanket. He began to sing. His voice filled me with longing and a sweetness which was heavy on my heart. I knew it was for me and waited for the translation. Sure enough, he tried, but soon gave up, saying that it is too difficult, nearly impossible to convey the true meaning. I said, just a hint will do, not necessarily the literal translation. Then he told me the couplet which was rather a long one. I'm not going to write it down here, for I didn't quite get the meaning; he was right, must be difficult to translate; will ask him in the evening if I have the opportunity. Could not see though how it could apply to my last night's problem and my trouble with the mind.

"Meditate on it; think it over," he said; **"the meaning will come to you."** Then I knew that he knew all about my last night's problem. He began a vivacious conversation in Hindi. I kept thinking about the couplet, how to understand and integrate it.

Then in a pause I said: "It seems to me that I have got the meaning: the mind has been turned in the direction of the Spiritual Life. I have to make a conscious effort to help; all irrationalities should go, and I must try to love His Creation as He loves it."

"Quite a good interpretation," he smiled, nodded repeatedly, and kept translating what I was saying. Then I told him how I discovered last night that there is faith in my heart, how the mind was troubling me in a sort of duality, how for the first time I solved the problem by myself, apparently without his help. He smiled, nodding, and continued to translate every word I was saying to others in Hindi, and he seemed to be pleased.

Later I asked if he knew who was the man in my dream.

"I told you, Great Beings will come in your dreams, very Great Beings, and the Grace of God will be with you!" He repeated this sentence twice, looking straight at me as if to emphasize it. I was not quite sure what he meant exactly, but I felt that I should not ask just now, though I had a feeling of great importance. Actually, the sentence: **"And the Grace of God will be with you,"** hit me. I knew it had to do with future work.

So, I only said: "While I was talking to you, you had a good look at my Heart *Chakra*." He laughed outright. I explained to the pandit sitting next to me, who looked very puzzled, that I knew when he looked at my *Chakras*, then switched over and looked at *Kama Rupa* (mental-emotional body); actually he need not look at all: he just tuned into it, and on the *Atmic* level, he just KNEW—no need to look or tune in. The pandit stared at me like a fish, and he, with his head thrown back, laughed his young and merry laughter. He sent me home about noon.

Slept in the afternoon, was full of peace. So, it was a test—last night's trouble—at least it looked like that . . . and he knew all about it. I wondered if he did something to my mind already, as he told me that he intended to do some time ago. Probably: otherwise how could I have controlled it by myself for the first time?

When I went there about half past four, he was sitting outside with the two men. He looked like an Oriental temple image, seated in his chair in such a twisted position as only Easterners are capable; their bodies seem to be made of rubber. Covered with a large blanket, he really looked like a temple *murti* (a temple statue). The two men sat in silence on the tachat opposite. He was in Samadhi—his expression was of the special, infinite, gentleness I loved so much . . . like Buddha, so unbelievably lovely. . . .

Took my notebook out of my handbag, and a pencil, in the hope of being able to ask him about the couplet, and looked at him. Enchanting, the light around him. . . . He must have felt my gaze, for he opened his eyes slowly:

"Yeees?" he murmured inquiringly, noticing my notebook. I asked if he could help me to check and verify if I understood the couplet well. I read it out to him. He shook his head.

"Curd is the mind; the churner is the 'real attention'," he said. So, I corrected it and wrote it down under his direction; here it is: The physical body is like a small vessel with curd in it. The curd is the mind; the churner is the "real attention." It means the mind is turned in the opposite direction, say from left to right, for instance, just to give an example. When there is real attention, the mind takes the turn to the Real. Everybody's mind is made on the same pattern, for it is part of the Great Mind, and every human being has attention. But the Real Attention is by nature suppressed. Only the Realized Soul can awaken it, i.e. the Guru.

"Why is the Real Attention suppressed by nature in the ordinary human being?"

"Dust covers the ground; under the ground there is Gold underneath."

"Oh, I see!" I exclaimed; "*Maya* suppresses it!"

"Right!" he said and laughed; **"quite correct."** And he translated my answer in Hindi.

"All the Knowledge will come to you, all at once, when you will be there; there is not the slightest doubt about it," he said, and he looked kindly at me. I closed my eyes; could not bear so much light; it was hurting. . . .

"And what pride can there be?" he continued; **"for we flow where we are directed. What pride can there be, if you execute orders only? Do not forget the formula; that's all."**

"What formula?" I asked.

"The last sentence I just told you," he smiled. I glanced at my notebook: ah, yes, they are like rivers: they flow as they are directed. He nodded in silence.

"All the knowledge you need will come to you automatically, not the least doubt about it," he said again later.

Now I know for sure that something was done to my mind; that's why I could control it by myself, for the first time. It was a turning point. One milestone more . . . here is the answer.

"Do you think it is advisable to make the effort to keep my mind on the middle road? Not to let it deviate, neither right nor left?"

"It will go right ahead like a slippery snail; right ahead it will go, neither right, nor left! Why not let it go where it wants to go? And see how far it can go?"

"Are you sure? Isn't it better to be on the safe side?" For I was a bit doubtful . . . the mind is such a devil after all. . . . But he nodded kindly—he seemed to be sure. . . .

Well, well: I expected something more dramatic to happen when he was telling me that he will do something to my mind. All I have felt was a head like a large balloon . . . no special vibrations, just the usual ones, and I have plenty of them anyhow. On the surface nothing very dramatic had happened that will considerably change things in the future; of this I am quite sure—it is bound to change at any rate.

Everything is achieved by weeping; we don't achieve things by laughing. Everything is achieved by effort, by pain. Everything has a price in this world.

"The self will not go in gladness and with caresses,
   It must be chased with sorrow drowned in tears. . . ."

He began to explain to others in Hindi how the *Satsang* helps and IS

THE CAUSE that the attention of the human being is directed towards Reality and away from the world of *Maya*.

"But surely *Satsang* alone cannot do it; you have so many people sitting with you, but how many are here whose attention is directed exclusively towards spiritual goals?"

"They flow as they are directed!" He laughed turning to me.

I understood: it is done when there is a Hint. . . .

26th November

DID NOT SEE HIM IN THE MORNING. And in the evening I saw him for one moment before he went for a walk with his wife. When he came back, he sat for a short while talking to Takur. Then he told me to go home.

27th November

IN THE MORNING HE CAME OUTSIDE wrapped in a warm blanket and talked to me for a while. Did not say anything of particular importance, only I told him what an uncomfortable psychological state it is to hate everybody . . . and last night there was a most wonderful sunset of glowing pink and gold, the sky full of feathery clouds. Previously, it would have filled me with sheer joy. Now I remained completely indifferent to it. He nodded and said it was good so. Speaking of the letters I will have to write to him, I asked how often I should do it. He said as often as I want to. L. wrote to him twice a week; he wrote to his Rev. Guru Maharaj every day, sometimes twice a day. I said that people will come to know that I was with him, and they will ask for help, and he said with a smile: **"As soon as you write it down, the trouble will be taken away!"** Wonderful! I thought.

"Not the whole day do you receive attention, but once a day something is done always." I asked if the separation from him will affect the training.

"Not at all." Time and space do not matter to him. Only those who have never seen him cannot concentrate very well their attention on him, but if somebody was with him for a while, he can be trained anywhere. Here must lie the explanation why some of his Shishyas hardly ever come to see him. They live in faraway towns and traveling is expensive.

"You are not here with me for many hours of the day; but does it matter? It is all the same."

"How will I be able to live without seeing you? With a kind of desperation like a drowning one, I look at you, when you are with us, and the day when I don't see you is a day lost for me."

"Yes, with a great love it is like this."

In the afternoon the mind gave me plenty of trouble with fears about the future. Went there about four. Saw him going out with the wife for a walk. Satendra and Virendra were fighting, a not very edifying thing to do for sons of a Saint. Told Satendra about it afterwards.

He came out when it was dark already. Sat there for a few minutes. **"Anything new?"** Told him that the mind gave me trouble. But I managed to control it. Tried to tell him more, but he went in Samadhi for quite a while. I kept quiet. Was wondering if he was teaching me now how to get out of trouble by myself.

"Don't sit here for a long time; I am going inside to rest."

I went, and as soon as I arrived home such a terrible trouble started with my mind that I cannot even describe it. He obviously put on the self in full power, to see how far it can go . . . . I was lying in bed torn by fear and worry, and the mind attacked him vigorously. I finished by cursing him and God, myself and the mind, everything and everybody, the whole universe. Then I hated everything and everybody including myself. And tried to hate God and him . . . but could not. . . . So I kept cursing them both because I couldn't hate them. . . .

He said yesterday that I will hate myself, and I told him that I do already, finding myself looking horrible and ugly . . . for the worries don't make anybody look more beautiful, just the opposite. I think I have reached the rock-bottom, hating, feeling dirty, unworthy, the least of all. . . .

I think I fell asleep and slept for about three hours until 2 a.m. Then the game began again, and in desperation I was looking up to the starry sky for help. Did not pray, could not, was in such a deep despair. In the morning while drinking my coffee, I realized why I was so attacked: my mind knows that I will go anywhere and do anything he wants me to, so naturally it will rebel. This is the whole trouble: the mind is fighting for its life, for I am committed and cannot help it.

This morning I did hope that he will come out. But the hope was in vain. He swept his room over an hour, then dusted it; he did not even lift the chik or look outside. I did not exist at all, and I knew very well that he knew all about my state of mind. I am left alone. Now I will have to see how far the self can reach. You are burning me, my dear . . . it hurts to be so neglected . . . and how is it going to be? I know nothing of his teaching, and what the Dynasty really means is not quite clear either, if it is not hereditary as he has told me. If it is a Dynasty, it should be hereditary, should it not? Worries, worries . . . endlessly, and no help from him at all. . . .

When I was sitting in his garden, I felt a great vibration in my heart, so I knew that he is switching the mind off again. He knew about the trouble, of course, and he tried to help, for there was no trouble in the afternoon, neither in the evening. He was not at home and I came back when it was dark.

"All right?" he asked.

"Yes," I said. Went home. Had a quiet night.

40

There is No Luck,
but only the Divine Grace

28th November, 1962

NOTHING NEW. All quiet. All vibrations seem to have gone.

29th November

IN THE MORNING after a peaceful night, woke up at four and the mind began to swirl about. This time the mind was attacking him, because he does not teach me anything.

"You will get a hint, it is enough," he will say, but to others he explains for hours and in many details. If I only understood Hindi well enough. . . . I finished by weeping with frustration, and he was telling me off for a long time. **"Things are done, and it is beyond understanding of the person to whom it is done. Who has the time to explain everything? Go on experiencing . . . go on writing it down."**

1st December

YESTERDAY HE WAS SITTING WITH US but did not talk to me at all. He looked so remote and unearthly beautiful. Prayed well last night, such was the stream of love that it was difficult to bear . . . and God is a Reality, so near, right in my heart. Today, I thought that he will not come out at all, but he did . . . looking rather weak and frail. A bit breathless, I thought . . . the heart is not working too well. . . .

"Bhai Sahib, I have a dream to tell you, and it is so clever and important. It is a lovely dream."

"Yes?" he said, and suddenly I felt that the dream which seemed so important to me, was not so at all. . . . Told him the dream and my interpretation of it. He shook his head.

"Wrong," he said, **"you are still full of the self. Don't you see that this dream is a hint? It is always 'I' and 'Me,' and 'I want' and 'I don't want.'"**

"So I missed the mark completely!" I exclaimed astonished.

"Quite wrong," he declared. **"Don't you see that even in**

354

conversation continuously the self is present? If you have surrendered completely, where are you? Where is the 'I'?"

"Good heavens!" I said full of dejection; "here I am trying so hard
to get rid of the thing, but it is ever present still!" He smiled.

"It is not so easy: it lived with you for over fifty years; if you live in
a house for so long, you would not like to go, would you?" I agreed.
"It will take time!"

"Could you not help me?" I asked full of dejection . . . "a little
help?"

"I could, but would there be any merit? One becomes a Wali
immediately when the ego goes. Then it would be like a father
taking the child on his shoulder, but the child must learn to walk.
Here you will not progress; the stars disappear before the sun." I said
that it was a lovely analogy. He smiled.

"Many more experiences will be there when you go . . . you will
see. I sometimes will write harsh things to you, like my Rev. Guru
Maharaj did to me, sometimes about things which did not happen
yet but will happen. Those letters you will not read to anybody else;
they are for you only."

"I wouldn't dream of reading your letters to anybody," I said
astonished.

"No, what I mean is that certain things should not be told," he
said. "Even now, I was harsh to you—sometimes I am so hinted. If I
don't tell you, how will you know?" I thanked him with folded
palms. "You made a progress in one year like others did not in
twenty," he said with a kind smile; "but still I have to be harsh
sometimes. Why those people don't progress, those Hindus?
Because they worship idols and they think what they do is right!
Even this man," he pointed to the *Sannyasi*, who was walking away.

"He is not intelligent enough," I said, "it is so evident."

"Let's leave this apart," he said with a quick movement of his
hand. "This is not the point; the fact is that they don't want to accept
anything apart from their beliefs; they don't want to sacrifice even
the smallest belief, not to speak to give away oneself. Who wants it?"

"Oh, but I do!" I said, and how, "I will pray that the ego should go,
for I can go on the wrong path if I have to go from here and the ego is
still strong." He smiled.

"The higher you go, the higher will the ego go too; but if you reach
the highest state, where will the ego be?"

Of course, how simple, I thought; when the ego merges in God, where will it be? Nowhere! "Oh, I will pray, pray, pray, and please help me!"

He looked at me thoughtfully.

"How deceptive the mind can be; I did interpret this dream in such a way as to reach completely misleading conclusions!"

"The mind . . . sometimes it hits the point; sometimes it is completely wrong. Dreams either show the future, how it is going to be; sometimes they show a stage one has passed, and sometimes they are worthless . . . just mind dreams."

"Was this one worthless?"

He shook his head. **"It was a Hint—that the ego is still very much there."**

Tasseldar came. **"Very difficult it is to get rid of the ego or self,"** he was saying in English (for my benefit). **"To my father, so often, my Rev. Guru was saying: 'You are still so full of the self?' And my father was the last and the least, and he never used to say 'I' . . . never. He always used to say: it is all due to my Rev. Guru Maharaj's feet . . . never to me . . . where am I? We are like a flowing stream— this is the formula always to be remembered. The Saints** (in the Sufi terminology, a Saint or a Yogi is the same thing) **are like a flowing stream: they flow where they are directed."**

"Your Rev. Guru, he never spoke in the first person also?"

"He was a Master, a maker of Saints," he answered quickly. **"He would say: 'Come here, I will make a Saint of you just now . . .' and he did! Just like this! If the iron is put into the fire and melts, the iron is right when in this moment it says: I am fire! But then it cools down; it becomes iron again. When one is at this stage, a maker of Saints, then it is a different matter!"**

"But there is no merit to be made a Saint in this way; you just have mentioned it, is it not?"

"None. It is better to get the experiences oneself!"

"That's why you send me away—to be tested and re-tested, and how difficult it is going to be!" He nodded and kept silent for a while.

"When you will be in difficulties, and people will puzzle you, you will pray and . . . it is always there!" He smiled gently. **"Here you won't progress—I told you already."**

"I think that I understood why you said to me that one never makes any prophecies; it is because of the self . . . is it so?"

"Of course," he said looking directly at me. **"This is it! There is much self in every prophecy, knowing better than the others: I told you so, I have foretold you, etc."**

To Tasseldar he was saying how people want him to go to London, but he does not want. L. called him and others too. **"One should be without desires to flow where one is directed. Sometimes all is ready . . . the taxi waiting; I have packed everything, and I don't go at the last moment. I got a hint that something is going to happen, or I should go another time. So, I don't go. I don't care. I do as I am hinted."**

When Tasseldar had left, he told me that now I can go home.

"You don't go anywhere?" he asked. No, I said, not today; I was with Pushpa yesterday.

"Yes, go home and stay home."

I left happy; it seems that I get much encouragement nowadays. Dreams, his statements. It sounded like music in my ears: you have progressed in one year more than others in twenty . . . sounds wonderful. . . .

Was full of stillness all day long. He went to a wedding tonight.

9th December, Evening

I WAS IN A STRANGE MOOD for over one week. I suppose I did the usual things, like eating, drinking, sleeping, doing the daily chores, going to his place—but I have hardly any recollection of it. Remember dimly that I was worried because he never came out all this time, but I seem to have lived on a different plane altogether . . . a place of great Peace, and of practically no memories of it.

To avoid boys who played cricket in the garden, I went around the corner of the house to sit behind the *nimbu* tree (lime tree). It grew outside the window of his room, and its green foliage used to reflect in his eyes and on his skin when he sat in the big chair near the window. Took three nimbus from it, just for the pleasure to have them from his garden. They were green and smelled fresh and spicy. Later I sat in front of the house in the usual place. People came, and then one of the men who was in the room came out and asked us to go inside. He was not well at all . . . it was very plain. So my fear that he was ill and that this was the reason why he did not come out proved to be correct. I sat for hours . . . Hindi was spoken. I just looked at him . . . and looked. His head was under a towel, and one could not see his face well. But in the brief moments that I saw it, I thought every time: how beautiful he is, my lion . . . even with the flu, even weak, always this light . . . too beautiful for words. . . .

Some people began to leave and he said: **"You can also go."** I got up, saluted him wordlessly, ready to go. But he began to talk, telling me that he was not well, and he does not know if he will be able to attend the *Bandhara*, explaining to me the difficulties of going there in his state of health. Then speaking of one of his disciples in Delhi, he said how much trouble he had—daughters became widows, one son died in an accident, the other lost his job, then died, and so it went on—but now he is better off than before . . . because he accepted it. For He alone is the real help; He looks after everyone; He is the real manager. . . .

"Who is without trouble in this world? Hardly any that I have seen, except my Rev. Father and my Revered Guru Maharaj—they were so happy, so wonderfully happy—nothing could disturb their happiness. That is how it should be," he said looking at me. **"Real happiness lies there—in acceptance."**

I said that I knew why he says that to me; it is the answer to what I have been thinking in the last few days.

"Yes, yes," he said kindly . . . **"no talk without meaning."** . . . **"I did not come out, I could not, those days I had fever; but it is seasonal, it will pass. I could not go out and talk to you, but it does not matter; it did not matter to you anymore . . . no more."** I said that it mattered because I knew that he was not well, and I was worried.

"You can go now." he said. I was standing before him all the time he was speaking to me. I went. I thought that he knew everything, and his talk was to the point. It is exactly what I have thought already: the state I am in now is the answer to all the problems. To live like this on some other plane of being—no worries, no desires, not really, and I will be with Him always . . . one with Him in infinite peace . . . good God, can it be true?—that I have reached You . . . reached You really? After such a short time? Difficult to believe. If it is true, how lucky I am, and how I have to thank Him for His Grace. Guru *Krepa*, the Grace of the Guru. . . .

"If I am well or not, this has nothing to do with the people; they sit and are benefitted; I do my duty always," he said, and don't I know it. . . . **"And who am I to say that I do it? If I say so, there is trouble. It is He the Doer, always He, never us."** And he looked at me and I knew why he was telling me this. It has to be my attitude from now on, always. I AM NOTHING, HE IS THE DOER. He is training me well, I must say. . . .

10th December

MR. CHOWDRIE WENT INSIDE in the morning, and I sat until eleven outside. It is all very well to say that I don't mind anymore to sit alone, but I am human after all, and not to see him at all for days, knowing that soon I will have to go, is hard . . . hard indeed. The hatred against all is tiresome. I have found that it is the best policy to let the mind run, and when it did run itself empty, then to conclude . . . and the conclusion is always against it, for love is stronger. . . .

The moon was shining on top of me; I slept badly . . . had a kind of nightmare . . . thought that I was going off my mind. In the morning I was serene. During the day though I did not see him; he has fever, so I have been told, and I can hear him coughing pitifully . . . I was serene. . . .

Prayed to Him who is Merciful and Generous and Infinitely Almighty, to be united with Him soon . . . to be surrendered soon. Sitting outside in the evening, had spells of such serenity as was not of this world . . . dying colors of the evening sky. The air transparent like crystal. And the large, infinite happiness, so all pervading, so great, so full. You who are Merciful, listen to my heart.

"*Tawadje,*" said Mr. Chowdrie, "is a sort of *Shakti, Shakti* Path, which is given by the Guru. It can manifest itself as vibrations in the physical body, its lowest expression, or as vibrations far beyond the understanding of the mind."

There must be urge from within (longing, keen desire), and engagement which is the RIGHT kind of effort—plus the urge within which will lead you to the realization of God (like voltage in electricity).

"You are lucky, very lucky," he said later, shaking his head, as I narrated some of the troubles and sufferings to which I have been subjected in summer.

Yes, I thought, it is all due to his lotus feet. Such a fool I am . . . so many doubts, so many troubles my mind gives me. And he is still kind to me. Never mind, if it is his wish, I will sit in his dusty garden forever and ever. . . .

12th December

I WAS SITTING IN THE GARDEN in the morning, alone. Nobody was there, and nobody came out from the house, so I was suspecting that he was very ill and became worried. Suddenly Satendra came out of his room and said: "Father wants you inside." "How is he?" I asked, and he said that he is better. I went in. He looked up and my heart melted, so frail he looked, and so pale.

"How are you?" he asked.

"I am well Bhai Sahib, but how are you?"

"I am better." He smiled with infinite kindness.

"Really better or you just say so?"

"Truly better." He looked at me, his eyes shining in a wonderful way. I sat down and he began to speak. Could not hear properly, for he spoke so softly, so I changed my place and went to sit in his father's chair.

"Jalal-uddin Rumi has written: I remain with those Saints who are faithful and obedient; if you want to realize Me, go to those Saints and realize Me through their hearts. From the wood of a tree a chair is made. It is the carpenter who has to make a chair, to polish it and make it beautiful and a useful object. The wood in itself is worthless. From iron the sword is made. Iron in itself is worthless. If I am what I am, if people admire me and respect me, it is all due to my Guru, my Revered Guru, Shamsi Tabriz.

"It is due to the Grace of the Saint if we realize God. The Soul is in the body from head to foot. When one realizes the Self, the body becomes quite stiff, so if the body is stiff it is all Soul, so go to those Saints whose body is the body of the Realized Souls.

"Christ was walking along, and it was raining heavily. A fox ran across the road and went into his den. 'My Lord,' said Christ, 'even a fox has such a dry home and I have none!' In one moment a golden Palace appeared and a Voice said: 'Go and live there if you want to!' But Christ understood and said that he was content to do only the Will of God.

"Golden Palace means also a purified personality. Worries purify and cleanse if there is *Bhakti*."

"Why do you say you had good luck?" said Mr. Chowdrie to one of my remarks.

"You Europeans are always too much on the mental level: why don't you say: Guru gave it to me? If he gives you trials, he also gives you the strength to bear them."

He is right. I must switch over from the mental concepts. Looking at a tree outside my bungalow, a sort of mimosa full of white flowers, only one year ago I would have loved to look at it. Now as soon as I saw it, I said to myself, how more beautiful are You than the reflection of Yours. And there was such a longing . . . and I understood fully what he said last year (and it did amaze me at that time): **"Your heart is like a hotel; you love this and that, only One can, must be loved."** Now I understand. One speaks from the level one stands upon, said Mr. Chowdrie yesterday. How true.

13th December

LAST AFTERNOON I WAS SITTING outside full of peace . . . such were
the vibrations of love. He must have done something to me this
morning, for the state of consciousness was very keyed-up. Like a
white flame on a windless day burns my love, trembling in the still
air. . . . And then I remembered a dream I had about five or six days
ago which I thought was not important, and I forgot it afterwards.
But now the idea came to me that it may be important after all, and
when the idea surges like this suddenly, I have learned already it is
better to follow it up because it may be a Hint. It was a dream about a
torch-light procession and a golden-yellow rose in a silver container.

Then Satendra came out and said that Guruji has a severe vomiting
condition since half past eleven—he took a little dahl, and then the
vomiting began. The doctor had been called and gave a medicine, so
now everybody hopes for the best. The fever is not high, only slightly
over 100.

I sat with Chowdrie and others and worried. Chowdrie attacked
me, because according to him I am too much on the level of the mind.
I did not react . . . was praying to Him who is Merciful. So many
worries he gives us, being so ill, our dear Guru Maharaj. . . .

At home, went to bed early and could not sleep until three in the
morning, worrying and praying. I fear so much that, if I don't
surrender by the time I go, I will end on the wrong path, the path of
Shaitan. . . . Proud I am, like Lucifer, and the self is still strong, and
with this hatred in me I am bound to do some wrong if the self does
not go completely. . . .

This morning some of us were sitting outside, and about ten
Chowdrie asked Satendra to open the door and let us see Bhai Sahib.
Satendra did it, and then called them in. **"Yes, you too,"** he said to
me—I was just about to ask if I too could go in. He was very weak
. . . breathless when trying to speak. I was deeply distressed. Soon
everybody had left. I also stood up ready to leave, but he made a
movement with his hand for me to sit down, which at first I
misunderstood, for I did not expect anything of the sort.

"You can sit down if you like," he said half audibly. He asked if I
knew the date of the *Bandhara* had been changed. I said, he told me,
and I knew. He nodded.

"It will take place one month before I go."

"Yes, it will be a month." And then he discussed the money
question, the amount which I will get from Pushpa now, and later the
check from Australia.

"Yesterday I was not in the position to speak to anyone."

"But you did so to me, and you gave me a beautiful couplet." He smiled kindly in response, pulling his blanket up to his ears. How radiant his smile in his eyes illumining his face and disappearing into the beard . . . and sometimes it is like sunshine breaking out from his beard, the eyes half closed. It is then that he looks most Chinese. . . . But usually the eyes begin to smile first, shining like stars.

Told him that it was not clear to me what he meant when he said that the body of a self-realized Soul becomes stiff. **"It is because of the vibrations: they become so strong that the body cannot bear it; at a certain stage of development the body is ill continuously. This is the secret people usually don't know. They think the more perfect one is, the healthier one becomes. It is so at the beginning, but not at the later stages. We must not forget we have an ordinary body meant to serve us in this world. When we are on the Path, at first we are still able to take care of the body and the mind, but later the body and mind are left behind as quite unimportant."**

I thought that it was an interesting statement. Later he said, when people make cutting remarks about you, don't answer immediately; tell them later in a nice way. Remember the couplet, if people make cutting remarks about you, give them a place of honor in your garden and treat them as friends. I said that I will remember it.

"What did Chowdrie say when you told him about your experiences?"

"I had the impression that he was jealous; he was not very friendly when I said that I considered myself to be lucky."

"He thought that I gave him the *Tawadje*, but I did nothing of the sort yesterday. Only when one is ill and weak, the mind remains in the body and the Soul is very strong. Somehow sitting here he tuned in into the line and went into a deep state."

He asked me if I was going to have food with Pushpa. I said that I was only going to see if she was here, but will not stay there for lunch; I don't feel too well; I have been having a vomiting condition for a few days. He nodded.

"It is like this; if I am ill, those who are near to me have to suffer to a certain degree."

I was glad that I was nearer to him; before I hardly felt anything . . . sometimes, but not much. I knew that my condition was not due to physical causes, only I thought that it was due to the vibrations. But it is better like this—to be so much part of him that one is affected by his condition even on the physical level.

"You can go now to Pushpa, and half an hour later you will go home and cook something for yourself?" I said that I would. He nodded. **"If the door is closed when you come, you just knock, or even better I will send somebody to call you!"**

I thought that was good news, and I thanked him.

"I am strict with everybody, with Chowdrie also. For the last seven years or so I realized that I have to be. My Rev. Guru Maharaj was not strict, but as a Teacher he was very much so. And how many people he prepared like himself ... it is difficult to prepare even one, and he prepared my uncle, my father, my elder brother to some extent, and his son, and I don't want to speak of myself. ...."

"But you were prepared more than anybody else," I said, and my heart was very still, but he did not answer.

"He was a great Teacher," he said at last and went into Samadhi.

I left rather happy. Pushpa was not at home, so I went to my place and had some boiled rice and raw tomatoes.

I forgot to write that I told him that my self is still so strong, and that I pray so much that it should go. I pray that it should go before I have to leave . . . and he looked far away without answering.

"It will go; it will go," he said after a silence. He also said that when the Soul is realized, it remains ALWAYS with the REAL MASTER, the Almighty, who is Himself part of the Absolute Truth. This is also an important information.

In the evening I sat there for a very long time; everybody went inside, but I was not called in. I was serene. After all, only his will matters; if he calls me, I will be glad; if not, well, it will be for another time. . . .

41

Living with God

14th December

HIS PRESENCE IS CONSTANT. To live with God as a living reality is a new experience. And even if I forget it, as one day I surely will, it will remain with me as a sweet memory, an encouragement never to be forgotten.

Great happiness keeps pervading me when I happen to think that from now on I will do His Will only; finished are the days when I thought I was doing things by myself, deciding things for myself. Somebody else will decide for me. . . . Told him this morning. He nodded with one of his softest expressions. **"It is easy to realize God: it is enough that one who is addicted to drink gives you the full cup after he touched it with his lips."**

Had a still and peaceful night. Such nearness to Him all the morning: not even nearness—oneness. Bhai Sahib looked very frail. He spoke for a long time to Sageji and the *Sannyasi*. He turned to me:

"*Swamiji* speaks very highly of you; he says that you are a first class *Bhakta*." I had to laugh.

"The trouble is that I don't know if it is *Bhakti* to the Master or *Bhakti* to God! I am trying to analyze the feeling for the sake of writing it down . . . seems an impossible task. Sometimes it is you, sometimes it is He, so, I never know if it is He or you separately or both together! Before I seemed to talk to God mentally—a constant mental conversation was going on all of the time; there was still duality; there was I and He in my heart. Now I seem to be part of Him." He gave me a look for the briefest of seconds.

That's why I asked him, I remember, if one surrenders to the Master or to God. As I feel it—I may be wrong, of course—one does not surrender to the Master at all, for in reality the surrender is to God THROUGH the Master. The Master is only the focus of attention on the physical plane. In other words the outer Guru points to the Inner Guru, the Self. In the night, for instance, one is resting in God—body, mind, everything. The body is included—this is an important point; it too is resting in Him, and this gives such a feeling

364

of pure physical bliss. It is like relaxing within the endlessness of love. . . . If one could only tell people: you don't need alcohol; you don't need drugs. If they only knew WHAT happiness it is to be with Him, they would not try to reach peace or try to get experiences by artificial means. . . .

"Yes," he said, "but in order to do so they have to undergo a certain training or discipline, sometimes severe. And who wants such a thing? Who wants Him as badly as that? It is a gift, but it is not given for oneself, it is given for others." He closed his eyes for one moment in infinite tenderness.

"At first love is created; it is not done to everyone."

"But don't you create it in the heart of every Shishya?" I asked astonished, because I thought that it is done with everybody.

"Not with everybody." He shook his head. "Not everyone's heart is made in such a way that it can be done. It is not for everybody. If there is much feeling quality, love is created. If the person lives on the mental level and there is hardly any feeling, first feeling is awakened and love afterwards. Those who do it, do it well, for the Master is directed. In the ordinary way love comes slowly; in the state of Dhyana, a state of pure being is felt first, then currents of love and bliss. But it is a slow process. It takes time. Things are done according to human beings, according to the necessities of every one of them. No two are alike.

"Surrender, I told you, has to be on all levels, to form a closed circle. If the mind is surrendered, the body is surrendered too, for the mind is the master of the body. So the body is surrendered THROUGH the mind. Completely, everything has to be included; surrender is surrender."

It seems to be quite a natural state to be with God all the time. . . . It may sound incredible, even crazy perhaps, but it is a fact; it is the most natural thing in the world. The simplest thing . . . you just live with Him all day long, talk to Him mentally all the time, do your housework, your shopping, and all the time the whole of your being is in the Presence of Something so real, so intimately near. And even sometimes it is more: it just seems that I am home; that there is duality, and sometimes there is none. I look into my heart and . . . it is there! It is the very core of myself! But this is not always; mostly there is this sweet duality. . . . I tried to explain it to Pushpa, but she looked quite blank at me. I could not convey the idea to her.

"Why do you say such things to Pushpa?" He looked annoyed.

"She is the public; if she understands, the others will too," I said.

"She is full of worldly things!"

"But when back in England, I will have to deal with worldly people!"

"Why not tell them only what they can understand, and as far as they can understand? We speak according to the state of evolution of the human being!" He said, looking afar with a bored expression.

The purely physical bliss in the night . . . the body is so happy. Every particle, every cell, is perfectly at peace, happy in its own right. He smiled. **"Yes, the surrender begins from the physical level—everything surrenders. It is a complete circle."**

Told him that the vibrations are of a higher order—how they are quicker. I can feel it, and only in the higher *Chakras*; I don't feel anything in the lower *Chakras* at all. "The frequency is higher; I feel it in the night."

"One can feel the *Chakras* sometimes," he nodded.

"One can notice it clearly; one can watch it actually happen—how the atmosphere becomes charged when several people sit here. As soon as they come through the gate, entering your influence . . . do you charge the atmosphere deliberately?"

"It is done automatically. Who am I to do something? The atmosphere is prepared for all there who are able to take it."

"Why is it that I cannot pray on some occasions? Sometimes it goes so well, and at other times it is impossible!"

"Sometimes the food is wrong—food is very important; sometimes too much talk, so many things can go wrong."

"Where is Bogroff?" I asked him in conversation. "Do you see him, is he with you?" He had this faraway look.

"He was with me; now he does not need to be with me; he is free. But he still sees me. It is due to him that his wife is writing to me. The time comes when one does not need the Master anymore. But reverence and love and gratitude remain always.

"Everything I do or say is for your benefit, never for myself—remember that. My father never punished people. He was so gentle. That's why, this is the reason he did not take anybody to a high state. You have to be hard: be severe with people, otherwise how will they learn? Those who obey are taken to a high state. It is so in our System. It is difficult to obey always. But they are taken to a high state, not immediately, but eventually they are. If you obey the Master, you cannot go wrong."

"About the Karmas, the question which was bothering me so much: as far as my actual understanding goes, according to your System, Karmas are accepted as a Law of Nature, the Law of Action and Reaction. But God in His infinite Mercy can overrule them at any moment; one need not bother about them; they are not important. The Teacher, by the Order of God, does away with them absolutely."

He opened his eyes wide while I was speaking, looking at me full in the face; then an infinitely tender smile crept over his tightly closed lips, and he closed his eyes again.

"If the human being comes to me in search of Truth, where are the Karmas?" he said softly, and went in Samadhi.

So it seems that I have hit upon the solution: Karmas are and are not according to how we look at them. . . .

He was telling me about his cousin who keeps losing his temper constantly.

"But why? There must be a reason?"

"Reason there is; he thinks that he knows much, and he is learned and knows better than others. He had eight hundred rupees per month, and now he has only fifteen—he keeps losing faith. He asks me to pray for him; I am praying, then he again loses his faith—so what can I do. . . . If one loses faith, one can come down from every level, from even the highest stage. But there is a stage when one can never lose faith, like a ball. If one would succeed to throw it high enough, it would never come back, so the Soul at a certain stage will go on and on to God, and one never loses faith."

"I hope it will be so with me from now on. I have lost my fear; I am not afraid; how can I be, if He is with me all the time?"

"No," he shook his head slowly, **"be not afraid. Never."**

I left happy . . . he was so kind today. Pushpa was in Allahabad, so I went shopping with Mrs. Ahuja and went with her to see her new flat, not far from where I live; her husband is ill, so I combined the visit and did both things: saw the flat and visited him. We spoke about Sufism, and I told him about my training, and the future he is preparing for me.

What I was doing during the last few afternoons I don't know. I am with Him constantly, all the time, and I don't remember a thing. I think I just lie on my tachat and think of Him. In his garden in the afternoon I was alone. Virendra passed by, and I asked him to go and ask his father if I could go in. He came and said that I can. He was lying on the tachat and told me that he had no fever.

"Now I am at the stage my Rev. Guru Maharaj was; he would be ill for a few days, then he would be all right again."

Later he said: "Let me get well again, and you will come to know many things. I don't answer questions on God and the like; some things I don't answer at all. But with you I speak . . . let me get well. . . ."

Then I told him my dream: There was a torchlight procession, and I said to someone whom I didn't know in real life: I'll go on the roof and see it. I ran up and saw a long procession going up the hill in the distance, winding upwards in the form of the letter S. It was a beautiful sight, all those torches in the completely dark night. From the roof where I was watching I saw many cars parked near the building, and they too were illumined, full of lights. Then I went down and passed an attic with many dusty objects. It was crammed with all sorts of things. Other people get rid of things too, not only myself, I thought, and said to the servant who stood there: "Take what you like—those things may be of use to you." Then I went down and saw an acquaintance from London; she was pointing to a lovely yellow-golden rose standing in a silver vase, a big beautiful vase of silver.

"Mrs. Tweedie," she was saying, "tell me how you grow this rose, and what is the name of the variety?"

"Her name is Mrs. McGreedy, she is not grown in the earth, but I keep her in a silver vase . . . can you see?" And because it seemed to me that she did not understand I repeated: "It is in a silver container, can you see?"

"Yes, yes, I can see that," she said. And I woke up.

"Has this dream a meaning?"

"It has," he said, "a very deep meaning. Maybe you will get such a chance one day. . . ." He fell silent. Rose is a symbol of devotion, and golden-yellow, may it be a Sufi rose? And the procession in the form of an S . . . could it stand for the word "Sufi"?

But he was in deep Samadhi; I knew I should not ask anymore. Went out soon. Felt he wanted me out.

"Yes, I was just thinking to go inside and have my tea," he said. I was glad that I anticipated his desire.

16th December

WHAT A LESSON OF SELF-DISCIPLINE it is: to be full of vibrations, dying to be able to speak to him, and it is not possible. For hours on end they discussed all sorts of things; he was so friendly, so kind to everybody; perhaps, I thought, perhaps I will speak to him. But they talked and talked endlessly . . . the objectionable Brahmin whom I cannot stand, and others. Began to weep silently out of sheer frustration, sending him mental messages that I wanted to speak to him. But more and more people began to come in—clearly I won't be able to speak to him at all. At last everybody left, but it was already nearly eleven. The wife stormed in; he, with annoyed expression, began to talk to her; she took his singlet from the hook on the wall. I understood that he wanted to change and stood up to go. He hardly acknowledged my greeting, nodded stiffly, and I went. So kind to others . . . he makes it difficult for me, I reflected not without bitterness. It is Your Will, I thought; I have to learn NEVER to want anything. Without speaking I got the answer—I am surrendering to His Will, but I am not completely surrendered; otherwise why would I even want to speak to him? Or be hurt, or cry? No need to talk. If one understands, one gets all the answers.

God Himself is showing to me that I am not at all completely surrendered. It is difficult to size up with the mind what happens to me; now it really is as if I were taken over by God. I say "God," because I really don't know what it is, but it feels like God; it has a numinous quality about it, a kind of awe . . . but really it is very simple: the human being is just taken over and that's that. That is all there is to it . . . I am with Him, so intimately near, felt like mad this morning, possessed by Him. It was absolute glory. Drinking my coffee in my tiny kitchen, I had the idea that all I have to do now is to wash my body, to feed it, to do my daily jobs . . . and this is really all I have to do: the rest He will do. I am His thing, and the clue lies in the small remark he made the other evening:

"Don't worry if what you say is right or not; it is not you who says it." And if what I say is not correct? Yes, the answer came, it can happen; the human instrument is not perfect. Then either you will be made to correct it, or it will be corrected by events—at any rate it will be all right in the end. Or it can also be true that what you say will be just the thing for this moment and the person for whom it is meant. Mistakes like this do not matter . . . I am not the doer here; this is the clue. Pride will go—everything will go, if one can keep this fixed in one's consciousness. . . .

How good the coffee tasted, sweet and strong. My washing swayed gently on the line drawn across my small courtyard. The strong smell of woodsmoke I love so much came drifting from the main bungalow of Mrs. Ghose. And my heart was burning . . . life was so good.

But I have proof that I am not quite yet there: I still want, am still hurt. Help me, You merciful, You generous, You infinitely almighty . . . help me for the sake of Your Love . . . the feeling of Belonging . . . such a glory . . . composed of non-being and stillness. Stupid old thing: do learn the lesson he is trying to teach you for so many months. Don't desire even to talk to him—only if he wishes to do so. Never mind you bursting with vibrations . . . by absolute obedience to the will of the Guru, you are learning to obey the Will of God.

18th December

LOGICALLY, BY NECESSITY OF THINGS, this state must lead to the realization of God. Nearer and nearer is He to me, and Guru Maharaj is closer. Realization cannot be a very long way off, this also I know. IT WILL BE SOON. One part of me is somewhere, in a different kind of time. At the beginning I kept losing this state when I concentrated on doing the everyday things. Now it is practically permanent. And if I lose it, I pray and I pray till I get it back. It is a difficult state, because it is so fluid. I seem to stand on water—all is movement; all flows from under my feet. As soon as I get hold of an idea, or an understanding . . . as soon as I grasp it and say: here it is, it is like that! . . . I see that it is completely different! So many things go on beyond the mind and come to the surface of conscious thinking only be reflection, and a distorted one in the bargain. It can be described only in contradictions: it is a state of perfect peace, but the vibrations are such that sometimes it seems to me that my head will blow off in the next moment. . . . Worries on the plane of matter are relative; how can it be otherwise? But there is such longing which is much worse than any worry. And love is like a huge, single, white flame rising as high as the sky and beyond. . . .

On the other hand, everything goes on as usual. The usual people. The usual talk. He is a bit better, but he is coughing all the time, and it hurts me each time he does it, as if I were doing it. Somewhere he is so near to me . . . somewhere, deep down . . . but where? Sitting there this morning, once he looked at me for a few seconds, and I knew it was a special message for me . . . but what, I did not fathom—and I had to close my eyes quickly . . . it was like piercing me with a ray of light right in my heart: You gave me Him, I was thinking. What can I give you in return? Nothing! Nothing at all! Except my aspiration, my devotion, my effort. If I would say: I will love you forever, even this love is not mine: you gave it to me. It is truly a GIFT, and everything ends there; one can say no more.

The most wonderful part is that it is such a natural state . . . our natural Home, the birthright of all human beings. Our heritage. Of everyone of us. But we don't know it until someone in his infinite kindness tears away, or rather burns away a few *koshas* (veils) from our deluded eyes so that we can see. . . .

The mind does not give trouble, not even a little. It must be in the real state of Real Attention, quoting Guruji's own expression. And, I am not going to God, but being blown to Him, a small straw in the strong breeze. . . .

19th December

MAN CANNOT REMAKE HIMSELF without suffering. For he is both the marble and the sculptor (Alexis Carrell, *Man the Unknown*).

There are whiffs of happiness from time to time, but not always, not 100%, because there is too much longing.

He created the greatest intimacy, without being in the least intimate. On the physical plane I do not form part of his living, nor am I even admitted into the intimacy of his family, nor is there any confidence or even exceptional kindness on his part. He is cold and aloof most of the time.

The moments of happiness, when they come, have a special quality—so light, so out of this world; they have no relationship either to my surroundings, my mood, or to what I am doing.

How I hate everybody. . . . Recently after I prayed for help, I thought there was less hatred. It was like a secret brotherhood somewhere, deep down, where I cannot reach it. Hidden somewhere, very deep. Glimpses of it far away. But I lost it soon. And now again I hate more than ever. It is very disturbing to be so full of hatred.

In the evening he came out looking absolutely wonderful, more slender after his last illness. He had the new golfer on, the one which I gave him. He walked up and down with it on the brick elevation very deliberately, too deliberately—I knew he wanted me to see that he was wearing it. Only too well I knew that perhaps tomorrow he will give it either to his son-in-law or somebody else and will go about in his old one, so worn out and so old that his wife refuses even to darn the holes in it . . . it would be a waste of work . . . no use. I tried, but it is of no avail. I cannot give him anything; he will give it away.

In the meantime he walked up and down with elastic step. Then he sat down on the chair. I began to reflect how it is that in everybody it shows when they have been ill, especially when they have lost so much weight. But not him, God bless him . . . he looks more

wonderful after each illness—a sort of spiritual, transparent look
about him . . . thin, emaciated, ascetic.

Prof. Batnagar translated a couplet for me:

"Go to the places when the wine is drunk, drink there day and
night.

At any moment someone addicted to drink may give you to
taste

the very dregs, the remainder of the wine on the bottom of the
glass."

I knew it was for me, the answer to my wondering yesterday, if the
statement I wrote down was not too bold, that the state I am
experiencing now will lead to realization of God . . . it cannot be far
away. Here seems to be the answer; I was quite to the point. At any
moment, someone may give you the dregs. . . .

This morning I asked Mr. Chowdrie if he had noticed how Guru
Maharaj is training me: he never chats with me as he does with others
on politics or other topics. I get hints only, and he only then talks to
me when he himself gets a hint from his Superiors. A preferential
V.I.P. treatment. I laughed at the idea of getting a V.I.P. treatment,
seems ridiculous, seeing how I am treated by him . . . a funny idea.

He said to me later that Guru's English is not perfect; something is
missing. So he does it in this way: by giving direct knowledge.

"It is rather a high state," he said. "Knowledge of the mind is one
thing, of the heart another thing, and the Knowledge of the Soul is
still another. This kind of training is called the *Shakti* Path in
Sanskrit."

Guru Maharaj came outside looking fine in his new dark blue
overcoat he had made last year. Told him that the first thought when
I woke up this morning about 3 a.m. was a sense of despair because I
am still full of the self. I think I brought it through into the physical
brain from the experiences in the night when we are out of the body.
Probably I complained to him about the self being still so big. He
smiled and said that now I understand myself and am helping in the
right direction. The first thought which comes into the brain just on
awakening is called in the *Yoga Sutras*, "the thought of truth."

He confirmed that the couplet was for me. I was amused this
morning to watch how he did the work of the *Shaitan*, and he knows
it. "Yes, yes," he laughed—by putting the irritating vibration on me. I
never discovered what it really was, but there is a kind of slow
vibration—I call it the brain-washing vibration—which produces
intense irritation, and sometimes induces me to speak out all the

poison which is in my mind. This time the mind did not give trouble, but I was afraid it would, and I was in near despair for a short while. Then I remembered that I was not alone anymore, so I prayed. The situation was much better now than in the previous months, when I was quite alone, no help anywhere in sight, and he was acting as my worst enemy. He laughed and closed his eyes.

So I prayed and prayed and got Him back again, not completely though . . . but the mind did not trouble me. Then he began to talk to Chowdrie, and so kind, so tender was his expression. How it always changed when he was alone with me; he would look bored and hard and annoyed. I was telling him what Chowdrie told me about Karmas; after all I must have good *Samskaras* if I am so interested and stick it out. The Guru, so he said, will not waste his powers on someone who is not worthy. Whether one is worthy is determined by *Samskaras*, etc. He gave me a few stony answers, some very good ones:

"You cannot go to a high state when you stick to your beliefs; let them go." He seemed to be annoyed. It is strange and interesting how he can look so tender and so beautiful when he talks to others, even to those who don't matter to him at all, like occasional visitors. And to me . . . it causes intense frustration to be treated so hard. Yes, I know it is infinitely more valuable to get all the knowledge via the *Shakti* path. What is speech, explanations, after all? They are still on the level of the mind. But sometimes a kind word is so precious. Frustrations, frustrations, no end of them. I offer it all to You, You Merciful, You Absolutely Almighty . . . all the pain, all the frustrations, for the sake of this Love. One day no pain will remain because there will be nobody left to be hurt. Told him that when Prof. Batnagar had said: "Then all the knowledge will come back, and you will become yourself again," I answered:

"I hope that there should be nobody left at all—it would be better."

"No, no, Prof. Batnagar has much deep Sufi knowledge; he knows what he is talking about," he said. **"The self will be back, but it will be an illumined self, not the same as you have now. It will be, plus the Knowledge of the Soul. There can be no life without the self—how could you exist?"**

I understood.

42

The Great Separation

20th December, 1962
AS SOON AS I WOKE UP this morning, the mind did rather funny things: when my eyes were closed, it was as if lights were jumping up and down, and there was much restlessness of thoughts. It looked as if there would be trouble. There was. Hatred was much increased—a dark, killing hatred, and I hated myself as well: the fool I am, ugly and old. Remembered all the frustrations I was subjected to since I was here. How I never could speak to him for days on end, and if I could, I had to wait till everybody else had finished, and everybody could interrupt me, but I was not allowed to interrupt anybody, and so on.

When I was at his place, exactly the same thing happened once more. People were there all talking—all these men I hated so much. For hours they were discussing, or he was talking, and it never had an end. As soon as I came in and sat down, he gave me a quick inquiring look, and by the expression of his eyes I knew that he was aware, of course, that there was trouble. I kept crying from time to time and was wondering if I would be able to speak to him at all. But the talk went on. Tasseldar came. When he went at last, I told him about our talk with Chowdrie.

"**Always the same thing: like an insect in the mud.**" His expression was full of profound disgust. "**The same thing again and again: Karmas . . Phoo! again you repeat it! Will you never stop?**" I cried in sheer frustration. He flicked his hand as if to say, it is all hopeless with you, and went out. I wept silently. He came back and began to pull on a clean pillow case on his pillow.

"Please do understand; there is so much misunderstanding between us: all I wanted to imply is that the fact of Karmas does not bother me anymore—I am finished with it!"

He shook the pillow in the air noisily, not listening. Here he goes, he does not even try to understand. Even if I have the chance to speak, there are always misunderstandings. He sat down in the big chair, and I told him what my troubles really are—too many vibrations, too much love, too much of everything. . . .

"It is not love," he interrupted me; "if there is trouble, there is no love. Love is joy always. . . ." And he closed his eyes blissfully. "Love is joy, peace, happiness—they are really the same thing. It only seems different. And if there is trouble, love is far away."

"But how can you say that!" I exclaimed. "Love is such punishment, such an intense sorrow! Since I have been here, I have known joy so seldom!"

"You don't know what love is. This is not love when there are adverse thoughts, when the mind, when the self is stronger than love. Why don't you ask your mind if it wants to be stronger than love? Why it does it? Make it understand."

"But I am trying," I said desperate; "what more can I do? How can I go beyond the enchanted circle?"

"One day, you too will go beyond the mind," he said very thoughtfully. "If the mind, if the self play up, they are masters; they are stronger. If the wave of love lessens, the mind takes over; it attacks."

"What to do? To pray?"

"Pray, try to convince the mind." He went into a short Samadhi.

"But I am going, that's why it is so difficult. I look at you as a hungry person looks at food, because I know that it will not be for long. . . .

"This is good that it should be so, but separation must be separation—it is necessary." He looked out the window with this mysterious tender smile I knew so well. The green of the foliage was reflected in his eyes, was like a greenish shadow on his skin.

"It is not forever; you will come back."

"But will I have the money to do so? And if not, I will never see you alive again—this is my fear!"

"Oh the mind, the mind, all these ideas; all you know is to worry about money! Money comes and goes. He looks after it; He is the Real Manager. Who knows what will be tomorrow? When Majnu loved Leila, he was wandering in the forest repeating her name. He was beautiful and she was ugly. Leila means night. She was black. People told her that he loves her so much and wanders in the forest like mad, so she asked for some parts of his flesh! When told this he said: "Take it! Take what you want!" When told, she said: "He does not love me!" After long years, again the question was repeated, and he took a knife and cut pieces of his flesh, threw it on a plate—'take them to her.' Then Leila knew that he loved her truly."

"Only now I understood the story . . . you told it before. But the meaning was never clear to me." I began to weep bitterly; everything seemed to be too difficult. Nothing seemed to remain, no belief, no mind, nothing. . . .

"But why do you say that nothing remains?" I looked at him. **"If the mind still gives trouble, how can you say it is not here; it did not remain?"**

"But how to get rid of the self?" I asked near complete despair.

"It is not a question of one day or two. It will go eventually. If one is so lucky that love is created in one's heart, when one is so fortunate that the self goes and the mind does not give trouble, this in itself can be called the Goal. What is the Goal? For a thousand years you can go on, and it recedes. What has been done for you is not usual; people sit here for twenty years and we don't even notice them. . . ."

"In a way it would be easier; I resigned myself to sit here for years, but things are done so quickly for me; every day something happens . . . vibrations, crises, moments of knowledge, separation . . . and everything is so fluid. I seem to stay on water; all is in movement; nothing seems to remain, nothing to grasp. It is as though you would walk quickly up a stony path dragging me behind you with bleeding feet . . . a very difficult state. . . ."

"This is not bad, quite good," he smiled his strange smile. **"Still, you should not complain. There can be no nearness when the mind is there. How many people reach the Goal at all? Training is not given like this as you want it to be. The year has so many days, and all the days will be all right, but once the mind will rebel. For long spells you are all right, but then . . . it all comes back. I like those people who never doubt once they are in."**

"But you are an exception—how can you compare yourself with anybody? There is nobody like you! You never doubted, but who is like that?" I exclaimed, and began to cry bitterly.

"You can go home," he said, and I went.

Cried in the evening sitting there. So kind, so friendly, so full of love he was talking to Chowdrie. Chowdrie was in Dhyana and did not even listen to him. What a waste of energy and time, I was thinking—to talk for hours on philosophy to people who don't listen or don't understand. Many who come here are not intelligent enough to understand what it is all about . . . and to me—who is supposed to write about it, who notes down every word, every single word by his own order, and it will be put to good use—to me not a word. Seemed ridiculous . . . unjust . . . and I wept silently. He did not stay for very long. When Chowdrie was about to leave, he stood up and said to me that I also can go. Thank you very much for the permission, I thought bitterly, and very quickly I went before everybody else began to file out. Cried in bed for a very long time. Bitter thoughts filled the restless, resentful mind. Fell asleep, woke up in the night . . . useless to protest. I am wasting my time. Surely he will not miss the opportunity to make the best of the situation and endeavor to get me a bit more down. . . .

21st December

SURE ENOUGH, HE CAME OUT and for a long time talked to Chowdrie and to *Sannyasi*. I did not speak at all . . . thought he will send me home as soon as they have left. But he began to talk on Jesus Christ and Christmas. Chowdrie, before leaving, asked if Christmas was the birth of Christ, and even what represented Easter. I was talking to Guruji for a while, but he seemed to be in Samadhi. "Shall I stop? What I have to say is not of importance; I don't want to disturb you!"

"Go ahead," he murmured, hardly looking at me. So I went on, but it was just for the sake of conversation. I was telling him about the Roman Catholic Church and the Order of the Jesuits. He seemed to want me to talk for some reason. I wondered, maybe if one speaks and the mind is occupied, he can do something to it or to the higher vehicles.

Yesterday he had the same look when *Sannyasi* was talking and talking on nothing. "Nothing of importance," he said this morning. Only when I remarked that sex and Sufism are on the opposite ends, like two ends of a stick, he opened his eyes and said with emphasis: "On the very opposite ends!" Later he said: "We want people to marry, but never, never do we want them to do evil!"

When at home writing down the story of Leila and Majnu, it seemed to me that I understood it completely. I say it seemed, because in the actual state of my mind it is difficult to know for sure if I understood something or not. So fluid, and changing so rapidly is the position. But to judge from the clue the story gives: the ultimate act of surrender has to be a conscious act of giving over, for the sake of love: to cut the flesh out of one's body, without condition . . . not because one is given something or expects something in return.

He will be more terrible now. The last act, the very last act is upon me; it looks like it. More than ever there will be frustrations. I only hope the mind will hold out. I always knew intellectually that it has to be so, but it is a very different thing, as everybody will agree, to know it in theory and to experience it as a living reality in the heart. But when one is full of vibrations, the mind not working properly, him acting as my worst enemy, the self playing up—it is difficult to have a clear vision. Merciful One, help me to check the *Shaitan* of the mind . . . . Just NOW I don't want any trouble: NOT NOW, PLEASE!

22nd December

So I TOLD HIM ALL THIS in the morning; my heart was aching so much. His face was severe. He was half listening, half in Samadhi. I had the feeling that I was boring him. He lifted his head and looked me straight in the eyes:

"Why don't you become a human being? Why don't you try to become less than the dust at my feet?" I stared at him; it seemed like an unexpected attack.

"Am I not a human being?" I was amazed and felt forlorn.

"What you are I don't know, but a human being you are not," he drawled, and it sounded like a growl. **"Only when you become less than the dust at my feet will you be balanced, and only then can you be called a human being!"**

C. G. Jung! flashed like lightning through my mind. In his writings, Carl Jung emphasized again and again the danger of what he calls "inflation," and our mental asylums are full of Napoleons, Cleopatras, Julius Caesars, not to mention even more exalted personages. I was always convinced that the process of Individuation is a preliminary step, a springboard, so to say, a starting point to something more, which I think would be Yoga or Self Realization. The individuation process makes the human being whole, complete, to be able to take his rightful place as a balanced, perfectly normal member of the human family. But Yoga is much more than that. And in Yoga there must be much more danger, consequently, of the so-called "inflation." At one time during the training the disciple is bound to begin to realize his divine origin, and then to say and to believe: I am God! It is then that one needs a Teacher. And the Teacher will say: no, be careful, with those lips not yet pure, with the heart not yet as limpid as the Waters of Life, it is a blasphemy to say that you are God! But a Great Teacher does not say it so directly—he simply teaches humility: **"Become less than the dust at my feet."** How can the inflation arise if one is made to be so humble?

But this is not all. From my own experience I know that the nearer one moves towards the Reality, the more one realizes the absolute oneness of all and everything. And if I am part of something so Great that my mind cannot even conceive it, of something which fills me with awe, where is the pride? And those two processes—the inner realization of absolute oneness and, on the other hand, the Teacher pushing one's nose into the dust, to put it figuratively—they protect the disciple from the greatest danger: of himself being inflated like a balloon bursting with pride. I think it is here where Yoga and modern psychology meet; the training of the disciples, devised thousands of years ago, and the psychiatrist's dealing with human problems use the same tactics; Yoga and science speak the same language.

He coughed, then got up, went further away a few paces, and spat out. After a few moments a crow which until now sat on a branch of the tree watching us, flew down, came hopping along, and swallowed the spit. An idea came into my mind and I asked him: if the crow eats the spit of a Saint, will it be beneficial for its evolution? He shook his head.

"Saintliness is only for human beings; how can it help the crow? And in what way? What do you mean by evolution? It is the function of the crow to eat all the filth it can find. Some people believe crows can be human beings; it is written in the Scriptures. Those who believe in evolution think humans were animals once, but it is nonsense. Animal is animal, man is man. Animal can never become man. They have no *Atma*. Realized people never believe in such a thing." He was dry, hard, and did not smile even once.

I said how should one understand the famous, very much quoted poem of Jalal-uddin Rumi:

"I died as mineral and became a plant,
   I died as plant and rose to animal,
   I died as animal and I was Man,
   Why should I fear? When was I less by dying?
   Yet once more I shall die as Man, to soar
   With angels blest; but even from angelhood
   I must pass on: all except God doth perish.
   When I have sacrificed my angel-soul,
   I shall become what no mind e'er conceived.
   O let me not exist! For Non-existence
   Proclaims in organ tones 'To Him we shall return.' "

"This is something quite different; the meaning of it is not what you think." He fell silent.

His attitude is quite unmistakably clear; it all will go on as it was; I have no hope at all; it all will go on until . . . nothing will remain. I really must try not to protest and just try to manage to surrender somehow, in spite of everything. In the evenings he does not come out now; it is beginning to be too cold, and tomorrow Chowdrie goes to Calcutta, so probably he won't come out even in the mornings. . . .

23rd December

WHEN I WOKE UP ABOUT THREE in the morning, He was not with me, and Bhai Sahib also was not. I was quite alone. Well, I expected it, really . . . deep was the loneliness. Yesterday when I was cooking my food, such was the nearness with Him that it was simply wonderful, and when my eyes were closed, I saw green flashes of light . . . such a wonderful green, and so much of it. I was so happy and now . . . nothing at all. . . . Was reflecting that everything is going, everything is leaving me; I am alone. Pondering about the theory of evolution, I thought God knows if it is true at all. What is true? Nobody knows. . . .

He came out looking very weak. The cough is worse; last night he was coughing so much, so I was told. Each time I hear it, it is like a knife thrust in my heart; it hurts me when he coughs.

Told him in what mess I seem to be—how disgusted I am with myself; how I begin to understand that what happens now is very wonderful; because all the beliefs have been uprooted, there is nothing which can be called permanent. But the human being must believe in something—even atheists have some kind of belief, if they believe in nothing else but themselves, or evolution; man can create a creed of almost anything. I believe now in Him, I KNOW He is a reality, a tremendous, deep Reality, and THE ONLY REALITY to seek after. If one tries to give up a belief by letting it go, by dropping it with an act of will, the belief doesn't really go. I experienced it. Beliefs hide; they don't go. But if the mind realized that it is not worthwhile holding them, then they go. Mind, at least my mind, wants the Truth; old beliefs obviously were not the Absolute Truth. They were worthless. But the mind is helpless; it cannot reach out to Him who is like the rising sun on the horizon of my Soul. . . . He, the only Reality to believe in, to strive after, He who left me alone and went away. And I remain confused, have nothing to stand upon. If you knew how I feel, you would be sorry for me, but no, you would not, because you don't really care. . . .

And if I am still in this state when I am not here? Here at least, I can tell you, hoping that you listen, though I am not at all sure of that. But there, what will it be? Dark night all around, nothing to hold on to, and I am so alone. . . . I have been thinking that in three days time I have to ask you for money again, and I wondered why I am not worried. Not at all, because I have bigger issues to worry about; money is nothing when compared to these. After all, if He wants me to suffer, to starve or to die, it is His Will, and I belong to Him. This represents a new thought to me: I am not important at all. Until now I thought that I was very important. Somehow, since I experienced the nearness with Him, I know that I am less than a speck of dust. Here is one more contradiction: one can speak only in opposites— the whole world is contained in this speck of dust—deepest intimacy and nothingness, this is it. . . . But I had to stop, for my heart was burning. . . .

He listened with a tender expression. I looked at him in silence. How can he manage to look like this, wondering at the beauty of the light around him . . . full of light . . . green and yellow light, hurting the eyes.

"But I am the only one who sees you like this." He nodded slowly and began to speak to *Sannyasi*.

25th December

YES, I AM IN A STATE of confusion, chaos . . . but out of chaos the Universe was created . . . on the level of the personality, not a very comfortable state. Three things seem to have remained only: the Love, reaching as high as the sky; the hatred, the shadow side of love; and He who is not with me anymore, who only remains as a memory to haunt me. He, like a rising sun on the horizon, beckoning, calling . . . the only reality, but gone seemingly forever. The hatred is dreadful, most disturbing, and it seems worse as the days go by instead of better. I hate his family, darkly, deadly; I hate all people who come and sit there; if I had powers I would have misused them, I am sure.

But the love . . . how can I put it? Something divine burning and burning, but what courage has he to say that it is all joy. He never lacked courage, not he. I only hope this state will not last a whole Night of Brahma, many cores of *Kalpas*, I told him, and he laughed.

"You know today is the 25th December?" I asked.

"I did not know; I thought it was the 24th," he smiled. He was especially kind today, smiling gently, and he answered even a few questions which is not always the case. He was full of light and was sitting in this fascinating posture on his chair with the legs so twisted that one had to study which way they were tucked in.

"You are full of white light; is it because of Christmas?" He did not answer. I knew it was a stupid question.

"What are you going to cook today?" he asked. I said rice and tomatoes; I don't celebrate; Christmas passes unnoticed in India. In the West they go crazy about it for commercial reasons; it becomes a sort of mass-hysteria. He smiled.

Later: **"My father and my Rev. Guru Maharaj never answered questions on the System; it is infused. You know only how it feels when love is created, but how it is done . . . there is the real philosophy behind it. One day you will know. . . ."**

"You had said that I am not trained according to the System, and you said love is not created with everybody."

"One cannot go against the System," he said. **"You are trained according to the System, but you are on the other Path. Love is created with everybody, but not everybody's heart is capable of holding it. So sometimes love IS created. There are different kinds of hearts. Everyone loves according to one's capacity. Things will be done through you. At first you will be the postbox; only later you will do things knowingly—you will know what you are doing. For some only One remains. . . ."**

He was silent for a while. I knew he meant me; there was this faraway look and the feeling of MEANING. . . .

"The followers spoil the faith always," he mused, and softly he added: **"I fear after I am gone it also will be spoiled. . . ."**

"Not everybody will do it," I said quickly, "not everyone!"

He did not answer but seemed in Samadhi. **"Nakshmandia Dynasty descends from the Prophet. The first Deputy was the father-in-law of the Prophet. He was the first. But Sufis were before the Prophet. Sufism always was; it is the ancient Wisdom. Only before the Prophet they were not called Sufis. Only a few centuries after his death they were called Sufis. Long before they were a sect called "Kamal Posh" (blanket wearers), and they went to every prophet. A tradition goes that they went also to Jesus. No one could satisfy them. Every Prophet told them, do this or that, and they were not satisfied. One day Mohammed said: 'There are many Kamal Posh men coming, and they will reach here in so many days and now at that moment they are there and there.' They came when he said and on the day he said. And when they were with him, he** only looked at them without speaking. **They were completely satisfied."** He fell silent, and I laughed and said that I bet I know what he did to satisfy them!

"**Yes?**" He looked at me inquiringly.

"He created love in their hearts; that's why they have been satisfied."

"**Yes, it was so; it is correct. Every Prophet told them this or that. Naturally they were not satisfied. But when love is created, what dissatisfaction can there be? So away they went, fully satisfied.**"

I thought that it was a lovely story.

26th December

HE DID NOT COME OUT in the morning. I was waiting because I asked him for money, and he said yesterday he will give it this morning. When he did not come out, I decided to go home. I will cook what was at home; there was not much but it will have to do. He obviously wanted me to be in trouble. O.K. But when I was going out of the gate, one of his disciples who was with him in the room called me back to stay, not to go. So I stayed. When everybody left, he called me in. He gave me the money and said that he had vomiting condition. He looked very pale and ill. I became very worried.

"**Pray for me,**" he said. Poor Bhai Sahib, my heart was so heavy.

43

Sitting Outside: A Self-discipline

30th December, 1962

THIS MORNING ABOUT SEVEN in the kitchen when making my morning coffee, I was thinking: my Revered Guru Maharaj, you have forgotten me; no vibration at all, all was stillness. But half an hour later the heart began such a wild beat, and it went on for hours. So I knew something new is being done; it was different from what it was before. Love was perfect . . . if only I can keep this state . . . I am praying for help. So near He seems to be sometimes that I feel there is only a thin wall left between Him and me. Perhaps I am mistaken after all. For after and behind this wall there will be another . . . perhaps forever. Never mind, at least I can have a good try. . . .

The physical conditions in his garden are very difficult. Sitting alone in the dust before a closed door would be difficult even for an Indian. And it is not only for one day or two, but over one year already . . . nearly overrun by incredibly dirty children noisily playing ball, or just throwing dust in the air . . . children coming in from the street and playing with the kids of Tulsi Ram. Dogs seem to come from everywhere. Sitting on dirty chairs covered with dog hair sometimes—I try to clean them when I come in the mornings. The servant forgets to take the chairs in, so they are left outside during the night, and the dogs will sleep on them. I sit facing the slum conditions of Tulsi Ram's shed . . . all this for many hours every day, with this longing in my heart; he will be inside with others, but I cannot go in without being invited. It can be cold, and I am sitting. It is windy, clouds of dust are blown in the air, and I am sitting. It is hot, and I am sitting . . . always, or nearly always, before a closed door. Often it happened that young men passing in groups in the street would stop at the gate and laugh at me. Probably they think it funny to see an elderly European woman sitting before the closed door of an Indian man . . . I don't care.

I wrote the above sitting in the garden this morning. However well intentioned I am, I am a human being after all, and the conditions sometimes become so difficult that I get discouraged. But he came out today, even if very late . . . it was nearly eleven. All went still outside me . . . I looked at him . . . nothing more existed for me; I saw nothing and nobody else. He was all wrapped in a white blanket, the head covered with a towel. He looked tired, hollow cheeks, burning eyes, like strange lights . . . like an exotic, old woodcarving with high cheek bones, so Tibetan, so Eastern. Such was the nearness, I thought the heart had stopped beating. I wonder how it is done, this nearness. On the physical plane he does not look at me; he is severe. But from time to time he will close his eyes in that infinitely tender manner of his, and though he does not look at me but speaks to others, I know it is for me. And what I feel is too sweet to describe. I am compelled to close my eyes too at the same moment. A tenderness, a sweetness, a complete sense of Oneness with Him. Not with the Guru, strangely enough. But with Him, absolutely final, complete . . . such a feeling of fulfillment . . . while the Guru does not even speak to me. He sat in the sun, but not for long. I noticed that under the blanket he has only his flimsy cotton *dhotie*; even Tasseldar objected, and said that he will catch a cold just before the *Bandhara*.

I was wondering why these difficult conditions did not matter anymore. Often it happened that when I had the opportunity to tell him about some difficulties, or even only wrote about them in my diary, they suddenly vanished or lost all importance and I had the strength to go on. Something new is being done to my heart. I feel it. Is it because I pray so much? Perhaps. The heart did beat tocsin in the afternoon, nearly all the time. The feeling of nearness was great, and I could not help wondering if the heartbeat was his and not mine?

He was talking to us about desire; he said that he wants to be completely without desires; he thinks that he has still so many desires, he said, speaking of *Sannyasi* who had just left.

"But he is a *Sannyasi*; he is supposed to be without desire," I said.

"Yes, he should, but it is very difficult; very few remain without desires, only the fortunate ones. The *Satsang* has this great advantage." He fell silent with the sphinx expression on his face, screwing up his eyes looking into some inward distance. . . .

"And here you are sending me away," I said, watching the flashes of light suddenly blazing out from his forehead.

"Yes," he nodded, "physical separation must be." He took the letter I prepared for Mme. Bruno and began to correct it.

"The sentence that the Trica Philosophy is a low kind can hurt her feelings; if they want this or that, I never answer; why should I say that they should follow me? Whatever they want to believe, they can believe; it is not my concern. Only those who are in earnest will follow me. One can speak harshly if it is necessary, but when one writes, one has to be careful. Written words sometimes look differently from what one intended them to be. If the heart is full of love, how can one hurt?"

"But I hate them all!" I exclaimed. "I hate them deeply, and violently! If I could poison them all, I gladly would do it! Why is this hatred in my heart? And why so constant and so violent? I simply loathe everybody!!" He looked at his shoes without answering and then went into Samadhi.

Yesterday people came in the afternoon; they all went inside; I was sitting outside alone. The longing was deep. The sunset sky was magnificent to look at . . . wild birds in crimson and plume helmets and tongues of flames dancing as if in a storm, all mingling together . . . the crimsons deepening on the background of pale watery blue. But it was over so quickly. How short the colors last here in the South. In England the sunsets last much longer, and the colors in the sky remain for quite some time. Soon I will see the English sunsets again.

"Every human being must work," he said yesterday. "You must go and do some good work. You will come back . . . it is not for- ever. . . ."

"But how can I go without knowing for sure that I will see you again? Just tell me that, if you know?" I asked, but he was silent.

Ahuja told me yesterday that he will buy my typewriter. O.K. Why take it with me? I can get a good price here for it and will buy another one in England. This one I have is too heavy for air travel anyhow.

How much I loved Him and prayed silently that I want Him so badly to come back into my heart . . . and the sky was a glory . . . the deepest feeling of belonging mingled with the greatest sorrow, and something was crying in me. . . .

1st January, 1963

IT WILL BE THE YEAR of the Great Divide . . . what will it bring?

He came out very late. Said that he still had some trouble with his bowels. Gave me a letter from Mme. Bruno, and asked me to answer it point by point and make a better job of it. But he did not tell me what he wants to be said. Well, I suppose, I have to capture his thought; it is not easy to be a postbox. Told him again that I am in such a bad state, that if he knew he would be quite sorry for me . . .

at least I hope so. I realized that I have built my castle on shifting sand.

"Everybody has built his home of shifting sands in this world," he smiled. **"Everyone in the System comes to the point where they lose all beliefs, and are confused and say that they are nowhere . . . you are not the only one. Until one forgets everything, *Samskaras* will remain. I never had this trouble. I, of course, had also my beliefs; everyone has, but Karmas and things like this did not bother me . . . I believed in Him alone."** He proceeded to tell me what a wild and violent boy he was until his Rev. Guru took him in his hands and his life was turned completely.

The Guru of his Rev. Guru said to his disciples: "Everyone has to die, life is short (he was 107 years old). I am sorry I could not take you to the stage I intended, but you work alone to reach there."

"This is always said so," he remarked, looking kindly at me. **"The teacher will never tell the disciple that the teaching is finished and he knows all that there is to know, in order that the disciple should not be proud."**

Speaking of Chowdrie, I said that he has an easy life.

"Yes, an easy life, easy and smooth, no family to worry about. We have to live our life in the world and be occupied with worldly affairs, and reach the highest stage in spite, or rather, because of it. For the greater is the limitation, the greater will be the ultimate perfection by overcoming it. Very few reach it indeed. It is very difficult."

"That's why you want me to go back, because you think that my life here is too easy!"

"It is not a question of easy or difficult," he said, **"but the human being has to work. You come here and go back; you make no effort."**

"Oh, I thought that I am making such a terrible effort! This morning I was weeping bitterly for a long time because my life is so full of misery in every way!"

"From my point of view it is nothing," he said, and went into Samadhi for a short while. Then he said: **"There things will happen much more than here . . . much more. . . ."** He went silent again.

"Bogroff when he was here was full of love. He was sitting here on the brick elevation where I used to walk, and when people asked him if he was hot—it was in June—he used to answer that he was all right. So full of love was he, he did not feel anything."

This is for me, I thought . . . I seem not to be quite there yet; more love is needed if I am still complaining. The day must come when I will be no more. But when?

I said it seems to me that only love is left, and its shadow-side, hatred, and the belief in Him like a rising sun on the horizon, and nothing more.

"Only one thing will remain," he said slowly.

"Is this thing love?"

"Only one thing," he repeated without answering my question, and then, **"even this will not remain."** He fell silent and closed his eyes. I wondered . . . it looks as if my going to London will represent the supreme test. I always thought so, but from the hints I get it is going to be terrible. Somehow I am not really worried. . . .

He went for a walk with his wife. I sat alone and prayed so much. I was not alone anymore . . . and in the night prayed and prayed in the fullness of love. . . .

When he returned from the walk and sat in the chair for a while opposite me, I told him that it looked to me as if Mme. Bruno is in a greater mess than myself, and we discussed her case for a while. "For myself I must say, I thank you, you helped me; this morning I felt as if beaten up severely; it is not easy to be a letter-box." He looked at me directly with an expression I have never seen before, so full of tender compassion, but I could hardly see his face in the dusk.

Told him that in the night it came into my mind that Sufis work from the *Atmic* level downwards—that's why it is so powerful. All the other Yoga Schools begin either on the physical level like Hatha Yoga, or on the level of the mind like Raja yoga . . . Buddhists, etc. At the *Atmic* level, no disturbances from the *Kama Rupa* level can reach; that's why it is so effective and quick results are achieved. He smiled so tenderly again, but now his expression was hardly visible in the darkness.

It seems to me that the state of consciousness is shifting. But I have so often thought of it in the past that I don't know how far this statement is correct.

This morning the chair is full of dog hair and dirt from the dog's feet. A dog slept in it during the night. The servant does not take the chairs inside at night, and often dogs sleep on them. I asked for a clean chair, and Virendra brought me one from inside the room. But I was not particularly upset about it. Some time ago I would have been resentful because I am expected to put up with such conditions. But somehow, it did not matter much. Sure, I would not sit on such an unhygienic chair, but it was soon dismissed from my mind.

The world looked more than ever like *Maya*, quite unreal. He did not come out but called me from the door, telling me to go to the Post Office and ask when was the last date for the Radio License. So, I went home early and did some shopping. The state of consciousness DOES seem to change—love seems to be deeper, and the feeling of nothingness before him is increasing.

All this being sorry for myself is sheer nonsense. I have to switch over to perfect love. Nothing should matter anymore. Not even the most difficult conditions. In England they will be even more difficult . . . it looks so to judge from his hints. It is so useless to be resentful, and still I am . . . incredible to say. . . .

I throw myself before You . . . I am crying to you from the uttermost depth of my heart . . . I want You so badly . . . I want to become one with You, but I cannot because the mind gives me some trouble. Not much, but even a little, creates a veil between You and me.

Again he came out dressed so flimsily; it seems he does it on purpose. It was bitterly cold and a sharp icy wind was blowing from the north. Told him that something is happening to my *Indrias* (senses); they seem to work in an unusual way, as if they were not able to record the impressions properly. Difficult to explain, but everything is like a dream, unreal, as if I were living on another plane altogether. And I AM living on another plane: He is with me and I am with Him all the time. And I pray, pray all day long that a Hint should be given to you (at this point he smiled) and pray for help, because if I can keep this state I will overcome the present crisis. He smiled again.

"The *Indrias* do not seem to convey the correct impressions because you are in a state of spiritual constipation; it sometimes happens like this."

"So it is bad?"

"No, good, very good," he smiled; **"spiritual constipation is a very good thing; it means you will make a jump forward after that."**

"I know that the only thing to help to keep this state is to pray; as soon as He is with me, I am all right. . . . Please do go inside; it is so cold; you give us all much worry dressed like this." He had an amused look.

"I don't call you inside in the morning because the room has to be cleaned." And he went in.

But later? I thought, and in the afternoon? And when the others are in with you? The reason you gave me is not the one; it is for the sake of training you do it, my dear, I thought. . . .

In the afternoon when I was sitting outside, and the room was full of people talking to him, I sat near the door to hear his voice and was thinking: to be content to hear your voice, my dear Bhai Sahib. To be content, bearing the loneliness and pain and longing. To be content with the *Darshan* you give me, without asking for more, without desiring more, that's how it should be. . . . The nearer the departure, the harder it is bound to become . . . but I must manage it. It seems the greatest possible effort to demand, but clearly it has to be. . . . Will pray . . . I feel there is only a thin wall between Him and me. And this wall has to be broken down. All my being I have thrown before Him, but He will not listen until the whole of myself is completely down before Him.

He came out, sat for a while (at least he had a warm pullover now), and I went quite still with wonder at the beauty of the light which surrounded him. Pure gold and flashes of an unusual green: I just stared.

"Why is this hatred?" I felt compelled to ask, to my surprise.

He smiled suddenly. **"It is because you have challenged me to produce love; this is the other, the parallel current."**

What did he mean by that? I felt I should not ask; he will not answer. He looked far away with a hard expression. No, I could not ask. . . .

"If people should ask you, how is it that you are so far after only such a short time, tell them, how is it that a woman becomes pregnant in a second?"

I said that I answered that it was Guru *Krepa* (grace).

"Yes, but there are people who don't believe in Guru *Krepa*; to those one can answer as I have told you!" I laughed. He was right.

"In our System the disciples become sometimes very jealous," he said when I told him that Sitla Prasad made remarks accusing me of pride.

"But not only in your System . . . I read that it happens in every School of Yoga—it is human nature! And I thought that Sitla Prasad was right; perhaps I was full of pride, not in the particular connection he was meaning, but pride I have enough. So, I did not answer him."

"Yes, let them speak. Often my school fellows came to me asking me, how is it that you are a Wali? How can it be? I am older than you, and I have nothing! You cannot be a Saint! So, I answer: you say that I am not, let it be! Why should I explain that my Rev. Guru Maharaj

gave it to me but not to him? Will I be less if he does not believe in me? It is of no importance at all."

Then we discussed desires, and I said I hope to be like him one day, wanting nothing; it is the Goal to which one should aspire.

"It is difficult; very few reach this stage." I know I will reach it. I SIMPLY MUST. There is no other way . . . he was leading me towards it steadily. . . .

"If I will be so inefficient and confused when I am in England, it will be very bad. How will I live?"

"It is because you are here," he said slowly; "when you are there, everything will be different. . . ." I wondered what he meant but dared not ask.

"You can go home," he declared, and began to pace up and down rapidly. I went, wondering if I will be able to walk, such were the vibrations. But I managed.

2nd January

HE ONLY LOOKED OUT from the room and gave me some postcards to post. "You can go home," he said curtly, and went with the two disciples inside.

Mrs. Ghose's dog woke me up; he barked without a stop for nearly one hour. At first I was annoyed, and then I just wished myself a Happy New Year. The prayer seemed exceptionally easy. I could tune in without the least effort. Did not analyze why it was like this. It was easy, so I prayed, and prayed, for his health in the New Year, for my progress, prayed with words and without, just in fullness of love. At about five in the morning the heartbeat, which until now was normal, changed abruptly to a new beat—the quicker and the stronger one which during the last few days I have had from time to time. I began to wonder if the state of nearness with Him and the new heartbeat had something to do with the easy prayer tonight. The mind does not reach there; it is not at all simple to check it. Then I suddenly realized what was the matter: He seemed to be PART OF MYSELF. To explain better: until now I was WITH HIM; now He was part of myself. Until now I had to make an effort, even if lately it hardly seemed one, so easy I could reach Him; but tonight I could simply take a little dip, a small step inside myself and, lo! There He was! Nearly effortless! I tried it again and again to be quite sure; yes, there was no mistake: He was part of me, so it felt. . . .

Now that is a very wonderful thing, I said to my mind; do you realize what a great thing it is? But the mind did not seem to realize it at all. . . . He was so naturally, so easily part of myself that it did not seem wonderful at all. . . . Even now, in spite of the fact that I thought it over, in spite of all this, I seem not to be able to realize completely the importance of this fact. He is myself, seemed to say my mind. HE IS ME. What is wonderful about that? Does one find it wonderful that the eyes are mine? Or the head? Or any other part of the body? It is simply part of me. Something similar I discovered some days ago: the why of the fact that in spite of the physical nearness there seemed to be no desire at all. How could that be, he being a man and I a woman? Well, it is too simple, really; if there is a sense of identity, how can there be a desire? For a desire you need two things, one desiring the other. But if you are ONE AND THE SAME, what desire can there be? One does not desire one's own body, isn't it so? I think that the identity with Him is because of the identity with Bhai Sahib. It is one and the same thing. It feels only as duality, Guru AND Him . . . but it is a mistake, there is a mistake somewhere. I have to watch this state carefully to discover where the mistake lies. . . .

Thank you for the boon you gave me last night, I thought, seeing him pacing up and down. It was my New Year's Gift. . . .

I was wondering if he knew exactly what had happened, or if he just puts on the vibration, or changes its frequency, or creates something to which the disciple reacts as well as he can according to his or her capacity. But his attitude showed me clearly that he knew very well what did happen, because he began to test me immediately without delay. When I gave him the letters I had written to some of his disciples, he was curt, criticized a few things, hardly looked at me, and spoke abruptly. But I was full of love and his unfriendliness did not affect me; it did not matter that other people were going inside and I sat alone as ever. Love seemed much bigger now, increased.

What he did, I think, is to stimulate the Heart *Chakra*. For the last few nights I felt it whirling; it seemed huge—at least it felt like that. And it was going round and round; the whole upper part of the thorax was affected. Also when I lay sidewise, I could even hear it spin. The heartbeat did change since Friday, five days ago. In the morning, when I was holding the mirror, my hand would shake; I had difficulty putting cream on my face. I knew that he was doing something different. I told him so and he nodded. Something very important is happening. I was thinking that I have to do it alone, that he will not help me, and I have to cross the crisis alone, and here he is not only helping, but I think that HE ACTUALLY DID IT, much more than myself. . . .

"And what had happened?" He asked severely, when I told him that I kept wondering if he always knew exactly what does happen, or if he just gives the vibration and the Shishya gets what he is capable of getting.

"I always give," he said one day; **"everyone takes what he can."**

I told him in detail what had happened, but he did not look at me and seemed in deep Samadhi. His face was very hard.

"And why so wonderful?" he asked harshly, when I was telling him how I discovered that He was right inside my heart. . . .

"Precisely; that's why my mind could not understand, for it seemed the most natural thing in the world . . . to have Him part of myself . . . just a small step inside and here He was. I think the mind cannot quite reach there so it just accepts it; it feels so simple—it is just that." I was not quite sure whether he was listening or not. We were alone for a change . . . he was half in Samadhi. I knew he remained sitting not for my sake; somebody was bound to come; he always knew that, that's why he remained. He always knows. He won't sit for me alone. Quite out of the blue, suddenly he said:

"It is for the very few. How many reach it? Very few take up the thread, and of those, few only follow it up. . . it is for very few." He fell in a deep prolonged silence. I waited for him to continue, but of course people came and general conversation began.

44

Suicide?

PLENTY OF PEOPLE were sitting this morning, and he paced up and down for a while. Then he sat down and the usual conversation began . . . he, nearly all the time, speaking and explaining. Then everybody left. Hardly looking at me with an impatient expression he said:

"Talk was going on that if the Guru gives all in a moment and makes one a Saint, it is for everybody. But it is not for everybody, it is for the few. One has to give time to it and effort, and time means effort. It is for the very few. . . ." I wondered why he had repeated it in the last few days. Something was brewing. . . .

He got up abruptly and went inside without a word. Then he came out with a stick and declared with a smile that he was going for a walk. I went home. In the evening he came out for a short while; people were there and he was telling that Saints when buried are not touched by worms. He himself saw with his own eyes that not even the shroud in which the corpse is enveloped was touched by worms.

5th January

TODAY IT IS ONE YEAR since he began the training. I was so full of vibrations this morning. Only the one-eyed man was sitting, and he left soon. He was pacing up and down on the brick elevation, and when he sat down for a moment I said: (I was afraid that I wouldn't be able to speak to him, so I spoke quickly) "Bhai Sahib, Guru Maharaj, it is exactly one year when I challenged you here, before this door, to produce love. You may not remember, you may not remember, why should you, with so many Shishyas you have, but I do remember, for it was a memorable day for me. And I said to you then: You who are the maker of Saints and know how to write on the back of hearts, write on the back of my heart one letter and one letter only: that of Alif, and let it burn itself out at your feet. . . . But what you did was to write your initials on the back of my heart, the initials of your name which I never could pronounce, and for some secret mysterious reason your initials and His were one and the same thing.

394

And you threw my heart into the sea of fire, to be consumed by flames. . . ."

He listened with half a smile, a ghost of a smile; his face was looking away from me in the opposite direction; he never glanced even once at me.

"A wonderful thing you did during this year, a terrible and a wonderful thing; you skinned me as one skins an apple, and my heart felt so full, so full, that I have no words. . . . Please do allow me to touch your feet, and I knelt and pressed my forehead against his feet.

"You spoiled your dress," he laughed; I saw that he was moved. I got up and began to brush my skirt; it was full of the dust of the soil. "Never mind," I said, "I had to do it; it was a big thing for me!"

He began to pace up and down.

"I never believed that you really could produce love just like that!" I said, when he reached the level of the chair on which I was sitting.

"Nobody believes!" he laughed.

"And you gave the greatest love to me, the very greatest!"

"It may be great for you, but for me it is nothing!"

"Oh, I know, it is nothing for you; but for me . . .," I fell silent, had a lump in my throat. . . . "For me it is the world." I said it half audibly, could not speak. . . .

He went inside and did not come out. It was very early when I went home, and in the evening he was sitting with his wife in the sun, his back was turned, and he went in and did not come out. But my mind was serene. All the vibrations which I had this morning and which made me feel as if my head would blow away at any moment, stopped. I was completely alone, could not pray, but the mind was still and peaceful. And I slept well.

6th January

SERENE I REMAINED also this morning. But He was not with me, and neither was Guru Maharaj. Could not pray last night; somehow there was dryness. Sitting in his garden I was thinking, why is there no trouble? I discovered it: it is the feeling of belonging which helps. I belong to Him, so intimately, so utterly, whatever he does to me, what can I do? I am a thing of his—he can hurt me, he can fill me with bliss—who am I to say anything? And I realized something else too; that there is no trouble whether he comes out or not, whether I see him or not; I remain calm and serene. Will it last? Who knows . . . it is His Will, so why worry? What will be, will be. Since that Friday, nine days ago, when he began to do something new and the heartbeat changed, since then there is practically no trouble. So I began to pray . . . Help me You Merciful . . . if this attitude persists, if I can keep this sense of belonging to Him, then, it means that the greatest trouble will be overcome. . . . Please, oh, You Merciful . . . please, please. . . .

He came out early; many people were there because it was Sunday. Gave me a letter from Gritty, telling me to go through it and reply. I did, and asked him what does he want me to answer to her complaints that she has many faults, and she would like to better herself and put all her energies into it.

"Tell her everyone has faults, nobody is perfect. It is a good thing to try to better oneself. She is a lady who is a chain-smoker, and for a lady it is not very nice. Ladies who smoke so much have other vices too."

"Shall I tell her to give up smoking?" I ventured.

"No," he shook his head, **"one must never injure people's feelings."**

"But if she is your disciple, you have every right to say anything!"

He shook his head again. **"No, I am not her Guru; she does not follow me."**

"She follows L. and L. follows you, so what is the difference?"

"No, I am the Guru only for those who follow me step by step. It is just a way of speaking to say 'he is my Guru, I am his Shishya'; it has no value. Guru is only for the very few. Only those who have faith have a Guru. If the Shishya is good in the morning because morning is a good time and bad in the evening, how can I be the Guru of those?"

"And some are even your accepted disciples and still they don't follow you step by step."

"Quite," he nodded. **"Guru and Shishya is a unique relationship. It is not for all. How can it be?"**

Once more he seemed to say what was in my mind this morning. If I only can keep up this faith . . . My God if I ONLY CAN!!

7th January

THIS MORNING SUCH WAS THE LONELINESS that I began to weep because the situation looked so difficult beyond belief. How can I go on? The thought and the mind began to whirl and to turn. He came out in a dark mood. His face was hard. My heart grew heavier and heavier. I did not want to tell him, not really, but somehow I got the desire to tell him, so I did say that I am discouraged because I am so lonely. He was very hard to me. Made me weep bitterly. Needless to say that there were endless interruptions—the *Sannyasi* suddenly got the desire to talk for hours, the wife came, the children, all had very much to say and to discuss and so it went on. Takur did not stop talking and in between I had to try to say something to which he either did not listen or gave me rude and harsh answers.

"You don't know how to love; this is not love. Did you try to serve me when I was ill? Did you sit up all night?"

I was horrified because of the accusation; how could I dare to sit up? "What would your family have said if I did? Once I tried to fan you, but the fan was taken from my hands; once I tried to massage your feet when you were unconscious, and was stopped immediately. What an unjust accusation!"

"I am never unjust!" He snapped. I was weeping and weeping. **"You are impertinent; go to another man to get instructions, one who is less rude to you!"**

"But I don't want, I cannot, and you know that I am helpless!" I sobbed.

Then he spoke of the importance of the *Satsang*.

"If the *Satsang* is so important, why do you send me away after only a few months with you? L. was more fortunate; you told me that she stayed here for three years!"

"You must make an effort there, and if one can work, one must work; and L. was clever; she stayed here only in the winter season; in the summer she went to Kashmir!" I wept because I thought that it was a horrible thing to say; he knew I had no money left to go. . . . When I said to him that he never subjects his wife or his daughters to such a treatment and such cruelties, he said angrily:

"You are impertinent! How can you compare yourself to my wife and my daughter? They are good ladies!"

"They are women like me; what's the difference?" And so it went for a long time, and I ended by being so desperate that I said to him that death would be better than this life of such a misery, and for a brief, intense moment I seriously thought to finish it; I will never make it anyhow, it is too difficult. I was a failure, and I felt a boundless desperation. . . .

"You have no pity for me," I cried bitterly, looking at him in despair. He was hard, did not even look at me, but kept telling me terrible and bitter things. . . .

"I am going inside!" He threw this sentence like a stone at me and disappeared behind the door which he closed with a bang.

I went home, and when I looked back when going out of the gate, I saw him in the room through the open door sitting slightly bent forward as if in deep thought. The light around him . . . so beautiful. At home washed my face, red from crying, and went to Pushpa. While there I was thinking all the time how really angry he seemed to be with me, how hopeless it all was. Never-ending torture. Never-lasting peace, never-lasting happiness. These ups and downs . . . I could not bear it anymore. Was too depressed for words. . . .

"What effort are you making here?" he asked. **"All the difficulties are solved for you!"**

I said that I thought that I was making a superhuman effort! Such was the loneliness, and the physical conditions so unbelievably difficult.

"It is nothing!" he said angrily. **"Nothing! What are you doing? A bit of hot weather you had to bear, that's all!"** I was weeping so loudly, could not control myself. . . .

Yes, it is the most difficult thing in the world!

"Ocean of fire, the greatest love! Phue!" He blew disdainfully and later: **"Why do you compare yourself with my Shishyas? You are not my Shishya! And you never will be at this rate! Never."** He shouted, **"Never!"**

Was thinking and thinking at home. Did not go in the evening. It is of no use. The depression was terrible . . . I had better finish with it all. It is of no use. I am useless, I am a failure, I will never make it. I cannot go on like this anymore. . . . There is a railway bridge over the Ganges. Though it is not the rainy season and the river will not be too full, still, there will be enough at this time of the year. . . . It won't hurt too much . . . I cannot, cannot, cannot go on . . . it is of no use. . . .

Went to bed too tired to think. Was exhausted with pain and desperation . . . went into a sort of oblivion, though I was sure that I didn't sleep. But I must have done so, for when I opened my eyes it was morning. Immediately the misery flooded me with absolute despair. Decided not to go.

8th January

BUT I WENT. Could not stay away. Such was the pull, and I was too tired to resist.

He was already outside. Many people were sitting with him. He was laughing and telling jokes in Hindi. Everybody was full of merriment. I greeted him without looking at him and sat down, a little to his right. You laugh, I thought. Go on laughing. You don't care. You never did. . . . The bridge . . . it won't hurt . . . was too tired, so tired . . . it is all in vain. . . .

Mind did not work well. Noticed at one moment that he threw at me a quick sideways glance. How far is it to the bridge? How tired I am. . . . Useless, useless, useless, sang something in my brain. . . . What is life?

Was like numb. Then I began to notice that one after another everybody saluted and began to leave. Is it so late? I thought, so I had better go . . . what's the use? What's the use . . . like an obsession repeated my brain. . . .

"Mrs. Tweedie!" I suddenly heard his voice. I did not look up. Was too disgusted with him. It's no use . . . "Mrs. Tweedie, look at me!" The tone was of command. I slowly raised my head and turned it in his direction . . . and . . . froze. He was full of blinding light, white shimmering light . . . I simply gasped . . . looked. Looked . . . so much light, by God . . . so much. . . .

"Mrs. Tweedie, when I see a human being for the first time and when the hint is given, I know not only the past but also the future of this human being. Mrs. Tweedie, I will never waste my powers!"

He got up. Stood there tall, slender, shimmering (or was the trembling shimmer a fault in my eyes?), and throwing the towel over his shoulder, **"You can go home, I am going to have my bath!"** and swiftly he walked away with elastic step; the chik fell with a swoosh behind him.

I stared. Well . . . and like an immense joy it flooded into my mind: You old cow! If you were really hopeless, he would NOT take so much trouble with you! He knows the state of evolution; he acts accordingly. He would never waste so much time with someone who is absolutely useless. So hold on! Hold on, for heaven's sake! And I went home.

Evening

I SAT ALONE TILL DUSK. Was tired. All was numb, all was still in me. Then somebody came; Guruji came out and talked to the man in the doorway passage. The person left soon and to my surprise he approached me where I was sitting.

"**How are you?**" He asked in a friendly way.

"Well," I answered, getting up; I did not know what to answer; he is not angry, I thought with relief. He sat down.

"**This is done for the sake of training; I am never really harsh, but harsh attitude is maintained with lovers. Otherwise how can I give a stroke if the mind gives trouble? It is done like this . . . this is the System. A stroke must be given when the mind rebels.**"

"Oh, I was thinking this afternoon that you are quite right: I am still full of the self!"

"**Why don't you say that I am** ALWAYS **right?**" He laughed his boyish laughter, young and gay, as if nothing had happened. . . .

"Yes," I nodded meekly. I would have said anything at this moment to please him, so glad I was that he is not angry with me.

"**Wait, I will open the door; we will not sit outside; it is cold,**" and he went inside, opening the door of the room from inside.

Sitting in his father's big chair he told me many things.

"**I am glad you are in a good mood again,**" he said, adjusting his legs in a comfortable posture. "**The trouble really started because you took objection about my statement that women cannot reach the highest stage in the same way as men. Men have a substance in them and women have not. It makes men absorb the very essence of the Master. But men have to learn to control** prakriti **in themselves, and for this purpose practices are given to them. Women, because they are nearer to** prakriti, **are fertilized by the Divine Energy which they retain in their** Chakras **and because of this, very few practices are needed. Women are taken up through the path of love, for love is a feminine mystery. Woman is the cup waiting to be filled, offering herself up in her longing, which is her very being. Souls go the way of the souls where they are destined to, for they have different qualities, and according to those qualities they are directed.**" I said that I did not understand, and he said it is not easy.

"**How can the Shishya reach the stage when the Master is still alive? There are exceptions; some do and go even higher than the Master; to those he gives something when he dies. I am sending you away because you must make an effort; you must write to me— never stop writing.**" I said that I will surely do so and very often, for probably I will be full of trouble.

"**And sometimes you will be so full of vibrations and the mind will not work, then you must not work. I happen not to work at times for months. You work again when your inner voice tells you to do so. One does not speak much to lovers. It is not necessary. If you** want to change, I can give you Dhyana and Samadhi, but those are gymnastics, I say, and you can play with them for the rest of your life. But it is not for you; I told you, hearts are different and the Teacher decides which Path is suitable for each particular heart."

"I don't want any change; I am glad I have to suffer; love is the greatest thing for me; I wanted it from the beginning."

"One should not want any change," he said screwing his eyes to a slit. Then he looked outside for a moment. The greeny shadows of the moving foliage in the breeze were reflected on his skin and in his eyes.

"My Rev. Father, myself, we have been trained like this; you challenged me; why? Because it is your character; human beings cannot help acting according to their character; and the training is given according to the character. I can give Dhyana to you in a moment; it is not at all difficult for me, but I myself don't attach any importance to that. . . . To produce love is difficult in other Schools of Yoga, not in ours; in ours it is easy. Love is a great suffering in the beginning and in the middle; later it is all joy; or nearly all. . . . In Dhyana or Samadhi, love is also created, but much later. Prof. Batnagar is wrong to say that you must write only when you have realized. Many people write books, and they know nothing; you have the experiences of love, many of them; your diary will help you."

I said that I pray that the self should go before I have to leave.

"No, no," he laughed; "don't give any span of time; don't limit the date! It cannot be! How will you make the effort? When you come back, then you will be united with me, then the self will go completely and forever . . . and your Greater Self will be with you! You will come back; stay with me for some time, then . . . you will see me alive . . . I got an extension; some important work has still to be done."

I said that I felt that he wants to go.

"Yes, I have no interest in this world; what can attract me? People say they merge in me; it means nothing. Merging in the Master is a very different thing. They just think of me, and they say they have merged. Thoughts don't reach me. You want to surrender to me, don't you?"

I said that it is my greatest wish, one of the few which still remained. "And I want it to be 100%. Please, don't leave even a hair's breadth; do it completely, as it was done to your Rev. Father and to you; otherwise my mind will never give me peace!"

"Not 100%, but 199½%!" he laughed. "No veil will remain!"

Speaking of knowledge he repeated what he said so often: "It is not given on the mind level; it is infused."

"Reflected into the mind?" I ventured. He gave me a nod and a radiant smile.

"You have such a way of talking to one that the heart is melting," I said, and he looked at me sideways and laughed merrily. Went home happy.

9th January

WHEN I WAS COMING THROUGH THE GATE, I saw him standing at the side door of his room. I went to him and gave him the photo Pushpa gave me. Actually Pushpa gave me two photos, both taken by the French woman archaeologist; one was of the whole of his family and the other was of him alone. He looks wonderful in it: he was just about to come down from the steps of the Samadhi, the clean, clear lines of it behind him in the background. His eyes are half-closed, for he came out into the sunshine, and he looks free and bold and tall, standing there as if hesitant, a mysterious longing like an aura around him . . . I think he was not aware that his photo was taken. At home I was looking and looking at it; it is wrong to keep it, I thought, but his children have many photos of him; I have none, and am not likely to get one . . . I will give him only the one with his family and keep this one for myself . . . I prayed that the Hint should be given to me that I can keep it . . . and if he will ask me, then I will tell the truth. I know he will speak to me this morning. I was thinking much in the night; there was a lot more to say. . . .

Giving him the photo I confess that I was afraid and felt guilty. "This one Pushpa sends you," I said. He looked sharply at me, my heart went quite small.

"How kind of her," he gave me a quizzical smile and went inside. Good God, let me keep it, I thought, I wanted it so much. . . .

He came out almost immediately; I hardly had time to sit down. We were alone, and there were hardly any interruptions. And he talked to me from half past nine to nearly one. To my inquiry if I will remain always with him, he answered:

"For ladies, perseverance is difficult for them. It is difficult for men too; very few achieve it. Ladies have *Bhakti* (devotion) and if they get it, they get it in an instant. Otherwise it takes time. You will be on the highest level, but there is such a thing as Character Roll. In it the character is marked, and all the doubts and the lack of faith, will be seen there. In our System we make no difference—hearts are hearts. But in our System no lady was sufficiently interested to go on to the highest level. . . . One has to leave the love behind . . . nothing remains. Not that the love has gone—one can get it—it does not mean that one loses it; one can get it at any moment. But one leaves it behind, so to say. Even of my spiritual brothers nobody wanted it; they are not with me; they are left behind; how can they be with me? Who wants to work? Why do you want to understand? It is not for you now; don't pray for it now; wait till the time comes. . . . Everything, every prayer has its time. One thing at a time . . . work is a wide term. *Bhakti* is such a state; the state itself makes it that one does not want to leave it. My Rev. Guru Maharaj took me to this state when I did not even know about it. Only much later I came to know. . . . Who wants this state? Nothing remains." He was silent for a while. All was still. I had the feeling that even the garden was listening.

"Even men want *Bhakti*," he continued; "it is a wonderful state. Bogroff also had trouble with his mind, but for a very short time."

"He was an exceptional man," I said. He shook his head.

"He had to complete the road in a short time; that's why. . . ." He was silent once more. A light wind sprang out from somewhere behind the corner of the house rustling the leaves in the mango tree. A bird whistled. "Love," he said musingly, "you did not recognize it when it came."

In the evening he came out, many of us were already sitting, and he spoke to them very highly of me; when asked to translate, he said it is not for me, it is for them. I smiled inwardly. The Teacher of Rumi, Shamsi Tabriz, was always rude to his disciple, but to others he spoke highly of him. History repeats itself—not that I want to compare myself with Rumi, but this seems to be the training. At home I kept musing that all the statements seem to be contradictory. There is only one road . . . this is clear . . . to disregard them all. HE WILL NOT tell me the truth. All his behavior shows it to me; that it is the ONLY road. I have to reach such a state of faith that if he should say: this chair is a dog, I will think, yes, it is a dog, and I had better not sit on it for it can bite me. . . .

45

Faith without Understanding

I TRIED TO REPEAT THE STATEMENTS to him in the morning, but he interrupted me:

"Logic will not help you; it is only a matter of lack of faith. If faith is great enough, it will carry you through. If not, mind will revolt always. . . . I never, never, contradict myself. We never do in our Yoga System. All my statements are perfectly correct, seen from different levels."

"Even if you say it is effortless?"

"How can there be effort with Divine things? They are GIVEN, INFUSED," he smiled gently, "and the Guru can NEVER be forced. If you will say so, you will deceive others and deceive yourself. Divine things can never be forced, however right, however correct is the attitude of the Shishya. It is given as a gift. Never, never can there be a question of forcing the Guru. One cannot force God. Yes, there is a connection between the Almighty and me for the sake of training. You must tell me everything, but if you don't, I come to know." I was thinking if he knew about the photo . . . probably. . . .

Much talk was going on about politics, and he sent us home early.

11th January

HE CAME OUT GRINNING BROADLY; in his hands were the two photos. "Miss L. sent me those photos," he said to me, "look! My children appreciated it very much!" I sat stiffly. He passed the photos around. Everybody thought that they were very good. Don't ask me for mine; I prayed silently.

"I am going inside, I have to work," he declared and went inside. Others and myself sat for a while, then we all went home.

12th January

LAST NIGHT I LEFT HIS PLACE about half past five. Felt so tired, am like a drunkard now; if there are no vibrations, the body feels tired and depressed. Ten to six I was in bed. So deep, so much longing there

404

was. It is a lovely feeling, no wonder the poets sing about it, but it is very painful. Slept well, which is unusual, perhaps because the body was tired. Usually I don't sleep more than a few hours, and the rest of the time I look at the stars. The moonlight was so bright that it woke me up—it may have been about midnight—pulled my bed into the veranda and fell asleep again until seven. The night was so fragrant. I will miss them in England—those southern nights laden with fragrance of some distant flowers, and shimmering with stars. . . .

Some men came, and he was very angry because of the sawdust they had delivered which was of bad quality; he was shouting at them and his wife was shouting too. Later he said that they were swindlers. "Cheats," he grumbled when they had left.

I said smilingly that I did not know that a Saint can get angry until I came to him. People say "a saintly man," when they mean that he never gets angry.

"The world is full of wrong ideas, and full of foolish people," he said. "A Saint is an ordinary man, only he does not indulge in anything. He has desires as every other human being. Only he is not after them. If they are fulfilled, there is no pleasure; if not, there is indifference and no pain. That's all. He is on the same platform as any other human being. People say the Saint has to be hungry, must not eat, drink only twice a week and so on." I said that the misconception has arisen because of Hatha Yogis who often do that, and the world thinks this is the highest thing!

"Hatha Yoga means one who has not been accepted; it is not a high state. The Almighty is full of desires; otherwise what was the necessity of creating the world? Nobody can ever remain without desires; they must be fewer, that's all. Some desires are needs, like eating, drinking, needs necessary for daily living. Understanding alone is not enough; if you have understood something, it must become part of your thinking. Part of your mind. Your mind is always revolting; it even revolts now."

13th January

DID NOT SEE HIM YESTERDAY; he seems to be occupied with the *Bandhara* preparations. The other day I complained that there were few vibrations; tonight I could not sleep so strong they were. The mind also was working well. But I could pray, and I prayed for faith.

There are two kinds of happiness: the dynamic one, the feeling "the world is mine"; the other composed of non-being and stillness.

Had both of them in the night, first the one, then the other. Both are different, but both are perfect bliss, each in its own way. One is full of joy, the other full of a sense of belonging.

And I was sure that after the prayers so deep in the fullness of love, my relationship with the Guru was different. . . . Somehow all my being was directed towards him in a single devotion, difficult to describe.

Somehow he fitted better in his surroundings, and I seem to hate them less . . . **"We Sufis are ordinary people."** . . .

14th January

MANY PEOPLE WERE THERE LAST NIGHT and he came to sit outside. Hindi was being spoken. As soon as he came out, I saw that his face was grey. "You are not well," my heart became heavy. . . .

"Who says so?" he asked sternly. **"Why do you think such a thing?"** I said that I had the feeling that he was not well, and I was worried this morning.

"What makes you think that your feelings are always right?" he asked ironically.

"Oh, by no means," I said, "by no means!" I remained silent. It is the second time he is unfriendly with me since yesterday, I reflected. He does not lose time, I must say . . . he is testing me . . . he knows that I am making the effort and am praying so he will test me. . . . Must be very careful now . . . all my attention must be directed NOT TO BE RESENTFUL EVER . . . whatever he does. Hindi was spoken exclusively. I just sat there looking at him, and suddenly I saw green light around the lower part of his face and flashing on the forehead . . . a very light-green and golden light. I closed one eye to test if I was not mistaken. No, it was still there, but later it disappeared. In a pause of the conversation I managed to tell him about it. He flicked a few rapid glances at me and gave me one of his radiant smiles. Later he asked us to come into the room; it began to be cool and too damp to sit in the garden.

"You too can come in." We all sat on chairs around the room and conversation continued. I asked him if I could say something.

"Yes?" he lifted his eyebrows. So I repeated the conversation I had with Sitla Prasad yesterday.

"This is the place of drunkards; people who want to drink come here!" said Sitla Prasad.

"How right you are," I laughed. "Two days ago I had to go home at half past five, so tired I was, and was in bed before six. All because there seemed to be no vibrations, and my body is so used to them by now that it flops if there are none. As a drunkard needs alcohol to keep him going, so we too need a stimulant, though of a different kind!"

"Those vibrations are only if he is pleased, and while he is alive," said Sitla Prasad. "As soon as he dies, they will stop. We, the disciples of his Rev. Father, were full of good vibrations; they have all stopped since he died."

"I did not say anything, but it does not seem to apply to you, since the death of your Rev. Guru Maharaj? The contrary is the case, is it not?"

He listened and then smiled: **"It is all a question of character; if during the lifetime of the Guru the character has time to change completely, to become like his, the vibrations will not stop after his death. On the contrary: after the death of the Master the vibrations are much stronger! But if the character is not formed yet, all the vibrations will stop unless one goes to the successor. Those people were puzzled and seemed lost; they had no faith in the System. The Master will die, but the Yoga System will go on forever. You ask why blind faith, without understanding? Why blind? Well, a blind man needs a stick, and without a stick he cannot walk. So, we too, without faith, cannot go on the Path. People want to know the how and the why and then they surrender, when they are satisfied. It is rare, very rare, as it was in my case, that one surrenders in the first second; then the mind does never rebel. Why should it rebel if there is blind faith? But it is rare, as I say. Until now I have found nobody capable of doing it. . . ."**

COUPLET:

"It is a strange thing with Love, that it is the Beloved who merges into the lover."

EXPLANATION: the lover is imperfect, so it is God, who is Almighty and Perfect, who merges into the Soul. . . .

15th January

WHEN I LEFT PUSHPA yesterday afternoon, suddenly in the street, I felt funny; it was as if I had a bang on my head, no pain, but a sort of emptiness inside my head. I kept walking, reflecting what could it be. . . .

Arrived at his place . . . to my surprise he was sitting in the door passage. He seemed to be waiting for me, stood up as soon as he saw me entering the gate, and spat out something. I thought that he will go in now, as he so often did when I arrived, but he sat down again. It was drizzling and not a pleasant place to sit, for it was draughty. I sat down on a chair opposite, and told him about an article in the Reader's Digest; it seems that the astronomers have discovered something like God. So many and such enormous vibrations in space were detected by the radio telescopes, and nobody can account for them or explain them reasonably. But his face was averted, and I was not sure that he listened. His expression was as if carved of stone. Told him how funny I felt. No answer. I wondered if something was being done to my mind, and he was sitting there just to be sure everything was O.K. Could easily be, but it is possible that he expected some reaction from me and wanted to test me. It was the mind, of course; every impression goes through the mind; perhaps he switched it off too quickly? But that could not be; he makes no mistakes. He knows exactly what he is doing. . . .

Went home very early, felt tired and worn out. Slept well. Woke up about four in the morning, was full of peace; the mind did not give the least trouble, but there seemed to be no feeling of love. But He was not far, even if not quite near. Prayed for faith without understanding. . . .

It was raining all night. And when I went there in the morning it was still raining. So, I sat in the doorway. It was cold and draughty. My feet were wet. For one moment I began to think whether it was right, whether it is friendly, to let an elderly woman sit in a cold doorway on a rainy day? What does it matter to him to let me sit in the room, and if he does not want me to sit in his room, could I not sit in the veranda encircling the courtyard? But I stilled the mind quickly. A dead body, if it is put in the rain, gets wet. If it is put in the sun, it is scorched. Can it protest? It cannot. Can I protest? I cannot. When in London, suppose I have to wait for a train in a draughty place—will I be resentful because of it? I wouldn't like it, that is sure, but very probably I would think that is one of those things . . . it cannot be helped . . . so here too. If he wishes me to sit in the cold, I will sit. I belong to Him, I am His thing . . . what He will do with me will be. The Guru is only His representative.

And so I sat there full of peace, full of vibrations, and then I went home.

And last night I was thinking that He loves me. He was in my heart. And as He loves me, so He loves others, all the Souls. For Him there is no difference. Not even a little. And suddenly I understood why Guruji said that one has to be careful how one speaks to people; they will not take it; they will not understand. If it is a Christian, then one has to take him the Christian way; if he is a believer in Hindu philosophy, I will not say anything against Karmas, or Shiva, or the like. Gently, by and by, things are infused . . . one has to lead His sheep gently . . . no matter by what road, one must get them nearer. And I understood how much humility is in this attitude: it does not matter what I think right, what I believe: it is THEY who matter only, and I am nowhere . . . I am only the instrument of His. And so full of peace I was. Deeply.

16th January

HE CAME OUT YESTERDAY AFTERNOON for a quarter of an hour. Sat in the doorway for a short while. Didn't speak to me. Went home early; it was cold and damp. This morning it was foggy and damp. I sat outside his door. And I pray and I pray all the time, day and night, for faith without understanding. I don't want to judge, or think, or understand . . . I want faith, please, help me to have faith, endless faith; I cannot afford to waste time any longer. Time is so short . . . it is running out. And that I should accept gladly whatever he inflicts upon me . . . that I should not be resentful, because I belong to Him.

It was so cold. I was freezing. Men went inside. The engineer came; he also went inside. Could not bear it any longer. Went home. Was crying when walking down the street . . . he does not care . . . Guru Maharaj, my dear, it hurts so much! Why does it hurt so? So deeply lonely I am. He is not with me, and there is no nearness with Guru Maharaj either . . . but I can pray. While I can pray, all is well . . . so give me, oh, Merciful, please, give me the strength to bear it. It hurts so very much! And I cried and I cried at home . . . oh, the feeling of loneliness . . . forsaken by God and by men. . . . My God, You who love me as You love Your Creation, help me to bear it without resentment! It is so difficult; I will never make it I fear. . . . It is really better to go back to England. Here this situation is unbearable sometimes. There are times when I am happy, but never often and never completely.

After I had a good cry, I made myself go there again and sat in the chair before the door for about one hour. Had to go home because I was trembling with cold. But I was not resentful anymore. . . .

17th January

DURING THE CONVERSATION this morning he said that I had no real interest whatsoever. The interest has been created.

"You were disgusted with life after the death of your husband; everything seemed empty, not worth living for. You had enough money, so you decided to become a Theosophist, to travel and to lead a simple life. Simple life is nothing. Many people lead simple lives. They are good people, but it is nothing. If you were really interested, you would not have wasted seven years. If interest is there, the opportunity comes; it is done like this. . . . But you took time, you came to India, you met L., the time has come, you came here. And here, if you were really interested, truly interested, you would not have wasted one year as you did. . . ."

I was full of astonishment and wonder, because HE WAS RIGHT. Here we are: If we want God as a drowning man wants air, we would realize Him in a split-second—it is said in one of the *Upanishads*. But how could I have wanted the Realization if I didn't believe in God? Belief had to be created. Interest, great desire, had to be created. Nothing is mine then? "Why me, and not somebody else, for instance?" I asked.

"This question everybody wants to know. People will come here for the *Bandhara*, three thousand of them. Anybody can ask; why me and not somebody else? This question I cannot answer; you will know it one day. Some people are guided, some are not. . . . He is so kind . . ." and he fell silent, his eyes veiled in Samadhi.

In the afternoon I asked questions on the same subject. I wanted to be clear what he had said. But the essence was that I was not really interested.

"You were disgusted; your life is clearly spread like that before me," he said with a smile. "Interest was created. If the desire is keen, you will realize, there is no doubt," he said, because I told him that I swore a big oath this afternoon to know the Truth one day, the Absolute Truth, and will have no rest until I achieve it. . . .

Was thinking of it for a long time and in the night too. Interest was created. Love was created. What is mine? Nothing, so it seems!

"At certain stages you must make an effort, otherwise you cannot progress. This is the ONLY effort . . . but otherwise . . . He is so kind to us. And we are forgiven and forgiven endlessly, even if we don't ask for forgiveness . . . for He is Love and Kindness." He smiled tenderly. The sun was blazing; we were sitting outside; he was very kind and talked much to me.

18th January
KEEP THINKING MUCH. Even interest was created . . . and I keep

praying for blind faith, without understanding, on the Road of Complete Sacrifice. . . .

19th January

HAVE THE LETTER FOR THE BANK with me. He said that he had no time to see me about it in the morning because many people were there, but he will discuss it with me in the afternoon. Arrived about half past three, thinking I would be able to see him before anybody arrives, but he was inside talking; I waited under the mango tree. He did not call me, and when he came out he sat talking politics, and I was thinking what a waste of time it seemed; it will take him only five minutes to discuss it with me.

Such an important letter and he says that he has no time . . . are politics more important? Seems so illogical to our Western mentality. Finally he got up and told me to give him the letter; he will give it to me tomorrow. It was dark already. I went home. No time . . . he never will have time for me . . . I had better make up my mind never to be resentful whatever happens. I am on the road of complete sacrifice. Self-annihilation in the Teacher is the complete sacrifice. Fana-fi-Sheikh . . . yes. . . .

20th January

THE MIND WAS PUT ON in full force in the morning. And the self. But as soon as they began to trouble me, I prayed. If I can pray, I will succeed, I said to him as he came out early. If separation is created and I cannot pray, then the trouble will begin.

"Pray," he said, "pray always. Help is always there."

"From certain people no complete sacrifice is demanded; but this does not seem to be my way."

"Spiritual life is sacrifice always; sacrifice is most essential. Complete obedience and faith . . . otherwise one gets nothing."

Then the black Guru came and he was talking to him.

"Lord Buddha was A Great Sacrifice," and he smiled tenderly. Later he was saying: **"First God created *Devas*, and *Devas* kept wondering why He had created the world. Man has been created last, and when this happened the *Devas* understood that the world has been created for man. Man is the leader. When I say leader, I mean that he has all the possibilities which can be developed to the utmost degree. On a certain point on the way of *Devayan*, *Devas* have to stop; they cannot go further, but man can. No limit for man. I said to you, man is the leader. Leader is a wide term . . . but don't**

think *Devas* are low; some are very much higher than man. All respect to the Devas! You must not think that they cannot realize God; but there is a limit for them; no limit is for man . . . man is the king; he has in him the germ of everything."

Later he said: "Book knowledge is useful to some extent. There are books written by enlightened people, scriptures, and so on. On the level of the mind you will accept this and reject that. But to verify what is written, one has to realize. Then one will *know* the Truth absolutely, only then. But until this happens, one has to be content with books."

"Are all men alike for you?" I wanted to know.

"All men are alike," he said slowly; he was in Samadhi nearly all the time. I looked at him. He really had a thousand faces . . . how cruel he can look, his eyes terrible, unseeing eyes. . . . Or he can look so young, like tonight . . . or Chinese, or Tibetan, or non-human . . . a *devic* quality about him.

The mind was so restless this morning, darting here and there, trying to get out of hand. I prayed. And prayed . . . and when sitting with Pushpa, suddenly there was such an unbearable longing. . . . Then I knew that the trouble will be over; he switched on love again. . . . As the monkey trainer has his monkeys, so do you have human beings in your hand, I thought.

And in the evening I was serene, looking at the light playing around him. No trouble with the mind.

21st January

LIKE FISH IN WATER so are we in Thee . . . nothing is mine. You have been kind to me, so Bhai Sahib said. And why to me? I will know one day. Like fish in water . . . and I was thinking how wonderful it is to reach this state of consciousness when all human beings are alike. The same as for God. For God is with them, and for Him all creation is one.

The sheets of my bedding were so fragrant this morning. I kept smelling them. There must have been much fragrance in the air in the night. Nights are so sweet nowadays . . . the sky was of a transparent bottomless quality, and such a stillness at sunrise. Golden clouds stood motionless as if in wonder suspended in the blue.

He came out with his mala, so I knew that I can speak to him. I came to sit nearer to him as soon as Chowdrie had left. The others chatted with his brother.

"I want to ask you something in connection with the man who came yesterday," I began, and he looked inquiringly at me with a smile. "Must watch you, how you do it with people; perhaps I will be doing it soon, very soon, maybe in May!" He listened, his head slightly sideways doing his mala slowly.

"Now, that man who came, you let him speak, and when you did not want to listen, you went in Samadhi. He is after the *Shastras* (sacred books); you did not correct him at all. For how long has he been your disciple?"

"He is not; he comes only for the last eight years."

"But eight years are a long time!" I exclaimed.

"But he comes only occasionally; he respects me, that's all."

"When is the time to tell the people one's own view?"

"I won't be such a fool to tell everybody: I speak as I am directed."

"This is a clue!" I was pleased with the explanation. One speaks only according to the inspiration.

"Here is another question: You said that the human being is the leader and the king; how is it that he is so ugly and full of sins? Surely God had created the human being pure and beautiful."

"It is only you who see all men ugly," he began, but I interrupted: "But he is full of sins! You cannot deny it! And I don't exclude myself; we are full of sins! How did man become so full of sins?"

"Have you ever seen anything in nature that equals man?"

"No, I did not, and if I compared men with anything else, it was always to the advantage of man!"

"Men are completely free to do what they like—free to do good or evil, to do any Karmas they like." I looked at him profoundly puzzled. He lowered his eyes and continued to pray.

"Yees," I said slowly, "but you criticized one of the women who came to you; you said that she is full of sins, so you don't approve, and still you say that men are free to do as they like?" . . .

"Free, yes, quite free. But because they are free, why should they choose evils? They can choose the opposite, can they not?"

"How simple!" I exclaimed. I was pleased again. "How simple you have explained it!"

"It is simple, very simple, and really quite natural," he said softly.

"And why is it that the human being is inclined to evils naturally; how is it that evils are much easier to do than the opposite?"

"Because his *Indrias* are made of the substance of the world and are attracted to worldly things." He said it very slowly, looking outside the window. Well, more clear than that, I thought, and was pleased once more. He was still praying.

"One more question," I said tentatively: "how will I know that it will be inspiration which will make me say something, or just the desire to speak, to express my own opinion?" He closed his eyes. "No answer?" I said softly. He shook his head, ever so slightly, still praying.

"Never mind, thank you," I said, and a little later I showed him the letter. "See the signature; my hand did not tremble. With this signature I was made a beggar! Never again will I have this amount of money, and if I should have, I will give it away as you do . . . I will be like you, from now on. . . ." His eyes closed, and his face was tender. His lips moved in silent prayer. My hand did not tremble, but I must confess that I felt strange, just the same. Never in my life was I without anything.

I challenged my mind to worry, and what do you know, it refused to worry! It just sat put and did not worry. Why? I wanted to know. It does not matter, said the mind, it will be all right. . . .

Was something done to the mind, or is it the result of all the events connected with training?

He was singing a couplet, then he explained it in Hindi. **"He will translate it for you very well,"** he said pointing to a man in Samadhi.

"He is asleep; surely he could not have heard when you were singing it."

"He is in a spiritual sleep from time to time."

"Can you not translate it for me, just to give an idea? It was something beautiful; one could gather that from the reaction of your audience." He nodded smilingly and continued to speak Hindi. Some more people came; I waited. But he greeted them and began a new conversation. He doesn't want to tell me, I thought, and was frustrated again, nearly cried. But looking at his smiling, friendly face, I reflected that after all it matters little. If it is his will, never mind. I will always be sacrificed to all the Alaci Baba's, Tulsi Ram's, Sitla Prasad's . . . I will always be the last. Does not complete sacrifice mean exactly that?

Later I told him this. He listened silently. Now it does not matter so much as before. He nodded ever so softly and began to speak to others very deliberately, as if to say that the listening session was over. I silently looked at him. Politics were discussed at length. I left to post the letter about twelve, when he stood up, took the towel and made a slight sign with the head which was the signal to go.

46

Quite Poor, Nothing is Left

WHEN LEAVING THE TINY POST OFFICE opposite our compound where I lived, I felt strangely light. Quite poor, nothing left, I thought. Stood for a moment in the street; it was a clear day full of fragrance as they are in this season now. What do I feel? I looked inside myself. I felt light, no worry, felt free. Am I not one of His creatures, completely His? Like fish in water are we in Thee, like birds in the air will I depend on Thee. Interest was given, love was given. You took everything . . . now I have to rely on You. It will make a great, a big psychological difference. It is good that it should be so . . . seventy-five percent I have forgotten, the other twenty-five percent I don't believe in anymore, and the new knowledge is sporadic, uncertain, from the point of view of the mind. The mind cannot rely on it, for it is and it is not. Nothing is sure, nothing definite. So the mind remains confused. And very insecure.

"Before, when you didn't explain, I was in despair. It matters much less now." He smiled. It is now as if there was a secret understanding between him and me on a certain level. And explain I cannot.

22nd January, 1963

LAST NIGHT I PRAYED but there were no words . . . just love, immense, no end of it. Did not pray for anything as of late. Stillness there was and a strange kind of happiness, but no words at all. And love, and love, and love, non-ending and infinitely serene. He did something to my mind last night. I felt funny just as I felt last week when coming from Pushpa. All was swimming around; the world seemed a strange, incredible dream, very unreal and very shaky. But when I left his place about six, I walked in the street all right. Nothing seemed to be wrong. There was a new heartbeat. He is probably doing something to my heart *Chakra*.

23rd January

YES, SOMETHING IS BEING DONE. The heart was beating tocsin strongly, and I was convinced that I wouldn't be able to sleep. But I slept, woke

415

up only twice in the night, and the heartbeat was normal again. Before falling asleep the mind was restless, no trouble, but it jumped here and there and interfered with prayers. Could not pray for a long time and gave up.

"Do you remember on the 20th of January you put me in this terrible trouble last year?" He smiled gently.

"People accuse me of so many things; you can also accuse me of that."

"Oh, sure I know now, it is all due to myself, but you know what I mean." He smiled kindly.

"Is it true that the heart *Chakra* is as large as the diameter of the chest? It seems to me that I can hear it spin in the stillness of the night. I can hear it even with my physical ears."

"Wrong conception," he said sternly. **"Heart *Chakra* has no limit, and to hear it spin like that is wrong again."**

"But is the heart *Chakra* not in the Etheric?"

"I told you it is unlimited; it is as large as the Universe," he said and looked annoyed. I was very astonished. What on earth did he mean by: **"As large as the Universe?"** He smiled a weary smile: **"You talk too much, you know. People talk and talk. All of them. For thirty years some of them are still talking . . . and the idea behind it is: 'How clever am I, how well I have understood,' and the Master thinks how backward he is. Mental things have no value for me. Luckily, most of the time I don't listen."**

How right he is, I thought; I too speak because I want to show off my cleverness, and my little self is full of pride. . . .

"Only in silence things can be assimilated."

"But you, at least you understood what your Rev. Guru told others; I sit here and just look, cannot catch a thing of what is said!"

"But no spiritual talk is going on; if you understand or not, what value has it?"

"Sometimes you explain details about your System and other things which would interest me and be of value for my book," I said getting desperate.

"But those things are infused, never, never are they explained! L. too had written many things in twelve years; what value have they? None! She does not understand our System and Trica philosophy became a great obstacle." He moved his chair into the sun. **"It feels damp in the shade,"** he remarked. He sat now near the wall in the sun. How completely unearthly he looked; in full sunshine his garment looked so white as if imbued with light from within . . . and the face unreal, so full of light, it radiated a kind of golden glow.

I began to cry. "I cannot do right; whatever I try to do, it all seems wrong. I understand: from now on I won't speak to you anymore if this is the only way!"

"But you cannot do it!" he exclaimed, "you are not the only one! Others speak too, and they are Indians, the same culture as mine. It has nothing to do with your Western mentality as you think; human beings want to speak!"

"I don't care what others do," I said crying, "I HAVE to do it!"

"But won't be able to! One cannot force those things! Let time come, go on as you have before," he looked puzzled now.

"No, Bhai Sahib, if you say something, it is always for a deep purpose; it means that at least I have to try. I will. If I will be defeated, at least I tried."

"I hinted it to you again and again that it is the only way?"

I nodded in assent. Could not speak, was crying.

"I hinted so often and you failed to understand. If you would have listened, you would have made such a jump forward," he smiled with great kindness, looking at me sideways.

"I am such a fool; I wasted so much time!" I cried bitterly. Felt absolutely defeated.

He fell silent, then spoke to the servant passing with a shopping bag.

"One day you have said that the Teacher is the best friend."

"I am not your friend!" He interrupted irritably.

"But in the Sufi terminology he is called the Friend." I was amazed.

"God is called the Friend, not the Teacher. How can I be your friend? Wrong conception, completely," he emphatically declared. "I am your taskmaster! Here lies the effort: to reconcile the Teacher as a person and the relationship with the Teacher which does not belong to this world. This is an effort, but Divine things are effortless. Did you notice how you always accuse me and never yourself?" He laughed ironically but not unkindly.

"So, I alone am to blame?"

"Of course!" he laughed; "why don't you try to be absorbed in me? In the Teacher? To surrender means COMPLETE sacrifice. My wife and children, when they think that I am an ordinary man, they come down; when they think that I am something more, they are on a high stage, on the highest stage," he said, watching my reaction.

"So I have to pray for blind faith and nothing else!". . .

"Blind faith, what nonsense is that again!" He nearly shouted impatiently. **"Never, never, blind! One has to test the Teacher thoroughly, and when he is tested and one is satisfied, then one has faith, but never blind!"**

"Blind faith in Him?" I ventured; because some days ago he DID say that one must have blind faith. . . .

"He is far away," he said quickly; **"why don't you try to realize yourself first, become one with the Master?"**

"From now on I stop speaking," I cried more and more . . . what confusion was in my mind! What is true? What is false? Where is he leading me?

"Not speaking is not enough; all the rest matters too. If the mind cannot be stilled, it is better to speak. Continue to do as you did until now . . . time will come. . . ." I wept.

"Now you have said that you are not my friend; but such things happen somewhere . . . such nearness, how on earth can I reconcile it?"

He looked at me, his eyes were deep with compassion. **"Love alone would be quite enough suffering, would it not?"**

I cried more. . . . He watched me silently.

"Reasons, reasons, you cannot progress by reasons, you know...."

"Oh, I don't try to find excuses, but it is not easy when the mind is not working, and the suffering is great, and you deliberately try to confuse, to perplex me." He said nothing, only looked at me severely.

24th January

LAST NIGHT AS USUAL politics were discussed. I sat. Went home early, when he went inside to have his tea.

In the night the mind was restless, but no definite thoughts about anything. He said yesterday: **"If the mind is restless, it picks up every current from the atmosphere."**

25th January

THE MIND WAS LIKE A SYLVAN POOL, dark and still. Like a shady pool in the woods. Full of secret thoughts. As if something was eluding me, hiding from me.

26th January

HE LOOKED AT ME OFTEN and yesterday he turned from time to time to give me a brief look. This he never did before. You are testing me, I thought, but I was quite determined not to speak. The mala of his Rev. Guru Maharaj was sliding slowly through his fingers. He looked very friendly. For a while he was silent.

"What talk was going on with Mr. Chowdrie?"

"Nothing of much importance, about cleanliness and hygiene."

He sat there smiling all the time. I was silent, answering only the direct questions. Vibrations were not many and I felt full of peace.

In the evening he was talking as usual to Chowdrie and others; *Prasad* was distributed because of a sort of purification rite of the Hindus: the hair of his daughter's baby boy was cut ritually.

I took the *Prasad* home and had it with my tea before going to bed.

27th January

PREPARATIONS FOR THE *BANDHARA* are going on. The marquee has been put up. While it was being done, we were sitting under the mango tree. From time to time I could see his profile when he was turning his head, for I was sitting against the fence behind him. In the afternoon many people began to arrive; I hid behind the nimbu tree because Babu and the boys played cricket in front of the marquee. Then I remembered that I had left my dinner in the kitchen. Fearing that the cat may come in and upset the saucepan as it did once, went home for a moment to put it away.

When I returned, a man came out from the room where he sat with many people. He said Guruji wanted to know if there was some trouble with me. Not at all, I explained; I went home because I forgot to put away my food. He went inside to deliver this message. Later a young man brought me some *Prasad.* He obviously told him to take some out for me sitting alone under the mango tree. It is quite a change, I reflected. Such peace was in me that I cannot describe it, since this morning . . . tremendous, eternal peace. Later he came out and many of us were sitting on chairs facing him. He was talking in Hindi. Much later, in the dark when nearly all had gone he asked:

"Are you all right?"

"I am well, thank you; but why do you think that I may not be well?"

"As a human being I inquired how you were, that's all."

"But you are not well; you are coughing again." I was noticing that he was breathless a little, and he looked tired.

"Yes, but not much; many people came, many ladies; I had to do my duty; they come to see me so I have to speak to them."

After a while he began to sing softly. His face was partly lit by a street lamp; his voice was a little hoarse (he has a cold, I thought), yet was sweet to listen to . . . it was lovely to hear him sing . . . concentrating on his voice, so peaceful, gave me a strange happiness. It was a song of Mira, and he translated:

"I will mold myself as my Spiritual Guide wants me to be. I want to become less than the dust at his feet. The physical body is nothing, so let it remain as a dust at his feet."

The word "impossible" does not exist in the vocabulary of lovers, he said once. And I see how help is given, and one is driven in the right direction all the time.

28th January

WHEN HE CAME OUT his face was ashen; it was clear to me that either he was not well or very tired.

"I had a vomiting condition in the night," he said as soon as he sat down.

"Oh it is because of the *Bandhara*; such forces are here that we are all like drunk."

"Perhaps," he smiled. In fact I was sitting there in the morning blown through with *Shakti*. My head was spinning. . . .

Later, commenting on a boy who was there and had a sign on his forehead, he said: **"Those signs, moles . . . if they are on the right side of a man and on the left side of a woman, are good. I had this dark sign on my forehead, so had my Rev. Guru Maharaj. That's why I remark on them. On the thorax they are good, but below they are not considered to be good."**

I said that I had one over my right eye; it was removed.

"Yes, I can see the sign left on the lid below the eyebrow. It means that from the worldly point of view, you have not many friends; you lose them. At the beginning they are friends, then . . . nothing!"

"Yes, I had only very few friends in my life."

"And if the sign would have been over the left eye, people would have followed you! But this is from the worldly point of view; we don't believe in such things!"

I told him that I had a sign on my left arm.

"Is it above or below the elbow?" I showed it to him; it was below the elbow, on the forearm. He nodded looking at it.

"Yes. It means if you have wealth, you will not keep it. Mind you, you will have money when you need it, and how much you need it, but it will not remain with you. . . ."

"Bhai Sahib, it means that I would live like you; what a bliss!" He nodded with a serious expression.

"And if you had the same sign above the elbow, it means you would be wealthy; it would not be a good sign for you." ·

47

Bandhara

29th January, 1963

LAST NIGHT I HOPED that he would let me stay until midnight. People were arriving all the time; I could have easily sat somewhere. He was seated on the *dharri* under the canopy and many people were with him. But he sent me away at quarter to eight. I felt so frustrated that I cried. Hated to go when he was standing at the gate greeting new arrivals, and I had to go home alone. Felt so lonely and unhappy, and I cried and cried and prayed.

Decided to remain awake till midnight to see if one feels the difference when the gates of the *Bandhara* are opened. Took some coffee to be sure not to fall asleep. Prayed much for complete surrender. And cried and prayed, and the stars were near and happiness was just around the corner, unreachable for me. . . . My heartbeat was very rapid, too rapid as if in high fever. I was thinking that it was the effect of the vibrations which were really something. Was waiting, lost the sense of time, and all at once the heart went really mad with beating. . . . Good heavens, I thought, I feel funny; so I got up and switched on the light to see what time it was. It was five minutes to midnight. So, it was very true. The vibrations increased immensely; my whole body was affected. Those were the doors of the *Bandhara* which were opened at midnight. Fell asleep soon afterwards.

This morning arrived before eight. The vibrations seemed normal, or nearly. Found a place near the carpet where he would be sitting . . . right in front I sat, to be able to see him well. He came out looking well and dressed smartly, sat down and the meditation began. He went into a deep state almost immediately. The light around him . . . could not stop looking. The vibrations increased and I prayed for complete surrender. *Prasad* arrived in a huge container; he prayed over it, and then it was distributed. Then he just sat there without talking; he obviously did not feel well. About two he asked me if I would like to take my food with everybody, and I answered that I would like very much. He smiled and sent Ramji to arrange for it.

"**I felt not at all well last night; high fever again. Vomiting condition too. Annoying.**" Now I know why the rapid heartbeat last night . . . got his feverish condition. . . . Had my food seated on the floor of the veranda with all the others; the food was served in little earthenware containers placed on the mats in front of us. It was good, simple food cooked by the servants and his wife and the female members of his family. While I was finishing it, he was just coming out. He asked if I liked it, and I said that I enjoyed it very much.

"**Have it here tomorrow too,**" he said kindly, passing by and followed by a crowd.

"**Go home and have a rest and be here about three,**" he said looking back, and disappeared in the doorway.

So I went home, had a rest and was there about quarter past three. Waited sitting there on the *dharri*. About five he came out. I was sitting in front again. He was flushed, feverish obviously, and intoxicated with God. For the first time I saw a Saint when he is full of spiritual intoxication. Wonderful spectacle it is. He sparkled, laughed, talked, sang. My heart stood still for a moment: he looked at me suddenly, and I saw two rays of light coming from his eyes, and this look was like a dagger right into my heart. Disciples massaged his feet while he was talking away. He was singing as I never heard him before. My heart kept beating and beating. I was fascinated. Flushed, lovely, tenderly smiling, he was full of inner fire . . . a Saint intoxicated with God . . . drunk with the *Shakti* (Power) of God.

For the first time I witnessed it, and for the first time I really understood. . . . Such was the love, that I kept having tears in my eyes all the time . . . this smiling expression which is a powerful call . . . a memory from somewhere . . . it makes one shiver for some reason. . . . When I looked up, I saw him still looking at me and I could not bear it, had to close my eyes. The next moment I looked he was laughing and talking to somebody who just came in. Could not help wondering if he did unite my soul with his in the moment he looked at me. . . . For the physical body knows nothing of this happening, so it might well have been. . . .

Stayed until ten in the evening. Then he went inside, his disciples helping him to get up and carrying his blanket. At home I simply dropped into bed and fell asleep immediately. Was very tired somehow. It was probably his tiredness I was getting.

30th January

I WAS THERE ABOUT HALF PAST SEVEN. It was the day of *Samadhi*. Great confusion was reigning. Nobody knew if the truck would be available; rikshaws were standing before the gate; people were milling about. He was invisible yet. I was thinking how great love was, how strong the vibrations. If I could keep this feeling, there could be no trouble with the mind . . . but I knew that it was impossible to keep it up all the time. I never could . . . it will go. But now at this moment it was like a rich, full song . . . difficult to bear the vibrations. The world unreal, but so beautiful. . . .

The truck, a huge one, arrived at last. Everybody filed in. He was standing directing everybody; I did not notice when he came out; saw him only when he was already standing in the street looking like a patriarch, every inch of him full of authority. There seemed to be no room in the truck anymore. The engineer came to me and said that I will travel with Guruji in his car. But somebody called me and I was accommodated in front of the truck near Mr. Chowdrie and a few others, the grandson of his Rev. Guru Maharaj and two old disciples. So I travelled in style, looking at the sunlit road while the truck, full to the brim with people, rattled along the road past the crowded streets, bazaars, factories. Seven miles of it. Then it was gathering speed on the road outside the city; right and left were sugar plantations, maize fields and the usual groups of mango trees in between. Lovely Indian plains so fragrant and so full of bad smells in places, with the sky of this indefinite blue above—how I will miss you when back in England. . . . Many people were already at the *Samadhi*, and it was full of the most dirty children who had left long before us, travelling in a tractor with a trailer. It was fun to see them leave, all gay and happy in holiday mood, trailer overflowing with children, puff-puffing along with a terrible noise of thunder which made the houses around tremble. The fragrance of spring was in the air. How sunlit the white mausoleum was.

He also just arrived in the engineer's car with the members of his family. Slowly he went inside; I was right behind him walking beside his brother. Took my seat nearly opposite him so that I should be able to see him well. Looked at him at his father's grave and prayed fervently, prayed hotly. . . . You who are generous, You who are merciful, help me to mold myself into the shape my Rev. Guru

Maharaj wants me to be. . . . My heart was so full; cold showers were running up and down my spine. He was transfigured with inner light, was talking to people, greeting everyone; many of the old disciples of his father were there; the graves of his father and mother were covered with flowers . . . yellow marigolds, mostly, and red roses, and no end of garlands. *Prasad* was put before him. Then he prayed. Children were running about as usual, but today they did not matter somehow; I was not quite here, my consciousness was somewhere else. . . . Could not help looking at him so infinitely lovely, the face so still, so deep with devotion. Behind him, all the old disciples, his sons, his brother, and in the background stretching away in the distance the sunlit plains, the groups of mango trees in the azure haze. I will not see that anymore for years, but for some reason it did not matter too much . . . things of external value; there were other problems haunting me now, more deep and more pressing problems. What was going inside me was new life . . . something of lasting value, and things of this world had little to do with it; the mind could only look on helplessly, not understanding much. By reflection new values of things came into the mind, but like a distorted reflection in a defective looking-glass. . . .

When *Prasad* was being distributed, I took two red roses from the grave of his father. Put them into the pocket of my coat. Red fragrant roses from the grave of a Great Sufi . . . they had a tired fragrance of dying roses, a smell so sweet and full of melancholy. And the plains were so full of sunshine, so radiant that day that it seemed absurd that something could die and decay.

When everybody was occupied with *Prasad* and he with blessing children who were brought to him for this purpose, I knelt down before the grave of his father, pressing my forehead against the cool smooth marble. At your feet I am, oh Father of my Rev. Guru Maharaj, I thought, help me, oh help me to be molded as he wants me to be. I cried and had difficulty to get up. Nobody noticed me except Babu who was standing to my left, and I noticed a long, thoughtful look, then he turned away. He was still blessing children and talking to people. Nobody saw me praying—incense was blowing into my face, the incense holder was just beside me. Still felt the cool of the marble stone on my forehead. He was writing something on a slate which somebody placed before him, then more children were brought to him. I had tears in my eyes all the time. Dear, dear, Bhai Sahib . . . so much love was there, so much longing. . . . Our truck left soon; he was still talking to some of the disciples. I was half-suspended in between two seats, squeezed in between men and children, most uncomfortable, bumping about, thrown about, but I did not mind a bit. I was as in another world . . . the whole body vibrating to some kind of inner rhythm, heart full to the brim with this burning Love. . . . The greatest, the most terrible Love, will I survive it? In London? And I was sure I would. . . .

At his place I sat and waited near his door. Children were fighting on the carpet as usual making a lot of dust. But it did not matter, and I did not dislike them as I usually did. He came out and sat down reclining on his carpet. I was sitting slightly sideways looking at him. He was rather still, spoke quietly with people, then began to hum a song. Chowdrie was making a speech. About two he asked if I had a meal. I said that with his permission I would like to have mine at the same time as he would have his.

"No, it will not suit you; I will have my meal after three, not before." So, he called out to someone and I went inside. Had my meal sitting on a tachat, had very little as I could not eat. While I was eating he came past me; I stood up.

"I have my food when everybody else has finished," he said. I answered that I would not have minded. He made an indefinite gesture towards my food to denote that I should eat and passed on. I saw him standing in the courtyard talking to some women and children. I finished and went home. Had a rest. The vibrations were such that I could hardly remain in the lying position. The heart was thundering along; I wondered if it could be affected by such activity. But I remembered that he once had said that Sufis get a very strong heart because of the vibrations which sweep through it constantly, and it gets used to that.

Went back about half past four. Had to wait a little, taking my seat right in front. He came out about five, and sat down. Somebody was singing beautifully, just before he came out, a young man with a lovely voice. He sang with deep devotion. The songs were continued for a while even when he came out. The advocate came, and important disciples, Brahmins, old followers of his father. They all made speeches, and *Sannyasi* too with his croaking voice. Then Guruji began to speak. He was not intoxicated as the day before, but very lively just the same, and he was explaining much. I distinctly saw light rays flashing from his eyes. He was in a belligerent mood; he picked out a disciple and ordered him to speak, but as soon as the man began, he obviously picked out some fault and began to tell him off. He asked questions and objected to every answer the disciple

gave; the disciple got hotter and hotter; I had the feeling that he was
sizzling; he tried to answer but was talked down every time
mercilessly. At one moment Guruji must have challenged him on the
question of *asana* and *pranayam*, because he sat in the kneeling *asana*
and demonstrated his way of *pranayam*. I saw him taking a short
breath and then becoming still, not breathing for quite a while.
Minutes ticked away, nobody stirred. The wind flapped gently the
canvas of the marquee. I was looking at him; his eyes were closed; he
was not breathing at all. He was more beautiful than ever. The Great
Yogi, I thought, but I began to be worried; he still was not breathing.
How long will he hold out? He is not well after all, and he is old, and
he had fever last night. . . . I hope nothing will happen to him. . . .
Ten minutes must have passed. More. . . . One could hear a pin
drop. Everyone seemed carved out of stone. Finally after what
seemed an eternity to me, he opened his eyes and said to the disciple:

"**Go on, do it!**" The disciple began to talk rapidly, shifting
uneasily, and Bhai Sahib lowered his head slightly, breathed out a
short, purifying breath with a sniff, and only then began to breathe
normally. All this looked so effortless, so natural, and I remembered
that somebody was telling me a few months ago that when he was
young he could hold his breath for half an hour.

He was talking now, telling the assembly that it was wrong to
mislead people. Obviously the disciple in question was teaching
wrong ways of *pranayam* or something of that sort. I know he is a bit
proud; he has been Bhai Sahib's disciple for the last thirty years, and
he has disciples of his own. Then Guruji was explaining something to
an old man who obviously had many doubts. He said at one time—
and this I understood though it was in Hindi—pointing into my
direction, he said:

"**She is here over one year, and she gets very little. Do you think
the guru gives so quickly? You have to attend** *Satsang* **for a long
time.** *Satsang* **is necessary; you have to come and sit here; in** *Satsang*
**you will achieve everything. If you want to fly, you cannot; but if
you pay the price for a plane ticket, you can. The price is the effort;
you have to make an effort, and effort is made by** *Satsang*.**"

I remembered that in his Guru's place he had to sit in the most
dusty place which was never swept. Everybody was commenting on
that.

"**He was testing us, for we are Hindus, and it is hard for a Hindu to
sit in a place considered impure. And we did not even notice it; you
have to sacrifice the smaller thing for the greater.**" This was the

answer I got when I was telling him about the conditions in his garden, and the dirt the family of Tulsi Ram was making everywhere.

"You may go home now," he said turning in my direction. Just at this very moment I was thinking myself that it is getting late and I had better go home. I felt tired. All those last days I was weak and headachy, I probably was getting his condition; it was clear to me.

"You may go home; it will be about ten now." I obediently got up and folded my palms in greeting.

"Go and have a rest; you had more than enough, more than enough," he repeated smilingly, looking at me with great kindness.

"Only Hindi was spoken. Nothing of what has been said today will be explained to you. But you have it all in your heart; not in your mind, but in your heart."

Two disciples were massaging his feet. I knelt down rapidly and touched his feet, my heart was so full with gratitude.

"No, no" he said quickly, and his disciples smiled. I got up and went immediately. At home I slept like a log. Till nearly seven.

31st January

IN THE MORNING HE DID NOT COME OUT. I was sitting with the grandson of his Rev. Guru Maharaj, and the grandson of the Guru of his father; children were fighting on the carpet making too much dust. Babu told me that they will arrange a music program tonight because of the *mundan* (the ceremony of the hair-cutting) of Guddu and his baby sister, the children of Durghesh. The vibrations were very strong; though the gate of the *Bandhara* was closed at midnight, it did not seem to have affected the vibrations. Left about eleven, had a good rest. Went there about four. He was standing outside with people and came towards me. His face was yellow, and he walked like a drunken man.

"How are you?" he asked, and I said that I was well, but he was not, it was very visible.

"Oh, I am all right, nothing much wrong with me, but the physical body is tired." He went inside.

I at first sat outside but, such was the noise and the dust so many fighting children were making, that I went behind the house near the nimbu tree near his room, to hide there from the dust. The courtyard was full of women singing and drumming the traditional songs which are sung by the female members of the family when the *mundan* ceremony was performed or a child is born. But such was the dust that I went home. Virendra told me that the program will not begin before six. I was a bit resentful, felt so neglected; there is no room for me to even sit. Oh, fool, why are you resentful? Don't you know that you will be sacrificed ALWAYS?

Began to write into my diary when at home. But had no peace, wanted to go back. The desire gradually became so strong that I obeyed and went. He was sitting outside on a chair with Mr. Chowdrie, talking. I took my seat opposite. I understood why the feeling was so strong to go there. He was outside and it was like a call. A great vibration started suddenly in my brow *Chakra*. A strong powerful vibration it was, going on and on and creating a special type of headache, radiating from between the eyebrows. I was reflecting that my brow *Chakra* was activated, the *Chakra* from where orders are issued, and also received. He said once that with ladies it is not done as a rule, but sometimes an exception is made. I kept touching my forehead from time to time, but he misinterpreted my gesture and said at one moment:

"You had better go home and have a rest, because I feel very much tired tonight. If you sit here for a long time, you will get it too." I told him that I felt tired anyhow all the past days, and please, may I remain for the music program. He made an indefinite gesture which I interpreted as a permission to stay. The music began. It was performed by local young men, some of them really good at Tabla and Sitar. I will miss the Indian classical music when back in London. I looked at him so weak and so pale and was wondering how long he will live . . . not very much longer, I thought, if his health does not improve. He is very weak and cannot recover properly. He got up about a quarter past ten declaring that he is going to have a hot drink and then a rest. I went home too. At home I distinctly heard the songs from the microphones in his garden and was thinking that he cannot have much rest; he did not sleep for two consecutive nights, so he had told me, and here they are making such a noise. But I suppose he could not say anything because the *mundan* was celebrated and at any rate he never thinks of himself. . . . He is always the last one. . . . Fell asleep full of peace and deep love. How he enjoyed the music. . . . How lovely he looked when in genuine delight he kept beating time with the music, clicking his fingers with the rhythm, and exclaiming from time to time: **"Wah!"** or **"Bohot sundar!"** which in Hindi means: "Very lovely!" It was a pleasure to look at him. So Oriental, so sincere was his reaction.

48

Took Some of His Hair

DECIDED LAST NIGHT to go to the bank this morning. The vibrations were terrific. Could hardly hold the mirror, my hands were trembling so much. But in the bank I managed somehow not to behave stupidly and asked all the questions I intended to ask. Went and came by rikshaw and had such a nice rikshaw driver. They usually are not, but he was so nice and gentle he charged me only six annas each way, but I gave him more of course. When the rikshaw stopped in front of his gate he was not in the garden, but I knew that he will come out to inquire why I wasn't there this morning. He did in fact do so after I was there not more than five minutes. Told him that I went to the bank and asked if I could speak to him before I forget what the bank official told me; my mind was not working too well, such were the vibrations. . . . So we stood under the mango tree; I could hardly stand before him. Fancy how I cannot stand in front of him; I feel like fainting all the time, my knees give way, and I can hardly talk so breathless I get. . . . I gave him the information I received about the postal orders from abroad, the money I can take with me and so on. Then we sat down for a short while. He wanted to know how the *Bandhara* was for me. I said that it was terrific; even the physical body suffered.

"Yes," he nodded slowly and seriously. **"This is the second time you have had the benefit of the *Bandhara*; the first time you did not understand. . . ."**

"It is not so much the question of understanding; even now I don't understand, but last time I was full of trouble, you remember . . . it made a barrier. All I knew then was that you were so transfigured, so beautiful, that I looked and could not help looking, and the vibrations were tremendous but that was all. . . ."

"Yes," he nodded seriously, **"yes, that was it."**

"May I ask a small question?" He nodded, looking at his shoes. "Do you transmit something through your eyes?"

"From every point of the body one transmits; it is not done deliberately, one gets used to it, it is automatic."

"But I think sometimes you do it deliberately," and I told him that I saw streams of light flashing from his eyes.

"Yes," he said slowly, "sometimes it happens like that," then he got up. And he went to sit with the two Mohammedans who were sitting near his brother's room. I knew he wouldn't come back. He did not. Panditji appeared and beckoned to me to go away because the marquee was being dismantled and was going to be crashed down. I saluted him from afar and went to Pushpa. In the afternoon he said in passing that he slept a little last night, just a few hours, and felt a bit better. I saw him coming and going; he had no rest at all in the afternoon. People were departing and Durghesh also left her children and husband when I was there. I went home early and fell asleep praying and full of love.

2nd February

WOKE UP EARLY. The peace was absolute. When I began to drink my coffee the vibrations started strongly, and when I was sitting in his garden it was remarkable how strong they were. I prayed in my heart that he should not cut his hair in the afternoon when I am not there. I wanted a bit of his hair. I believe it will protect me when I am away. He was talking to some people who were still here from the *Bandhara*. Half an hour later the barber arrived. Well, my prayer was accepted. When the barber began his work, I watched if some hair fell on the towel the barber covered him with. Yes, some did. When a few larger bits fell off on it, I took a piece of paper, it happened to be the program of the *Bandhara*, stood up and went to his chair:

"May I take those?" I asked, pointing to the bits of hair on his knees. "It will protect me when I am not here." He gave me a brief smile.

"Why do I need to give you the permission?" He asked with half-closed eyes, for little bits of hair were falling from his forehead, covering his face, while the barber was clipping with his scissors.

"So I may take them?" He nodded. I picked up the hair with the paper without touching it with my hands. Put it in my bag. Was very pleased. I wanted it. It will help me. As soon as the hair was cut, he went inside. I offered to pay the barber but he arranged it differently. The barber left. I understood; he wanted it to be a gift; I must not pay; if I would not have taken the hair pieces, perhaps he would have allowed me to pay.

In the afternoon when I came he sat with his family and the few disciples who are still here from the *Bandhara*. I went to sit under the mango tree. All the time I was sitting there I noticed a great activity in the brow *Chakra*. It gave me this special type of headache radiating from the middle of the forehead. An uneasiness was there, the vibration was going strong in it, a sort of ant-creepy feeling was in it too, and a kind of tension. I was watching it with interest. The pain in the head was not much, rather of a nagging sort. I also noticed a vibration to a lesser degree in the throat *Chakra*. In the morning the vibration was in the heart *Chakra* only. Nowadays the vibrations are never in the *Muladhara Chakra* as before. They never are below the waistline. Until dark we were sitting outside. He was dressed very smartly in white narrow Indian style trousers and steel-blue *kurta* in which he was photographed. Two Brahmins came and he stood up:

"Do you prefer to stay here or go home?" I said that I would like to stay if he allows me. So we all went into the room. He looked radiant; he obviously felt better. One of the Brahmins was singing songs of Kabir. He was praising the Brahmin and was exclaiming : **"Wah, wah!"** Later he put both Brahmins in Dhyana. It must have been for the first time, I think, because he behaved just as he did, when in summer, he put one young man in Dhyana. Sitting cross-legged and looking at their higher vehicles, from time to time going off into a deep state. Seven men were in the room—all of them were in Samadhi, some of them were disciples. I watched everything with interest and wondered. . . . New calendars were on the walls. I noticed that the freshly painted wall was badly scratched in one place near the ceiling and I wondered what had caused it. When the Brahmins had left, he chattered for a bit with Happy Babu, then asked him what time it was.

"You can go now," he said. I stood up, folded my palms, and went out without a word. The vibration in between the eyebrows was still strong. Fell asleep tired but happy.

Woke up before five. The peace was eternal. Endless was the love. It was still quite dark, and the constellation of the Great Bear was just above my head. It is seen in the mornings nowadays. The fragrance in the air was so remarkable, so much so that I got up and went outside to investigate from where it came. But in the Ghose's garden was no fragrance whatsoever. It obviously did not come from the garden but from somewhere else. My courtyard was full of it. Never before was love so burning at this time in the morning. It was blazing. Early in the morning, there is usually only a feeling of great longing and deep peace. Never such a current of love. The vibration was not very intense, but the love was really tremendous. Prayed looking to the stars, had such a longing for Him, such a tender longing. The stars were huge and near.

When sitting in his garden could hardly bear the influx of *Shakti*. The body suffered and I had to sit bent forward to be able to bear it more or less. All around everything seemed so strange as if I had never seen it before. . . . When he came out, the vibrations increased, as usual. He began to speak on Buddhism in English and said that the Europeans don't know anything at all and he never knew one who could know something. Even the learned Buddhists who were here could never answer a question properly. The first question one asked them, why did they embrace Buddhism?, they cannot answer.

"I can answer that, but only for myself: I was attracted to Buddhism because I did not believe in God, and the idea of the Eternal Law appealed to me. A personal God seemed a laughable conception; the idea of just a Law, of the Void, was so much more satisfying." A discussion on Buddhism followed of which I can't remember much. The mind did not work and I said so when he asked me a few questions. He laughed.

"Never mind, don't bother," he said kindly.

Later I told him the dream I had before the *Bandhara*: I saw him dressed this time in a dark coat (unusual, because in my dreams he always wears white), and he was telling me in a stern way:

"You must stop using lipstick."

"I know, I know, but I am so used to it," I was answering.

"From now on you must be quite simple," he was saying in my dream.

"Well, and did you stop using it?" he asked.

"No, I still have it as you can see," I said, feeling guilty. "But I did not think that the meaning could be interpreted literally; I thought that it meant something else." He nodded.

"But why use lipstick? If you don't want to attract men, why use it?"

"But we don't do it to attract men; it is a question of habit; if the face is not made up somehow I feel as if I would not be properly dressed."

"I don't ask you to stop using it, but I don't like it. Women in my household don't use it."

"I understand habit is not a good thing; I will stop it from tomorrow."

"No, I don't ask you." But I knew that I will stop it. . . .

Surrender means: everything must go. . . . He looked at me
thoughtfully.

**"Man must be man for his family and his surroundings; man
must be man for his disciples; man must be man to kill the self."** Of
course I understood that he meant the human being, not particularly
the male sex.

One by one they pass, the golden days, full of the fragrance of
spring. . . . How I am going to miss your luminosity, the sky of
delicate blue, the sleeping in the middle of the courtyard, the
sunshine day after day, the smell of the wind coming from afar,
sweeping thousands of miles of plains. . . . How homesick I will be
. . . I know it. . . .

In full moonlight, until seven, we all sat in the evening. He did not
speak to me save once when he remarked that Swamiji was saying
that the flow of Grace was such for a few days, that no matter where
one was, one could feel it. I said that he was quite right. The
vibrations were very strong and I was enveloped in currents of *Shakti*
all the time. And this too I will be missing much, I know. . . .

Translations of the songs the young man had sung during the
Bandhara on the 31st January:

"I leave my boat in Your hands, and it is safe with You. . . .
    You can take it into the stormy waters or in a lagoon, I have
    no claim, I do not ask for anything. . . . You take over, I
    surrender to You, and You guide my boat, wherever You
    like, wherever it needs to be. . . .

"Do not mind my sins, for it is said that whoever comes to You
    trustingly and stands before You in surrender, You will not
    look at his sins. . . . You are like Pars (Pars was something
    which could make iron into gold, but he could not explain
    what Pars really was. I imagine it must be some kind of
    Philosopher's Stone), You make iron into Gold. You make
    into Gold the iron which comes from the temple of knives,
    and also the one with which flesh has been cut. And the
    more iron there is, the more Gold there will be. . . .

"Other sinners may have come to You, but I am the greatest
    sinner, so my qualifications are the greatest. This is how a
    Bhakta speaks to His Lord. . . ."

And a little story from the Scriptures:

A man was walking down a path and suddenly he noticed that
    the earth where he was just standing had a wonderful fra-
    grance.

"Oh dust," he addressed it, "why is it that you smell so nice? Are you a special dust?"

"No," said the dust, "I am just as any other dust, but once a tree stood here and the flowers used to fall to the ground. I was permeated with fragrance, but it is not me, I am just the same dust as any other. . . ."

And he added that "all good things come from the Guru and all the bad things are my own." And he smiled. He was so thin and good looking; on his hip he was carrying a baby—he had six already, he told me, and he is a poor man. They are in a hurry to make children in this land . . . .

3rd February

I FORGOT TO MENTION THAT YESTERDAY sitting there in the morning, the heart went simply crazy. Went inside the room and asked Babu for his watch. I counted 120 pulse beats per minute. He did not believe me so he checked first the right then the left wrist. It was correct. Bhai Sahib wanted to know why I went into the room. Told him that my heartbeat is twice its usual which is a little more than sixty per minute. So I asked Babu to check it; I could not believe it. He laughed. But said nothing. I think he did not notice that today I had no lipstick. He would not notice a thing like this. . . .

4th February

HE WENT OUT EARLY to visit a dying woman and I went home. Had to write letters. Could hardly bear the vibrations, cried with love. Went to his place about three, sat in the shade of the mango tree; he came out about five. Cried all the time there was so much love, so much longing. And could not stop. Feel pale without lipstick. How a habit can imprison us. Of course he noticed that I was crying, and I hoped that he should not think that the mind is giving me trouble. I really did not know why I was crying; it seemed to me because the waves of love were so strong. . . . If the body is well, one can bear it, but if the body is weak or not well, it just becomes too much. . . .

He began to tell me that he went to see a woman but she was dead by the time he arrived. Told him that I did not feel too well and asked him if he had fever, perhaps I am catching his. No, he said he had no fever, but it seems to him that I have. I was shivery in fact, so probably I will have fever. I got a thorn into my toe when walking through the gate into our compound (I wear open sandals), and did not notice that it remained inside—I only felt a prick. Sat there yesterday and had pain, so when I went home I examined it and found that there was something still inside. Could not get it out so deep it was, and it was giving pain, so I fomented it. Got it out at last and it was nearly one quarter of an inch long. Dirt was still inside and those small shivers could mean infection.

"Don't take any notice of me," I said. He was looking at me quietly. "I don't cry because I am worried. . . . Not at all . . . it is . . . you know. . . ." I did not want to mention in front of everybody that there was too much love. He nodded and sent me home soon, and I cried and cried at home and could not bear it. . . . Beloved, I thought, there is so much of it, so deep it is, so tormenting, so endless, cannot bear it. . . . Like a desperate one I cried sitting in the kitchen having my meal; the tears were dropping into it; it tasted salty. Then I stopped, fell asleep after having fomented my foot; it didn't look too bad, only the toe was a bit inflamed. Fell asleep with such a longing for Him. Had a peaceful night.

Woke about four. The heart was going like mad. Such was the beat that the whole body was vibrating from head to foot. The stars of the Great Bear above my head were huge and shimmering like diamonds, winking.

Got up, had a cup of coffee, felt hungry suddenly. Fell asleep.

5th February

IN THE MORNING I BROUGHT THE LETTER with me which he said he will look into. Many people were sitting. Plenty of talk was going on. *Sannyasi* with his horrible croaking voice was getting on my nerves. Tulsi Ram was smelling like a goat. Began to pray. Help me to have faith. . . . Be merciful with me. . . . Prayed because it seemed to me that the mind wanted to take over and give trouble, the love seemed less. So I prayed and prayed and the mind had no chance . . . it did not trouble me. I waited for him to see the letter but he kept the *Sannyasi*, and when he wanted to take leave, he engaged him in a conversation and encouraged everybody to talk a lot. He is testing me. . . . Finally his wife came out telling him that his bath was ready. He took the letter from me, read it, nodded.

"It is all right," he said, **"I am going inside to have my bath."** I went home. Here we are, I was thinking. No use to be irritated, he WILL keep doing it. I will always be sacrificed to every man with smelly feet, to every *Sannyasi* with a horrid voice, to every Tulsi Ram. . . . I am on the way of sacrifice and should be really grateful for the opportunity instead of being resentful and irritated. Yes, grateful for the opportunity. . . . This was it. . . . And I felt light, and I felt good suddenly, as if a light bulb was switched on in my mind. Grateful to him for doing his duty, grateful always. . . . And I felt deep peace. . . .

In the afternoon the vibrations were terrific when he came out. Sat there bending forward and pressing both hands crosswise over my heart. It seems to help a bit. He does not speak to me, I have no desire to speak to him.

Later, towards the evening the beat was so strong that the body gave a jerk at each heart beat. Was wondering if it would damage my heart. But he said that Sufis get a very strong heart. But surely the whole body must resent the quickened beat. If the blood rushes more rapidly through the veins, everything will be quickened. Metabolism, digestion, everything. Nails will grow quicker, hair, the skin cells, etc. Something seemed to go through the nose. A kind of current. The brow *Chakra* was working. When he came out he gave a searching look at my head and then looked more intensely as if wanting to reassure himself of his findings. I know this look; he always has it when he looks at the higher vehicles. His eyes have a different expression. It is a sort of vacuous look, the eyes seem to be swimming slightly. He glanced repeatedly at my head. Some changes must go on there, I thought. The vibration was so strong that I had to sit bent forward. The world around was so funny. When the brow *Chakra* is spinning, the world seems to change. There is a great happiness and great peace. Love is non-ending. The surroundings not only become unreal, like a crazy *Maya*, but also look different, somehow. My own hand looks not mine at all, not belonging to me. He is of such beauty that I keep staring at him and he is full of light. Inner light, just white light. He sent me home just when I was thinking that I had better go, for I felt funny in my head, a headache began in the region in the middle of the forehead.

When the brow *Chakra* is going strongly, sometimes one feels the head spinning and there can be a dull pain in the bone above the nose and when one presses there it is very tender, and something goes through the nose which makes you sniff. The colors around become of great intensity and the world is very beautiful in its unreality. . . . The brain does not work properly; it is as if one would switch over slowly to another state of consciousness.

When the throat *Chakra* is activated, there is less trouble, only perhaps a dull pain at the back of the throat; one feels the heart-throb in the thyroid and a sort of tenseness is there too. I constantly keep touching my throat, feeling a kind of tightness as if I had a high collar.

And when the heart *Chakra* works with intensity the heart begins to do strange things, like missing out beats, fluttering like a dying bird in agony, racing at the maddest pace, or one has two hearts. . . . And the mind does not work at all, and the love seems of no end, and the longing is killing. Before, love came in waves; it was not always of the same intensity. But not now. Now it is more stabilized. It is always the same. I love and I love and I think of Him in the night, and I talk to Him with the same deep tenderness in the day, always.

Slept well all night which is unusual, woke about seven. Quite a feat. Woke up several times in the night owing to the pumping of the heart, but had not time even to think, so quickly fell asleep again. Throat was aching a little.

49

A Saint has always a Light over his Head

7th February, 1963

THE VIBRATIONS ARE SUCH that the mind seems to stand still, cannot think at all. . . . Oh, the love, how strong it is! How it burns inside! How I thank You, oh, Merciful, for the Gift You gave me!

"He is so kind," he said once. **"Why some people remain far from Him and others are brought quite near, you will know one day."**

Why me, my Beloved? Why me? One day I will know. . . . The sky is of such a serenity this morning . . . and such peace is around . . . eternally . . . and forever. . . .

He came out rather early because somebody important came. He knows who is to come even if the door is closed. He just knows, so I was aware that he will come out early. The feeling of oneness was tremendous. It was lovely, I was resting in Him. Later when I went to Pushpa, I was as in a lovely dream-state. Found her crying and she was telling me about her dear friend who died—she committed suicide. I was sorry, but really it did not affect me a bit. It was all on the surface, all the thoughts, and all the happenings. I understood that while I was in this state nothing could really affect me. I was with Him somewhere and things of this world did not matter a bit. In the evening we first sat under the mango tree; he was late to come out. The fat Bandhari Sahib was with us.

Ram Prasad told us a nice Persian story: One man from Afghanistan, a Pathan, came to visit Kabir. Kabir was not at home, only his wife. So, he asked if he could see Kabir. He is out, said the wife. Can I see him? asked the man; I came from so far away! Yes, said the wife, he went out with a funeral only five minutes ago, you can catch him. But how will I know him? asked the man. You will see, said the wife, that all the people who go after the body will have a light over their heads. When they reach the burning Ghat the light over their heads will be more dim. But the light over Kabir's head will remain bright. Then you will know that this is him and you can talk to him. The man did as he was told. And when going back he saw the bright light over an old man's head; he knew it was Kabir Sahib and he spoke to him. He asked all the questions he wanted to ask and then he said: "Please tell me why it is that the light over everybody else's head dimmed and yours remained?"

"It is because when the people go after a funeral they all think it will happen to me too and they all remember God. When you remember God, there is a light over your head. But when they go back they forget God again and begin to think about the matters of daily life. Only a Saint remembers God all the time and he always has a light over his head."

I sat facing him and the bliss was such that I felt weak and the body was tired. . . . Great bliss hurts, and tires the body. He kept glancing at me all the time briefly, as if trying to assess something. We all went home early because some Muslim ladies came and he was called inside to see them.

In the afternoon Babu came and sat in his chair; he does it usually when he knows that his father will not come out. But he came. Babu left rapidly, leaving the chair free; he sat down. I felt I could ask a question and I began by saying that Ram Prasad told me to ask him. "I tried to get some information from him telling him that I cannot speak to you until spoken to, and he told me to ask you because he could not help me." So I told him about sensations the vibrations create in different parts of the body and if it is a normal occurrence. He said: **"Yes, headache can be if one is not used to the vibration, and sometimes a sensation to which the body is not used to is interpreted as pain, like the pain at the back of the throat, which is probably not a pain at all. You feel strong vibration in the whole of the body."** I said that it was true. I feel them much in my feet too, like last night I had to sleep with my feet uncovered though it was cold. He smiled and looked at his own feet poised in his usually graceful way on the chair opposite his.

"At this stage, if one does not cross it, one can become a first-class debauchee. One can meet people, men and women alike in other Systems, who were not made to cross or did not, or could not themselves cross this stage of vibrations, and they became first-class debauchees. Vibrations are vibrations, they have to be crossed, everybody has them at one time, every stage represents a barrier to be crossed. At this stage, it would have been better for you if you had a married life, but it won't make any difference, never mind, all that means is that it will be a bit more troublesome. That's all. You will cross it just the same. This stage will be crossed just as all the others were, just as well. In our System this stage is crossed without fail."

He fell silent and made a movement with his hand to denote that it is of small importance.

Rasputin came into my mind. He was supposed to be a Saint but he certainly led a very immoral life. . . . He probably had nobody to help him to cross this stage. And how many Yogis suffer from the same predicament?

If one does not progress with a Guru like him one is a fool. . . . After what he had said it becomes understandable why a Guru is needed. . . .

"Such are the vibrations lately that I don't seem to walk, I seem to fly." Told him about the feeling of oneness.

"Every part, every cell of the body becomes a heart, the heart is everywhere, all over the body are the vibrations." He closed his eyes for a second. Here is the explanation that I felt such a happiness in every little bit of my body; every cell was happy in its own right. Every cell is a heart, then . . . how wonderful! Told him that the vibration at the base of the spine is very strong too, but no trouble like last year.

"No, you will feel them everywhere; you are at the stage of the vibrations."

People came, much talk was going on, on all sorts of topics, and I was thinking that he had said that every stage is a barrier to cross. . . . How true, and how one has to hurry to cross each stage and not play with peace and bliss states like so many I know here. . . . He turned to me as if approving of my thinking, nodded softly, his eyes tender, and he closed them and went into a deep state of Samadhi.

9th February

WAS TIRED LAST NIGHT and fell asleep soon. Slept well. Did not even pray. This morning the vibrations began before seven. The head was reeling and before they began there was a pressure in the heart like a dull pain. Lights are jumping before my eyes. I feel swept from my feet and the base of the spine *Chakra* is humming. I sat there all the morning and the love was painful. Love can be a great suffering, physically I mean, when the vibrations are so intense. One feels a kind of excitement all the time: one feels like being swept away. Life is not easy, and of course there is this longing . . . love becomes an endless longing. . . .

He was beautiful. Gracefully sitting there and talking with animation. His hand movements are full of rhythm, as of a dancer.

His feet always poised gracefully, never did I see him in an unsightly posture like any other human being. Either sitting in an incredibly twisted posture, Indian way, or his legs on his own chair, or feet poised on the chair opposite; there is always such a grace about him. And when he is laughing or being animated, such charm he has. And he is so full of light. Never, not even once, did I see anybody who had such a quantity of light around him.

At home could not do anything this afternoon, was breathless with vibrations. Could lie on my bed and think of God, just that, nothing else.

Went there about four, he was outside, a man whom I did not know sat with him. He commenced immediately to ask Bhai Sahib who I was and what I was doing there, from where I came, etc. He did not speak English. Bhai Sahib was telling me that this man is very much hen-pecked by his wife and she even beats him. While he was telling me that, he was full of hidden laughter. Full of mirth, laughing inwardly, I did not often see him like this.

"I have to remember you like this, talking to people, never hurting their feelings—how much have I to learn from you!" He was grinning in a most delighted way. I think this man amused him with his chatter. For a man full of virility, such a weakling must have been something to laugh about.

10th February

IN THE PAST THE VIBRATIONS usually came on in the morning just before I went to him. They would fade out during the day and at night they were practically nil. Now they are always with me, day and night. The heart is thumping along, or pain in the head or some other sensation is felt constantly due to them. Love is so hard to bear that I keep weeping, such is the longing and the pain of love. . . . How much I love Him, and He is sometimes so near, and sometimes He forsakes me completely. . . .

11th February

HAD A LONG PEACEFUL NIGHT. In the evening Ahuja and his wife dropped in when I was preparing to go to bed. Had a meal full of raw garlic and was very conscious of bad smell. We were talking banking business and I fell asleep late reflecting over all sorts of worldly things connected with bank, money, and my return to England.

At his place I cry every time nowadays. Just look at him and start

crying. . . . Heart is aching too much . . . I cry silently and he talks
to others. It is so cruel to send me away. . . . It is a difficult life.

Did not go to Pushpa; felt the need to be much alone. Besides I
keep weeping all the time; it is embarrassing to have to give
explanations. . . .

12th February

WANTED TO TELL HIM what Ahuja had told me. He did not come out; I
sat alone. As soon as I saw the poet standing outside the gate I
thought, now he will come out because the poet knows English and I
won't be able to speak. And so it was, the next moment he came out.
A soft click of the chik and out he comes with a silken-like swoosh
of his *longhi*. **"Aia, aia!"** he shouted to encourage the poet and the
Nigam to come in. They came and a lively conversation began, on
politics, on Pakistan and what not. In a pause I managed to say that I
saw Mr. Ahuja and would like to speak to him about it. He nodded
and then I sat there. If I cannot speak, never mind. Felt listless. When
everybody had left, he turned in my direction and I was able to tell
him about some money matters, the information I got from Ahuja.
Then he went in. Sat alone for a long time. I heard him speaking to
somebody near the door. Did he look at me through the chik? Quite
possible. I wondered if he knew about the deadly feeling of hatred I
have? It is so disturbing to hate so much and so deeply everybody,
and for no reason at all. . . . Just hate them, that's all. . . . Listened
to his voice telling something to Babu. He must stand behind the
chik, I thought, and then suddenly I was aware that the hatred had
gone. . . . I looked, surprised, within myself, there was no hatred at
all anymore; it was gone completely, as suddenly as a smoke
disappears before a gust of wind. . . . I was astonished: such a
strong feeling of hatred, gone completely, without a trace, as if it
never existed. . . .

Only peace remained. While occupied with analyzing the event, I
saw him coming out with the wife. He looked smart in a new green
longhi.

"I am going for a walk," he announced. **"Keep an eye on my
house!"**

"If they all go out, they can leave the key with me," I offered.

"Oh, there are plenty of people inside, just keep an eye," he
smiled and was gone, the wife walking behind him. I was still
reflecting what he meant by **"keeping an eye,"** why should it be

necessary if his family is at home? Satendra came out; he squatted beside my chair and we talked.

"If you are a Guru one day, will you make me one too?" he asked, and I said, yes, I will if I should become a Guru, and we both laughed at the idea. . . . Babu joined us, I talked to them, felt friendly, had no hatred in me at all. . . . They were human beings like everybody else, rather distant from me, but I was not unfriendly to them . . . and while talking I was still full of wonder, how such a hatred could disappear so completely.

Shortly afterwards he came back; he looked grey and weak and he coughed. Sat in the room in front of him while he was resting and my heart was very heavy. Kept worrying looking at his tired face. Then he glanced quickly at me and got up.

"I am going to rest in the courtyard, will not come out; you can sit or go, as you like."

"You are not well," I said, my heart heavy with apprehension.

"Not too bad," he answered casually and went in. I sat for a while and went home.

When in bed I prayed much but fell asleep soon. And slept all night until dawn. Lately I sleep well and sometimes until late; I think the body gets tired with the strong vibrations. Woke up about four; it was still dark. The waning moon illumined my courtyard with a pale eery haze. I looked up to the stars. God was near. . . . Began to pray for Guruji's health. The longing was such that it was hurting my heart physically. I began to think how little money I had in London, how difficult it is going to be. But in reality there was a certain indifference, it is all up to You; if You want me to be in trouble, I will be. I will pray as I am doing now, full of love. Infinite peace was with me . . . peace and tenderness to Him who guides our lives. . . . The Real Master is He, I thought, repeating Guruji's words. And it was wonderful how tender the love to Him can be. I never suspected that it could be so tender, like the sweetest human love . . . the most tender feeling in the world. . . .

13th February

THE VIBRATIONS DID NOT SEEM TO BE SO STRONG this morning, in fact I hardly felt them at all. But when sitting in front of him I was one with him. It was such a glorious feeling. Could not help wondering how it is done—how this feeling is provoked, and if I really am one with him at this moment, somewhere; or is it just an illusion, of no consequence?

When he came out, my heart stood still for a moment. He looked so immaculate in his long, white *kurta*. He was pale, and the light around him increasing all the time. So beautiful, so transparent, he did not look like a human being but a being from another world . . . I looked and looked. He sat down and began to do his mala. *Sannyasi* was there too and from time to time he said a few words to him. But most of the time his lips moved in silent prayer. I sat there full of bliss. How to describe it, I wondered . . . resting in your inutterable stillness and peace. . . . Words are completely meaningless. What I never could reconcile is the difference between the happenings around him and his behavior on the physical plane and what happens within myself. Here he will shout at servants passing by, talk about politics, discuss household matters with his wife, and Munshiji and I will be one with him. So completely, so sweetly is the feeling of belonging. And he will not even speak to me, or be harsh to me, will not even once look at me. It is puzzling indeed. It is the most difficult relationship, because it is not a human relationship at all. It belongs to the "other part of me." On the human level it is hard and terrible. But somewhere, where the thinking cannot reach, it was wonderfully lovely.

"Babuji loves you too much," said Satendra to me yesterday.

"He does not; he treats me badly," I answered.

"But this is a sign of love," said he. "I know the System. If he treats you badly, he has much love for you!"

He was right of course. And his words made me glad. Maybe he was talking about me with his family, I was thinking. *Sannyasi* went. But he remained sitting. He organized some work for the sweepers, gave some instructions about the sweeping of the garden, then went into the room, and I was convinced that he will not come back. But he did. Sat down again, always doing his mala. This sort of light . . . as though transparent, I was watching it. I had tears in my eyes, the bliss was difficult to bear. . . . Who will forget the way you sit, the slender legs drawn up, the elegant way you hold your head. . . . How I will miss you. . . . He seemed to wait for something. I had this feeling. He sat there, prayed and waited. For what? I wondered. The wife, who went in the meantime to have her bath, appeared. She sat down and he was talking to her in a special, extra kindly way. Children came. Poonam with the grandchild in her arm. His voice had a thousand inflections; it was so tender. He was talking to them and they all had their little ways and smiles for him.

I understood. It was meant for me, to irritate me. I had to smile. It was amusing. It went on for a while. He was talking softly with them and once gave me a quick and searching glance.

"You can go home now," he said coldly, "I am going inside." But when I was leaving he was laughing and playing with the child still sitting, and it did not look that he will go inside.

At home in the kitchen, while cooking my meal, I thought that it was a bit naive, the whole behavior; he clearly wanted to make me see the contrast how he treats his family and me. It was so deliberately done it made me smile. But then I stopped dead in what I was doing: I remembered that this summer he did the same, being extra kind with the family and the disciples and I suffered hell. Now I do not . . . this is the difference. Now I can smile. It is *not* a naive behavior; it is my not understanding the why and the how of the ancient training.

The vibrations in the feet were strong when I lay down to rest after my lunch. Intended to rest for only one hour and, though I am sure that I did not sleep, I must have lost consciousness, for when I looked at my clock it was three; two hours had passed. The vibration in the heart was very strong. Summer is here. Today I saw the first wasp in my courtyard, so I know, summer is here again. It is windy and warm. The sun begins to be rather hot.

He had fever in the night, so he told me. And when I answered that I prayed for him, he murmured something and continued to pray. I was silent, he did not want me to speak, it was clear. I was beyond talking anyhow, such was the bliss. . . .

16th *February*

SPOKE TO HIM ABOUT MY IDEA to keep the flat. I am afraid that I will not find accommodation when I come back. Pushpas's place is not at all suitable for spiritual life.

"Why you Europeans always think of the future?" I said that we are brought up like this. "Then you have to stop it! You still don't want to change?"

When at home I spoke about it to the landlord, but he was not very enthusiastic; he said that in a flat not inhabited for a number of years white ants appear, it cannot be done. I was thinking of arranging it with L., but it did not seem a practical proposition and he was against it, it was only too clear.

"We never think of the future. If you think of the future and make plans, you don't trust in God. Never think of tomorrow."

He was right. The future is in His Hands. Why should I worry?

But there was a nagging fear in my mind that I will not find accommodation when I come back. I must confess it. . . .

Decided not to write to L. after all. When told about it he said: **"For a few days you were after the flat and not after the Reality. If we have a desire, we are after the desire and not after God."**

"Is the sense of oneness a reality happening somewhere and coming down into the mind, or an illusion?"

"It is an illusion. A superior kind of illusion. What one thinks, what one tries to explain or what one speaks is an illusion. There are superior and inferior kinds of illusion. When there is a feeling of oneness, how can the mind give trouble if it feels itself one with the object? Many are illusions, some high, some low."

I said that I did not mind; it was a glorious illusion full of bliss, and if the mind does not give me trouble I want it every time; never mind it being an illusion! "Illusions will remain until the mind goes completely; but what about your mind? Is it gone? It seems to be very much here, very much perfect!"

"What a useless question! You don't know how to talk to the Elders!"

"It is of no use blaming me for something I cannot know!"

"It is not a question of blaming; the culture of this Line is not for everyone. Only for the few. Who will accept it? Even Hindus don't accept it, or know nothing about it. By and by, never mind, you will understand . . . let time come. . . .

"Why don't you listen more carefully to what I say? Why don't you try to grasp it? For the third time I say to you: when there is a little interest it can be done! If there is interest and if they are ready to make a sacrifice . . . without a sacrifice how can it be? Europeans are materialistically minded, but so are Hindus. I never said that Europeans are hopeless! Why do you jump to hasty conclusions? We don't differentiate; for us Christians, Mohammedans, Hindus are all the same. We are not narrow-minded. Why do you say that you are discouraged? It only shows that you are at the mercy of discouragement! Like a straw tossed by the waves! Emotions are nothing; they are not at all a sign of spirituality! If somebody would hear you talk like this, he will say what an idiot you are to waste one year, and what an idiot I am to train you for one year! We never discourage anybody, never deceive, never lie. . . . If I am angry, the person will not even come to my gate because I don't want it. . . . I may do things for the sake of training; this is another matter.

Never think that I am angry or displeased, it is a wrong conclusion."

"You have said that I never will progress here." He nodded seriously, his lips tight.

"You are sent back to atone for the life you have led previously, and which was not justified. If there is search for Truth, there is an URGE from your side and SWIFTNESS from the side of Truth. . . . If you want the Truth, Truth wants you . . . Truth will be after you . . . and then you are quickened."

50

The Pain of Love

"PEOPLE LAUGH AT YOU," he said. I nodded.

"I know, and they will laugh at me in England; because I will be intoxicated with God and I will speak of love."

He had said that the nearness to the Master is an illusion. But if everything which goes through the mind is an illusion, and the nearness represents a higher kind of illusion, then it is nearer to Reality, is it not? So, it is welcome, a thousand times . . . illusion or not. . . .

In the evening he did not come out. He was coughing and I left soon, could not bear to hear his painful cough. In bed prayed for him and how. . . . Deep down the fear that I won't see him again . . . how much I want the Truth . . . the longing was terrible . . . how much I want You, so deeply, so endlessly. . . . Truth, hurry up, help me to You! I am small and silly and not worthy of You! But I am prostrated with longing for You. . . . Help me to get You. . . .

HE CAME OUT IN THE MORNING. Sat there motionless, pale, coughing painfully. Ignored me completely, and my heart was heavy with concern for his health. He left soon, went to see a sick woman who had fever. Vibrations started strongly. I was glad that Munshiji went with him so he was not walking alone. In the evening he did not come out at all. Sitting near his door at sunset, so serene and full of drifting clouds, I heard his voice from time to time and the chatter of his wife. Looking at the sky, all in gold and grey, I began to sing softly. My repertoire is not great; mostly folk songs, from Italy, Germany, Russia, everything which came into my mind at this moment. It gave me a kind of sad comfort to hear my own voice. One melody after another I sang, marking the time on the armrests of my chair. It was like a drive, an urge to sing, and to sing to the setting sun and the fading colors of the sky . . . to sing in unison with the vibrations deep inside my heart aching with longing for Him and His Glory.

In the afternoon I had had some trouble with the mind. The usual story of discourtesy to a woman and sending me home because I have no money anymore and he has to keep me. . . . L. will be welcome, she has money, and so on. . . . But in my heart I knew that it was wrong to think like that and it was not true. And now sitting here and singing to Him I was ashamed of it. So I sang to be forgiven, sang my longing and the restlessness away and the deepest, sorrowful love. And my heart was full of such yearning as I looked up to the now dimly lit sky. At one moment I heard his voice near the door, and wondered if he came to have a look at me and if he had heard my soft humming and singing. When it became quite dark I went home. Passing his door, with the light inside the room, saw him sitting near the door, in the big chair, something he never does. And I could not help wondering if he did it because he listened to me or was watching the ironing man iron his garments in the garden. Probably the latter was the reason, but I preferred the thought that he was listening to me.

He looked up when he saw me passing. I quickened the step. But this look from behind the chik remained in my heart. Love flared up, and I went to bed aching with it. Noticed that there was a difference in feeling quality. It was more painful. The longing, always difficult to bear, was killing. So I prayed to Him who is Merciful telling Him aloud how much I wanted Him. I want You, I want You so much . . . terribly . . . endlessly. . . . I am small and silly and I was a fool to waste my life. I am nobody and You won't even look at me. But I throw myself before You, imploring You to love me for myself. My whole being went out to Him in unending sorrow, to Him who knows and guides our destinies. Could not fall asleep because of the vibrations. The heart was a wild thing. I wanted to get up and run about, but did not. What's the use of it? . . . perhaps I am hungry, but no, I was not hungry at all, so that was not the reason why I could not sleep. Heard the hours chime in the big bungalow, and at last fell asleep. When I woke up, the longing was still there like a torment throbbing in the background, and it made me moan in sheer pain. The pain of love, the terrible, tormenting pain, which the poets say is even superior to the feeling of love itself. . . . And they are right . . . it is. . . .

20th February

THIS PAIN . . . how it burned inside today . . . restlessly, endlessly, an unceasing torment. . . .

The other day I said that I did not care if I had success when lecturing.

"No, you have to care!" he said. **"You must want to be successful. If you do something, you must want to do it as best as you can! You will be letting down the superiors, you will be letting down Sufism if you don't care!"** He is right of course. Another time he said: **"At the beginning and in the middle one wants to work, to share, to teach. Later this desire also goes. It is then that one really begins to teach. If you feel the need to teach, you are not ready to be a teacher. Wait till the need is no more; then you can teach, and only then there will be success.**

"The road to Him is to forget all knowledge, to leave all preoccupations behind, to forget; put yourself into His hands, trust; and YOU WILL KNOW."

To be after knowledge is to create a veil between Him and me. Even this has to go. The less one desires the better. It is the desire which prevents us from perceiving the Hint. It clouds our perception.

"Were the Church Fathers not very wise after all to suppress all the ideas of reincarnation? Because otherwise we will not make the effort in this life! Why not realize here and now in this life? Why think of later? Only the moment of NOW matters; the future is far away. . . . True, we all work for the future, ultimately, what else?; otherwise you wouldn't be here but think of NOW ONLY; forget the tomorrow." How right he was again. . . . And the longing, the longing, oh, how it burns today. . . .

When I came, he was standing in the doorway talking to some people. Then he came out dressed in a thin *longhi* and a singlet. Cold wind was blowing. It had become cool for the last few days. I was horrified and asked him if I could bring a blanket; he had fever for three days. No, he said, he wanted no blanket. And he sat there for two solid hours, listening to a horrid, ugly, selfish man who kept talking about his courtcase like a machine gun. And he sat there dressed in nothing to speak of, the wind playing with his *dhotie* and blowing it around his feet. Finally I could not bear it, stood up and asked him to move his chair in the sun or to allow me to bring his blanket. No, he shook his head. **"No, I don't want one."** You make my life an agony, I thought sadly, and went to buy bread. When passing by I saw him still sitting in the same place in the shade, in the cold wind, the man still talking and talking. . . . Went home in utter sadness. Oh, the longing today . . . burning high. If I have it like this in England, there will be no danger that the cold ashes of everyday life will ever bury this fire. . . .

21st February

HE DID NOT COME OUT last night, of course. He had high fever. No wonder, after having been dressed as he was, sitting in the cold wind in the morning . . . I sat there full of sadness, and Babu told me that his father will not come out, so he is sending this message for me. But I did not expect him to come out at any rate. So much longing was in the night, and I prayed for his health. But He does not listen to me when I pray for his health, even if I offer my own in exchange for his. . . . Obviously he has to suffer to some extent. Great is the nearness to him and to God and I don't know who is who . . . the Great Beloved or the Guru??

22nd February

DR. BANNERJI CAME TO SEE HIM this morning. He keeps having fever since the 28th of January, Virendra told me. But he came out shortly afterwards looking not too bad. I gazed at him, wondering how can a human being look so glorious. . . . Pale, ashy, his color was so delicate, as if transparent with inner light. Was thinking, looking at him, that something was done which made love different. There is a different dimension about it. Either he again increased it or some more veils were removed so that love can shine through. For it is somehow different. Such a restless longing which is like nagging pain. And the weeping when I am in his presence gets worse. Cannot help it and cannot stop it . . . like a compulsion . . . so full is my heart. . . . The nights are shimmering with stars; prayer is easy. He is near, quite near, and I can talk to Him, and I ask Him to make me realize Him soon. And it is a dialogue as if of two lovers, and the longing and the love, and then the mind goes somewhere and I am not.

This morning the impact of *Shakti* was such that I began to cry as soon as he came out. The light of my eyes, you are, I was thinking, and I have to go soon. As beautiful as the morning star and I won't see you. . . . What punishment is love. I did not want to speak to him, did not want anything from him, just to be able to look, to impress his image in my mind. . . . I have to tell him my dream but there is plenty of time . . . if I have the chance. Today he will not speak to me; he will go inside as soon as the man will leave. And so it was. When the man had left, he sat for one minute or two, looking far away; he was very much aware of the fact that I was thinking how wonderful he looked. His face was expressionless, very lovely. A *Deva*, I thought, not a human being at all. . . . Then he got up and went inside. I too went to write this bit down; today I am with Pushpa, so will have no time to write in the afternoon. Some trees are flowering, giving out a delicate and subtle fragrance. And the call of the woodpecker is going on ceaselessly.

I put on my nice velvet twin set and the pleated skirt; when I go to Pushpa I had better look decent. Spring is in the air. Rather summer. And the longing is such that it pains the physical heart. And You are near, and You are far and You are all I want, all my world, my only longing. And I don't know who is who . . . Guru or God??

I had better write down my dream; I don't remember it well. I only remember that I was telling other people pointing to a thick book: "In this book here is everything about his System. He gave it to me, I need not worry!" I knew in my dream that he gave me the book; it was mine and I need not be concerned about knowledge. But how he gave it to me is not clear. Only the book was clear; it was a thick volume bound in hardboard cover with heavy lines of yellow and it seemed blue. And it was new, which is surprising, really, a book on his System would be an old one, would it not? And I was pleased in my dream about the book which was mine.

Also a few days ago just as I was waking up in the morning, I saw the sun in the shape of an egg. The upper half was of the color of the sun, that is golden, but the lower half was of the most glorious magenta red. It is surprising, the vivid colors one sees like that. But as soon as I became completely conscious, and the mind took over, I was surprised to see the sun like that and it vanished of course immediately. But when I closed my eyes again, such was the light inside my eyes and inside my brain from the sun which was no more there, that everything in my brain was illumined by it. When I opened my eyes there was, of course, no light, just the dawn as it always is. I wonder what meaning can it have to see the sun like this?

In the afternoon when sitting there I saw a youngish man arrive on a motorcycle. He had a small bag under his arm and I thought that he looked like a doctor. He was. He came out after half an hour, much talking to him in the room. The wife was also inside. With great noise the motorcycle went. Quite suddenly I felt enormous peace . . . such peace . . . all will be well. . . . He is going, it is true, he is fading away. But he will not die until I come back; he will finish the training. All will be well. . . . I was full of stillness. I want You so much, can it be that You let me down? No. It cannot be. He cannot go if the training is not finished. I will see him. Went home early. Longing was so great in the night. . . .

23rd February

HE HAD HIGH FEVER all day long. But at least he takes some medicine now. At least, so Virendra told me.

So much longing. . . . Last night he had 102°. My heart was aching. What an agony it is to sit outside and hear him cough the painful dry cough . . . am sick with worry and apprehension. . . . Chowdrie did arrive. Saw Guruji pottering in his room in the afternoon.

25th February

SENT THROUGH MUNSHIJI the *chit* (note) about money to him. How I hated doing it, God knows, but I have to pay the rent . . . left soon. At Pushpa's place such a heartbeat, and such longing to turn the heart inside out. . . . When I went to him in the afternoon, the wife made me a sign to go in. Went in and was horrified to see how weak he looked and how grey; he was lying on the bed, a wet compress on his forehead. My heart fell. He quickly gave me the money, but Babu rushed in to see why I was called in and began to talk, and the wife talked and I stood there looking at him full of pity. . . .

Then I said that I hope that he will be better soon—"Yes, yes," he said. Babu was talking, so I went out, sat down and cried. Satendra was making stupid remarks trying to be witty. And the wife was talking and some Indian ladies went inside. Poor man, he never has a moment for himself. . . . Did not sit long in the garden. Preparations for a wedding were going on opposite; tomorrow hell will break loose from the microphones. . . . Poor Bhai Sahib . . . he looks dying now! How CAN he survive for the years I am away????

26th February

HAD A PEACEFUL NIGHT. About eleven had a CALL. The usual one. It is such a delightful feeling; the whole body relaxes and I go to sleep in a moment. In the morning was thinking of him so pale so breathless. The vibrations were moderate.

He came out this morning. I did not expect it. As usual my heart at first stood still as he suddenly appeared. He was very pale, and he looked absolutely glorious. And then the wild heartbeat started. I went and sat in the shade of the mango tree, a bit further away. I wanted to look at him from not too near. The light around him was so interesting, I wanted to assess it from afar. A ghost of a smile appeared on his lips, as if he knew why I was sitting away from him. I knew that he was sitting there just to test me if I wanted to speak. But I had no such intention. Wanted only to look at him. He kept combing his beard with his fingers as he does often when he is thinking. When everybody had left, he was still sitting there thinking his quiet thoughts. Do sufferings make one more beautiful? I wondered. In his case it seemed so. . . . Peace remained with me. I felt happy. Looking to the right and to the left, he was not in Samadhi. I was smiling inside myself; I will not address you, I thought, I know what you expect. . . .

In the evening sitting there, Peace was mine. Sweetest peace, and I touched just the fringe of the most unbelievable happiness . . . just a little of it. There was no end of it, and one day it will be mine . . . mine forever. . . .

A wedding was going on, two bands were playing, the loud-speakers were roaring, but it did not bother me. Such was the Peace. Satendra came and asked me a question: "God can create anything?"

"Yes," I said, "anything absolutely!"

"So he can create a stone?"

"He can."

"Can He touch it?"

"No, how can He? He has no hands!"

"Good answer!" he said: "God is a Power, how can He touch it?"

In the fading evening light, with the moon two days old in the sky, I sat there enveloped in a musical din, full of peace . . . full of tenderness.

Somehow the idea that He is a Power made me feel so tender. You a Power, a Great Power, the Power whom I love and Who loves me.

Many people were inside the room. I heard him talk and I heard him cough, his painful dry cough. But he seemed to be without fever because he was sitting in the chair and not lying as he does as a rule when he is not well.

Guru Maharaj . . . my deep reverence for you. My dearest, my glorious Guru Maharaj. . . . He was right: the Guru is not a friend, how can he be? Not a father, never a beloved. Guru is Guru, the Great Master . . . and nothing else. Not a human relationship at all.

27th February

HE HAS FEVER IT SEEMS. I get really discouraged. Did not see him.

Evening

THE LONGING IN THE AFTERNOON WAS TERRIBLE. Those Sufi Masters, they know their job . . . to put such a longing into a human heart . . . it breaks the bones. When sitting behind the nimbu tree, trying to hide from the noise of the wedding, I felt such a peace and such longing that the heart was streaming out endlessly. There is a special peace in this corner near his room; the side door and the windows face this side.

Please, don't die. . . . I want Him so badly . . . what will I do if you are not . . . I cannot reach Him by myself. But once I am one with you, your death will not matter too much. I will be able to reach you always. . . .

At first there was such a pain and longing, then such love. I was burning with it . . . it was as endless as the sky. Lovely peaceful corner, so secluded. Went away when it began to be dark. The music was too much and the drums. He seems to cough less. He came out for a moment and looked at the sky. I stood up. He made a sign with the hand to sit down. Went inside immediately. He looked so grand, so smartly dressed, all in white. . . . Please . . . don't die . . . wait for me . . . when I come back . . . don't go without me. When I become you, then you can go, then you will be free. . . . Do not go now, dear Guru Maharaj. . . .

Vibrations are strong tonight . . . but not too strong.

28th February

IN THE MORNING WHEN I WOKE UP ABOUT FOUR there were no vibrations at all . . . strange. I am used to so many of them. It felt funny to hear my own heartbeat slow and soft. And I was thinking, looking up to the brilliant stars, that such was my desire for Him that I will accept anything from the Guru without rebellion. This egg business, for instance. Mrs. Ghose gave me one egg every day from her hens. I brought it to him, thinking that he will need it more than I do. The hens stopped laying and only now I came to know that he does not take eggs. But nobody told me so. I deprived myself, brought it to him with such pleasure thinking that he will take it and it will help him for he is so weak. But some of his too well nourished children probably got it every morning. . . . My diet is so scanty, I think I would have needed it more than they. . . . But no, it is a wrong attitude . . . sacrifice is sacrifice. What is an egg? Thousands of pounds went, and I will grudge an egg? It is a little thing. Let them eat it.

I was continuing to think on those lines sitting in his garden. I won't cheat. Everything will go, every sacrifice will be made . . . even to the people who don't need it, even if I am not allowed to do it for him. . . . He wants it so I will do it. I won't cheat God, and I know He will not cheat me, when the time comes. . . . And in this moment the heart made a thump. All of a sudden the world became a crazy dream, so I knew that it was a spiritual constipation as he told me some time ago, and each time after that I will make a jump forward. While I was still reflecting upon it, the servant appeared with his chair. He came out in fact immediately. He was pale yellow, with hollow cheeks. Looked so thin and tired. He began to talk in Hindi, but mostly he kept quiet because his brother never stopped talking, on the Chinese question, frontier incidents, politics. . . . I was looking at him; he looked around with a vacant look. His eyes had a glow like burning coals, deep-set and fiery. Did not feel like speaking to him at all . . . simply because everything has been said. And I had nothing to ask either, even the desire for knowledge is a veil between him and me. Those are the reasons, so it seemed to me, but perhaps something was done that it became like this. Love has drowned it, perhaps.

Had to move my chair and go further, because the garden was swept by a *jamodar* (sweeper) with a large broom making the most dreadful dust. So while it lasted, I took my chair and sat behind him. Such were the waves of love that he must have felt it I am sure. Deep, tremendous, endless. . . . Then I sat again further away from him when the *jamodar* had finished. He did look at me from time to time, a long, earnest, unsmiling look. Nigam came and gave him a small rose. He took it, smelled it, and was holding it in his hands. I wanted this rose and was wondering if he will give it to me as he did this summer. . . . But no, he will NOT give it to me. It was a small pink rose. He was turning it between his fingers. From time to time I had to close my eyes. Was thinking that it was interesting how the feeling of nothingness seems to increase as the time goes on. I had it more or less always with him, but now it is deeper. Sweet it is . . . the great nearness to him, like a secret complicity of which nobody knows. I want to be nothing. The greatest bliss is in Nothingness. . . .

Everybody left one after another. I remained sitting where I was. He got up, moved the chair into the shade, and then stood not far from where I was sitting for a short while looking at nothing in particular. Then he threw the rose into the dust, turned and went inside. I got up quickly and took the rose before he could open the door of the room and catch me doing it. It smelled sweet, and I was holding it in my closed hand feeling the cool petals against my skin. Sweet smelling flower . . . he had it in his hands. He knew, of course, that I wanted it—that's why he threw it away so deliberately.

How wonderful he looked, so thin, but I heard him cough again, and I went home with a heavy heart. . . .

Evening

BEHIND THE HOUSES on the other side of Deva Singh Park the sun was setting serenely in a sea of gold. Inside the room I heard others talking to him. I was sitting outside his door, looking at the light fading in deep yellow and the first stars appearing. A happiness, vast, complete, endless, was with me. Thank you, my dear, for sacrificing me like this. . . . Sacrifice . . . how sweet it can be! Old girl, do you know what Glory this sacrifice could mean for you? Old girl, do you know what future he is preparing for you? What he wants to do with me, I think I've known since March a year ago . . . though it only sank deep into my consciousness now. . . . Thank you, my dear, with all my heart. With all the deepest respect and love I say: Thank you! No words will ever be adequate to express what I am feeling at this moment. A happiness so great, so limitless, a completely new kind of happiness. A never experienced joy of COMPLETE sacrifice . . . and no resentment, and no regret. . . . Thank you, in stillness with folded hands, I thank you. . . .

This happiness is like the sound of an organ, a tremendous fugue, full and rich. Since I have been here I have experienced for the first time this kind of rich happiness . . . to be sacrificed for love . . . it is great, it is complete. Do you know, old thing, do you know where you are going? Where you are being taken?

Did he do something to my mind last night when I woke up with the idea that such is my desire for Him that I will accept anything? Or was it the result of days, months of longing?

It is a fugue of Joy. I am going with you. I am going to You in full understanding this time. This time I seem to KNOW.

There is a young moon in the sky. The dusk descends slowly, gently, the sky is still pale orange in the west. Old girl, do you know? Whispers my heart . . . yes, I know. Have you any words left for gratitude? No, I have none. . . . And so it came that the suffering of the sacrifice became gratitude and joy. The suffering was the fire, the sacrificial fire. Go ahead, Bhai Sahib, the more the better . . . I hope it will not hurt anymore. . . .

Above the mango tree stood Orion in all its splendor. What date is it today? 28th February. Today is an important day; I feel I have passed a turning point. The road turned once more. Now (I hope) I will go like a slippery snail, right ahead . . . right to the Goal. It happened in the silent, darkening garden: the first impact of happiness, risen like a Phoenix from the ashes of pain. . . . Two people were sitting in Dhyana, no noise, no music . . . all was still. Only dogs barked far away and the traffic went as usual. I heard him sweep his room; later he sat near the door talking softly to his wife. I KNEW that he knew. . . . Of course, after all, he gave it to me. I was thinking that he will proceed to test me now. . . .

I will pray. . . .

51

Forebodings: The Killer Instinct

2nd March, 1963

HAD TO FLIT THE ROOMS because they were full of sleeping mosquitoes. And while I was flitting, I began to think. His tone was harsh; he insisted on his illness as if to cause me worry. And he is breathless when he speaks, to the extent that he is forced to stop, unable to continue. But when people come, he speaks to them for long hours, tiring himself out. With me he insists on his illness; perhaps he thinks that I cannot rebel with a sick man . . . or perhaps to cause me more worry. But why should he do that? At first I thought it is improbable, but then I wasn't so sure. . . . Anything to cause suffering will do . . . and this is a very effective thing—he knows how concerned I am because of the state of his health. God knows, I had better be careful . . . and never forget, for goodness sake, that it is a test! And suddenly, quite out of the blue, I had the idea that he may send me away in angry mood . . . must take everything without rebellion. Not everybody is treated like this . . . it is for the few. . . . For Lord's sake, remember it, old girl . . . don't make a fool of yourself! He may be quite rude, quite in keeping with the ancient tradition, where the Shishya is thrown out for no reason at all! Careful! God will help me! He will do EVERYTHING, old girl, everything with you now. Better be careful as never before.

In the afternoon such were the vibrations causing a vomiting condition. Decidedly it is a difficult day for me.

Yes, it is a bad day. In the evening sat there for a long time. Many people were inside; I heard much laughter. People like the horrible Pandit who don't mean anything to him, who don't even respect him properly. . . .

He complained to me that he has to speak; and I constantly heard his voice, telling jokes, laughing, just being merry. . . . Heavier became my heart . . . I resolved to sit it out and wait till they had left. They should see me sitting outside alone in the darkness before the closed door. . . . They came out and pretended not to see me, passed by, talking to each other. I hope they felt guilty. Behind them he closed the door of the room with a bang. He saw me, of course, sitting there in the moonlight. . . . Went home and cried. . . . I say the more the better; but when he does even a small thing to which I should be used to by now, I cannot bear it. So difficult it seems. So, I prayed much in the evening, to be helped because I cannot do it alone. . . . So much I want you, so much. You know how sincere my heart is; still love is not great enough, otherwise I would not suffer. . . . Such are the difficulties with my small self that I cannot do it alone. Help me! Oh, help me . . . I cry to You. . . .

4th March

IN THE MORNING I KILLED THREE MOSQUITOES which got caught into the net somehow. They have been eating all night. . . . The depression was great, the pain of love so deep and of no end. Kept thinking, how will I live without him for years? It seemed impossible. . . .

I was thinking that there are two definite things: one is love, and the other the pain of love, the longing. Just when I wake up, before the mind takes over, I always know which of those two is "ON": either love, tremendous, breaking the heart with its power; or the pain of love, which is such a longing, such a distress; it tears away all my inside . . . I seem to bleed.

As soon as the mind takes over on complete awakening, one of those two states in the waking consciousness is present in a subdued way, as it is usual in the physical consciousness, that is, in the brain. Outside the physical awareness, outside the function of the brain, the feelings are so strong, so exaggerated, if one may put it so, the vibrations of love or the pain of love are such that they cannot be tolerated for a long period of time in the physical body without damaging it; they are far too strong.

This morning the pain of love is being switched on . . . and . . . oh dear, it is quite something; the human being is helpless in its grip. Helpless, swayed with all sorts of feelings, it can only submit and tolerate them. In this state, I think there can be no question of free will. One is dominated, like possessed. . . . What power he has . . . for it is the Teacher who regulates the influx and the intensity of this Power. . . . Or is He, the Real Master? He the Infinite who, because a few veils have been removed, can flash His Ray into the Soul? Who knows? Sitting in his garden I prayed. It was all I could do. I am unable to do it by myself . . . please, help. . . . The heart was so full of the deepest longing. . . .

When he came out he was severe and indifferent. One of his young disciples sat there staring at me. I felt annoyed. Then I began to think how will I live for years without my Teacher . . . a mystery to me. . . . I was filled with terrible hatred against everybody remaining here with him who would be able to see him, and I was banned from his presence. Only looking at him one became worried; how will he survive, reduced as he is? And I sat there hating deeply and darkly. Chowdrie left. I quite expected that he will get up and go inside, but he remained sitting. All of a sudden my heart began its acrobatics, so I knew something was being done to it—that's why he was still sitting there. . . . The feeling of loneliness began to deepen noticeably. He called the ironing man who came into the courtyard, and he went inside taking his towel. I sat alone and began to weep. Terrible was the loneliness. Such a life of deepest misery. After a while I noticed that he was standing behind the chik. Was he sizing me up? Of course he knew how I felt . . . he always does. Wept for a while, then went home. And I prayed and cried, breaking down with nameless despair. Did some sewing just to do something. Made some entries into my diary. Like a monkey in the hands of a monkey seller, I am. . . . What is done to the human being? . . . if only people knew. The idea people have of spiritual life . . . if they only knew how much sorrow, how much heartache. . . . Went to Pushpa and the whole afternoon felt terribly lonely. Guests were there from Lucknow; much talk was going on.

At his place stayed for a short time. Could not sit in the garden . . . the dust storm began. His room was full of laughing men. Heard his laughter ringing with merriment. You laugh, I thought, and how will it be for me in London when the Western life will close tightly around me? How will I live?? Lonely and miserable, I went home. The storm filled the streets with the dust; the eyes were smarting. Went to bed without food. The body was tired and weary, a nagging pain in the heart. . . .

5th March

THERE ARE HARDLY ANY VIBRATIONS this morning. He was inside and did not come out. In the afternoon a storm was approaching. Love was like hot iron inside my heart. Kept crying. Chowdrie said to me: "You keep out? One does not need permission to get in!" I said that in my case it was different. What do they know of the treatment I get; what do they know of burning. . . . The lightning began, all went, and he said to me: **"You can also go."** I cried going home, thinking if he had any pity for me. . . .

6th March

NO VIBRATIONS. He came out early; I went there at half past eight and
he was already walking up and down. He hardly nodded distractedly
when I greeted him . . . and went inside. I don't remember the
afternoon. I did not go to his place; a storm was blowing and I was
lying on my bed.

I don't know where the hours have gone.

13th March

THERE WAS NOTHING TO TELL except terrible pain in the heart . . .
longing, and longing again so terrible that I cried non-stop. And he
was inside with others and I was outside, and I felt like a lonely wolf
howling to the moon. . . .

Was sorry when Prof. Batnagar came and went inside, for he
speaks English, and when he is here I have the chance to speak a little.
He is sympathetic and interested in me. Sometimes he asks how I am
and I am glad of a little attention; it is difficult to sit, unloved,
unnoticed. . . . But he remained inside and I sat outside the door.
Much merriment was inside, much laughter. It is useless; the less
rebellious I am, the quicker it will be over. It is not long anymore
. . . soon I will be gone and the burning days of Kanpur will be over.
The professor came out when it was dark already, and Guruji came
out too. He was coughing and moaning softly, and I was thinking
sadly, don't speak and laugh so much and you will cough less. When
he talks so much (and he does it against the doctor's orders), he
coughs . . . so why does he do it? He looked unfriendly, spoke for a
long time with the wife, and she never stopped talking.

Hatred against everybody was terrible. Dark, deep, killing hatred
. . . at home I wept. Could murder everybody. I knew that he came
out when it was dark purposefully, that I should not see him. Felt
resentful, and cried in bed. I was tired of the same story . . . ill-
treatment for over a year . . . tired and weary. The same story of
harshness and of hurting. Always. Will it NEVER end?? and I cried,
and the pain in the heart was such, and so endless was the despair,
that I could not bear it.

I sat up panting. I will die of it, I surely will . . . so I cried for a long
time looking to the stars. A crazy thing this love: the incredible thing
. . . could it be called spiritual life? If it is, what do you know of it
. . . oh, all of you, who speak so glibly of spirituality and spiritual
life? What do you know of the pain of it? "And the glory of it," said

the heart softly. . . . So incongruous, so strange, so out of the usual from the point of view of the world . . . and to explain it? How can one? Who will believe it?

Then I felt some peace and fell asleep. After all, I love You who live in my heart so much. You will do with me what You like. Can I really protest in earnest? I cannot. But there are moments when it seems so difficult, almost unbearable to bear . . . when the misery of everything connected with this incredible love overcomes me. The miserable life, the pain of unending sorrow. He said that in my case he behaved differently, for sometimes they don't look at their disciples for years. . . .

How can they bear it? They must be very strong; perhaps for the Orientals it is more easy, for us it is more difficult . . . who knows?

He is helping everybody. He helped Bogroff, so he said, therefore he had very little trouble with his mind. . . . But he does not want to help me . . . it is evident. . . .

This morning he did not come out at all, was pottering about in his room, arranging the shelves, dusting the books. Hardly a hygienic occupation with this cough of his. . . .

Left soon . . . will go to the hospital in the early afternoon to get injections. Got a letter from the bank yesterday telling me that the money has already been sent to India.

So events march on, in steady progression. And I am so full of misery that even to try to express it or to write it down is useless.

When entering my semi-dark room, still blinking after the blinding glare of the courtyard, I caught a glimpse of a mouse scampering under the bed. A sudden fury seized me. Wait, I thought, that will be the end of you. . . . I quickly closed the doors to both communications rooms. Got hold of a broom. In a vain attempt to escape, the mouse was wheeling around the room jumping up the walls, squeeking, while I was chasing it mercilessly. But the more it tried to escape, the hotter my hatred, my fury became. Beside myself, I kept hitting and missing and hitting, till at last it fell down, but I kept beating, hammering at it lying there already dead, till it was reduced to a bloody poultice on the concrete floor. . . .

Only then I stopped dead. Horrified. I looked at the mess. Why? Why this uncontrollable fury rising in me, and for what?—for a little mouse who entered my room perhaps in search of food, in the hope to find something . . . because like everybody else in India I keep all my provisions in tins and there was no food for it anywhere. The magnitude of this feeling was disproportionate to that occasion; it had absolutely no justification, if there could ever be a justification for fury. . . .

The truth was that I became afraid of myself, of my own reactions. For a long time I stood and stared, almost afraid to move . . . then fetched a rag and a pail, some disinfectant, and began to clear up the mess. Washed the floors of both rooms and the veranda . . . the acrid smell of disinfectant made me sneeze. And then stood for a long time staring at the broom, the cold water from the tap running over it. . . . How much evil is hidden in us? . . . I realized, of course, that the intensity of feeling was such that I could have easily killed a human being . . . and with the pleasure of destruction into the bargain. And for no reason at all, just as there was no reason to generate such a cataract of emotions all because of a tiny creature caught in my room. . . .

I suddenly realized that I knew nothing of me, of the real me, somewhere I could not reach with my conscious understanding. And I was ashamed. Perplexed. And very much afraid.

Must tell him. Why did it happen at all?

14th March

HE CAME OUT THIS EVENING. He was praying silently. I sat there full of misery. Have no strength to resist, to fight the depression. . . . Physically was also low because of the anti-cholera injection. But gradually, sitting there I began to feel a kind of sorrowful stillness, a sort of resignation. I was sure he did something to my heart, but I did not feel any vibration, nor a different heartbeat as it usually happens when he does something.

The night was full of restless dreams.

15th March

I SAW SATENDRA STROLLING TOWARDS ME soon after I arrived. "Father says you can go home if you want; Poonam has smallpox."

I said that I was vaccinated, and I remained seated. I was alone. Nobody came. Soon he came out looking very pale. I asked how Poonam was, and if she will be sent to an isolation hospital. He lifted his eyebrows.

"She will be all right; I gave her a glass of water."

But he himself looks as weak as a kitten. He will die. Only God knows with what feelings I will go back. . . .

Told him about the mouse incident. He nodded gravely.

"Sometimes it happens like that. Certain powers are aroused in

the human being, and they bring out all the evils, like dirty bubbles of foam appearing on the surface of the water when the mud at the bottom is stirred up. It is not bad," he added, continuing to pray.

Not bad . . . good heavens . . . I could have killed. I know now I CAN KILL, and he says that it is not bad. Of course I knew what he meant; it is good that it comes out. This is the way how to get rid of it.

Was under the nimbu tree, the room was full of people. My heart was so heavy. The day will come, the day is bound to come when you will speak to me alone . . . when you will be alone with me, as a Presence in my heart. . . .

But this day is not yet. . . . One day there will be no people with horrible voices, no family members interrupting, no servants, no crowd. You and I will be together, in silence, alone . . . and the door will be closed for everybody. . . . Only I am not sure that the language you will speak to me will be the language of this world . . . and the door will not be the door of this world. . . .

He came out when it was dark and I did not see him. Mosquitoes kept biting me . . . went home leaving them all still sitting outside. No vibrations. But the mind seems to be all right; it does not give trouble.

16th March

TODAY I TOLD HIM ABOUT THE HATRED which bothers me and worries me; it is so deep and so strong.

"It is pride. You think yourself better than the others and you hate them."

And here I was thinking that it is the other side of love; the parallel current of it: and it was simply pride! How deluded one can become! But what to do?

"It will go away," he smiled. "Things are done slowly." And left it at that. "I speak only as I am directed and only as much as I am told, not a word more. When does Gold Ore become pure Gold? When it is put through a process of fire. So the human being during the training becomes as pure as Gold through suffering. It is the burning away of the dross. I told you that Suffering has a great redeeming quality. Like a drop of water falling on the desert sand is sucked up immediately, so we have to be: nothing and nowhere . . . we must disappear."

Evening

WENT TO THE BANK WITH HIM. He wanted me to come. The money

arrived telegraphically, so he had forms to sign. Waited for him outside for a long time. He is so weak. . . .

He was talking to me kindly this afternoon. For one month he did not do so. One month . . . it did pass and it did not matter, really . . . it is better so. Told him my dream and the vision, the sun egg-shaped and half-gold, half-magenta red. But he did not comment on it at all. In conversation he said: **"The little you know, it will be enough for you to speak on it for years. Like the child who sucks the milk of its mother and becomes strong and grows, so the disciple absorbs from the Guru. The disciple is nourished with the essence of the Guru. You will know when needed."**

He was pacing up and down and I was walking beside him for a while. People came but he was talking to me telling me about Chowdrie. When I remarked that he has not much love in his heart he said: **"Yes, those who lead no family life become a little dry. But he sticks, so he has been taken to a certain level. People are taken to different levels."**

Later he said: **"Yes, you have work to do. Training is something which you acquire; talent or ability is something which you cannot help having, as a cock cannot help crowing. But training is something different—it changes the human being. Some sort of doubt will always remain. The mind is made this way. . . ."**

This morning, before we went to the bank, a woman was sitting there, and she had the most horrible voice, never stopped talking. It is incredible how much they can talk, Indian men and women! And the voices they have! I rarely heard a good speaking voice.

17th March

I WONDERED WHERE LOVE WAS. It seemed not to exist . . . yet there was no trouble. But I was alone and could not even pray. This morning the teacher next door came to have a chat with me. Guru came out as soon as the teacher came. When he left, he did not say anything to me. Neither did I, the speaking interlude seemed to have ended. Only in the evening, when he was pacing up and down, he admitted that he felt so weak. I said that he should try to eat even if I should bring him a woolly, but he refused. I became more and more worried. Sitla Prasad never stopped with a voice like a hoarse crow. A cold wind was blowing. He will catch a cold. I told him that it is dangerous, and his brother has a warm woolly on. So he got up at last, and I went. But he was still standing there when I was already turning the corner. I was worried and angry with him. So unreasonable! He weakens his body with non-eating and then exposes himself to the cold—how will he live? Wept with frustration.

18th March

SOME KIND OF VIBRATION WAS IN MY HEART this morning. Guruji was already in the garden when I went there, though it was early. He was writing *Yantras*, and I wept in silence. He is writing *Yantras* for people to protect them; he chats with everyone; all can be with him; but I am sent away alone, thrown out not only of Kanpur, but from India altogether. . . . And I wept . . . the pain in the heart was dreadful. What a punishment it is. . . .

52

"Never Hurt Anybody's Feelings"

NOTHING MUCH TO SAY. The same story: pain, loneliness, worry. . . .

Snatches of conversation I remember: **"Surrender? Surrender does not mean conversion. L. thought that I wanted to convert her to our way of life, and she began to wear saris, but I told her our Rev. Guru did not convert us, so why should I? We are not like that. We are broad-minded . . . surrender is something else. Beliefs can be great traps, they imprison us; and facts are not reliable, we outgrow them. But there is such a thing as a Supreme Fact, only to that we must arrive by a long road, and it can take a lifetime.**

"One does injustice to people by comparing them. Nobody can be compared to anybody else. Nothing can be measured by the same time measurement. The time of a cell in your body, your own time, the time of the Solar System, are different and equal in proportion.

"And always remember that some sort of doubt, some sort of imperfection will always remain. . . ."

22nd March

HE WAS RELATING TO US SOME HAPPENINGS which occurred in his household recently—a death of a relative in the North; the wood which was delivered was not of a good quality, etc. I was looking around. We were sitting in the garden. It was a beautiful morning; it was already hot, but the leaves of the trees looked so fresh, trembling in the breeze.

Somehow or other during the conversation I came out with the remark that he said a few weeks ago that God is full of desires. Otherwise, why should he have created the universe if he had no desire to do so?

"God is full of desires?" He looked at me in surprise. **"I am supposed to have said it?"** I told him that he certainly did; it was when we were discussing about the desires of a Saint and him not getting angry. I noted it down in my diary as I usually do. He also added then that I must not say it ever; nobody is going to accept it in the form it was presented.

"God is full of desires . . ." he mused, stroking his beard thoughtfully. "I must have been in a strange mood when I said so . . . I don't remember it at all. Yes, He has Qualities, and functions of those Qualities. Perhaps it is here that one can say that He is full of desires. But the Supreme Power has nothing to do with it. How can we know why He created the universe? The world?"

"YOU know," I said smilingly, "you are one with Him."

"Life springs up without a seed . . . things come up," he said, ignoring my remark. "It does not mean that the earth desires them to come up. When there is mucous in the eye in the morning when you wake up, it does not mean that the eye desires it. If God is full of desires, why, what's the use of getting rid of ours? Why should we try to get less desires then? Fewer and fewer desires? True, it is said somewhere in the Hindu scriptures that *Ishwara* (the creator) sees the *Parabrahm* (absolute reality) through the veil of *Maya*. That is, immersed in *Prakriti* (matter), His vision is somewhat blurred. This is the reason why I told you once that in order to reach the Supreme Reality we must renounce the fruits we have gained in Samadhi. The state of Samadhi is still within the limits of *Prakriti*."

Later he said: "You don't always catch my thought; I didn't say women cannot reach the highest state; I said they can . . . only the road is different."

I answered that all I want is to be with Him always. I cannot bear the idea not to be with Him forever. He smiled faintly.

"There is a question of speed," he said. "Even I cannot be with my Revered Guru Maharaj." He fell silent.

"But I want to see you, to be able to reach you from time to time, as you do with your Rev. Guru," I said with a sinking heart, looking at him hopefully.

"That can be done, it is not so difficult," he said slowly. "Follow the System and you will remain with me. The System will remain ALWAYS; individuals come and go. And as to why there is suffering in the world, it is all due to ignorance, *Avidya*. ALWAYS REMEMBER THAT YOU BELONG SOMEWHERE, THEN YOU CANNOT GO WRONG."

In answer to my question he said: "If we have to use the yogic powers, it means we come down to the level of the individual." So when he is training somebody, he has to come down to the level of the disciple, and it cannot be always easy. It was as if a light went on in my mind, the explanation of many things happening since I have been here. . . . He had to come down to my level. . . . I looked at him; his face had one of those strange, mysterious expressions and a very still smile. How magnificent they are, the great ones, I thought . . . that a divine being is a human at a certain stage of evolution. But his face was very pale today, and he looked tired.

"I tell only as much as I am allowed to tell, and only the strictly necessary, no more," he said, smiling again imperceptibly.

Later he made a few remarks on differences of civilizations, and how one must always give a good example. We are judged by the life we lead. We teach by being what we are.

"And when I come face to face with evil and see people doing evils, as it is surely bound to happen at one time or another?"

"Then say it as gently as you can. Truth which is not said gently is not Truth. Why? Because the person in question will not accept it. But if they persist in evil, then you can hit; but NEVER if you have any personal advantage from it. When duty-bound and there is no personal advantage for you, then there is no sin; and if they get offended, it is just too bad. . . . If the doctor operates, and cuts and hurts the patient, does it mean that he will injure himself? No, he is duty-bound. If duty-bound, there can be no sin, even if they get offended. You can say or do what is necessary, but you have to clear the point as well as you possibly can, otherwise you will injure the feelings. If you make yourself understood, the feelings will not be injured.

"You never injure the feelings of others when you have merged. Then you will know that all souls are one; you will know why he did it, how he feels about it, what he thinks, and you will put it in such a way as not to injure his feelings. And I repeat: NEVER SAY ANYTHING FOR THE SAKE OF PERSONAL GAIN AND ADVANTAGE. Be careful about that. This is a guide, a platform to stand upon and from where to start; one cannot go wrong."

He smiled. Fell silent for a while.

"Even Yogis, in spite of everything, sometimes injure people's feelings. If for instance the Yogi has a disciple who is a gambler, and he comes and asks permission to gamble, or worse still, asks the Guru to come with him just for once? What would you do?"

"I will tell him as nicely as possible to get out of such ideas," I said with amusement.

"First of all, your behavior must be of such a kind that nobody would dare to ask you at all, and still it happens sometimes even to a Yogi."

When asked in what way one injures oneself when one injures the feelings of others he answered: **"To hurt others is to hurt yourself, because before you do it, you think badly of them, so you hurt yourself."**

"If I had come to you when quite young, then there would have been less trouble?"

"There would always have been, but less, much less, a fortnight or so. . . . But when one is old, it takes time; it is very troublesome.

"Yes, it was done with the Kundalini . . . Kundalini is full of sex."

I think I omitted to note down that the *Bandhara* for his Revered Guru Maharaj, which is always celebrated around Christmas, has been postponed this year due to his ill-health. It was decided that it should be in spring when the days are warm, so it is going to be in April, just before I will go. . . . We will all go to Bhogoun, and I will see his grave. . . .

He came out in Sufi dress, long *kurta*, white pajama trousers . . . so radiant, so immaculate. I closed my eyes; could not bear to look at him. He got up, went to inspect the irrigation ditch in the garden behind the trees, and then went inside. I had time to recover. He came out and sat down, his small pale green jade mala in his hand. One bead after another began to slide through his slender fingers. The attitude full of grace. Golden skin. White garment. Green mala. Face radiant with a light difficult to bear. What a sight, I thought, my heart aching. . . . I wish I would remember it forever. . . .

I had the letter from Madras, but was thinking that I will not tell him unless he begins to talk to me.

"Have you written to Madras?" he asked after a while, giving his mala a flick with a movement of his wrist. I answered in affirmative and gave him the reply. He read it in silence.

"Well," I said when he gave it back to me, "well, there remains nothing to do anymore, except to send the money and get the ticket; everything seems to be settled." He did not answer; his lips were moving in soundless prayer, an occasional click of the beads; an ox cart passed, rattling by.

The end is approaching. A new page in my life will be turned soon.

24th March
WENT TO THE HOSPITAL to have my last cholera injection. Three young doctors were sitting around and we began to talk. I suddenly

began to speak about him, had a definite feeling that I have to talk about him, that I was directed to do so, what to say and what not. Sometimes I felt: don't say that, so I did not; or I had the urge to say something, so I did. When I left, strangely enough, I forgot everything and did not remember exactly what I had said. After returning from the hospital, went to Guruji's place and told him about it. It seemed to me that I have been talking too much. He shook his head:

"**Never think that what you have said is wrong**," he replied. "**If you feel the impulse to say, say it. To act on inspiration, without a particular desire, is the thing.**"

"Please tell me: why do you suffer? I have seen you suffer greatly; even if you don't complain, it is evident that you suffer much, and often I wondered why should you suffer so much? You have no sins, so why should there be suffering for you?" He smiled subtly:

"**Who tells you that I have no sins? Imperfections are everywhere! I did hurt sometimes people's feelings, so I have to suffer for it. Sometimes I did hurt your feelings. . . .**"

"Oh," I interrupted, and his wife laughed. "Even your wife is laughing; you did not hurt my feelings, you crushed them, you left nothing behind!"

"**If it is done for the sake of training, all is good and well; but sometimes I don't do it for this reason only, so I have to suffer. Never, never hurt anybody's feelings . . . never**," he added, and fell silent for a while. Told him about the fear I experience when waking up, in the very moment of waking up, a terrible fear like a panic, and it seems beyond my control.

"**It happens sometimes; we have much fear in our unconscious, an immense heredity of fear. Does sex bother you?**"

"No, not at all, just this fear every time I wake up and it worries me."

"**Then don't worry, it will go.**" When asked what to do in England when a *Yantra* is needed, he said that as soon as I will write to him, the trouble will go.

"**You will have to gain experience; sometimes you will deal with problems yourself; sometimes you will write. But the trouble will go; you will come to the stage,**" he added. What he meant was not clear to me, but I didn't ask further.

"**You will be protected from evils. Others who work are the same; it is done this way.**" I asked how is it that before, when I prayed, nothing ever happened, but now I am in constant communication

with Him . . . with this Power. I pray and He listens to me. I get the
answer in the form of direct knowledge right into the heart, and
when I make a stupid mistake or a blunder, He even smiles and He
forgives and He forgives, endlessly. . . . At this point he closed his
eyes with such tenderness as if he would give thanks to this Power for
me. . . .

"Not all things can be answered, as to why and how," he began
softly. **"It is all a question of surrender . . . if you have faith, if you
are surrendered to His will . . . His will becomes your will. And
what needs to be done will be done. People say: why should I have
faith? It is silly to think this way. Even to cross the street we need
faith. If you say to yourself: I cannot cross this street; you will not be
able to do it. But experience has shown you that you can cross the
street. Experience has shown you that you can go from one room
into another and pick up an object, for instance. But just convince
yourself that you are not able to do it and see what will happen."** He
looked out of the window. A sparrow pursued by another flew into
the room chirping noisily; they saw us seated there and disappeared,
continuing their quarrel on the tree opposite. He followed them with
his eyes and then said quietly:

**"Now I will tell you the secret of the creation. Sex is the same in
men and women; the ultimate moment of ecstasy in sexual
relationship is the same in both. It may vary in intensity according
to the temperament and mood, but it is of the same stuff. It is
Ananda, the only moment of real _Ananda_ on the physical plane in
existence. It is the sweetest thing on earth; nothing is sweeter than
that. And it is given to men for the sake of procreation."**

Bhai Sahib gave us a detailed explanation of the creative energy
coming down into manifestation from the highest spiritual plane. I
understood that the sacred creative gift which manifests in human
beings as the bliss experienced in sexual union is but a reflection of
the bliss experienced at the atmic level; indeed, that the physical state
stands no comparison to that which is the very essence of the divine,
creative dynamism, the exalting and shattering power that quickens,
nurtures and dissolves, the divine _will-to-be_ which can only be
described in terms of _fire,_ and which in every creature expresses itself
as the desire for existence; hence, that bliss and life-giving or
procreative energy are one; that this descends and is mirrored in one
way or another throughout all the planes of manifestation,
interlinking them all through that one _will_ which is _bliss_ because it is
at the very core of every creature, every thing, every atom . . . it's

life-giving fire, it's alpha and omega, it's Heart of heart. Then did I remember a forgotten phrase read somewhere: The heart of things is bliss. And there flashed through my mind the thought that, in surrendering ourselves to that Heart of heart, we partake of, indeed, we become that divine bliss. The great renunciation signified, in human terms, the great atonement, and therefore the conscious receiving and the conscious radiating of the divine *grace* of the Heart of heart.

Guruji went on: **"When the period of renunciation is passed, no words can describe what can be given, no imagination. Now you are one-sided, and you pick from the atmosphere all thoughts which are on the same current, the same line as yours. They are sorted out, and the one which is your own you are made to renounce it. That's why you are sent back. There you will come in contact with people who know you before, and if you have everything but don't care about anything and are indifferent, people will wonder and they will respect you and follow you. When you have renounced everything, what cannot be given? . . .**

"Faith and obedience are only possible if there is great love. Very subtly the Master puts you against him, before testing. . . . Sometimes the test is impossible, too difficult to fulfill. But if one thinks: what can happen—I cannot more than die—and one accepts it, then the test has been passed and one is ready for the high stage."

I was listening; the feeling of meaning was here as a kind of inner warning. . . . Puts the Shishya subtly against him. Hm . . . I had better be careful. . . .

Later he said in answer to my question: **"When complete control of the mind has been achieved, you will know which thoughts are your own and which you pick up from the atmosphere around you. And you can keep the ones you want to keep and throw out those you don't want. Then one becomes the master of the mind and not the helpless play-thing of it as most human beings are."**

"May I have an explanation of a few sentences from the *Idyll of the White Lotus?*" He nodded. "There are Three Truths which are absolute, and cannot be lost, but yet may remain silent for lack of speech. 1. The Soul of man is immortal, and its future is the future of a thing whose growth and splendor has no limit."

"Correct," he nodded briefly.

"2. The Principle which gives life dwells in us, and without us, is undying and eternally beneficent, is not heard, or seen, or smelt, but is perceived by the man who desires perception."

"Correct."

"3. Each man is his own absolute lawgiver, the dispenser of glory or gloom to himself; the decreer of his life, his reward, his punishment."

"And where does God come in?" He looked at me ironically, stretched himself out on the tachat, and went into Samadhi.

I had my answer. And I felt it was the only correct one. . . .

26th March

WHEN WAKING UP AT DAWN, before I could even think properly, I felt a sharp physical pain. The longing is just like the roar of the sea, just as powerful and never ending, on and on it goes. And suddenly, still with my eyes closed, I saw the sea, an endless expanse, grey at dawn . . . the surf beating ceaselessly the foaming waves against the shore. And I heard the roar of it, the rhythmic flux and reflux. . . . I opened my eyes and there was the grey dawn, my courtyard, and the sky beginning to lighten in the East. The longing was tremendous. Really endless as only the sea can be. . . . I was one with Him and the Teacher and all the Superiors. And it was such a bliss and a peace, so I prayed without words, suffocated by the fullness of love. . . .

When I went to his place, the rich man from Calcutta was in the room. But he soon left and Bhai Sahib came out. I prayed ceaselessly, full of peace, and the world once more was a crazy dream. But afterwards it passed, and all seemed normal once more. Until eleven we sat; finally he got up. **"I am going,"** he murmured half audibly, taking his towel. He was in a deep state nearly the whole morning. The peace and stillness persisted, and He is so near. Last night I prayed to His Rev. Guru Maharaj; the prayer went exceptionally well, though there were no words at all. But I realized something: He and the Teacher and his Superiors were all one and the same thing. Until now there seemed to be a sort of duality or even plurality—to feel one with Him or with the Teacher. It must have been a mistake, a lack of understanding, of being able to have a clear conception of it with the mind . . . to bring it clearly into the consciousness. For the first time, clearly, I could see no difference whatsoever. I was one with them all. . . .

This evening he came out dressed as in my dreams, all in white, long *kurta*, wide pajama trousers. He had a stick in his hand, so I was thinking that he may go for a walk. But he sat down and began to talk with Chowdrie and others. They talked and I was looking at him. Set against the wall, his face looked as though carved out of pale yellow stone, a face out of a dream . . . and he was full of light, very pale yellow light radiating and changing in intensity. I was spellbound. His expression changed constantly, vivacious and tender and smiling; they were discussing all sorts of things. The tremendous energy emanating from this wonderful human being was like a powerful flow; all of us were enveloped in it, all of us partaking of it . . . it was glorious.

Chowdrie left; it was dark already. Guruji got up and began to walk up and down in the garden in front of the house. To remember you like this, I was thinking, walking swiftly with elastic step, as if obeying an inner rhythm. . . . Slender, tall, a white figure in the moonlight, crossing from patches of light into the shade, up and down. Swift, unreal he looked, so ancient, a priest of days gone by, a mysterious, arcane being of far away, of half-forgotten dreams. And my heart followed him as he walked on, like a thing of faith walking behind him. . . . He sat down for a while. Somebody came, so he talked to him. But when the person had left, he began to pace up and down again, the stick tucked under the right arm, and he looked so old, older than my remotest dreams. . . .

Prayed well in the night, without words, in an endless, unceasing stream of love. . . .

53

To Become like Him

27th March, 1963

WOKE ABOUT TWO. No vibrations. No longing while waking up. Kept thinking of him walking in the garden last evening . . . a mysterious figure all in white. You priest of my far away, long forgotten dreams. . . . And all of a sudden there was an urge to BECOME LIKE HIM. A strong urge like a flowing stream, endlessly pouring out from the innermost depths of my soul. . . . From somewhere, terribly deep . . . to be like you . . . but how can I? How can I ever hope? You mysterious, glorious, impossible to understand . . . are you for me? I am destined to become less than the dust at your beautiful feet . . . what hope has the dust to be able to understand? To be like you. . . . There is nothing small in you. To be like you, so free, so unique. You have faults, for you are human, but they are rather faults of your environment; you are imprisoned in tradition, the custom of your country. But it is not you. To be like you, so free, so unique. . . . You one with Him, for whom I long more than my own life. . . . Kept thinking of his voice, slightly metallic, a refined sort of voice. He sang for me. When I close my eyes and keep the mind still, his voice comes from the depth of myself. Is it part of some memories? Who knows . . . stirring voice . . . an echo. . . .

That's how it is done with a human being . . . this new sort of longing. . . . I never had this irresistible urge to become like him . . . it is a new development. Did he not say some time ago: **"Why don't you try to become like me?"** Here we are. It is put into me now. And it is not new to me: something has been awakened which was *always* there. . . . I was ignorant of it; it was brought into my conscious mind. Is it the outcome of the longing which never seems to decrease? Is it the result of the prayer? If you want the Truth, the Truth wants you, he said.

About 6 a.m. the longing began. And the heart began the tocsin-beat. The longing, the love, the restless pain of love . . . to be like you . . . somewhere I am part of you already . . . I always was. To be like you in stillness, merged in peace . . . forever, my dear. . . .

Again the feeling that I have entered a new and important stage enveloped me.

Chowdrie said this morning that he is going to the hills in a few days. When I arrived, Guruji was walking in the garden, mala in his hand. He gave me a friendly look just as I was entering the gate, acknowledged my greeting and went inside. Came out shortly afterwards and sat there in deep Samadhi. There was no talk this morning. Everybody who came was in Dhyana. How unusual a human being looks when in Samadhi: so pale, clear lines of the noble forehead, such a gentle expression around the mouth. I closed my eyes and put my heart mentally near his feet . . . and lost the sense of time in utter peace. When Chowdrie had left, he remained sitting leisurely reclining, the feet poised on the chair standing in front of him. I knew that he was testing me: if I had the desire to speak to him. I had none. To sit like this forever . . . the image of him, all in white before me. . . . The wind blowing strongly from the west smelling of dry, hot, earth, cow-dung, and God knows what . . . this wind is already the beginning of *Loo*. . . .

To sit like this forever in utter peace . . . wanting nothing, desiring nothing except the One Thing. He got up, and wordless he went inside throwing the towel over his shoulder. I went home. It looks as if I had passed the test. But he is bound to test me again in different conditions; it is not finished, by no means. And going home I was reflecting that the same factors which caused great unhappiness and frustration before are the reason for intense happiness now. I am satisfied like this—him not speaking to me, ignoring me. Nearer and nearer I come to him, and the peace is such that it hurts. . . .

28th March

PRACTICALLY NO VIBRATIONS THIS MORNING. He came out early and today he looked at me much and often. Look out, I was thinking; he is putting the mind on, it will mean trouble. When he looks at me like this, there will be separation . . . it can mean big trouble. On this Yoga Line the Power is transmitted mainly through the eyes, and all the time he kept glancing at me. The love and the longing were such that the heart was hurting. At one time such tocsin-beat began that I knew for sure that he was doing something to my heart. . . . He was testing me again . . . being especially friendly with others, explaining something from the *Koran* to Chowdrie, and from his System to others. But I was thinking that, though it is a pity that I am deprived of hearing it from himself which is life, and when I want to know it I have to look it up in the books, never mind. . . . How much nicer it would be if I could learn it from him; still I have no desire, neither to ask nor to speak to him. To be one with you is all I want; desire for knowledge creates a veil, a separation, between you and me. I want to be like you . . . everything else is of no importance. . . .

When Chowdrie left, he got up immediately and went inside. People were inside in the afternoon when I came. I heard his voice and his laughter. Later he came out looking so radiant, laughing and talking with men trouping behind him. What charm he had! And what a youthful laughter. Now and then he kept glancing at me . . . I had the feeling that there was a separation already. . . . But he went into a deep state and suddenly I was so near Him . . . kept my eyes closed in perfect bliss.

It became dark. As soon as Chowdrie had left, he made a sideway movement with his head in my direction, and I knew that it meant that he was going inside and I can go home. Without a word he got up and went inside. I went home. It was windy. Slept in the veranda very badly, had much pain in the liver. I wonder if the pain was mine or his. . . .

29th March

COULD NOT PRAY LAST NIGHT. Liver pain interfered and there was separation. Was quite alone. And this morning the longing is killing and I am so lonely. . . . The suffering of the longing was great enough, but there was the fear in the mind, the fear of what it is going to be in London. . . . Alone . . . without him. With this terrible longing . . . and him dying, perhaps no prospect to see him again.

Went there in the afternoon. He was in the room with others. I was thinking if I could borrow the hot water bottle I gave him, for one night. So, I went inside and with the help of Babu explained to the wife that I had pain and could I borrow the hot water bag. Then I sat outside. Chowdrie came out telling me that I am wanted inside. I lifted the chik and went in. I greeted him; he was sitting in the big chair and my heart stood still so radiant he was.

"What is the matter with you?" he asked, and I explained. The wife came and gave me the hot water bottle. I remained sitting and watched him talk. How he can laugh with those hazel eyes of his with the most delightful expression of mischief. He kept his audience spellbound with stories. I hoped that something will be translated for me, but the horrible *Acharya* came. We all went outside and the *Acharya* talked for two solid hours. I kept thinking that there will always be somebody to talk for hours with a horrible voice and Guruji will say: **"Wah!"** and **"Bohot sundar"** (very lovely) with the expression of the greatest delight, though we all knew that he didn't really care. . . . The screechy voice, loud and almost shouting, went on; I could not bear it any longer . . . had pain in the liver. It was dark already and I went home. Had some tea. Went to bed with the hot water bottle. Was so full of peace that I didn't even pray. Why pray? I am with Him anyhow . . . I belong to Him and He is in my heart. . . .

Got up about one a.m., filled the hot water bottle once more. The pain was still sharp. The peace was endless. . . .

30th March

THERE ARE NO VIBRATIONS ANYMORE. I seem to have crossed the stage of vibrations. They are bound to appear later sometimes; it is all a spiral, the spiritual life repeating itself on a higher and higher level. The peace was endless. When I went to his place, he was already sitting outside with many people. I went inside to the wife and gave the hot water bottle back, then sat down with others. Chowdrie wanted to know how I was and I told him that I was better. Guruji looked weak and yellow. The waves of love were very strong and steady. I sat there looking at him talking to others. Then he began to sing, and he sang for a long time. I was crying . . . and could not explain why it was that, when he begins to sing, I can hardly bear it. And then in a flash I knew: it was because he was calling my soul . . . that's why the physical being reacted with tears and endless longing. From the depths, of which the mind cannot know, came his voice; all went still in me; it was a CALL . . . such endless sorrow and longing and pain, surging up from the dimensions beyond ordinary understanding. . . .

Later I sat in the shade of the mango tree and reflected why it was that I had such a deep peace. Only now I understand the saying: "Peace which passeth understanding," for it is the stillness of non-being.

I want nothing from him anymore, neither to speak to him nor any teachings. Just to be here, just to be able to see him so full of light, to hear his laughter . . . to look at him. Nothing more . . . and it is peace . . . I am nothing, I want nothing . . . and it is peace. It must be the Great Surrender—at least the beginning of it? The Great *Samarpan?* I wonder. . . .

He asked me in a friendly way if I had pain and I said, yes, and I will go to Pushpa and get from her some homeopathic medicine for the liver. He only nodded. I knew that he did not want me to talk to him, so I was silent. Somebody came and until eleven we sat, I looking at him from afar, the wind from the plains full of fragrance came from behind, ruffling my hair, and it seemed to me that it was the wind that was bringing the peace. . . . Such peace, impossible to describe, peace from beyond the mind, surging endlessly, peace charged with love and serenity . . . oh, what a peace!!

Never felt anything like this before! It surpasses every description and imagination . . . the whole of me, floating away in an endless stream of non-being which is seemingly a non-ending peace. . . .

31st March

CHOWDRIE SAID, ANSWERING MY QUESTION, Kabir was not a Sufi but on Sufi lines. He was a Hindu, and both Hindus and Mohammedans claimed him as their own when he died. The way of training of Sufis is not exclusive to them alone; in the *Gita* it is described in a similar way. But they developed a system of *Tawadje*; this is the only difference.

He came out when it was already nearly dark, and he did go inside when it was not yet seven. So, I did not see much of him. I had pain in the night, could not find a suitable position of comfort to be able to fall asleep. Kept twisting and turning, but was full of peace and could pray.

"You have peace," he said, looking at me. **"It is good. Try to keep it with you—not to lose it."**

I was tempted to say that it did not depend on me . . . but said nothing. After all . . . perhaps he is right; I alone am the cause of losing it. . . .

Prayed so much that I may become like him, so balanced, serene, mysterious, leading people with secure, steady hand wherever he wants them to be. . . .

Fell asleep, woke up in the night because of pain, and then had bad dreams of which I remember nothing. . . . Dimly I remember to have dreamt of his father sitting cross-legged, framed in a window, the light behind him. He was giving a music lesson, but his disciples played very badly. I put the instrument away when they had finished, and it had this shape: it was a string instrument.

Went to Pushpa and told her that I was without pain this morning; her medicine had helped. Then I went to his place and saw that guests have arrived from the station; luggage was carried through into the courtyard. So I knew for sure that he will not come out. People went inside; I heard the sound of many voices. Chowdrie had left, so from now on he will seldom come out. Went home early and the longing was great. There seemed to be no vibrations but the world looked unreal, and this was unusual because that kind of unreality happens only when the vibrations are strong. Mind was nowhere, once more. . . . If it is like this when I am in London, how will I live?

Last night, when I was going home, the waning moon was low on the horizon; it looked so beautiful coming up from behind the trees. The dimly lit bungalows in our compound seemed so mysteriously unreal . . . the still trees, the shadows beneath, as in a dream. I stood still for a while looking at it all and reflecting how lovely our earth is. . . . Let's look at it, let's enjoy it; once I have left it, when I die, I won't come back, I was thinking. There will be other *Lokas*, other marvels and worlds, but here, to this beautiful earth of ours, I will not come back. I will not see it anymore, not like this, so fragrant, so lovely. There was so much scent in the air, and every night I become as though drunk with the sweet smell of some flowers. . . . Something is flowering nearby, but I could not discover what it was.

1st April

WHEN I PASSED HIS WINDOW carrying my chair, he asked me about the fan which needed some servicing. Then he turned to talk to Bandhari, and I went to phone about the fan, and as I came back I wanted to go in for a moment to tell him the result, but he saw me coming, got up and went out from the room. So, I sat in the garden; it will be for tomorrow, never mind. He does not want me inside. The vibrations were very strong and began before seven. Bandhari was inside and he was reading something to him in Urdu. Later Bandhari called me in. I approached the door and looked at Guruji seated in the big chair with a stony face. "May I?" I said timidly.

"Yes, yes," he said briskly. I went in thinking that when Bandhari called me he probably was told to do so. As soon as I went in, he went out of the room. *Sannyasi* came and his shrieky voice went on and on, non-stop. Endlessly. . . . I was sitting full of such peace; if it is your will that I shall suffer, I will, it does not matter. . . . And it did not matter . . . Guruji came in and fell into deep Samadhi, sitting on his tachat. The atmosphere became so charged that at one moment I could not bear it and began to weep. Bandhari was sitting in front of him and later he told me that he did notice how much power there was. When he went out, I also did so and sat for a while under the tree.

In the afternoon Bandhari again asked me in as soon as I came. At the door I looked at him inquiringly: **"Yes, yes,"** he said abruptly; he was lying on the tachat. Bandhari told me to sit down. I was not sure he wanted me; I think he did not, but I sat down. But as soon as I did he turned over, face to the wall. Bandhari wanted to begin a conversation asking me about my progress, but I hardly could answer, was so near Him at this moment. It was sheer bliss. Then Guruji turned and began to talk to Bandhari. He looked young, clad only in a thin *longhi* and singlet; great light was around him.

Could not sleep in the night until four a.m. Such was the nearness to Him, such was the bliss, I seemed to die every instant the sweetest death. . . . Near to Him and near to Guru Maharaj . . . I was in the Land of Nowhere where Nothing eternally IS.

2nd April

WHEN AT HIS PLACE HE ASKED ME about the fan; he was standing in front of the mirror combing his hair after his bath. I told him that it will soon be ready. I sat down . . . the vibrations were strong. He began writing postcards and letters . . . not a word was spoken.

This morning the ladies came relatively early. And he put them in Dhyana while talking to Bandhari.

"It is done automatically; in Patanjali's *Yoga*, Dhyana is explained, but until now, nobody who was doing this *Sadhana* ever got Dhyana. One cannot do it by himself."

I said that one of the ladies told me she cannot do it at home.

"No, of course, she cannot. We don't do things in a hurry. Can you fly without an airplane? There are many ways of training according to the character and the heart. Really in our System Dhyana is not always used. It is more a Hindu way of training. We use the Way of Love. It is quicker. But it cannot be done always and not with everybody. In our world of pressures and manifold responsibilities a gentler but slower road is used. Dhyana is this road; love is created gradually; it takes more time. The Path of Love

creates a great psychological upheaval; not everyone can be subjected to this pressure.

"You will come on the stage; all will be well," and he dismissed me coldly and abruptly. This was his answer to my unspoken question. . . .

Slept in the afternoon because had hardly any sleep last night. Asked him in the evening if he could give me the usual thing tomorrow. **"Let tomorrow come,"** he said, unfriendly. I sat down and was thinking that perhaps he will not give me what I need for the sake of the test. Then I stopped worrying and was serene. He will do anything before I go; every test will be given . . . so, I had better be careful. . . . Everybody had left and he remained seated for a while. I sat there so full of peace, could not move. No need to worry ever . . . I belong to Him, He will look after me . . . my love went out to Him in a steady stream. Orion in all its magnificence stood right above my head, clear, big, near . . . so near. . . .

"You can go," I got up and went.

54

"Try to be Absorbed"

I HOPE HE WILL GIVE ME WHAT I NEED . . . I have to pay the rent . . . I tried to chase away my concern about the rent, but it kept coming back. . . .

As soon as I came the wife came out, gave me the money, turned away and went inside before I had time to say anything. I was much relieved.

Yesterday went to the bank, made out a draft which I sent to Madras to the Air India Office for the ticket. In the afternoon told him about it.

"So all is finished?" He smiled.

"Yes, the last job was to send the money; now I have nothing to do but to look at you. . . ." He smiled quietly.

"Satsang," he said with a nod, **"very important."**

We went to his father's *Samadhi* in the morning. Only two cars were going because the truck did not come (the traffic inspector wanted a bribe to give the permit; conditions of India!!), so there was no crowd of dirty children to run about when meditation was due. Only his family, Durga Shankar's mother and two children, and the brother's family; it was quiet, no noise. In a bluish haze were the Indian plains, and I wept so much because it was the last time I will see the grave, for years to come. . . .

Prayed for understanding, trembled when prostrating myself before his father's grave, blinded by tears, could hardly get up. . . . When I did finally, tears still streaming down my face, I saw he was looking at me. His face was still and cold. I went to the car; our car was the first to leave because it was Pushpa's. I saw his tall figure standing at the railing looking at our departing car. White as snow, in full sunshine, his garment seemed to emanate light, and I knew that he stood there because he wanted this picture to remain in my memory . . . the Mausoleum, the heat, the sunny haze, the palest azure of the distant plains, mango trees, small huts far away, and fields endlessly stretching away seemingly beyond the horizon . . .

and his shining figure in the foreground. . . . Cried so much all the journey back, and went home because could not sit in his garden shaken by sobs as I was. . . .

But I was there in the evening. He came out and looked very pale. I was told that he had fever. He had no food Satendra told me, and he suffers from a vomiting condition. Will I see you again? I thought sadly. Will I see you alive? What a parting. . . .

In the night could not sleep until two a.m. So strong were the vibrations in the soles of my feet. Needed a blanket, for the night was fresh, but kept the feet stuck out, they were burning. Ssss . . . it went, I could hear the sound even. Then the vibration at the base of the spine began strongly, and I just lay there watching the light circulating within. There was a sense of a very great peace, and of physical pain in the whole of the body. It was literally aflame.

5th April

THIS MORNING HE CAME OUT IN HIS SUFI DRESS; Satendra brought his writing material. Ahuja's sister came; his nephew came. She was nearly all the time in Dhyana. I left about eleven.

Tonight many people came. It was a soft, fragrant evening, full of moonlight and huge stars. It had been very hot all day. But now it was delightful.

How difficult it must be to live in the world AND be just a drop of water absorbed into the desert sand . . . difficult it must be. . . . Still, it has to be done; it MUST be done. The very loud talk was disturbing me. Sometimes it is so restless here. People make it so. And he not only tolerates it, no, he encourages it, himself talking a lot. Clearly it must be so for reasons I don't understand. . . .

6th April

THIS MORNING WHEN I CAME he was working in the garden. Later when people came and we were sitting, I asked: if for instance the Master says this chair is black. I must think: he says it for a certain purpose and I must accept it.

"No," he interrupted with a smile, **"If the Master says: this chair is black, you MUST SEE IT BLACK."** I understood. But it seems incredible that one can reach this degree of surrender. . . .

He was telling me off because I talk too much to Pushpa about the Training and myself.

"You think that you did much, but from my point of view it is

nothing; nothing at all. We served our Rev. Guru Maharaj for so many years and we thought it amounted to nothing by comparison with what we are given by him."

Then he made an ambiguous statement, intended to upset, to confuse my mind and create trouble. When confronted with it, he at first pretended not to understand what it was all about. Then he twisted and turned it, then denied three quarters of it, and paralyzing my mind, so that I could not think clearly sitting there before him . . . I knew no more what is what and which is which. . . . When he speaks to me in a certain way, it is sometimes as if a strong wind would blow through the whole of my being, making me feel as if I would take off at any moment. . . . And I don't remember a thing about it. . . .

On the other hand, when he speaks to me kindly so that my heart is melting, there is always poison hidden somewhere underneath.

In the night the mind gave me terrible trouble. Deceptions, falsehoods, contradictions. Either he does not speak to me, or if he does he frequently confuses me with denials and contradictions . . . makes statements immediately to be contradicted—about his culture being the only right one, and ours a bad and an inferior one, or inferiority of women and the like—all sorts of statements which I know well he does not mean, cannot mean at all. And of course the next day he will say exactly the opposite, or deny the lot.

Maddening. I was so furious that I cried. In the evening a storm was approaching with much thunder and lightning. He came out for a moment. **"It is going to rain,"** he said. The storm swept down in this very moment with gusts of wind whisping up clouds of evil smelling dust from the unpaved streets. We all went into the courtyard and I sat there on a tachat feeling miserable in the whirling dust. They were all in the room. At last the wife called me inside. He was squatting on the tachat.

"Yes, yes," he said mechanically, contemplating his toes, **"Yes, yes, you can come in."** I sat down on the chair; the fan was whirling around uselessly, bringing no refreshment at all. Outside, the storm was raging, and the yells of the kids of Tulsi Ram were heard amongst the howling of the storm; they rejoiced about the green unripe mangoes falling from the tree. I was crying silently; he was talking to his wife, chatting to Satendra. Once I caught his thoughtful glance; he quickly lowered his eyes when he saw that I noticed it. Then the wife and the other lady present became aware that I was still weeping. They commented on it.

"My wife wants to know what is the matter with you?" He was still looking at his toes.

"Ask Guru Maharaj," I said blowing my nose.

"When the doctor operates and hurts, does he listen to the protests of the patient?" I shook my head. "And who is always blamed?"

"The doctor," I said. He kept looking at his toes.

I took the air ticket from my bag and gave it to him. He read the letter and examined the ticket.

"So now," he said slowly, "there is really nothing more to do. . . ."

"Only three weeks are left, three miserable weeks . . . such a short time!"

"Three weeks are short, so are three months, or three years, and so short are three hundred years. And in one split-second the world was created, and in one split-second it will disintegrate. . . ."

"So Sufis also believe in *Pralayas* and *Manvantaras*," I said looking at him squatting there, all in white in a thin *dhotie* and singlet, his face radiant with light. He nodded.

"Yes, only the terminology is different, and we don't speak of it. Many things my father and my Rev. Guru did teach me. I never tell it to anybody. People are idiots; they will not understand. Not everything can be said, only the strictly necessary. Until the human being reaches the stage, no teaching is given."

Then he told me that the life of the physical body is one hundred years, the life of the *Manas* (the mind) is five hundred years, the life of *Shukshma Sharira* (the body of the higher mind) is twenty-five hundred years—3100 in all.

"We don't believe that we come back again and again. The *Atma* is supposed to be immortal because after millions of years we know of people still in existence here."

"Do we go to other Lokas?" I asked. But he was in Samadhi. The wife came in telling him to come; supper was ready.

I left. It was a clear night after the storm. But as it did not rain, the air still smelled of dust. A little rain came later in the night, and I had to move my bed from the courtyard into the veranda.

Was thinking practically the whole night. I will try to attempt the seemingly impossible; there is only the one way: to accept everything at its face value. He said that all I did was nothing; all right, I offer my effort, my suffering to Him as a flower. . . . Bogroff was sitting on hot stones for half an hour not feeling the heat, Guruji commented. I was without a fan for twelve days, not to speak of other discomforts, but he says that it is nothing. All right. I understand that until I give up the idea that I did something of great merit it will represent an obstacle. So the sooner I forget about it, the better it will be. And when he says that women are inferior, all right, I will, or rather I WILL TRY to accept it. I cannot haggle about what he said or did not say, what I can accept or cannot. One cannot surrender to a Great Being directed by a higher power and criticize the man as imperfect. He will say things, then he forgets them; it is up to me to understand. He throws them before me to be picked up, to sort them out. I should rather accept everything, as it comes. . . . So if one day he will say: **"You are cow-dung,"** I must think of myself: though I don't look like one, there seems to be a slight difference; if he says I am so, I am . . . he knows better. . . . Only by accepting everything in this way there is a slight hope to surrender this devil, the mind. . . . Otherwise I will haggle till doomsday and get nowhere.

The vibration in the feet and at the base of the spine has been going on in a terrific way since Sunday.

In the morning plenty of people were there all knowing English. He said: **"The regard in our family is such as is in no other family to the same extent. My father NEVER talked to his elder brother, and answered only: 'Yes, Sir,' when spoken to. So did I to my Rev. Guru. My son cannot speak to his wife before me. Cultures are different, but where the Truth is, one has to find out by oneself. We Sufis lay great, primary importance on regard for the Guru. When my Rev. Guru made me his disciple, my uncle hinted to me that if I regard the Guru and please him, he will give me everything. I was a small boy; I did not understand them . . . later only I understood; something more is necessary as well. It was clearly a hint. If you regard him, he will give you; you are not yourself doing it. The disciple is nothing, can do nothing."**

I understood it only when I came home. In the meantime he was talking all the time on all sorts of topics so that I should have no chance to open my mouth. I was crying, feeling very rebellious. . . . At eleven when the others had left he said: **"It is eleven; you can also go home."** Only at home I understood the wisdom of it; it was useless to talk to him accusing him of this and that. . . .

The way is clear: the GREATEST reverence to the Master, and acceptance without murmur or doubt, or criticism—only then can I have some hope! So my mind went still at last and I had peace. In the evening I asked permission to go home early. Felt tired, could not bear horrible voices going on endlessly. . . .

7th April

IN THE NIGHT WAS MUCH BOTHERED by my feet, for more than three hours. Got up, switched on the light, sat in the room for a while keeping my feet in a bowl of cold water. Then drank some cold water. Fell asleep after midnight, and in the morning it was a bit better. The vibration went on strongly. He must have noticed that I had trouble, for in the afternoon the vibration was not there, and there was hardly any in the night.

9th April

HE IS FEVERISH and had a vomiting condition last night. And I was thinking that perhaps he will not die after all. It did not matter really what he did.

Later he said: **"A child is afraid to leave the arms of his mother, that's why I am sending you away."** In the evening he was talking "nineteen to the dozen" and it was very hot. Went home at half past eight. He was still talking to others.

10th April

ONLY LESS THAN THREE WEEKS . . . and the mind gives so much trouble. Packing for Bhogoun. Will pray at the grave of His Rev. Guru Maharaj. . . .

16th April

OF BHOGOUN I REMEMBER PRACTICALLY NOTHING. There was a long, tedious, hot, train journey; somebody payed for my ticket. A stranger joined our party in the carriage and spoke to Guruji in such impertinent, practically derisive way, arguing endlessly. Bhai Sahib answered him gently with infinite patience. Nobody spoke. I sat there boiling with indignation. At last I could not bear it any longer and asked the young man if, being an Indian, he did not learn from his parents how to respect the elders. He stared at me in amazement, but Bhai Sahib attacked me most viciously, telling me how could I dare, being only a woman, speak to a man in this way. He practically shouted at me. I was so taken aback and so deeply hurt, I only sat there and said nothing. The young man was also amazed at Guruji's outburst—perhaps feeling somewhat guilty because he was the cause

of my ill treatment, or perhaps realizing that he really did lack respect
for an old man—kept quiet from then on and got out after a few
stations.

All I know is that it was hot, oh, so hot. All I remember is that I
prayed so ardently as never before in my life. I think we stayed at first
in the house of his aunt where the lavatory was arranged in such a
way that I suddenly noticed that a crowd of boys looked at me from a
nearby roof when I was in it, so I didn't dare to go. Very little
consciousness was in the mind. Then I remember that we went to
stay with a Muslim doctor who sang most beautifully his prayers at
four in the morning, his magnificent baritone voice ringing far and
wide across the village . . . the procession of us all to the group of
trees across the cultivated fields where the two small Muslim graves
of his Guru Maharaj and his son were found. And that's all. No
memory of anything else. I think that we stayed three days.

In the evening he translated many couplets: **"Those who love
always cry, where is deep love there is always separation. Beauty has
a reason, but love has no reason for the mind knows it not. . . .**

**"It is easy to come with me: I am standing in the middle of the
bazaar and shouting: Come with me! All you need to do is to burn
down your house and come with me! It is easy to come with me: take
off your head and follow me!**

**"If I am happy I forget You; but if full of sorrow, I think of You! So
give me sorrow only that I may always think of You. . . ."**

17th April

"GURU BHAKTI IS DIFFICULT (devotion to the Guru)," I said and he
nodded.

**"The lane of Love is narrow, as narrow as the edge of a sword; two
cannot walk on it. I have shown you the room where I was sitting for
years. And in front of the room there was no veranda as it is now.
And I was standing before the door in the sun when it was closed,
and I did not feel it. And you know I cannot sit in full sun. But then
I did not feel the heat or the sun. It was his greatness. And you have
been thinking all the time that you have been getting harsh
treatment. You have been sitting here in the garden all the time . . .
it carries no weight with me. . . ."**

"Yes, I am afraid I did think so," I said.

"It is my failing."

"Oh no!" I protested, "it was my foolishness, my lack of
understanding. Because the conditions in your country are different;

in my country pigs live better," I pointed to Tulsi Ram's shed. "I never sat on chairs where mangy dogs were sleeping."

"But in your country you will not find people like me." He smiled faintly.

"Yes, you are right; here lies my foolishness; I should not have been distracted by non-essentials."

"No," he shook his head. **"It was my failing. My Rev. Guru was much greater than I. He would have taken away those ideas as he did with me; they would not arise at all. Culture has nothing to do with it. He was much, so much greater than I; I am only dust at his feet, and even so, I am fortunate to have absorbed what I could."** He fell silent with the most tender expression in his eyes.

"Even now, he is the greatest; he gives orders; nobody can be like him." He looked thoughtfully at his feet, slender, brown, perfectly shaped, stretched out on the chair in front of him. And I was thinking that history repeats itself—nobody is so great, nobody is so beautiful or perfect as he is for me . . . and still my mind keeps rebelling. . . .

"Those lotus feet of yours. . . . I must make them famous, at least I will have a good try. . . ." One tear rolled slowly down his cheek and he closed his eyes softly and tenderly. I knew it was meant for me and I began to cry.

"It is because you have challenged me on the 5th of January to produce love; that's why you have to go. Otherwise you would have been like L."

"No, I think you would have done it anyhow. I have a proof of it: you said once in November: **"I will take you in a gallop by a short-cut."** He shook his head slowly.

"I don't disobey the order but it can remain with me for years; I don't disobey it, but it is up to me when to execute it. You challenged me; so it was done quickly."

"You mean that I precipitated the events. I understand; but was it bad?"

"No," he said, **"not bad, but you could have had it like L., coming and going. I would not have sent you away so soon. . . ."**

"But I did not want unconscious states for ages to come! Those who are in Dhyana, you see where they are—nowhere! This is not for me! I want love, I want suffering! I even asked your Rev. Guru for more suffering! . . . and I will get it, you will give it to me!" He nodded very, very slowly.

"Let's go into the room," he got up. There he left me for a while and went out. I began to cry, thinking will I see him alive?

"I hope to see you alive," I said when he came back and sat in the big chair.

"Who knows what the future will bring," he murmured with tight lips. I cried more. It seemed such a cruel answer. He looked at me thoughtfully.

"Where will you live in London?" I told him that I will take a room. **"A room?"** he inquired.

"Yes, I will have no money to do more than that. Besides, probably I will be very little in London. I will be sent into the provinces to lecture."

"Very troublesome life," he looked at me with an ironic smile. **"Difficult life to travel and to talk all the time. . . ."**

"But this is the idea, is it not? That's why I am sent back; to have a difficult life to travel and to talk, is it not so?" But he did not answer; he went into Samadhi. After a long while I got up. He suddenly opened his eyes.

"When you are alone," he said, looking at me with those strange eyes half in Samadhi, **"When you are alone, you should try to be absorbed. . . ."**

"In you?" I asked.

"In whom you like," he smiled. I went out.

In the evening I asked him what he had meant exactly. Was it a hint? "If I try to be absorbed, will I not remain on the level of the mind? I will not reach you!" He smiled tenderly, his head turned sideways, a strange soft smile illumined his face.

"This," he said, **"is to be understood, not to be explained in words. . . ."** His eyes were shining in the darkness like two blazing stars. The wife came out calling him for supper.

Slept well. I wish I knew what he meant, how it worked. "Is this the state of nearness?" I asked before leaving, but he did not answer and went inside.

55

One Must Be Able to Sleep in the Street

18th April, 1963

THIS MORNING LOOKING IN THE MIRROR, just when I got up, I noticed with surprise that my eyes were blazing like two huge stars, so shiny. The Light of the Guru, I thought, examining it. Those are not your eyes, neither are they beautiful ones . . . but what light in them . . . his Light! And I looked at them for a long while. Grey eyes full of cold, brilliant, unearthly light. . . .

Here we are; the disciples get the training according to the will of the Guru, according to the character, and according to their own liking. I challenged him. The character was there; order was there—all the three factors. So I am taken to Him in a gallop . . . I am a lucky old girl . . . what am I complaining about? Pushpa told me never to fear, not even for a moment; he will not die, she feels it for sure. He smiled one of his infinitely tender smiles when told about it. And he looked so incredibly young, so radiant. How many expressions he has!

19th April

GREAT PEACE. Bliss unbelievable since Bhogoun. The vibration goes on.

20th April

SLEPT WELL. But in the morning woke at dawn to a Great Separation. Complete emptiness. Felt so lonely, and the Longing began. Wondering if the mind will give trouble again.

He was sitting cross-legged in stony silence doing his mala. I just sat, had no desire to speak. Everybody had left, we were alone. My birthday today—56. Am an old lady, but the body feels young and healthy and full of energy. And the heart is full of this terrible Thing which people call Love, but I would call it Longing.

He got up abruptly, took his towel and went inside without a word. I sat for ten more minutes. Then I too went home. Began to prepare for packing.

How will I live? And my heart was heavy. How will I be able to
survive? How to become a drop sinking into the desert sand not
knowing if I ever will see him again?

21st April

THIS MORNING THE VIBRATION began strongly and became quite
something as soon as he came out. He asked me only about the socks
which I try to shrink for him. In the afternoon the heart-vibration
was very strong.

In the evening he translated a couplet from the Persian:

"The Beloved gave me some dust from the backyard.

Why are you so fragrant, oh, dust?

I am a dust people tread upon,

But I partake of the fragrance of the courtyard of a Saint.

It is not me, I am just an ordinary dust.

So if people praise you, you must say that you were just near a
**   flower,**

but you are an ordinary dust. And it is all due to His Lotus feet.

Speak up, that I may follow you," he said and I repeated.

"Yes, this will be a correct answer, if you always say like that!"

"Only eight more miserable days," I said. **"Yes,"** he answered.
Only one week left and he will be a memory. . . .

22nd April

HE DID NOT COME OUT THIS MORNING. He is not at all well, vomiting and
coughing much. So, I went home early.

The greatest happiness in life is the conviction that we are loved,
loved for ourselves, or rather loved in spite of ourselves, said Victor
Hugo.

I was with Pushpa and we were talking all the time about him. My
heart was so full of the sorrow of parting that I could not speak of
anything else. "I will surrender before Thee and Thou willst love me
for myself," Pushpa translated from the *Ramayana*.

"How are you?" He asked suddenly. His face was in the darkness,
dimly distinguishable, only the eyes blazing, looking straight at me.

"I am all right," I breathed. Wondered if he had fever. A
tremendous stream of power emanated from him; he closed his eyes
and so did I. And I was not, and lost the sense of time, and I think lost
consciousness too.

23rd April

HE SENT US HOME EARLY LAST NIGHT. Slept well, and this morning love is burning sky-high, and the longing is killing. I am going, and a kind of panic is in me. I am going, no time to bother, to speculate about the state a woman can reach or not. No time to bother about anything anymore . . . I am going and I will have to live without you. How will I? This tremendous sorrow to have to go makes my being numb with pain. The vibration goes on softly. It is like a sorrowful ecstasy, a kind of higher state of consciousness . . . a sort of exaltation mixed with panic. . . .

Told him that I had my birthday on Saturday, and it was the most lonely birthday of my life. Last year I asked for a boon on my birthday. I did not get any boon. "And this year you throw me out, not only out of your town, but out of India altogether. What a wonderful birthday present on my 56th year! An old lady! . . ."

"A woman is never old; sexually she is ever young. A man is supposed to become old."

"But I am not after sex," I said.

"No, never mind if one is not after sex; what I say has nothing to do with it. If women became old, the whole creation would disintegrate. The physical body becomes weaker; this is the law," he smiled faintly.

"Do you mean that *Prakriti*, Matter, is eternal, ever-young?" I asked. He nodded. "But *Purusha* is also ever-young?" I wanted to know.

"*Purusha* is composed of many things. *Prakriti* means: 'to work with.' If there were no *Prakriti*, there would be no Light. The more sex-power the human being has, the easier he will reach God or Truth. Impotent people cannot have *Brahma Vidya*, men or women. Great sex power is a great help in spiritual life. The outcome, the emanation of *Brahma Vidya* is coming down into manifestation as *Virya Shakti*, the Creative Energy of God.

"On the lowest plane of manifestation it appears as seminal fluid in men; in women it is preserved in the *Chakras*. That's why the yogic training on the etheric level for men and women is different. For men I give sometimes many practices; for woman it is only necessary to get rid of her greater attachment to *Maya*, because she is made by nature nearer to matter. In her the ties to material things like children, possessions, security, are very strong, stronger than in men."

"You said that one day even love has to be renounced; it is going to be a sad day, because love is the only thing I have left."

"Love will remain always," he answered. **"One day the self will go, then only Love will remain. . . . You will not say: I love. Where will the 'I' be?"**

"But how could we live without the center of the 'I'? There would be no consciousness, like in sleep, for instance."

"Yes, one lives in the self; in my case I can go out of the body at any time. When in the body the self is present, one suffers, feels like everybody else."

"But your self is not the same as in others. It must be of a different quality."

"The Real Self belongs to the Soul; once one is established in it, the life on the physical plane becomes of small, relative importance."

24th April

TOLD HIM THAT THE VIBRATION is softly going on, but there is no trouble. Only a kind of restlessness in the body.

"Should not be there," he looked at me thoughtfully. And there was none this morning. He took it away.

Even with my mind paralyzed I keep weeping all the time. Woke up at four a.m. A thunderstorm was fast approaching. Amongst the gusts of wind and clashes of thunder the voice of a newborn kitten was heard miauling loudly and helplessly. It was thrown behind the fence to die—somewhere nearby, I assume, but could not locate from where the sound came. Listening to this desolate sound of anguish made my heart even heavier than it already was. . . . What will become of me? How will I live? Without you? Without the hope of spiritual achievement?

The storm passed at a distance with lots of lightning. There was much barking of dogs for a while. About 5:30 the voice of the kitten was heard no more. Swallowed up by some dog I presume. . . .

25th April

IT IS SIMILAR TO A KIND OF HIGHER STATE of consciousness, a sort of enthusiasm. Sharp feeling of panic each time I remember that I am going. And I remember all the time. The heart keeps aching.

Told him that he, as a little boy of fourteen, was so much wiser than I, a mature woman. He knew that he had to love only, and I, in spite of clear hints again and again, kept fretting, causing myself endless suffering. Wanting this and that. Only now I have reached the stage that I want to love only, but now it is too late. I have to go. And surrounded by worldly preoccupations in London, what will become of my love, of my spiritual aspirations? He only smiled gently but said nothing. A newcomer came, a young man.

"I will go into the room with him," he pointed to the young man. **"You can remain seated outside or go home, as you wish."** His expression was dry and hard. They went in and the room was closed. Could not help feeling bitter. It was only a quarter past nine, still so early. I am going away for two-and-a-half years and he is grudging me the few remaining hours. . . .

Went to the electrician to arrange my ceiling fan to be taken down. I am giving it to him as well as all the furniture. The last night will sleep with Pushpa. When I came back, he was drinking at the water pipe in the garden.

"You can come inside." The newcomer was in Dhyana. He sat himself cross-legged on the tachat. Looked him over with such an expression of deep love. **"It is enough,"** he said suddenly, and with a start the man woke up. He was talking to him kindly for a while, then Guruji sent him away.

Sat in his big chair. Gandiji came. He began a long talk explaining something about the System, and I heard mentioned the word Bhogoun, and he was talking now about his Rev. Guru Maharaj. And I cried because my heart was aching too much. . . . Left after twelve and he was still talking.

In the evening the old Vahil was there, and he translated what he was telling him in Hindi: when there is deep peace, even music disturbs; one does not want any distractions.

"We don't encourage music even. Nothing. We rest in peace."

26th April

"MAY I ASK A QUESTION?" He bent forward with one of his beautiful smiles.

"Yes?" he said encouragingly.

"You said yesterday: **"Let it be!"** when I mentioned that London has a bad atmosphere; does it mean that one gets a protection when one is sent out into the world?"

"Why should London be worse than any other place? People say this town is a very bad place. The world is the world; good and bad are everywhere. One should not dwell on it and it will have no effect. A beautiful flower has a thorn. People pluck the flower; they

don't touch the thorn. I walk in the street, so do many people. I am not concerned with the street, nor with the crowd which passes by."

"Does it mean that Sufis should notice good things around them?"

"With Sufis it is different. They are absorbed somewhere all the time; they don't notice good or bad. We were in Bhogoun. No fans were there. We all slept on the floor. Were we affected by it? Certainly not. We should be able to sleep in the street when there is no other possibility. Why not? the street is also part of Him, made by Him. Sufis don't say: I do this or that. THEY DO IT. It is the Sufi way. If you think you did a great thing, then it goes; it has no value. Why not think you did it because it was your duty? Duty has a permanent value. Never think you did something great, something special. Think you did your duty only."

"You told us that your Rev. Guru was short-tempered with you and spoke to you only briefly, only to give orders as if in angry mood?"

"Yes, so it was for years, it is true."

"Did you not suffer very much . . . you must have!"

"Why should I?" he asked narrowing his eyes.

"Well, if one loves, a kind word is so precious, so desired, so necessary. You must have suffered greatly!"

"Why should I?" he repeated looking straight at me.

"I am afraid I don't understand what you mean." I was puzzled.

"I was after him, not after the suffering," he spoke slowly. "I wanted to please him. Why should I have suffered?" His eyes were resting on me quietly. What an answer, I thought . . . .

"I am afraid I DID suffer; very much so. . . ." He did not answer. He was in Samadhi.

His eldest son came out. He wrote down a few *Yantras* and was explaining to him how to write them and how to fold them. Then the newcomer came and he sent his son inside the room.

"He will put him in Dhyana. How interesting!"

"In our System it is not difficult; if I give an order, anybody can put anyone in Dhyana."

"Does he know what he is doing? Because L. told me that she does not know what she is doing; it just happens."

"L. is after the Trica Philosophy and her own *Kundalini*; one cannot ride two horses at once. My son saw it since his childhood; he was in it. He knows what he is doing. I am preparing him," he added, narrowing his eyes to a slit.

"Are you preparing him for the System?"

"This I don't know," he said with his eyes closed. "God knows who will take it. But I am preparing him; he is a silent one; he does not speak very much. And he is afraid of me."

Later when the newcomer joined us he said: "To be intellectual, to have much knowledge is a hindrance. For people who are not, it is easier. They know all the rules, what is written in the scriptures, but they are not able to lose themselves. They may get up at four a.m., go to the Ganga, do this exercise, this *Abhyasa*. They don't understand it is only an external thing, not at all important . . . for instance if I am a vegetarian and he is not," he pointed to a man sitting there, "why should I say: be vegetarian, do this or that—and hurt his feelings? The time will come when he himself will know what to do. Why should I bother? Intellectuals split themselves into so many exterior things; but the only essential is to be able to lose oneself. To be absorbed somewhere. . . ."

"Here are clear and definite directions how to behave when I am away," I said when I sat down. "To think always that I am only an instrument, never the doer, to do what is my duty and to try to be absorbed all the time." And I told him that since last Sunday it is like resting in Him. I am with Pushpa amongst people and I rest in Him in infinite peace. . . . At first, months ago, it used to happen like a stream, a Call from Him. Now I can "tune-in" so to speak, when I want to. Guruji never gave me the answer when I used to ask if it has to do with the nearness to Him. And for a long time I tried to understand it. And now it seems that I have the inkling of it: it is He merging into me through the mediation, the Grace of the Teacher, and now I begin to learn how to "tune-in" to His stream, or influence, which is probably always there . . . only the disciple has to learn how to get into it. In other words, the Teacher has to come to my level at first; later when the speed has been increased, I can do it myself.

All the while I was speaking, no words can describe the quality of the radiance, the tenderness of his smile. Then I knew that what I told him was correct.

7th April

AND IN THE EVENING HE CAME OUT when it was dark already. There was no talk to me, only in Hindi to others. Oh, yes, he did say that he does not believe in any kind of medicine; doctors know nothing. All depends on the Will of God, and our body is a wonderful instrument; the doctor can give it a little help, that's all.

And this morning I am waiting for the electrician to remove the ceiling fan. It is already half-past-eight and he is not here yet. One hour lost . . . I am at his place already at half-past-seven as a rule.

And my longing is endless, the longing for Him. This is going to be my permanent state; it looks like it. But in stillness, in infinite longing, I am with Him. I hope I will be able to keep this state of being absorbed. But I am fool enough to lose it like so many other times.

The electricians came about ten a.m. What could I do? I was so upset.

"The parents of everybody are great; and I mean of absolutely everybody. The parents keep for you the Gate of Heaven open. Respect is due to them. Otherwise when you are dead and come face to face with the Absolute Truth, it may ask you: You did not even respect your parents? Then it can become really difficult. Respect your father always," he turned to me. I showed him photos which I received yesterday. **"He is a very good man. I like him very much. A very fine man. I have seen him once or twice, so it seems to me."**

"Pictures of people come sometimes into the mind; you must have seen me surely also before you knew me. When L. wrote to you about me, you knew about me already; she showed me your letter." He smiled. "How will I live without seeing you," I said with a sinking heart.

"One answer only: keep me in the heart of Hearts."

"Keep me with you, don't forsake me," I said looking at his face full of light. He had a sphinx-like, stony expression.

"Only two days," he said slowly as if savoring the words, **"only two days and the physical nearness will be no more. The physical nearness,"** he repeated.

"Your physical body will change much; you will not be the same," I said thinking of his illness. He smiled faintly.

"I change every moment; every second I am not the same."

"Everybody does, but in your case it will be much more." He lowered his head.

"Time passes and nobody can assess time. It passes forever . . . one cannot bring it back."

Later he said: **"We discourage everything which has nothing to do with the Absolute Truth. Anything. Only THIS has to be THE GOAL."**

56

Mounting Irritation

27th April, 1963, evening
"I HATE SMOKING BUT I DON'T HATE THE SMOKER. **Otherwise how will he come round, give up?"** I asked what he had meant when he said that nobody loves like a mother, and if mother-love is not also a *Moha?*

"**Mother-love is not quite *Moha*. When the mother has one child who loves her and respects her and another who does not, she loves them both alike.**"

This is not a proof, I thought; a mother will always do that. "But what I want to know is does this love remain? No? then it is all *Moha*! And is father-love *Moha* or not?"

"**Don't criticize parents, otherwise you will criticize the Master!**"

He is evading a direct answer, I thought, but I only said: "I criticized you so often."

"**You did not know; now you know, so don't do it! Parents are the first Masters; don't they teach you: there is one God; look towards Him! Never, never criticize parents!**"

Speaking of love, later, he said: "**I cannot love anyone except only my Master. At least not in the real sense. But there are people who are convinced that I love them very much.**"

"But you will love a disciple by reflection, when he comes on the Line."

He shook his head. "**Two swords cannot be in one cover; in the heart there is room for only One. . . . In the real sense I cannot love but like this. . . .**" And he made a gesture towards the room, "**Many think that I love very much.**"

"What a pity; what a lonely road it is . . . I did hope so much one day you will love me." He shook his head.

"**I loved my Rev. Guru, my Father. They did and they still do much for me. I can say I love them, but as to say do they love me, how can I know? And if you say 'I love' it remains on the level of the mind; it won't reach them. . . . But those people are very great; no one knows what they can do.**"

"I would be satisfied even with a reflection, even with an illusion," I said, looking at him with aching heart. In reality I did not understand his answer. . . .

28th April

HAD A PEACEFUL NIGHT. One more day is left. Tomorrow there will be hardly any time left with furniture removing, shifting to Pushpa and so on. And I know, his statement is not at all correct. It is probably correct in the strictest sense seen from his own level. On the mind level there is no love, so much I know. But by reflection he must love me; he loves me already. He must, to be able to put me on the Line. But he is a great Teacher; he knows my character: put an obstacle in my way and I will make a greater effort to overcome it. He sends me away saying: I will never love you. And I say: try! You will have to! Because my attitude will be such that you won't be able to help it! If you unite me with you as at the end of Yogic training the Teacher does, you will have to love me. . . . **"I do only my duty, I am duty-bound,"** he said. He will love me BECAUSE he is duty-bound, for to unite my *Atma* with his, how can that be done without love?

This morning I was sitting alone for a long time. Then the horrible *Sannyasi* of last year came. It is the last day; surely he will attract the most disagreeable types to give me the last bit of torture. For hours I listened to the croaking of the *Sannyasi*. He came out almost immediately as soon as the *Sannyasi* arrived. And he was friendly. And he was radiant. Tenderly smiling, inciting the *Sannyasi* to talk. I cried a little. You don't change your attitude to the last, I thought. Kind to everybody but me. Then I saw him closing his eyes and becoming still for a few seconds. He is putting into the *Sannyasi's* head to go, I thought; he had enough of him. He was in Samadhi for a few brief moments. And sure enough the man got up and went. But the old Maharaj kept calling him back, praising him about a lecture, talking to him, asking questions. At last he left.

"Finally I managed to get rid of him," he said with a sigh of relief.

I laughed. "How you flattered him, encouraged him to talk; but you put it in his head to go. I watched you doing it!" I told him what I saw and he looked blank.

"You do it always!" I laughed, "and you put the idea into the head of your wife, or other members of the family, to come and interrupt when you don't want me to speak, attract all sorts of people to create disturbance, when it suits you! Yes, I am accusing you of it, but you know that it is true!" He gave me a still smile, his face looked radiant.

Then I thought that I increasingly felt a mounting irritation against him. How irritating he can be . . . but in spite of that my heart was so heavy; tomorrow, tomorrow there will be hardly any time left, so many things have to be done. . . .

29th April

HE SENT SATENDRA AND SITLA PRASAD with a handcart, and I got annoyed because they were so clumsily banging the wardrobe against the stone wall so that the varnish got scratched. I lost my temper with them; they were worse than little boys, the two of them. At last the wardrobe went and the tachat. I remained behind to collect a few things which could be useful in his household, like a plastic bucket, soap powder, a broom and a few other things, and took them to his place.

When I was entering his gate, I saw him sitting outside alone; he looked dark, his eyes flashing angrily. What's on? I thought, a fear sprang up from somewhere deep. I saluted and was about to enter the courtyard to deposit the few belongings I brought when he stopped me.

"How did you dare to speak in such a way to my son? He is a man and you only a woman! And Mrs. Ghose's daughters laughed because you lost your temper with him!"

"But they both handled the wardrobe in such a clumsy way, banging it against the wall. If you will examine it, you will see it is badly scratched; if you were present, you too would have lost your patience!"

"What do I care about the wardrobe! You idiot old woman! I am glad you are going at last! You have no respect towards my children; you are good for nothing, old and stupid! Prof. Batnagar was here when Satendra complained about you; what will he think of you!"

I was so taken aback at this quite unexpected attack that I sat down stunned. I don't remember even if I cried or not. Was like paralyzed, could not understand. Saw Satendra standing in the doorway regarding the scene with evident satisfaction, saw his brother looking at us from his side of the garden. He went on like that for quite a while. I think I cried, tried to justify myself, but I really don't remember . . . it is completely effaced from my mind.

"Go!" he shouted, **"I don't want to see your ugly face again! Go away!"**

Then I went, and when in the street looked back. He was still sitting in the same place, bent in two as though weighed down by a heavy burden. And this was the last impression of him which remained in my mind. . . .

When at home, I collected my last belongings mechanically, took a rikshaw to go to Pushpa's place. When passing his premises, had no desire to stop and go inside to say goodbye.

Pushpa and family saw me off to the evening train to Delhi. The journey was uneventful. Pushpa's relatives met me at the station. They were pleased to have me with them, and I spent a lovely day; in the night we all slept on the roof. It was very hot. I cried practically all night.

My last night in North India. . . . In the morning all the family including the grandmother came to the airport to see me off. And all the time while the plane was flying to the south I cried and cried, so that the lady sitting next to me finally asked if I was well and if she could help me. I told her that I was upset because I was leaving India where I had made good friends, and she was most sympathetic. Joyce met me at the airport in Madras. Her flat facing the river is so lovely, and I spent two days packing and talking about Bhai Sahib and him alone. And Joyce told me that she never felt such a deep peace as when we were together. Those were two lovely days, hot, full of fragrance of flowers—all the shrubs were flowering around the windows. And my longing was as endless as the sky. On Friday at six in the evening, Joyce took me with the car to the airport. In Bombay I learned that the schedule of flight was changed; instead of waiting until one a.m. for the London plane, it left at half past ten. We were rushed through the customs and we were off. Also, instead of flying via Cairo, Rome, Geneva, Paris, London, we went back to Delhi and the route was: Beirut, Geneva, Paris, London. When the plane was three-and-a-half hours from Delhi in the night, I was thinking that we must be somewhere above Persia or the Arabian Desert. And I began to cry. It was the sacred land, the birthplace of Sufism. . . . Thrown out by a Sufi, going towards a dark and, very probably, a terrible future, I cried desperately and complained to Him about my Teacher who turned me out. . . .

It was dark; all were asleep; we were cruising at 30,000 feet altitude.

In London, Maritje (whose daughter is in Bombay) met me at the airport, and I went to Andrée who could not come because she had a bad leg. Very swollen and painful. I stayed with Andrée. Was trying so hard to find a room, but it proved to be very difficult. I wanted to be near her, and Kensington is an expensive district and I was very poor. After three weeks I felt that I overstayed my welcome; it was evident from her attitude.

I was so desperate; even asked a policeman if he knew something, and he said that I should try in Holborn district because here all accommodations are so difficult to find and are expensive. But after two days I saw a notice on the board of the tobacconist in Ladbroke Grove: a flatlet to let, £2.10 per week. I immediately inquired. He looked at me and said: "Madam, I don't think that it is for you; it is very small, rather for a student." But I asked to see it. The flatlet consisted of one room five by ten feet. A bed, a tiny dressing table— there was no room for even a chair, only a small stool; inside a built-in cupboard in the wall was a wash basin, a small cooker and a very small wardrobe. The small room was literally sticking out into the traffic. On the first floor, corner Ladbroke Grove and Holland Park Avenue, the roar of the traffic was deafening. And his words came into my mind: **"You must be able to sleep in the street; why not? Is the street not also His?"** I would be sleeping as if in the street here, and the branches of the large beautiful plane trees practically touched the window panes. . . . So I took it. The price was all I could afford. For the moment it was the right thing for me. And what a discipline it would be . . . after that, every other room will be like a ballroom for me . . . to learn how to live in such a small place is a great lesson. And one month after arriving in London I moved in.

On the 16th of May I wrote a letter to him . . . a letter of recrimination and reproach; it was a bitter letter. But I doubt that he ever read it. I said in it that probably I won't write to him; it won't be welcome. But on the 22nd May I began to write to him regularly two or three times a week. I could not help it. Told him about my work, my life, everything. After three months I got a letter not written by him but dictated to somebody, that he was very ill for two months. He had an amoebic abscess on the liver which burst, and he nearly died of it. So my letters must have accumulated; he probably never read them; his children probably did.

His letters were few and far in between, mostly dictated to others. They never dealt with important spiritual matters, only his family affairs . . . chatty, insignificant letters. But I was not put off. I felt that it was deliberately done. It was a test. Such a man am I; you still want to come back? He seemed to imply. But I kept writing for two-and-a-half years. I never got a direct answer to any of my letters. Just a few lines from him about unimportant matters. And very rarely in the bargain.

Then I met H. And the sign was given that here is work to be done. By now I knew how it worked, the Hint, so I became interested in her.

And then one day he told me in one of his letters to bring her with me when I will come back in '65. But this was much, much later. And in fact in December 1965, we both went to India to him. But in the meantime I had to put her through a definite training, and after four months she had the state of Dhyana by His Grace. . . .

PART TWO

THE WAY OF NO RETURN

57

Return

THOUGH WE ARRIVED HERE, H. and I, on the 15th December, it is only now that I begin to make entries into my diary. But before I commence to relate the events in chronological order, I had better note down what he said yesterday concerning the Yantra. When we came to him yesterday afternoon, about 4:30, he was sitting outside, a man sat in front of him, a thin man, obviously very worried. Bhai Sahib was writing something on small pieces of paper.

"The children of this man, four in number, are suffering from smallpox," he said to us, looking up with a kindly smile when we were sitting down. **"I am giving them Yantras. And it is absolutely sure, without any doubt, that the children will be all right. When this Yantra is used, death cannot come near; death goes away. I am thinking how to teach you this Yantra."** He looked at me smiling kindly, his eyes narrowed to a slit. **"But how can it be done? English language is written the other way round from Persian."**

"Perhaps I can learn it by heart how to write it?" I ventured, thinking what a great service to humanity it would be if one has the power of this Yantra. . . .

"I am thinking . . . I will find the way," he laughed . . . this laughter of his, so young, with the bell-like, metallic ring in it. He continued to write. We sat quietly. He lifted in the air one small piece of paper covered with Persian writing: **"This is the Yantra."**

"I was thinking that a Yantra is rather a Symbol; like a five- or six-pointed star or a syllable, something like that."

"Yes, it is usually so. But I was left completely free by my Rev. Guru Maharaj; I can do as I like. And I prefer it this way. I am quite, quite free," he added with great emphasis and a faraway look.

If he is free, he will find the way to teach it to me, even in a language foreign to him, like English, I thought, watching how he was folding the paper. I even stood up and went behind his chair to see how he did it.

"This Yantra is against smallpox, cholera, plague, typhus, typhoid fever, and other things. And the person does not die if the Yantra is

tied on him. Cannot die. Death keeps away." I asked where one
should tie the Yantra.

"If it is a question of children, it is tied around the neck, but in the
case of adults it is tied under the left armpit of a woman and under
the right armpit if it is a man. The Yantra is dipped into the wax,
then put into a cotton cloth and then tied on. So if one takes a bath
or is washed, it is not spoiled or damaged. Never, even for a moment,
should the Yantra be removed. If it is removed, the person dies. So if
a person is intended to die, somebody will remove the Yantra. You
see, two orders are running parallel. Somebody is destined to die. In
this case one of the family, or friends, or perhaps someone present
will remove the Yantra. While the Yantra is there, the order is there
and he cannot die. So it is bound to be removed. Sometimes people
come and ask and I don't answer. I keep silent. If they insist I say:
"Yes, if you like, you can remove it." This is the end, of course. . . ."

"Is this Yantra against T.B. also?" asked H.

"No, not against T.B. There is another Yantra for that. But if T.B. is
at the initial stages, no Yantra is needed for that. The illness is made
to go away without it."

He gave the completed Yantras to the man who left touching his
feet.

"Never, never, charge anything for this sort of thing, not even a
nayapaise (a small Indian coin). If I would have charged, I would
have been a millionaire. Many people came to me to have a Yantra;
all are helped, it never fails; but it must be given free, as a service,
without a charge. Tell them to give something to the poor after they
have been healed, but never an even number, always an odd one.
Either one, or three, or five, or seven, or whatever they can afford—a
coin if they are poor, or a bank note, or several, if they are richer."

We stayed till 7:30. He made me speak as he sometimes did
before, and explain to Tandem some Sufi tenets and historical facts
about Rumi. Then he spoke for a long time to them in Hindi. And
lastly he went into a prolonged Samadhi. I felt nothing at all. So, I
thought that he was giving H. a sitting like the day before yesterday.
But today I am not so sure of that. Strong vibration in my heart
started. And I was thinking that the trouble he announced several
days ago has begun. . . .

Had a good sleep last night. This morning he said: "Let's walk,"
and he, H. and I were walking up and down the garden. He told me
that he wanted the car the day after tomorrow and told us a few
things of no significance about some of his disciples. But I felt such

impact of his Shakti and had an unpleasant feeling like a premonition that my trouble will begin soon . . . they will start all over again.

We arrived by plane on the 15th of December. Babu and Satendra with their new wives were meeting us at the airport with the Sharma's large car. They took us to see some temples and some city sights. Though I was glad that H. had the opportunity to see that, my heart was longing so much to be at the Guruji's place as soon as possible. He came to meet us, and I fell at his feet and was so moved that I nearly fainted and was much ashamed about it afterwards. H. was wide-eyed, looking at him in wonder. We were accommodated with Mrs. and Mr. Sharma, Guruji's disciples; he was an important city functionary, and we had a lovely room on top of their bungalow. Mrs. Sharma had a sort of fay look, the slender, elegant Indian ladies sometimes have.

Around Christmas we went to Bhogoun. I only remember that we stayed at the house of the doctor where we stayed when I was there for the first time. Remember his prayers sung with a wonderful baritone at four in the morning. Remember that we all slept on the floor, that we had meetings under a marquee in front of his Rev. Guru's house, that H. took some photos which turned out to be lovely (later she sent Guruji some copies) . . . but I remember very little of anything else. My memory failed me again like last time . . . I think Guruji gave a lecture in Persian, though he does not know this language to such an extent as to be able to give a learned lecture . . . that he was congratulated on it, and he was laughing about it and very amused. Remember the two small Muslim graves in the fading, soft evening light, and the vultures who were settling on the trees for the night. Remember dimly our walk across the cultivated fields, the heart sick with longing. And this is all. Nothing more.

2nd January

"IF YOU ARE ADDICTED TO MUSIC, there is no progress. Why? If you cannot go in Dhyana or Samadhi without music, it means that you are addicted to it, cannot do without it. It becomes an obstacle. In our Yoga System nothing is needed. My Rev. Father was of Chishtia Dynasty, but even then, because His Guru was not of this Dynasty, he gave it up."

Later he said: "Perfection cannot be. Some imperfection must always remain. As soon as we become perfect, we cannot remain in this world."

I had to answer some questions to people who were there, while he was having his tea inside. When he came out, he talked to them in Hindi about me, then he said in English (it was intended for my ears): **"I gave her a training I could give to nobody else."**

A few days before he said in conversation: **"The Prophet is the Master of Time; but the Wali is the master of the people of the time."**

When we came this morning, several of the old disciples who came from the province were there. He pointed to one elderly man who was sitting with folded palms and downcast eyes in his presence.

"He is the son of a man whose place here is still vacant. He was an old man. He came one day, he was over 60; it was in 1923, and he knocked at the door. And he kept knocking. I was not at home; my father was on the roof terrace. Nobody opened it for him, but he kept knocking. You understand, it is very symbolical. Finally, my father said: 'Whoever it is, let him in.' He came in and never inquired about anything. Why? Because his Master gave him directions what to do and he did it in utter obedience. He died when he was over 80. And he left it in his will that nobody should touch his body until I came. I was at that time in Lucknow. Suddenly I knew I had to go home. There were no trains. But somehow by the Grace of God it was done and I arrived at 3 a.m. My father told me that it was good, in fact, that I came. But he did not say anything else to me. At 5 a.m. the sons of the dead man came and I was told."

He translated a couplet from Hafiz:

> **"Wine is not considered to be a good thing. But if your Spiritual Guide orders you to drench the carpet on which you meditate with it, you must do it without questioning, in utter faith. Guide can be only one; he is the Guide amongst the guides** (it means an old link from the past for you)."

H. was told by Guruji last evening that he will come in the night to visit her. This morning she told me on awakening that she woke up three times during the night with the feeling of a great and wonderful Presence and felt great bliss. It happened three times, and she fell asleep and woke each time with the same feeling.

He saw us as soon as he came out and he asked: **"How are you? H., you are VERY WELL!"** And he laughed. He knows, I thought, of course. . . . Since yesterday there is such a deep love in me . . . and I pray to Him, the Eternal, with such deep feeling of utter nothingness . . . nothingness which is the deepest bliss. . . .

"SINCE I AM HERE, my heart is singing, singing before you. It seems to me that I can even hear it sing; it is going on all the time, ceaselessly, when I am before you or at Sharma's place; it is just singing." He nodded slowly.

"It is good, very, very good."

"Can I ask one question?"

"Do, by all means," he smiled at me.

"Is this singing the constant remembrance of God? We are supposed to remember God at every moment of the day; if my heart is singing to Him all the time . . . when I am praying it is singing to Him, when I am here it is singing to you . . . then there must be constant remembrance?"

"It is," he nodded. **"But later, the remembrance will be there all the time, and one will not notice it. And this state can last for many years."**

"In my case, probably it will last for a short time, because the states with me change quickly."

"With a Wali or a Saint, the states last for a long time, then they change. The progress is infinite, the Knowledge is infinite. It goes on endlessly."

I told him that I used to give an example of a musical instrument in my talks. We bring the instrument; the Master is the Musician to tune it and to play on it. In other words, the Teacher cannot change or increase the capacity of the cup, the size of it—he can only fill it.

"Oh no!" he exclaimed, **"The capacity can be increased by the Teacher. Everything can be done by the Teacher; the Teacher is one with God. What can God not do? God can do everything! The Teacher can also do everything. There are laws and regulations; God made those laws and regulations. Because He made them, why should He change or transgress them? But still it can be done. But not with everybody. Munshiji, for instance, was a drunkard and a gambler. There is no harm that he was so, from the spiritual point of view, if he would give up the tendencies. But he does not, and he has been with me for the past forty years. Not everybody can surrender. It is not done with everybody. Why should one do it?"**

"One could quote here the words of Christ: 'Many are called, but few are chosen,' " said H. He nodded.

"The sayings of Great World Teachers are the same always. They are only expressed differently; the meaning is the same."

Already a few weeks before our departure for India, all became so stale for me. H. gave me hospitality for the last two months because the rent of my room was increased and I could not pay it. All in me seemed to be empty; I had nothing to say to anybody. I disliked everyone; they all went on my nerves. I had finished my song, my heart was waiting. . . . On the day of our departure, in the morning I was so tense that I could hardly bear myself, and it must have been very difficult for poor H. . . .

4th January

H: "WHAT IS THE DIFFERENCE between a Saint and a Sage?"

He: "A very great difference. A Saint, a Wali, is taken up to a certain stage, is made like his Master. Then he progresses automatically; he goes with his Master. He does not come back. A Saint is pure Love. They do not give laws like Prophets. They do not rule. They obey and are content with the Will of God. They are Instruments of God. If a Saint commits a mistake, God always will give the opportunity to correct it, because he is completely surrendered; he has no will of his own except the Will of God. But the Sage, if he commits a mistake, he has to come back. . . ."

5th January

YESTERDAY SPEAKING OF A DIFFICULT ATMOSPHERE in a certain place, he said laughingly: "Why don't you change the atmosphere? The atmosphere can be changed by you people. Try! Pray! and if you cannot change it, ask for the help of the Almighty. Don't think that it is difficult. Don't dwell on the difficulties; get it out of your mind! Change it! You can do it!"

In the evening he said: "You should pray in the night; pray for the dead. Then they will pray for you, and the nearness to God will be more and more. . . ."

This morning when he came out, the great vibration in the heart began. Since I am here I kept wondering how is it that I don't feel strong vibrations in his presence as I used to have before, and can speak to him calmly. But this morning it began strongly, the irregular beat in the heart and breathlessness just as before. He is not well today. He looks angry. Perhaps he will give me a test; the heart activity would account for that.

Early in the morning I woke up. It was still dark. H. was sleeping peacefully. Remembering what he said about prayer, I began to pray. Prayed for him, for everybody, for the whole world. Tears were running down my cheeks; the whole of my being was one endless stream flowing out to Him without ever diminishing.

In the afternoon we sat for a long time under the tree near the papayas at the bottom of the garden behind the shrubs. He was not too well and was resting. I kept thinking of G. and that I had better ask him about her. When he came out, it was after half-past-five and during the conversation he asked about her. As usual he knew what was in my mind, and he gave me instructions what to write to her. My mind gave me a little trouble this morning, but as soon as I saw him, it all melted away as the mist in the Himalayas before the rising sun.

Speaking about Ragunath Prasad, he said: **"Whoever asks Ragunath Prasad about spiritual life, he answers that all that is needed is to merge into the Master. He always knows when I am not well and either sends a man, or writes, or comes himself."**

"Merging into the Master," I said, "Fana fi Shaikh, then Fana fi Rasul, and the last stage Fana fi Allah." He nodded.

"And the first stage is the most difficult of all. Most difficult," he repeated nodding thoughtfully. I kept thinking in the meantime that I have to pray so much, so much that God gives me this Grace. . . .

6th January

"LOVE IS QUENCHING THE THIRST on the physical plane. This is not love. The human being is love, and Love loves the human being. To realize Love is to realize God. If we sit before an open fire, it warms us. There is no effort on our part. Those who have realized God are like this fire. Keep in their company. God realized Himself in the heart of Hearts of the human being. Example of the ocean and the waves. They disappear and are here. When we realize, Love disappears. We cannot give shape or name to Love. The deeper we go, the more it disappears. It radiates from every part of the body. And the last transfer which takes place from the Master to the disciple is from the heart to the heart. Where the trouble comes from, help is also there; people forget it, that's why they are in trouble.

"Everything is done with spiritual power on our Line. But if the receiver is not a good one, then one tries the mental plane. If this is not enough, one has to come down to the physical plane.

"I know nothing; I flow where I am directed. The river does not know if it is flowing. If we know something, we have to throw it away, to throw it back; we have to forget it for it is worthless.

"Only He knows everything; REMEMBER: WE KNOW NOTHING. If

people speak highly of you, beware of pride. Pray. If people do so, IT IS ONLY HE WHO SPEAKS HIGHLY OF HIMSELF. If they flatter, they don't flatter you, really. It is He who in their shape does it. He flatters Himself. If you are abused, it is the same. He is abusing Himself. We should not abuse people; we should bear it. We can be angry only with people who are with us, who follow us step by step. Not with others. Disciples are guided. Their errors are pointed out to them by the Teacher. Otherwise they will be misguided. It is a chain of love, the love to the Master. From the bottom to the top. It never disappears. It becomes complete; no difference between bottom and top. Later, nothing but love will remain. Later still, even that remains behind. It is an airdrome from where one has started.

"Forgetfulness is the greatest qualification; one is sure to pass the examination; you won't come back to this place. They who have gone don't come back and even don't send their messages to us. They just do you services without a reward or return. They leave their grace and bliss; it remains with us."

While he was speaking, just before, I felt a tremendous bliss. Somebody was here . . . a Great Being. . . .

"The relationship between the Teacher and his disciples can be compared only to the relationship of a father to his children. Only a father wants his son to be more than himself. Elder brother will help you, yes, but he does not want you to be more than himself. The Teacher knows no envy; there is no jealousy in him. He is glad when the disciple is on a higher stage than himself."

8th January

WHEN WAITING FOR ME TO GET READY to go to the Guru, H. had a mystical experience this morning. She was standing in front of the picture of Padmapani painted by Mrs. Sharma. Her experience is in her diary.

When I called her to go, I saw her standing in the middle of the room as in a trance. She could hardly walk. I saw that she was in a good state. It passed after several hours. As soon as we arrived, Guruji asked her how she was; he was dressed for a walk and we went to the park. She was as in a dream.

When speaking to him in the evening, I said that I am such a beginner. He replied: "Nobody is a beginner. Or we are all beginners. I am a beginner from my stage; you are a beginner from your stage. Swimming in the Infinite ocean, who is nearer the shore?

We are all beginners, of course. . . . One day I will tell you how to help people and how they are helped, how they receive it. There is a way to come before an audience and by one glance to know the mind of the whole audience. A higher stage is, for instance, if you have a friend in America, and want to help him and do it, and know everything about him. But this is still not the highest stage; it is a high one, but not the highest. The highest stage is when you can transfer the powers to another human being. This is the highest stage. Only great people can do that. The most difficult stage is *Fana fi Shaikh*. If this stage is completed, without any doubt one becomes a *Wali* (a Saint). You understand what I mean?" I could only nod.

Then we had a long discussion about H. He sent her away for a walk. When I was leaving he said: "**When you are hurt, never show it to her. She does not understand. Never show it, and throw the thought of it out of your mind. Those who are guided by us are forgiven so much. But sometimes, but only very rarely they are not forgiven, accordingly.**" And then he added: "**We all have some difficulties to overcome; everybody has. I am always with you, so why should you care?**" I bowed down with folded hands, my heart was suddenly so full, my throat was choking, the words of Jesus were ringing in my mind: "I am with you always till the end of the days. . . ." And I walked quickly out of the garden in order that he should not see that tears were running down my cheeks. Walking home, I cried and I prayed, and so much love was in my heart that it seemed to want to burst. . . .

9th January

IN THE NIGHT I PRAYED SO MUCH. When I woke up I prayed and repeated His Name, and it was like a song in my heart. The sweetness of His Name. The pleasure to repeat it. The nearness . . . I prayed to be united with the Master. He said that the Mediator, or Representative who is the Master, is most necessary. So I pray that I may achieve the most difficult stage, the oneness with him.

H. who was just now sitting with closed eyes beside me said: "It all happened again like yesterday. . . ." Her eyes which she opens from time to time are as if in a wondrous dream, eyes like dark pools of deepest wonder . . . and I pray . . . and I pray . . . for the Grace.

10th January

"PEACE CAN ONLY BE HAD in the most peaceless state which is love."
I introduced H. yesterday to the judge, one of his disciples. I got a

warning flash from his mind. It was against the etiquette; it is not done in the presence of the Master. I apologized today. He smiled.

"Those things are forgiven. Again and again, endlessly. I don't look at these things. I don't consider you my disciples; if I would, then so difficult would be the signs of respect and reverence one has to observe that it would be impossible for you. I myself was never able to do it completely. All that is needed is complete obedience and faithfulness. It is very difficult to please the Master, in order that the Master should make you like himself. It is the most difficult thing in the world."

Speaking of special peace at the grave of his Rev. Guru he said: **"The peace at the grave of my Rev. Guru is unbelievable. There is also great peace in the Samadhi of my parents. But in Bhogoun it is greater. Of course. He was their Guru. He was the Great Teacher."** He fell silent for quite a while.

"It is perfectly true," I said softly; "when I was sitting at his grave, I kept thinking what a difference this time is from the last time, nearly three years ago. There was a great difference. Then I was heart-broken; I had to go; I did not know if I would see you again. I wanted spiritual life; I wanted God so badly. Desperately I prayed. And now? I looked within my heart, analyzed my feelings. It seemed to me that this time I wanted nothing . . . nothing at all. What is spiritual life? Perhaps it is also a delusion. It is Maya. One more Maya. To desire something is a delusion. The only thing which seemed to remain now is my love, my desire for God which is Truth. Only that is Reality; only that I want even more than before. So I just sat there full of peace, desiring nothing, except God, and all around were the plains and the palm trees, vultures settling on them for the night, and the sky of the special mother of pearl azure. And later the sun setting in the glory of yellow and gold, the infinitely serene sunsets of the plains, full of majesty, the calm ending of a perfect day. . . . And when you were all already walking away, I remained behind, and I prostrated myself before His grave, my heart crying out to him. . . . I did not want to be seen doing it, and nobody saw me; they were all around you talking; nobody noticed that I remained behind. I soon joined you all."

While I was speaking, he closed his eyes. And such a stream of love, like a current, flowed strongly from him towards my heart . . . I knew that he was pleased. . . .

11th January

WHEN THE SERVANT BROUGHT US THE HOT WATER in the morning, he told us that the prime minister Shastri died. Later we knew from Mr. Sharma that the news came through at one a.m. He was in Tashkent, and a good agreement was reached between India and Pakistan. He was due to arrive in Delhi today. He died from a heart attack. There was such a restless atmosphere; people were standing around, and all were discussing excitedly how he died and what will be. I was on edge. How restless it can be in his place . . . and the horrible orangutang face was talking his head off. . . . He did not speak to us at all the whole morning, and in the evening we sat in the dark room and he was with his family in the next room. I could just see his profile, the white beard, looking like a prophet with his grey topi. It suits him. But about seven, Sharma came with some other men. So, he came out hurriedly. The same story repeats itself again: he will never come out for us. If others are there, we may benefit from his presence. But if we are alone, he lets us sit in the dark room . . . and he does not care that H. will be here for only two more weeks. And she made such sacrifices in order to be able to come. . . .

58

The First Cloud

I MUSN'T FORGET TO MENTION what happened two days after our arrival. He turned to H. and said: **"I want you to go to the post office and get me a few inland envelopes and some stamps. You don't mind going to the post office?"** He looked at her sharply.

"Of course not, why should I mind? Tell me how many you want and I will bring them to you!" I looked at her thinking that she does not know how different the Indian post offices are from the ones in our country. The jostling, pushing crowd of men can be disagreeable to a woman. Very seldom I saw an Indian woman in a post office, mostly servants. As soon as she left, he asked me about her. I told him what I knew about her background, how I met her, that she reached the first stages of Dhyana after being with me for four months in my little room filled with the roar of the traffic of Holland Park Avenue. She used to come every day at four p.m. and stayed until nine or ten . . . all things I wrote to him in my letters, but probably he wanted to hear it from me.

"And when she comes out of Dhyana, she does it quickly and her mind takes over clearly and efficiently?"

"I think so, at least I hope, but you will be the better judge of it." He said nothing. "There is only one problem, if one can call it a problem; she is unable to do it in a seated position."

"Oh? And why so?"

"Because she has an abdominal condition which prevents her from sitting still for any length of time."

"Hmm . . . that should be corrected. . . ." He was thinking for a while, his lips tightly pressed, the eyes narrowed to a slit. **"How long can she stay?"**

"About six weeks, till the end of January. She has her property to look after; it is her living, her business." He seemed to ponder.

"Hmm . . . what can one do in six weeks? Six weeks are nothing. I cannot subject her to what I have subjected you—she will go off her head. You will help her in London as well as you can."

I looked at him. He knew what I was thinking.

522

"Yes," he nodded, **"I know. It is a great responsibility to guide a soul. And it can be painful to the guide and to the guided. Still, we have to do our duty, and she will be part of your responsibility. You will get help; help is always given."**

I said nothing. What could I say? So I began to tell him how to my surprise the quick vibrations of the traffic not only did not interfere with meditation states, but proved to be helpful. And the day came while meditating, I began to realize why the Spiritual Life, or Yoga, is a question of speed. He said it himself, I remember, one day. "Life in the world, civilization, is speeded up constantly; everything is going faster and faster. Our children for instance are much faster than us; they live quicker. The pace of life, the pressure of it, the blaring of the radios, the noise of the big cities, does not disturb them, but it disturbs us, because we are much slower. New discoveries, the sciences, inventions, follow each other with hair-raising acceleration. And the day must come when the Spiritual Life and the life as it is lived in this world are bound to meet; they are like two ends of the same stick; they will meet in the middle and become one."

He listened to me with attention. **"Write it down; write down everything. It will be helpful."**

H. returned. He told Satendra to take what she brought into the room and told her to sit down.

He began to talk in Hindi; several men were seated around, listening. After a while I turned to H. and saw she was in Dhyana, seated on a hard, wooden chair (and it was an uncomfortable chair, I knew it, for only too often I had to sit on it and I could never do it without shifting my legs or my body from time to time). But she sat motionless, completely relaxed; her face was serene and she looked very beautiful.

At one moment Jagan Nathji noticed that she was in Dhyana. "Oh?" He remarked inquiringly, pointing at her, "She is here only for the last two days? And already in Dhyana?"

Bhai Sahib nodded slowly. **"When there is faith, everything can be done,"** he said. The men were talking now about an incident which happened recently in town.

I was watching H. I did not know when it began, for I did not look at my watch, so I did not know how long it lasted, but I think it must have been at least one hour. Then Guruji gave her a sharp look, and at once she opened her eyes looking at him with those soft brown eyes of hers, this wonderful look I know so well; the Soul returning from far, faraway. . . . She kept looking at him. For the first time she could do it seated, I was thinking; what can a Sat Guru not do?

And the lovely quotation came into my mind: ". . . and the Prophet loved perfumes and lovely women, and the shining of eyes in prayer." The shining of eyes when the Soul looks through them, just returned from the Spiritual Plane . . . its own domain . . . a look of Divine Purity.

Great is your might, Bhai Sahib. Wonderful is the power of a Sat Guru. . . . He looked at me quizzically.

"What is the difference between a bad Teacher and a good Teacher? A bad Teacher will always behave how his followers expect him to behave. The conventional idea of a spiritual Teacher is that he is always kind, benevolent, compassionate, dignified, wearing robes, or garments which distinguish him from the ordinary mortals, uttering at all times wise, profound sentences. So he will behave accordingly . . . because he is after personal prestige, or worldly possessions, or even money or honors. But a good Teacher obeys a law of which the world has no notion. Do you know what is *Swadharma*? It is a Sanskrit word and it means a Dharma, a duty which is innate in the thing itself, imbedded in its *Swabhave* (true nature). For instance the *Swadharma* of the water is to be wet and fluid, that of the fire is to burn and to consume, of the wind to blow. They cannot help it; it is in their nature. And so it is the Sat Guru; he just IS. He may do things which people don't understand, or may even condemn. For love does not always conform to the conventional idea people have made of it. Love can appear in the shape of great cruelty, a great injustice, or even calamity. In this respect, one could say that the Sat Guru is similar to God. He cannot be judged or measured by worldly standards. Shamsi Tabriz was said to be rude and abrupt; he used to address his audience as 'oxen' and 'asses.' Nevertheless, he was a great Teacher and Rumi dedicated a whole book of poetry to him."

He was silent for a while, following with his eyes a sparrow hopping along the brick elevation. Then he said: "My kindness will not help you, but my severity will."

I sat very still, listening carefully. So, it looks as if my tribulations are by no means over. At that moment the future seemed to be very dark. But no, there is, there MUST BE a light at the end of the tunnel, however black, however long it may be. . . . A Light, so glorious, so much longed for, so much mine, mine alone, but only because it must be shared, given to others. . . .

12th January, 1966

"I AM LAZY," said Mrs. Sharma this morning. "What prevents me from repeating the Name of God? Nothing. But I prefer to think of something more pleasant." What can be more pleasant than the Name of God?, echoed my heart, as she was saying it. . . . And in that moment I suddenly realized something important and I told H. about it while we were walking along to Guruji's place.

"Mrs. Sharma said that she prefers to think of something more pleasant than the repetition of the Name of God. Here lies a mystery. Unless the Name of God becomes the sweetest thing to us, we are nowhere and nothing will happen. If we repeat it as a unpleasant duty, we are nowhere. Like myself, I was repeating it and repeating it, and it had only a meaning of a hard duty. But later, gradually, from time to time, it became sweeter and sweeter. This feeling came and went. And when it went, I stopped to call on Him and waited till it came back, and then began the repetition once more . . . and now it is the sweetest thing in the world. And my heart goes there automatically, when I am alone, at any moment of the day, when it has the chance to do so. And then one can pray tremendously, as never before, and the nearness is there, more and more. . . . To put it differently: if our Religion remains on the surface, we are nowhere. Only if it becomes part of us, of our innermost being, then we draw nearer the Infinite Truth. The Soul of man will not do anything in which it is not interested; it is useless to force it; the mind will prevent it. It will create a barrier. And the Interest is an Act of the Grace of God. It is given by the Guru as an act of Grace. Through Love you repeat the Name of the Beloved which is the sweetest thing in the world! . . ."

I was like you Mrs. Sharma. I got bored by repeating His Name endlessly. I preferred to think of something more interesting. Life has so many interests . . . but then the moments of great nearness came from time to time. . . . Then to repeat His name was of greatest sweetness. So I used to wait for the nearness in order to enjoy repeating His Name. And now it is the sweetest thing in the world; nothing could be sweeter. And now things do happen. And as soon as I begin, such peace is there, and my heart is only happy when I can do it. . . .

"If you come to know something about people, either the future or the past, or sins, or other things, help where help is needed, and then forget, throw it behind you. And do not disclose it, otherwise this knowledge will be taken from you. People will be afraid of you;

they will not follow you. They will say she knows everything, and it is frightening to have to deal with somebody who knows so much. Perhaps intimate, perhaps secret things . . . knowledge comes through the heart . . . from the heart to the mind. Knowledge is always good. But if one discloses it, discloses the good things and then the bad things, because one comes to know both, and speaks about it to others, in the absence of the person, one becomes used to it. And the self will never go. And if the self remains, there can be no spiritual life. But by throwing away, you are not the doer. Samskaras don't remain. Throw away everything."

"It is frightening to the mind—the mind likes to know why and how, especially the Western mind.

"There is no such thing as Western mind and Eastern mind. There is only one mind. And how can it understand the how and why if those flashes of Intuition are not from the mind? The whys and hows are in the mind. By and by you will understand. For such things the Master is necessary."

So, I began to understand while walking down the street of Aryanagar, after having bought him a small cake. By throwing things away—resentment, knowledge, everything—the self will go. There is the past and there is the future, he said, the present is nothing. I must try to understand what he means.

Throwing away means to be completely in the Hands of God . . . relying on Him completely. Sometimes this feeling of bottomless abyss is frightening to the mind, when I think of it. . . .

To throw it behind . . . how simple. So simple that I wonder how is it that I didn't think of it myself. . . . Now I will practice it. But to be able to understand it, to practice it, one must be ready for it, one must be ripe. If the memory of the resentment, of the offenses, is thrown away, where would the resentment be? One would live without the memory . . . one rejects it. It would mean to live in the NOW in the Hands of God . . . a tremendous thing, difficult, if at all, to be understood. I looked at him when he came out and saw that he did not want to speak to me. So I kept quiet.

Earlier, speaking of clairvoyants he said: "They are at the lowest level; they don't even go beyond the mind."

Leaving with the Vippin ladies who were giving us a lift in their car, I remained a few steps behind, thanking him with my eyes. He bowed slightly with a smile; deep understanding was in his expression and his smile.

"I really know nothing, but I will say or do the right thing for every occasion."

That's why he is constantly repeating, since I am back, that forgetfulness is the greatest qualification—not in the sense of forgetting what one knows or needs to know, but in the sense of *forgetting what ought to be forgotten.* Will I be like him then? Heaven knows. . . .

In the evening he sat there as serene as eternity. Cranes were returning from the Ganges, as I have seen them so often in the past years. . . . A large bluish star was hanging in the west, on the fading pale-yellow horizon. Perhaps it was Venus. It became dark quickly. I saw his face, his eyes light up, as he was talking to a man sitting beside me. We were only four in the garden, he, this man, H. and I, and nobody else. My heart was singing to him. Great Teacher. Gently he guides us. Each time a little more, a little further. . . . This morning he pointed to the next step: Throw behind you . . . everything. For this is the Way. . . .

13th January

HE HAD A SEVERE VOMITING CONDITION in the night, so he told us. It was like death. He could not catch his breath for several minutes. We did not see much of him. Went to the bazaar with Mrs. Sharma. What a waste of time. H. was choosing some saries.

59

What is Nearer—the Source or the Delta?

14th January, 1966

HAD A BAD NIGHT . . . bad dreams which I could not remember. Kept worrying about his condition while awake. The mind was restless.

"Some very pleasant things are going on in unpleasantness," he said, and added that he felt much better today.

"Last night you both remained for a long time with me. Others were here too, but you both remained for a long time. . . . Day and night, things do happen in dreams, in experiences, and the mind knows nothing about it."

"You say that we remained with you for a long time. But if I understood well, Sufis work from the *Atmic* level—that's why they are so powerful. And on that level there is no time or space, only oneness, so how can it be said that we remained somewhere, and for how long?"

"Yes, it is so. When one remains in the Heart of Hearts, one is nowhere. It is said that when the disciple is ready the Master appears. What does it mean? It means that when the disciple is ready, he is with the Master. And the other way round: the Master is with the disciple. That is the Law. We are all on different levels. Some are not at all on the high level. They cannot reach there. So the Master will come down until the disciple can go higher."

"It cannot be that now I am further away from you than I was at the beginning; it is just not possible after more than four years."

"It is so, you are right," he said.

"So, how can it be that I never know that you suffer? The night before last you vomited and suffered so much, and I slept and felt nothing. L. feels, Ragunath Prasad feels and always knows, and I know nothing. Does it mean that it is done this way, that I shouldn't know?"

"Oh, no!" he laughed. "But we approach the Great Trunk Road from different directions. Now imagine the Great Trunk Road: some come to it from the plain, some from the hills, some from towns, some after crossing the rivers. Who can say who is nearer and who is further? But we all have to go on the Great Trunk Road to arrive at our destination. **Here is the river Ganga: the river Jamuna joins it at one point near Allahabad. Jamuna is lost in the Ganga. Its name is not mentioned anymore. It has disappeared. The water of the Ganga is changed; it is fuller, deeper, but Jamuna is no more; it is merged into the Ganga. Who can say that all the rivers which join the Ganga are further or nearer? What is nearer—the source or the delta? Our roads are different, as I say.** If you don't feel the physical condition of the Teacher, as some others do, it only means that perhaps you did it sometime in the past, or you are on such a level with the Master that you cannot know the physical condition. If you knew sometimes, and sometimes not, then you could be blamed. But if you never know, how could you? Besides, when you were in London, most of the time you knew, and here you do not!"

"Yes, it is very true," I said.

"You see! It is as I say," and he smiled gently. "You cannot know when you are here. It is impossible. The stars do not shine before the sun. Even if you would try, you will never be able to."

"I think one should not try. One should remain in the hands of God and not try to do or be anything."

"God is nowhere. God can only be known through the Master. If you are being merged into the Teacher, you will know God. Only the Teacher is important for you. Only the Teacher. The Divine Master is complete in every way. By simply becoming like him one becomes complete."

"The most disappointing thing is that the mind knows nothing of the high states."

"For some time the mind has to remain dipped. It receives a big dip somewhere. It must be so. Keep your thoughts occupied with important Ideals, but for the rest let it be empty. When it is empty, something can be infused into it, can be given; that's how it is kept in control."

15th January

"TO WORRY ABOUT A HUMAN BEING is a pleasure. If you worry about yourself, it is suffering. Then the pain one experiences is stronger than the pleasure. If you are helpless to help, you pray, and the prayer is always accepted. Prayer is done by the Heart of Hearts. If your heart had heard it, the Absolute Truth has heard it. Everything comes out of it, of the Absolute. One should go beyond words like God, Om, Ram, Ishwara, etc. Only Absolute Truth is Real. The doctrines of Islam are the best. I mean the metaphysics of it. But the superficial Islam is not. Much hypocrisy crept into it. Said Mohammed: Never think yourself superior to yourself. Why? Because you get the same reply. If you say that you are pure, people will hate you. Make people pure by your company; don't advertize it."

This morning my heart is full of such love for Him. It is singing and singing. Full of deepest reverence. The love to the Teacher is sheer reverence, but the love to Him is more, for He is the Beloved. . . .

"If you are training a human being, you must be able to accept being hurt by him. You must give a place of honor to all who hurt you."

"To all those who hurt and abuse you, speak ill of you,
Give them a place of honor in your garden."—Hafiz

16th January

ANSWERING H.'S QUESTION, rather her remark, that she thinks that one can reach Reality without the help of a Guru, he said:

"We say Love is God or God is Love, and we have to love each other and so on, but it is a mental concept, is it not so? Do we really know that God is Love and Love is God, and do we really love each other? One needs only to look around to see how little understanding there is and that we are far from loving each other. You say that the Grace of God is needed, but the Grace works through the Guru. It is he who helps you effortlessly to Realization. After a certain realization, then, some effort is needed. You may say, and what about those millions of people who never will find a Guru? But one could ask, do THEY WANT a Guru?

"The Soul of man comes into Manifestation to have certain experiences. We get so deluded by them; we are covered by so many sheaths of all kinds of delusions. If they are satisfied with them, they will never want a Guru. But if you have 'lit the lamp' as it is said in the Scriptures, if you want a Teacher, as soon as you are ready he will be there for you. I told you before, it is the Law and it works on all the levels right through from the lowest to the highest. When we call out, the response will be. The words of the *Upanishads* hold good always: it is like putting Spiritual Life into a nutshell:

"If you want the Truth as badly as a drowning man wants air,
You will realize it in a moment."

"But deluded as we are, who wants the Truth as badly as that? That's why the Guru is needed, to give us a hand, so to say. If you want to fly up in the air, say, two miles high, can you do it? Even to fly up ten feet you need something to pull you up. If you want to fly, you need an airplane, is it not so? Something to take you up, to carry you along. It is the same when you want the Truth. Try to pray with the heart, only then God can hear it.

"Pray for forgiveness; say, please God (or whatever you may call him), forgive me if I injured the feelings of anybody and give me the power that I should avoid it in the future. It is called in Persian, 'TOBA'—repentance, a promise not to do it again, a vow, a resolution. If you don't pray like this for the power, if you don't do the *Toba* you will fall back again and repeat your sins. But if you pray like this, there will be progress."

17th January

"I have broken the laws of Islam; I became an idol worshipper,
I am helpless, I have left myself in the hands of a man
Whose eyes are so drunk and the eyes are the main door of the
   heart.
No pride is in me, he likes a man to be humble.
If you call anybody to have food with you
And he did not come in time and you reproach him—
No, let him be free to come as he likes.
And I have left myself in the hands of such a man in complete
Surrender (Iman—complete surrender)."—Sarmad

"Blessed is the Poverty when it comes smoothly,
The Poverty of great Saints left in the Hands of God."
How his eyes were shining. . . .
"Since the very beginning, since I have met you, I was always staggered by the expression of your eyes and the special light in them. Somehow, it makes me tired to look at you when you are talking; the physical body gets very tired." He smiled.

"Something is given through the eyes while talking. This is so done on our Line."

He was speaking for a while about different things, his family, and the coming Bandhara and the wedding of his nephew.

18th January

"THE MASTER SENDS HIS DEVAS, his disciples, into the world to do his work. But he remains."

Plenty of people were coming through the garden gate. He greeted everybody, much talking in Hindi was going on, much laughter.

"The days of the Bandhara are testing days for a Wali. Therefore those who live in the world and have worldly worries reach a much higher stage. Not to be affected by the worries, one has to live in both worlds, this and that. You sit here and you don't see what work is done. It goes on, and if one cannot manage, He is here to help. He is the Doer. We are only instruments."

19th January

"THINK OF A BUNGALOW in which the electricity has been installed—the wires are there, the lamps and switches are there; all the bulbs are in their place. But there is no connection with the power house. For this a medium is needed, which in this case would be the engineer. In Spiritual life it is the same. A medium, a connecting link, is needed to get the power from the power station. Therefore *Satsang* is of utmost importance; it is essential. Do you remember Diana who came here from the Pondicherry Ashram and stayed here for thirty-two days? She was a guest and was treated as a guest. A guest is given. When she asked me if the spiritual states will last, I said: for a while; it cannot last! If she would stay here, that would be another matter. But she has other Gurus. So what can one do?"

He went to a wedding last evening and today he is not at all well. People press him; he overtires himself, and then he suffers. I understand it was difficult to refuse; it was the marriage of the son of one of his old disciples. He did not sleep all night and had a severe pain in the heart, and fell asleep only about six in the morning. I have restless nights full of restless dreams which I don't remember afterwards. But such peace is in me, eternal, endless, and the heart is singing to Him. He asked us if we pray. We do. And prayer flows from the heart as a stream of love. This peace I have, and the singing inside me . . . peace, in the most peaceless state which is Love.

"At the root of every virtue is courage. Live in a way that you are everything and you are nothing. Faith can also be given and is given."

To my question as to what determines that faith is given to the one and not to another, he replied:

"Faith is given by the Teacher to whom he wants to give. He is free. One should try to please the Teacher. The Teacher can be pleased in many ways. Right attitude, service, obedience, right living—those things please the Teacher. Dhyana is not given to everybody; it is not for everyone. It should be effortless, otherwise it is hypnotism or mesmerism. If one sits for it, it is only exercising the will power. There are many ways by which the mind can be stilled. Those states are not Dhyana. In Dhyana one experiences such kind of bliss which is not of this world. In cases when the Master makes the disciple like himself, Dhyana is very helpful."

I said that I knew what he meant by that . . . a very high state, not the ordinary kind of Dhyana. He nodded with a smile and continued:

"In the *Bhagavad Gita* great stress is laid on Dhyana. But Arjuna could not remain in it; he had to fight. Dhyana is not for everybody. There are many other ways to train people. You will stay with me for a while, you will see."

20th January

"HAVE YOU SEEN A CAT waiting for a mouse at a mousehole? How alert it is. Every glance, every muscle of the body is full of alertness. The human being is supposed to be like this."

"What is the difference between a devotee (*Bhakta*), and a disciple (*Shishya*)?"

"A great difference," he answered. "A disciple is following the Teacher in order to acquire knowledge. The duality always remains. There are always two of them: the Master and the pupil. Among the disciples are a few devotees. Among those there are even fewer who stick and are faithful. Even less do follow the Line. And among those, perhaps one can find only one to continue the System." He fell silent. Some more people joined the group already seated around. He continued:

"Between the devotee and the Master the duality disappears. Devotees have to sacrifice themselves. Completely. When there is duality, there can be no realization. To surrender all possessions is relatively easy. But to surrender the mind is very difficult. It means one has no mind of one's own. One is like a dead body in the hands of the Teacher. How is the dead body? It cannot speak, it is washed, it is burned; if you put it in the sun it will stay there, if you put it somewhere else it will remain there. It cannot protest. A disciple can sacrifice himself only to a certain degree. If you want something, the duality always will remain. A devotee wants nothing: he is pure love. . . ."

"How perfectly things are done; I came to you for knowledge, but it was changed because I wanted God. You diverted my attention towards you, and then you threw me out and pointed to God. . . . You set my boat in the right direction; you blew on the sails and you let it go!"

He closed his eyes in infinite tenderness. But his smile was sphinx-like, and though he looked at this moment as gentle as a dove I had a moment of anxiety like a hidden warning. . . . He remained like this for a while, smiling gently.

Dolly: "What is attraction and what is repulsion?"

"This is easy to answer," he smiled. **"Attraction is what attracts you. If it is an attraction without reason, it is profitable. If one knows the reason for attraction, it is an obstacle. Love is without reason. What is repulsion?—it is no good. We think this or that is not good because it is contrary to our conditioning, or education, or ethical values, or our code of behavior. Repulsion should be welcomed. Why? Because if we overcome it, we make a jump forward."**

While he was speaking, I kept thinking how he used to put all the appearances against him in order to teach me acceptance in spite of everything. . . .

Last night we went to the wedding of his nephew. I was in such stillness and such bliss. Was sitting or standing all the time beside him. He and I alone in stillness . . . and around was the noise of many people and the usual a-do of an Indian marriage. There were samosas (fritters of flakey pastry filled with spices and vegetables) and tea in a bungalow which was made empty for that occasion. H. and I stood outside for a short while and I drew her attention to a crimson and scarlet sunset behind the coconut palms and the graceful silouhette of a temple. Those serene, magnificent sunsets of the Indian plains. . . .

The torchlight procession through the dark, dusty streets . . . people at the balconies were watching. H. and I were decidedly white elephants and aroused great interest and curiosity amongst the children. How nice these children were, just standing and staring at us with huge, dark eyes, or walking along with us. Music was good and the four drummers were wonderful. Especially one was an artist. He would have made a fortune in the West if engaged by a band. He was walking as if in trance, swaying his body in a kind of rhythmic dance, graceful, slight, his eyes closed as in ecstasy, throwing his drumsticks in the air, turning them around, catching them; his drum was very small and he was beating it incredibly fast; it is almost unbelievable how human hands can achieve such a speed; one could hardly see them. It was delightful, and noticing that we admired him he became even better, showing off, completely lost in his rhythm.

I was in such a peace. . . . H. told me at home that she wants to speak to Guruji privately and I am glad. Now I know all will be well and her problems will gradually come to an end. She was increasingly difficult lately for the last few months. When we were looking at the sunset, H. was joking with Surendra, telling him to look at it—it is the last sunset while he is still a bachelor. And I was thinking that it is the last sunset for H. in the state she is in. Tomorrow after speaking to Bhai Sahib, it will be different and never the same again. We had a meal in a marquee at the bride's house. It was very good. We were sitting at the table with others near Guruji's tachat, where he was installed on the cushions, together with the bridegroom. The custom was that the bridegroom must sit with the eldest of the family. The only disturbance were the dogs wandering under the tables. One mangy one with no hair at all, covered with sores, brushed against my coat. I was horrified. But H. reassured me that it did not matter. We went home in a truck . . . and the night was cold and full of stars. The Great Bear stood on its head, tail up in the southern sky, not at all as it is seen in Europe. And my peace and serenity were without description. . . .

21st January

GREAT AND IMPORTANT THINGS HAPPEN within me. Not that it does not happen all the time since I am with Bhai Sahib. I have the impression that all the time great and important things happen constantly. But now, what is it? Very difficult to describe it. It is like a feeling of warmth in the depth of the heart. But not in the physical heart. Maybe it is the love which is growing, increasing? And with love faith will grow, and the greater the nearness will be . . . and the greater the nearness, the less doubts will come to the mind. . . . But lately there are very few doubts if any. Only, will it last?? Who knows. . . .

Like a trembling within . . . crying out to Him who is Infinite. The only Friend. . . .

H. asked to speak to him when Dolly and I were leaving. I went home happy, knowing so well that all will be all right now.

What he told her I don't know; she did not tell me, and I did not expect her to do so. But her attitude had changed as I expected it would. And she looks at me once more with those eyes full of wonder, eyes filled with dark light. . . .

"Two men wanted to test who of them is the greater. They put some burning coal on their thighs. One man was burned badly, the

other was not. Who was the greater? The one who was burned. Because he was in such a high state that he did not feel it. The other wore it off with his will and was not burned at all."

"Mr. and Mrs. V. complain that they never saw you in deep Samadhi," I said. "I answered to them that it is because they don't stay for a long time. If they were here all day long, they would see it."

He shook his head slowly: "They come here for a talk and I talk to them. It is all they want. They don't come for me. Everybody gets what he wants. And at any rate, how would they know that I am in a deep state?"

"It is very evident."

"Yes, but how would THEY know?" he repeated. And after a pause: "My good wishes are with them and my sympathy," he smiled his radiant smile. "People want different things; they are after different things. They get it. Never more than what they want."

Later: "Be like a hunter: alert . . . a hunter watching his prey."

22nd January

MY GRANDFATHER AND THE GURU OF MY REVERED GURU have learned that a great Saint had come to live in a town nearby. They went to him with the intention of staying there for ten days. After four days the Saint inquired from them why they came and what they wanted from him.

"'We have heard that you are a Great Man of our time,' they answered. 'And as we are without guidance, we would like to ask you for a sitting and we would like to stay with you.' After fifteen or twenty minutes the Saint said:

"'If I direct my attention towards you, you won't be able to bear it. My look is so powerful that if I look at a stone, I split it in two.'

"They went out and searched for a stone, the largest they could carry, and brought back such a heavy one that they could only carry it with difficulty. It was put before the Saint. He looked at the stone and with one glance it was split in two. The Grandfather made a deep bow.

"'Sir,' he said, 'we have met a juggler and a magician under the disguise of a Saint.'

"'Why do you speak like this,' said the Saint obviously displeased. 'People say that I am a Great Man.'

"'Surely you are a great man; it takes a great power to do such a deed. But with all your power you cannot split a human heart. We are simple people. But we can turn the heart of a human being so

that the human being will go on and on, where nobody can even imagine it.' And so they left."

28th January

BANDHARA CAME AND WENT. There were the usual preparations—flour, rice, kitchen utensils kept arriving, borrowed from diverse people. He was busy and did not speak much to us. Only Hindi was spoken and much of the time he was inside and we sat alone. During Bandhara I noticed that I felt much less power. I remember before I felt it tremendously, it was like being in a power house; the head seemed to fly away. But this time I felt a great influx of power only when we sat in meditation on the first day, at eight in the morning. Then for one moment I felt like fainting. But I suffered from great giddiness and the sensation of being drunk. H. felt the same. . . . She left yesterday.

I asked Babu Ram Prasad how to practice *Shirk* with breath. I hope he explained it well. I will ask Bhai Sahib when the opportunity arises. But at any rate when I practiced it this morning, vibrations started. So, it cannot be very wrong; I think I understood all right. This morning I had unbelievable peace. He came out late, spoke only Hindi; many men were sitting who remained after the Bandhara for a few more days. Talk, talk, talk . . . endlessly. And I will be sitting again, for weeks, for months, waiting . . . waiting for something which seems never to happen. . . . He will probably subject me to boredom . . . to all sorts of tests of endurance.

"Not the same trouble . . . this is in the past, but there will be some trouble." So he said, I remember, soon after we came. I keep praying. He is near, but not too near anymore.

60

Faith and Love are One

"CHISHTIA MEANS 'GALLOPING'—they realize through vibrations of music. Nakshibandis do the Sadhana in silence. Naksha means 'impression.' Where? In the heart. Hazrat Harun was the founder of the Dynasty. He had a Pir, a Guru. His Guru loved him very much, therefore the other disciples had a grudge against him; they were jealous. One day the Guru had to go away and he ordered Hazrat to paint a certain quantity of pots, black, with the inscription 'Allah' in white. But Hazrat, owing to many devotional practices, forgot to do it. When the Pir arrived, the other disciples immediately informed him of the forgetfulness of his favorite disciple. The Pir asked him: 'Did you paint the pots as ordered?' 'Yes,' said Hazrat. All the disciples were furious. He is not only forgetful but a pukka liar!, they said. Pir went into the room where the pots were standing. Hazrat by profession was a pot-painter. But as Hazrat glanced at the pots standing there, owing to his great devotion and the Grace of God, all the pots were standing black with the white lettering as ordered. Since then, his Guru gave him the name: 'Nakshibandi,' the 'impresser.' "

I was sure that he would take me in hand after the Bandhara. He began today. Verily he did not waste any time. Since H. had left, the very same evening he changed his tactics completely. Again he does not speak to me and his face is severe. This morning they all went inside; I am sitting alone outside. He talks exclusively in Hindi. I come and go hardly being noticed. This morning in bed the vibrations were tremendous, especially in the heart. I seemed to fly; the head was light, the same feeling as one has in the rarefied air of the high altitudes in the mountains. So, clearly he had begun again. He promised troubles. I do the Shirk to transmute feelings which may arise.

30th January, 1966
HE SPOKE TO ME FOR A LONG TIME about tremendously important things. And I cannot write it down . . . my mind is nowhere and no memory of it remained . . . everybody had left. Bhai Sahib went

inside. I am sitting alone trying desperately to remember. Vultures circle in large sweeps high above in the clear azure of the sky. The dry, dusty garden is full of fragrance. Fragrance of what? Heaven knows. Some subtle fragrance, impossible to define. Somebody was playing the bagpipe next door. My heart was at peace. Mr. Vippin came and we discussed the Spiritual Path and the training. He came out later and soon we went to the home of one of his disciples for lunch. The disciple also invited me; I told him that I never go anywhere, but as Guruji goes, I will come too. After lunch I was looking at him while he was talking and listening to people. His eyes . . . he was in a high state of consciousness. I know it by the expression of his eyes. He was not here at all; and still he spoke and laughed and answered when spoken to. He looked perfect to me in this moment.

But I had better try, at least partially, to put down what he said this morning.

"In a few days you can write to R. After such a violent death, explosion and burning alive, there is no peace for a while. Last night he was not quite at peace. That's why I told you yesterday to wait for a few days for an answer. Perhaps tomorrow or the day after he will be at peace. We will see . . . then you can write. They go out by one way. Everybody goes out by one way. But if for instance you throw out a bundle of wood through this sky-light, what will happen? You break the sky-light and the wood will crash to pieces too. They have no peace for a while after such a death. I saw people burned to death; it cannot be imagined what terrible suffering it was . . . how can there be peace after that?"

"And what about Great People like Christ or Mansur? Did they also have no peace?"

"One should not compare Great People, for they have died before the physical death. Such people are made to die, not once, but many times. That's why they are beyond comparison. You should not ask such questions."

I was standing while we were talking. How difficult it is to stand in front of him; I feel like fainting. Sat down opposite him and he began to say many things of which I remember nothing. But in substance he affirmed that the Guru is absolutely perfect. I denied that, saying that only God can be absolutely perfect. Perfection is impossible within limitation.

"If it fulfills its purpose, it is perfect," he was saying, pointing to the iron chair standing in front of him. **"This chair is perfect because it fulfills its purpose."**

I said that it is functional but not perfect. "It is unstable, for one leg is shorter than the others and it is very uncomfortable and too small. So it does not fulfill its purpose properly, the purpose for which it was made. Can man make absolutely perfect objects? I don't think so. You, for instance are perfect when working in the higher vehicles out of the physical body, but as a human being you are bound to have imperfections."

"The Master is perfect because he can make others perfect," he said.

But I said that there are degrees of perfection. The degree in the Master is greater, for he is nearer to the Truth, less subject to the law of opposites. But I could not accept the concept of absolute perfection on the physical plane.

31st January

HAVE BEEN THINKING OVER what he was telling me yesterday and this morning. I understand why he said it. It was one of the tests. Three years ago such statements would have disturbed my mind very much. Not now . . . he can say what he likes. It is of no real importance. The knowledge I won't get from his words. It comes from somewhere, by itself, when needed. I saw how it worked in London. He will tell me nothing. And if he does tell me something it is mostly done to confuse me and to test me. He said that the mind has to die. He gave me this hint again during the conversation:

"One thinks the Master is this or that; what sort of a man he is, I myself know more, etc. etc. Doubts take a long time to go completely; that's why one has to remain for years.

"IF THERE IS NOT ONE DOUBT LEFT, ONE HAS ACHIEVED ONENESS WITH THE MASTER."

"Absolute faith IS SURRENDER. One accepts absolutely. No difference remains."

Then he proceeded to disturb my mind, telling me something which was not correct, and he knew that I knew that it was not correct, and could not accept it. But didn't he once say, long ago: **"If the Teacher says this chair is black, you MUST SEE IT BLACK."** I am still not at this stage. . . . But at least the mind did not give me trouble. This is already something. . . .

And in the evening when he came out, he kept glancing at me as he usually does when he suspects some disturbance. But there was none . . . he saw it. And later in the room he went into Samadhi, and such waves of love were flooding my heart that I had to fight back the tears. . . . What is done with the human heart is nobody's business. . . .

I remember now that he said during the conversation: **"My Father and my Rev. Guru Maharaj kept testing me in every way, but never I failed."** And later he added: **"If one loves and then loves not, this is not love. Love must be constant, no matter what happens."**

One of Pushpa's tenants asked me about my experiences; we had a long conversation about training, the Nearness and the experience of living with God, and the feeling really is that He is within and without and there is nothing but Him. . . .

"My Father and my superiors answered questions of that kind IN A GUARDED WAY; NEVER **told it was their own experience."** I understood.

"When you go on a journey, you make all preparations; you take all the necessities and money and food, and you send a message to those who are at the place where you go, to meet you, to look after you. When you go on the last journey, no preparations are made.

> **Man, do prepare yourself for the last journey**
> **Do prepare yourself in time.**
> **When your Beloved will call you, will there be time to prepare?**
> **When your Beloved comes to fetch you, you cannot stay**
> **You cannot say: wait till I am ready. . . .**
> **When you are dead, all your relations go behind and cry for you**
> **And call your name; your palanquin goes behind you**
> **But you go alone, ahead, to face your Beloved. . . .**

"Did you get the idea?" he asked smilingly.

"Very much so," I said. "It means we must learn to die while alive. Yesterday, you said that the Great Ones die many times before they finally go."

"They go on dying," he said nodding slowly. **"Dying all the time. And when they go, their Grace remains. . . ."** And after a pause: **"The Master is the keeper of the Grace of God on earth. Only he can give it. There are exceptions. But they are very rare. Only very, very few can reach The Reality without the Master."**

DREAM: a long one in which I was with him all the time. I don't remember the whole of it, only one situation. But the feeling of the dream was of serenity and of "being together." The situation, the only one I remember, is the following:

He was sitting about fifteen feet in front of me, not exactly in the dark but in the shade. His back was turned to me; he was sitting in Sufi posture, knees drawn up. He was covered with the brown blanket he usually has; on his head was his white topi. I was sitting on a large tachat covered with a white sheet and was dressed in white pajamas. I also was sitting with my knees drawn up, and seeing that he was in Samadhi I also closed my eyes and forgot myself in meditation. When I opened my eyes, I saw that he was sitting beside me, to my right scarcely three feet away.

"I thought that you are there," I said pointing to the place I saw him first. "I did not realize that you are sitting near me!" He only smiled. He sat without a blanket, his knees drawn up, and behind him was a large window full of sunshine.

"Can I tell you my dream?" I asked in the morning. **"Later,"** he said. They all were talking Hindi. After a while some of them left, and he told me to tell him the dream. I did and said that the meaning is clear; it does not need an interpretation.

"No, not at all," he mumbled, his eyes veiled with Samadhi.

I am always there about four . . . and I sit alone under the mango tree. He does not come out before six. Then they all sit and talk or go in Dhyana. The sky was paling; it became dark. Suddenly he turned to me: **"What is faith? Explain it!"**

Taken by surprise, I said: "Faith is something one must have in spite of all adverse circumstances, in spite of all deceptive appearances. Faith only comes when one loves." And I was thinking what was done to me and how I had to have faith.

"Faith and Love are one. Faith is not belief, and it is not action either. If it is action, then there is a strong attachment—it need not be faith. Love and Faith are one and the same thing."

"Oh, but I thought that faith comes only when one loves first."

"Yes, at the beginning love is separate; faith is separate; service is separate. But the time comes when all is one. Only one remains. Later this one also goes."

How simple, I thought. Too simple for words. Until now, I was not quite clear what was meant by absolute surrender; the concept was somewhat hazy . . . confusing. I never knew what to make of it. Only now, after years, he expressed it quite clearly.

But at this very moment it seemed not at all difficult to me. . . . "It is not difficult," I said, looking at his eyes shining in the dark. "If there is great love, it is not at all difficult."

1st February

I MUST SPEAK TO HIM about the mark on my forehead. I have the feeling that it has some significance. Noticed it since I came here; it is gradually increasing in size, becoming deeper, and very often in the mornings it is red. It looks as if it was made with fire, my small finger actually fits into it . . . as if a fiery finger had been pressed against the skull—the impression is in the bone which has a deepening there, and the skin is red. It was not very noticeable before; it seemed to me that I saw it in London faintly, but I am not at all sure. At any rate it was not so marked to that extent, and it goes on increasing, becoming clearer and clearer. I drew H.'s attention to it a few weeks ago.

He is sitting in a deep state, and everybody around is likewise in deep Dhyana. I alone am wide awake, writing, looking up from time to time. He has an unearthly look about him when in a deep state. Two chipmunks are chasing each other around the trunk of the mango tree. Two magnificent, pale grey oxen, huge and with large humps are passing majestically in the street, trailing an oxcart behind them fitted with lorry tires. A tiny old man is excitedly shouting at them swinging a thin rod. He looks so funny like Jack in the Box, jumping up and down, and the oxen impassively, placidly, ignore him. . . .

I wonder why he said, when he spoke of perfection, affirming that the Master is perfect on the physical plane: **"You will understand it one day, not now."** He repeated this sentence twice.

I wonder why, for he cannot mean it . . . or it must have a different, perhaps esoteric meaning, which is beyond my under-standing for the moment. . . . The Master is perfect somewhere, but on the physical plane he is subject to limitations. The limitations are here, but great love can make us overlook them. One does not see, does not notice them. They are not in the least important. Is the meaning of his words to be interpreted that love should increase to such an extent that all else becomes irrelevant?

My heart is singing all the time, endlessly, in great peace and utter stillness. But I am aware that he is trying all the time to confuse my mind, and I confess for a moment an acute sense of irritation came over me. Not again! I thought. But with the speed of lightning a thought flashed into my mind: he is trying to help me! All is done to get me quicker to the Goal . . . and the resentment vanished. . . .

"The Master is the sole dispenser and keeper of peace. The nearer

you are to him, the greater the peace and bliss will be. If there are disturbances, you are still far away. . . ."

But he certainly does his best to disturb the mind; there is no doubt about that. . . .

The last few days were like a song. And this morning is the most peaceful state, sitting here, a light wind in my face ruffling my hair. It is still very early.

Told him about the mark. He asked if I feel any trouble there, an itch, or a pain, or a pressure. I said no, I did not. The skin looks healthy apart from this reddish color and there is no pain at all. I added that I felt that it had a significance. He nodded, his eyes as if veiled with bluish light, as always, when he looks at something beyond the physical. I suggested tentatively (hoping for an explanation) that this mark has nothing to do with the physical body. Perhaps there are happenings somewhere which can have a reflection upon the body? Have I been marked somehow, by something, or somebody? He did not answer. When his consciousness came back, he turned to a man seated next to him and began a conversation in Hindi.

Soon he retired, telling me to sit until half-past-twelve. It was only 11:30, so I sat. One by one the others left.

2nd February

"WE ARE ALWAYS TAUGHT: think before you speak. This is for others; it is not for us. I never think beforehand. I say the first thing which comes into my head; the first thought is from God."

He was luminous last night. At one time he asked what is Chishtia and what is Nakshmandia, and I told him what I have learned from Babu Ram Prasad.

H. rang from Delhi; she was at the airport coming from Adyar, waiting for a plane for Tel Aviv. She sounded like a little girl without a mother. Forlorn and lost. Fancy to want to come for one day . . . crazy. . . . It took me time and effort to persuade her to continue her journey. And the line was so bad I had to shout and could hardly understand her. Poor child. . . .

As soon as he came out, I told him that H. phoned from Delhi . . . and she sounded distressed. It is becoming more and more difficult to speak to him, especially when I have to stand before him. The body began to tremble, such were the vibrations. I was breathless, could hardly get out a few words; my mouth was dry. Asked him for permission to speak to him about H., when he had time. He nodded severely. All the time, while I was sitting, he kept glancing and looking at me periodically. My heart stood still each time, such was the power of his eyes. The body was under suffering. Then he went in very early; it was only half past ten. Even now I am still trembling while writing this. I am under pressure again. It is more evident. Great changes are taking place in the body, I feel. Some transmutation is taking place? Or something was done to the mind? Only he knows.

3rd February

HE CALLED ME INSIDE YESTERDAY MORNING. Told him about the phone call from H., but was incoherent, could not speak to him. Something like a tremendous storm was blowing through my heart, could hardly catch breath. It was like fighting against high wind when walking in the altitude. One cannot breathe properly. The mind stops working in complete blankness from time to time, periodically. One cannot make coherent sentences. Then he sent me out and told me to sit in the garden till twelve. I did.

He was in his room lying on the tachat; he felt not well and wanted to rest. While I was sitting, I suddenly knew that H. was all right and happy. She was in Tel Aviv with her friends whom she loves, and Guruji sent some help to her. She was full of peace. . . .

In the evening he did not come out at all. Babu Ram finished telling me about the superiors.

There is a spark of joy, somewhere, deep within. So deep that one cannot trace it . . . it springs up like a sudden, silvery laughter, to die away instantly. It is and it is not, nowhere and everywhere, light sparkling, drops of water dancing in the sunlight in the fountain of joy . . . and life becomes good. I remember fear was like that: deep, deep somewhere in the blood, part of me, springing up from nowhere this fear, terrible, uncontrollable, a kind of despair, gripping me by the throat like a fiend. . . . I had it for years. . . . Has it changed into this joy? Was it transmuted, or simply dissolved like snow before the rising sun? Heaven knows. . . . A few days ago, the mind was working clearly, sharply, but now it does not. Not at its full capacity, and sometimes even less than that. . . .

"The Lane of Love is not near, it is very far off;
But some people have a certain substance in them
Which will take them into the Lane of Love.
I search for him far and wide, do not think me mad;
Sometimes I stand, sometimes I fall; I am not here nor there . . .

Everyone who is on this Path thinks he is near the Goal but he is
   not. . . .
I am nowhere . . . it is an endless Ocean which has no end.
I took a dip into it again and again
And there are currents where you go in and cannot go out
And the Pearl is there; I dive in, again and again.—
Oh God be kind to me, the water is becoming unbearable,
Give me strength to bear it. . . .
No doubt I am a great sinner, that's why I am under such
   suffering;
Then I have to sacrifice myself and all my belongings. . . .
Have mercy upon me; give me this wine by which I can come
   near Him;
Those who have this longing don't want peace; peace is not for
   them;
People call me his disciple and him my Master,
But I want to become his slave and he be my Master by the
   strength of his wine. . . .
I am in need of this wine to be a slave of his forever. . . .

—Rumi

God is perfect in every respect,
Guru is perfect in many respects,
Disciple in one or two,
Man in the street perfect in one thing only, if at all . . .

God is Chief Engineer,
Guru is executive Engineer,
Complete (perfected) disciple is engineer,
Disciple: driver of his own body-machine.

These things he said in Hindi to others the same day when he was
telling me that the Master is perfect. I noticed that he was looking at
me ironically from time to time, as if to say: see what I am saying, but
I didn't take much notice of it, only when Babu Ram told me
afterwards what he had said. He began by telling them that there is no
perfection except with God. . . Thank God my mind did not give
me trouble. . . .

   Yes . . . I had better pray for this wine . . . and keep praying, till
the Milk of His kindness boils up, to quote Rumi again. . . .

61

The Story of a Wali

4th February, 1966

"ONE CANNOT HAVE FAITH; until time is ripe, nobody can have faith. Complete surrender is absolute faith. He is Absolute; so faith must be absolute. Such a complete faith must be that one never says: why did my Master say or had done something; I would have said or done it better. . . . Very difficult," he added after a silence, "*Fana fi Sheikh*. The most difficult stage. I have been given complete *Adhikara* when I was twenty-seven. But I was nothing. And until his death, till the last moment before his death, he kept testing me. He said: 'Now you have caught the thread! Now you can give to anybody you like!' The Power of transference was given. The Teacher is free; he is not in trouble. But the disciple must be, must sacrifice, must tolerate, must endure. . . . There are many ways to please the Teacher."

When I stood up ready to go home, he asked: "**And how do you feel?**" I said that I was very well, and what difference it is to sit alone in his garden with the feeling of luxurious peace in my heart. He misunderstood.

"**Longing, you mean?**" I said just the opposite: peace and happiness. He nodded. "**I see, but you will get it.**"

"And the greater the nearness, the greater the longing will be." He nodded in agreement.

"**Yes, it will go on according to the state you are in.**"

This morning when I came he was already out; an excise officer was there talking to him. When he left, he read a bit of Urdu poetry and went into a deep state. Everybody was in Dhyana. And I was sitting and watching.

The grandson of his Rev. Guru Maharaj came, saw him in Samadhi, and sat quietly down. Babu Ram and the grandson were obviously in the state of deep bliss. He was giving them a sitting. And my heart became heavy; I never had a sitting. My path is a different one. I have so much longing and pain always, and when there is peace and bliss he will immediately promise that it will pass and I will be back where I started; pain and longing . . . and so heavy my heart

547

became that I could not stop tears coming into my eyes. Have mercy on me, I was thinking. I had so much pain and worry already. . . . Complete faith you want from me . . . but must I have so much worry as well?

He opened his unseeing eyes from time to time; he was in a very deep state. . . .

You are so kind to everybody, Bhai Sahib . . . to me you have been, and you are, so cruel, and nobody is tortured as I am. . . . It will all start again with frightening regularity. Probably even more than before . . . endlessly . . . and there will be heat and flies and suffering of the old body taxed by climatic conditions. And when in London, away from you, I was dreaming to come back to you to see you, I who feared I would not see you alive again. . . .

5th February

HE IS NOT AT HOME. He received a phone call that his eldest son was wounded (his nose was broken), accident or fight, it seems not clear from what they say here. He left by car. The car was at his disposal, but there was no driver. One driver was found; he turned up at two a.m. At four a.m. Guruji and wife and Bhim, the youngest son, left. I feel like an orphan . . . sat there for one hour in the morning. Went to Moti Jheel for a walk. But it was hot and too much glare. Went home, rested, and had lunch. Went there in the afternoon. Sat until seven.

6th February

HE IS STILL NOT HERE. Nobody knows when he will come, as usual. . . . Sat in the morning till twelve. And in the evening until seven.

7th February

HE CAME LAST NIGHT ABOUT EIGHT. The incident with his son was serious. Some rogues wanted to murder him, to throw him into the well. He was beaten up and his nose was broken. The culprit was arrested. It was a case of mistaken identity; they took him for somebody else, against whom they had a grudge.

Paramatma mahan hai—God is great.

Paramatma samip hai—God is near.

The last two nights I woke up many times. I think it was the longing tearing my heart to pieces. God is near this morning.

Practiced *la-il-llillah*, and have been thinking that I want Him now more than ever before. . . .

In front of the large veranda in Sharma's garden where we take all the meals stands a nimbu tree (lime tree). It is covered with flowers . . . small, waxy flowers, of five petals, white with yellow center . . . and the fragrance is very similar to the wild cyclamen which grow so freely in the Alps and in Tyrol. It is perhaps my favorite scent apart from roses. It is light, elusive, is here and not here, with the whiff of the breeze. For a long time I stood and looked at it. Sparrows sat on the branches and picked at the flowers. Many flowers were lying on the ground; the tree had too many to fruit them all. If the tree had consciousness and could think, it surely would hope that every flower will bring fruit, because fruit represents fulfillment for the tree. But it cannot know which flower and on which branch will bear fruit. . . .

Evening, 7th February

WHEN HE CAME OUT, he looked drawn and tired.

"Any letters?" he asked as an opening. I said there were none. And he spoke about Sharma, about his son and the attack . . . about his journey and the difficulties. In the tank were only twenty litres of petrol. Seventy miles were each way, and 50 miles they did while coming and going on diverse business. And when coming back after a few miles, everything went wrong with the car which had been in perfect condition. The dynamo did not work for no reason at all, and the tire went flat on the side on which he was sitting. And he said to the members of his family: "Talk amongst yourselves, but don't talk to me." The driver went on driving. No petrol anywhere. One car was standing at a petrol station since two a.m. waiting for petrol. No petrol. They drove on.

"Only by His kindness we reached home; how I don't know. Life is full of trouble on every side. We have to trust Him absolutely."

Speaking of one of his disciples he said: "He speaks of irrelevant things. On our line irrelevant things are not said. One must NEVER exaggerate." I said that this was one of my faults; when I get enthusiastic I exaggerate.

"You may think that I know everything, but really I know nothing."

I said that after all he has a physical brain; he cannot know everything. But he can tune in at will into the Universal Mind and he will know what he needs to know.

"Yes, it is so," he said. **"And in a way you are right to say that I know all I want to know, but to be a master of it, more is needed."**

"What is *Adhikara?*"

"*Adhikara* is the PERMISSION TO TEACH . . . for instance to teach in the primary school, or college, or university. But COMPLETE or FULL *Adhikara* is to be MADE A DEPUTY . . . a permission to teach everything according to the need.

"My family, when I came back, did not speak for five minutes. Nobody spoke; they only looked at me. Of course they think if something happens to me, the next day there is no food. Nobody earns a decent salary. But on the other hand it happens to everybody. People think parents provide, but in reality help is given through the parents. The Provider provides. He alone. Nobody else."

Two letters arrived, from H. and from J. It was the letter from H. that he expected, that's why he asked. How right I am when I say that he knows. . . .

Gupta came into the room; his son-in-law had an accident. Guruji came out with him to the waiting rikshaw. He told me about it in detail afterwards. **"How many troubles are in the world. The world is full of trouble."**

How right he was. . . .

8th February

WAS RESTLESS ALL NIGHT. Did the *la-il-llillah* practice. Fell asleep towards the morning. Noticed that the whole body was trembling with vibrations. He seems to send vibrations early in the morning, I noticed. Especially in the back, at the shoulder blades. This I began to notice increasingly since I am back, but never before so strong as this morning. But it did not cause either heat or suffering. It was quite bearable.

When he came out he looked less tired. **"How are you, anything new?"** I told him that there was a letter from H. **"No other news? Everything all right?"** he asked again. I said everything was all right. He spoke for a long time with his brother and his son about some cement and some building work to be done. Then he spoke to me for quite a while. And here is what he said:

"We went for fifty-seven miles completely without petrol. How was it? A car cannot go for a few yards without petrol. And we went

for so many miles . . . it was done." Then he spoke of the accident of Gupta's son-in-law who is very nervous and whose sister is seriously injured. Then he wanted to buy some Amruds (guavas), for which I asked the permission to pay. Afterwards I mentioned that Babu Ram told me a story which seems quite pointless to me.

"Which story?" he wanted to know. I told him it was the story about the Guru of Raipur who beat a man to death and then resurrected him and made him a Wali.

"I was present then, when it happened. I was there, and my Rev. Guru was there, and others too. The boy was the son of a disciple and the whole family were disciples of his: father, mother, uncles, all of them. They were all sitting there, and also the Master, the Teacher of the boy. The boy had a natural smiling face; he seemed always to smile, like my Rev. Father . . . he also had this expression. The Master looked at the boy and said: 'Why are you smiling?' And the boy kept smiling. At that time everybody used to have a stick. I still have mine today; you never saw me go out without a stick. So, with the stick in his hand he began to beat the boy till the stick was broken. The boy kept the smile on his face. When the stick broke, he grabbed the heavy piece of wood with which wrestlers practice, and he continued to beat and beat till the head entered the shoulders and the shoulders into the body. One could not recognize who it was—nothing was there, just a mass of broken bones . . . flesh and blood were everywhere. Then he stopped and said to the relatives of the boy: 'What is this? Am I not at liberty to do as I like?'

" 'Yes,' they said, 'we belong to you for life or death; you can do with us what you like.' 'Yes,' he said, 'I can do what I like,' and he went inside. Some say he was sitting and chewing betel nut. Then he came out. 'What is this?' he asked. 'Who is lying here?' And, pointing to the mass of broken flesh which once was a human being, he said in commanding voice: 'Get up!' And the boy got up and was whole, and not a scar was seen on him. And he was told by his Teacher that from now on he is a Wali. He was a Wali all his life. He was a land proprietor. When people were grazing their cows and cattle happened to trespass his property and ruined everything and some complained, he used to say: 'Let it be! They have to eat somewhere!' And the crop used to be twice as much as usual. Every year he brought *seers* and *seers* (a weight measure) of sweetmeat to his Teacher, and grain and all sort of fruit of the earth. 'You have come?' asked the Teacher. And after five minutes he sent him back. Yes, he was a Wali all his life. . . ."

I said that it seems pointless to kill a man and then to make him a Saint. Why commit such action?

"**Oh no,**" he said with vivacity, and how young he looked, when he was like that. "**You see, to make a Wali, it takes thirty or forty years. The physical body, the heart, the mind, is subjected to great suffering to clear out all the evils which are in the human being. And here the work was done in half an hour.** How many evils were cleared away completely through such a terrible suffering. **The boy loved him so much, always was sitting and looking at him. Never spoke before him. And was killed. Of course he was ready to be a Wali. Things are done in different ways according to the time and the people of the time.**" He concluded and fell silent, narrowing his eyes looking into the far distance.

After a while I said—and I felt some reluctance to speak . . . did not want to interrupt the silence, such peace was enclosing us: "The Saint can make anything perfect, but he always will wait for the order of God."

"**Oh, no, not at all!**" He turned his head quickly, looking at me. "**One does not wait for inspiration; all is within, is contained within. One can make gold from iron.**"

"Every iron?"

"**Every iron,**" he said emphatically. "**But one cannot make it from brass or lead. It must be iron. There are Souls who are made in this way, and the Master selects them. They have the capacity to become Saints.**"

"It was Attar who said that every Soul is born with a Light within, and this Light is kindled within the Soul."

"**In the dynasty of Attar many years ago they attached great importance to the Light. But we do not. What is Light? You can say that you see Light in me, Light in my eyes, but it is only an effect of something else. It is the Bliss within the Soul—the Soul is made of Bliss, and one can describe it as Light. Light per se, is nothing. If by capacity is meant Light, then it is correct,**" he said, when I told him that according to my understanding this is the meaning of it.

Then I told him that when I practice *La-il-llillah*, a vibration usually starts approximately near the shoulder blades where the lungs are.

"**It is a very nice practice; you can do it, but I didn't give you any practice to do. With ladies we send vibrations of love, that's all. But it does not mean that ladies never need any practice. It is according to the necessity of each human being. If I would teach you *La-il-***

llillah correctly, the world will be yours. The human being becomes very powerful. Power can be abused . . . what then?"

"One should want to do only the Will of God." He nodded.

"*La-il-llillah* is so powerful because it was given by a living Soul. If you repeat "Aham Brahma Asmi" for instance, nothing will happen, because it was not given by a living Soul. Sometime, very long ago, it was given, but there is no succession, no continuity." At my inquiry if I should continue with it he said again: "It is a nice practice; you can do it if you want." But from this answer I gathered that it is not absolutely essential in my case.

"What is a sitting?"

"It is what you have seen being done to the Mohammedan."

"But I thought that one must be alone with the Master . . . and nobody to disturb."

"Yes, this is the usual way," he agreed. "But one can give at any time, anywhere. You have seen he was in a deep state, and people were coming and going and even talking. He will get more; it is his, it is not mine. It is his," he repeated. Then he got up. "Did you get the idea?" I said, I did, but I also told him that it is difficult to remember everything he tells me—with the strong vibrations and the mind not working.

"Never mind," he laughed gaily. "It is all being registered in the brain of brains!" And how right he was. In London how often I remembered something he said which I thought I had completely forgotten. So, the Mohammedan had the capacity, for it was his . . . and in his young days he never worked, never studied, went here and there like the children of the Guru, so Babu Ram told me. . . . How can we judge who is great and who is not?" He said once.

To be like the nimbu tree, knowing nothing, to grow as the flower grows, unconsciously—the beautiful words from *Light on the Path*—I was thinking when walking to the post office on my way home. . . .

In the afternoon he came out about six. He was talking all the time with his brother and a Punjabi man on the subject of politics. Before leaving about seven I told him that Mr. Sharma spoke to me about himself and him.

"You will tell me tomorrow," he said at first. Then he asked: "Is it anything good?"

"Not really; he lost faith." Then he got up and walked with me to the gate away from others; he clearly was interested and did not want to wait till tomorrow. I related the conversation with Sharma.

"I love him," he said. **"It does not matter if he lost faith. Faith comes and goes; it takes time. Think of him before you fall asleep."**

I answered that I always pray for people.

"No, think of him before you fall asleep; it is done this way." With a smile he made a gesture with both hands like a swimmer before diving, the fingertips together.

I tried to think of Sharma before falling asleep. Very difficult to have it as a last thought. Practiced much *la-il-llillah*. Had a very restless night. So many vibrations. The body is restless. I am thinking of his words yesterday: how much suffering is still in store for me, physically and otherwise, before becoming a Wali . . . and he said weeks ago that I will be one. . . .

"Go on tolerating, go on accepting, and without the slightest doubt you will be there! There is not even the smallest doubt about it!" And I clearly remember how my heart made a jump and then stood still for so long that I thought that it had forgotten to beat. . . . Great joy pervaded me, remaining like an echo reverberating in the very depth of my being. About the Mohammedan, I was thinking that he was so worldly and now he will be a Saint . . . and what about myself? A worldly woman with no other interests but dresses, enjoyments of this world, parties, excursions . . . especially with my first husband who was in the banking business—we lived for three years in Switzerland in an elegant hotel. Every night we had food with friends in another restaurant, to taste one or the other specialty, dancing in the evening . . . intensely selfish, intensely greedy for life. Now too, I am greedy. The human being is greedy by nature. The soul comes into this world to gain experiences. So we are greedy to experience, and now I am greedy and selfish again: greedy after Truth. But this kind of selfishness is a good kind of selfishness. As long as we are in the physical body and there is the sense of the "I," selfishness will always be—it cannot be avoided. At least there should be a good kind of selfishness leading us towards the Goal. . . .

62

Rebuff to a Bore

"IN DHYANA THE MIND IS THROWN SOMEWHERE. Where does it go?
The smaller is supposed to be absorbed into the Greater. And what
is this Greater? One should not say God, not even Almighty. It is
Absolute Truth. Truth as such is absolute and it is everywhere. The
mind itself forms part of this Absolute Truth. Imagine an earthen
jug—air is contained in it. When the jug is broken, the air will
merge again into the surrounding atmosphere. If the jug is mended,
some air again will be imprisoned in it. But will the surrounding air
be affected? Surely not. You have seen how it is done. (He put a
newcomer into Dhyana just before this talk.)

"In the *Bhagavad Gita,* there is a hint: *Param Para . . .* it means
'from the heart.'"

I said that I thought that *Param Para* means "succession," as in the
Sufi Dynasty.

"Yes, it is the same thing . . . from heart to heart, a succession."

The man who was with him had a very disturbed mind; everything
was falling away from him. He had a good position (Home Secretary
of Mattar Pradesh), a car, good food, friends, influence, everything.
And everything was a burden to him; he wanted nothing; his life
seemed so useless. After he had left, Bhai Sahib commented:

"*Viragya* (detachment) **without love is a burden and very
troublesome; it gives no satisfaction.**"

When I told this to Sharma, he said: "It is the detachment from the
particular and attachment to the Universal. And the Universal is
Prem (Love). It is at this turning point that one needs a Guru." He
was right. I had this experience in the past. I was traveling in India
and, as the time went on, I kept thinking: what for? One more town,
one more valley, or river, or mountain. It all seemed so useless. . . .
Darjeeling . . . Chandigarh . . . Kashmir . . . so pointless . . . so
boring . . . and it was then, that I met Guruji. I was ready, and when
the disciple is ready . . . well, we know the rest.

This morning the longing was strong. But as I sat in his presence,
there was everlasting peace. And I could hardly keep my eyes open

. . . even the body was so completely at rest that I lost myself somewhere. . . .

He was dressed all in white, kurta and trousers, and looked so young, and so gay. Partly he was dictating letters to Bhim his youngest son, partly he was talking and laughing with the usual crowd seated around. I was looking at him. Bhim with the eager, sensitive face, is really getting very handsome, I was thinking . . . and so like his father. . . .

11th February

ON THE FRONT OF MRS. SHARMA'S BUNGALOW there are two creepers coming high up to the flat roof terraces. One—orange, large, tubular, flowers; the other, rich scarlet. Poinsettia is flowering at the bottom of the garden, and the beds are full of roses. A large, scarlet creeper is tightly hugging one of the columns of the veranda near the table where we take our meals. It is such a lovely thing—covered with bunches of rich scarlet, dark green glossy leaves. Early in the morning the sky in the east was robed in the colors of the dawn, grey stripes of clouds cutting across it. The Moti Jheel Park was just beyond where the garden ended. One could see the street lights, the lit windows of the houses behind the trees at the other end of the park and, far on the horizon, the dome-shaped temple standing like a sentinel watching over the just-awakening town. From where I was standing, one could not see the chimneys of the factories as from the flat roof of Pushpa's house.

I sniffed the wind—the gorgeous smell of India's endless distances. Sky everywhere, and the daily drama of sunrises and sunsets. . . . I cried in the afternoon and my heart was very heavy because Mr. Sharma had said to me that he asked Guruji point blank what H. had achieved. And apparently he had said that she had achieved nothing.

"I gave her something to encourage her, but she is still in *Dal-Dal* (morass)."

I did hope so much that H. did get something. For her it was such a sacrifice to come here . . . sitting there in the afternoon, Hindi was spoken, and Guruji answered questions on Atma, Dhyana, the function of the mind, and so on. And I could not help thinking bitterly, that Bhai Sahib, sitting for so many years with his Rev. Master, at least had the advantage of listening to what he was saying to others—never mind that he did not speak to him or very seldom.

When Guruji got up and went inside, pandit Meva Ram said to me: "We are speaking about you. We are saying what an advantage it is that you don't understand our language. So the mind remains without distraction and you can concentrate on one thing." I said there is not much concentration—the mind wanders and I get very bored. In this moment he came back.

"**Bored, why?**" he asked. I explained that it is a very hard punishment not to understand anything . . . month after month to sit here from morning till evening. . . .

"**When I was with my Revered Guru,**" he interrupted, "**I never could follow what he said. The mind was not working . . . God knows what was happening. I never could follow him. All I knew was that he was speaking; that was all. Also my Father and my uncle, as far as I could see, did not understand. Sometimes he used to ask: 'Munshiji, did you follow?'—'Yes Sir!' he answered; that was all.**"

I laughed in astonishment: "So we are in the same boat!" The idea amused me. "But at least it was your language; from time to time you must have understood at least something! It would be so wonderful to get the meaning of your many explanations, at least something, even if I am not able to absorb all of it. I am sure it would be helpful!"

"But you benefit from non-understanding!" said Meva Ram.

I shook my head in disagreement. "I am a human being after all; it is bitter to sit here mute and dumb for months on end. . . ."

"Change the patterns of your days; give yourself a change," suggested Meva Ram.

"**Yes, there will be a change,**" said Guruji, and he fell silent thinking of something.

"But the change Bhai Sahib must make," I said, "I cannot. I cannot do anything else but what I am doing. It is impossible! It is like a compulsion to come here and to sit, and if I am even ten minutes late I am restless! I simply HAVE to come here; it is an urge and a necessity for me."

He kept looking at me thoughtfully, thinking something, and I had once more a split-second feeling of panic, like a premonition; it passed. . . . Happy Babu came, the wedding album was brought, and I pointed out to him the photos of Bhai Sahib I would like to have for H. and for myself. His brother is a professional photographer; he took all the wedding photographs.

Later it was nearly seven—I was thinking that I will go home soon. It was dark already. Suddenly he asked: "**Are you depressed?**" I told him, not exactly; but my feelings are hurt because Mr. Sharma told me what he had said about H.

"About H.?" he repeated. "I don't understand." So, I came nearer with my chair and told him. He shook his head in disapproval.

"I never discuss anybody except only when I have to say something favorable about them. And if people ask, I give such answers that they will not ask again. That is how Sharma understood it; it was his interpretation of my answer. Certainly not mine. If you believe what people say, how will you protect yourself? Who will protect you if I am not with you, or if I am dead? People ask me: have you realized God? Have you realized the Self? I have not realized the Self. I have not realized God, I answer."

"Bhai Sahib, this is a lie!" I laughed. "It is not nice to tell a lie!"

"Why a lie? If I am nowhere, how can I realize something? To realize something there must be somebody to realize: if I am nothing, if I am nowhere, how can I have realized something?"

I was amused at the cleverness of the answer and how philosophically correct it was. . . .

"I often say to my children, to my brother: 'You are nowhere.' It is a nice thing to say—it is helping people. My Father used to tell me: 'You know nothing; you are nowhere!' I don't remember to have had a talk with Sharma about H., but if I have said that she is nowhere, as he says, so he did not understand what I have meant. That's all. You should not let your mind to be so easily disturbed. Keep it quiet and still."

I left. And walking home I was thinking how subtle the training is: a passing remark, a sentence here and there sometimes said in a casual way and easily forgotten when not written down, and even then I don't remember it because I don't read what I have written. Sometimes it is clearing a point . . . like today . . . taking his stand in a definite way, but more often confusing my mind with contradictions.

13th February

ON THE PHYSICAL PLANE, or the worldly platform, as Guruji likes to put it, the Sufi training is chiefly a test of endurance. How much one can endure for the sake of love. How much and how long one can tolerate.

Yesterday morning when I came, he was already outside doing his mala. He was dressed in white. And I wondered why he has his mala again. When he is in his official Sufi dress, all in white AND doing his mala, it means he will subject me to some tests or something of the sort. Usually I saw him in this apparel when he had to test me or gave a sitting to someone, in other words, when he was on "official duty."

What a beautiful sight it is to see a Saint praying, I was thinking, and as his slender, strong, fingers passed one bead after another, I began to repeat *La-il-llillah* mentally. So we both did it together, only he held the mala and I kept his rhythm. At one moment after a while he gave me a glance as if to say: I know what you are doing, and then changed the position of his legs in such a way that the left knee hid his hand and the mala. It made me smile inwardly and I continued my practice following the rhythm of his wrist which I could see from where I was sitting. Soon Sharma came and he got up and went inside. As soon as he left, one of the new men, a droning bore, began to talk. And he talked and he talked in Hindi, an English word thrown in from time to time (probably for my benefit). A large, chauffeur-driven car brought Mrs. Sharma, and she also went inside. The bore kept droning. He kept afflicting even the fat Bandhari who from time to time kept closing his eyes. The Sharmas were inside for already more than two hours. At one moment I could not stand it any longer. The bore was droning now about concentration and its benefits.

"How can you concentrate if you don't stop talking?" I asked. "For over two hours you did not stop for one moment, and you prevented us from concentrating. How can you benefit if your mind is working like this? This is not a place for talking—that you can do elsewhere. Here we come for something else. Bandhari Sahib does not talk; he absorbs in silence!"

"Thank you, thank you!" said the man, obviously infuriated about my remark. But he fell silent at last and I gave a sigh of relief. Only I noticed that Bandhari did not appreciate my interference. Strange mentality have the Indian men; a woman must not speak up in their presence, and as to pulling up a man—this is unheard of! A woman is a woman and should know her place. . . . After a few minutes the Sharmas came out and we left by car. When I was walking with them to the gate, I heard his laughing voice from inside: **"Aia, aia, come in!"** and saw the bore and his colleague go in. Bandhari remained seated. Poor Guruji, I thought.

Later his son told me that last night they stayed till half past ten, and this morning they came at seven and remained so long that he had to tell his father that it is already late for lunch. The bore did not like it. I hoped that he will not come this afternoon. He did not. But

Bhai Sahib, as soon as I came, went inside. I saw only his back disappearing through the door. He closed all the shutters and went to rest.

Later about six, a stream of people began to arrive. They all went inside, at least most of them. The rest were sitting where I was, under the mango tree, shouting their heads off on the topics of the day and politics.

Bandhari came and asked aggressively: "Can I sit down?"

"It is a pleasure!" I smiled at him sweetly. But after a short time I had to leave because his booming voice covered all the others and it became unbearable. They all shouted now, each trying to prove his point. So I began to walk up and down in the garden and then took my chair and put it near the wall of the bungalow where the empty chair of Guruji was standing. People came, one after another, and in twos and threes they all went into the room. Vippin came, and his wife and daughter and her child. I sat outside, this time alone; all went in. It began to get dark. My heart was heavy. Ten minutes before seven his brother opened a chik a little and said: "Yes, you can come in!" So, I went in.

The small room was full of shouting men. The smell of feet was strong. My head was already aching from listening to shouting all day long. As soon as I sat down, he gave me a look. I lowered mine; I felt like crying, so exhausted I was.

"I will be coming back," he said, and went out to take his tea. The men shouted all together, arguing. I waited for ten minutes. Then I went home. And I cried all the way home out of sheer exhaustion and frustration. Had no food. Could not swallow anything. Felt so sore and tired and cried myself to sleep. . . . There is complete separation from Him. Sometimes I look at Guruji and think, full of wonder: this nearness. A tremendous, intimate, nearness somewhere . . . like a haunting memory in the shadow of my dreams where the mind could not reach. . . . But when he is testing me like this, there is complete separation. He looks even evil to me, in a way, and I am afraid to go to his place; it becomes a place of torture and evil. . . .

14th February

IT WAS RAINING TONIGHT. And this morning it was dark and stormy. The sun rose amongst threatening grey clouds in blood-red and crimson. My room was filled with red light. It was quite uncanny. I will go there now. It will be cold and uncomfortable . . . sitting in the draughty doorway probably. . . .

As soon as I walked through the garden gate the brother told me that he was not well; shortly after I had left last night and he was having his tea, he got a heart attack, or a weakness; as usual, nobody knew for sure what it was. Bandhari came almost at the same time, and Virendra came out and asked us inside. The sound of singing came from the room as we were approaching. He was lying on the tachat. At his feet on the floor in kneeling *asana* was the young man who was singing so beautifully at the Bandhara. It was he who was singing now. And his voice was so tender and devoted that it brought tears to my eyes. Several men were sitting. They all listened with closed eyes. I looked at Guruji who, as soon as I saluted him, beckoned me to sit in the large chair in which he usually sits and which belonged to his father. So, I could see his face from where I was. A strange face. Pale. With large nostrils as if hungry for air . . . the same face when he was so ill a few years ago. His eyes, veiled with Samadhi, were full of tears. Ragunath Prasad came. He probably felt that he was ill, and came from Lucknow as he usually does when it happens. He took his pulse. Later I was told that he had hardly any pulse, such a weak one, like a child. He opened his eyes for a moment and said something in Hindi to his son. The latter took a sheet of paper from the recess and gave it to the singer. The singer began to recite it in his soft, vibrating voice. Bhai Sahib opened his eyes and looked straight at me. My God, what eyes!!

"In this couplet it is said that Love is not found in the market," he said with a half-audible voice and closed his eyes again. The singer continued for a while, and when he finished he asked Ragunath Prasad to translate it for me. But he refused saying that it was too difficult. I was sad. I would have liked so much to know the couplet.

"Let's go out," said Meva Ram, "he must rest." And we all went out. While I got up and greeted him, he looked at me with a smile . . . in it was so much pity, understanding, compassion, love, that I felt my eyes filling with tears and I quickly went out. Outside I asked Meva Ram to translate me the text which the singer gave me. As far as his English goes, here it is:

> Love does not grow on the trees nor is it found in the market.
> Saints are seldom found as also lions are; not many and not everywhere.
> One must learn how to respect them, how to love them.
> And how to increase the longing which takes one near them.

I will ask Sharma to translate it. Perhaps it was meant for me. . . .

He did not come out in the evening and I spent a serene day. I don't mind not to see him if I know that he is resting. But to watch a procession of indifferent people go into the room, knowing that they tire him out and not being allowed even to see him, is too frustrating for words. . . .

A saying of his came into my mind: **"Where is demand, there is a lack of supply. If you demand, it must be given to you, because there is the need in you . . . and it is given at the appointed time."**

Some heavenly fragrance was coming with the wind from the neighboring garden. Like the one I smelled yesterday when he was doing his mala, dressed all in white, looking frail, and I looked and looked at the light coming from him. . . .

This morning he came out soon. I did not expect to see him and my heart was glad. He looked weak and ill. When asked, he told me that he felt better.

"Not in the sun," he said when I was bringing his chair, so I put it in the shade. He sat down. He began to speak in English and the short time he was out he spoke in English only.

"It was serious; my heart kept thumping and stopping. I gasped for air. The *jiva* (soul) is in his place within the heart. When the *jiva* has to go, all the members of the family stand around and they call the name and all are alarmed and the doctor will give an injection or do something else. But if the time has come nobody can do anything. The best thing is to close the eyes and let them do it. The time will come to everyone; we all have to go." And he looked at me and my heart went quite small from anxiety, so much more because I saw that he was somewhat breathless when speaking. . . .

"It is a weakness of the heart," he continued, saying that the man who was there the day before till half-past ten and the next day till half-past two in the afternoon, he was drinking before he came to him, and it is very bad for him if people who drink sit with him.

"But excuse me saying so," and he smiled at me, "why don't you go inside?"

"This man is nothing to you; you cannot help him; but look what harm he did to you and what anxiety it caused all of us!" He nodded kindly. Then he said that he had heard that I told him to be quiet. I repeated the account of what had happened and what I told him. Bandhari was sitting there listening. Bhai Sahib laughed.

"I wanted somebody to tell him; I am glad you told him." And I was glad that he approved and that Bandhari was there to hear it. I feared that he would be displeased because the man clearly did not like my remarks. He approved, so all was well. . . .

Then he went inside. I also left with Ravindra by rikshaw. We went to the manager of the Allahabad bank to whom he wanted to introduce me. When I came back, a man was in the room talking loudly and he and his wife were answering. I left to buy some Flit—too many mosquitoes lived in my room—went to see Pushpa for a moment and then went home. I told the Sharmas about his illness and I was deeply worried, and I prayed so much. . . . If there is any justice, he cannot die, until I am near to him. . . . Oh God Almighty, help! Listen to my prayers! Such is the longing, such is the pain in my heart! Let him live! But after all, nothing can happen without Thy Will, so Thy Will be done! And I cried . . . and while I am writing, my heart is crying; a drunken man can obsess him for hours . . . but I cannot speak to him, neither can I see him, only sometimes. . . .

He said that Sharma does not believe that anything can be given, and one cannot keep it: **"But I put it this way: It can be given, but it has to be given again and again. If you plant a flower, you have to water it. Otherwise it will die. Krishna gave Arjuna in the battlefield—he made him an Avatar. It is the *Param Para*, the succession from heart to heart. But who will believe it, if in all the books it is said that it is only our own effort which takes us there? Those who have the Succession are not many in the world. Fortunate are those who find them. . . ."**

15th February

HE BEGAN HIS TERRIBLE WORK ON ME giving me this great worry . . . it WAS a heart attack. He is very weak, and we can lose him just like that at any moment, so the doctor said. I don't believe it: a Saint of his calibre KNOWS when he will go and will arrange his work accordingly. . . . Still . . . perhaps it is the Will of God that my training should not be finished. . . . Who knows ? . . . And now I have this fear in my bones. . . .

The whole afternoon I was sitting in front of his door; a few people were there too. He was inside, resting. And when at home, waiting for my supper which the servants were late to bring because Mrs. Sharma was not at home, I sat on the steps of the veranda, facing the dark garden fragrant with night air. And I was thinking and thinking. . . . And in the night I cried, repeating the Name of God so desperately till I fell asleep. Woke up about three. Began to think and such fear was in me that I began to cry out loudly; such was the agony that I HOWLED like a wounded dog to the moon. . . .

I knew nobody could hear me on the top in the room on the flat roof. It seemed to relieve a little the agony to hear myself cry out. All the time this agony remained, though at last I had to stop howling out of sheer exhaustion. I went to him in this mood and he soon came out and he talked and talked in Hindi. I kept thinking that he will get tired. His son told me as soon as I came that he was dusting his room and doing all sorts of little jobs. He thinks that it does his circulation good to be active. And he never stopped talking. The thin arguing man came, he who was the other day in company of the drunkard. And he talked and argued and how! Guruji kept answering. At one time he began a lengthy explanation about Nakshmandia and Chishtia and their practices. I kept praying. Oh, God don't let me be sorry for myself! Let me only want the Truth! To want the Truth as badly as a drowning man wants air, let me only want the Truth! To want it. Every moment of the day . . . this is the essence of Bhai Sahib's Teaching. . . . At one moment I could not hold back any longer and I said to Bandhari that Guruji will be tired. . . .

"Shall I tell him that he had a heart attack?" he asked. I nodded. He told him in Hindi, but the man folded his hands, respectfully bowed to the Guru and continued to talk more than before. Guruji himself seemed to encourage him, telling him that it was nothing, that he is well. My heart fell . . . they went on for a while. Bandhari said again that he should rest.

"What time is it?" he asked me.

"Quarter to twelve," I lied—it was half past eleven.

"Right. I stay until twelve, another quarter of an hour!" and he continued.

Then he said suddenly in English: "Evil does not exist; we have to throw the evil out. All the evils are in the self. Be courteous and polite at least, as you are to yourself." (I am not polite to myself, I thought quickly.)

"Be always courteous," he repeated. "It is like that that the self will go. If you want to get rid of the self, throw it behind." Then he continued to speak Hindi. His wife kept appearing at the door time after time; seeing that he was talking, she went out again. Finally his eldest son came out. I winked at him; he nodded and told the father to go and rest. When Bandhari and the thin man began to talk to each other, I got up and went to Guruji's chair and said to him:

"You say evil does not exist, but you were a victim of evil; an evil drunkard came and you got a heart attack and nearly died. And I was thinking that evil can NEVER affect you, that you are beyond evil."

"**This,**" he said with a slight impatient jerk of his head, "**this we can discuss another time.**"

I sat down. "I am very perplexed, you know," I said in a very low voice, but he did not hear me; he was talking Hindi. His tenant came . . . more discussion with loud voices.

"**You can go now.**" Bandhari left and the thin man got up. But he was still talking to Guruji standing there when I was walking away. And I just saw his gentle profile, his gentle expression he had all the time while he talked to this man the whole morning.

63

Training of the Jinn World

16th February, 1966

IN THE AFTERNOON PROF. BATNAGAR'S huge bulldog bit me while I was passing in the street. I went inside and told him what I thought of him to have such a dangerous animal running at large in the street. Then I went to Guruji and asked Virendra to put some disinfectant on my leg. He rubbed it with alcohol. The skin was not perforated; there were a few scratches and teeth marks. But the huge thing nearly knocked me over jumping at my back. Guruji came out after a few minutes and was standing in the courtyard while Virendra put alcohol on my leg, but he did not say anything, neither did he seem to notice me. He was talking to his wife. Then he came out. I told him. He said that nothing will happen to me, but the dog is dangerous and should be kept away from the streets; this dog bit Gandiji several times. In the night my mind was so restless. So much anger is still in me, hatred, resentment. . . . How much I dislike everybody. . . . To throw it all behind me, to be polite always, seems hopelessly difficult. Help me, oh Infinite God, I cried out after my mind was so full of restlessness and confusion for many hours. I was awake since two a.m. But there was darkness around me and I knew God did not hear. . . . As though wounded I was lying alone in the darkness. . . . Then, later, there was suddenly like a wave of light, and it carried me along effortlessly. It did not depend on me; I did not cause it; it just came. All the confusion was gone. Oh, Infinite One, help me to see the Light, I thought gratefully. It was all over, my darkness, the helplessness, the restlessness. The light within which is His Light helped me, and my heart rested in a clear pool of serenity.

Mrs. Sharma told me when I said to her that it seems to me that all evils are in me, every possible evil, that once Guruji told her that before the doors are closed all the doors are thrown open.

Bhai Sahib came out dressed elegantly in sandy beige kurta and narrow Indian style trousers. The topi was of the same color. He asked me how I was. Told him that I was quite well but my mind was restless last night. When I told him that it was like a stream of light and all the restlessness was over, he said with a smile:

"You see, the door opened. This is the way of progress. How would one progress if there is blockage? It is cleared away like this. Go on praying. And do the practice of *La-il-llillah*. Even when you walk or sit here in the garden."

Later in conversation he said: "My Father was so surrendered, as I have never seen anybody else. Not a shadow of doubt, ever. And he never injured anybody's feelings. Only to me he spoke roughly: 'he knows nothing,' or: 'you don't pay me the due respect.'

"I sometimes injure people's feelings. But never for my own benefit. Perhaps I am made like this, I don't know. But I never injured anybody for my benefit."

I told him that perhaps it is a question of temperament; he has a lot of fire in him.

"My Father had more fire, oh much more, but he conquered it all. . . ." Then he got up: "I am going to have my bath, now, after my massage. You please, remain seated, if you like. And never think that you are here alone. I am with you." I only folded my hands; could not utter a word. Too full was my heart. I knew what he meant. And when he left, there was peace. And the heart was singing. The longing was over. The nearness was here. . . .

When I told him that by practicing *La-il-llillah* with the last utterance of La!, with breath one throws the self with all the evils out of the heart, he said: "La-nothing, it means that in Arabic. When there is a heart attack, the jiva goes out, then it is returned. I was hinted to keep my eyes closed though all my family members wanted me to look at them. My father kept having heart attacks for eleven years. . . . But before the last one he said to me: 'If I have this trouble again, this time I die,' but I did not believe it. I thought he is such a great man, he will not go yet."

"I will die if you go. I cannot imagine life without you. I will lose the will to live."

"Then pray that I should stay," he laughed.

I asked him how it was possible that the drunken man could affect him so much with his evils. I thought that he could not be affected by any evil whatsoever.

"You see," he said, "I have a physical body, after all, and it can be adversely affected. Bad smells make me suffer very much (me too, I thought); a drinking man smells badly. Smokers too smell very badly. My Rev. Father and My Rev. Guru Maharaj used to smoke, but either there was such a faith in me that I did not notice any bad smell from them, or they did not smell."

"Probably both," I remarked, and he nodded quietly.

"Do *La-il-llillah* when you are walking, but so that nobody should notice what you are doing."

17th February

I WENT OUT ON THE TERRACE this morning at dawn. The sky was of an ominous dark red color in the east, like an underground fire of a volcano beyond the horizon. The dome of the sky was deep purple full of stars. A young crescent moon was shining unusually brightly in the east against the deep red and not far from it was an outsize star like a large diamond. It could be Venus: probably Venus is a morning star this month. . . . Fresh wind was blowing from the west. Soon this same wind coming from the deserts of Pakistan will become Loo. . . . Blissfully I sniffed the air. Oh, the glorious smell of Indian plains in the mornings, at dawn . . . exhilarating freshness in the air, the smell of coal fires and the slightly bitter, pungent smell of burning cow-dung cakes which they use here as fuel.

Last night he came out looking a little tired and frail. And as usual I lost myself looking at his wonderful face full of light. . . . Then he began to speak in English after a while and mentioned a name of a well-known writer who wrote many books. He said that this man in 1943 wrote a letter to his Rev. Father asking him if he could come and see him. But his Father said that he did not want to see this man, so he did not answer. I said that this man was last year in England and people say that he is a God Realized Soul.

"Is he still alive?" he remarked, **"and as to be God Realized, such and other things are said about so many people. But how could they know? This gentleman,"** and he pointed to the thin pandit sitting beside him, **"this gentleman said that he met in Bareilly a Sufi by the name of Jelebi Baba. I also know him. Many young men were sitting with him; he was teaching a special kind of Pranayam: *La Ilaha il Lillah*, to take the breath from the navel right to the mind and to the Brahmarandhra if possible, then to the right, and then to throw it out through the heart. It causes vibrations. Vibrations must be; they purify the vessels. If the vessels are not pure, how can one see the Light? My father used to practice this Pranayam very much; he believed in it. One day some people annoyed him greatly, so much so that he did some things which he thought were not right, after which he did much of this Pranayam. But then My Rev. Guru came to know about it after a long time, and he said, one Tawadje would do it, and he did it and my Father was all right. It is all**

gymnastics. The one who could say it 101 times without taking breath becomes a Wali at once. The Teacher says it once and the Shishya does it and becomes at once a Wali. But only a very young man and a completely innocent one can do it."

"It must be very difficult," I said, thinking how long one must hold the breath in order to do it.

"Difficult, yes, but not impossible," he said thoughtfully. "But the one who becomes a Wali through his own effort is not complete. Complete, one becomes only through the Grace of the Guru (Guru Krepa). Either the Guru loves so much or there is complete surrender. . . . Of course, if there is complete surrender, the Guru must do it; he cannot help doing it." He smiled looking at me. "I think it was St. Augustine, if I remember well, who had said that the Kingdom of Heaven must be taken by storm. God must be forced; such must be the attitude that he cannot help to grant His Grace to the Devotee." He kept smiling. "I am not such a great man as he was and I cannot put it in such a way. I said it in my own way. The meaning is the same," and he smiled again.

I had a dream about four a.m. A strange one. I was together with a child; at first it seemed to be a little girl, then it was a little boy. We went to a room which looked like a dining room, and the boy sat in one corner facing the wall which was covered with dark blood-red wallpaper of some brocaded design in darker color. I noticed a strange, dreamy expression in the boy's eyes, full of bliss at first; he was staring at the wall. The boy is seeing something, I thought. Then his expression changed into a deep suffering; he pressed his hands to his body murmuring: No, no, as if in anguish. It is a Jinn! I thought, and he is trying to do evil to the child! I became suddenly angry, and pointing my finger at him I said with emphasis: "Go in the Name of my Master!" As I was not sure that it would obey immediately, I repeated the order: "Go in the Name of my Master!" And then I said to the women who were in the room: "See, the child is sleeping! The Name of the Master is the greatest Magic, nothing can resist it!" And I looked at the bed covered with a white sheet where the child was laying, but I saw to my surprise that instead of a child there was lying an umbrella. But I knew it was the child and I continued to speak.

Then I saw myself in a room full of women, dressed in gaudy, colorful, Oriental garments and jewelry; they were dressing, putting on perfumes, lipstick and cosmetics, and I was thinking: I have cast out a spirit in the house of prostitutes! What power has my Master! But I must tell them that it was not I who did it; people already say that I did a miracle. And I began to tell them how powerful my Master is, how nothing can resist him. I spoke with fire and enthusiasm, but they continued to dress; nobody seemed to listen.

When having my bath, I was thinking that this dream was a mind dream; surely, I need not tell him about it.

It was a windy day. He came out early dressed in white. Nobody was there as yet and he asked me how I was. I said that I was very well.

"A Wali has depressions sometimes; restlessness can be; but we must know how to control it; we must be above it."

I said I had a dream (taking advantage of the fact that we were alone), but I don't think that it was important.

"Don't say so, you cannot judge. Even if it is a mind-dream, it shows the state of mind." So I began to tell it.

"How old was the boy?" he inquired.

I said five or six.

"Continue." Then he asked again: **"Did you feel a Jinn, or thought that it was one?"**

I said that when the child seemed to suffer, I realized that it must be a Jinn. He nodded. When I came to the point of the umbrella he asked again: **"You mean to say that the umbrella was transformed into a child?"**

"No, rather the boy was transformed into an umbrella."

"Then it was a Jinn," he said firmly. **"It was a Jinn. It is a good dream. I explain it to you."** And he fell silent. I thought that he will explain it sometime later and was silent too.

"It means," he said looking attentively at me, **"it means that the training of the Jinn world began. Your dream shows that. How to guide them, how to control them—they will obey your orders."**

I asked him what about the second room which was full of women looking like prostitutes?

"It is so; Jinns often come in this shape to the ladies."

Hosla, the mischievous servant boy, appeared from the door and Guruji began to tell him off loudly about some mischief he had committed previously. I waited.

"But not to all ladies surely?" I asked, when he ended and Hosla walked out of the gate into the street. "Surely I have no Jinn?"

"With you they come in another shape." I saw he had no desire to explain. So I kept quiet. **"They cannot come unless you allow them to do so."** The old man arrived with his wife by rikshaw. **"We talk about it later."** As usual, I thought not without irritation. . . . At

the most interesting moment an interruption comes and I have to
wait patiently for an explanation which perhaps will never come. . . .

The drunkard came. Mrs. Vippin came, and we all went into the
room. The wind began to increase carrying clouds of dust as it swept
along the streets. Later he went to the doctor and I am writing this
down sitting in the garden. When in the room, talking vivaciously
with sparkling eyes, authority and sense of humor, I could not help
thinking that he is a great Master, every inch of him. . . .

19th February

THE USUAL SANNYASI WAS THERE, Vippin came and went, and as soon
as he had left the drunkard came. I looked at him with apprehension;
what if he harms Guruji again? But he did not come near him but sat
on the tachat standing near the large doorway. I saw Bhai Sahib going
into Samadhi; nobody spoke. I looked at his face. My God, how
young he looked; not one day more than thirty . . . and the
expression of infinite mercy, the lips softly curved in a kind of
mysterious smile. As my sunglasses dimmed the colors, I pushed
them down a little so that I did not have the glare and still could look
above them. If I could paint this wonderful face with its golden skin, I
would put brilliant light-blue in patches on the forehead which is the
reflection of the sky. And deep green on the cheeks, especially on the
left one which has the reflection of the Amrud (guava) shrub, and the
shade of the mango tree. . . . I could not look enough. He was
breathlessly beautiful, incredible, how beautiful a human being can
be. . . . And there must be a crowd of invisible people, or Devas
present, because he kept looking rapidly from left to right and from
right to left, and above, everywhere, and then he quickly glanced at
me. I was so fascinated by the spectacle of the split-second change of
consciousness, that I did not notice at first that he did something to
me.

Then I became aware that the feeling of love and admiration
increased and kept increasing in waves. It was of such power that at
one time I thought he must feel it. It must affect him; how can he bear
it? But he was in Samadhi, and there you bear easily quite other
things than just that. . . . And he did not even notice it, so it seemed
. . . but I felt it, and how. . . . At one moment I had to press my
hands tightly against my chest, deep was the pain in the middle of my
chest, and I did not feel my heart beating at all. Then I saw by the
expression of his eyes that he came down to the physical plane; he

looked at me for a second, then went off again. And he kept looking and glancing at me, with those tremendous eyes in deep Samadhi, like shimmering brilliant light dancing in them. Tremendous eyes. Not human eyes. Unseeing insofar as this world of matter is concerned, looking at something else, seeing other worlds beyond our imagination. . . . What do you see, oh, Glorious One? Where do you roam? Then a noise from the street attracted his attention; he came back to his mind-consciousness. How clear it was visible, the change of expression in the eyes—they became human, soft, lovely eyes. A rumbling ox-cart passed by loaded with clattering iron bars. He turned away and looked above my head and then all around me. Does he look at my aura or somebody standing near me? I could not guess. At one moment such were the waves of love, that with both hands I clung to the seat of my wooden chair, clutching till the fingers ached. I noticed that the mind seemed to work well. I was sharply aware of the surroundings, of my feelings, and especially of him. At one moment I looked at the drunkard; he seemed to be in Dhyana with closed eyes, or at least he was in a drowsy state, so he did not want or could not speak, or even move. I tried to analyze what was happening. First of all, I knew that it never happened before like this; it was for the first time: was it *Tawadje*? I wondered. And it seemed not to come from him; it was as if from myself. These powerful waves of love came streaming towards him. Love is the greatest magic; he seemed transformed. What an experience . . . a thought crossed my mind . . . of course I understood that it was he who had created the condition or did send some power that something in me responded to it with a resonance like an echo. **"What time is it?"** he suddenly asked. I tried to answer but could not speak so he asked again.

"Ten to twelve," I managed to say. Then he looked at the drunkard and the man opened his eyes. The man from Mathura was fast asleep; all the time he was snoring softly. Did he give me *Tawadje*?—this thought crossed my mind again. Now he was engaged in conversation with others. I felt distinctly the power subside, less and less, as the waves in the ocean after a storm come slower and slower and smaller and at longer intervals. One of his young disciples came.

"It will be twelve?" he asked in Hindi. The man assented. I will not move from here until he tells me. God knows if I will be able to walk. . . . I felt an impelling overpowering desire to fall at his feet. I must do it before I go, I was thinking, so full is my heart, I simply HAVE to do it. . . .

At quarter past twelve he nodded his usual nod which means: you can go now. I simply sat there and stared at him.

"Yes, you can go now," he said not looking at me. I got up, not quite steady on my feet, and fell at his feet touching his left foot clad in a black shoe with my forehead. I remained so for a second and a wave of deep tenderness crossed my heart.

"One can die of it," I said softly standing up and dusting my skirt. "It was difficult to bear . . . will I be able to walk?"

"You will; walk slowly."

And it went much better than I thought: I felt like dancing down the street. The wind was blowing directly into my face. Life was good.

And at four when I came, soon he came out.

"I am walking," he declared laconically, as I stood up. And walking up and down the garden, he gave me twice a sharp inquiring look. Probably he wanted to see how I was. In the evening just before seven he suddenly remarked: "Mrs. Tweedie, is the Soul masculine or feminine?"

I will try to write it down tomorrow, when the mind is working better. At home, when I came out on the terrace before going to bed, some distant religious music came from the direction of the temple. The wind smelled fresh. A lovely, rich, tenor voice was passing by singing something which may have been a love song. My God, life was good!! Imprisoned splendor, imprisoned splendor we are, I thought, and went to bed.

64

Tawadje

20th February, 1966

DEEP AND SERENE IS THE LOVE. Flowing peacefully like a steady stream towards the sea. Like the Ganges here in the plains. Nothing could be more serene, more peaceful; a large river winding lazily amongst the fields. . . . The mind is very still. I can keep it completely still, effortlessly; just stop thinking; that's all. The thoughts revolve serenely around familiar objects and activities. Washed a few socks, some underwear. Looked at the crows having a morning bath in the pool in the park, shaking and preening themselves on the large tree on the opposite side of the garden. Unearthly silence within. Does not belong to this world. The mind works little, the memory is weak. I will try to remember later what he had said yesterday, but I doubt that I will be able. Pity. Perhaps it does not matter much. Somewhere it remains and it comes up later.

Fancy how completely conscious I was during yesterday's experience. The mind was working well then. Was aware of everything. A few boys passing in the street, laughing merrily, for one moment attracted his attention too; I saw them pass by. Fragrance in the air. The wind. The birds, and the drunkard sitting there in silence as if half asleep. And him . . . glorious . . . unique. Full of mysterious light, sitting gracefully, one foot resting on the knee of the other leg, in his familiar pose. My Teacher. So great, so aloof, so impersonal and so deeply, intimately near, nearer to me than my very neck-vein. . . . I remember four years ago—February was perhaps the most difficult month. It is gone. . . .

"Throw it behind you, don't try to remember." I will have to remember it though, when I will write it; the book, I mean. . . .

"Yesterday I could not see you well; is my eyesight failing? Or has it to do with the *Ajna* (brow) *Chakra?*"

"It happens like that. I remember, sometimes I was hard of hearing; sometimes it was like a dark cloud and even during day light I didn't see well. It should pass after a few days. If the eyesight is weakening, then one should see the doctor. But if it passes, it does not matter. The eye nerves have connection with *Brahmarandhra.*

So have the ear nerves. If there is some heaviness in the *Brahma-randhra* and the Brow *Chakra* is also closely connected with it, then it usually happens."

"Sometimes when I have to ask you something, it is like a barrier within me. I know I should not ask. Now, for instance, I wanted to ask you something very badly. People were coming and going; then when your son was sitting there alone, I said softly, 'Bhai Sahib.' I looked at you and got a clear: 'No!' mentally. I know you did not want me to speak."

"The self; this is the barrier. If you want it badly; who wants? The self. If you have no self or the self is diminished, you can ask. There will be always the chance then. But for me," he continued, "for me you are always the same. I authorize you to ask what you want."

"But you know that now I will not ask and will be very careful how and why to ask." He gave me one of his faintly amused smiles. We sat in silence. And the same thing happened as yesterday, only it was less strong, and only for a few minutes. His wife came. The son came. A shopkeeper came. After they had left I asked: "How can you bear it? It is so strong, such a terrific power, you must feel it, for it has to come through you?"

"I can bear so many things," he smiled. He did not look human, but a delicate being from another world. He is so much thinner now, transparent sometimes.

In the afternoon we have been discussing the male and the female aspect of the soul. I quoted the theory of Inayat Khan: when the Ray comes into Manifestation it touches first the angelic plane, etc. He confirmed that it was correct.

"First is the Sound, then the Light, then Love. Sound is the *Akasha*. Sometimes during the discussion something is concealed, not the whole Truth is told. Now the moment has come to say it! There is the right moment for all things!

"Surrender is twofold: Absolute faith, plus a conscious contribution (or effort) from the side of the disciple."

Otherwise why should he have told me: throw everything behind; forgetfulness is the greatest qualification; and, be courteous and polite always, otherwise the self will never go.

"You will not digest it if the self does not go." Meaning, one cannot absorb what is given if the self remains.

"One should only give a hint and NEVER directly. Direct hint is never given, otherwise the feeling may be hurt. If one feels that one should give a hint, one gives it in a way indirectly, and if the person

understands, it is good, but if not, the hint was given just the same. You did your duty, and sometimes the hint is given again."

I asked that once long ago he told me that his Rev. Guru punished the people, that the Saint has the right to punish. How does this statement tally with the remark of not injuring the feelings?

"It works this way: if one comes to the Saint and the Saint is pleased, he will clean your room. What is your room? Your heart. And the cleaning means that the *Samskaras* are being pushed. This will cause great suffering. People then will say: he is punishing her. But in reality it is not so."

21st February

JUST BEFORE AWAKENING in the early morning, I clearly saw him sitting in his chair, while I was walking up and down. He was attentively looking at me. Then I knew that he was looking at my mind. When awake it was clear to me that he knows about the resolution I took last night.

1.   I will not ask any questions anymore. **"When you begin to ask questions the mind formulates another, and there is no end to it."** What he tells me I often forget; so why ask at all?

2.   Surrender is the acceptance of everything WITHOUT exception.

Ergo: I ACCEPT. I will go to the end of the bitter road. Will sit, endlessly sit, and ask nothing anymore. And now because I accept it voluntarily, the mind will not give me trouble and restlessness anymore. Not from this side, anyway. Acceptance of "everything" means: acceptance of falsehood and cruelty, to which he treats me freely; "everything" would mean in spite of all appearances which are sometimes deliberately distorted, in one word: the lot. Did I not tell him once, long ago, I could not understand the meaning of complete surrender unless he does evils and I am able to accept it? Only then it would have a meaning for me. Otherwise it is only half a thing. And I will never be satisfied with half a thing.

And so, this morning I was alone with him and asked nothing. And he looked friendly, as if to encourage me to speak. I kept quiet. There were no vibrations, only a deep peace. And a very faint nearness. "I am sure you know the poem of Jal-ud-dim Rumi which begins:

   We are sitting in the garden Thou and I,
   Two bodies but one heart, Thou and I."

For one split-second he closed his eyes and nodded slowly. I kept quiet again. Then some people began to arrive including the drunkard, and later he said in English:

"**Books are all mud. It is us who create books; books do not create us. Everybody reads and they say it is written in this or that book. Only they don't agree amongst each other. Secret things cannot be communicated. Secret remains secret. How can it be told? It is like trying to explain the taste of sugar and its sweetness. Therefore if one has a good Spiritual Guide, one must stick to him and forget all book-knowledge.**" And discussions are also mud, I thought. Amen. . . .

And now it occurs to me that he gave me a hint. He said the other day: "**I am not of such a nature, but I throw sometimes your mind into confusion. If I would not do so, how will you get the pearl?**" I thought then that he meant the actual conversation we had at that time and said that he tried to confuse me twice. He laughed. Actually he twisted and perverted my question on equality of feminine and masculine principles, then gave an answer on a completely different topic concerning Sufism and the training and the *Chakras*. He evaded the answer of the theory of Karma, then denied it completely, and then spoke in such a way that I did not know where I was. And this conversation which caused confusion was the hint to give up everything.

How difficult is this fact of the hints . . . how subtle. This time God helped me; I did the right thing first and then remembered the hint. . . .

22nd February

THIS MORNING A SIKH CAME, the same who came yesterday for the first time. Bhai Sahib told me that three years ago he had a hotel and was a proprietor of two trucks. But he came into the hands of some Brahmin Gurus who advised him so badly as to make him penniless. Now he has no food, neither he nor his family, for days sometimes. Guruji gave him breakfast.

"**I will give him five rupees,**" he said; "**the family shopping is done for today, this money is over, I will give it to him.**" Then he gave him kurtas, pajamas, trousers and clothes for children.

"**You see, Mrs. Tweedie, this is my life. Always has been like this. I cannot take food if there is somebody who approached me for help and is starving . . . People see me dressed like this** (he pointed to his snow-white kurta and immaculate narrow trousers of the type one saw Nehru wearing on all the photos, his clean black shoes), **and they think that I am perhaps a wealthy man. It is good that they should think so. If they would see me miserably dressed, or gloomy, nobody would come for help. Let them come. . . ."**

Tulsi Ram with his horrible urinating family had left last year. In his place he has a tenant who has a shop of fodder. But when I came this year, behind the nimbu tree I have found a simple hut with tiled roof. It was occupied during the Bandhara by his disciples. Now for the past two days a family lives there who was turned out by the landlord.

This is his life. The life of a Sufi. Never to refuse hospitality.

Yesterday he said as if casually: **"I am thinking of taking some walks again in the park; the season is suitable."**

"As you wish Bhai Sahib," I said. It is not good for him to walk passed through my mind; after a heart attack it would be better if he rested. He was watching me. Probably he was thinking that I am so keen to walk with him as L. used to be. But I was indifferent. I am not too keen on walking. And with him one is bound to meet a man or two who will walk with him shouting their heads off deep in conversation, and I would be trotting behind like a dog trying to keep pace with them. Not a pleasant prospect at any rate. Then he said:

"I am thinking that you should give Poonam English lessons from tomorrow. She is at home now since December; I don't let her go to school. She is a strong, healthy girl. She could improve her English."
I agreed.

I suggested that it should be between four and five. "But please, do realize that I am not a teacher and I don't know how to teach . . . I never did it. I will do my best though. Only your children are not very keen on study. I am sure you know that, still, I will do my best." He did not comment, listened quietly. "There is much to learn by heart, if one studies a language. If she does not study, I can do nothing." I was thinking of Babu three years ago. . . .

He sat still, thinking something. I knew he was watching me if I was disturbed. I was not. I accepted anything. I know by now that he will not make life easy for me. But I don't care anymore. The mind is very still. No vibrations at all, anywhere.

When I asked him the other day what was this experience, he answered: **"The same thing I gave to Bogroff and he gave out a loud cry. What he experienced only he knows. Two years later he died. He had to die,"** he added thoughtfully. I had to laugh.

"That does not sound very reassuring, but I will not die, at least not of that. But all I wanted to know: was it a sitting? A *Tawadje?* Never mind," I said, seeing that he remained silent.

The next day he said: **"Secrets cannot be communicated."** So, one day I will know by myself. . . .

23rd February

HE CAME OUT LAST NIGHT looking tired. But then he talked much and sang. And when I left he was still talking, and it was cold. About six people were sitting. I wish the mind were not so restless. Thousands of thoughts . . . milling in my head. I sleep little; at two or three a.m. I am awake, and the mind begins like a wheel turning madly. Kept worrying about him. Perhaps he is not well. It was so cold last night, and he was dressed so lightly. Kept worrying about H. Ideas, ideas . . . tiring. . . . When I do the *La-il-llillah* it is all right for a while, then it starts all over again. About four a soft vibration in the heart began. Stopped soon. And when I came at nine and sat alone, a strong vibration started.

He came out looking very tired. I remembered a couplet which somebody translated yesterday:

"The diamond does not say himself how much is its value,
    Its worth is judged by the people."

Then I remembered he said the other day answering Mrs. Sharma: **"Perhaps this Saint was under vibrations; then one is irritable."** So, when one is under vibrations, one is irritable. So, that's the reason for my constant irritation and perhaps even anger. . . . He never admitted it to me, but don't I know it! Only I didn't know that it was due to vibrations. . . .

A strong wind was blowing this morning. Clouds of dust were sweeping in the garden. Soon my face, my hair, and my black skirt were covered with dust. A dense wall of evil-smelling dust came from the other side of the road, from Deva Singh Park. It is called a park; a large notice at the entrance proclaims it. But it looks like a waste-ground, not a blade of grass; boys play football there all day long, and a herd of buffalos is driven there every morning to stand in the sun the whole day. When there is a wedding or a festivity, a marquee is erected there and ear-splitting music will come from there through the microphones. Whoever invented these devilish things, I hope he will never have peace in the grave . . . and children and adults of the whole neighborhood use it as a latrine.

I watched thick clouds of dust rise high in the air from there, being swept with the gusts of wind across the road into Guruji's garden. Nobody asked me inside. I was sitting. My heart was so heavy with longing. I will drink to the bitter end the cupful of sorrow. He will see to it that my life is as difficult as possible. When he came out, he looked tired; he had a towel round his head to protect himself from the dust, and it made him look like an Arab. It suits him. His face acquired a remote nobility, and the curve of the lips hardly seen through the beard seems more gentle. Soon we went inside the room; it was too dusty for him. In the room it was cool and dark. He was talking to Vippin and to the Sikh. Then Vippin went and he told me that he was last night under fever. My heart sank . . . he looked at me several times and went into Samadhi. The heart activity began. The longing became deeper and deeper. Great, powerful longing. The Sikh was talking with mournful voice for one full hour without stopping for one moment. He pretended to listen. From time to time he answered something but he was in Samadhi. Then he went out. The Sikh tried to talk to me. This time I thought that it was fortunate that I don't speak Hindi. He came back and sat in the big grandfather chair. The Sikh was still talking and began to massage his feet.

"May I go now?"

"Yes, yes," he answered gruffly. I left. And at home was full of such misery and depression, full of foreboding. . . . Something is approaching . . . something frightening . . . but what??

24th February

A FEW DAYS AGO there was a new crescent moon. The new moon in India at certain times of the year is different; it is not upright as in our sky; it is floating like a silver boat, and it stood against the fading dull orange and mauve of the evening sky.

"Two days old moon; the moon of Shiva, very auspicious," I said to the man sitting next to me. Guruji, who was talking to his brother, turned suddenly in my direction:

"Nonsense! There is nothing auspicious or non-auspicious. Those are man-made superstitions! They are made by us and we entangle ourselves in ignorant beliefs! Sufis are free from them. . . ."

He was not well last night. I was sitting outside and talking to Meva Ram. Then we were called inside. Fancy, I thought, I am called in. . . . He was lying on the tachat, emaciated and tired. Meva Ram began to talk about me, telling him what I had told him—I understood so much of Hindi to gather that. I saw that he was pleased. Heart activity began. I had such longing and so much sorrow. . . . May God give him health. And when at home prayed so much and prayed well. . . . The nearness . . . how sweet it is. . . .

Did not sleep since two a.m. Kept thinking about the infinite Truth. Kept up the practice. When I say: *La*—it is like a Void—the mind vanishes. It is a lovely feeling of Nothingness.

I don't want Yantras. Not really. I am not after Samadhi, or Dhyana, or even states of bliss. I don't want powers. I want only Truth. Truth alone. . . . And my heart was at peace, and the hours passed swiftly.

He came out about ten a.m., but before that I sat alone; clouds of dust were whirling around me. Was thinking that it mattered little. The mind did not seem to work much. There was such peace.

The Sikh was there sitting in the doorway with his two sons. Lovely boys. They were barefoot, no shoes, so poor they were. Bhai Sahib gave him some money. He asked me to count it; it was sixty-one rupees. The man nearly cried. They all left soon after touching his feet. He got up. **"I will walk for a while,"** he remarked and began to walk on the brick elevation.

"Meva Ram was telling me last night how much he was impressed with what you have told him. I said that she comes here for the Truth, not for talking, like so many."

"Oh, I don't know why he should have been so impressed; I told him the difference between joy and bliss."

"Is it not the same thing?" he asked.

"Oh, no," I answered; "joy is a positive, dynamic feeling; bliss is a passive state. I prefer joy. To lift the world upon my shoulders . . . I concluded."

"Very good, very good," he laughed. Then he sat down.

"I said that the human being, being the crown of Creation, should aspire only to the highest, the best, the greatest Ideal. To put one's ambition high, so high that one can hardly reach it. Then try to reach it. To want the Glory without limit and the singing Joy." He laughed again, his young laughter.

We went into the room. He took the book of Guru Nanak from the shelf and began to read sitting in the big chair. The door was closed. A strong wind made the curtains fly, and opened and closed the wooden shutters with a bang from time to time. Children of the family to whom he gave hospitality shouted in play, and the little one cried. It did not disturb at all. There he was sitting, and here was I at the other end of the room, and there was oneness and great peace.

His wife came in. She took no notice of me. Strange, how lovely it is not to be. To be absolutely nothing is the greatest, the loveliest thing on earth. . . . On earth only? No, everywhere. There is such a power in being nothing . . . a latent Power like a tightly wound-up spring. About quarter past twelve I went home. The mind was peaceful all day. Got a letter from H. and I was glad.

When I went to him in the afternoon, he gave me a letter from H. and I was a little worried because I thought that she had troubles.

25th February

SPENT A PEACEFUL NIGHT. Was awake as usual about three a.m. Was thinking quiet thoughts and doing the practice.

When I arrived he was already in the garden. Read to him H.'s letter which I received. He was walking up and down on the brick elevation; talking to him I had to keep pace with him.

In the afternoon two microphones installed in Deva Singh Park blared two different kinds of music at the same time, so loudly that if one had to speak, one had to shout to be heard. Some kind of children's fair was going on. Could not write, not even these notes, not to mention a letter. Just sat there thinking bitterly what a difficult country India is for us coming from the West. Dirt, horrible dogs, diseases one sees in the streets, dreadful beggars, and the climate. He came out late (who could blame him!) and went after half an hour to a wedding nearby.

"Will be back soon," he said. But I knew he wouldn't. So, I went home. And even at home, I heard the blare, though not so loud for it was quite a distance away.

65

Time Runs Short

26th February, 1966

HE CAME OUT LOOKING TIRED. Talked for a while to his eldest son. He looked at me with a hard distant look. I knew he was observing the state of my mind. When his son said that it was ten a.m., he murmured: **"Time . . . Hm . . . some old people, but very few, begin to understand the value of time. The young ones do not. Time . . . how precious it is. . . . If it is gone, it is gone forever."**

It was for me. And he could not have said anything more appropriate. I am obsessed with the idea that time runs short, that he will go, and the training will not be completed. . . .

"That's why Sufis don't encourage irrelevant talk, it being a waste of time." He was in Samadhi. He probably did not even hear. . . .

27th February

TODAY IS SUNDAY. Many people will come as usual on Sunday and much talk will go on. I arrived half an hour late. When I saluted him (each time I salute him it is like burying my face into fragrant flowers, my heart begins to sing), he laughed.

"Yes, yes; sit down!" I explained that I was late because the night before there was a party at Sharma's place, and so I came down for breakfast late, thinking that nobody will be up yet. Then I was talking to Mrs. Sharma.

"You are never late!" He laughed. **"Never! One is late only when the heart is late! Do you understand?"** I said that I did. But secretly I wondered if he meant that my heart is never late? Was it??

Plenty of people were sitting already. I ventured a question: "At the party Mr. Vippin told me about a new man who came to you yesterday and he told you that one corner of his house seems to be haunted; it has a very bad influence. This bad corner affects the whole house. All the time somebody is falling ill; his daughter died recently, and all sorts of misfortunes happen to everyone who lives there. Mr. Vippin said that your answer was as follows: **"If you think as you seem to do, that there is a grave underneath this corner, dig it out, take whatever you find there to the river and throw it into the** water. Take some earth from the river bank and fill it in. You will see all will be well. But if it is a grave of a Venerable person I can do nothing."

"Now, my questions are: Firstly: why can you do nothing? You can do everything! All of us seated here, we know it! And secondly: A venerable person can never do evils, how can that be?" He smiled.

"There is evil and evil. How do we know what evil is? Those people say that there is evil. But we also know that some persons have to suffer evils. They call it evils. But who knows. . . . And as for you saying that I can do everything; it is you who says so. It is your faith. I will never say so. I always say that I know nothing, and I can do nothing. If one is nowhere, one has to speak like that. Nowhere, meaning everywhere, of course. . . ."

I understood; in substance it was the same answer as he gave me about healing years ago: "We can heal everything, but we cannot heal everybody." The Saint, being one with God, knows if it is the destiny of this particular person to suffer and be afflicted and if it is allowed to be taken away. . . .

Then he began to speak of faith: "There are few people who can be faithful; those who smoke, those who drink can never be faithful. Why? Because they are not faithful to themselves! What happens when it is smoked in the room? The room gets black. The same happens inside the human being. It becomes black. Bad smell comes from the mouth, from the skin, from all the orifices."

"If somebody sends evil to a Saint, it cannot affect him. Does the evil return to the doer harming him?"

"Only if the Saint orders so. Otherwise it is absorbed. If a disease is to be cured, it is absorbed. As for you in London, you had to ask for help because you were affected by some evils belonging to another person. It was because you were not yet capable of absorbing. Not yet. . . . One absorbs effortlessly. If one asks for help, it is absorbed somewhere else. Yes, you are right; there is a direct connecting link with the Master. I will not always know your thoughts unless you are completely absorbed in me. When one is absorbed, it is on all the levels." I said that I always believed that help is given, and now in the case of a certain woman after so many years he still does not know if it is a woman or a man. . . .

"Help is given from the Universal Reservoir of help. You asked for help and it is given either direct from the Master, or as in this case through you, because those people do not know me, never have seen me. One does not need to know if one who asks is a man or a woman.

I asked just now, only because in the case of a man the reason why the accident happened is a different one as in the case of a woman. That's all."

Other talk went on in Hindi. Then he got up to go.

"Did you understand the meaning of all I have said?"

"Yes, but still many puzzling things remain. . . ."

"Which one?" he asked becoming suddenly earnest, and sat down again.

I told him that one of the Sufi tenets is to avoid irrelevant talk. Ninety percent of the talk done here is irrelevant. And if people come here only for such a talk, then it is all right. But what about the Sharmas? They complain that they want spiritual talk and they get worldly talk from you. They come for bread and they get stones. "If your child asks you for bread, would you give him a stone?"

His expression was difficult to describe. He smiled . . . his lips were tight as if in tense expectation.

"And if the child asks for poison will I give it to my child? The Giver knows what he is doing. Who comes for absolute Truth? Very, very few . . . hardly any. The Giver knows what to do. . . ."

In the evening he did not speak English at all. The Giver knows. . . . Until now I accepted it because my reason accepted it; the understanding came that it was done for this or that purpose. But the stage has come to accept it because I have faith in his superior Wisdom. And it seemed to me at that moment that it will be not too difficult; so many proofs I had of his greatness. . . . I must take a firm decision. . . . Please, help!

28th February

DREAM: I was dressed in black as for a lecture. I looked in the mirror and I saw that I had a beard . . . a white beard around my face, as Muslims have. No other hair was on my cheeks, only the beard about three inches long, like a white, soft halo around the lower part of my face. Strange, I thought. I touched it; it felt like my own all right. . . . Strange, that I go on lecturing to large audiences all over the world and nobody laughed at me, nobody called me a woman with a beard. Nobody seems to notice it. . . .

When I came down, Mrs. Sharma said to me, "I play for you a new tune, I have composed this morning. The words are from Bahadur Shah, the grandson of Aurangzeb. He composed it while he was in prison where the English put him. It is the song of a bride, apparently, when she leaves her parents' home.

"I have to leave soon. Soon four men, four bearers will come, they will call for a palanquin and they will carry me my feet forward. And all which belongs to me and which belongs to others I leave behind."

I told Bhai Sahib that he is after regard because he said about Mr. Vippin: **"He pays me regard in every possible way."** He preached to me harshly for over an hour. Either he made confusing statements, or my mind was confused; I don't remember a thing. . . . In the evening he came out smiling and he asked me how I was.

"Not too good, I had trouble with my mind in the afternoon."

"But if there is such a link, such near relationship, why should there be any annoyance?" It suddenly occurred to me how right he was. How simple it all sounded. . . .

"I hope after that you will make a jump forward. Such things are necessary in order to push us on. One must have a keen desire to reach the goal. If the keen desire is there, where is the mind, how can it give trouble? If it gives trouble, the desire is not keen enough. Where love is, nothing can remain!"

"How difficult it is to control the mind!"

"No, it is very easy!" he said with a smile. I suddenly understood what he had meant.

"That's why you said in the morning, that love is easy, surrender is easy; when I come to know it, it is the easiest thing in the world! It was a misleading statement, but you tried to help me! Why didn't you rather say: it is the most difficult thing, but I expect you to do it just the same!"

"Oh, no, THEN, I would mislead you! Why not take a short-cut and say: it is easy! If you think that it is difficult, you yourself create an obstacle! Look at the Goal! Let everything else go! If you continue like this, where will you be? Trouble with the body, with the money, is nothing; if people don't respect you is nothing . . . but trouble with the mind—you become yourself an obstacle. You cannot go on. Throw it behind you. Look at me: I have no reaction because there was no action."

I asked him what the action was that I may avoid the reaction.

"Don't listen to letters from another culture," (what the deuce does he mean, I didn't get any such letters). **"Answer such letters but don't dwell on them. Not to take food in different places. Not to do irrelevant talk. Did you ever hear me speak about my superiors in the way you talk to me? How can a man who did not dare to ask his Teacher even how he felt or how he was, how can such a man**

tolerate your attitude? Why don't you try seriously to control your mind?" He said that, obviously displeased.

1st March

HE IS RIGHT, my desire for Truth is not keen enough. Otherwise the mind would have had no chance to give trouble. I have to renounce the mind, the doubts, the criticisms . . . as simple as that. Simple??

"I have to throw out such thoughts," I said to him in the morning.

"No; don't let them come in . . . then you will save yourself the trouble of throwing them out."

"But will I be able to keep it up?"

"Of course! This love is easy. It is the worldly love which is more difficult. For worldly love you have to waste time, energy, but here? Here is not waste. All the energy is concentrated on One. For you, love is not difficult at all. It was; but not now, not anymore," and he smiled a secret, tender smile. **"Love and faith are not difficult for you, now. But physically and mentally you are not surrendered. And people will notice that you are not surrendered. People cannot be deceived. It is felt. Love is in the heart of hearts but the mind is covering it. The control of the mind is the effort of the disciple. Love is created. Created effortlessly . . . but the mind one has to curb oneself."**

This evening when he came out, he began a friendly conversation with me on all sorts of topics.

"I will go soon to my superiors," and I closed my eyes in pain and the heart was aching. We talked about graves and cremation, and answering my question he said that the body of a Saint can remain intact for several hundreds of years and the skeleton sometimes for two or four thousand years. I said that his father and mother must still be intact. He confirmed it. Then he said:

"Try to go deeper; every day there will be something new." I said that knowing my character I was not sure what my mind will do.

"Don't try to do it with the mind."

"But if the mind does not give trouble, there will be no obstacle." He only nodded. I asked about the interpretation of the dream with the beard. He smiled again.

"I did not say much yesterday—but don't think of me too much."

"But how can I help it! For more than five years I do nothing else but think of you, or events and happenings connected with you!"

"Don't think too much," he repeated. But I said that this cannot be the meaning. The meaning must be a different one. Perhaps he does not want to tell me. Sometimes the dream may not be destined for me but for him. It happened in London several times; people told me dreams and it was not for them but for me who was guiding them. He nodded repeatedly.

"Usually the hints are not given directly, but sometimes my Father was talking directly and would say: you cannot do that or, that you will do. Or he will say: do like this—how will you be a good guide if you don't pay attention?" I thought that was a hint for me. . . .

"This body of ours is composed of five elements. But I don't look at the body but at something else. By the way: don't trust yourself, but trust where trust is. It means don't trust the mind but trust the Higher Self." Those words he said to me last night and told me to think them over; this morning he explained them:

"Try to go deeper every day now, there will be something new." And he said it casually in conversation. Such a tremendous thing expressed so casually. . . . And going home I was thinking so much, prayed and longed so much. Is it possible that now I get some kind of reward? I don't like the word "reward," but could it be that at last I will see some light? And I was going over the conversation we had.

"The body of a Saint is so purified that it decays slowly. There is decay, of course, but a very slow one. And the body of a Saint should be buried; it is a blessing for the surroundings." Speaking of the physical suffering:

"I should not say that they are my Samskaras, but suffering must be. . . ."

"They are Samskaras of others," I said tentatively.

"I should not say so, but they are not mine," he repeated. **"Saints are dhobies (washermen)."**

"Oh no; sweepers, sweepers of humanity!" He laughed heartily.

"At the beginning love was difficult for you, but not now." And he made a sideways movement with the head as if throwing away something. **"The way was cleared."** What wonderful words they are . . . and so glad was my heart. I must remember those words. . . .

"And what a wonderful thing is love . . . created without effort. And one cannot help loving. Even if one would like to stop, one cannot. . . ."

I said it was so true . . . (did I not know it?). And even if there is cruelty, one cannot help; one loves. . . . The story of Leila and Majnun . . . but do I need to go so far? Don't I know it from my own experience?

2nd *March*

LAST NIGHT WHEN WRITING MY DIARY I felt much vibration in the solar plexus. Went to bed and listened to it. It was just bearable. Otherwise it can cause a vomiting condition. Fell asleep. Woke up in the night; it was still there, but not too bad.

In the morning, my first thought was: is it still there? It was gone. When I came, I learned that he was not well in the night. Soon two people came, husband and wife, and they and myself were asked inside by Munshiji. He was lying on the tachat. Took no notice of me saluting him. Talked to the two people till they went. In the courtyard was a great noise and commotion—decoration of a room was going on, the room of his nephew. A heap of old rubbish, old boxes, old furniture was thrown in the middle of the courtyard. The wife came in, sat next to me and talked and talked. I gathered that something was worrying her; there was a problem, but my knowledge of Hindi was too limited to understand what it was all about. Something to do with decoration, presumably. Then the smallest child of the eldest son sitting in the big chair began to cry. Poonam took it out into the garden talking to it soothingly.

"Hm," he said. "**Everything wants sympathy. Everything wants care and attention which is a form of love. This tachat, this chair wants sympathy, to be dusted, to be looked after. . . .**"

"But things have no Soul!" I said.

"**Light, they have Light, this is the Soul in them. If you live in a shed, this is a place for you . . . you don't know better.**" This was the only sentence he spoke directly to me. I mentioned that on the 31st will be the General Election in England. A few words were exchanged on that, then he turned to the wall. Talked to his wife from time to time in monosyllables when she kept coming in and out. Clearly she was worried about something. . . .

The meaning of the Dream is: (I got it in the night in a flash between sleep and just awakening). I will be merged in him, when back in the West, i.e., into the System. It is a "future" dream.

At home had strong vibrations.

4th *March*

YESTERDAY MORNING I had such a strong vibration. I remember in the past this kind of vibration caused an intense irritation. I used to call it brain-washing vibration—one has an impelling desire to talk of all the doubts, all the tribulations of the mind. Will see what it will do to me now . . . it is the first time since I am back. It usually makes one talk too much. . . .

In the afternoon when I was sitting near the irrigation ditches regulating the flow of water, trying to distribute it evenly amongst the poor half-dried plants, he lifted the chik and said that I can come in. I washed my hands, dirty with mud, and told him that I received lovely photos of him and the Bandhara from H. He looked at them, and his wife and sons passed them from hand to hand. His room was arranged differently, much better . . . one large tachat was taken out and a settee and chairs put in instead.

In the evening I prayed, prayed desperately for Truth. This morning too. Some restlessness of the mind . . . I am hungry . . . hungry for Truth. . . . And I pray that this hunger, this longing for Truth should increase so much that I cannot live for one moment without it.

Told him about H.'s letter in which she mentions that he foretold her a car accident. She had one; only it was not on an icy road as he said then, but in rain and fog. A lorry smashed into the back of her car. Insurance will pay for it, but it is a nuisance.

"That's why I am sometimes reluctant to tell the meaning of a dream," he said thoughtfully, stroking his beard.

"The dream was about roses and plants."

"Never mind what the dream was about. IT IS FROM WHERE IT IS COMING, that alone is of importance. From where it comes. . . ." I told him that I know the interpretation of the bearded dream. He gave me an indirect hint, but those are things about which one should not speak.

When he came out this morning looking well and happy, he opened the conversation like this: **"The other day I deliberately spoke to you harshly in front of everybody, without telling anything beforehand. Without warning."** I smiled at him.

"Oh, you did it before . . . it is not the first time, and it did not do anything to me or very little. Besides, I remembered nothing of it afterwards."

"'That might be so, but like these things which are in the brain of brains they are washed away. As the things which are in the heart of hearts are gradually washed away, so from the brain of brains it is washed away when one is humiliated and people don't respect you." (What does he mean by the "brain of brains?" Perhaps the higher mind?)

Later: "The real *Ahimsa* cannot really be practiced on the physical level: not completely, at least, and not by everybody. What about regions in which nothing grows and one has to eat meat or fish? What about insects we crush unknowingly under our feet? The germs we swallow or destroy; they are life also. It is the mental *Ahimsa* which has to be practiced, and by everybody and completely so.

"Never to say evil things, never to wish evils to anybody, never to injure people's feelings. Never to injure or put in prison yourself by creating habits. This is real *Ahimsa*. Non-killing is too simple and limited a concept of *Ahimsa*, for it is much more than that.

"The Self is within and without. By injuring others one injures oneself. It is, for instance, like in a room around which are many mirrors: in one mirror you look thin, or broad, or with distorted features. But it is all YOU. And the shape depends upon the nature of the reflecting medium."

5th March

SOME MORE SAYINGS:

"Don't trust yourself; when you trust, trust is there. Meaning: don't trust your mind, but the Trust is in the Soul, the heart of Hearts. One should speak to the audiences just a little higher than their understanding. For instance: I may say Kanpur is the largest town in U.P. And then I say, but Bombay and Calcutta are much larger. Everybody will understand me. But if I would say: Kanpur is the largest town in U.P., but Paris and Berlin are much larger, many of my audience may think: what is he talking about? We have never heard of Paris or Berlin; where are they?"

Mr. Sharma told me that he read in a scientific magazine the following: Light consists of seven prismatic colors. If an object absorbs any color, it does not reflect it. If all colors are absorbed, then it is black, which is no-color. You see here in the garden many flowers of lovely colors. If the flower is red, it rejected, it renounced red color, but absorbed all the others. And so it is with every other color—blue, yellow, white. White means renouncing, rejecting all colors. So the flower gets its beauty through Renunciation. . . . What a lovely thought. . . .

I wonder if the custom of mourning in India—the widows wearing white only—has this meaning: renouncing, rejecting, everything? The ancients had so much more wisdom than we have; they knew the esoteric meaning which we have lost. Only now science begins to confirm certain things of ancient beliefs.

Sufis who have completely renounced the world wear black garments. One day I will know the meaning of all this. . . .

Last night much talk was going on about a new gate. The carpenter was there making drawings and discussing prices. The drunkard kept giving unasked-for advice and instructions. The villager who came in the morning smelled so badly that I had to get up and walk for a while to get a breath of fresh air without addition of sweat and worse. Before seven I saluted him.

"You want to go?" I said that it was nearly seven, but seeing that he seemingly wanted me to stay, I sat down again. Soon he got up and went inside. I walked. Then he came out through the doorway and I saluted. **"Yes, you can go now."** Spent a peaceful night. Mind was tranquil.

In the morning Mrs. Sharma came with me; they talked for an hour. Then when she left, he asked me into the room and left at once. I sat there. The villager came and sat opposite. This is too much, I thought in utter frustration. In the room I cannot get away from the smell. . . . But the door was open . . . there was a draught, so it wasn't too bad. He came in, took his mala and began to pray. Though I saw it so often, each time I became enchanted anew, for nothing is more beautiful than a Saint in prayer. I looked at his face full of light and watched the beads slide through his fingers, one after another rhythmically. And I felt like crying suddenly; all the heaviness, all the sorrow of those difficult years was upon me. And I cried. How much one has to swallow for the sake of Truth . . . hoping to get it one day. . . . Suddenly my crying stopped as quickly as it came. I kept looking at him. He was still praying. And then again as once before it began to come in waves—tremendously powerful feeling, waves after waves, from me to him . . . it was the greatest sorrow and longing. Longing to break the heart . . . I want the Truth, I kept repeating in my mind. I want it so badly, more than my life. . . . At one moment I nearly cried out loudly; it was as if my very life-blood, all my innermost being was torn out of me . . . as if my heart was torn out of my breast. It was such a painful experience, physically painful . . . something was trembling inside me . . . and kept trembling and trembling, ceaselessly, and something was crying desperately within me. I seemed to shrink on my chair. He kept praying. When he finished, he sat up in his chair and was talking to the Sikh. I heard him say that he has prepared for him ten kilos of flour. **"It is our ration, part of it; we don't need so much—it is for you."**

Then he asked his son what time it was. Quarter to twelve was the reply. **"You can go now."** He was right . . . I was all right again. The giddiness had passed. And going out through the courtyard, I saw him giving the Sikh his bag of flour. Spent a peaceful afternoon doing absolutely nothing. Was burning incense and thinking.

And in the evening he came out. Again there was this forceful stream of feeling from me to him, but not so strong as in the morning. Went home at the usual time.

66

People Judge by Appearances

6th March, 1966

WOKE ABOUT FOUR A.M., I think. Prayed so much . . . and last night too. When I pray, there is nearness. And the power which I feel in Guruji's presence flows towards him crying for help. I curb my mind, but it is restless. At dawn went on the flat-roof terrace outside my room and, looking at the clear sky and fading stars, prayed so much for help. Prayer is such a relief nowadays . . . for how long? Then I won't be able to pray again and will be alone. . . . So much . . . what a life. . . .

"The pandit sends you his *pranams* (greetings)," I said as soon as he sat down. "He was sitting here and went away about a quarter of an hour ago."

"Good. I don't care about people who come and go."

"But if he asks me to give you his greetings, it is my duty to do so."

"Quite. But some don't go further than to salute me, that's all. All that I care for is that I never should be careless."

"You never are." In answer he gave me one of his radiant smiles.

"Some people don't know and don't understand, even if they are here for years, through which Channel the Bliss and Grace comes. (I wondered if this was a hint for the judge who just came and sat down, or did he mean the pandit who has also been here for many years?)

"And those who understand . . .," he made a quick movement with the right hand, **"they come on the Channel. . . . Some people don't know how to pay respect. I don't like my children if they don't pay respect to my daughter and my son-in-law."** He remained silent for a moment. **"Yes, I don't like them if they fail to do so,"** he said slowly.

"Why such an importance is attached here in the Orient to paying respect?"

"Without regard, nothing can be done; even if you go to a shop to buy something, you have to pay respect. If you are rude or quarrelsome, you will not be served. Now, look at yourself: You deduct a sum from your pension to help your father." The wife came in at this moment and began to talk on household matters.

"The sum from your pension," I helped out, when she had left, so that he shouldn't lose the thread.

"Yes, and why do you do it? Because he is old, and only in this way you can show your respect. When for the first time you told me about it, I said to myself: she is right. First comes her father; it is her duty."

"I wish I could do more," I said.

"This is another matter," he said emphatically. **"If there is an impossibility, nothing can be done. If you try to carry this tachat, for instance, you cannot do it. It is impossible for you. Then even if people say: look here, she cannot do even such a little thing, then it does not matter. Let them say what they like. If you did your duty, if you have peace, then it does not matter what the world says. But you must have done your duty, you must have peace, otherwise it will be better to listen to what people say, if they criticize you."** In this moment the wind brought a specially large whiff of dust; he got up and told us to go inside. We all went.

Speaking of his Guru he said: **"I gave myself to him in my lifetime."**

Later he said: **"My uncle was the rising sun, my Father was the midday sun—he was shining just as radiant as the midday sun. Who will be the setting sun?—God only knows,"** he added.

"Do you mean to say that then it will be the end of the System?" I asked, thinking that by the setting sun he meant himself.

"Oh, no?" He laughed, **"How can that be? Never! If there is no sun, there is the moon!"** I went all cold. Such a clear hint, I thought. . . . By the expression of my face he must have gathered that I understood the meaning. He gave me a quick glance and then looked out of the window for a few moments.

"Sun and moon eclipse; stars never eclipse."

"How is this to be understood?"

"Saints undergo obscurations," he amplified, **"undergo great sufferings, lose the respect of people."** Then he went out.

I was half thunderstruck, thinking his words over. A hint?? Who knows? . . . In the meantime I made myself more comfortable in the kneeling *asana*. He came in, took the mala from the recess. Oh, I thought delightedly; I wasn't sure I didn't say it aloud. Now, I will have the pleasure to watch him pray. All in white he was today, seated in his usual posture; he prayed. Bluish light played on his forehead and his cheeks, flashes of lovely green around him. Today it was not the usual mala of his Rev. Guru, but the delicate Muslim mala of pale greenish jade with a red tassel.

"This mala is a beauty," I said when he interrupted his prayers for a moment to talk to Sharma's son who just came in.

"It shines in the dark." He asked one of his disciples to close all the shutters. In the now dark room his mala was shining with bluish light, like the phosphorescent numbers on a wrist watch. Now, I don't know if there is such a thing as a phosphorescent jade; and I don't think that it can be made phosphorescent artificially. I prefer to think that it became so by the use of the slender fingers of a Saint. . . .

And then it began . . . actually it had already begun softly when we were sitting outside. And it was increasing all the time as soon as he began his prayers, and I knew that he will give me a sitting . . . or was it one? Or something else to which no definition can be given? . . . and waves followed upon waves, stronger and stronger. At one moment the physical body was as though under great suffering, the tension hardly bearable. I had to press both hands to my chest as hard as I could, so much was the pain. He flicked a sideways glance, noticing my gesture, and continued to pray closing his eyes. The mind was not working. Wave after wave followed. It was such unbearable pain, such longing. . . . I began to do *La-il-llillah,* following the movement of his fingers. When after a while he put away his mala and began to pray lifting both hands in the Muslim fashion, I too prayed ardently, asking for illumination of my mind, for Wisdom, for Truth. . . . He took up the mala once more. The dim light in the room. His posture in Teaching *Asana.* I saw it sideways; this gave his body a graceful twist. His face, serene in prayer, eyes half-closed in deep concentration, the bluish light on this face which I seemed to know always, from somewhere. . . . Children were shouting and crying outside. Strange, at other times I would have been annoyed at the noise. It did not seem to disturb today. He prayed like that till quarter past twelve, then he talked to Sharma's son. The waves began to subside. He sent us home at 12:30.

He said: **"I try to use the words 'Absolute Truth' whenever possible. One should not even say the Almighty God. Many people object to that. But to Absolute Truth, nobody can object; it is everywhere . . . everybody accepts that, from whatever religion. Zarathustra was the first to coin the word 'God.' Since then it is in use. 'God' is a good word. But 'Absolute Truth' is better."**

A disciple of his asked me how long I will remain here. I answered that it depended on the Teacher. Going back into the room I said to him: "I have been asked how long will I stay here; I just arrived, why should one think of departure?"

"It is because people think that Europeans cannot stay here in the hot season—that's why they ask."

"But I can; I did!" He nodded.

"Great sacrifices are demanded from one who wants the Truth. Sacrifices can take many forms. Physical, mental, all sorts of great sufferings are necessary and are required!"

7th March

BECAUSE OF THE LINK which binds you and me like an arc of a glorious Rainbow thrown from one Eternity to another; in the Name of this Old Relationship which always was and always will be and which gave you the right to do to me what no one can do to a free human being without paying a high price for doing it; because of this Love which you have lit like a Sacred Torch in my heart; because of all that, I am controlling my mind. . . .

You know it is not easy. I live in an atmosphere of doubts and suspicions, and to keep my mind fixed firmly on the Point of Light, still so far away, is so much more difficult, is a gigantic task and a full-time job, from morning till evening. . . . But I am not alone; you are helping me, by saying the right word from time to time. . . .

God is helping me through you, by giving me this endless longing. . . . Last week I told you about the new vibration which feels like powerful waves of love and great Longing from me to you. In the past, always, the vibrations seemed to come from outside myself; from you to me for instance.

Now it seems the other way round: it is FROM ME TO YOU. And so strong it is that something keeps trembling inside me, and the physical body can hardly bear it. . . . Because it is He in me who wants Himself. . . . But all this I did not tell him; what for? I only wrote it down. . . .

TODAY IS HOLY FESTIVAL and I don't go to him in the morning. I suffer from great Longing. . . . Yesterday morning he sang a couplet which was translated to me; it is of Bahadur Shah:

"After having given him the *Diksha* (consecration) his Master asked him the usual question: What do you want? and he replied: 'I want to be one of those candles which are lit on the graves; they are lit in the night, and are extinguished in the morning. Like one of those I want to be before you!"

"It means complete surrender," he laughed his young laughter. Then he told us a story: "The chief police inspector sent his son to my Rev. Guru Maharaj for study. But my Rev. Guru wrote to the father: take your son back; he is not very intelligent; I cannot teach him anything. One day the police officer and his son were sitting there and I was also there. Somebody asked a question: 'How long does it take to learn Urdu and Persian?' 'About one year,' he replied. 'Oh, so long?' asked the questioner. Then he said: 'Oh, about nine months.' And as the discussion went on, it became six, three months—it was less and less until it reached the stage that to know Urdu and Persian will take half an hour. Then the police officer got up and said: 'Here is your slave and here is the son of a slave!' 'Ah?' asked Guru Maharaj, 'don't you see that this talk was going on for your sake? Come here!' he said to the boy. And he covered his head so that the ears were covered with the square of cloth men wear in the district of Ferruchabad. It is done like this, if the Guru wants to give something, and for ten minutes he explained the meaning of Alif—why Alif is Alif and the First and not 'B' and so on. And for the first time we all heard this explained and we were very interested. After that the boy fell unconscious. He was unconscious for three days and then it took him another three days to recover. And after that whatever difficult works in Urdu or Persian were put before him, he could read and explain them. It was the most perfect example of a powerful *Tawadje*.

"One day the relative of my Rev. Guru was lying here in the room upstairs. His temperature was not at all high, hardly any fever at all. So my Rev. Guru asked me: 'He has hardly any fever and you are worried, why?' So I told him that the man has to live only for ten days. 'How do you know?' asked the Guru and laughed. I told him that I knew it by counting the pulse; he told my Father how to do it and me too, but he forgot it. Later my Father told me that I lacked regard to my Guru by answering like this. I felt very badly about that. So next day my Guru told me to go upstairs and tell him how long he will live. I did not like it. I went and this time I only told him: 'Do you want him to remain here or be transported to Ferruchabad?' And Guru Maharaj said that he should be transported to Ferruchabad—that was all. And how is it known by the pulse? One counts the pulse; it is and is not."

"Do you mean irregular?"

"No, somebody else who counts will say that it is quite regular. There is a way to know if a person will die in ten days. I did it to my

Mother and my Father and then forgot it. So their death took me by surprise."

Later in the evening he said speaking to the drunkard: "Forgetfulness is one of the greatest qualifications. What we know, we have to forget."

I waited till the verbal diarrhea of the drunkard subsided and asked him what he meant by this sentence which I repeated: "All our knowledge, all we have learned, we have to forget it, it is a barrier."

"The memory is a barrier—how much can the brain hold? We don't need the memory at all. It is all here when we need it; you experienced it in London; experience is better than any explanation."

"Does it mean that, if our cup is full, nothing can be put into it?"

"This is another matter. On our line we have to be emptied completely in order to get something. If your cup is full of water, how can I pour anything into it? We have to be empty. We must be able to close our doors, all our openings, and remain alone with somebody. Even if we are not alone, even if we have no room for ourselves, we can still close our doors and remain alone. Only, there can be non-cooperation from within, but this is another matter."

"But if there is cooperation?"

"Then," he said, "then one is blessed. In this case half of the work is done already!" He abruptly interrupted himself. Many men came in and the room became full, and general Hindi conversation began. At half past seven I got up.

"I must go," I said saluting him.

"You must go?"

"It is half past seven; we have dinner at Sharma's place at eight."

"If you must go, then you must!" He laughed, and when I was already at the door he added: "Keep in mind where you are going and who has to go!" I looked at his slender figure seated in the usual teaching Asana under the lamp; the room was full of people. I muttered something to the extent that I understood, nodded, and lifting the chik quickly went out. I had suddenly an acute feeling of special meaning, and my heart was beating fast.

8th March

HAD A RESTLESS NIGHT. Keep in mind where you are going and who has to go. . . . If on the back of my mirror of the heart is written "Alif" and the face of my mirror faces my Sheikh, where am I?

When I came this morning, he soon came out.

"People were sitting till late, till ten. Good talk was going on. I put to them three questions. I often do that, then I leave them to discuss it between themselves. They all said something and nobody was satisfied with his own answer. The questions were: King Janaka has sent his son to a Rishi to be trained in Spiritual Life. The question is—a man sends his son to be trained by one greater than himself. Janaka was said to be the greatest of his time. So why did he not train his son himself?

"Second question: this Rishi did not exist in his physical body, not in his mental body. He had many wives and even prostitutes. How is that?" I leaned forward; the questions seemed to me easy to answer.

"And what did you say?" I asked guardedly.

"I said nothing!" he laughed. Then he looked at me. Does he want me to answer? I thought. I leaned more forward balancing my chair on its forelegs:

"It seems to me if I am right," I began hesitantly (I wasn't sure that I did well to answer), "it is only natural that Janaka did not train his son himself, however great he might have been. How can a father, who is after all a human being, how can he subject his child to the sufferings and hardships the Teacher has to subject a disciple, if needed? Could you put your child through the trials you had to put me? Impossible! You would do it if the order was given. Anything is done and can be done if the order is given, but it will break your heart. . . ." I looked at him, his face assumed a tender expression. Narrowing his eyes to a slit he seemed to look into an empty space before him; around his lips played a mysterious smile.

"A doctor does not treat his family members. He will ask another doctor to treat them. With the Guru it is the same."

"Quite correct," he nodded, "it is so."

"And to say that the Rishi had wives and prostitutes has no meaning in this case; if he didn't live either in his physical or in his mental body, he probably was not even aware of them!"

"And the boy did not have faith; he did not want to go to the Rishi. 'Why should I go to such a man?—he is not great,' he was saying: he was disgusted. He saw him sitting, and one prostitute was massaging his feet and he had his head on her shoulder. So the third question is: was he justified to be disgusted?"

"Not at all. He was not even conscious of his body because the mind wasn't there; he was probably talking, or rather being in perfect oneness with the Prostitute on the Atmic level, that was all. People judge by appearances, how can they know?!"

"**Quite, quite correct,**" he said, and I saw that he was pleased with my answer, so I continued: "When I showed Mrs. Sharma the photos H. had taken, I told her that I never saw you in Samadhi on any photo. Those were the first."

"**Yes, H. was the first to do it,**" he said thoughtfully.

"But Mrs. Sharma wanted to know how do I know that it was Samadhi? It could be concentration. I told her, she needed only to look at your face—it shows so clearly; this is the face when you are in Samadhi . . . there can be no mistake. Only it seems to me that I see more than many other people—I should not say it, it might sound like pride. . . ." He shook his head.

"**No, no,**" he said softly, "**it is not, but one has to reach a certain understanding in order to see many things.**"

"To put it in plain English: in order to see the beauty of Leila one has to have the eyes of Majnun! A certain understanding is needed to see correctly."

"**Quite, quite correct!**" And then with a strange smile: "**Nobody knew when my Rev. Guru Maharaj was in Samadhi, but I always knew it.**" Then he asked about a postcard I had to answer for him, dictated a few final words to it, and went inside. Came out shortly with a mala. A different one this time, a long one of blond Tulsi wood. And for one-and-a-half hours he prayed. I did *la-il-llillah* practice for a while following the rhythm of his slender fingers. And thought. Reflected. Felt no waves of power. All was still in me.

In the afternoon wrote my diary and finished the letter to G. Then, when resting on my bed, I noticed great heart activity . . . a vibration in the heart. Before it used to make me always very apprehensive—a change of state is always announced like this and that could mean trouble. Only this time there was no apprehension. Come what may. I am controlling my mind. Now I am more the master of my mind than before. And was full of peace and serenity. But soon adverse ideas came creeping persistently in. The body became tense with the flow of fiery light. But it was not too bad. Could control it without difficulty. And sure enough, when I was sitting and writing these lines, he came out with his mala. And the flow of tremendous Power began as before . . . I could hardly breathe. . . . The physical pain of terrible longing: I never thought such a thing to be possible, that longing could cause such acute physical pain. . . .

67

The Divine Thread

GO ON CONTROLLING MY MIND. But only just. Two major difficulties confront me—one is memory. Sitting in his garden, many situations occur which remind me of the past sufferings. Resentment creeps up. The other difficulty is that I live in an atmosphere of suspicion. Thoughts of doubt and suspicion surround me; I cannot help picking them up. They reflect in me. So I have to fight not only my own mind but protect myself from other people's thoughts. And which are my own, and which are other people's, is difficult to distinguish. . . .

It is a two-fold process, as far as I can see, the controlling, I mean—to keep the eyes fixed firmly on the goal—and secondly to relate everything to it. For example: my mind gives me trouble only in connection with him. So whatever he does or does not, I must think it is done for the good, to help me reach the Goal quicker. Or I must say that for the moment I don't understand it. But one day I will. So, I accept it for the moment as it is, *without* understanding. In other words: it is a question of ATTENTION and of RELATIONSHIP.

He said last night translating a couplet:

"The Divine Thread is so subtle and thin, not easy to see
Not easy to catch. It is not for everybody.
Only for those who can sacrifice. Not the physical possessions
are meant here, this is not a sacrifice.
It is relatively easy and is only part of it.
Sacrifice means merging into the Great Man of the time,
Who is the Sat Guru."

He continued to speak in Hindi, giving more explanations about the couplet. I kept quiet for a while, then taking advantage of a pause in conversation, I asked: "What is the Divine Thread?"

"I told you, don't you see it? It is for what you come to the Sat Guru. For what did you come?"

"Oh, I see; the term 'Divine Thread' confused me."

"It must be understood; but it cannot be understood completely. Only partly. The greater part is beyond understanding. As far as we

live in this world and as far as this world is with us, we understand it. Beyond, there is no understanding anymore, but Realization.''

As far as I can see, for the memory there is no other cure but to accept everything that happens as the Will of God. And in reality, it is so, of course. And as to thoughts which don't belong to me, it is a question of keeping them away, I suppose. . . . Heaven knows how it is not easy at all—not always can I recognize which is my own thought and which is not. . . .

HE CAME OUT LOOKING GREY AND TIRED.

"How are you?" His voice was friendly and warm.

"I am all right, but you are not well," I answered while I was saluting him.

"I was under fever last night and had a trouble to some extent." And he went to the water pipe to wash his face. Then he returned into the room. A few moments later Satendra called me in. The room felt cool. He was sitting in the big chair and he had a mala in his hand. The jade mala. I call it the lady-mala. It must be of feminine gender, those pale, smooth beads, alive as it were, shining in the dark. It is so beautiful . . . all the other malas of wood, especially the shining black one belonging to his Rev. Guru, which he had yesterday, are male malas. They are solid, masculine, larger affairs. He sat quietly. Somehow I felt that I could speak, so I said: "For the last eleven days I have managed to control my mind. And I see that it can be done." A flicker of a radiant smile passed like a ray of sudden sunshine over his tired face.

"Gooood," he said cheerfully, drawing out the "oo's."

"But I find that I encounter two major difficulties. The first is the memory."

"How is that?" he inquired.

"You see, by sitting in your garden, there are many situations which crop up and remind me of the past sufferings. Terrible things have been done, and they come up and stand before me like ghosts. I was afraid that it might happen, and I wrote to you about it from London, I remember. It happened as I feared. Then the resentment comes. Now, to get rid of the resentment, one has to remember that it was, and it is, the Will of God. Then the resentment goes. But the other obstacle is the fact that I live in surroundings of suspicion. How to know which doubts are mine and which are somebody else's reflections?" A shadow of compassion showed in his eyes. He picked up his mala which was lying pale and shining on the armrest of his chair.

"At last I am beginning to master my mind . . . am less a slave of it . . . am not completely helpless. I see that I can master it, even if only just."

"Thoughts come and go," he said softly.

"Yes, but they should not come at all; you yourself told me that. But by being able to control it at least partially, I feel a deep satisfaction within."

"A great satisfaction and peace will come when one controls the mind," he said slowly, beginning to pray. I settled down comfortably to pray too, watching him. Suddenly I had the feeling that he prayed for me. Such was the intensity, such was the concentration, his deep devotion . . . it was touching to see. And it occurred to me that for a fortnight he had the mala every day, and I remembered that when I was under pressure he also had the mala every day for many months. And today I was 100% sure he prayed for me . . . and so I sat there praying with him. When he finished, he stretched as if in exhaustion; his body felt tired—one could see it. And he fell asleep reclining in the big chair. I changed my place and went to sit not exactly opposite him, but near the wall at the head of his bed. There I could see him better. There was a deep peace . . . what a peace, I thought. No other feeling but the deepest peace.

The branches of the guava bush outside the window moved in the breeze. Sparrows were chirping, a myna sang in a tree nearby. The melodious call of the Indian woodpecker was heard; I call it the sugar-mill bird; it sounds like the sound of the press of the sugar mill, a kind of rapid "too, too, too," endlessly going on. Bluish light on his face. Green light on his magnificent forehead. Some silly little sparrows were trying to stuff some straw in the upper part of the ceiling fan. They want to make a nest there . . . poor silly things. When the fan will be used in a few weeks time, they won't be able to approach it, and the eggs will be lost.

I reflected on the feeling of oneness. Here we are, two different physical bodies. Not even sitting near each other. There was a bodily difference, of course. But already on the mental level there was some intimate feeling of belonging. And somewhere, deep, deep down, there was absolute oneness. . . . I don't disturb him at all, I was thinking. His wife came in, wanted to talk, gave him a look, saw he was sleeping, and went out. A few seconds later he opened his eyes.

"What time, please?" he said in a friendly way.

"Half past eleven; do you want me to go?" He shook his head and closed his eyes again. I don't disturb him . . . how can I? We are one somewhere.

At half past twelve I went reluctantly. Could have stayed forever in this place, but it was time to go home for lunch.

12th March

IN THE AFTERNOON HE DID NOT COME OUT. A procession of people went into the room. I was not asked in, so I sat outside alone. It did not matter much. I was with him alone in the morning, and there was a sense of deep oneness.

Woke up in the morning about six . . . very late for me. Hurried to open the bathroom door for the servant to bring the hot water. I was just in time.

Had two dreams last night. One was: two chairs were standing near each other separate from other chairs further away, presumably for other people. The one chair was his usual one, and the other, the exact replica only smaller, had an orange fringed cover, and was for me. I woke up and was thinking that it really does not need an interpretation. Fell asleep again and dreamt that he and I were sitting on the chairs close together in the middle of an empty street. Beautiful houses and trees were on both sides of the street, but the shutters and all the doors were closed, and no people in the street except one European man who passed by and kept looking back curiously at us sitting on chairs in the middle of the street. I could not make out what it could mean.

The feeling of belonging and great peace is still with me. This morning after breakfast, sitting at the table and reading an article on Razia, the queen of India in the thirteenth century, I suddenly felt like a stab and then a gentle vibration in the heart. The feeling of love and belonging increased, and I was reflecting that for the last twelve days, while I was engaged in the task of controlling the mind, there were not many vibrations. Only very few and for a short time. I was left seemingly alone to cope with my mind. Seemingly. Help is given, of course. The human being cannot do such a formidable task alone. But I probably will never know to what extent it is given.

This morning I was thinking: the greatest proof for me that the Spiritual Life is a TREMENDOUS REALITY must be AND is, that a man, a COMPLETE STRANGER, takes such trouble with me. For what? To train a human being is a hard, difficult work; it requires time and effort. Why should he do it if not because of some received order? Orders

from Whom? Orders for what reason? Here lies the answer of the
reality of it. . . .

When I analyze my feeling, for the first time I notice now that the
nearness to the Master is of the *same quality* as the nearness to God.
When I pray, the feeling is the same. Only the Master is much nearer
than God, or shall I say Truth? This is the only difference. The
difference is in the *distance* of feeling. God is more distant.

He came out and I did not notice it until he passed me by going to
his chair. I got up and saluted him hurriedly.

"Strange, that for a few times I did not notice you lately." He had a
ghost of a smile for an answer. I remembered, ten days ago, as I was
coming through the gate I was aware faintly, as if on the edge of my
consciousness, of somebody at the other end of the garden, but I
realized that it was he when I heard his voice and saw him standing
near me.

"How are you?" he asked, and I was startled, so unexpected it was.
Another time I was also startled when I was taking back the bucket
into the courtyard after having watered the plants. I did not see him
sitting with his wife who was talking to him in a low voice. I am so
deeply aware of him always and he is surely not a person to be
overlooked so easily at any time. It is a strange phenomenon. A fault
of the mind? Of the eyes? Or is my consciousness being abstracted
somewhere else? At any rate it seems to me to be strange.

He had the little ivory mala. After a while I asked him if it had a
special meaning that he held it sometimes in the right hand and
sometimes in the left.

"Just for the sake of convenience; it has no other meaning."

The whole morning he was sitting there, at first praying, but not
for long, and then in Samadhi. This feeling of perfect peace . . . one
is quite simply resting in his heart. Or is he resting in mine? There is
an utter stillness within, which for the mind is a vacuum, for it
understands it not. The merging into the Master is obviously
accomplished by degrees . . . and in utter silence. . . . He looked at
my forehead twice or three times when opening his eyes. All was
peace. Even the garden was still. Even the traffic . . . as if from very
far away came the usual noises of a busy household.

13th March

HE CAME OUT LOOKING BETTER, and for a long time he was talking
Hindi. From time to time he gave a friendly nod in my direction. He
must have noticed that I was somewhat depressed. It was hot already,

and I was thinking of the heat in the months ahead. After glancing at me in a kindly way he asked:

"**How are you?**" I said that I was well and was glad that he was better. "**Better, yes; hard times are ahead.**"

"Hard times?" I echoed alarmed, thinking he was alluding to his state of health.

"**Please, don't sit always outside, come inside at any time. You can sit in the room. Go inside, don't even ask; nobody is here to check you. I myself sometimes don't come into this room for hours.**"

"Thank you," I said, and then with a smile I added: "This is a great change . . . you know what I mean." His smiling eyes said: Yes, I know, and he nodded. I was alluding to the past when I could never go inside, heat or no heat. Then he talked about the coolness of his room, the cross-ventilation, due to the three doors and two windows. The windows in all the rooms in his bungalow have no window panes, only wooden shutters.

"**Last night when you left, the advocate Bhalla and the others were speaking so highly of you. They were saying: she is coming every day sitting here for many hours, or she will do something in the garden. And she does not know why and for what she is coming, but she sits. . . . But we know about *Brahmavidya* and we come here to have a talk only. We don't want to sacrifice, we don't make any efforts. . . .**" In this they are mistaken, I thought. I know much more than they imagine . . . *why* I am here. . . .

"**And when people speak like this, I feel ashamed,**" he continued.

"But why should you feel ashamed?" I interrupted, profoundly puzzled at his conclusion.

"**Had I been a greater man, I would have taken you**—and he made a gesture as to indicate infinite horizons—**God knows where I could have taken you, but I cannot do it.**"

"Good heavens, you cannot do it because of my limitations! What can you do if I am still full of the self!?" While he was speaking, all the time he was looking me straight in the eyes. He wants to see if I am resentful that he is not taking me higher, I thought; this talk is a test. . . .

I was talking to Durga Shankar and to a pandit who is here from Tundla. Then I noticed that they did not listen because they were in Samadhi. He is testing me all right—if there is resentment in me because I should have been given more—flashed through my mind. He was not with us; he went to have his bath.

This morning he has a small, new mala, made from Tulsi wood.

When he came back, he began to pray, the mala slowly revolving in his hand. Leaning forward when he looked up I said softly:

"Bhai Sahib?" He turned his head in my direction with a smile. "When will the self go?"

"When the smaller merges into the Greater," he answered, **"will the self go."**

I shook my head. "People speak highly of me and I don't speak highly of anybody. I sit here and dislike people, am full of criticisms, have resentment, am irritated, dislike this and that—the self is still very much in evidence."

"Something will always remain; I told you this before. Even in Great People something *always* remains; so that people will say: 'Look here, how many faults are there!' While we are in the physical bodies, something *must* remain."

When walking home I was thinking much of what he said to me. I am sure it is myself which is to blame if there is a lack of anything.

When I was resting after lunch, the wind already smelled of the hot breath of the Indian plains. It is the forerunner of Loo. Hot, unbearably hot, is the breath of the plains, for they stretch for thousands of miles. When flying to Madras in '63, I saw them: ochre-colored and endless, tiny villages with a few trees lost amongst this arid vastness. . . . How can they live?, I was thinking; what life of privations it must be. . . . The bougainvillea on the terrace on the right, seen from my wide open window, is a glory. I looked at it for a long time, feeling the hot scorching breath of the wind on my face. The crimson and scarlet of it! I know that if I will see one like this in the future, it will always mean India to me, and all the longing and the heat of the plains, all the smells, all the memories will come crowding back with unbearable yearning. The wind sweeping through all the open windows (the room has windows all around and a large double door, all glass, opening on the flat-roof terrace), the dome of the temple in the distance, the trees of the park . . . and the longing, the longing . . . Oooh. . . .

14th March

LAST NIGHT HE EXCHANGED a few friendly words with me. And then I sat in the darkening garden, listening to the Hindi conversation and looking at sudden flashes of his eyes when they caught the light of the street lamp. The feeling of nearness was perfect. I was thinking that before, when I dreamt of him most of the time, many people were present. Lately, when I dream of him, we are alone either sitting near each other, or he is telling me something, or sometimes I do. I wonder, could it mean that the merging began? Last night I was very lonely. There is a kind . . . a kind . . . a foreboding? I am not sure. . . .

The water was running from the pipe for irrigation. The sound of running water is a blessed sound in India. The air was sweet and heavy with the scent of the Queen of the Night (in Hindi, *Rat ki Rani*)— it is a shrub, and it flowers at this time of the year. There is one, a small one, in Guruji's garden.

16th March

YESTERDAY HE TALKED TO ME in a friendly way in the morning. He was squatting near the water pipe and the Sikh was cleaning a sickle. I just stood there quietly. We both were together in deepest peace.

When the Sikh departed, taking the sickle with him, he got up and said: **"I gave the sickle to him. When the human being is in trouble, who will help? Even animals help each other. Shall we be less than animals?"** He began to walk up and down. I sat down near the wall where the chairs were standing. He beckoned me to him. I approached. He talked about plants, irrigation, simple everyday things . . . just as in my later dreams, was the feeling. Just being together, together in the deepest peace. There was oneness, and I never experienced it to such an extent as today. Infinitely lovely. . . . The garden was sprinkled. People came and went. He was sometimes inside talking to his family, sometimes outside directing the sweeping. The Sikh came back and began to sprinkle. A lovely smell of moist earth was in the air. Then the chairs were put out. The usual crowd arrived and the usual talk in Hindi began. I sat there in perfect peace. And when I left I touched his feet, as I have been doing lately for the past few days. "Good night," says my heart. "Sleep well."

Had a restless night. It was so hot and stuffy. This morning when I came out on the terrace at dawn, the sky was perfect in pale yellows and tender mauves in the zenith. A waning crescent moon was to the right, and a large star was in the east. I stood there in the coolness of the morning . . . how my skin enjoyed it! Tried to analyze this peace. The deepest peace can be had only in the most peaceless state which is love. . . . Yes, but the love beyond conflict is not of this world . . . where did I read it? *Kama Sutra*? Welling from within, a feeling so rich, so full and of no end . . . stretching into the Always. So still, so deep, that I cannot express it in words, not even in clear thinking

. . . cannot say and, what is more, don't care even to try to say it . . .
nobody will ever understand. And he knows about it, for he gave it
to me, so no need to say anything to him either.

Is this merging?? That's why he told me sometime ago: **"Write it all
down; every day there will be new things."** At any rate HE KNOWS.

When I came, he was already sitting outside talking to a man in
English: **"Prophet Mohammed ordered that nobody should bow
down at his tomb, that nobody should be inclined to worship it.
And nobody ever did it. Pilgrimage to the Kaaba is not a worship of
it. Nobody can kill a mosquito; nobody can say a bad word; nobody
must even say, this is good and this is bad. This is Pilgrimage. Only
this."**

Then the man left and he told me that I can sit in the room where it
is cooler and dark and there are no flies, and he in the meantime will
have his bath and massage. So I sat in the semi-dark room. Could not
help being pleased because I saw the drunkard sitting alone under the
mango tree. For one moment I felt inclined to tell him that the
Master will not come out. But I refrained from doing it. After all, it is
not my business. And it does him good to sit alone for a change.
Sounds of some songs on the radio were pleasant, heard from the
distance. He kept coming in and out. I felt deeply at peace, deeply
happy inside. Each time he came in, I got up as usual. At one moment
I had the impression that it somewhat embarrassed him so I said:

"Please, allow me to get up each time you come in; it is a pleasure
to me, no bother at all."

"Hot season is coming," he remarked for an answer, took a singlet
from the hook on the wall and went out. How priestly he looks, his
brown torso naked and the longhi reaching down to the sandals. . . .

Some of his sayings: **"Luminaries set, but when the sun has set,
the moon shines like the sun. . . ."**

Speaking of a letter full of doubts which arrived from London:
**"One should always answer letters of doubts. Always try to disperse
doubts in the human being. When the doubts go, then there is
progress."**

Speaking of the brother of one of his followers who just died: **"If
he is faithful, he will be helped; if not, why should I bother? I am not
the Lord of the World!**

**"*Tassildar* (the drunkard) went on talking last evening about
advocate Bhalla. He was saying that the advocate does not pay me
the due regard, and this regard is due to me and everybody should**

know it. And he went on and on . . . but I don't listen. Who can listen to every nonsense!"

"Couldn't you tell him that one should not speak like this about others?"

"What for?" he retorted. "People don't listen to one, not to speak about acceptance. They don't listen and they don't accept. Until the time has arrived, nobody accepts anything. But when the time comes, only a little hint is needed and the human being accepts. . . ."

"Who has renounced, God will provide for his needs."

Mrs. Vippin was asking about somebody who was considered to be a Saint, but he was such an angry individual, so easily aroused.

"If a Saint is under vibrations, he will be very irritable; his condition may be due to that."

"GO ON TOLERATING, go on renouncing; and without the slightest doubt," he said emphatically, "You will be there!

"I am sorry that she is in financial difficulties. I will pray for her. But if she will follow you, that is, if she remains with you (he corrected himself quickly, and it made me smile, for the disciple should never have the opportunity to become proud!), and you will be strict with her, and she will stick in spite of that, then she will never be in money difficulties, and neither will you, WHEN YOU HAVE SURRENDERED."

68

Testing Period

17th March, 1966

KEEP PRAYING FOR FAITH . . . faith in spite of everything, faith endless, faith to move mountains. Faith is the door to Truth . . . the desire for knowledge must go. One must desire faith only. But how can the desire for knowledge go? The very purpose of our coming on earth, is to KNOW, to EXPERIENCE. Every Soul wants to KNOW above all. . . . Still, the desire for knowledge can be given up for something greater. . . .

18th March

HE CAME OUT LATE, some people whom I never saw before were present. They were from another town. Soon we all went into the room. He was in the big chair, had the small mala of blond wood. The drunkard was there too, but he is not a drunkard anymore; he gave up drinking, so Bhai Sahib said a few days ago. So I will call him Tasseldar; he is some kind of magistrate, as far as I understood. I sat near the door because it is the coolest place . . . nice draught in the room and it felt pleasant. Was thinking of the last evening—how I cried sitting in the dark while all of them were busily talking . . . an ocean of despair was in my heart. . . . He had hurt me by twisting my words, by accusing me of something I had not done . . . I was perplexed and could not get at the meaning of it all. He was ironical, made sharp, cutting remarks; then he said something which I knew was not true and contrary to facts, twisted his statements, was sarcastic and then denied everything. . . .

Why on earth does he drag himself into the mud before my eyes? Here are no more contradictions; he is untruthful . . . and he did it repeatedly till I was reduced to absolute despair . . . and I cried in hopeless frustration. Then I began to think: who is hurt? The self, of course. Let it go! I did . . . and was at peace.

When saluting him when leaving, **"Everything all right?"** he drawled ironically. I mumbled something in assent in profound disgust. Of course he knew that I was crying, and how hurt I was, and he was laughing at me. . . .

But I had peace that night. I should know him better by now and not fall into the trap, for I know why it is done . . . go on lying, I thought. My heart does not believe that you mean it. I know why you do it. All this I was thinking sitting in the cool near the door. He finished his prayers. Lifting his head, he gave me a hard look right into my eyes. I looked back at him: I don't believe that you are such a twister, I thought, and repeated this thought clearly three times to be sure that he gets it. I don't care. Go on twisting, denying—go on hurting me. I wonder if the feeling of despair is caused, "done" deliberately, to increase the suffering, or if I myself cause it. I wonder . . . I was subjected to so many things, to so many pressures, that nothing would surprise me anymore.

While talking to Tasseldar, he got up and came to sit on the sofa, next to my chair. I had a slight surprise and then a sense of alarm. I remembered that he did that once in the past—he came to sit near me—and then I had terrible trouble with my mind. I watched him with suspicion.

He told us two stories of Ajaz, the first of the Slave Dynasty: **"The King had a slave, Ajaz by name, and he loved him much and he trusted him. The courtiers were jealous of him. They tried to accuse him before the king but with no success.**

"One day the king learned that a troop had crossed the frontier of his kingdom, so he sent Sardars, the pillars of the kingdom, to investigate from where they came and what they wanted. And he also sent Ajaz to do the same. The Sardars came back the same evening reporting to the king that those people crossed the frontier by mistake and they had left already. Ajaz remained away for three days. The courtiers and the Sardars began to whisper to the king, 'What is he doing so long? He is wasting his time. We investigated and came back in one day.' After three days Ajaz came back and the king was angry with him: 'Give me the report of what you have done, you unfaithful slave,' he shouted at him. 'Those people,' said Ajaz, 'were sent by the enemy to spy and to prepare for the invasion. They crossed the frontier at this spot. They spent the night near this village. They put some obstacles at the strategic places.' 'Why didn't you arrest them?' asked the king. 'This was done,' answered Ajaz. 'They have been arrested and are in prison awaiting your orders.

"The king came back from a war expedition which was very successful, and he was happy and pleased. He wanted to make his people happy, so he put part of the booty in an enclosure and issued a proclamation that whoever comes can take whatever they like.

Crowds of people came and took young slaves, and treasures, and carpets, and silks. Ajaz was sitting in the middle and did nothing and said nothing. 'Well, Ajaz,' said the king, 'you don't want anything?' 'I did not quite understand your orders; please, repeat them to me,' Ajaz replied. 'Everyone who lays hand on anything in this enclosure, anybody who touches it, it belongs to him; these are the orders,' said the king. Ajaz stood up, bowed deeply before the king and put his hand on his shoulder. Ajaz was the successor to the throne after the king's death." Guruji laughed at this point. "He was the only one to want that! He wanted the king! Nobody thought of it but he alone!" This story is for me; he is going to test me more, I thought. I had better be careful. . . .

Some of his sayings: 'I should not have the desire to buy this perfume," I said, when he told me that he wrote to Lucknow to have it bought by one of his disciples.

"A minor desire," he said, with a brief movement of his head. "We cannot help to have some desires. If it can be fulfilled, why not? Man or woman, makes no difference; a human being is a human being, soul is soul; only here on this plane is differentiation."

19th March

HE WAS SITTING OUTSIDE when I came at nine a.m. He was dictating letters to one of his disciples. Then Tasseldar came hobbling in, sat down and began to talk. And he talked . . . and he talked . . . and he grated away with his horrible voice. At one moment I could bear it no longer. Bhai Sahib seemed to be interested, encouraged this verbal diarrhea. How kindly he can listen, and with what interest! And with me he will pretend not to understand, will ask people to repeat what I have said, misinterpret my words. . . . I got up.

"I am going to the bazaar."

"Yes, yes," he said distractedly, listening to the machine-gun talk.

After half an hour I came back. Nobody was outside; the room was open. Already from the bottom of the garden I could hear the monotonous croaking of Tasseldar. Oh, no! I thought, oh, no! Guruji listened, encouraging him with provocative remarks of approval.

"Yes, yes," he mumbled with bored expression when he saw me. I sat down near the door. The croaking went on and on . . . I cannot bear it! A terrible feeling of hopeless despair seized me . . . he does it on purpose! It is a refined way of torture! Chinese torture, I thought. I will go in a few minutes. Anything is better than to have to endure this. I looked at him. He looked straight at me; an ironical expression I knew so well was in his eyes. I think my eyes must have conveyed to him my feeling of despair. I cannot bear it! My mind cried out to him. Help me!! He slowly took up his mala and began to pray. His expression became distant. Tasseldar went on. Guruji kept nodding distractedly, clearly making him understand by his attitude that he wanted to pray. Gradually Tasseldar understood . . . became quiet . . . went into a state of torpor . . . could not imagine that it was Dhyana. But he clearly got something, and it was not for the first time. The room became very still. The Saint, with a stern, stony expression I also know so well from the past, went on praying.

Quarter past twelve I left. Going home I was reflecting that I am passing a period of tests. Possibly very severe. I had better look out. He knows that from the 1st of March I am controlling the mind. Now he begins to test how far I have gotten. When I make a move, he makes a counter move . . . he does not waste time, I must say. . . .

20th March

MUNSHIJI BOUGHT ME A CHARPOY (a rope bed), so when I get four bamboo sticks, I will be able to sleep outside on the terrace. He is hard; he does not even notice me. Sitting there for hours, unseeing and unnoticed, can be very depressing. When I salute him, he keeps talking to others, and even if he does not, he ignores me completely. Irritation, naturally, begins to mount gradually in me. I just pray, that's all . . . pray for help. . . .

I showed him the charpoy before taking it with me in the rikshaw and asked him if I can take four sticks. At the bottom of his garden were lying some bamboo sticks which did not seem to belong to anybody. **"Take, take,"** he shrugged. So I took the sticks and with the rikshaw took the charpoy to Sharma's place.

21st March

"ABSOLUTE FAITH, SURRENDER IS THE GREATEST THING; it is for the greatest people only. It is not for everybody; it is only for the few. Because it is the easiest thing, it is the most difficult to do. Constant tranquillity, constant peace, bliss and grace, those are states of being one with Brahma. Like Mansur who had said: 'Ana l' Haqq, I am the Truth. Aham Brahma asmi.' . . ."

"Is it the highest state?"

"No," he replied, **"according to our System it is NOT the highest state."**

Later: **"If you say there is nothing but One, you insult Him and you insult yourself."**

And in the afternoon I cried, lying in the hot room under the fan . . . cried desperately in utter loneliness. Cried loudly and prayed to Him that the Teacher should be kind to me. . . . Oh, Bhai Sahib, be kind to me! Oh Lord, please, tell him to be kind to me! I talked to him about H.'s letter, about people who need help in London. He seemed hardly to listen. Tasseldar was there sitting, hating that he could not get a word in. Then about quarter past eleven he got up and I hoped that he would go, but Bhai Sahib engaged him in conversation, and each time Bhai Sahib spoke to me he interrupted and made loud comments. I lost most of what he had said because of the loud comments of Tasseldar.

And last night I prayed and prayed, and now my heart is broken with pain. Good Merciful God! You who know everything, tell him to be kind to me! He is so cruel! When he wants, Tasseldar is quiet. When his wife talks to him for hours on household affairs, there are never interruptions; when people talk irrelevant things, nobody interrupts. Tasseldar is never interrupted. So, it is clear that he wants me to bear Tasseldar and his horrible voice for hours, and he will be listening with interest. So I will have to bear it. Will I be able? I don't know. . . . As it looks to me now, it seems quite unbearable. . . . May God help me. . . .

22nd March

AS SOON AS I ARRIVED Tasseldar came. I saw him wobbling through the gate. Oh, no! I thought in sheer despair—not at nine in the morning! How will I bear it for so many hours? Bhai Sahib came out soon, looking grey and not at all well, and after a few minutes went inside. I went to see the cementing of the courtyard, how it is progressing, and when I came back, Tasseldar was not there anymore. I was glad. Bhai Sahib came out a few moments later.

"He has left?" he asked. I could not help feeling a certain bitterness—he came out for him . . . he turned to go inside. **"You can come into the room,"** he said with the most bored expression he puts on lately, when he talks to me. I went in and he went out through the other door into the courtyard. After one hour Mahabir Nigam arrived and the Sikh. He came and sat in the big chair. I was so thankful that Tasseldar was not there. He was talking to the Sikh all the time about Guru Nanak. The grey tired look was gone; he was full of radiance; he seemed to sparkle. About quarter to twelve I told him that I was going to the dry cleaners to get his suit which I took last week to be dry-cleaned. To my horror the beautiful pale beige suit was completely ruined! They must have dyed it by mistake, or heaven knows what had happened; it was greenish and patchy and stained with machine oil. I became terribly upset. . . . I went back to him; he was still talking to the Sikh.

"Your garment has been completely ruined," I began.

"What? What? What government?" he commenced his usual, bored, non-chalant inquiry.

"Listen," I said infuriated, "don't you see that I am so upset that I am hardly able to speak! For God's sake, at least try to listen!"

"Why do you confuse yourself? And if it is ruined? We are not ruined are we?" I told him what had happened. Took Satendra with me, went to the cleaners, got the suit, brought it to him and asked if he can wear a thing like that. . . . He admitted that he could not. Munshiji was sent back with the garment.

I did not care. It was out of my hands now, out of my responsibility. I was furious with him . . . listens to every nonsense for hours, tires himself with people who talk rubbish. And when he sees me upset about something which is not even mine, but his, he does not even care to listen. . . .

When I came in the afternoon it was terribly hot. I went into the courtyard and sat on a tachat fanning myself. My room, surrounded by the boiling flat-roof terrace, was hell. He passed through the courtyard to the bathroom.

"You can come into the room," he said very quietly, very bored. Sat alone in the half-dark room. At least it was peaceful there. Then people began to arrive and he came too. I noticed a great weakness, like a torpor coming over me. It was the stillness of nothingness, of non-being. It was like being dead in deepest peace.

Slept outside. It is much better than in the room. Towards the morning there is always freshness and ventilation, a cool breeze, lovely. . . .

23rd March

WAS PRAYING, BUT NOT TOO MUCH. Had a great peace. In the morning decided to ask him about the letter I have to write to Babu Ram Prasad. He came out early looking not too well. Bandhari was there too. I asked about the letter. He began to twist my words and to turn them as he always did when he wanted to irritate me. But I put my foot down. I told him that I have nobody here to ask. He listens to everybody's nonsense. But when I ask something, some work I have to do for him, there is boredom, misunderstandings, or he tells me off. The least he can do is to answer politely when I ask politely. It was lovely to watch his technique—how at first he attacked hard, and twisting ironically like a clever lawyer he confused me completely . . . then doing his mala with a face carved of stone as if he would not even listen, but I knew very well that he jolly well did. I was partly speaking to Bandhari. Then I sat for a while. He was speaking Hindi to him, and I was thinking that I will go to Pushpa or home, but then I said:

"Can I go into the room? It is too hot and dusty." And I went in. And he and Bandhari followed immediately. He began to speak in English relating the story of a saint in Delhi.

"A rumor reached the king that the Saint is preaching to huge crowds, and the emperor sent a message that he is coming. The Saint replied: 'Delhi is far away; you will not reach it.' At eight miles from Delhi, the elephant on which the king was riding went mad and ran into the palace in which the reception for the king was prepared; the palace came down and the king was dead, buried under it."

Then: **"A great man is needed to break a wild and wicked horse."** (That was I, presumably—the wicked horse.)

Then he asked me with just a suspicion of irony in his voice if I was satisfied with the session. I said that I appreciated that he spoke English, and I keep praying to God that he should be kind to me.

"Am I not kind to you?" He laughed his young laughter.

"Yes, but I hope you will be even more kind, and if you like I can put it differently: I pray for more faith, to be able to bear more."

"Now you put it correctly," he smiled. **"You can tell me anything. I am always the same for you,"** he said at one moment in conversation. I nearly answered that after what he said and did to me, I really can tell him anything. . . .

Was very peaceful in the afternoon.

"Nanak means the very smallest.

"A perfect man is the one in whom all desires have dried up. Desire itself is designed to remove the sense of personal imperfection in the individual. We naturally revolt against imperfection. Only the Perfect can satisfy us."

So in our mistaken craving for perfection we want more and more, forgetting that Perfection can only be had from within, I thought.

"The sense of possession gives pain and sorrow.

"A Saint is the one who is always, at all times, contented."

When I came in the afternoon, I was asked by the wife to go into the room almost immediately. He gave me H.'s letter. When I asked if the state of bliss she is in will remain, he answered that no state remains.

"But the Saint surely remains in one state?" He had the faintest smile hardly moving his lips, looking through the mail just arrived.

"This cannot be told."

Had a restful night. It is lovely to be able to sleep on the terrace under the mosquito net, the Indian sky studded with stars above. A gentle breeze is always blowing from somewhere. The sound of a Kirtan across the park of Moti Jheel. Moti Jheel means the "Pearl Lake." A small lake is in the distance, and two ponds nearby . . . a great open space with some trees and some flower beds, and an expanse of grass for people to walk and sit on. Dogs are not allowed in, so the grass is clean. It is very much used in the mornings; then one can see fat and elderly men doing their morning exercises, walking briskly with swinging arms and swaying dhoties.

Woke up about four. The great morning star stood high in the sky in the east. When I was waking up, such a pain of longing was in the whole body that it was even a physical suffering. How well I know this feeling of pain just on awakening! And I kept thinking of Him. There was such a feeling of deep surrender. To be like the Teacher . . . what a bliss, what a glory it must be . . . serene like him, so wise like him, so . . . oh, so perfect like him!

Great love, full of peace, is in my heart this morning. Truly peace can only be had in the most peaceless state, which is love. . . .

69

Renal Colic

25th March, 1966

WHEN I CAME, Munshiji told me to go in. I was informed that he had some difficulties with breathing. Could not help feeling guilty; here he was suffering and I felt nothing—I slept well.

Again I felt the same tremendous peace. I tried to analyze it. It comes from somewhere, very deep. It does not come from the mind, but the mind is resting in it. The body is very tranquil. The mind too. It is like nothingness, like a state of non-being, and I still don't know if I like it. It seems like the state of Pralaya, a negative state. It was windy in the night. Woke up with a terrible longing. Painful. Like in the days gone by, when I was here. . . .

It was a fresh morning and he came out. I had no opportunity to tell him about the heat flashes I have when in his presence. Starting in the chest and back and mounting to the head . . . the whole body instantly perspires. And the tic on the lower lid of my left eye . . . it disturbs the vision. While writing this I just had one of those flashes . . . had to stop and fan myself. Rather troublesome, as if the heat conditions were not enough! . . . Truly I am destined to have it always the hard way!

26th March

LAST NIGHT I PRAYED . . . and fell asleep praying. The nearness to Him is quite impossible to describe. It is as if it were the very essence of my being. The deepest. The nearest. Prayed for surrender without understanding. Just for surrender because of great love. To become Nothing as He is Nothing. Like Him: Nothingness. That no obstacle should remain in the heart of Hearts in the brain of Brains. . . . And the whole of my being was a song, one single sound of offering. In the morning woke up and began to pray. . . .

It occured to me how broad-minded he is. Never have I noticed even the slightest narrowness. This, of course, is the line taken by the Nakshmandia Dynasty; they never try to convert anybody. They open the door to everybody, he said once. The Ancient Wisdom in all Religions is one and the same. No need of converting.

"The human being is trained, and we have devised the easiest way of training."

It is like a passion, this longing, this praying . . . like a hunger, a hunger for Him. Yes, it feels like a tension, like an emptiness waiting to be filled. A hunger for Truth. Restless, unquenchable. . . . Let me, oh, let me be like him! Never quite like him . . . how is it possible? But like a small part of him, his devotion, his compassion, his great humility. . . .

When I came out he was outside.

"You are well?" he asked, giving me a sharp look. **"You sleep outside. No inconvenience of any kind?"**

I said all was well, only the physical body is under suffering; such is the nearness to Him that it seems too much for the physical body. He nodded gravely.

"One can hardly bear it," he said softly. Then he began to speak in Hindi to Bandhari. At one moment he said:

"The physical, the astral, the mental bodies must be made one." He continued again to explain in Hindi. In a pause of the conversation I asked what he had meant.

"When the body is full of vibrations, once they have stopped, it is most essential to repeat His Name. Then every particle of the body, every atom will echo it." And smiling, he made a sweeping gesture as to indicate the infiniteness, the all-embracing quality.

"When you walk or sit here, wherever you are, whatever you do, repeat His Name. But do it silently."

"La illaha il Allah? Or just *Allah?"*

"Yes, this," he nodded. **"La illaha il Allah should be repeated in the night after midnight. Then when one knows how to do it, one becomes the master of the world."**

"I don't think that one should want such a thing. All I want to be is slave of the One and servant of people." He nodded slowly with gravity.

"Yes, this is right. One should not want. But one will get it if one wants it or not; it does not depend on the disciple."

Then we went into the room. He lay down and went into Samadhi. I looked, fascinated. His face was that of a young man. Unlined and innocent, soft as if not touched by life . . . around his lips played a ghost of a tender smile. A little later he called Ram Singh, the servant, who began to massage his feet. I came to sit at his head and watched that the flies did not bother him. The Sikh who came in with his wife sat down and eagerly tried to speak about his affairs, but he hardly opened his eyes and soon turned his face to the wall. The Sikh, realizing that he cannot discuss his problems, left soon followed by his wife.

I don't like this man—he has greedy eyes. I feel he is fleecing Guruji; he does not want to work . . . and gets money and other help from him.

28th March

"I THINK WE ARE AT THE LAST STAGES of what is called the Crucifixion," I said to him on Saturday, and he nodded gravely with the still luminous expression in his eyes.

"How long this stage will last, of course, I cannot know, but as things are going, it seems that we are at the last stages of it. From the first of March I am controlling the mind. And I see that it can be done. I cannot say that it is easy. But you from time to time gave me a direction to follow, and if I follow it to the letter, things begin to happen." He kept nodding slowly while I was speaking.

"Since Saturday I have been repeating Allah all the time . . . mentally all day long. Yesterday morning on awakening, my mind tried its tricks on me. It was resentful because it has no time to think of anything else. It becomes dull, it was saying; it will become stupid. There are so many interesting things to think about; the world around has so many interests. But it seemed to me so ridiculous that it made me laugh, my own mind rebelling, so to say, against itself."

When Guruji went out for a moment, Bandhari told me that he asked him to help him to remember God at any moment of the day.

"But this only Awwaliya (Persian: Saints) can do," answered Guruji. Well, I am not a Wali. Let's see how far I get. . . .

4th April

MANY THINGS HAPPENED and I don't know where to begin. The obvious is just to continue my diary from where I have stopped.

On the 29th I went to Bhai Sahib, in the morning as usual. But immediately after lunch I felt great discomfort in the bladder. While I was wondering what it could be and what I shall do, while lying on my bed, all the windows open and hot wind sweeping through the room, I suddenly felt a severe pain in the right side. The pain increased rapidly to become unbearable. A liver attack . . . the symptoms seemed to indicate it. It was two p.m. I could not go down to Mrs. Sharma for help for I knew that she was resting. So I bore the pain, did some Jap (repetition of a sacred word), but could not keep it up . . . the pain was too severe. It slowly increased in spasms and it was really unbearable. About four I went downstairs. Mrs. Sharma was surprised. I got the hot water bottle; she phoned the doctor. I spoke to him on the phone. He said he will come in the evening; it is the end of the financial year, so he has much paper work to do, but he will send the medicine in the meantime. I was installed in the bedroom next to the Sharmas, to wait for the doctor. The medicine arrived—tablets of Spasmidon to be taken every hour, and a red liquid. But soon I discovered that one tablet of Spasmidon did not ease the pain, so I took another and felt a little better. Then repeated one every hour. But the effect lasted only a short time and I was in pain. Finally about eight the doctor came. And he said immediately that it is not the liver but a kidney colic—the symptoms are very similar. I protested, telling him that I never had anything wrong with my kidneys. I am not so sure of it now. Perhaps many things which I attributed to liver conditions, were due to kidneys after all. . . .

Told him that the tablets have a very brief effect and he gave me an injection which practically knocked me out. I was like paralyzed. But the pain began after eleven. I was trying to do my *Jap*, listening to the pain inside me. If it increases, to become like in the afternoon, what will I do? But it did not. It remained stationary. In the morning when I collected urine for analysis in a jar which the doctor left me, I noticed at the bottom a small dark object; thinking that an insect fell into the jar, I fished it out with a stick. It was a small stone with very sharp edges. Well, if I had this thing inside me, no wonder that it created such a havoc. . . . The urine analysis showed blood and traces of albumin. Clearly the doctor was right: it was a case of renal colic. I stayed in bed in the room downstairs and Mrs. Sharma sent a *peon* (message) to Guruji to let him know. His son came in the lunch interval (he works in the bank opposite) and told me father wants to know what is the cause of the complaint. I told him and about five he came telling me that his father was coming in about half an hour. The car was sent for him. He came. Looking splendid as usual, all in white. And he stayed nearly until nine p.m. They all were sitting around my bed. The eldest son brought his children, but they were like little lambs, did not even move . . . they just stared with enormous eyes . . . Babu was also there. The neon lamp was shining into my eyes, I was full of dull pain, and I began to wish that Guruji should go. His presence is always difficult to bear for me physically. I get so tired, and when the body was ill it was even more difficult, could hardly endure it . . . but he was sitting and talking as was his usual. I looked at him and my heart was very still. Kept thinking that in the night when I was lying half-dazed and in pain . . . there was such love in my heart. Such peace, no fear at all. I offered my pain to Him with all my love, and that was all. . . .

Next day, already, I went to Bhai Sahib in the morning. Gave him thirty rupees for the transport tomorrow; we were going to the Samadhi. Stayed only half an hour. Was resting all day long and the next day was at his place with Sharma's car. We left in two cars before eight. Sitting sideways, squeezed between his wife, children and the door, I began to think that in March '63 I also went to the Samadhi. I cried so much then, thinking that I never will see him again. And I prayed so much to his father, and the friendly old Saint helped me. I came back after all. . . . And I will pray now that nothing should remain in the heart of Hearts. . . . May he help me that his son should be kind to me. And suddenly I began to cry . . . I did not know why I was crying . . . it was as if my very heart was wrung out of my breast in terrible agony of pain.

Arrived at Samadhi. I sat at my usual place opposite him. Kept crying, could not help it, could not stop, before the eyes of everybody . . . was just sitting and crying. It was a cool morning, as lovely as usual were the bluish distances, the cultivations, the pale morning sky. The smell of the sun-drenched Indian plains. Help me . . . wept my heart, and tears were running down my cheeks. Help me to become nothing . . . and I cried all the way back without being able to stop. The car stopped at his gate; all went out, but he came to the car window, stood still, looking distant. I cried hopelessly looking at him, not understanding why I was doing it. He nodded reassuringly, then told the driver to drive on. And I still cried when the car brought me back home to Sharma's place. As soon as Mrs. Sharma saw me she said: "You are full of Guruji's *Krepa* (Grace)." I thought it was a fine way of putting it. I just thought that I was full of misery. . . .

Next morning I went to him as usual. His wife asked me into the room. He soon came, looking very weak and severe . . . had his stony face. He can look very hard when he chooses to do so and usually when my heart is breaking and I want to speak to him. I asked what did happen, what was done that I had such a crying fit. Could he tell me—perhaps it may help the understanding? But he shook his head. And all the time I was speaking he was in half-Samadhi with stony face. I told him that I repeat the Name of God all the time and I can do it now. Clearly, things must be done at the proper time; when in London I could not do it constantly—such vibrations started that it was difficult and I had to stop it. Others also cannot do it, Bandhari for instance. He, without changing his severe expression, said:

"It is because they have no faith in the System; that's why they don't do it, and don't understand."

Here was a pointer for me: I only need to listen carefully and follow to the letter; it is quite easy. It is clear: think of all the Superiors while you are doing *Jap*; once more he is pointing, as so often, in the direction to follow. . . .

70

Blessing of a School

IN THE EVENING MRS. SHARMA gave a literary party. But in the afternoon Guruji and myself were invited to a performance of *Ramayana* in a girls' school in a poor district—cotton mills and mostly children of the workmen. Pandit Butchly founded it four and a half years ago. The car came to fetch me and we drove first to Bhai Sahib's place. He was not ready; we had to wait in the garden for quite a while and it was very hot. My body felt very weak. Finally he came. The school was very far at the other end of the town. The dust on the road was frightening, whipped up by the hot wind. A large, low, red brick building—all school rooms of raw bricks, but full of air . . . fans in every room and dimmed light filtering through windows protected from the glare. The building stood in an empty waste ground, clouds of dust were milling and dancing about. The singing was already in progress when we arrived. We were garlanded with red roses—they smelled sweetly and fresh—and were led into the room by the head mistress, a young woman with shining eyes, dark intelligent face. We took off our shoes.

In front of a picture of Ram a large crowd of children were sitting on the floor chanting the *Ramayana*. It was the usual kind of *Kirtan*, with tabla, harmonium, and small cymbals. For a few seconds Guruji stopped at the door, with one sweeping glance took in the whole room, smiled and went to his chair . . . and immediately plunged into Samadhi. I saw him looking at the group of singing children with unseeing eyes. It was evident . . . he was blessing them all, and the school, such tenderness was in his expression. I was sitting at Guruji's left, the photographers came, and we were photographed. I thought with amusement that, garlanded as I was, I felt like a prize-cow at an exhibition. I was tremendously aware of his deep state. I had better try to look as saintly as possible I thought, as this situation seems to demand, but I don't think that I succeeded; later, when I saw the photo, I found that I looked only old.

Then I was asked to go and sit amongst the children; they squeezed together to make room for me, and we were photographed again. I enjoyed the atmosphere, and when I turned my head and looked at Guruji I saw him staring at me with those terrible eyes in deep Samadhi, and such light, such power was in them that I had to look away quickly.

We were served Coca Cola as a refreshment. When I saw ice in the glasses, I asked to have my Cola without ice (knowing what treatment ice gets in India), so the ice was thrown out and the little boy who, with a flourish was opening the bottle of Cola with a small bottle-opener, had his little, very dirty, finger inside the bottle and then wiped the neck of the bottle with the hem of his shirt. I winced mentally and only prayed silently that no dysentery germs were present just then at the time. . . .

We went home by hired car as we came. And though I had to sit practically squeezed against him, there was not the slightest feeling of nearness . . . for this nearness has nothing to do with the physical vehicle. . . .

He was talking to the Pandit, not taking the slightest notice of me and probably completely unaware of my presence.

"Don't come in the afternoon, will see you tomorrow morning," and he quickly went out of the car and, followed by the Pandit, disappeared into his room.

I had no intention of coming. I wanted to see the party, and it was a lovely one! Mrs. Sharma is a wonderful hostess. A large podium was made of eight tachats covered with mattresses and white sheets. When I came, many men in white dhoties and beautifully embroidered kurtas were already sitting there. A few ladies came afterwards with their husbands. The poet in whose honor the party was given was Dinkar, reputed to be the best contemporary Hindi poet alive. Later the men queued for refreshments at the buffet, and the ladies and all the others who were invited for supper conversed in the large sitting room. Later, about ten, the supper was served in the dining room, and it was excellent . . . lovely Indian food; everybody helped themselves at the central table. Then somebody called me to be introduced to the poet.

"You are studying Yoga?" he asked. He was a large, burly man with wonderful eyes. "What is your Teacher teaching you?"

"Nothing."

"Nothing?" He echoed thoughtfully, looking at me closely.

"I sat for years before a closed door," I said. He pondered for a while.

"Great Teachers of India never taught anything. There is a tree and under the tree is sitting a little boy—he is the Teacher of a Teaching which is not imparted," he quoted.

I would have liked to know from where the quotation was taken. Was it his own? But I seemed to remember dimly that it is from some Hindu scripture. (Actually I wrote to him a few days later asking him to tell me from where the quotation was, enclosing a stamped self-addressed envelope. But I have never received a reply.)

Next morning I was telling him about the party. And then asked: "Where does the mind go when one is in Dhyana?"

"Aha, you want to know where the mind goes? Where can it go?"

"Is it being absorbed into the Greater Mind?" I said tentatively.

"Yes!" and he laughed, young and gay. **"Yes, the mind is absorbed in it, the mind which belongs to the world of Maya. One day you will come to know who you are and then you will give your self away.**

"Hypnosis or self-hypnosis is something entirely different. Hypnosis is imprisonment, limitation, is subjecting the human being to a stronger will. Dhyana is a liberating practice. It will lead to freedom. . . ."

This morning I could not look at him. Even his garment was shining with blinding light. He was like a dream image of days gone by . . . frail, elegant, with sparkling eyes, a being not belonging to this world. . . .

Could not stay long in the afternoon. Had trouble with my bladder, needed to go to the toilet every quarter of an hour. It was tiresome. Went home early, it was dreadfully hot. Rested. Had my food, went to bed with hot water bottle on my kidneys. Under the mosquito net outside, it was a hot moonlit night, but it was not too bad. Hot water bottle helped, fell asleep. Then I heard a voice:

"Mrs. Tweedie, Mrs. Tweedie, are you asleep?" At first could not make out from where the voice was coming, but then looking through the mosquito net I saw Mrs. Sharma standing on the roof, her slender, elegant, silhouette outlined against the sky. I still thought that I was dreaming; fancy dreaming about Mrs. Sharma standing on the roof . . . but then I realized that something must have happened. Came out from under my net and, while putting on the dressing gown, I learned that the son of the chief medical officer (the one who is treating me) is dying of tetanus in the hospital, and Mrs. Sharma came to ask if we should go to Guruji. I looked at my watch; it was ten p.m.

"Definitely . . . if somebody can help, Guruji can!" I said. We went by rikshaw. The small side-gate was still open; Satendra was standing with two young men in the street. He went inside to tell the father. He came out immediately.

"I was expecting you," he said to Mrs. Sharma who told him about the case.

"Oh, noo," he drawled. His face became very serious and he asked the name of the boy. I could not help looking at him all the time, standing in full moonlight against the dark garden. Munshiji and all the others were already sleeping on their charpoys in a row under the trees. And when he walked with us to the gate, he stood there as the rikshaw was pulling away, slender, erect, his face dimly lit by the light of the street lamp. It all looked like a painting—a luminous being against a dark background—and Mrs. Sharma said: "He looked like Christ, standing there." And I thought that she was right. . . .

Could not fall asleep, so much love was in my heart and so much compassion for the boy and his parents. . . . Heard a clock striking somewhere . . . midnight. Practiced, and the practice was easy. . . . All was love, He was near, and the mind was not. . . . Woke up feeling much better.

Practicing and practicing, suddenly since yesterday there is a feeling of great urgency. Do not miss a moment . . . every time I say His Name I am a step nearer to Him . . . something is whispering in me. I seem to rest in Him, in His very Heart, where is eternal peace, non-ending love. It is the answer to all the problems, fears, ills. For the first time I have something in hand, where by my own effort of exertion I can get somewhere. Until now I had to submit, to tolerate; only recently I realized that I am able to act. And the more I do it the more I want to do it. For I know now that this is the way.

71

Dhyana?

I AM FORGETTING MYSELF somewhere in deepest peace. He did not tell me how to do it; it came by itself. . . .

"My Rev. Guru Maharaj and my Rev. Father were so well equipped that they could transfer perfectly and they never failed. To transfer the Power is difficult, but they did it in a most perfect way."

"According to my understanding, spiritual life is a question of speed. The disciple is "quickened" by being in the presence of the Master: *Satsang.* And the quicker he becomes, the nearer he is to the Master. It seems to be an automatic process. Why, then, is a transference necessary?"

Answer: **"Yes, it is an automatic process, but also the transference is done. Those two things go on parallel. Both are necessary."**

7th April

"GO ON DOING THE PRACTICE."

8th April

"Why should I say that I am your Guru? If you consider me one, then I am; if you don't, then I am not."

DREAM: A wrestler was pressing my shoulders hard on a black and white chessboard. Guruji who was standing beside me said: **"Throw him off!"** I could not, however hard I tried; he was too heavy. I simply could not lift an inch; he was pressing my shoulders down and I felt the hardness of the board hurting my chest.

"I cannot now," I said, "I know I will later, but now I can't do it."

VISION ON WAKING UP: I saw him from profile; he had the hard cruel expression seated in teaching *asana.* He looked like a horrible wild cruel animal. The face was not human. Toh! I thought. I believed him to be so beautiful, but he is not—he is so ugly! And long after waking up completely, I remembered this terrible face and wondered, and there was fear. . . .

9th April

AND SO HE TOLD ME that he is not my Guru. Mind gave me trouble. He kept attacking me. I was contradicting him, telling him that there is no greatness in being so harsh and I cannot speak to him—the usual story of rebellion when the mind gives trouble. . . .

At last he had enough, took up his towel, went out and closed the door. I left . . . and at home I cried. What a difficult path! Treated with harshness, cannot speak to him when I want, and he is not my Guru. . . .

Then I remembered a quotation from some Buddhist scriptures (I have forgotten from which one):

"I have no home, I have no father, I have no mother,
    I have no Guru, I am not a disciple; all is taken away from
        me. . . ."

Nothing will remain at the end. . . . It is Easter . . . I had forgotten it . . . and in the night under the stars calling to Him in loneliness and longing. . . . The neem tree nearby was so fragrant . . . strong, sweet smell which came with the whiffs of the breeze. . . .

10th April

"OUR RELATIONSHIP TO GOD is something entirely different from what we usually imagine it to be. We think that the relationship of God and man is of duality. There is God and there is the man who will pray to God asking for something, or who will worship, or love, or praise God. There are always two. But it is not so. I have found that our relationship to God is something quite different. It is a merging, without words, without thought even . . . into something. Something so tremendous, so endless, merging in infinite love . . . physical body and all, disappearing in it. And the physical body is under suffering; it is taut like a string in this process of annihilation. This is our experience of God and it cannot be otherwise.

"What you have said," he nodded gravely, **"is absolutely correct."** He is not well.

11th April

CALLING, CALLING ON HIM . . . all the time. . . .

12th April

HE IS NOT WELL. He ignores me completely. When he sat in the garden before others came, I asked him how he was feeling. I saw that he was breathless and gloomy. He said that he was not well.

"No wonder, you can never be well. You talk too much. Every doctor will tell you that a heart patient must not speak much. And you talk for hours. And for what? And to whom? To people who are here only for discussion." He did not answer but turned away. He looked disgusted.

Sweet are the nights of the waning moon full of strong fragrance. I am calling on Him day and night. . . .

14th April

SOME GLIMPSES OF TODAY'S CONVERSATION (of nearly two hours).

"Between you and what you are doing, your practice, there is a veil, a barrier caused by the flood of ideas which bring confusion into your mind. The flood comes, the flood will go . . . but you cannot wait. . . . To turn against the Guide is to cut off the link. . . . The wiring is there, the bulbs are there, but there is no current. . . .

"When you eat a sweet, for instance, what happens? When you swallow it, the taste is gone, but the memory of it remains. So it is with the desires of the mind and of the body. Even if the desire is not here anymore, the memory is still there, and the mind can give trouble. Every human being is full of desires, of the body, of the mind. The training I am giving you is of such a kind that in this life you will be away completely from your body and your mind. . . ."

Actually I began the conversation by telling him how troublesome it is for others when some people don't wash. They don't wash their dhoties, their bodies; they smell. A man had just left—he was so dirty I think he never changed his clothes. . . .

"Yes, this is true, it is very troublesome. But there are people who are dressed nicely and clean, and they are full of inner dirt. Greed, vanity, sex, and other things too. . . . They come here and sit, and what shall I say who am the sweeper of everybody. . . ."

I felt small. . . .

"Yes," he repeated kindly, "you have only that—the physical smells—and I know it is very disagreeable. But myself, what shall I say? And I will not hate anybody, because if I hate him, how can I help him to better himself? I cannot stand cigarette smoke, also the smell of drink, but if I hate them, will they give it up? No, never."

"He is a nice man," I said when Mr. Vippin had left.

"Every human being is nice, provided he is a human being and not an animal in human shape."

"In some the light is so hidden that it hardly shows."

"Every human being is nice," he repeated softly, looking very far with his strangely shimmering eyes.

"I ask God that I may die. Owing to our relationship, I won't be able to live when you are gone." He smiled a tender, mysterious smile.

"When I am not here, you will have me through the System. This body will go, but I will be always with you. Do you think that I am not with my Rev. Father, my Rev. Guru Maharaj, always? If I train you for a certain work, you will remain. . . . We go, the System remains. . . .

"The other day you asked me if I am your Spiritual Guide and I told you that I will not answer such an absurd question. It is up to you to know if I am your Spiritual Guide or not. . . . If you think that I am, then I am your Spiritual Guide. If you think I am not, then I am not. If a lady comes and asks me if I love her, what shall I say?"

"Just a moment," I said, "you here in India make a great distinction between men and women; if a lady should come, I know what you will answer, but if a man should come in and ask you this question, what will you say?"

"I will say, no, and I will throw him out," he said. "The only distinction we make in our line is because ladies are of the other sex; we will say it guardedly; with men we will say it directly. If somebody would have dared to ask such a question of my Rev. Guru Maharaj or my Rev. Father, whether he was their Spiritual Guide, they would have him thrown out.

"My training which I am giving you, I told you, is the one that in this life you will not be in your physical body nor in your mind. And now, if I am trying to get you there, you yourself interrupt. Be not concerned about your kidney condition; it is troublesome, no doubt, and will remain so for a while, but not at all fatal in your case. I was trying to do something, but perhaps I was doing it without the order; there was no Will of God; it did not succeed. When the pain increases and becomes unbearable, it goes forever. This is the law. But you yourself have interrupted. So it was not to be. . . ."

When I was about to leave yesterday, he was alone in the room. Seated cross-legged on the tachat, he was writing letters. Vippin had left; others were sitting outside. When I got up and saluted him, he looked up with a smile:

"DO NOT CARE ABOUT ANYTHING EVER: THE GRACE OF GOD IS IN EVERY SHAPE AROUND." It was like a greeting, like an admonition for the future. Perhaps it was intended as one, who knows? . . . I kept thinking of these words walking home and long, long afterwards. . . .

In the night a sudden wind sprang up. A few large drops of rain woke me up, and the wind was tearing at my mosquito net. I thought it would die down. But sitting up I saw great clouds of dust approaching. I had scarcely time to rescue my mosquito net when the storm began to shake the bungalow. I closed all the windows and bolted the doors. It was quarter past eleven and the storm lasted not more than a quarter of an hour; it was soon over. But I did not go out, thinking that it would come back. So, I spent the night in the room, as hot as an oven in nightmare dreams, the fan humming uselessly above my head. When I woke up in a bath of perspiration from the restless sleep, it was very still outside. The time was 4:30. I went out. It was a lovely warm night. I took my bed and put up the mosquito net to have at least a few hours coolness. Mrs. Sharma must have left already. She was supposed to leave for Delhi at three a.m.

15th April

NOBODY WAS ABOUT when I came down at seven. No servants. No hope to get a cup of tea. So I had half a glass of water and went to Guruji.

Soon he came out and walked up and down for a while, and then sat down to write letters. His wife was reading letters to him which he answered there and then. I felt tired and depressed after a hot night.

He spoke to me about one hour in the semi-dark room waiting for his wife to get ready. They wanted to go to town and she was having her bath. He talked on all kinds of topics: Indian politics, the Muslim rule of the past and how it influenced the Indian culture and the laws of the country. Then he came out with a saying which was a jewel:

"Before, there was no divorce in this country. A woman could never divorce her husband. Now even a woman can get a divorce. But still, there are men who are reluctant to marry a woman who belonged to another. Why? Because they say that she is impure. But the woman is like Gold, she is like the Earth, she is never impure. . . . Gold, even if it falls into the latrine and is taken out and is cleaned, it is the same, and its value is not less. The Earth purifies everything—the changing seasons . . . the Earth is always pure . . . and the woman after every menstruation is pure. So, they say, the Gold is pure, the Earth is pure, but the woman is impure . . . how ignorant they are. . . ."

When it became quite dark, mosquitoes began to bite. I got up, came to his chair and said jokingly alluding to a remark he made two weeks back: "Every mosquito has four wives and all of them are biting me!" He laughed his young, sonorous laughter, obviously amused.

"Make them your friends, then they will not bite!"

"To make friends with the devil as you told me three years ago?" I smiled at him.

"The devil," he said suddenly becoming serious, **"the devil is much greater than the Devas."**

"Does the devil exist?"

"Yes."

People came; salutations began; he immediately began to speak in Hindi. Always, always, at the most interesting moment, interruptions begin. . . . I would have loved to know more. Something in his voice when he said **"Yes"** made me prick my ears . . . and I was thinking about it in the night, wondering. . . .

The fragrant nights of the waning moon . . . and thousands of swallows at dawn competing with bats in chasing the insects who have their last meal before retiring to sleep . . . the sky tenderly pink with a few soft, streaky clouds. The dawns and the dusks of India— heaven knows, how much I will miss them when I am away. . . . But let this time be far, far off. . . .

16th April

"MANY THINGS YOU WILL UNDERSTAND only when I have gone. I myself understood so many things only when my Rev. Guru Maharaj was not alive anymore. As for a child the cradle is the whole world, then the room, when it begins to crawl, then the veranda and the garden, and so on . . . so for the disciple also, the understanding comes gradually."

"When you are not alive anymore, I would like to go too . . . I cannot remain here; it would be unbearable."

"Somebody has to remain; the System must go on. The training I give you is to continue my work. . . ." Clearer than that, I thought, the hint cannot be given. . . .

"One should always remain in prayer; one should always

remember His Name. And in the time which remains, one must serve. Serve human beings, animals, trees, all living things. But human beings come first. They are most precious to the Almighty. . . .

"Sufism is as old as humanity. It is the Ancient Wisdom. The Sect of Kamal Posh (the blanket wearers) went to every Prophet of the time, but no one satisfied them completely. But when they went to Prophet Mohammed, they were completely satisfied. So they remained with him . . . because the doctrines of Islam, not the Religion, the doctrines I mean, are the highest, the most perfect Teaching. . . . 'There is only one Allah, and nothing else beside it.' The way it was presented was so perfect. . . ."

Since midday I am in a strange mood. Doing my practice while lying under the fan after my bath, I could not help thinking of all the Lines of Superiors who went before us for hundreds, no, for thousands of years. . . . Like Great Luminaries, rising each one in turn, shedding light on the humanity in darkness . . . each one doing his duty and then passing on the Power and the Path to the successor. . . .

If I could keep my mind merged in the Master, and through him in all the Superiors, and through them to God, then my mind would not give me trouble anymore. Tomorrow at the grave of his Father I shall pray for that. . . . The car will be here at seven to take us to Samadhi. I learned a few days ago that he wanted to go and arranged for the car with Mrs. Sharma. I did hope he would take me too; he told me yesterday that I was coming with them. I was so glad. I know, I must pray so much. . . .

17th April

I WAS THERE WITH THE SHARMA'S CAR and the driver, at quarter to seven. About half past seven we left with two cars, the other was of one of his disciples. Our car had to wait in the bazaar for Guruji who was in the other car. I hoped so much to go in the same one as him, but no, I had to sit with the daughters-in-law. While we were waiting, the kid, Pappu, was jumping in the front seat making an awful lot of noise. And I kept thinking I am always sacrificed. . . . He took with him the smelly old Pandit and I was confined amongst giggling daughters-in-law and a jumping child. . . . Why can't anything go smoothly with him? Why are there always unnecessary sufferings and frustrations? But great peace was with me and I felt that it would be my day . . . it was. After a while Guruji's car joined ours and we proceeded to the Samadhi. Guruji's car went into the compound. Our car stopped at the gate. So I made it in a way that I was walking to the Samadhi alone. Wind in my face . . . and I was glad that there was the wind I love so much . . . smelling of sun-baked earth, a bit of dust, giving the feeling of the vastness of the plains. I noticed that the distances were hazy with dust. Then I entered the Samadhi taking off my sandals, sat down at the usual place, facing him, a little to the right. Between him and me were the two graves. We were only twelve people and the driver. The only child was Pappu, but he kept quiet. Wind in my face . . . the blessed wind. . . . He went into a deep state immediately. And I prayed. Prayed that my mind might be absorbed into this mind, my heart into his heart, and through him in all Superiors, and through them in God. . . . How I prayed . . . so much.

I knew that he prayed for me. I felt it. And I thought of all those who went before . . . the glorious procession of Param Para, culminating in him, the great man of the time. And if God is gracious to me, I will form part of this chain. I prayed and prayed and my heart was so full, but I did not cry . . . there was infinite peace. Few people and silence and only the voice of the wind. Now he was talking to the smelly Pandit. I turned my face to the wind. It blew and tore on my head-scarf, winding it around my neck. Merciful God . . . help me. . . . Merciful Saint, tell your son to be kind to me, for I have to surrender. Blow wind, blow, smelling of freedom. . . . And when we came back there was still peace. Help me, oh, help me, You who know everything! Alone I cannot do it!!

18th April

"IF ONE IS AFTER THE ABSOLUTE TRUTH, one cannot be after people. Two souls cannot live in one body. The richest people in town at one time or the other come to me. What for? If they have five mills, they want eight. I am not a mill owner; they should go to the mill-owners. I am polite to everybody; this is another matter. And if people come for help, help should be given. But I am not after anyone. They should come and merge themselves. Divine Providence will guide them to me. . . .

"Anger, the real anger cuts us away from Reality sometimes for months. For years I did not get really angry. But sometimes I make myself angry and look at myself if I am after a thing or not. . . . It is beyond the power of the human being to control anger. But after the anger, look at it: from where it came, why and

how it came, and what it did to you. You might learn many things. . . ."

Speaking of the struggle with my mind, I said again that the difference between our two cultures was making it more difficult for me, but he shook his head:

"No, culture has nothing to do with it; it does not matter. All those thoughts of distrust and doubt are in the atmosphere. Now you will pick them up ten times easier than before. If the mind is vacant, they can crowd in. Keep your mind merged always, either in the Absolute Truth, or in the Great Man of the time, who is the Sat Guru, the Spiritual Guide. When the mind is merged, nothing can come in, nothing can disturb it. . . ."

"Even when the disturbance comes, it is less than before."

"Yes, it is quite true. But if this lesser disturbance comes after a long time, it has great power and would disturb much. Don't let it come in at all. Prayer, meditation, and the remembrance of the Name are the only things worthwhile doing in this world, because you will not stay here forever. In the night pray. Pray much. And on the roof walk up and down repeating the Name. This is the idea. . . ."

Speaking of the necessity of having faith in homeopathic medicine, in order that it should help, he said:

"Yes, faith is needed for everything if you want to be benefitted by it. One does not need to surrender oneself completely before every doctor, but if you have not a certain faith, how will he be able to help you?"

Reclining leisurely on his tachat, he was discussing Indian food, clothing, the way of life.

"In England people are chain-smokers and even here many are, and they eat boiled meat. Boiled meat can be useful for some human beings, but it gives out a bad smell. Here it is not so bad because here is so much sunshine. In England there is not enough sunshine; this great power is lacking. Here in India we would be all dead if we did not have this power which cleanses all."

I forgot to say that when I prayed at Samadhi, great vibrations began in the heart. When I was doing *Jap* sitting alone in the dark room in the afternoon, very great vibrations suddenly started. Something was going on, something was preparing. . . .

WHEN AWAKENING the vibration was still going softly at the base of the spine. Then it became much stronger. Aha! I thought, he is going to grill me again. There was no resentment. I thought the situation over. Going to be difficult in this heat and the kidney trouble. Took bicarbonate of soda last night. This morning the urine was clouded with deposit, and later there was pus, greenish bits of mucous swimming about. Took off the mosquito net and prayed looking to the pale, bluish-grey morning sky. You made me as I am with this powerful thing in my body, I prayed. You must take me out of it! I will tolerate anything for your sake and Guruji knows it, so he will give me the lot. . . .

When I got up, I noticed that I was under strong vibrations. Well, I am in it . . . God help me now!

GREAT VIBRATIONS. They went on in the afternoon. He did not even notice me at all.

72

A Birthday Present

MRS. SHARMA AND I WISHED EACH OTHER happy birthday this morning. We had *pokoras* in the afternoon about five, waiting endlessly for the cook to make it. And consequently Dolly and I went to Guruji after six. Such a waste of time. . . . In the evening, sitting on the lawn in the dark, under the tree (all the chairs and the drawing room table are now put on the lawn in the evening, which is very pleasant), Mrs. Sharma told me that she has a big wedding on the 29th, and I must try to find something, because the room and the terraces upstairs are needed. And I felt very lonely and upset. . . . Foxes have holes, birds have their nests, but the daughter of man has no place whereon to rest her tired head. I cried in the night looking at the immense sky trembling with the shimmer of stars. I am not welcome anywhere . . . I am not his disciple . . . he is not my Guru. What next??

23rd April

DOING MY JAP ALL THOSE DAYS. He does not notice me. Not even a little. And last night he had another attack. A terrible one, apparently. He is very breathless and can hardly breathe, and I am deeply worried. . . .

24th April

HE BROKE MY HEART THIS MORNING. I was discussing the situation with the Sharmas before going to him. And I went there by car; the driver was given orders to bring the message about Guruji's condition. He was already sitting on the charpoy in the garden looking frail and very pale, dressed all in white. He talked to the driver himself. When the driver had left, I said:

"You know, Mr. Sharma also thinks that it is cardiac asthma." (I told him yesterday that I was sure that the breathlessness comes from the heart.) "And if you don't see the heart specialist and don't do something about it, it will carry you away in less than one year!"

He who was standing in front of me suddenly gave out a laughter which sounded almost cruel:

"He is right!" He turned away to go inside, then stopped for a moment before going into the doorway passage.

"He is quite, quite right!" He emphasized the words, laughed this strange laughter and disappeared inside. I was like stunned, felt cold, was staggered by this statement so brutally thrown at me. Sat down alone. All the chairs were standing in semicircle in front of his empty chair. A cold despair seized me . . . he intends to go before the year is over. . . . I will never make it . . . never. . . . What can be done in a few months? In Sufism are four initiations; and it takes time to become balanced after that . . . and I began to cry. It was one of those crises of hopeless crying when I could not stop. Such a terrible despair, of no end. . . . It was embarrassing to sob like this in front of everybody in the garden. I went inside the room, sat there alone under the fan, and I must have cried till after ten. Stopped out of sheer exhaustion. Then he came in, without taking the slightest notice of me, changed from Kurta and pajama trousers into more comfortable singlet and longhi. Indians have a way of changing in front of everybody, trained by the lack of privacy that is astounding. L. told me once that five men came into the room and changed completely without taking the slightest notice of her; and it was done rapidly and discreetly, no exposure whatsoever. Fantastic.

Suddenly it occurred to me while he was changing, that each time he has to test me, or do something important from the point of view of his Line, he is always dressed in white; now he changed because he will not speak to me, less important work is coming. And in this moment the car came with Sharma and another man. Sharma stayed till half past twelve. I sat there. Did not cry, was too ashamed to do so. Trembling was my heart, with sorrow . . . and he sat there cross-legged in Sat Guru Asana, talking vivaciously, his eyes sparkling, his sonorous voice, his laughter, ringing in the room. . . . Gone was his tiredness, his weak look, his breathlessness. He was all alive telling stories, and I wondered from where the Yogis get this boundless energy. . . .

At lunch Sharma told me that he is disappointed in Santiji; his talk is reduced to anecdotes. As so often, I repeated again that Guruji will never teach anything directly. Those stories and anecdotes ARE the Teaching—one has to understand them. But it was of no use. . . .

Cried so much in the afternoon lying on my bed, the fan endlessly revolving over my head . . . it is every day over 42°C and sometimes more. . . .

25th April

AND I CRIED THE GREATEST PART of the night. I will never make it. . . . I simply have to accept everything. . . . It is useless to think why he does this or that. However contradictory it may seem, however wicked or unreasonable it may look, I HAVE TO ACCEPT IT. The time is getting desperately short. . . .

Went to him in the morning in a very tired condition. The eyes were burning, the body felt like beaten up.

26th April

MY JAP IS DISTURBED. Cannot pray. Yes, I have and WILL accept everything. The only trouble will be if he puts the vibration on very strong again. This makes me usually very resentful. What to do? I have to accept this too. . . .

Mrs. Sharma again told me that I must go. A few days ago I went to Nigam asking him to help me to find something. He promised, told me to give him one week time. I have not much hope.

When I came, the Hakim Sahib, the Muslim physician, was there at seven a.m. He only touches the pulse and tells all the symptoms and gives an herb medicine. It is apparently the ancient Greek method. He prescribed the medicine, said that there is no enlargement of the liver as all the doctors said until now, and the heart is also all right. But there is a catarrh in the bronchials and with this medicine it will clear up in five-six days. All this Guruji told me laughingly . . . seemingly very pleased.

The Muslim is impressive, tall, about the middle forties, dressed in a kurta and tight long pants, the typical Muslim dress; but what is more important, he is clearly a very spiritual man . . . Nakshmandia Dynasty, as Guruji told me.

Later, I told Guruji that I noticed that each time he has a duty to perform according to the training, he is dressed all in white.

"You are quite, quite, right!" he laughed, clearly pleased and amused at the same time.

Did not want to go in the afternoon yesterday but still went before five. And today too he spoke nothing to me in the afternoon. I sit first under the fan in the dark room, while he, the wife and some others play cards in the next room. Then the place is watered where the chairs are put out by the servant; the gardener who works part-time in the evenings arrives, then he comes out and we all sit outside. I never stay longer than 7:30. It is so hot, the body seems to be weaker now than it was when I first was here a few years ago. And to sit and sweat amongst perspiring men, listening to endless talk, seems too much.

Go home, eat something. The kidney is a little better. Apart from Mrs. Vippin's homeopathic medicine, I take a tea of Kulti, an Ayurvedic remedy. A kind of Dahl. It is given to horses as fodder. It is to be boiled and the water taken, two glassfuls of it, one in the morning, one in the evening. Makes the urine alkalin. I had the analysis done again. It was not bad. Many germs have been found but no blood and no albumin. Told Guruji about Mrs. Sharma wanting me to go. But he did not even listen. He does not care. . . . The nights are very hot, but after midnight it is getting cooler. I cry so much. Unwanted. Alone. And if I have to move, I have not even money to do so. One week ago £5 arrived from H. I gave it to Guruji, of course. . . .

27th April

IN THE MORNING HE ASKED ME what about my having to leave before the 29th of this month? Told him all about it.

"You had better go to Nigam Sahib." But I told him that he will let me know; he asked me to wait for one week.

In the afternoon I was walking to Bhai Sahib thinking that to walk for half a mile now in the heat four times a day is becoming quite a burden. We have now nearly 43° Celsius in the shade, practically every day, and it will be much more in May. The Loo is blowing hot, the breath of the deserts, and it will push up the temperature even more.

Suddenly somebody blew the horn repeatedly. If it would happen in London I would look, thinking that some friend passing in his car wants to attract my attention, but here I never thought that it could be for me. The car stopped abruptly right at the curb; out jumped Nigam Sahib. It was so sudden that it made me laugh. He said that his wife succeeded in finding an accommodation for me, and we agreed that I would go to him tomorrow morning at 8:30. Well, I thought, it looks as if I will be out before the 29th after all. . . .

28th April

SO I SLEPT FOR THE LAST TIME on the romantic terrace overlooking Moti Jheel. Saw for the last time the dawn, the pale dawn of the hot season. Lately I take the mosquito net away when the sky gets just pale . . . and watch the sky getting pale pink. Bats are flitting around, small dancing ones with the jerky flight, black against the sky. At first they are the sole masters of the space, except the great chorus of the croaking crows flying with much noise from the trees in all directions. Then the bats are joined by the black Indian swallows darting swiftly with piercing cries; they sail high, higher than the bats fluttering jerkily.

So many trees are in flower. The glory of red and scarlet of the Flame of the Forest; many tall trees are around with bunches of rhododendron-like flowers, mauve and pink and yellow. A lovely sight. But the best is the Flame of the Forest, called here the Golden Mohar, deep gold, orange, crimson and scarlet. To see an alley of those trees in full flower is a breathtaking sight. . . . Many gardens have it too; near Guruji's place is one dominating the view down the street with its large umbrella.

The birds at dawn are lovely. There is one magnificent fellow— bright yellow tummy and chest, jet black wings, and the head is attractively marked in yellow and black. He has the sweetest voice and sings only at dawn . . . an insect-eater obviously, with a long beak and the size of a blackbird. Several of them used to gather on the tree in the middle of the lawn which just begins to flower in bunches of pink flowers.

From the terrace one has the impression that all the trees make an effort to flower; so many yellow ones, a few mauve patches here and there; one is deep pink like candles on a Christmas tree.

Birds of the morning, goodbye. . . . Jet black ones who don't sing, with forked tails similar to the astrological sign of Aries, ♈ , blue-black they are with a metallic sheen. Grey ones, with lovely voices, so many. My friend the woodpecker is mute now. I don't hear him anymore.

Goodbye, Moti Jheel. I am glad to go. I hope the room is not too bad where I am going, but it never will be as beautiful as this terrace and this view I am bound to miss.

Went to Bhai Sahib who sat already in the garden. Last night told Mrs. Sharma that I have found something and will be going. She was clearly relieved. The first guests are already arriving for the wedding.

At half-past-eight went to Nigam Sahib, and he, his wife and myself went to see the room. And where was it? At Mrs. Scott's where I lived before I came to stay with Mrs. Ghose last time when I was in India. Not the same room I had then, next to it, smaller. It was newly built, the cement not quite dry, and consequently not yet white-washed. I took it and was grateful . . . had no alternative.

Returned to the Sharmas . . . she was so pleased that she offered me the car. And by 10:30 I was out. Had tea for lunch at Guruji's place; brought some bread and butter. And in the evening made for myself some potatoes, and parval (a kind of small gourd). What a blessing to have food without chillies!

29th April

OH, THE NIGHT OF NIGHTMARE, the fan humming its maddening song, all closed in in an oven-hot cement box! For the room was that: a cement box . . . one door and one window opening into a crowded courtyard . . . the courtyard so small full of sleeping people . . . The sheet under me wet with perspiration . . . like lying in a pool of steaming water. . . . Had to borrow from Guruji's eldest son fifty rupees—had no money at all. Because I did not sleep all night, I was tired and listless in the morning.

30th April

DID NOT SLEEP. Sweating. Oven-hot, hot, hot, hot . . . could not do even *Jap* properly, such was the suffering of the body. At Guruji's place: unsang and unnoticed.

"You came here to suffer; so suffer . . .," he said yesterday when we were discussing the money question. And he said it softly, his eyes full of compassion, dark and sorrowful. . . .

1st May

WHEN I CAME AND WAS WALKING towards my usual place, I saw that he was in deep Samadhi. When I was a few yards from him, he opened his eyes and stared at me approaching. When he is like this, he does not see the physical body but something else. He raised his hand in automatic gesture acknowledging my deep salute, staring at me all the time . . . and closed his eyes. I sat down spell-bound; what an expression his face assumes! Soft are the lips, tender the face. Deepest peace. A face not human in its infinite, eternal, loveliness. . . . Suddenly it seemed to me that this is the face he will have when he is dead . . . pale, tender, the nostrils whitish, transparent. And peace eternal, mirrored in the countenance of his features . . . and my heart felt small and sad. . . .

He talked much with his wife who kept interrupting his deep state. With his children. With Meva Ram who came later. And I prayed and did *Jap*. And just looked at him, grateful to be able to see this perfection which one does not usually see in this world, even if I was unnoticed and seemingly completley forgotten. . . . My heart was sad but full of peace.

At one moment he got up and, still in Samadhi, began to walk up and down in the garden. He had a most beautiful ankle-long kurta of transparent cotton with embroidered stripes on the shoulders and around the armholes and also down the front, and a simple white longhi. Tall, emaciated, he looked like a priest belonging to some ancient rite of long ago. And the face so pale, transparent, not of this world. . . .

In the afternoon I sat alone in the darkened room; he was having a game of cards with his wife in the courtyard. Suddenly he came in and lay down on the tachat. I felt a slight surprise; he never came in like this for my sake alone. Then a great activity in the heart Chakra began. Aha! I thought. Something is being done! He was lying on his back, the eyes closed. I was listening to the somersaults of my heart . . . the soft hum of the fan, noises from the street. In the room was great stillness and peace. Then he got up and, as quickly as he came, he went out. Not once he glanced at me and not a word was exchanged.

2nd May

DOLLY CAME TO HIM in the morning. She wanted a male child; she was ten weeks pregnant. She came at seven a.m. He made her wait for a long time, talking to people, and in the meantime coming and going in and out. Then about nine her car came to fetch her. He called her into the next room. I hoped to see something, got up and peeped inbetween the door and the curtain. He came into the room to take his towel, saw me standing and, going back, drew the curtain in a way that I could not see anything. I felt hurt and humiliated. The room was made dark, Dolly told me later; he made her lie down, put his towel over her navel and made some passes over it; it seemed to her that he outlined the shape of the baby. His wife was present; she was sitting in the corner. That was all. Then he told her that all should go well now . . . it will be a boy.

Next day I told him that Mr. Sharma did a bad service to his daughter by telling her that it was all humbug and most unscientific. He shook his head thoughtfully.

"Faith is needed. If she has no faith, it will be a female child. Divine Power is not magic; for magic no faith is needed. Also with the Divine Power it can be done if there is no faith, but one has to come down. And why should one come down?"

I said that at the beginning of the training he also must come down to the level of the disciple and he said:

"This is for spiritual purposes and it is not difficult. But for worldly purposes, why should one come down? Sometimes people do. Why? Because they want to serve the public. My Rev. Guru Maharaj sometimes said: 'Yes? There is no faith? But I wish it to be and it will be!' Money is never charged for a thing like that. Divine Power can never be sold. Clairvoyance is a worldly power. Magic is. Yantras have to do in part with the Divine Power. Also NEVER can money be charged for it. It is a service free for all. Yogic Powers, as a rule, also are not a Divine Power. They can be acquired by Yogic practices and will power. Divine Power is a Grace given through a Great Man of the time, who belongs to Param Para. There are not many in the world who can claim that. . . .

"So if she has no faith, it will be a girl. . . ." He was silent for a while; and then with a beautiful smile: "But she has faith; it will be all right. . . ."

He came out in a singlet and blue and white chequered longhi. There was laughter in his eyes. He began to walk up and down.

I slept on the roof with all the members of the Scott family; it is infinitely better than in the room. Just the sky above, ventilation, and it becomes cold towards morning; one even needs a light blanket. Saw the dawn rising. The street below looked romantic in the bluish semi-darkness before the dawn, the street lamps still on and the sky just getting rosy. I looked in the direction of Guruji's bungalow; it is quite near from here, hardly five minutes to the east. There was great peace. The atmosphere is much better here in spite of so many people living crowded together. They are a large family, Mr. and Mrs. Scott, their sons and daughters all married with children. They are Christian Indians, like Mrs. Ghose. They will have their worries and problems, of course, and they seem to quarrel too, but it is all far away from me. Here is no atmosphere of suspicion created by the minds of those where I stayed previously. Even the servants were resentful. Here are no servants. It affected me so much, and though the physical conditions are here much more difficult, in every other way it is easier for me. I told him so and he smiled and agreed.

DREAM: I was walking towards him; he was talking to a man. How kind he can look when talking to others, I was thinking with some sadness. Then I saw him lying on the naked earth and I knelt beside him. His body was buried in the earth; the ground was completely level; none of his limbs was showing above—they were hidden underneath. Only his head was above the ground and he was small of stature, had no beard and delicate Chinese features. How beautiful he looked even like that!

"But who put you here into the wet mud!" I exclaimed. "You will get ill and catch your death!"

"It is entirely my own responsibility," he answered, suddenly sitting up, **"I alone am responsible for that!"**

Waking up I thought that they will give him plenty of hot water to wash all this mud down. That was all.

When he came out, only Sageji was there. I asked if I could tell him my dream. His face was aloof and severe; he nodded gravely. Told him how this dream disturbed me and filled me with a kind of fear, and that I hoped he would tell me the meaning. But he made an indefinite gesture as if to say, who knows? and went into Samadhi.

He remained in this state until 9:30. People came, sat there quietly. I went to the market for a moment, came back; he was still sitting in Samadhi. How unearthly he looked. . . . After ten the Vippins came and he began to talk with them. They soon left and I asked permission to go home too, said that I was disturbed because of the dream and felt like fainting all the time. Must be something wrong with my nervous system. . . .

"What?"

I repeated.

"Some dreams have no meaning; why be disturbed because of a dream?"

I left rather puzzled . . . didn't he say some time ago that dreams have ALWAYS a meaning?

SOME SAYINGS:

"Help is always given to the human being; we humans are always surrounded unknowingly by the Help of God. The question is to realize it; when it is not known, it is of not much use. . . ."

"The rose does not say: I am fragrant. The fragrance reveals itself; it is its very nature. The God-Realized Man will never say: I realized God; it is NEVER done. All he needs to do is just to be. His very being will reveal what he is. . . ."

When I told him that I cannot remain standing when lecturing he said:

"I also cannot stand. I can speak extemporary for hours when seated. But standing is troublesome for me. . . ."

"You don't get the Beloved with smiles; you get the Beloved with tears. . . ." (Persian couplet).

"If He wants to give you something and you don't want to accept it, you will have to accept it through whipping" (Hafiz).

"If you want to know the secret of bravery, you must learn from the mosquito; it makes a sound before it bites" (Persian saying).

"Sing not the song the others have sung; sing what you yourself have realized in your heart. And it takes only a great man to break a wild wicked horse." (I think the wild horse was supposed to be me; he sang this couplet to us after he conquered one of my acts of rebellion.)

"When the Master makes the Disciple like himself, he takes a deep dip and the Disciple not so deep. . . . The Ocean is limitless; by and by the Disciple learns how to go deeper . . . by and by. . . ."

(Thinking it over, I am sure it is a hint. He is referring here to the state of Dhyana. He never does a thing without giving a hint. One can follow the steps the training will take by noticing the hints he periodically gives in advance.)

"When you remember Him every moment of the day and don't forget Him even for one second, then you are there, you have arrived. . . ."

"The three doors of Maya: Money, Sex, Property. . . . And still there are people who live in the world but are free from all those things. Only apparently they seem to be subjected to Maya. And to know that they are not, one has to remain in their presence for a long time; only then one comes to know and understand."

"Cruel to you? Unjust? Why do you say so? I am never cruel, never unjust. It is your mind which makes you see so. . . . I change my mood, that is all. When I seem cruel, I am most kind to you. . . . You see it crooked. That's why you speak so. When people come to me I am always polite. Otherwise they will say: we come to him and he injures our feelings. I change the mood; this is another matter. And it is done for some extraordinary training. But cruelty? No! A Saint cannot be cruel! Never!"

73

The Test of Hunger

5th May, 1966

UNSUNG AND UNNOTICED . . . and I must admit that I admire the control he has over his eyes. . . . I was sitting opposite him in the room; he was lying on the tachat facing me; I was scarcely three feet away from him. Not even once, not even by mistake did he happen to glance at me . . . it is very difficult. How often had I decided not to look at somebody in the audience when lecturing, but for some reason my eyes wandered there to my annoyance. . . . I was often quite angry with myself because I did not remember to be careful. But it never happens to him. Even if I sit in front of his very nose, so to say. . . .

He does not speak to me. Nor does he ask about my financial situation. On Monday after having spent two rupees and four annas on the rikshaw—I had to bring the fan from Mall Road, he wanted his fan to be serviced, and one rupee was bad which was given to me in a shop—four rupees remained. Today is Thursday; I still live on those four rupees, and it looks as if I will go on living on them if the money does not arrive tomorrow.

There was a question of me touching the water jar without taking off my shoes. He remarked on it rather severely and then began to tell me off when I took some water for drinking. I was puzzled. "But I did not come with my shoes even near the jar!" I protested. Could not understand what sort of hygiene it is when the servant, when he fills the jars, keeps his dirty fingers in it . . . but I cannot have a glass of water standing as far as possible and not touching even the brim.

"This is our Aryan culture," he declared, throwing a card on the table. I saw that even his wife gave him a disapproving look and made an impatient gesture. Even she seemed to think that he was too hard on me. They were playing cards, as usual, in the afternoon at this time of the year.

In the evening I told him that I will come later, tomorrow, because I have to go to the Sharmas to see if the registered letter is there. **"And if not?"**

"Then I will have to go another time, later."

Stretching himself comfortably on the tachat in the garden—it has all been watered for it was dreadfully hot—he began to talk to me kindly. I came nearer to him on an empty chair and told him how lately I have strange feelings when I am with him or even just thinking of him.

"And what precisely are those?" He was drawing the words out, ironically. Told him that it becomes more and more difficult to look at him. I have a sinking feeling in the stomach and feel like fainting . . . it is a kind of not-being, very bewildering. . . .

"This is quite good," he said slowly, **"it is rather very good, it is. . . ."** He stopped and sat up.

"It is excellent," I mentally completed his thought.

And he began to talk to me for one and a half hours. On the importance of time. On wasting the time. Who wastes time? Those who don't catch the thread, or those who love not.

"If you have adverse ideas, what happens? The thread is cut completely. Even if the wiring is in order and the bulbs are good, the connection with the Power House is cut."

I tried to explain some states I am in lately, but the mind was void. I stammered and could not formulate the sentences properly. And he talked about so many things. . . .

"Did you get the idea?" he kept asking. At that moment it seemed to me that I got it and said so, but already at home in bed, when I tried to remember, I could not.

"If a golden chair is put on auction, what happens? People will bid for it, and whoever offers the highest price will get it." He was alluding to the training, of course.

"When you are before the audience, you are the master, you are the sun—nobody can shine before you. Before my own Guru I was an idiot," he smiled, looking at me closely.

I complained that I cannot speak and cannot think two coherent thoughts in his presence, and he laughed.

I know he gave me a few hints, but I don't remember them. . . .

6th May

WENT TO THE SHARMAS IN THE MORNING, but the letter was not there. She promised to send it with the peon to Guruji if it should arrive.

Sat there alone till ten a.m. Bhai Sahib was in the room talking to his tenant . . . asked his permission to come in and sit under the fan.

It was so hot already. They all went out and Guruji went inside. But soon he came back and sat on the tachat. I felt the pleasure of the cool air on my skin and sat there in stillness and peace.

"No letter?" he asked after a long while. For a while we talked about the Sharmas and things of not much importance. Again I attempted to express what I felt.

"Bewildering. This perhaps is the best definition of it. Rumi describes some sort of bewilderment, but it seems of a different kind than this one. The mind does not understand. It seems to be gasping and gets hold of this and that like a drowning man. It is the nearest state to dissolution. And after all you are a human being (true, to me you never were a human being, but something much more)—still you look like a human being and behave like one. Why I should feel like this before you is beyond my understanding."

All the while I was speaking in disconnected hesitant sentences, he kept nodding quietly. And suddenly I knew that I am not afraid because somewhere he is holding me. . . . I should have fear, but I have not because there is faith. Dissolution, non-being, is death for the mind. The mind should be afraid, but it is not . . . strangely enough. . . .

Then the wife came. Then Tasseldar came but soon went, and he told me to close the door and the windows which I did. He turned his face to the wall and went into Samadhi. And watching him closely I saw that he did not breathe. Then I remembered that he said lately that breathing sometimes disturbs and prevents one from going into a deep state.

"So I simply stop it. It is called *Ghat Pranayam,* the 'inward breathing.' I sometimes don't breathe for hours. The heart goes on beating. . . ."

Still was the room . . . a Yogi in deep Samadhi . . . and I, mindless, bewildered, but full of great peace. . . .

"Yes?" he said suddenly, sitting up and turning to me: "Please, open the door!" As I went to do so, thinking that he probably heard somebody outside (though I did not hear anything), he said: "Collector Sahib." But nobody was outside. I went out, looked around; empty chairs stood in semi-circle in the sun.

"The garden is empty, nobody is here," I said returning. He sat cross-legged, blinking in the light which came through the open door. At this moment a car stopped; Collector Sahib got out. I laughed.

"You knew it before it happened," I said.

"This is nothing unusual," grinned Babu who was having his lunch in the next room.

For some reason which I cannot explain, I had the uncanny feeling that the training is taking on a different form; some turning point is ahead. . . .

8th May, Sunday

TESTING TIME. He does not speak to me. Nor does he ask anything. When I lived at Sharma's place, he often asked me if I was short of money. Then he knew perfectly well that I wasn't. Everything which arrived I gave to him, or nearly everything, because I needed so little . . . had a roof over my head, and food too. At that time I confess that I was surprised why he was asking me. Now I understand why he was asking then. Because he knew that soon the time will come when he will not ask, and the contrast will be greater and more painful. Of course he knows, even if I didn't tell him that I had to borrow fifty rupees from his eldest son when taking the new room—had to pay the rent in advance. He knows that the registered letter with the money did not arrive. His not asking now and ignoring me must have a special meaning, only I cannot for the moment understand the purpose of it . . . I live on potato soup. The little bit of rice I had at home was finished a few days ago, as well as gram flour. Have still some sugar left, and a little tea. The last half-kilogram of potatoes I boiled with the skin on to avoid waste, and I sucked and chewed the skins before spitting them out to get out all the nourishment. But then I decided to eat them when I was finishing the last lot; after all, they cannot do any harm and they will fill the stomach.

On Friday the temperature was 44.5° C, and yesterday it must have been even more. It was quite unbearable last night when they watered the place where the chairs were put out. I kept wandering up and down avoiding the servant throwing buckets of water. Hot steam rose from the sun-baked soil. Bhai Sahib, squatting on the brick elevation, was organizing the watering and gave directions to the gardener. The gardener, by the way, was Mr. Sharma's—lent to Guruji for a while. I left soon. Had a bath. I ate the last three boiled potatoes with all the skin on, and finished the last small gram-flour pancake. There was wind on the roof. My skin, made soft with constant perspiration, was grateful for it. Prayed to the blinking stars. My heart was full of Him. . . . Soon the wind became stronger and about nine p.m. became a dust storm. Clouds of dust whirled in the air. I looked at the others; nobody moved. So, I remained where I was, covered my head completely . . . could not face the idea to go down into the oven-hot room. And there too it will be full of dust. The whole night the wind blew in strong blasts. In the pale dawn when I was collecting my bedding to go downstairs, the sheets were grey with dust. I managed to shake some of it off. My face and hair were full of sand. I needed a good wash which I had later. Had some tea, and two cold boiled potatoes left from yesterday. The feeling of nothingness seemed to affect the physical body . . . a slight vomiting condition, like a weakness, when I think of Him or pray. And I think of Him all the time. . . . And the mind does not work at all. . . .

When he was talking to me a few evenings ago, I asked him why was it that at the Bandhara this time I did not feel the tremendous vibrations as in the years before.

"It is not my business to answer such questions; why don't you try to know yourself?" To know myself . . . with the mind in such condition? . . . the most difficult thing in the world! How can I hope to achieve it? When I told him that the more I try to know the more confused becomes the mind, I realized how little I know and that I will never be able to catch the thread. . . .

"You caught it," he said in a very low voice, nodding gently. **"Otherwise you would have run away long ago. . . ."**

I came later this morning, about eight. Had to wait for the bathroom. Everybody was full of dust like myself and needed a long bath.

He came out almost immediately. He gave me a sharp look and a faint smile. I knew that he was pleased with the state of my mind; he was watching for trouble. There was none. We exchanged a few words on the dust storm last night, on cold nights in the desert, and he began to organize the gardener, which plants he wanted to be watered, and how many buckets for each.

"It is surprising how many blisses India has in store for us: there is the bliss of cool stream of air from the fan, the bliss of water enveloping one like a cold sheath from head to foot from the shower . . . the bliss of water running on one's hair because the skin feels itchy from perspiration . . . and the bliss to sleep under the starry sky and to be able to pray to Him under the light of the moon, fresh wind in one's face."

"Each climate has its own bliss; cold countries have their pleasures, so have the hot ones." But I hardly listened. Like ice before the sun I am melting before you, I was thinking, looking at him seated in his usual pose, knees drawn up . . . just as I have seen the snow in the crags near the glaciers in the Himalayas melting, when the midday sun reached them . . . melting, becoming soft, and then running away in small streams making their way to the nearest brook. . . . Like that am I before you . . . just like that . . . and my heart sang. And he looked stern, a little bored organizing the gardener. Somebody came, a Hindi conversation began. Then Sharma came. We all went into the room. At first I sat near the door, but the pandit smelled so badly that I changed my place and came to sit near his tachat at his pillow. There I could feel the fan a little and could not smell the pandit.

A man came saying that his ten children are all ill of smallpox, asking for a Yantra. He told him to sit down. It was interesting that he kept the man waiting and talked for over an hour with Sharma on worldly matters. Only when Sharma left he took some paper and proceeded to cut it in small quadrangles, giving some to his son Ravindra to do likewise.

"Is there smallpox in your country?" I said there are some cases, but rarely.

"Nobody can die of smallpox, if given this Yantra. It is more than magic. It is magic helped by the Divine Power. Children under twelve must have it tied around the neck; over twelve, under the right armpit for the boys, under the left armpit for the girls."

He gave half of the bits of paper to Ravindra and he prepared them. Then they were blessed by blowing on them, folded properly and given to the waiting man. Bhai Sahib told him to give for each child three or five paisa (uneven number) to the poor. In the meantime the son of the pandit arrived and fell immediately in Dhyana. Later his wife and the little boy also came. The young wife touched the feet of the Guruji and began to cry.

"Enough, enough," he said gently. She was made to sit in the big chair. There I saw that she seated herself cross-legged and almost immediately went into Dhyana. I watched her; she knitted her eyebrows from time to time as if wanting to cry, her face perfectly still otherwise. She remained like this for one-and-a-half hours. Conversation was going on. Not once did Guruji look at her. I said something to him at one moment, I don't even remember what, and he suddenly had this flickering, radiant look when his consciousness is not on this earth. My heart stood still . . . so much radiance, such tenderness. My stomach felt empty. But I did not go. He began to recite and to sing poems of Kabir and Persian songs, marking the time with the left hand on his ankle. He was seated in Sat Guru *Asana*. His voice . . . and I remembered how a fortnight ago I could not bear to listen to his voice—it was too much for me and I kept running away, going home or to the bazaar, so disturbing was this feeling of non-being before him. . . . Most of those present were in Dhyana. Only two or three listened. I wanted to see what will happen when the woman will come round. Finally the husband sent the little boy to the mother to wake her up. But she did not. I told Guruji:

"He cannot wake her; look!" But he did not look at her and his expression was tender. The husband got up, came near her, shook her; she began to tremble.

"She is trembling, she cannot wake up," I said again, and his expression deepened. He called his wife and asked her to take the girl to the room inside. She left, led by the wife, hardly being able to walk, like drunk. I leaned forward:

"With your permission, I would like to go home." He turned his head in my direction, and again this tremendous flickering Samadhi look, which pierced my heart like a sword with its power and awe-inspiring magnetism.

"Yes, yes," he smiled, but I knew it was an automatic reaction; he was not here. . . . I got up, saluted, touched his left foot which was within my reach, and walked to the door.

"My feet are full of dust; you took the dust with you!" I heard his laughing voice. Almost at the door I turned around. He was radiant . . . I stopped dead looking at this divine countenance. . . .

"To become less than this dust of your feet—this is the right thing, is it not?" I said slowly, like one hypnotized. I heard the murmur of assent and approval from those who were present. I did not know if I answered correctly; I did not know what he meant exactly by his sentence. . . . I left with the ring of his kind laughter in my ears and the light of his eyes haunting me. . . .

And walking home I was thinking that this feeling of non-being must be the physical surrender. And suddenly I was glad. So that is it. . . . It comes swiftly from somewhere where the mind is not and neither can reach there ever . . . and I was glad and grateful that it was so. . . .

9th May

IT WAS FAIRLY COOL IN THE NIGHT. Between one and two a.m. a strong wind began to blow for about one hour. I was lying awake much of the night—one does not sleep much with an empty stomach. Last night I asked him if this young woman was put in Dhyana for the first time.

"Which woman?" I told him. He shrugged.

"I really don't care. The atmosphere was there so it happened."

I told him that it seems to me that he has much more Power than a few years ago. Before, people had to sit in front of him and sometimes there had to be silence. Now the talk is going on; he seemingly takes no notice, even of a particular person, and things happen. He did not answer. His face was stern and stony. Felt a slight bitterness thinking it over in the night. Nothing is explained. He does not give me the slightest satisfaction. . . . I had money just to buy half a kilo of potatoes. Again potatoes? I felt nausea only to think of them. I had better buy some nimbus (limes) and have them with water. Potatoes in this heat must be poison . . . so I bought nimbus . . . and had mugs of water with half a nimbu in each, eight in all, and I thought that would be good enough. Noticed that the kidneys worked well—as long as I have enough water, I can hold out. . . . I have only headaches, but not unbearable ones. Guruji does not look at me and does not speak to me. I hope he will not ask anything . . . the Test of Hunger. The whole situation and his attitude seemed to point clearly that this was it. . . . It is quite according to the ancient Tradition of Yoga training. The Test of Hunger, and then the next one of the Acceptance of Death. What does it mean? Complete surrender, of course. The Test of Hunger is not the very last one, but it is one of the last. I have to hold out, at any cost. Help me! Help me not to be resentful! Help me to pass it! I am determined to persevere. . . . Today is holiday so the post is not being distributed. At the earliest the letter will come tomorrow. So I cannot get the money before Thursday. It would mean four days of complete fast, only water. Okay. And sitting alone in his room this morning I suddenly remembered his words before I left for England:

"The Master will put the Disciple very subtly against himself; then he will subject him to a severe test. And if the disciple thinks he cannot do more than die, then he has passed the test and is ready for the high state." Well he did it once, before he threw me out of India. I had better look out. I wonder if history is repeating itself?? One cannot be careful enough. . . .

10th May

LAST NIGHT IT WAS UNBEARABLE. I left soon. On the steaming soil, on boiling hot chairs. . . .

"May I go?" He was sitting on the tachat, his brown torso nude.
"Go!" he laughed, "and have a bath; I just had one!"

I left. Had water and half a nimbu juice. It was a hot, hot night. Did not sleep much. There is no feeling of hunger, only the head feels light. Went there this morning about 7:30. He was not in the garden. But while I was walking towards the chairs where they were left standing last night, I saw him coming through the door passage. His face, stern and serene, was like the face of a prophet. My heart flew to him and I bowed low. He gave me a searching look.

"Yes, yes," he said, turned and went inside.

Ravindra came. Said it was unbearable; it will be certainly 50° C today, in the shade. I agreed. The air did not stir; it was like a boiling hot oven. He came out about eight. And soon I asked his permission to go into the room to sit under the fan. I was wet and itchy. A little later they all came in. He dictated letters to Satendra. About eleven I asked him what time it was.

"You can go, it is eleven." And then he added: "You cook your food?" I looked at him.

"When cooking your food, don't do it in late hours." I stood up and saluted without answering, ready to go.

"How long does it take you to prepare your food?" He looked up at me gently.

"Very little time," I answered.

"Good, go now!" I left slightly puzzled. He gave me an opening, in case I could not bear it. He tested me, or was it pity? But no, it was a test. If I would have said that I have nothing to eat, then it would have meant that I did not accept the situation. He would have offered immediately some food. But no, my dear . . . I offer it to you, the Test of Hunger, one of the most important Tests of the great Tradition of Training. And I will go through it, whatever happens. I will not die. And if I do, in this condition, it would mean Salvation at once. I will have won in any case. No headache. Feel very light.

11th May

LAST NIGHT THERE WAS A GREAT DUST STORM. As soon as I went on the roof at 7:30 and began to arrange my bedding, it started. I quickly dived under the sheet, covered up my head completely and remained like this. The storm was shaking the bed, tried to tear off the sheet; I had to tuck it firmly under me. It went on like this for at least two hours. So much dust was in the air that the opposite houses were hardly visible. The strong wind lasted until about one a.m. Then it subsided and I fell asleep. About four a.m. it began again. While I was lying covered up completely with the sheet, I kept listening to the noise of the storm and the falling of grit on my sheet.

"Undisturbed peace there must be," you said to me, my Sheikh, when you spoke to me last Friday evening. . . . Undisturbed peace there is . . . absolutely. . . . The fasting goes on well. No headache, no feeling of hunger.

"You are happy, yes, I know; enjoy it. The tests are here to cause some suffering because nothing should remain in the mind of mind. If something remains, what sort of training is it? But undisturbed peace must remain always. . . . How much you have got, what a Grace you had; you will know only when I am not alive anymore. I also did not know, could not know, while my Superiors were alive." All this he told me. Little by little I do remember what he had said. And now, listening to the voice of the storm, I became aware of something else within myself:

There was a deep happiness. Serene. Very, very still and even. . . . Happiness in this world we always associate with something; I am happy because I love, or people are good to me, or I am in nice surroundings, or have security, or simply because the sun is shining and it is a lovely day . . . but here was a noticeable difference—it came welling up from within like a fountain, on and on . . . serene, still, continuous, so light, so ethereal. It had nothing to do with my surroundings, nor with me as a physical being. It came from somewhere, remained for a while, and went as it came: gently. I had no control over it; I could not provoke it or keep it. It comes and goes independently from me as the Grace of God . . . and it is not the first time I have it—many a time since I have been with Guruji. Only this time it is much, much deeper. . . .

"Happiness is within only," he smiled at me the other evening. **"We who live in this world, because our senses are directed outwardly, we think that the happiness is without. We forget that it cannot be so. Only on the Path of Return we discover it."**

So light. So serene. And it is like the wind which bloweth where it listeth. . . .

Decided to go to Mrs. Sharma to inquire about the registered letter. Went this morning. The letter wasn't there. Verily there must be close cooperation between Paramatma and Guruji; the outer circumstances are adjusted in such a way that a Test is possible. . . .

If H. had posted the letter as I asked her to do on the 30th of April, it should have been here last week. . . .

74
Another Heart Attack

12th May, 1966

WHEN SITTING ALONE IN THE DARKENED ROOM under the fan in the afternoon—he was playing cards with the members of his family in the next room—I thought I had better ask Babu who works in the municipality and deals with the post, if by any chance the registered letter was received but was sent back because somebody wanted to be too clever, knowing that I was not at Sharma's address anymore.

So, about six, when the garden was being watered, I got hold of Babu who was organizing it and inquired from him. No, he said, the letter was not received, definitely. While we were talking, I saw him coming out rapidly through the middle passage.

"What, what? What talk is going on?"

"I asked Babu if it was very unusual that a letter from England takes such a long time."

"Yes, it is. I think something has happened to it on the way. As a rule, a letter from England takes six days, no more than a week." And then he suddenly said: **"You are not in trouble I hope?"** I answered that I was not; I can go on. . . .

"Not in a financial difficulty?" he repeated. It made me smile.

"Ask not; let it be as it is, I can go on. . . ."

"No, you should not be in trouble; you should have told me."

"As you ask me directly, I must answer." And I told him that on Monday the 2nd, after having paid the rikshaw and deducting one bad rupee, I had four rupees left . . . pulled on as long as they lasted, and then began to fast—water and some nimbu juice, and from then water only.

"But let me go on. It is no hardship. I have no sensation of hunger ever. I had no intention to tell you, if you wouldn't have asked."

"No you should have told me. I forgot completely."

"I cannot believe it, and I don't believe it," I laughed. "If you are a man I know you are, you must have known. There were little signs that you knew. So if I would believe what you said just now, I would lose faith . . . in order not to lose faith, I must disbelieve you."

He was observing the servant watering.

"Go to my wife. She will give you something to eat, and tomorrow I will give you ten rupees."

I went into the courtyard and the wife put before me vegetables, dahl, chappathies. I had only one chappathie and a little dahl. I know, after the fast and in this heat, to overload the stomach would have been dangerous. Besides, I was not hungry. . . .

From the ten rupees I bought some necessities of life and will go on till the money lasts. In the meantime I wrote to H. She should send me the June money immediately; even then, I will be in great difficulty until July.

I cannot bear to look at him, it hurts so much . . . hurts somewhere. . . . Then I have to run away and go home, and when I stay away I want to go back. . . . There are times when I cannot bear to hear him laugh, and hear his voice, loud and clear, laughing so much . . . it disturbs me. But sometimes I cannot go away, like this morning, when he is in Samadhi practically all the time. He has these eyes . . . the eyes I saw in London when lecturing . . . eyes of Samadhi, wide open, glittering with strange, unearthly light, unseeing eyes, unaware of this world. . . . And while talking to others he looked at me from time to time. Serious, deep look, right into my soul . . . and each time this look made my heart stand still for one second. . . .

This feeling of non-being before him is so disturbing. . . .

13th May

HAD A RESTLESS NIGHT. It was cool and pleasant, but I cooked myself some bindis (ladies fingers) yesterday so badly—they were so hard. It upset my digestion. When I woke up in the morning, I knew that he spent a bad night.

Went at seven as usual. Sat alone. Meva Ram came.

"And how are you fareing in this terrible heat?" he said passing by, and went into the room where he remained talking to Meva Ram for a long time.

Later he came out and sat down.

"Becoming thinner and thinner . . . you look old, you know," he said looking directly into my eyes.

"There are signs of old age in your face, owing to the heat."

"Yes, owing to the heat," I echoed; my heart aching so much . . . unbearable the longing this morning. . . .

When I went inside later, he was on his tachat in Samadhi. Others came. About ten he came round, went out and said when he came back:

"How are you?" I said that I was well.

"I was not well last night."

"I knew it, when I woke up this morning." A sudden smile lit up his face.

Told him that I too, a few days ago, noticed that I looked so old and ugly, but I don't care; nothing matters anymore. On this occasion too, just a suspicion of a mysterious smile passed like a flicker of a sudden lightning and died away. It was a smile of such a beauty, so tender and enigmatic, and I don't know why the story of Jussuf and Zuleika crossed my mind. Now even others notice how old I look. . . .

When Zuleika was so old and poor sitting in the streets and begging, Jussuf passed by, noticed her, and took her to him, and she became young and beautiful and his queen forever after. . . .

Yes, I must be at the last stages . . . there are signs. . . .

                                                          14th May

WHEN I SIT BEFORE HIM I look and I look . . . his expression when he talks to others . . . such is the light in his eyes. When he talks to me, I have no chance to notice it, first of all because the mind stops working, and I have to pay greatest attention to understand anything at all, but also as soon as he addresses me he assumes a stony, bored expression, so I just shut up and am still, like stunned. . . .

But when he talks to this dirty Pandit or anyone who comes here just for the sake of discussion, when I say that he is unbelievably beautiful, I have said nothing. When I say that there is an unearthly light in his liquid eyes, liquid-like drops of water dancing in the sunshine, strange fire suddenly flashing in them (he has hazel eyes, rare in an Indian), eyes of a Mystic who has seen the three worlds . . . when I say that I look and look because it is as if a faraway memory would haunt me, a memory I cannot get hold of or define, and which is so much more disturbing because of that; when I say that the feeling of nothingness before him grows deeper and deeper: if I said all this, it is correct, but I have said nothing. . . . All I feel now—love, longing—everything is COMPLETELY beyond words . . . like sinking into an abyss of non-existence. Neither pleasant nor unpleasant feeling; just nothing of nothing, just that. . . . But every night under the stars, God is near and prayer was never so easy. I pray that my sins, of which I have so many, may be forgiven. I pray that nothing should remain in the mind of mind. I pray for his health, and I pray and I pray. . . .

The registered letter arrived this afternoon. So the trouble seems to be over for the moment. This morning he was dressed in white, so I thought that it will be testing time, but he only looked deeply bored while he was alone with me. As soon as somebody came, he changed into a comfortable singlet and dhoti and began a lively conversation looking perfectly radiant. Could not take my eyes away from him. . . .

15th May

HE WAS DRESSED IN WHITE. He was already standing outside the gate when I came, because a demonstration of laborers or Communists was passing by. As soon as he saw me, he quickly went inside and sat down. I suspect he was afraid that I will greet him with my usual deep bow in the street. He asked me how much money I would need because he knew that it will take a few days; the money which arrived had to go through the bank.

"What you can spare. I am not in the position to dictate how much I want. I am in the situation of a beggar and have to accept what is given to me."

"Still, it is easier if you tell me. I can arrange it with my wife."

So, I said seven or ten rupees will do.

"Don't thank me, do not say like that; I am duty-bound. If something happens to you here, you fall ill, to whom shall you go? You are here for me. . . ." I just looked at him, my heart was too full to say anything. No, I am here for myself . . . for my own sake. Nothing, nothing in the world can repay you what you did for me . . . but I only looked at him . . . so radiant, all in white, and said nothing. . . .

A young man was there talking about his troubles. Later in the room he said:

"This young man has many troubles. The greatest is that he keeps seeing before him faces of certain ladies. Since his birth he always was in female company; no illicit relationship was there. But he keeps seeing them. So, I told him to sit outside, and when he came in I asked if he still saw them. He said, yes, to some extent. Then I went out and when I came back I asked if he still sees them, but he could not see them anymore; into this room they don't come. Now try hard to see them. But he could not, they were gone."

"Are those Jinns?" He shook his head.

"No, Jinns would have gone at once; it is something else." He stopped. I waited for him to say more; I was so interested to know. But he was silent.

"Perhaps those were his desires which in some way became visible," I ventured, saying the first thought which came into my mind. "Some sort of vision."

"What is vision? It is desire which becomes visible."

Here we are, I thought, that's how he teaches. He stops speaking and lets my intuition speak. This is his Teaching . . . and my gratitude to him was deep and full of reverence.

He sat, not on the tachat, but on the sofa next to me. Could not see his face. He was facing others at the other side of the room. I saw Pandit Butchly for the first time in Dhyana.

16th May

HAD SUCH A RESTLESS NIGHT full of bad dreams. When I woke up at dawn, I only remembered that he said in my dream that he is sending me back to England and I was desperate. And I was worried because the thought came into my mind that Guruji was not at all well during the night. But I chased the thought away. Why imagine always bad things?

I am still after beauty . . . I asked him yesterday when we were talking about visions that I used to see lovely plants and beautiful gardens just before falling asleep.

"You are after beauty. It can be unconscious" (it is conscious, I am afraid), **"and plants and gardens have great natural beauty, so you see them."**

And I live in such ugly surroundings, so difficult for me, with so many people, hardly any privacy at all, that when I see a flowering tree, or stars in the sky, my heart becomes glad and I praise God . . . I am still after beauty . . . I am. . . .

Yesterday he explained at length about Atma to the garrulous Pandit. I was filled with sadness because I could not understand.

"What is understanding of a language? The essence of it remains with you, even if you don't understand."

Yes, I know . . . but what a pleasure it is for me to hear him explain; it is life, it is joy. Nobody can explain like him . . . but I am STILL after knowledge . . . I know I have to renounce everything and still I want this and that . . . and I became so sad and disgusted with myself.

Went there at quarter to seven. His brother came out immediately and informed me that he had a severe heart attack in the night; oxygen was given. It was the worst one he had until now. I asked if I could go into the courtyard. He was lying on the tachat in the middle of the courtyard. His face was pale, full of the deepest peace. He seemed to be asleep. My heart flew to him in mute sorrow. I looked at him. Around the large household, life was going on. Satendra's wife was making tea, nearby dahl was sorted out for the lunch . . . and he was lying in the middle of it all—still, pale, infinitely dear. . . .

Satendra was telling me how they got a car from Sharma at midnight and brought the oxygen in twenty minutes. Everybody was pale, everybody was deeply worried, nobody slept at all. His wife had the look of such anxiety in her dark eyes that I felt deep sympathy and sorrow for her. Poor woman . . . her front teeth were taken out last week, and she is more beautiful; her face acquired gentleness without the large, dark, protruding teeth.

Sitting there I suddenly felt great peace. I know he cannot go yet. And I told Satendra so. He cannot go. Not now. He will go soon, but not yet. . . . And while writing this down I feel peace and great nearness to him which is the same as the nearness to God. Now I will go back to his place; it is nine a.m. The doctor will be there soon to take the electrocardiogram. Went to do shopping and went home to write all this down.

There was an atmosphere of tragedy all day in the courtyard. He was taken into the room where it was cooler; somebody was massaging his feet in semi-darkness. I was hanging around, then went home.

And if he dies after all? I know, my heart tells me it is not possible; still if he goes and I won't be able to reach him, what then?

This in theory I know: God does not cheat. If a human being is prepared to give everything including oneself, he must get at least something. Until now I got nothing; so he cannot go now. This is theory. But theory and practice don't always agree. . . . And if . . . and if he goes after all? Such a deep despair seized me—there are no words to express it. . . .

In the evening I went there early. Went into the room under the fan where Bhim was resting. Passed Bhai Sahib lying lifeless, pale, Satendra massaging his feet. And I cried so much, sitting there, as silently as possible, so that the sleeping boy should not notice.

He was brought out into the courtyard at dusk. He was very very pale . . . installed on the tachat in the middle of the courtyard which was swept clean and watered abundantly, in order to give coolness in the night.

Then he turned his head in my direction and beckoned me to him. I approached.

"You are all right?" he whispered half audibly. I said I was. My throat was like in a cramp, could not speak . . . he nodded.

"My wife and my children will look after you," he said, and turned his head to the other side. I stood for a moment, profoundly puzzled by this statement.

"You will be all right," I said quickly, not knowing what to think.

A little oxygen was given to him in this moment. The doctor has ordered that it should be given from time to time in small quantities. One doctor was expected soon to spend the night at his bedside. I asked if I also could stay. Ravindra said, yes, of course. Ram Singh, the servant, will go with me and bring my charpoy, but I soon saw that there was no question that it would be possible. Ram Singh was occupied with massaging his feet, and I could not very well carry my own bed and the bedding myself even with a rikshaw. So, I went home about 9:30, thinking that I will come in the night. Did not go on the roof. Would disturb if I want to leave in the night. Lying in my boiling room, under the blow of the humming fan, I was so terribly worried. What did he mean? That I would be in such a state to need help? But he must know that if something should happen, I will take the first plane as soon as I can to go back to England. What help will I need? It is I who in all probability will help them. . . . About two a.m. could not stand it any longer. Dressed quickly. The streets were full of yapping dogs. Really dangerous to go at this time without a stick . . . they follow you in packs coming nearer and nearer. At his place all was peace. Munshiji slept in the garden and the servant too. I slowly opened the door into the courtyard but could not manage to do it quietly enough; the thing cracked, the wife heard me, asked who it was. I said it was I. . . . In the courtyard all was still—everybody seemed to be asleep.

I sat down near the door against the wall in the Sufi praying posture and began to pray and do *Jap*. And the thought of what did he mean, did not leave me at peace. . . . About four a.m. the doctor got up, measured his blood pressure, gave him a medicine and left. I heard Guruji asking Ravindra:

"When did Mem Sahib come?" He answered at two a.m.

"Let her sit here," he said, and I went to sit on a chair near his bedside. He turned to the other side with his back to me and fell asleep. I left about five a.m.

17th May

W AS AT HIS PLACE AT SEVEN A.M. He was already in the room. Stood at the door and looked at him for quite a while from afar. He slowly turned his head in my direction and gave a long, deep look. I turned away and went quickly. I was choking; tears were running down my face. Such was the longing. . . . Do not go, prayed my heart. . . . I will go too—what will become of me? The whole day passed in anxiety . . . all the time I was with them, the whole morning. The doctor came about twelve. Took an electrocardiogram. In the afternoon Ravindra brought me the money from the bank. He asked me if I gave back the money to his son, which I did of course, and told me to give the money for the photos little by little; it means he wants me to save it from my food. Good. Will be done.

75

The Test of Acceptance of Death

18th May, 1966

WENT WITH RAVINDRA TO THE HEART SPECIALIST. There I learned that only the right side of the heart was working, and that he is seriously ill. . . .

"It was a hopeless night," he said yesterday.

What did he mean, what did he mean? It does not give me peace . . . keep thinking of it all the time . . . must have a special meaning: **"My family will look after you. . . ."**

Turning and twisting in bed, in the middle of the night, the real meaning of this sentence flashed suddenly into my mind, and I was so aghast that I sat up in bed feeling ice-cold. Of all the cruel things he said to me in the past, this was the most cruel one. It meant: I am going; I am giving you nothing; my family will look after you, and here my responsibility ends. . . . It was so cruel that it made me smile.

No, my Sheikh. I know what you mean by telling me that . . . but it will not work this way . . . God does not cheat. And your behavior shows it to me. . . . You don't look at me; you hardly notice me when I salute you from the door, in the morning and in the afternoon, when I come and go. You want the longing to increase to a fever. My heart is crying for you . . . probably it is not enough. . . .

Made a notice in block letters: "By the order of the Doctor no visitors are allowed"—and fixed it on the wall near his door with Ravindra's help. Let's hope that it will be respected . . . in India here, I doubt it. . . .

19th May

WHEN I SEE THE LARGE SHINING STAR rising in the East, I know dawn is near. And I look in the direction of Guruji's bungalow; seen from here it is right in the East where the sun is rising . . . and the large star above it—it is symbolical . . . I watch the sky get livid and then pink. . . . As soon as I open my eyes, the longing leaps up like a flame, burning. . . . the terrible, terrible, yearning. . . . Since his attack I pray to his Father and all the Superiors . . . make him well, make that his heart softens towards me!

Pray under the shimmering velvet of the Indian sky . . . and that pain in the heart, I can hardly bear it. . . .

20th May

SOME WEEKS TICK AWAY HURRIEDLY, as if set in motion by a nervous clock. But some days creep and creep, no end of creeping . . . so it was with this week. It seemed never to end. . . . Yesterday the temperature went up to nearly 47° Celsius. The nights are hot, hardly any refreshment. Can sleep but little, due to the worry and partly to the heat.

21st May

EVERY DAY I SEE HIM in the morning and in the afternoon when I come. See him for a moment from afar, salute him . . . he solemnly nods, sometimes ignores me. Then I go and sit either in the doorway passage or somewhere where I can find a bit of shade. A scorching wind is blowing; it is unbearably hot. . . .

22nd May

COULD NOT SLEEP even for five minutes last night. Caught a nasty head cold, cannot breathe. . . . In my desperation went under a shower for a long time in the afternoon. The hair wet, sat under the blow of the fan. Oh, was it hot! And the result: am very miserable now, nose running, the body aching, am acutely uncomfortable . . . and the maddening hum of the fan. . . . It is hot, oh, so hot, so hot . . . hot . . . hot. . . .

But how much must he suffer under the heat in his condition. If I could take some of his suffering upon me. . . . Make that my misery relieves his, at least to some extent. . . .

Thinking . . . all the time . . . I MUST and I WILL get the Truth . . . at any cost. There is one possible factor—perhaps I won't be able to get it now while in the physical body, in case he would go. I may get it, when dead. True, I should get it, because I give myself away . . . but should he die—and people do die, such things do happen. And if it should be the Will of God that he goes without me being able to achieve at least a crumb of it, I will go too. . . . I will not return to the West—what would be the good of it? I will be a failure. Everybody has something to hold on to. His family—they have each other, they love each other. When he goes, it is only a beloved father gone. . . . It is the law of life that parents should go before us. L. has her attachment to her Kundalini—all the disciples have something or somebody to hold on. Who has his bad health to nurse, who has family, and so on. But I have nothing left. I pointed everything on one card. I gambled; I have lost. The whole world fell away from me . . . it has no value. . . . No, I will not return to the West. Will go to the Himalayas, live in a cave, dress like a Sanyasini not to arouse curiosity, go on a periodic fast and starvation diet. Dysentery and malnutrition together with the climatic conditions will see to the rest. I know, it will mean dying by inches; it will be a life of suffering, but I know it won't last long . . . what alternative have I got? A failure . . . I don't deserve a better fate. . . . And perhaps because I will do it for His sake, He will have mercy upon me, and when I will come before Him, face to face, He will allow me to be near my Sheikh. . . .

23rd May

THINKING . . . AND THE DECISION cuts deeper and deeper into my mind. . . .

The night was not too hot. There was a little breeze. Mind very restless. Pray to all the superiors—may he soften his heart towards me. . . . I saluted him from far away, he being seated in the courtyard, having his breakfast. I think they feed him too much, and all this fried stuff they have for Indian breakfasts. But I can say nothing. I pray that it should not harm him. Sat in the inner room and he was resting in the front room. The life of the household was going on as usual. Breakfast finished . . . shopping inspected . . . cooking being done for lunch . . . Durghesh, who is here with the whole family, busily talking to her brothers and sister.

Then I was asked to go out because he was going to have his bath. And when I was leaving and saluted him, my heart nearly stopped its beat when I bowed low, so much sorrow I felt, and so much pity. . . .

He acknowledged my greeting, and the expression on his face was strange. . . .

24th May

YESTERDAY I WAS A LITTLE BETTER in the night. Suddenly remembered that I had some phials of Eucaliptine, so I took some in the afternoon and evening. It had its effect and cut the headcold down at once.

When I arrived before seven, he sat on a chair, his feet drawn up. Several tachats were still standing in the garden; clearly people slept there during the night. When I was approaching, my heart was trembling. He looked as weak as a kitten and deadly pale. He gravely acknowledged my salute.

"**How are you?**" he asked hardly audible. I told him that I was much better and sat opposite him on the tachat.

"And how are you?"

"**Better,**" he retorted. He was nodding softly, his head reclined to the right. He was so weak . . . and he was in Samadhi. So full of light . . . such a beautiful human being, such nobility in his face. Tears came into my eyes. He soon went inside walking with difficulty; he nearly fell at the threshold of the room. Ravindra sprang by to help him. A few minutes later I went to salute him. He was lying on his back moving his hand as if following an inaudible rhythm or melody. I left without disturbing.

Bought a small melon and a few nimbus. Had a little boiled rice with melon and nimbu. Cannot face food in this heat. . . .

25th May

HAVE A HEADACHE, a dull pressure on the top of the head, nearly all the time but especially in the afternoon. Mind is working badly and the body feels very weak. I have no energy left at all. Every afternoon I listen to the song of the boiling fan humming along. Merciful God . . . I pray. Please help somehow . . . it is all I am able to think. . . . Everything is hot. The key and the door-lock, and my mirror, and the comb, and the water from the shower . . . I dream of cool rain . . . of the snow and the drifting mist in the Himalayan mountains . . . I dream of a bit, of the smallest bit of happiness, a little crumb of kindness . . . it is so lonely . . . Merciful God. . . .

And the physical heart keeps being painful . . . feel like vomiting all the time. Merciful God. . . . "**Unbelievable suffering of the mind and of the body are necessary in order to become a Wali,**" he said a few weeks back. "**Absolute Truth is difficult to attain**" . . . and: "**In a subtle way the Master will put one against himself and then puts the Disciple under a severe test. And if he accepts it, thinking he cannot do more but die, then he is ready for a high state.**" The test of hunger, then the acceptance of death . . . like in the story of the *Upanishad*. Life is the dearest thing for every living thing. If one can renounce that too, one is ready. . . . Merciful God . . . how lonely is the Road. . . .

26th May

YESTERDAY AFTERNOON WHEN I CAME, the room was full of people, all
his sons, the son-in-law, and the garrulous Pandit and the Pandit
Batchly. All around him, all talking. But one by one they began to
leave, and his son-in-law told me to sit in his chair.

"I go into the next room," I suggested.

"No, you sit here." He also got up and went out. So, I sat at his
feet. The ceiling fan was gently humming; his feet, so thin now, were
only a few inches from me. I stretched my hand out and very very
gently touched his right foot . . . the Lotus feet of the Guru. . . .

He was lying on his back. I took advantage that he didn't take the
slightest notice of me. His body was restless, I noticed. I prayed all
the time. . . . Merciful God . . . make that he has time to help me
to be able to reach him when he is no more. . . . He obviously is
going . . . but what's the use of crying to the Merciful God? If I
didn't get the Truth, it means that I didn't want it badly enough.
Hundreds of times I told from the platform the story of the
Upanishads, that if you want it as badly as a drowning man wants air,
you will get it. . . . I must want it terribly, like a fever, and I must
pray . . . to God, to all the Superiors, I must pray. . . . All the time
I was praying. I wondered if he was conscious enough to know what
was going on in my mind. But he gave not the slightest indication that
he noticed my presence at all. I left after seven, when he was already
installed in the middle of the courtyard.

And I prayed so much in the night. Woke up after one with the
feeling of some calamity, and prayed and prayed. It was not too hot;
clear was the sky. I did not see his face this morning. But they say that
he is all right, though his blood condition is deteriorating. The anti-
coagulant has been increased to a double dose. How very, very
worrying. . . . Remembering what it did to Andrée. . . . Oh
Merciful God . . . I don't see it good at all! He is going . . . and so
will I. . . . What's the use of living without him? He was my only
hope to reach the Truth. . . . Nothing is left. If I cannot reach him, I
will go too. Perhaps there, somewhere, by his Grace, I will be able to
reach him.

I left about ten a.m. All flocked in and sat down in the room where
I was sitting. I felt they wanted me to go. So I left. I will cry to Him till
I will get Him, no matter if I am dead or alive. . . .

27th May

WHEN I ARRIVED BEFORE FIVE yesterday afternoon, they played cards.

The wife made me a sign to go into the next room. There I sat under the fan; Poonam was sleeping on his tachat. From where I was, I could see him well. Noticed that he was not sitting (probably doctor's orders), but reclining, his back supported by several pillows. How pale and noble he looked . . . how the Divinity shone clearly in him . . . and a sudden gladness sprang up in my heart . . . I will be a fool not to surrender. I could not do better than to do it completely, unconditionally, without any reserve, without the slightest regret . . . to be nothing before him. And it seemed easy at that moment, the easiest thing in the world. God knows how many weeks he has to live . . . it will not be many months, I am sure. . . . And they feed him the wrong food and I can say nothing. . . .

"Badam (almonds) **are good for me,"** he would say, and **"badam is useful to old people; badam was very useful to my parents; I gave them badam milk every morning till their death."** Perhaps it is good. But he is getting all fried stuff, pokoras, and so on, every morning because guests are here; his daughter and her husband, and everybody likes it, and they always did it. At midday puries are fried, so he will eat puries in spite of the prohibition of not only the one doctor, but of every doctor. . . .

But on the other hand this practice went on in India for thousands of years, and probably they dispatched each other to the next world much quicker in this way. Is what we do in the West better? To keep a body alive indefinitely? My worry will not change the custom . . . and he definitely knows what he is doing, so he will do what he likes.

All I can do is to pray, pray desperately, because if he dies, nothing will remain for me but to die too. . . .

Gazing at him, I was wondering how can a mortal look so divinely perfect, while he was thinking, looking at his cards, or throwing one on the table in the course of the game, or studying the situation, knitting his brows in concentration. I prayed. Yes, there is ignorance, and one may wonder why and how a man at this stage of evolution should submit, or even apparently partake of this ignorance. . . . He alone knows. He has to fulfill his destiny—he knows . . . and he will live his life in full knowledge of its purpose. . . . I will never know. . . .

Then when the garden was being watered, I went out because tortured by thirst. Went to drink at the pipe of running water. Not very cold, but water, and I drank a river, so it seemed to me, endlessly, from my hand as small boys do or thirsty wanderers on the dusty, sun-baked roads. Tachats were put out in the garden. He was to sleep outside. He came out slightly unsteady on his legs and as pale as death. Not looking at anybody, he went directly to the tachat and lay down. I went home.

In the night it was not so hot. I slept well, was very tired in the morning. Prayed much before falling asleep . . . and I have increasing peace now, as the days go by. The more firmly my decision takes hold of my mind, the stiller inwardly I become. . . . He dies? So will I. And it sinks deeper and deeper this resolution. And becomes quite natural. I know, it seems strange, but it is so. . . .

He told me that the time will come when I won't live either in my physical body or in my mind. It means that neither does he. That's why he is apparently involved in this physical life; but it is deceptive; he is not. I know that he can listen and talk and answer, and he himself is not here at all, and nobody notices it. He is a very great man, all right. . . .

28th May

HE WALKED A LITTLE, but he is unsteady on his feet. Then he was in the other room in deep Samadhi. At one moment he opened his eyes and saw me. I stood up and folded my hands in salute. A sudden, beautifully kind smile lit up his pale face like a swift ray of sunshine. That was all. But it was enough for me . . . I had peace. Deep peace. I shall watch him die and then go to the mountains and do the same. There is no worry for me anymore . . . I was alone with him. All those people, the whole world was a small insignificant thing. I was with him alone in eternity forever . . . it was a beautiful feeling. . . .

In the afternoon they played cards. Stayed less than one hour. Bought some sugar, a few vegetables in the bazaar. Was so full of peace, just went home. There was nothing else to do . . . I am at the end of the road. I can put a full stop at the end of this incarnation . . . everything was all right. Such peace, such peace . . . how can such peace be possible? It was. . . .

29th May

LAST NIGHT LOOKING AT THE STARS, I had the feeling that glittering peace, like Manna, was raining on me; all the stars were showering me with their glory. But it was a terrible night, so hot it was. The Scotts installed a fan on the roof, but it did not bring any relief. Hot. But it mattered little. Since last Wednesday (today is Sunday) the temperature exceeds 49° Celsius in the shade. Poor Guruji . . . they do what they can to make it bearable for him; still, in his condition it must be terrible. Never, not a word of complaint, from him. He is practically all the time in Samadhi.

There was heart activity; it usually means trouble. I wonder, what is coming? I have very few vibrations nowadays. So this heart activity could easily mean trouble.

30th May

YESTERDAY AFTERNOON I went there as usual at half past four. They played cards. The wife made me a sign to go into the front room. The room was in darkness. I sat there doing my *Jap*. Suddenly the servant came in and barred the outer doors and the windows. I could not comprehend what was happening. I heard Guruji's voice ordering to close everything, and in the next moment I felt the impact of the storm on the bungalow. The building was hit as if with a bang and trembled; in a moment it became quite dark. Tropical duststorm, I thought. I wanted to watch it outside, so I went into the next room hoping to get out. But the door was closed and they sat and played cards. I stood there uncertain what to do; to my good luck Ravindra came in.

"Did you see? It became as dark as in the night!" I said that I saw nothing, but I very much would like to see it.

"Come out with me!" and he held the door open against the impact of the wind. In the courtyard, already covered with dust, it was completely dark, and the sky was strangely deep red—a threatening dark-red light which very soon became bright yellow. In a moment I was covered with dust; my eyes were smarting; I had difficulty to breathe; clouds of thick dust were whirling so dense, showering my skin with grit and sand. I was thinking that I had washed my hair this afternoon . . . will have to wash it again . . . this here is too beautiful, too unusual to miss. Ravindra, myself, and a few others went into the front garden. The impact of the storm on the trees was tremendous. The Ashoka tree was bending and shaking dangerously; so dense was the dust that the houses opposite were invisible. The whole world was a madly whirling grey chaos. It was difficult to breathe—the skin inside the nose seemed to split, hurting and burning with dryness. Beautiful and very frightening is a tropical dust storm. Ravindra was telling us that he was in the garden, the sun was shining brightly, and it came in a matter of seconds, without any warning. I was so fascinated that I didn't care how covered with dust I was, only I remembered that my window was open, and how my room will look, heaven knows. . . . The storm seemed to subside a little. The gusts of the wind came in intervals as if in waves. Durghesh and the children came out too. We were watching it together and everybody was hoping for a cooler night.

I left about seven, half choked with dust, but glad that I saw it. Quite an experience . . . it was the biggest storm I saw until now in India. The night was cooler. But I had no benefit. When I wanted to go on the roof, the storm was still raging, though much less, so I stayed in the hot, hot, room under the song of the fan. About two a.m. I got up to drink some water and saw that the night was still, cool, and full of shining stars. Regretted not to have waited and gone up with the others . . . now it was too late.

When I was leaving, he was in the front room squatting on the tachat, clasping the sides of his head with both hands as if in pain. When one is not well, all those upheavals in nature are felt much more. I was worried for him and hoped he will sleep well.

When I arrived, he was in the courtyard. I saw him through the open doorway passage. His face was stony, ironical, hard, when he lightly acknowledged my salute. This expression, so hard, made the longing in my heart leap up. Oh, Sheikh, I thought . . . have mercy on my poor old heart. . . . And I did my *Jap*. . . .

Children came out. An airplane was circling low which caused a lot of shouting and great excitement. I went into the room. He was resting in infinite peace, in deep Samadhi, lying on his right side. His face was deeply serene. I sat down, resenting the noise outside. For some reason my heart was so terribly sad that I began to cry. Mrs. Sharma came.

"Are you upset?" she said, and sat down in the big chair, asking Guruji how he was and telling him and the wife the latest news about her own children.

They all come for worldly purposes . . . they are all satisfied. . . . I alone, who am here for the Truth, I alone, perhaps, will go away with empty hands. . . . This is not possible! cried out my heart in agony. And I cried more, full of longing, so much, so much. . . . She left soon, asking me while she was passing my chair what was the matter. I put my finger to my lips and she quickly went out. . . .

I left soon. The brother, seeing me pass by, asked why I was upset. "Sometimes the longing is too great for a human heart," I answered, and he said that he understood. We exchanged a few words on my midday meal and the food prices in general.

76

Resigned to Die

31st May, 1966

WHEN I CAME YESTERDAY he did not even respond to my salute but continued to play (they were playing cards in the courtyard). I quietly passed into the front room where I sat down under the fan. Later the post arrived, and I heard Ravindra reading a letter to him in English. I wondered if it was one from France. And the fact that he didn't give it to me to read or to answer showed that he did not want to speak to me at all. It made me glad. It means that something important is going to happen; the bolts are being tightened more and more. Since his illness he hardly spoke to me and most of the time ignored me. But I am glad—it does not hurt me as it usually did before. Do not speak to me, do not treat me kindly and humanly, but tell me the word one day, the only word which is my whole desire. . . .

Later, about quarter to seven I went out into the garden. In the next room the wife just finished chanting the *Ramayana*. I switched off the fan and quietly passed by without looking at anybody. In the garden the brother and his family members discussed yesterday's storm: apparently eighty miles per hour, and in some places in the province it reached ninety miles per hour, and it caused plenty of damage.

After a while when all around was watered, his tachat was brought out and Ravindra and Satendra carried him out on a cot. I looked at him. How sorrow grips the heart when I see his face . . . stony it was, expressionless. How pale he is . . . I had the feeling that he was listening to my thoughts. He aged since his illness. But also in '62 when he was so ill, he looked old, and later he looked young again. He gave me a fleeting look while I was standing there and he was being carried past . . . a blank, hard look. When I sat down, he turned to the other side. My heart was glad.

Left soon afterwards about half past seven. And in bed I felt very thankful and rather happy. He is being kind to me . . . he is testing me . . . something is being prepared. My heart was at peace and I fell asleep.

Once during the night, I woke up with a delightful sensation of cool air blowing into my face. How lovely, I thought, cool air from the fan. . . . Then completely waking up, I realized that it was a breeze from the east. I was on the roof and there was no fan. I always put my charpoy in such a way that I face the east, facing Guruji's bungalow. I cannot see it from here, hidden as it was by other houses. But I see the sky at dawn getting rosy behind it, and now the cool air is coming from there. How good, and I fell asleep. From time to time kept waking up feeling the soft cool blow on my face. Perfectly lovely. . . .

How many blisses has India in store for us. A joy like this coming from heaven . . . the bliss of cool nimbu drink, the bliss of a chilo (a whole chilo!) of golden mangoes, a chilo of sunshine . . . and the bliss of the southern sky above—deep, endless, full of stars so near, that it seems that one can touch them. India, I love you!

I forgot to mention that since his heart attack in February his voice had changed. It became more veiled, more cavernous. And now it seemed even more so, an old, broken voice—it has not the usual metallic ring in it. Yes, my dear Sheikh . . . if you should die without me being able to reach you, when you have gone (Heaven knows, it seems such an impossibility!!), then I don't return to the West. I will go to the mountains and there fade away like good soldiers do. But at last I have learned to love the King and it is not a small feat. And for that, my Sheikh, my very deepest gratitude to you. As the nearness increases, my gratitude grows, for I know, what looks like cruelty is the greatest kindness. . . .

1st June

HE WAS IN THE ROOM. When after sitting outside for a while I came to the door in the hope that I can come in (it was unbearably hot already at eight a.m.); he was squatting on the tachat and was having his breakfast. He made a movement with his head to indicate that I can come in. I sat down near the door. A table stood in front of him and on it stood a huge glass of almond milk, tasty rice fritters, pokoras, dried grapes . . . all the wrong things. Not my business, I thought. I tried not to look. My heart was heavy . . . they are ruining him with this kind of diet. . . .

"Did you get the living quarter?" he asked in a soft, old voice, munching the crisp rice fritters. I said that I did not.

"Why?" he wanted to know.

I told him that I went to Mrs. Ghose on the 27th to know the position, and was told that though the husband of her tenant will be transferred, the wife refuses to leave because the children should finish their education here, which will not be until December.

"There is a close cooperation between you and the Almighty," I said, watching his expression. "How much the human being can take, how much tolerate. . . . The circumstances will be just right; advantage is taken of every situation . . . as in a wine-press, one is screwed tighter and tighter."

He closed his eyes gently and slowly nodded assent.

And I began to cry terribly and helplessly, all the while I was speaking to him. There is a quality in him of a special tenderness and compassion, and as soon as I feel it I begin to cry and cannot stop; this seems to be my reaction to it. Sometimes I have the feeling that he avoids looking at me because of this tenderness. And he knows that I will burst out crying.

Told him about the difficult conditions I live in, and the heat and the terrible longing which is burning up my body. He listened, continuing his meal, the wife coming in and out, wanting to know what was the matter.

"She did not get the flat," he said. She went out and he stretched himself comfortably on his back and went into Samadhi.

For a long time I was sitting. He was resting. My heart was full of peace.

In the afternoon they played cards. I went to get a Coca Cola and, waiting to be served, saw myself in the mirror which hung at the back of the stall. My God, how old I looked . . . an old woman, grey and haggard. . . . I went home. He was resting. All the family was inside the room with him—sons, grandsons, the wife, daughters-in-law, the lot . . . discussing, laughing . . . there was no room for a fly, not to speak of me. Complete rest is a sad myth in India. . . .

2nd June

HE VOMITED THREE TIMES in the night and once in the morning. Satendra asked me if I would come with him to Dr. Ram Singh because he does not know the way; I went of course. The doctor was not at home, and Satendra said that he knew that he was at a wedding in Lucknow. When we came back, I realized that Babu did not want to go and therefore sent Satendra and me. I found him lying on the tachat in a languid, artistic pose talking to his sister. I told Babu that the obvious thing would have been to phone first, to find out if the doctor was back to save time to go so far. He mumbled something to the effect that the phone is often not answered. This lazy fellow never wants to do his duty; he is always sending others. . . . I did not stay . . . my heart was heavy, his room was closed. In the garden was the usual noisy, discussing crowd, and all the howling children. . . .

In the afternoon they played cards. He looked so weak. Vomiting continues. I think all the drugs he was given did upset the enlarged liver. It will pass. . . . And in the night which was fresh and slightly windy, how I prayed . . . there was no end of loneliness. . . .

3rd June

SEATED IN THE BIG CHAIR the wife was reading *Ramayana*. A disciple from Agra was massaging his feet. A truly traditional Indian scene, the pale light coming from the doors and the windows wide open, for the sky was covered with thin clouds. The voice of the woman, the ringing rhythm of the chant, the deep devotion of the young man, the buzzing of the large flies, the chatter of the chipmunks . . . and the smell of India—dust, some distant exotic fragrance of incense and flowers. . . . India—dust, some distant exotic fragrance of incense and flowers. . . . India, how, oh, how I love you!

He did not seem to notice me when I saluted him. And he did not see me at all when I left about half past seven. The heat was intense.

This morning he was still lying in the garden when I came. He was resting. A faint smile appeared on his face when I saluted. The vomiting was no more. Hakkim was there last evening and he prescribed a medicine. Later, about eleven, he was taken into the room. A woman was led in by Satendra; she did not stop talking; she was a fat, old Indian woman, full of worries she was. Guruji also talked a lot. At last I could not bear it, went into the room where Babu and others were merry-making with the radio, and told them that this is not the complete rest according to the doctor's orders. The wife laughed; Durghesh said something in Hindi. I went back, sat there listening to the voice of the woman coming from his room. She soon left. He asked for another fan which was brought in; it was very hot. He was restless. All the doors and windows were closed, and I sat alone with him under the cool bliss of the ceiling and the table fan. His back was turned to the fan in the obvious pleasure of coolness. It was dark. Voices of children came from the courtyard, voices from the next room. And I was in deepest peace with him, resting. . . . This sense of oneness—there was an activity of the heart, soft and rhythmic. (I forgot to mention that in the last two days there was a strong activity of the heart, and I feel no pain, only indifference at the thought that I am resigned to go if he goes.)

And I was thinking that the relationship with the Master is the most difficult in the world, because it is a fantastic super-human relationship, encased, screwed into, so to say, the most banal surroundings, amongst most ordinary people, involved in their petty, daily affairs, greeds, quarrels, worldly desires. And one has to reconcile it all with the transcendent feeling of oneness. With this terrible non-human longing. With this love which is not of this world. . . . The difficulty lies in the contrast: he, the Great Being, and his surroundings. . . .

"To know the pain of too much tenderness, to wake at dawn
        and give thanks for another day of loving.". . .
says Kahlil Gibran.

And around you would be the yapping of the quarreling voices, the noises of the children, and he, apparently interested only in his family.

The money did not arrive. Did H. send it? God knows, I am worn out with those financial troubles . . . what is she doing? Or is it the fault of the post? Destiny wants me to be in every kind of trouble. . . . Could not pay the whole rent. Feel bad about it. . . .

4th June

YESTERDAY AFTERNOON SAT ALONE for a long time in the darkened room. He was in the next room. The wife was reading the *Ramayana*; the disciple from Agra who looks like a bearded prophet was massaging his feet; Munshiji was sitting on a chair at his feet, the knees drawn up to his chin, listening.

I looked at Bhai Sahib's face in the dim light. Surprisingly young, ethereal, a strange, not even a human face. As a rule one cannot call his face ethereal; he has rather powerful features. But in the yellowish light coming through the veranda door he looked so different from the usual . . . incredibly delicate, almost boyish—a being from another plane of existence, which perhaps he was after all. . . . Then a man came and talked for over an hour in a loud, aggressive voice. Guruji also talked a lot. I was in agony. What suffering it is to know that every Dick, Tom and Harry are just being led in to talk and to talk and to tire him. He will die, I thought, and I will die with him. I am not going to say anything this time or in the future. . . . Oh, Merciful God, give me the strength to bear, to tolerate this torture!

I left after the man had left; it was nearly dark. He was lying, his face turned to the wall, and I stole quietly past him and left for home. And went to bed. The night was hot but not too bad, a light breeze was on the roof. We saw three satellites pass between eight and quarter to nine. They were like bright stars, traveling rather quickly. And I woke before three. Could not sleep worrying why the money did not arrive.

But this afternoon a letter arrived from H. telling me that she had sent it on the 27th. So it will be here next week. What a relief.

In the morning when I went there my heart was so heavy with some sort of feeling of impending disaster, a kind of fear which made my heart tremble and shrink. My body felt so weak; I had strong nausea. He was still on the tachat in the garden. Many people, his sons, his brother-in-law, some disciples were sitting around with funeral faces. I saluted. My heart shrank even more seeing how pale and ill he looked. Learned later that the vomiting condition began again. The medicines they were giving him for his heart condition upset his enlarged liver, I am sure. He gave me a long, long, look when I sat down on a tachat nearby. Felt like crying. Please, please, I repeated mentally, but did not know why I was saying, "please," and for what. . . . Something in me kept trembling and I began to pray. Often he looked at me. Long, searching, serious look which made me feel like nothing at all before him. . . .

Later he was taken into the room on a cot. We all sat in the room. But I soon left with others as he was to take his bath before nine.

Did not go to his place in the afternoon. Felt such weakness, could hardly stand on my feet. The body, the limbs were full of pain as if I was beaten up. Nausea and headache and some giddiness. So I decided to stay at home. The stream of boiling hot air from the fan was almost pleasant on my aching limbs. Went to bed after seven. It was still hot on the roof and orange-yellow was the darkening sky after sunset. Many kites of all possible colors were fluttering and buzzing like oversize insects in the evening air. I saw four satellites, two of them especially large, like stars, all passing from the west to the east. But of course, I was watching the sky looking out for them.

5th June

IN THE MORNING went there at a quarter to seven. The weakness persisted. I was giddy and already tired before the day even began. He was lying on the tachat in the middle of the garden. He acknowledged my greeting and murmured hardly audibly:

"How are you?" I sat down quietly.

"Father wants to know how you are," said Babu. They were all sitting around him looking at me.

"I am all right, thank you," I answered. His wife said something in Hindi in a low voice.

"What was wrong yesterday?" asked Babu again. I said that the physical body felt weak; I couldn't walk. Later they all left and I came to sit nearer to him on another tachat nearby. He gave me a long, deep look, right into my soul. I could not bear it and began to cry. When I feel his compassion and pity, I cannot bear it and begin to cry, and to cry. He was reclining on the pillows looking very tired and very pale. My heart is trembling when I see him like that. . . . Later I was called into the room, and not only that but the wife pulled the chair nearer and adjusted the cushions. I gave her a tired smile. Left about nine when his bath was being prepared. In the afternoon he was in the front room, Ravindra massaging his feet. Wife told me to go in. He told me to write to L. not to come. She wants to come here with some friends in June. And the £20 have to be sent to Cambridge to Sharma's son. I promised to write immediately, secretly glad of the opportunity to tell her that I will stay here in winter. Passed a restless night. Sleep badly lately.

77

His Anger

6th June, 1966

WROTE TO L. AND POSTED IT. He did not look at me nor see me this morning. When I left, he did not respond to my salute. In the afternoon he vomited most painfully and I saw that it was yellow dahl. Cannot understand why he is given this heavy food; he cannot digest it. He was squatting there vomiting, and I was thinking sadly that perhaps it is a blessing . . . he will be getting thinner . . . he is being overfed—they try to fatten him up and then he gets a heart attack. . . .

Later the wife, Babu, and Munshiji came into the front room and they began to play cards. The little boy of Durghesh was also there but kept quiet for a change. Watching his family, I wondered why they seem so huge and noisy—I don't mean physical bodies, of course, though those are also loud and noisy. He is not at all like that, though he is also from a physically dense family—one needs only look at his sister: a kindly face, a fat, coarse middle-aged woman like millions of others with dark lips, thick and flabby, and heavy eyelids. He is so different. . . . Suddenly I understood the why of it . . . they all carry their big selves with them, wear it like a garment. He has no self, and I try to get rid of mine. Because I am in the process of discarding mine, being so conscious of it, that's why they seem so huge to me, so noisy. . . . All at once many things became clear; this is the focal point to keep in mind when the conflict arises, and probably in the near future many conflicts will arise, so I had better keep in mind that the reason for disturbance and suffering lies in the fact of being too conscious of something I am already discarding.

Yesterday afternoon he was in the front room and Ravindra was massaging his feet. He asked me if I have posted the letter to L., and he wanted to know what I have written. When it came to the passage about Cambridge, how the money has to be transmitted, he said I should not have told her so directly.

"Write immediately another letter telling her that you did it on your own account; I did not order you to do so."

I was bewildered. Told him that three weeks ago when the question of Kiki's request was discussed he said:

"It is beyond your power, I will arrange it," and I wrote accordingly. **"Yes, yes, this is another matter, but you should not have committed the mistake to write like this; I never ask money from anyone,"** he said. Wife came in hearing us talk.

"What, what?" she asked rapidly; she did not want to miss a word. I said that I wrote to L. the account of his illness. Ravindra in the meantime brought the record player, and the sound of lovely classical music filled the room. Wife sat there watchful in case something should be said which she might miss. I was partly listening to music, partly hoping for the wife to go, so that I can ask him what and how he wants me to write. He was resting with closed eyes obviously enjoying the music. At last the wife went, because the children were fighting and howling in the courtyard. While Ravindra was changing a just finished record and I saw that he had his eyes open, I said softly:

"Bhai Sahib?"

"Yes?"

Told him that I don't know how to word it now; it must be done cleverly, otherwise she won't do anything, and Mrs. Sharma asked for it, and on the other hand the money is needed here. He smiled and I came nearer, kneeling on the floor to hear what he was saying because the gramophone began to play again.

"Tell her I am in a really great trouble owing to my illness, but she should do what she likes. And . . ." he paused, **"that is all,"** he added with a kindly smile.

Later Ram Singh, the servant, was sent with me with the heavy kerosene tin to my room, and Satendra was cracking rude jokes in the courtyard about my false teeth and the toothless mouth of his mother. I did not care. It is of no importance. It was stifling hot. Lying in bed in the night which was so sultry, not a breath of air, I was reflecting that there must be a mystery in his System which I don't understand. L. is supposed to be his disciple. Why can't she be asked directly for a small amount like £20? For her it is nothing. She earns a lot of money, has properties, was never asked to renounce anything. . . . I know when there is need a Sufi can ask, so why should it be wrong in this case? Mystery . . . my heart was heavy . . . but one day I will know. . . . The last will be the first one day. . . . But in the meantime the body was under great strain due to the heat, and I felt sick.

In the morning he was on the tachat in the garden alone. I expected him to ask about the letter. But he did not. I sat there feeling very weak and giddy. The heat was terrible. Soon he went inside and I saw that his bath was being prepared; it was only after eight.

Wrote a letter to L. with a sting in it. Will post it this afternoon.

8th June

IN THE AFTERNOON HE ASKED ME if the letter was posted. As soon as he began to speak, my mind stopped working abruptly. Had no time to open my mouth to answer as the wife came rushing in, nearly shouting in excitement about a quarrel this horrible spoiled child, Durghesh's son, had with the other children. All children were howling in chorus in the courtyard. Had to wait for quite a while until some kind of order was restored and she went out. I waited . . . he was silent. Then seeing that he did not say anything, I tried to remember the exact wording of my second letter to L. When I came to the passage: do what you like, but please write when the operation is completed, he interrupted sternly:

"What do you mean by that?"

"Oh dear," I tried to speak, a panic seized me, an inexplicable panic. I tried to compose a sentence, thoughts began to flee in all directions, like frightened mice. Began to stammer trying to explain.

"She will never do it without my order," he said angrily. **"In two letters you made a mess! First you say to send me money. . . ."**

"Oh, but I did not!" I exclaimed desperately, "not like this!"

"Then you say to send it somewhere else and why should she write?"

Nearly choking I said that if she does not, how will we know?

"How will we know?" he echoed. **"What a mess you are making!"** He looked furious. I lost all courage completely . . . began to tremble and to choke, was breathless.

"Don't be angry with me. Please, please, no! My heart is breaking day and night as it is!" I had to repeat this sentence twice, so choked I was. He was lying there, his face as hard as stone. Losing control completely I began to sob desperately. Tried so hard to get control over myself before the wife who came in.

"What, what?" she wanted to know. He said something in Hindi.

The small table was brought in, Munshiji came in, Satendra, and they began a game of cards. I went to sit near the door. Munshiji took my chair near the table. I was trembling; my body seemed to be breaking with endless despair. Such was the feeling of absolute desperation and hopelessness that all I wanted was to die, nothing else. God, oh, Merciful God, have mercy on me! I just cannot go on!! Then it dawned on me that I am making a very bad atmosphere; he must feel it, and so must all others in the room, this boundless sorrow, this endless despair which I was unable to contain or control.

In fact, after a few minutes he threw the cards down.

"**Ufff,**" he said in a muffled voice several times, then added something in Hindi. The table was taken out, Munshiji and Satendra left, the window was closed. The game of cards was over. I wondered if the wife felt resentful—she loves a game of cards. Perhaps she was, but she only put her hand under his pillow, took out a homeopathic medicine which was kept there, gave it to him and silently went out. I suddenly felt that I should go—I was disturbing him, he was not well, so I went too. Hurried to the post office to post the letter which I had forgotten; it was still in my handbag. When it was done I sat in the doorway crying so bitterly, so desperately . . . it was the end of the world for me. I did not understand myself why I was so desperate, but to know him angry finished the world for me. . . . The Loo was blowing scorchingly hot. The temperature was over 48°. Munshiji was lying quietly on his cot behind me. I was sitting on the servant's charpoy at the entrance of the doorway. Babu kept passing to and fro trying not to look too curious. Durghesh pretended to go to the gate; they all came out to see me cry. And I did not care . . . have no self-respect anymore, have nothing left, must look horrible, face swollen with tears, hair dishevelled, and still I did not care. . . .

Ravindra came from work with his briefcase tucked under the arm and a shopping bag.

"Why are you sitting here? What's the matter?" he inquired anxiously, seeing in what state I was. I told him that his father was angry with me.

"Why?"

But I said that I didn't know why, only my heart was breaking because I could not bear it. . . .

"Don't say anything," I asked him, and he went inside. Then Babu came, and I asked him not to ask me anything; he is also a disciple, and he must know that the Guru gets sometimes angry without reason, and he also went inside. I cried nearly until seven . . . then I thought it is useless to cry here . . . I can do it at home, cannot sit here indefinitely. Had nothing to eat. Went to bed immediately. Cried much before falling asleep, looking at the stars. There was some amazement in me about this terrible, boundless, despair. Why? Nothing had really happened. Why does his anger send me in such a fit of absolute hopelessness?

Slept badly.

9th June

IN THE MORNING AT FIRST did not want to go there. I cannot face him. Let him send somebody to see why I am not coming. But then I suddenly decided to go. When I arrived, he gave me a beautiful, kindly smile. Prof. Batnagar was talking animatedly with him; he offered me his chair, and another was brought for him. Nobody ever even dreamt to bring one for me; I always had to fetch it myself. I began to cry immediately as soon as I sat down. He was lying on his back, one leg resting on the knee of the other. Clearly he felt cooler this way. His face was expressionless.

Prof. Batnagar asked me how do I bear the heat. "Even we feel scorched," he said. I had only the strength to give him a smile, tears were streaming down my cheeks. He became silent after having given me a surprised look. For a while there was silence. Nobody of his family members, who were seated around, spoke. I cried silently. Prof. Batnagar got up, saluted and went to the other end of the garden followed by Babu, Ravindra and the brother. There they stood talking. I know, Batnagar was bound to have asked why I was crying. I don't know what Guruji told them, what they told him. Soon he was carried into the room on a cot and I left. Had a splitting headache and nausea. The heat was terrible. Took aspirin and was lying under the boiling blow of the fan all the afternoon unable to do anything at all.

When I came into the darkened front room where he was lying, the wife went out and he asked me in a friendly way about the letter. I explained that I did my best and if it is not to his satisfaction he should forgive me, my mind was not working. He was lying there still perfectly relaxed asking friendly questions from time to time and commenting on nothing as he seemed to be satisfied. Then he turned to the wall. I sat there merged in nothingness, my heart full of peace . . . only my head was aching so much from the heat and yesterday's crying. It is surprising what a few kind words can do, I mused, and did my *Jap* in greatest peace.

In bed, in the night, I reflected that not once, not even for a moment did the mind give me trouble. I did not think that he was illogical, did not think that it was unreasonable to get angry when I only followed his instructions. I only knew that he was angry, and to see him angry was worse than death to me, and I even did not query as to why and to how of it. This is something, I thought. There must be much understanding, much acceptance already. . . .

10th June

DEEPEST PEACE. I nearly fall down, when I salute him, lately. The feeling of nothingness before him represents such deepest happiness, such deepest peace. He will be resting, his eyes open or closed, mostly not even in Samadhi. I sit bent in two (this is the most comfortable position for me when I am in his presence since I am back), under the blow of the two fans, he and I alone somewhere, where nothing is but peace . . . wife comes and goes. The spoiled child disturbs sometimes, storming in, howling because he wants this or that or for some other reason. And I keep wondering why there are such disturbances around him, always—children with violent desires, people full of quarrels or animosity to cause intense suffering to me. But he seems to be unaffected by it all, an oasis of peace. . . .

Oh, I know it will pass, and never again in life will I suffer from such things to such an extent. The very physical child . . . how brutal and violent he can be, getting hold of a stick at the slightest provocation and boxing his mother even. They just laugh. They think it is funny. And he, how he loves this child. . . . The tender expression on his face, when he looks at him, the inflection of his voice when he speaks to him, and the child responds always . . . I think he must adore his grandfather.

11th June

YES, THIS FEELING OF HELPLESS DESPAIR when the Beloved frowns is described by the greatest Sufi poets . . . I remember it now . . . the relationship with the Teacher is a preparation for the Relationship with God. . . .

Now I know how it feels like. . . .

Today too, I sat there in the morning for hours with him. When I came, he slightly nodded. Later when I approached the door when he was already in the room, he pointed to my usual place at his pillow on the divan. He was sitting in the big chair. Wife kept coming and going. The child rushed in several times howling fiercely because he did not get what he wanted, or wanted something else and could not get it, or God knows what. . . . Later Ravindra brought his radio and there was a good program of classical music. I left about ten. Could not go to the post office, the wind was whipping up too much dust in the air, my eyes were smarting. Will go tomorrow to see about this registered letter. In the afternoon as soon as I came, he asked if I was at the post office. Told him why I didn't go. A few days ago I told him that I intended to go and he remembered. He never forgets, and if he does he IS MADE to forget. Later I just sat there bent in two . . . once more alone with him somewhere where nothing is all and everything. . . .

Later he wanted to rest and I went out into the garden. There Durghesh and others forced a grey-looking drink upon me. I tried to refuse saying that I am not thirsty, seeing that the kid was practically washing his hands in it by mixing sugar and ice with both hands. But in vain I had to drink it. It tasted sweetly of caraway seed. I went home and took immediately two entero vioform and prayed to God . . . ice is so dangerous, and combined with dirty hands it can be fatal. . . . Will take two others tonight . . . and another two in the morning. That probably will do the trick.

This feeling of nothingness . . . at first it was just nothing. Neither pleasant, nor unpleasant; just nothing, and nothing is nothing. It was very perplexing and I kept running away, I remember. A human being is never "nothing." One is alive, one is an entity, a being. But lately it becomes increasing lovely. Deep happiness welling from within, from the deepest depth. . . . Also at home when I think of Him it comes over me . . . soft . . . gentle. A bliss of non-being, not existing at all. It is difficult to believe, unless one has experienced it, that it is so glorious "not to be."

On the fourth of June, for the first time since April, I heard in Guruji's garden the voice of my friend the *pachta*, the Indian woodpecker, the sugar-mill bird.

78

Born of the Spirit

12th June, 1966

IT WAS A NIGHT OF HOT WIND . . . not much sleep and a lot of perspiration. But when I was sitting in his room near the door (the fan was not on), the wind was blowing my hair about. It was warm, not yet too hot; it was still early, only after eight. I let it blow in my face. How I love the wind. . . . The sentence: "The wind bloweth where it listeth, and thou hearest the sound thereof but canst not tell whence it cometh nor where it goeth, and so is everyone who is born of the Spirit," kept recurring again and again in my mind. Mechanically my mind kept repeating it while I kept my face in the warm blow. Then I looked at him. He was sitting in the big chair. Still, pale, old looking. Born of the Spirit . . . the mystery about you . . . who can know you? Who can say from where you came, what you are doing, where you are going? Like this wind you are . . . born of the Spirit. . . .

In this moment the horrible Pandit came.

"Aia, Aia," said Bhai Sahib encouragingly, and he came in, took off his shoes and put his unbelievably filthy feet on the chair cushion covered with white linen, and began to talk non-stop. Guruji also talked a lot and I began to pray exasperated. . . . Why, oh, why, does he encourage them, though they cannot mean anything to him nor can he be interested in the nonsense they talk. Luckily the wife came in and I saw her murmuring something in disagreement. She sent in Ravindra and Babu and they told that the father now must have his bath. But the Pandit did not listen; he was talking nineteen to the dozen. I got up.

"Guruji must have his bath," I said very firmly to him and went out. He soon followed me and sat outside where Ravindra told him that the father must have complete rest, etc.

Went to Nabab Ganj sorting office. The registered letter was there, but not the one I had expected. The July money arrived (I wrote on the 2nd and it arrived on the 11th, very quickly this time), so the June money which she was supposed to have sent on the 18th of May is lost—it looks like it. Went to Allahabad bank with the

691

postal order, because the International Monetary Fund has not yet fixed the rate of exchange after the devaluation of the pound. Well . . . I really am intended to be in trouble. . . . Even if the money is here, it cannot be paid out. Truly there must be a close cooperation between Guruji and the Almighty . . . every possible kind of trouble I am supposed to have. . . .

He vomited this afternoon. Got some oranges for him; his wife peeled one for him, giving it to him in small pieces—and he vomited it all after a few minutes . . . poor Guruji. . . .

It was a night of hot, hot wind. Woke up in the middle of the night in a pool of water, my own perspiration. Shifted away from it and tried to go to sleep again.

13th June

IT IS SUNDAY. When I was going to his place turning the corner of the street, I thought: Please God, give me the strength to bear all the suffering, the horrible child, the horrible people. . . . The suffering cannot last forever . . . one day it will cease. Let this day come soon that nobody should remain to suffer when the self is gone. . . .

But I was in stillness with him all the time. He did not acknowledge my greeting either when coming or when going.

The night was full of whispering hot wind. Felt very tired in the morning. Wrote some letters in the afternoon. I was aware of some kind of irritation. When I came into the dark room where he was lying under the blow of the fan—coming from the sun-lit garden one cannot see a thing—I slowly and carefully groped my way to the usual seat near his pillow. Some kind of irritation persisted. He was lying quietly. Of course he listened to my thoughts—he always knew what I was thinking especially when he was preparing some trouble for me. An interesting fact was that though I came there at 4:30, it seemed to me such a short time when he asked for a chair and went to sit outside. It was seven. I wondered where the two and a half hours had gone . . . passed in a flash, and I was not asleep, I knew it for sure.

Soon he asked for a basin and vomited. Dahl again. . . . They give him dahl though he cannot digest it . . . seems quite incredible. Somebody told me once that dahl is nourishing, and they try to fatten him up, obviously. Seems tragic. . . . All his family members grouped themselves around him. A wind, not too hot, was blowing strongly from the west. Felt low, dejected, so lonely that no words could describe it. High above, in the sky, was dancing a peacock-blue kite with a long, graceful tail. I watched it for a while—swaying, turning swiftly, like in a dance, in a kind of jerking rhythm, in the sharp breeze. It was so lovely, so alive, so happy it looked, the tail fluttering in a long, trembling stream. Somewhere there is happiness . . . somewhere there is laughter, like in this dancing kite . . . easy, carefree laughter, and golden happiness. But for me there will be unbelievable suffering, much of it, and goodness knows for how long. I did not see the light since I have been with him, and it is years now. I seem to have forgotten what laughter was. . . . They all have something—bliss, Dhyana, Samadhi, wonderful states. They all look at him with the eyes of unearthly longing. I don't think that I ever looked at him like this. His son-in-law too, seated here this afternoon—his eyes sad, deep, just looking and looking. They all have this look—one can see it during the Bandhara—the look of supreme wonder. . . . And I? Have nothing. Not one good thing . . . and I am not even his disciple, and he is not my Guru, so he said. . . . To what am I surrendering? Is it all an illusion? No, I was sure it was not. And I am sure than I am being unjust, for I too got much, only it is always obliterated by so much suffering and longing. Something in me KNOWS. But proofs I have none. . . .

I saluted thin air when I went. Unnoticed by anybody. In the night was intermittent slight rain. Had a splitting headache, wanted to sleep, but rain kept waking me up. Got fed up. Went to my room. Took some aspirin. Without any result. Kept turning and twisting, unable to find a comfortable position, thinking how fresh and cool it must be on the roof.

14th June

IN THE MORNING IT JUST STARTED TO RAIN when I was leaving the house at 6:30, and I arrived quite wet at Guruji's place. Washed my feet at the pipe in the garden, for they were splashed with mud. Then I went into the doorway where I saw he was lying. Saluted. He hardly nodded, with an angry, stony expression. I sat down on Munshiji's cot. From time to time he briefly looked at me, then turned away. A little later the wife came telling him to go into the room. He never goes immediately; also, when they bring him water, he keeps them waiting for a long time. With the wife it does not work—she will impatiently tell him to take it or to hurry up. But with all the others, if he has to go, he refuses to be hurried. If he has to go on the cot to be carried inside, it is a long affair. He would be lying there impassible, thinking something with vacant eyes. And they will wait in silence. To a Guru one cannot say anything.

Later I went to the door of the room hoping to be able to go inside. There was such a glare in the garden; it was beginning to get hot. He was sitting in a big chair.

"May I come in?" I asked timidly. He made an impatient gesture with the hand and said something. I came near him: "I am sorry I didn't understand what you said."

He looked at me with irritation, pointed to the seat and mumbled something I could not understand. I went out. No use to sit there and irritate him with my presence. Be still my heart . . . it is not the first time I have been treated like this, nor will it be the last. Be still. Be not hurt. He is bound to do this and other things too, because the self has to go. I will sit in the glare till nine, then I will go. But after ten minutes the wife beckoned to me from the door and, seated opposite me, looked at me with much curiosity. I wondered if he told her something and if she wanted to see if I was hurt or even crying. I was not. There was much peace. The heart was at rest. Left about nine when he was to have his bath.

15th June

IN THE AFTERNOON, as soon as I sat down, he asked me if the second registered letter had arrived. I had to ask him to repeat it, as the blow of the fan carried the sound away, for he spoke so softly. I answered that no, it did not arrive. Must have gone astray because it was posted on the 18th of May. Told him that I wrote to H. to take the necessary steps and also to the senior superintendent of the post office to look into the matter.

Seated under the fan I was reflecting that there was a great difference in my attitude as compared for instance with the time I was here a few years ago. It was difficult to formulate the thoughts properly, but seated there quietly—he resting with closed eyes—I was so much aware of the feeling of belonging. I had the leisure to analyze it. It was a wonderfully rich, full feeling. It is security, it is peace—one seemed to stand on a rock forever . . . belonging to that in me which is part of That. For life or death. Forever. It cannot be put into words. Not really. But it is a deep bliss, welling from within, coming from the center of oneself. And it seems to me that this deep awareness of non-being comes from the same center which is responsible for it. I cannot put it clearer. To put it differently: the non-being is part of the very make-up of ourselves. Without it, surrender is impossible. But when I feel less than a grain of sand, what criticism can there be? I am bound to accept anything, so much more because the mind is in such a bad working order that I know that I cannot rely on it, and what it tells me can very well be wrong. I try to describe it so much in detail, because if somebody one day happens to read these lines, I want to convey to him the conviction that non-being is nothing to be afraid of. For the mind it may be a frightening prospect, but what can the mind know of NOT TO BE? It is absolute, incredible, bliss. . . . Hours passed like this, me seated there trying to formulate the thoughts as clearly as possible in the mind which worked at half its speed. . . .

Later the gardener began to dig, and I opened the door wide that Bhai Sahib should be able to watch the earth being turned over. It is a lovely sight—I have the feeling that the earth loves being dug. Later I sat outside on a tachat, thinking. The secret is not to say that it will pass; the secret is to say, and BELIEVE, that it does not matter . . . does not matter: the gross people surrounding him, sometimes unbearable conditions. Only he matters . . . to whom my heart flies in mute prayer to help me to the Truth . . . and this wonderful feeling of belonging, of nothingness, of deep, mysterious beauty, like a song far away. . . .

A golden cloud was stationary in the sky. I looked at it. . . . When? I thought. How long? How long will this suffering last, when will it finish? And it was like a voice in my heart: not long anymore, said the Voice. It is nearly finishing; it is coming to its end. This suffering will finish soon. The Great Suffering, the Longing, will remain forever . . . for thousands of years. But this one will soon go. With the first clouds of Monsoon. . . .

I forgot to note down in my diary that all the time I had the feeling, since I have been here, that it will be in July when he will do something, initiate me, or something of the sort . . . that he considers the months of May and June as a test, as a sacrifice. . . .

The golden cloud floated and changed shape—it was nearly transparent now and melted away gently. Yesterday's kite was trembling high up in the azure. It had lost its tail. The wind took it away, probably. The tail which made its beauty, its personality . . . the wind carried it away. And the wind of the spirit is carrying something away from me too . . . just as it does from this kite. . . .

He came out. Looked at him from afar, pale and delicate. Fresh wind was blowing. Went home as usual about 7:30.

The night was delightful. I discovered another bliss: cold feet. When I woke up in the morning after a night of pleasant sound sleep, my feet were cold. What a nice feeling it is to have cold feet! And there was such peace in the heart.

When I went to him, he was washing himself at the pipe in the garden. I sat near the door and, when he finished, went to salute him. He bowed his head slightly, and I had to support myself and then stand still for a moment . . . was so giddy. Then I just sat there . . . head empty, much giddiness. The heart was somewhere, suspended in peace. When I opened my eyes, he was turned towards me, lying on one side supporting his head with one hand resting on the elbow. His eyes were closed. By the rhythmic movement of his lips I saw that he was repeating a mantra—it must have been only a few short words which he repeated continuously. When a Saint is praying, it is a beautiful sight. . . . I too began to repeat my mantra, or tried to, because my mind was completely empty. Later he got up and went into the room. When he got up and walked away slightly swaying, supported by his wife, he seemed old and weak. Dispenser of Glory and Gloom, I thought, and went to the bazaar. When my shopping was finished, I returned. Ragunath Prasad was sitting in the room; the wife beckoned to me to go in. I was pleased. Ragunath is one of his best disciples, so the atmosphere would be lovely and we won't be disturbed. And it was so . . . all was peace. Left after nine when he was to have his bath.

Together with Mrs. Scott we gave a bath to the new white cock, just bought from the bazaar and which was in unbelievably filthy condition, and to the dachshund. It was fun, and children were delighted.

16th June

WHEN I WENT THERE IN THE AFTERNOON, he asked what time it was. I said it was quarter past four. Stood for a moment at the door of the darkened room.

"Yes, yes," he said. I went in and could not see a thing after the bright sunshine outside. Sat myself in the big chair because the wife slept on the floor lying on the mat under the fan. But soon she got up and went outside. Where I was seated the air from the fan could not be felt. It was very hot. The temperature for the last few days was lower, but the humidity was high, over 80, so it was sultry and very humid. Why not sit on the mat? I did. Took off my sandals and sat in the Sufi posture on the mat in front of him, under the fan. At 4:30 his son-in-law came with a large volume of *Ramayana*. He began to recite. The very rhythm of the recitation, which is really a chanting, creates a special atmosphere of devotion. From time to time I looked up at his face. In his hazel eyes, looking far ahead into the distance, was an unspeakable longing . . . could not bear to look at him. It was the most deep, the most tremendous longing the human eyes can express. It is true: his eyes are special eyes, like nobody else's, and still . . . it was unbearable . . . his very Soul was crying out. I felt tears running down my cheeks. *Ramayana* fills the atmosphere with Bhakti and great love. It went on until seven. His son-in-law has a kind face and lovely eyes. Only he is far too fat for his age—he is still young and already so heavy. From time to time he looked at me in sympathy; I was crying.

At seven the door was opened. I rolled the chik up and went outside. It was cool and pleasant. The temperature was noticeably cooler. Heavy monsoon clouds were hanging low towards the east, grey and saturated with water, but they dispersed soon. Then the sky became quite clear, full of gossamer clouds of delicate rosy-pink. Again he sat in his chair, his overpowering family all around him. When I saluted when going home, he gravely nodded. Going home I was thinking that it was a lovely afternoon. When I went to bed, had hardly any food, was not hungry (but I never am now). There was lightning far away in the east, the Lucknow side. Perhaps the monsoon, I thought . . . but it may pass, need not come this way. Perhaps we will be lucky to have a quiet night and rain will come tomorrow. But about half past eleven it began. I woke up a few minutes before I heard the thunder, and the first impact of the wind began. This looks like the real monsoon. Coming from the east, this is not the local rain. No use to hope that it will be a few drops only. Went downstairs into my room. Had hardly time to reach it when the rain began pelting down—as it only can pour down in the monsoon period, like buckets of water. Was lying in the hot, hot room listening to the rain outside.

The monsoon has arrived . . . will my situation change? Or will it be the endless waiting as before . . . waiting for what?? Ennervating waiting, endlessly, day after day, in the sweltering heat . . . may the Infinite God help me. . . . It rained all night. In the morning the air was warm, very damp, and full of bad smells in our courtyard, of wet chickens, urine, and God knows what else.

He was not on the tachat in the garden as one could well imagine. I saluted; he gravely responded. I noticed when I sat down that I could not see well, could not focus properly, and was giddy. The overpowering family did everything around him, so much activity was going on. Babu was cleaning his throat at the water pipe; all the six children howled in chorus and kept running about. He went into the room. I waited till eight. It was getting hot so I got up and went to the door of the room. Wife was facing the door seated on his tachat; he sat with his back to it. She did not answer, kept talking to him. All right. Clearly I am not wanted inside. But soon he came out and sat in the chair. His face was friendly and he spoke to Sageji to whom he usually does not speak. The drunkard came and he talked with him in a friendly way. Keep still, my heart. . . . Merciful God, give me the strength not to cry, to bear, to bear, endlessly. . . . The Longing was terrible. Yesterday when he prayed, he had a strange *devic* face of sharply cut features, the kind of face which disturbs me because it is like a memory from somewhere . . . but today he had his usual face. And so kindly he spoke to the grandchild, to others . . . how tender he can look, how kind he can be. . . . This kindness was never for me, not even once. . . .

Keep quiet, my heart. . . . Perhaps I will manage somehow, not to cry. . . . I don't see well. Some kind of visual disturbance. The drunkard left soon, thank God. He sat there for another half an hour. I sat on the tachat because all chairs were wet and dirty with children's feet. Later he got up. I hoped he will tell me to come in. But he turned away and went inside. I sat outside. Will wait till ten a.m. Perhaps, perhaps he or his wife will call me in . . . to sit with him alone in deepest peace. I heard his voice in the room talking to his grandchild who was howling once more, then the rapid machine-gun talk of his wife. The rest of his family came out of the big room. Durghesh kept slapping Babu noisily in jest; all were laughing, loudly. In the courtyard all the children were howling, offended about something, a quarrel perhaps. My God, help me to bear it . . . please help. Monsoon is here, but the suffering seems to increase instead of diminishing. Left about ten. Could not bear it anymore. Had very little food. Looked at myself in the mirror; how haggard and grey my face has become. I aged considerably in those few months.

In the afternoon there was a powerful vibration in the heart for hours . . . and then in the solar plexus Chakra. I understood why I could not eat today. This particular vibration used to make me feel sick. I wondered what trouble is brewing for me. When it begins like this, something is being prepared for me.

In the afternoon he was resting, so I went inside silently and sat down. Only later, when the wife came and spoke to him, I got up and saluted. He gravely responded. Soon the son-in-law came and seated himself opposite on the divan. He kept looking at me with his soft, brown eyes with the look of compassion. And I thought that I must present a sorrowful spectacle to his family. A sad, old woman, getting thinner, paler, looking increasingly old and haggard. Nearly always red-eyed because of constant crying . . . my hair looks untidy, because I let it grow, hanging in white, floppy strands around my face. And with this sort of reflection in my mind, the endless longing burning in my heart, I began to cry . . . and I cried. His wife came in; she stood there and looked at me. He was resting on his back. Impassible. Then he said something in Hindi. Son-in-law went and fetched the *Ramayana* and began to recite. I did not experience yesterday's atmosphere; I was slightly bored. So, I began a sort of game to amuse myself. There is a rhythmic verse which keeps coming up from time to time and which is chanted in a different manner from the rest. I began to count these verses. It occurred to me that however many verses there would be, so many days there would be to the First Initiation. I did not mean it seriously, or course—it was a game. I counted them, beginning from the first of June, and when I finished about seven p.m., I arrived at the 18th of July. So, that should be the date according to this improvised oracle . . . I know it is nonsense, but it helped to pass the time.

He came into the garden later and sat in his usual chair with his feet drawn up. I could not help thinking how non-human he can look in the fading evening light. A being from another world . . . a Deva, I thought, observing the light which seemed to radiate from his skin. As soon as I formulated this thought, he gave me a quick sideways glance and looked away. He knew, of course, what I was thinking. His wife, seated beside him, kept talking. I left soon. And going home it occurred to me that there was in my mind a sort of irritation which prevented me from enjoying the *Ramayana*. For his son-in-law recited it very well. I began to pray lying in my bed.

"Are you asleep?" asked a voice. It was young Mrs. Scott. She sat on my bed and we had a chat. When she had left, I realized how silly it was to dramatize something which was of no importance. Truth, I want you more than my life, I said, looking at the stars.

"Do you?" asked a little voice within my heart. "Because if you really do, you would not discuss and question every little thing. . . .

Surrender is surrender . . . it is a blank check. You have to comply with his conditions—never ask, never rebel."

I was at peace and fell asleep. There was no rain after all, and I woke up to the rosy, transparent dawn.

17th June

THERE ARE DAYS WHEN HE LOOKS so incredibly young and of a loveliness which cannot belong to this world of matter. Today was such a day. He always looks special when he is in this kind of double consciousness—one part of him somewhere . . . and still functioning efficiently in this world, in his physical body.

He was reclining on the tachat. In a graceful pose resting one foot on the knee of another, hands clasped behind his back. Sat down not daring to breathe . . . could not look at him. The unearthly light . . . hurting. . . .

One day when complete acceptance is here, there will be no suffering. This feeling of nothingness, as soon as I come into his presence, is a bit disconcerting. But it should increase; it must be more; it is clearly not complete. . . . Why is there suffering? Because of the resistance. I myself am causing it. After all this superhuman effort, all this sacrifice, and privations, to see how others are given what is denied to me—others, who did not even do the tenth part of what I have done—to get nothing and to be content, not to desire, not to rebel, is not human. I am expected to achieve a thing which is against human nature . . . not to desire. . . . Here it is—the very fact of desiring the knowledge creates an obstacle. That's why from the disciple a devotee is formed; the disciple comes for knowledge; the devotee loves and wants to do the Will of the Beloved only, and nothing else. The Teacher is the representative of the Beloved on earth. By doing the will of the Teacher one learns how to do the Will of the Beloved. That's how one becomes like him, merges in Him. The disciple for the time being loses himself—his will becomes the Teacher's will, and by doing that he learns to lose himself in God. . . .

It is the only way. And he repeated it so many a time. And I know it. But when he begins to put all the appearances against him, I forget . . . fall into the trap each time. . . . What to do? . . .

Later he got up and sat in the chair. His body was perfectly still. No breathing was noticeable. His eyes were closed. What peace, my dear God, what peace! How can a human face express such an unearthly peace?!

Then he went in. I left; it was nearly ten a.m.

When I went there about 5:30, the son-in-law was reading from the *Ramayana*. But the child of Durghesh was in the room, shouting and making such a noise, wanting all the time something, so restless. The atmosphere was disturbed, for he had to constantly be pacified. Persian poets are so much lovelier than the *Ramayana*. I wonder why he lately prefers this scripture . . . there must be a reason . . . perhaps it is the rhythm and the special atmosphere it creates. After all, he is a Hindu, and some conditioning pertaining to this culture must be in his make-up.

Later he came out into the garden and sat in his chair. About 7:30 the Sharmas came. I left about eight. Kept thinking all the time. The cessation of desire, all kinds of desire, will represent the cessation of suffering. This is the core of Lord Buddha's Teaching. All the Great Masters teach the same thing.

Lightning was on the horizon in the early evening when I went on the roof. But soon the stars came out and it was a lovely, fresh night. Today the papers say that the monsoon will arrive in our province in forty-eight hours. What we had was only a pre-monsoon shower.

Slept well.

79

To Endure and to Endure

18th June, 1966

COULD HARDLY WALK when I was going to his place. The vibration in the heart was strong and I was giddy. He was sitting in the big chair in his room, his knees drawn up.

"**Hm,**" he murmured when I came. Could not look at him. Feeling of nothingness is increasing. How perfectly lovely he looks for the last few days. Healthy and alert. Soon he went inside. When I was walking up and down in the garden, I saw him in the courtyard squatting on the tachat having a huge breakfast. All fried stuff, as usual, I suppose, and probably almond milk in the bargain . . . the fattening-up continues—with a heart patient, it is unbelievable! Soon the trouble will begin again—the heart will break down, the liver will rebel to the heavy, oily food, will refuse to tolerate the medicines, the vomiting will start, and so it will go on . . . God help him and me. . . .

I asked the wife a little later if I could go into the room, but she made a sign to wait. I waited. Went in about 8:30 when he was already seated in the big chair. He looked so young. It is quite incredible how young his face can look in spite of the grey color of his beard.

Soon he fell asleep seated there, his feet resting on the arm supports of the chair . . . and his young look was not there anymore all of a sudden. He looked haggard and pale. The drunkard came. He kept shifting restlessly, seeing Guruji asleep.

Then I got up and went, hoping by doing so to encourage him to do the same. In fact he left too.

19th June

HE WAS RESTING. I was sitting behind his pillows. When the wife came in, he asked her who was in the room.

"Only Memsahib," she answered.

I winced. . . . He needed to ask if I was there . . . so far am I from him that he does not know that I am here. Or?—could it be?—that such is the nearness that he is unaware of my presence? I hope the latter is the case. . . .

In the afternoon the son-in-law was reading from the *Ramayana*, but his child, who was sitting on the divan pulling garlands of flowers to pieces, disturbed so much. He came to my chair with a tube of penicillin ointment which he kept squeezing. This was too much for me; I went to sit in the big chair. And as he kept being noisy, making remarks about me, I went out. Sat outside. Luckily I soon saw the child running to play with others in the garden. Then I went in. The wife gave me a searching, curious look. I sat down and later the cousin came in. He brought with him the atmosphere of unrest. He is the son of the elder brother who died many years ago, and he says that he is a Mahatma because his father was one. A self blown-up balloon he seemed to me, an insignificant fat Hindu, pleased with himself and vain. Now they will have to divide the property. Guruji will have a difficult time in the next few months. God give him health to bear it all. . . .

Later Guruji came out and sat on the chair. He asked me if I have got a reply from the postmaster. I said, no.

"You should have taken the signature, otherwise there will be no reply."

I got up from my chair and came nearer trying to understand.

"Take the signature from whom, and what for?—I don't understand," I said helplessly standing before him. Strange how the mind behaves in his presence—it can be bewildering. Could not make out what he meant, thought he said something; could only make out that he was speaking but could not get the sense. Somebody came, he interrupted himself, began to talk to the newcomer.

Only when I left half an hour later, I suddenly understood the meaning. Coming out from his garden it flashed clearly into my mind. He meant that I should have registered the letter and got the receipt, otherwise they would not reply.

Passed the night full of longing and a strange, peculiar restlessness. About twelve had to go down into my room as it began to rain.

20th June

PRAYED SO MUCH. Prayed for help to bear it all. . . . Children, all six of them, made such a noise, squealing like rats and howling. I tried to tell myself that it did not disturb, that it did not matter and it didn't make me suffer, but not with much success. Luckily they soon went inside. When I came, I saw the swing hanging from the neem tree. Thank God, it will mean that all the noise will be confined to the furthest part of the garden.

He came out and sat in the chair. After a while he said gently: **"It is much cooler now."**

"Thank God," I said, and felt deep relief realizing that the temperature is really pleasant. In the papers it is recorded daily as 36-37° C.

"I meant to say yesterday . . ." he began.

"Oh," I interrupted him, "I am sorry not to have understood! But it came to me as I left your place: you simply meant that I should have registered the letter and got a receipt. You see it is a question of language barrier . . . with the mind not working, it becomes a hopeless undertaking!" He nodded.

"They don't reply if the letter is not registered." He smiled faintly. Then he began to speak to others. The cousin came with some men; they talked and later he went into the room. I sat in stillness until the drunkard came. Bhai Sahib turned his face to the wall. I left.

In the afternoon the wife was reading the *Ramayana*. He had tears in his eyes. Later he sat outside. All was still. Children were out with their parents. I asked how long Durghesh will remain. He said three or four days. Thank God, I thought, but I said:

"Only?" He gave me a sideways look. I said that I thought that she will remain till the end of July. He shook his head. The horrible pandit croaked non-stop and I prayed to God to give me the strength to bear endlessly. Dolly and Rani came. Dolly said that I looked better, perhaps because it is cooler. I doubted that she meant it.

Left about 7:30. He was talking to a few men. I nearly fell saluting him, and one of them said that I am getting weak.

"No, only a little giddiness; it happens sometimes," I answered. Felt guilty. It won't do to fall; it would look so silly. . . .

21st June

IT WAS A COOL, LOVELY NIGHT. Slept well. And the longing was great and endless in the morning. God is so far . . . non-existent. Vibrations are lately more frequent and begin to be more intense. Something is being prepared. . . .

When I arrived, one of his disciples who stays at his place as his guest, for he does not live in this town, told me with a grin to go into the room.

"But it is early," I said, "he will still have his bath or his breakfast."

"Oh, no," he answered, "he is all right; he has already performed all these things."

I approached his room, looking first inside before entering. The grandson of his Guru was seated in the big chair. I went in and saluted. He hardly noticed me. Soon his wife came and brought some sweets. After that he asked for water and she brought the glass. He made a movement with his hand. I knew what he wanted, so I bent down and put the basin in front of him, taking it from under the bed opposite my chair. He washed his mouth, the wife went out, I took the basin, emptied it and washed it at the pipe in the garden, brought it in and put it back under the bed. He kept talking to the Mohammedan. I wondered if it was done deliberately before the Mohammedan to show him that I serve? Or to test me if I would do so before others?

Later I asked him if I should put the big chair back; it was not standing in its place, but opposite the tachat.

"No," he shook his head. But a few moments later the disciple came in and put the chair in its proper place.

I expected him to tell him to leave it alone, but he let it be, only looked at the chairs; they were not standing quite in a row, as he likes it. So I got up and corrected it. When the Mohammedan was here, he squatted on the tachat talking to him with the wonderfully soft expression he assumes when he is doing some spiritual work. I could not help thinking that he will give him much today. Who knows if he was not ordered to come on purpose. Keep quiet, my heart. . . . Others get. . . . You get nothing. Don't desire, my heart . . . His Will shall be done. . . .

People came. Pandit made a remark that the fan was not on. He ignored it and turned to the wall. They soon left. The homeopathic doctor came. They all streamed into the room including the noisy child. I was left alone in the front room. I sat there in peace . . . the vibration was going on softly.

In the afternoon he hardly noticed me when I came. The wife was with him all the time talking. He took an exceptional interest in every word she was saying, encouraging her to speak with his attitude. Later he lowered his voice, so that the others in the next room could not hear and began to discuss something with her almost in a whisper. I detected the word "Memsahib," so they were discussing something concerning me. Listened with all my attention but could not understand a word to my regret. Could only hear that he mentioned the word "*shishya*,"—perhaps he was telling her that he would make me his *shishya*? But, no, I don't think so. He is just testing me, all right. His face bears this look I know so well by now, a bit cruel and slightly ironical, when he intends trouble for me. From time to time he will look at me, a long, deep, serious look, then he will quickly avert his eyes. He also looks friendlier as if to encourage me to speak. But I had no desire to do so.

Had an afternoon of partly unconscious state. When he came out about 6:30, his son-in-law came too with the volume of *Ramayana* under his arm. He began to recite. Guruji listened and from time to time made a remark—it seemed to me in an ironical way. I asked the disciple who was seated next to me, what was the joke everybody was laughing at. He said that many people came to see Ram in the forest; Guruji wanted to know where they lived. Of course under the trees, the disciple said with conviction, and I thought that it would be quite easy, knowing the Indian conditions, to live under the trees, except in the rainy season; but this cannot last long and, provided the wild animals were kept at large, it could be done. Ram being an Avatar could do this easily with his powers. Later Bhai Sahib interrupted again: this time because it was said that there were 720 women and Sita had to touch the feet of all of them.

"Nonsense!" he said and laughed.

So, he did not accept the *Ramayana* after all, as I have been thinking. . . . And very probably his remarks were intended for the disciple who was a Brahmin and a bit fanatic. Great man as Bhai Sahib is, he will accept only parts of it; every religion is correct in some ways and incorrect in others. None of the religions and philosophies reveals the whole Truth. This must be realized. Consequently none should be understood and accepted literally.

More people came later. An endless discussion began. I went outside. Satendra was sitting alone in the garden looking dark.

"What's the matter?" I wanted to know. He said that he went to his father and told him that he did not like the Brahmin disciple who stays with them.

"He is not a good man!" he added, "he is too proud! But father said: 'Don't speak like this, Satendra! He came here to be changed; this is the place of change!' "

What an answer! I thought, and told Satendra that all Brahmins are proud. Never mind. If Babuji says that he will be changed, it will be all right—is it not so?

But he just sat there looking darkly in front of him. I understood. For the boy the present situation mattered; something in the present arrangement clearly disturbed him. We talked for a while, then I went home for it was eight already.

A lot of lightning was around the horizon in the night. It began to drizzle lightly, but we all stayed on the roof and it was all right. A lovely fresh breeze was blowing all night and the dawn was all orange and gold with greeny-blue patches of sky in between, of most delicate ethereal beauty. The display in the sky lasted for a long time. It was the loveliest sunrise I saw for many years in India. The most magnificent was in Bombay when for the first time I saw the soil of India. . . .

While looking at this loveliness, feeling good in the coolness of the morning I was reflecting: the realization of God is only the beginning. In other Yoga Systems it is the ultimate Goal; in this System it is the first step. And I wondered how the Initiation will be? Will he make me like himself immediately, or are there stages to go through, or what? How will it feel? How will it manifest itself on the level of the mind? And will it feel like Initiation, like something ADDED to me? Or will I be less?

To be taken into the arena . . . but discipleship does not necessarily mean that. People can approach the arena by themselves, by renouncing everything, so he said once. To be taken into the arena is to accept the Path of the Master. No initiation is needed.

God knows how long it will take for me. . . .

The Mohammedan was there; he obviously slept there. Bhai Sahib's cousin, many others came. Property matters were discussed. It was very hot already and I was seated very uncomfortably on a tachat, one leg of which was missing. So I went into the room and switched on the fan. He was in the garden on his tachat on which he slept during the night. Sat under the fan, the heart heavy with longing. A very restless atmosphere was in the air. In the next room they were all talking together; it was a dreadful din. How can they converse like that? It is impossible to understand each other at this rate. The spoiled boy was howling periodically and all children howled after him, all in chorus or one after another. It was a difficult morning. . . .

Decided to sit it out. The heart was aching, aching physically in longing and pain. I sat bent in two, resting my face on my knees. About 9:30 he came in. I got up but was so giddy that I nearly fell. He lay down on the tachat face to the wall. Great peace descended. For some reason I could not even hear the sounds coming from outside. The wife was coming and going, clearly giving him some detailed information of what was going on in the courtyard. As far as I understood, the property was being divided amongst Guruji's family, the brothers and the young cousin, the son of his elder brother; he had one room for himself. He also wanted to bring his wife and children, so I have heard.

It seemed strange to me, why Guruji was not present at this important occasion, important to his children and his family as a whole. But he was lying there, apparently completely indifferent and detached, half listening to his wife. Strange. . . .

The drunkard came. But the servant brought buckets of water in. I went out with the remark that he will have his bath now. The drunkard also went. Lately he has his bath in the room. I think the din in the courtyard is getting too much for him.

Somehow I have the feeling that he is winding up his earthly affairs. Have no proof . . . it is just a feeling. I try to chase it away. Cannot believe it . . . not really . . . but the thought comes back persistently . . . strange.

22nd June

WHEN I ARRIVED, he gave me a letter which was from L. She has sent £20 to K. in Cambridge. L. wants to come here in August or in winter. While I was reading the letter, he was lying on his side looking at me in stony silence. Then the son-in-law came in with the *Ramayana*. I hardly listened. Turned in my mind the possibility that he will send me away again. . . . She was here for two winters while I was away; why does she want to come again? And I began to cry bitterly, hopelessly . . . this longing . . . will it ever stop? This torment? Longing for what? Truth, I suppose, or is it just a terrible feeling of hurt within the heart, which burns up my body. I cried for a long time . . . ran short of hankies though I had three with me in my bag. The chanting was going on. The rhythm of the verses, the flow of the beautiful language. . . . He was lying on his back smiling faintly. I don't know if he did it because of the passage of the *Ramayana* which was just recited, or because I was crying so bitterly. The son-in-law kept casting startled glances in my direction. Later Sharma came. Then we went outside where I sat till 7:30. I shall fall, I thought. I will fall; I won't be able to stand up . . . and sure enough when I got up and saluted him, I fell down at his feet hurting my wrist a little. Was very embarrassed. Sharma looked very startled and I nearly ran out from the garden. . . . Next day I wore a light bandage around my wrist. Did not sleep well. Fell asleep in the early hours of the morning, looked at the moonless sky, the Milky Way, so clear and bright. Fancy! To think that we are on the very edge of it, our little earth . . . seems incredible. Was thinking of the hatred in me which represents a great obstacle. How every dark patch in my character, one by one, came on the surface like foam on the water . . . and gradually was removed. . . . But still there is a lot of it.

This morning when I came, he was taking his bath at the pipe in the garden. He will catch a cold, I thought. A cold can be his death. . . . I went in when two men came, but they soon left. I remained till nine, till I went to Sharma. This hard, cold, stony face . . . this is always for me, or most of the time it is. Smiles and kindness are for others . . . this face only, is for me. And he was dressed all in white . . . perhaps he was thinking that I would want to speak to him. But lately I have no such desire. He is all right as he is. Have no questions to ask, no comments to make. Looked at his face so forbidding, and my longing grew and grew. Managed not to cry . . . I had to go. Sharma gave me the check. Went to the bank to cash it and then to Guruji to give him the 420 rupees. Was so glad to be able to give it to him. He counted the notes with deliberate slowness, one by one. And I saluted and went to my lunch of mangos and boiled rice.

80

Hard Times Are Passing Away

23rd June, 1966

A KIND OF IRRITATION . . . cannot put my finger on it . . . have an urge to speak to him . . . I watched his face. He looked stern but not unfriendly. Perhaps . . . I will try. . . .

When we were in the room, we were alone. I leaned forward. He was sitting in the big chair and I near the head of his tachat.

"May I speak to you?"

"Hmmm?" He turned his head in my direction with the vacant expression as if pretending not to understand, his usual way when he wants to make it difficult for me. I repeated the question softly and clearly. He nodded with the stoniest expression. Instantly my mind left me and went somewhere . . . I managed to get hold of it somehow and began to speak. When I have this urge, I HAVE TO SPEAK—it is like a compulsion. I was aware that my voice sounded strained, not natural.

"It is this pain . . . this terrible pain which is drying up my body. The longing day and night causing even physical pain, and it makes me feel so weak. I cry all the time; it is a kind of pathological state." Tears came into my eyes and my voice choked. Somebody appeared at the door, stood there for a moment and vanished. "Cry nearly all the time; cry here before you, cry at home, cry in the night." Somebody else appeared at the door, stood there and vanished, letting the curtain drop. His face was still . . . a face immobile, of pale marble. . . .

"I wanted to speak to you because, when I am in this state, it is a relief to be able to do so. I am not complaining. Not at all. Sometimes I pray to God for help, sometimes to your Rev. Guru Maharaj. I know it is a weakness; we don't get more than we can bear. If I am given trouble, it means that somebody, somewhere, knows that I can bear it. Somebody has faith in me. This Somebody must not be disappointed. So I HAVE to bear it.

"Then there is this feeling of non-being. You remember perhaps that at the beginning, when it began to happen, I used to get so frightened that I was running away. To get out of your presence, to the bazaar, to Pushpa, anywhere. It was so confusing. I was frightened by it—confusing because the human being is never 'nothing.' One is always 'something,' the body, the mind, the 'me' and the things which are not me. When somebody says, for instance: I am nothing before you, you are so great—it is not that; it is not what I mean. This can be flattery, the self is still there. But in this feeling of nothingness there is . . . NOTHING! Just that: nothing at all! A void! I cannot explain it better. When I speak to you, as I do now, for instance, of course I know that I am speaking to you. But when I just sit there in silence, at one moment I notice that there is only you—nobody else seems to be here. A frightening experience. I used to pinch my fingers to see if I am not dreaming." Durghesh and Babu, faces tense with curiosity, appeared at the door. I looked at them, continuing to speak. They dropped the curtain and vanished.

"I suffer from great sudden fear, a sort of panicky feeling . . . cannot account for it; it grips me suddenly; it is most disconcerting. Please, tell me: is this surrender?" Munshiji came into the room, stood at the door, saw that I was talking and went out.

"Perhaps it is not surrender, or only partially. I will be so grateful if you would explain." And I went on like this for a while but most of it I don't remember now . . . after a while I fell silent . . . feeling that I had said enough and should not say more. He remained absolutely motionless during this time. Soon afterwards Satendra came in. Bhai Sahib said something to him and the boy brought the mala. I saw it was the one he used on special occasions, belonging to his Guru Maharaj. Clearly something is being done. When I was full of trouble four years ago, he used this particular mala every day. I think he is praying for me when he uses it. . . .

He remained in complete, stony silence. Slowly the mala began to slide through his fingers. I am not even sure that he has heard everything or was in Samadhi. I am glad though that I told him. It gives me a sense of relief. The terrible longing, the pain is less. . . .

27th June

I HAVE LOST THREE DAYS. A complete blank. A hole in my memory which is getting too hopeless for words. . . .

This morning his breathing was difficult and his voice raucous. He caught cold, he is so unreasonable! He never wants to listen to anybody. This morning, for instance, he stood in the doorway in full draught, clad only in a thin singlet and a very flimsy longhi.

Later I sat in the doorway because it began to rain once more. He was inside the courtyard on the tachat reciting his prayers, the pale green jade mala sliding noiselessly through his fingers.

My body feels very weak.

28th June

YESTERDAY WHEN I CAME, he was resting turned to the wall. My torturer, I thought sitting down. Heart was aching unbearably. He turned on his back, and I was just thinking, shall I get up and salute him, as he seems to have awakened, when the chair on which I was sitting made a few jerks sideways, like a ship. An earthquake! flashed through my mind. He quickly sat up.

"Did you feel it? An earthquake!" I said, getting up and saluting him.

"Open the door!" he ordered. His wife came in. She felt nothing apparently. We all went outside where he squatted under the mango tree. The brother came. He also felt it; people arrived; everybody was discussing it. But he was immersed in thought; he was not interested.

The longing, the longing for Truth . . . it was burning unbearably in the night . . . and the body was on fire again. . . . Rain began to pour down like yesterday. Slept in my room as in the last few days. During the night my left eye was itching very much, and in the morning it was so swollen that I could not open it. What could it be? I felt no pain. When looking in the mirror this morning I was thinking that I was looking dreadfully old. The face quite wrinkled, tired, the skin sagging around the mouth, and the neck scraggy. Old, old woman of eighty. . . . What six months with you did to my body, my Sheikh. . . . Poor old body. Felt sorry for myself. But chased this idea away; it is of no importance, not really. Other things are much more important; this is nothing. Still, felt a bit sorry; could not help it. It was raining heavily when I went to his place. The door was open, the room empty except for Ram Singh, the servant, sweeping the floor. Sat down when he finished. He came in. Got up and saluted. He distractedly nodded. Pointed to my wet raincoat which I had hung near the door.

"This," he said, **"outside."** I took it out and hung it on one nail of the chik outside.

A young man came in. He is quite new, has come only for the last few days. He seems to be very nice, educated, clean, and has the right attitude of a good Indian disciple before the Guru—of silence and recollection. When for the first time he came, Bhai Sahib, who was talking to Durga Shankar, suddenly interrupted himself and then said in a very friendly way:

"Come in, come in!"

This morning the young man came in, quietly touched his feet and sat down. Bhai Sahib who sat on the tachat began to talk to him. The wife came in, offered tea to the old Brahmin who lives next door and who was sitting there too. He accepted and got a glass. She asked if I wanted some. I declined because I had two cups already at home.

"Just look at this," I said to her lifting my face. She looked at the swelling and said something to her husband.

"What, what?" I got up and knelt beside his tachat so that he could see for himself, telling him that it does not hurt at all.

"It will go away by itself; it is probably a poisonous insect bite. You can consult a doctor," he added.

"I will consult nobody. I consulted you," I smiled.

He continued to speak to the young man. By the few words I understood in Hindi, he was explaining the Path; the word *Atma* occurred frequently, and *Abhyasa* and *Sadhana*. I listened, trying hard to understand at least something. Alas! My Hindi was too poor to understand a conversation of this kind. My heart became too heavy for words. For me there was nothing of the sort. So few explanations were ever given . . . all I got was stern silence, and heartache and all kinds of trouble . . . and darkness, and so much suffering, and this is going on for years . . . and I began to cry. The despair I felt was so boundless, inexpressible . . . it never seemed to end. . . . He glanced at me while talking.

"You should consult a doctor. Dr. Bannerji will give you a dose of homeopathic medicine. It will cure you; why suffer pain?"

I swallowed heavily with tears.

"There is much pain, but it is not in my eye."

"One should use a remedy when there is a possibility," he said, glancing at me and looking quickly away. He continued to give explanations which seemed to be so interesting because the young man was quite agog with attention.

Left about ten a.m. I am a fool. I should stop trying to understand. He does all this deliberately, because I am still after knowledge. I should forget about it, should not want it even. But I still do. . . .

29th June

WHEN I CAME HE ASKED about my eye.

"You had said that it will become better by itself, and so it will be. I am not worried." He murmured something which sounded like assent.

Told him about a letter I received from London about a friend who is so ill-treated by her husband. He nodded slowly.

"Sometimes ladies suffer too cruelly. A woman can never be so cruel as a man. A man can be terribly cruel to a woman." He fell silent, sighed and turned to the wall. The nice young man came and sat there looking at him in silence. The wife came in, asked if he was in pain and began to massage his head. Later he went into the other room and had some food. Then he came and I went because it nearly stopped raining. At home had only one *chappathi* and some tea. Had a restless night, full of longing and waking up each time my heart cried to God. It was raining heavily non-stop. In the morning it became a drizzle.

Went as usual at seven a.m. Sat in the doorway. Later I noticed that he was in the courtyard, went to the half-closed door and saluted. After a while Poonam came and said:

"Father calling."

I went into the room. He sat in the big chair. I sat down near his pillow. We sat in silence. Bhai Sahib was resting. Ravindra came in. I heard how he asked Ravindra to arrange an overdraft for me. My postal orders cannot be cashed because of devaluation. They discussed it for a while and Ravindra turned to me and said that he will do his best. I told him that my position is serious; I have arrears of last month rent to pay, the rent is due again, and I have to eat. He promised to get me 150 rupees. I hope he will. When he left, Bhai Sahib began to tell me about the difficulties of maintaining such a large family.

"The trouble is that your children seem to think that you get money quite effortlessly."

"They are right, I could. But we don't use such means. There is a way to attract money from all corners of the world, but it is improper to do so." Then he said that some of his disciples helped during the crisis of his illness, and then told me not to worry; my situation will be arranged. I was grateful, and told him so.

"I am in every kind of difficulty since I left Mrs. Sharma." At this moment Babu came in to listen to every word.

"But it is better for you now, since you left her," he said kindly.

"This is true, only the physical conditions are difficult, but I am getting used to it by now, and people with whom I live are so kind to me." He leaned forward, took his diary from the recess in the wall and began to write. Babu was drumming with his fingers on the armrest of the chair. He raised his head and looked at him. Babu stopped. After a while he went out. It was very still in the room . . . the scraping of his pen, an occasional movement of the chik caused by the wind.

"**Hard times,**" he suddenly smiled, "**in one way or another are passing away.**"

My heart gave a quick beat of joy.

"But it seems to me that hard times are only beginning. . . . This increased longing is leading somewhere . . . this terrible longing which is drying up my body. And it is not the climate. The climate was responsible for it to some degree, but no more . . . now it is all right, it ·is less hot; besides, the body gets used to climatic conditions."

A quick, kind smile passed over his face, like an unexpected ray of sunshine. He began to talk in Hindi to his son who came in from the garden. Then a discussion began with his wife and Munshiji who joined him. I left. The rain had stopped. Could it be? Could it be, that really hard times are passing, as he said? Seems too good to be true. . . . Joy filled me. . . . Streaks of first light of dawn are showing on the bleak sky of my destiny. Still pale, livid, very faint, but my heart was telling me: the dawn is not very far off. . . . Strange how he always finds the right word. Yesterday and this morning I lost all hope. Was thinking out some means to force him . . . it seemed all so hopeless going on endlessly. . . . No change at all. . . .

The street was full of noise, traffic, people, the pavement very wet, every puddle reflecting the colors of the sky. Tried to avoid being splashed by passing cars. But it was all lovely, so full of life. I felt so deeply happy. . . . In the west the sun was setting in the sea of shimmering golden clouds. The whole world seemed to be illumined by this vivid gold, was transformed by it. I had to cross Chowraha (circus, where six streets were meeting) to get to the baker's shop. I very rarely have bread, mostly make chappathies for myself, but today I hoped to get some brown bread. Before entering the bakery I stopped and looked back; this lovely golden light—the Great Painter delighted Himself to paint the busy streets with His magic. And I saw that right across Chowraha was a magnificent rainbow . . . so clear, vivid and bright, against the golden sky, and I must have walked right under it. I must have, if it is right there where I was passing . . . I stood for a while enchanted. There is a Russian saying: when one walks under a rainbow, it means that if one has a wish or a desire it will be fulfilled. I could not believe it . . . passed under a rainbow . . . and my Master told me that my troubles are passing away. . . . What an omen. . . . I don't think that I ever was so happy in my life . . . with this special happiness, never experienced before . . . passing away. . . . Passing away . . . and I had difficulty to fall asleep out of sheer happiness.

June 30th

SLEPT FAIRLY WELL. Woke up about four a.m. It started pouring with rain. We all hurriedly, clasping our bedding, scrambled downstairs into our rooms. Began to think about my financial situation—the rent which was due tomorrow—and wondering if Ravindra will be able to arrange to get me some money. I was lying on my left side, knees drawn up. All of a sudden I felt a very strong vibration at the base of the spine. I didn't have it for a long time and it was unusually strong. Thinking that perhaps I am mistaken, and it is the air from the fan blowing in my direction which is causing this impression, I got up, switched off the fan and lay down in the same position. Sure enough, after a few seconds the sensation repeated itself. And it was so strong, as it was when I had those troubles four years ago. I was lying still, fearing to move in case it goes away. I wanted to study it. Yes, at a few seconds' intervals it kept repeating itself. Then I turned over on my back and it was gone. Well . . . unusual. The activation of the dangerous Chakra . . . very strange. Had a cup of coffee. The body felt weak and tired. Later while I stood under the shower, the water running over my body, the vibration began again. Strong. And this time it stayed with me. There was no feeling of heat nor feeling of pain, but this usually comes after the Chakra had worked for a while. Even sometimes for days. I was a bit alarmed. Went to him. It was raining softly. It was like an English summer day. Sat in the doorway; the room was still closed. The nice young man came. He also sat in the doorway and I gave him some additional hints about the Path. Some days ago the young school teacher was there, and Bhai Sahib ordered me to talk to him. I did. Difficult to speak in Guruji's presence. At one moment I noticed that he stared at me with those tremendous eyes which don't look at the physical body but at something else.

"I cannot speak further," I said helplessly . . . Guruji . . . the mind went completely . . . complete blank. He looked away. I managed to continue, starting from the point where I stopped.

Later this young man came, and Bhai Sahib told me to acquaint him with some aspects of Sufism. He went out then, and I talked to the young man. Later he came back and lay down face to the wall. We continued to talk in a low voice. This morning he wanted some additional explanations which I tried to give him as well as I could.

Later we were called into the room. He was praying and we sat still. Then I saw him looking at me.

"I think I will die of it," I said, meaning the longing and the vibration. He shook his head in a very definite way.

"Hard times come, sometimes are necessary, but they pass, are passing."

Feel great nervous tension. Had only mangos and water. The longing is very great. Some uneasiness at the base of the spine. Is something brewing??

1st July

HE CAME OUT DRESSED in white kurta. People came bringing flowers, money and fruit. When I asked if there was some kind of festivity, he said that it was the Guru Pooja day. He began to talk to me. The opening was a statement of how difficult it is to achieve on this Path, to become a Deputy. I kept thinking why is he talking like this. Lately the mind was tranquil; all went well: will he begin again? To apply pressure? Sure enough, he began the old story of my bad behavior, how I don't know how to respect the Teacher, my ignorance, and so forth.

"But, you said it yourself, that you don't remember evils, so why do you keep repeating those old stories of years ago?"

"No, evils are not remembered, but faults are always remembered and pointed out." What? I thought, but in this moment the mind went and all I could do was try to follow as well as I could what he was talking about. Satendra sat there as though glued to his chair. Then he went inside and fell asleep face to the wall. I went to the bazaar, tried to get nice fruit, but only mangos were available. He will get plenty of those today, so I bought a box of glucose bisquits; they will keep and he can eat them when he is not well. Went back, gave him three rupees and the box of bisquits as an offering. Touched his feet like all others, then sat down and cried bitterly. The road seemed so hard, the goal so far, so immensely far away, and he has no pity on me. He always will say or do something to arouse my mind against him. Now he is trying to appear revengeful. What a statement that faults are always remembered . . . and I got such a fit of despair. My heart seemed to burst. Unbearable. What is the matter? Why is it that the mind gives trouble always? Because it looks to me that I have created a conventional image of a Christian Saint, and if he did not conform to this image, the mind rebelled. And it is the same story for years and I still fall into the trap. He WILL put all the appearances against him; he will appear full of faults and all kinds of defects. He shows himself to be just the opposite of the ideal I created of him. If I don't destroy this image, this idol, the mind will give trouble forever. He will do everything he thinks necessary for the sake of training.

"Training?" he nearly shouted in reply to one of my remarks. **"Nothing was done with you; I did not even begin!"** True. Because it is all preparation. Because, clearly I have to surrender first. Then the way will be easy, if I can make it. But the goal seems to recede . . . it seems more and more difficult to achieve. . . .

I simply must remember that. Why is it that I constantly keep forgetting it: he will do what he likes and it will always be the opposite of my conventional Saint. Kept thinking it all over. Went to him, saw that he was reading my mind. I know by now so well this look he gives me. I also knew that he expected me to talk. He sat opposite me on the divan. But I kept quiet.

2nd July

WAS THINKING A LOT IN THE NIGHT. Must tell him about it. I bet he is already outside waiting for me. He was, and I began to talk immediately. He attacked me in a hard and angry mood.

"I don't want to listen. You are full of impurities, your mind is," he hissed at me. **"You will never progress, NEVER, NEVER, NEVER progress! I tell you this in the most definite way!"** He was really angry. He was hard.

"It will take you years. You are too much for me!" He said with a grimace of disappointment. There was a moment of panic in my mind. There is NO TIME LEFT! Something cried out in me, in such a distress that I became ice cold. The mind worked so badly. I tried to compose myself . . . tried to explain, but all I could do was stammer. Ravindra came to sit there and listen. Never can one speak alone, all is in public. . . .

I left at quarter past eight. I thought that he understood nothing at all. He thought that it was an ordinary mind trouble. I could not explain that I have discovered the root of the trouble so it seemed. Rested at home, kept thinking and thinking . . . am so confused.

In the afternoon sat there—he was sleeping. His wife kept looking at me in a strange way. I wondered; perhaps she thinks that I am disturbing him? Perhaps I do?

3rd July

THE DAY WAS QUITE UNEVENTFUL. He ignored me completely. A Saint cannot be unjust because God is Just. Is He? What about the couplet of Rumi:

"I am the theft of the rogue, I am the pain of the sick."

And in the *Gita*:

"I am the gambling of the cheat."

4th July

TRIED TO TELL HIM QUIETLY my reflections as above, including the couplet of Rumi. His wife was shouting at the servant, children were crying. And he listened in stony silence.

5th July

THINKING DEEPLY and the body is very tired. All I can do is to drag it to Bhai Sahib's place. Then to drag it to the bazaar. There I look at the vegetables and cannot face the thought of food . . . don't know what to buy. Then at last I decide on something. Go home. Cook. Eat or not, accordingly. Often I throw away good food to the chickens outside. Am so tired. Body gets thinner and thinner. . . .

If one looks at it closely, this fact of the mind not working, being switched off, is quite an interesting phenomenon. I clearly remember that once in the past he said that the mind is paralyzed in order that the Buddhic qualities have the chance to come through.

One walks in the street as though drunk. All one is able to do is to try not to be overrun by the traffic. One can see only what is immediately in front, but right and left is as if one had blinkers; one cannot see; all one does is distorted, as if one were drunk or drugged.

I remember vividly, in summer when I was staying in Mrs. Ghose's flat, in '62. Came home, put the key into the keyhole, turned it, opened the gate into my courtyard. Locked it behind me, automatically. The courtyard was filled with blinding sunlight,

hurting the eyes, as hot as an oven. I stood near the door. Helpless . . . what have I to do? Ah, yes, I am hungry; I have to eat. To
eat? Then I should cook something . . . cook, cook . . . looked
around. Potatoes . . . must have some potatoes, somewhere. . . . I
looked at them, but it took time to realize that those were potatoes.
Aha! Here they are! A sense of relief. But I have to peel them . . . to
peel . . . I would need a knife. A knife, a knife . . . I was looking at
it, but it took time to understand that I was looking at a knife. The
mind worked as a kind of slow motion picture, causing delayed
action. And so it went on. It is quite painless, but life becomes
difficult. Luckily this acute state never lasted long. Perhaps only a
few hours, never more than half a day. And it never happened in
London when I was away from him, though the mind was sometimes
abstracted as if working at a quite different level.

A psychiatrist told me that those are symptoms of schizophrenia,
in this case created artificially by the Yogic Power of the Guru. And
she added that spiritual life and spiritual understanding are difficult
for somebody who is rational, perfectly normal, standing firmly with
both feet on the ground. But if there is something NOT QUITE RIGHT
with the mind, if it is just a little out of focus, so to say, spiritual states
are easy. I suppose that's why the Guru creates this state of "mindlessness" in order to help the disciple. . . .

81

The Pressure Increases

"YOU WILL NOT PROGRESS," he said. The Goal is so far, so far away, and I cannot pray and I am alone. . . .

YESTERDAY THERE WAS AN AYURVEDIC DOCTOR there; his age is 81. He just took his pulse, told Guruji all that was wrong with him, and gave him a diet. He wants to be admitted to the Path. He will succeed. He has the right attitude. And didn't he say once that He in His Mercy is so kind to old people? They get every possible help and opportunity.

Bhai Sahib gave me G.'s letter which he had received. I read it while at his place. He came out looking stern, chewing something. When he finished chewing, I asked him if I could read G.'s letter to him. He said no.

"Only a few sentences I don't know how to deal with," and I read the sentences to him. He shook his head when I told him that G. wants a Sadhana.

"But you give practices to so many people. Why can't G. get one?"

"He will never be able to do it. He is a worldly man and must be treated as such," he said, his face stony and hard.

"Everybody is worldly at the beginning." I was perplexed. The worldliest people get the V.I.P. treatment from him sometimes . . . why this answer? Decided that he wants me to deal with the case, and the harshness is deliberate that I should accept the unjust treatment. All right. I will deal with it as well as I can. I will get help. And one day God will help me to understand. Will He??? I feel so tired . . . it is all so hopeless. The goal is further away than ever. . . . Lovely letters full of hope and faith I receive from so many people in London . . . and I feel that I am letting them down. I myself don't get anywhere, nor is it sure that I will. They hope, poor souls, and I am letting them down. . . .

Dear God, will you help me? Dear God, PLEASE!

8th July

WHEN THE HUMAN BEING IS DRYING UP with the terrible longing, crying day and night, Truth cannot be far away. . . . A few nights ago I was crying: Truth: hurry-up! If you don't come soon, you won't find the physical body . . . I am getting weaker and weaker. . . .

Yesterday I wrote down the sentence: I will accept the unjust treatment. And the word "unjust" gave me a clue; injustice is the worst thing for me. That's why he is testing me with the emphasis on all kinds of unjust treatments. And I became full of peace. . . . If I am able to accept it, a great step forward would be made. All became still in me. And the irritation, I noticed, was no more. . . . Somehow, I felt this irritation was not mine. Probably it was "put on" for the sake of the test. It wouldn't be for the first time. . . .

This morning he came out about quarter to eight. Looking dynamic and ironical, as I know by a certain crease of his lips in quarrelsome mood. In fact he told Ram Singh off, told Hosla off, and both servants were sent to do something in the courtyard. And he sat there chewing vigorously. The Ayurvedic doctor prescribed a medicine which he had to chew for a long time, so he was sitting and chewing. He is going to test me every day now, I thought, and began to pray to his father, to his Rev. Guru Maharaj, to Him, whom I wanted so much . . . Him, the Infinite, the Truth . . . help me all of you! I hardly have any strength left to go on!

Ravindra just bought from a peddler some aubergine (eggplant) and put them temporarily in the earth to be planted in the evening. I thought he put them in the mud in the irrigation groove, but when I looked later, I saw that he put them in dry earth in full sun. By this evening they will be stone dead, so I got up and went into the courtyard, got a jar from Ram Singh, and passing him to go to the pipe I said: "He put them in full sun. They will be dead by the evening, so I will water them." He made a grimace. I could not interpret the meaning of it—he was still chewing. I watered them and went to get another jar of water, for it did not seem quite enough. While I was passing him, he said with irritation:

"Why do you meddle with affairs which don't concern you? Always useless talk, useless actions!" He gave me an angry look.

"Yes," I said meekly, lowering my head not to look at his irritated expression. Smiled faintly, hoping it would pacify him, turned back, went into the courtyard and returned the jar to the servant. Then sat down on a chair not far from his own. He was chewing violently with an irritated absent-minded air. Here we are. A test. I looked at my mind. As still as a mirror . . . and he is right. Why do I meddle, even if I mean well? While I was fetching water, I was thinking that the fellow is not much of a gardener. That might be true, but still it is not my business, and if I would have pointed it out to him, even jokingly, that he should have watered them, I would have hurt his feelings probably. Soon I asked if I could go into the room. It was unbearably sultry, and flies were sticky, not letting me in peace.

Soon he came in too, rested at first on his back, then he turned his face in my direction. I sat bent in two with the hand covering my eyes. But when I raised my head, I saw him giving me a few rapid glances. Then he went out and I left for home.

9th July

YESTERDAY AFTERNOON THEY PLAYED CARDS in the next room. I sat in the darkened front room sweating under the fan; it was very hot. Then I heard loud music from the courtyard; it sounded like a radio. Those were records played by Ravindra, and he and his brothers listened, as well as a few of his disciples. All of a sudden Virendra came running into the room, stopped dead, looked at me and ran out. A few seconds later he came running back, dashed into the room where I was sitting, switched on the light and stared at me in not a very friendly way. I just sat reclining in the chair, looking at him in surprise. He switched off the light and went quickly out. I thought that it was a strange sort of behavior. Later, after seven, when we all sat outside with Guruji, I saw him passing by, staring at me. He went to the pipe where the servant Ram Singh just finished his bath and began to say something about me. They looked at me and laughed, and Virendra was telling him something about my head. I understood it by the gesture he made with the hand around his head. They both laughed. I must be careful. He often uses his family members as pawns in his game of training people. He did it with L. and with me, many a time. Resolved to be careful with Virendra.

When I was lying in bed before falling asleep, I suddenly noticed a feeling of heat and burning far up in the throat, higher than the palate. Something seemed to run down from the sinus into the throat and the nose. I have no head cold, so what could it be? The burning and the dry sensation was like a cold, deep inside, but I was sure that it was not that. Later I blew my nose and found a slightly painful sensitivity in the left nostril. I seemed to breathe only through the left nostril, but the right one was not blocked, so how was it that it did not work at all? It was strange. It must have to do with the Brow Chakra. At any rate I slept well. But it was a very hot night.

In the morning he did not look well. I waited for a test. We were sitting in silence. My heart was at peace. I keep praying all day calling on Him. Help me, help me to go through with it! And I prayed sitting before him. About eight I went inside under the fan. Helped Ram Singh to make his bed. He remained outside. I heard him talking to the wife and somebody else. About nine he came and sat exhausted under the fan. I left with the remark that he is freer when I am not there; he can relax better; this heat is affecting him.

In the afternoon they played cards. It was dreadfully hot . . . and not even a little breeze. The air was perfectly still. The worst possible weather for somebody who is not well. He looked pale and very tired. I left soon, could not sit there much longer. He was in the courtyard under the fan. I did not want to go and sit there—only his family was with him; I would intrude. On the other hand, I could not sit in the garden, so I sat in the doorway. It was unbearable. Could not stand it for much longer. Left for home. It was still very early.

10th July

TODAY IS SUNDAY. One week has gone since he spoke to me, since he provoked the crisis. Then came the astounding discovery that it was not an ordinary disturbance; it was due to the discovery that all my troubles are because I made an image of him which was completely wrong.

A discovery is always disturbing. Then two tests came: this time I hope that I passed them both. And I pray, pray, and pray all the time that I may be tested quickly soon—one blow after another, while the iron is still hot . . . but perhaps he cannot do that. After each test the human being is getting something, something is done to push him on, and on, further on the Path, and one must get time to recover.

When I told him that I had to go home yesterday evening, because it was unbearably hot, he was squatting on the tachat under the fan in the courtyard.

"Yes, yes," he said, hardly glancing at me. But there was for a split second a fleeting expression of such deep tenderness and compassion that it was like a stab right into the heart. And I cannot forget it. I don't remember that I have seen it before . . . never . . . and it was so quick—it was, and it was not—that one could easily think that one is mistaken. But I knew that I was not. . . .

This morning he looked tired. Seated opposite him I kept praying. He wore his devic expression. I just looked and looked . . . how deeply noble, inhumanly dynamic his face becomes . . . of unearthly beauty . . . and my heart was crying to him in an endless stream of loneliness.

Later I went into the room. He was talking to his tenant about some arrears of rent. It was unbearably hot again and I went home. The night was hot too, but I slept not too badly. While I am writing this down, there is a strong vibration which began after lunch. And the feeling of nothingness, so difficult to bear . . . it makes the body feel so weak, so tired. Seated before him this morning, I was thinking that I have three helpers: Love, Longing and the Feeling of Nothingness. . . . They are my stand-by. And I need only to sink into Nothingness to be able to bear anything and everything. But who will bear? There is nobody to bear surely, if Nothingness prevails . . . it is a familiar feeling somehow. I seem to have known it always . . . only for the personality it is new. . . . It must become familiar for the personality too, otherwise how can one surrender? And it is of such sweetness. . . . At first it was neither pleasant nor unpleasant; later it was like a sorrowful happiness, a stillness, a peace in it. Now it is bliss; it begins to be glorious . . . to be not . . . for ever and ever . . . not to be myself, but a part of him forever. . . . It is a transcendent feeling, a kind of ecstasy perhaps? Difficult to know. There is a strong vibration. Something is brewing??

11th July

IN THE AFTERNOON THEY PLAYED CARDS and I sat sweating profusely under the fan in the dark front room. Later they finished and all went into the courtyard. I was very thirsty. So I opened the side door and went to the pipe and had a long drink. When I returned, my heart stood still for a second; he sat on the tachat looking bad-tempered. I did not expect to see him there; a moment ago I heard his voice in the courtyard. I felt apprehension, a sort of dark fear . . . went in closing the door behind me.

"Why do you close? Leave it open!" he said irritably. I opened the door, pulled the chair on which I was sitting in line with others, and turned the seat cushion.

"Why do you turn it?" His voice was harsh.

"Because I was sitting on it, I thought I had better turn it in case somebody else would want to sit here. But if you wish it, I will not turn it." I put the cushion back as it was before, went to the window

near the front door and opened it because I know that at this time of
the day he wants it to be open. Then I pulled the armchair nearer to
the fan, but he gave me an irritable look, so I put it back again and
came to sit on the divan. Looked at his profile for he was sitting
sideways. My heart was burning with sorrow and pity. He was
transparent; he seemed not to be here, so weak he looked. . . . At
one moment he turned his head and gave me one of his deep, long
looks, right into the soul. I was watching my mind. It was very still,
and I continued to pray all the time thinking that he will continue to
test me, but he turned to the wall. Three tests in one week, I reflected,
The pressure increases—he tightens the screws . . . hmm. The most
surprising thing is that it did not hurt at all. Not so long ago I was
desperate when he was angry with me: the world seemed to crash to
pieces—the sky was falling with fear quite disproportionate to the
occasion. And now, nothing! Some help must have been given; how
much, I will never know. Has the feeling of nothingness something to
do with it? There is simply nobody here to be upset. Or perhaps I am
more detached since I have understood that I have made a sort of idol
of him, a kind of illusion which does not hold? So all in me crashed,
went to pieces . . . I hope it will last. . . .

When I walk to his place, I pray. I seem to pray all day long. . . .

11th July

"LIKE A TREE struck by lightning, I crashed before Thee;
Like a star which falls from the sky its light spent forever,
So I spent myself before Thee like this star. . . .
Like a stone thrown into the lake by the playful hand of a child
Goes down into the utmost depth never to come up again—
So I went down before Thee, once and for all. . . ."

Have been reflecting upon those lines of this Persian poem, sitting
before him; he was resting face to the wall. . . .

The night was a nightmare of sultry stillness. The flame of a candle
would not have moved, when lit, all night . . . I was lying in a pool of
perspiration. All I could do to make it bearable was to pray and to
pray to Him, offering my discomfort to Him and thinking of Bhai
Sahib, how difficult it must be for him . . . there was no question of
sleep.

In the morning I thought that he will test me again and I prayed
much. But he did not.

H.'s letter which she sent about the middle of May arrived—by sea
mail!! She must have forgotten to put airmail stamps on it—how

careless! And she caused me so many weeks of trouble because of that!!

12th July

IN THE AFTERNOON YESTERDAY TWO WOMEN and two youngsters were sitting there. They seemed to be glued there forever, and he talked to them kindly. I thought that they were his disciples; but no, he told me today that they came for the first time, are cotton-mill owners, and full of the most terrible trouble.

"**Why do they come to me?**" he added thoughtfully.

The electric current failed and I fanned him for more than fifteen minutes with my hand-fan. He was glistening with perspiration; his breathing was uneasy. He told me that he had a vomiting condition due to the heat.

"**Heat is unbearable for me lately,**" he said. At six p.m. I stood up, and saluted him. Such heat in the small room full of people all talking! I could not bear it anymore. . . .

"**Where are you going?**" he wanted to know. I said that I was going home to have a bath (the sixth since this morning). I did not feel well due to the heat.

"You don't mind?"

"**No, no, I don't mind at all,**" he said in a friendly manner, and I left. Had my bath and slept in the room under the fan hoping that it would be better than on the roof heated all day by the sun. It was not, and I hardly slept at all, twisting and turning, the body itchy and wet all the time.

This morning he came out to have his bath at the pipe just when I was arriving. He looked magnificent—his torso naked to the waist standing there glistening like a bronze statue, pouring water over his body. Slender, majestic, bearded face, stern, serene. . . .

When he sat down I told him about H.'s mistake.

"**Don't be hard to her; she cannot bear it just now,**" he said. "**All human beings are not alike; just point out the mistake to her. . . .**"

Later he said: "**My Rev. Father and Mother were of the Chishtia Dynasty. They only followed my Rev Guru Maharaj. But the Dynasty remains in the blood always. Chishtias are like a magnet. Many things are done through the physical body so it becomes magnetic. They are for the public.**

"**Body attracts body, but with us soul attracts soul. For us the physical body is of secondary importance. We don't care much about it; it does what it can. The ways of working are different. We rarely come down to the level of the public. But sometimes we do; it** is service; otherwise why should we come down? When people came to me I told them: go to my father! My Rev. Guru Maharaj, he remained inside, he did not come out and people were sitting. Ninety-nine percent went away. Those who want to remain will remain."

When I told him that I pray practically all day long he said:

"This is the way how to do it. Pray, pray, much. And another thing; when you are alone in the room and nobody sees you, bow down. If one bows down before the superiors, what happens? The heart of the Superiors melts. If the human being bows down before the Almighty, Grace and bliss stream down. Only in the Muslim Religion they bow down five times a day. . . ."

Was telling him what H. wrote to me: that Andrée met the son of Inayat Khan in America and learned from him that he, Bhai Sahib, is a well-known Sufi Saint. He listened, not particularly interested. At my remark that people who knew Inayat Khan say that his successor is not at the same stage as Inayat, he said:

"He will be, he will be, before he dies. It is not so easy . . . it takes time!"

Mrs. Sharma was here in the afternoon and he was talking to her in Hindi. At one moment he said in English, repeating it twice with emphasis:

"There is nothing but Nothingness!"—then continued to speak to Mrs. Sharma. I knew it was for me. Mrs. Sharma told me afterwards that she knew it too; it had nothing to do with her, nor with the question she was asking and he was answering.

To be free . . . because born of the spirit like he . . . as free as the wind . . . to achieve the indifference of complete freedom . . . to be united with Him is the only freedom, the only thing which matters . . . the ONLY thing. . . .

82

Nothing but Nothingness

13th July, 1966

"THERE IS NOTHING BUT NOTHINGNESS," he said yesterday. And the way he said it, repeating it with emphasis, and the echo it awakened in my heart, made me think that it was meant for me. It struck me as the most wonderful sentence and it made me glad. . . .

"When you said it, I suddenly knew it was a special message for me."

"It was . . . you are right, quite right!" He laughed; it was evident that he was pleased.

In spite of the heat, this morning he wore the white kurta again. I suspected a test. But he was talking to me instead in a friendly way. I had the opportunity during the conversation to tell him what I wrote down a few days ago. Speaking of this astonishing state of nothingness, I said that at the beginning it was just Nothing; later there was like a kind of sorrowful happiness with much longing in it, but now it was just wonderful. Why it was so wonderful I could not say; this feeling is too new and difficult to analyze. All I know is THAT IT IS WONDERFUL. When at home, I realized that the answer is contained in his statement of yesterday: there is nothing but Nothingness, and it represents a perfect state—that's why it is so wonderful. . . .

"I sometimes suspect that this feeling of not being can put the body to death."

"The body can die; you will never die," he replied.

He said important things about the Nakshmandia Dynasty. To my question if in Chishtia Dynasty they also have Param Para, he replied:

"Yes, of course, they have. And in all the Sufi Systems the surrender to the Teacher is demanded. Chishtias are very magnetic, because many things they do through the physical body. So the body becomes very magnetic. It is the body which attracts the body, and through it the Soul. In our System it is the Soul which attracts the Soul, and the Soul speaks to the Soul. They need music, for instance. Without music they can do nothing. They use ceremonies, some-

times, breathing practices, and other things. We need nothing. We are not limited. Music is bondage. Ceremonials, worship, when done collectively, can also be bondage. But we are free. We go to the Absolute Truth in Silence, for it can be found only in silence and it is Silence. That's why we are called the Silent Yogis. If some practices are given, they are performed always in silence."

Then I asked if in Chishtia Yoga System love is also created like in our System.

"No. This is done only in our School of Yoga. Nobody else has this method."

Later I told him that, he not being well, this powerful stream of love is perhaps difficult to bear; he must feel it in his disciples. "And if this is the case with me, please do tell me to go." He looked at me.

"Where to go?" he said severely, frowning at me. Again I felt that this was a message. Of course I had nowhere to go, but in this case I only meant to go home. But all I said was: "What an answer," and left it at that.

"Sufis never attract the attention of the disciple to the physical body."

I told him that he said once that he never deceived me; but does he remember that he stated that a woman can never reach a high state?

"If she does not get rid of her limitations as a woman, she is more limited by Prakriti than a man."

"But I think this is the case of every human being, man or woman. If they don't get rid of their limitations, they cannot reach Reality," I retorted.

"This is correct, this is so. My Rev. Father was woodland and rustic. . . ."

This expression made me smile . . . very descriptive and original.

"What did you say? Please repeat it," I asked.

"Woodland and rustic," he replied. "It means like an animal. It has to be controlled. If it is controlled, it is all right. He had to suffer very much for many years. For men there are many restrictions, for women only one: to get rid of her limitations as a woman."

"Are those limitations acquired, or are they from birth?"

"With a woman it is always from birth."

14th July

HE HAS SENT ME HEADLONG into deep apprehension last night. We were already outside and it was dusk. Fresh wind was blowing after a hot and sultry day. It was very pleasant. The new old man asked about me, and offered me his chair.

"No," he said, "she is used to sitting on this wooden chair; she wants to lose herself in every way." Then he proceeded to tell him that the first time I stayed with him for nearly two years.

"Then she was sent back and did much work then. . . ." He smiled his strange, enigmatic smile. "There was something in her and she had to come back. Now she will stay with me, till. . . ." He stopped.

"Till she is perfect," the old man said. He shook his head softly.

"Who am I to make anybody perfect? Only God can do that. No, till the fruit is ripe, it does not give out a sweet juice."

Aha, I thought. He means I will stay till the end of the training this time. Good.

"Who is perfect can make others perfect," I quickly got up, knelt before him and touched his foot with my forehead.

"Why that?" He smiled.

"You said that you are not perfect and it hurts me, for I know that you are!"

"It is your faith which makes you say so," he said with great softness. Then he began to talk to me and I was all ears, but the old man kept interrupting. His brother came and began to talk to the old man. I was glad.

"You talk to me and I don't come down," he continued. "Sometimes I can answer and I do not. Go on talking; something will remain."

I said that I have the feeling that there are times that I have to talk to him, it helps me to clear my mind. But he does not need to listen, because he knows it at any rate already. He laughed kindly.

"But I don't want your mind to be clear; I want confusion. If you are in the mud, you try to get out."

"In other words, speaking figuratively, if I sit in a comfortable chair, I will do nothing." He laughed gaily. "Sometimes I am in such a despair that I feel like committing suicide, and I felt like this several times."

"Go on, show me how you commit suicide! One cannot!"

"Cannot?" I repeated. I was astonished, not being sure what he meant.

"Cannot," he repeated. "If He does not want, how can one

commit suicide? I was in this state many times with My Rev. Guru Maharaj. He never spoke to me in a kindly way."

"Many times?" I echoed.

"Many, many times," he laughed. "Now I can laugh, but then . . . it was not a laughing matter."

I told him that this time it is not an ordinary trouble of the mind. I understood what was happening, and if one understands, one tries to cooperate intelligently.

"No, no, you understood nothing; one cannot understand!" (I can still see his face when he said it . . . seated under the mango tree we were, a feeling of great Meaning seemed to be in the air. . . .)

"One is made to forget. It is done like this. When the moment comes, you will say, what is this? And if you don't hate the Guide, you hate yourself. . . ."

"Trouble is ahead," I said turning to the brother. "Did you hear the hints?" He nodded with a smile.

"As I said yesterday, where does one go? I was not angry last time; the mood was made so. You can ask me anything, always, if the mood is right." He lifted a finger warningly. "If not, it will come again and again to the same point. . . ."

"Does it happen to everybody?"

"No, not to everybody." He made a grimace of disgust and began to drink the medicine brought by Munshiji.

"But it happened to you, and this fact is enough for me; it gives me courage and consolation," I said, closing the conversation. But I remained disturbed. He talked Hindi with others, I left soon. And did not sleep practically all night, so worried I was. . . . It was a cool fresh night. A crescent waning moon stood in the eastern sky spreading ghostly light at three a.m. Some shrubs were flowering; sweet fragrance reached me with gentle whiffs of fresh wind. Merciful God! Didn't I have already enough? It seems I had more than my share of suffering. . . . I prayed to Him the Great Beloved, to his Rev. Guru Maharaj, to his Father who suffered so much, probably more than myself. . . .

And in the morning when seated in his garden (he was walking up and down), I suddenly knew what it would be: very probably the Dark Night of the Soul. Each Soul has to pass through it again and again on the Path before one is given anything. . . .

"Go on abusing; such people do not care," he said yesterday.

The hints: "Where will one go?" And "You will hate yourself

even if you don't hate the Guide." Many a time it happened to him—the desire for suicide; it is all described in the works of the Mystics; it all sounds very ominous. . . .

17th July

THERE WAS NOTHING TO WRITE in those last two days. I go there, sit immersed in Nothingness. And this evening he was in a very deep state. How the Divinity shines through the human frame when he is in Samadhi. . . . It began when Mrs. Sharma was there, when she left and the old man came. At first he was resting and then sat outside. It was hot. I could not take my eyes from him. It was magnificent. When leaving I knelt down and touched his feet with my forehead. But had to come back. He gave me an astonished look as if to say, what is the matter?

"Another five minutes," I said. "I cannot go away." He nodded. I stayed for a short while, then left with regret. The old man kept talking stupidly, disturbing him all the time. The fool—he understood nothing . . . he did not even notice in what state Bhai Sahib was. . . .

18th July

AS EVERY DAY IN THE SUMMER SEASON, this afternoon too they played cards. Later he came into the room and had to settle a quarrel between Poonam and Babu. He was in an angry and irritable mood. Something is brewing for me, I thought. When the two had left, he was squatting on his tachat and his lips were moving in a silent prayer. Then I was sure something was coming and my apprehension increased. He was praying either for me or that all should go well. . . .

Ravindra brought the 250 rupees. And I asked him to give it to his stepmother. This triggered it off. He began to attack me. It was useless to tell him that I asked him beforehand a few days ago if I can do it; he twisted everything and came down on me when I tried to explain.

"What is there to explain when the action is wrong?" he said and kept talking and thundering. At last I could not take it anymore and burst out crying. Not enough that I give every penny to him, and am myself in difficulties, but he is rude to me in the bargain. Then I stopped crying. He was talking to his wife now about Ravindra. She was talking rapidly, excitedly, clearly complaining about something.

Then we went outside because some people came. Munshiji brought water, basin and all the paraphernalia needed to take his medicines. Then he said kindly:

"Do you understand that you have committed a mistake?" and he began to explain how I don't understand such trifling things. I apologized and said that he was right, that it was an error of judgment on my part, but my reasoning and my judgment are distorted, and when he says sometimes that I am an idiot, he is right. . . . But here he interrupted me by turning to speak to someone who just arrived . . . it was the old man.

And it was wonderful to watch how his mood changed in a moment as soon as I accepted everything. He had his sparkle and his usual laughter; his conversation was lively. I watched his facial expressions; he was unearthly beautiful. . . . He becomes more and more beautiful, I was thinking . . . is it he who is changing, or is it me? The night was cool. I was restless though . . . and I prayed much, looking at the stars. . . .

19th July

IN THE MORNING WE WERE SITTING opposite each other in perfect silence. He wore his devic face and I just looked and looked, speechless with much reverence and awe in my heart. Later in the room he spoke a few words to me, and this gave me the opportunity to say:

"You know, Sheikh, this feeling of Nothingness deepens and deepens. It must be a rare, unusual experience, which one can have only with a Great Master. And it is so deep that I need only to keep myself in it consciously; I mean, to keep my mind consciously in it, and you can cut me to pieces and I will say nothing. I may cry though, if it hurts too much, but this will be all. . . . I try and struggle to express it somehow, but with little result . . . it is beyond description." I glanced at him and saw that his eyes were closed; his face was carved of stone. A sign for me to stop talking . . . I did. Reclined my head on my knees and remained like this bent in two. . . .

In the afternoon the Sharmas came before six and stayed, and when I left they were still there. And Mr. Sharma kept arguing, I thought, so foolishly, making bad atmosphere; arguments are so useless. I went outside into the garden for a while, could not bear it. . . .

Later we sat on the chairs and I just looked at him all the time. He seemed to be full of the Grace of God, sparkling . . . and in the pause of the conversation he suddenly looked at me with a smile, such a smile, like never, never before, so kind, so radiant, and so much love was in it. My heart stood still for a second, then gave a thump of deepest joy. I faintly smiled back and had to close my eyes. Such unspeakable happiness pervaded me. . . . And the Great Painter painted a splendid evening sky, of tender turquoise on the horizon and transparent blue overhead and feathery streaky clouds of orange and soft pink, and great big fat ones, greeny-grey with fluffy pink edges. . . . I looked at it and my happiness was perfect. . . . Something big is BEING PREPARED for me: the Nearness is too much. . . . After such Nearness the Separation would be dreadful. . . . And I just kept looking at him, laughing, talking, full of the Grace of God, kindness, and sense of humor. . . .

20th July

IT WAS A WONDERFULLY COOL NIGHT, and no mosquitos because of the breeze from the southeast. Slept without mosquito net. And prayed much, looking up to the shimmering stars. And so great was the Nearness. . . . During the night I was very restless. I had many dreams charged with agitated images which I don't remember. Before falling asleep an unusual heart activity began, very different from any I had before in all those years. And waking up at four a.m., there was a very great vibration in the heart which lasts until this moment. I feel light. Full of strange excitement. Impossible to describe. Something big is being prepared. I had better be careful, recollected . . . such a heart activity is quite unusual. I am used to all kinds of vibrations by now, but this is something quite different. It feels as if it came from a different direction. And love and Nearness are great . . . Heaven knows to what it will lead. . . . Oh, what a feeling of lightness and deep, deep happiness . . . and the heart races and races on and on, like a restless bird in a cage. . . . God help me . . . Rev. Guru Maharaj, help me . . . please. . . .

Lately he always sits opposite me on the divan under the fan, and I at the head of his tachat. I sit bent in two. Impossible to sit erect; the body is like broken in the middle, impossible to look at him. We sit in silence. When I happen to raise my head, I never meet his eyes. But I feel his eyes on me when I am bent down. The idea came into my mind that something is given, that it is a "sitting" because nobody ever seems to disturb or come in. And the peace? There are no words for it. . . .

On the 15th, in the afternoon, I tried to tell him the result of my

conclusions that it is going to be the Dark Night of the Soul, a
troublesome state each Soul has to go through again and again,
encountering it as on an ascending spiral when one is after the
Absolute Truth.

He listened to me (or did he?) wrapped in one of his icy silences
and half in Samadhi, so I don't know if my assumption is correct or
not. . . .

On the 17th in the morning he came out in white kurta and topi, a
stick in his hand, and I saw the wife dressed up, so I thought that they
were going out. A car came driven by one of his disciples, and I
understood that they were going to Samadhi. It suddenly passed
through my mind that I will be going too . . . and if not, I will do my
shopping, will go home early to write my letters. He got up.

"You can also come in the car if you like," he said indifferently.

"You are taking me with you?" I asked delightedly, "thank you!"
He did not answer. We all piled into the car. There was only his wife,
the youngest daughter-in-law, Poonam, Ravindra's two children, the
driver-disciple and myself. The ride was lovely; once more I had the
feeling that he went there because of me. It was a windy day with
chasing clouds; it was still cool at seven in the morning. The
atmosphere was wonderful. And I prayed to his parents, whose
graves were in the mausoleum, that I may be taken soon into his Path.
We remained less than fifteen minutes; he had to leave because of a
giddiness which overcame him. We were home at his place before
nine. And later he sat in the chair, as if nothing had happened and
seemed well again. The whole day I felt good because I love to go to
Samadhi, and this time it was somehow special. . . .

I am in a strange mood today; there is a restlessness—half
irritation, half resignation, and the latter was complete and absolute,
to my destiny. He looked hostile all the morning; the heart activity
was strong from time to time. More and more it looks to me as if
something is brewing. . . .

Now at home, the longing is great, so much, so much, it hurts
inside. . . . Dear God, help me! Guru Maharaj, help me!

The drunkard came about 9:30 and Bhai Sahib was reading to him
from the newspaper . . . court cases, politics, weather conditions
. . . God knows why he does it . . . seems such a waste of time. To
read aloud and tire oneself. . . . I left in disgust to do some
shopping. Praying to God. I leave him in Your Hand. If something
happens to him, it is Your Will. . . . God, dear God, WHY does he
do it?

83

Death

IT IS THE THIRD DAY since my Sheikh has left his physical body . . . and I still cannot believe it. . . .

When I am at his place, it seems that at any moment I will hear his swift step, his ringing voice, his laughter. . . .

A few days ago, I was thinking that since he had his last heart attack, his voice has changed. I was thinking it in the morning, listening to his voice in the next room. But in the evening he was singing Persian songs to the old man, and his voice was clear and bell-like as I always knew it. . . . And I looked at him hoping so much, so ardently, that he will translate something to me, but he did not. . . . It was the last time. Never again. . . .

But I had better write down everything in chronological order. I came on the 20th in the afternoon, as usual. They played cards; it was very hot. One window was a little open in the front room, so it was not so dark, the fan was humming. About six it began to rain. And as it became cool I opened the two windows and the two doors to let the cool air in from the garden. In the room it was unbearably hot and I was wet with perspiration. While I was opening them, I hoped that it will be all right and he will not object to it nor tell me off. They finished playing shortly after six, he got up and went into the courtyard. Thinking it over, clearly now, I can see that until the last moment he did the usual, ordinary things. Nobody at this time had even the smallest hint of what was going to happen. . . . Soon he came back from the courtyard, talking to the wife who was closely behind him. He went directly to the front door and stood in the cool breeze, still talking to the wife. I stood at the other door looking at the lime tree, so fresh and fragrant after the shower. I stood there for a while. When I turned and entered the room he was not there; the wife alone stood in the doorway. The rain stopped completely. It was very cool and pleasant. When he came back into the room, I was thinking what a profile he had . . . so young. He wore his devic face. He often had it lately. Dynamically beautiful.

Some people came. He went out into the garden and stood there talking to them. The chairs were not put out yet; it began drizzling softly. I was walking up and down looking at him from the distance; he was standing there laughing and talking. The sun came out; it was still drizzling. There must be a rainbow under these conditions, I thought. I looked for it; and here it was seen between the trees, towards the southeast.

"Sheikh, Bhai Sahib, please look!" I shouted, "Look at the beautiful rainbow! Please, come here, from here you can see it!" He smiled and came to stand beside me. He looked at it with a smile, saying something in Hindi to others who all commented on it. The colors were very vivid.

"There are two rainbows," Virendra said, "a double rainbow!"

"Let's go on the roof, from there we can see it better," I told him, and we—myself, Virendra and Poonam—ran quickly upstairs. It was lovely and fresh on the flat roof; a cool breeze was blowing; the cement was still wet from the rain. Right across the sky towards the southeast were two magnificent rainbows; they seemed to span from one side of the horizon to another. One very clear and bright, and the other above, paler, delicate, ethereal, but both complete, parallel to each other.

I did not notice anything unusual; it did not occur to me to look if all the colors were there, but Satendra next morning told me that his father went into the room for a moment and said to his wife:

"See, the Great Painter, what wonderful colors he paints. . .but the yellow color is missing. . . ."

And in the night when Satendra was massaging his feet, he suddenly sat up, his eyes blazing and said as if speaking to himself:

"The yellow color was missing. . . . My color was gone. . . ."

From the roof I called down to him as he talked to others standing under the mango tree:

"Bhai Sahib, please, look! Two magnificent rainbows!" He smiled, turned his head, glanced at them and continued to talk. We remained for a while on the roof, and I was telling Virendra that the rainbow is believed to be very auspicious by the Russians, and I think it is so in every country. And two rainbows must be even more auspicious, though I really don't believe completely in such things. And I told him that two weeks ago, when he told me that now my troubles are going away, right over Chowraha where I passed a moment ago was a magnificent rainbow. I was so happy to see it, thinking that it was a good omen. . . .

We went down. In the meantime the chairs were put out, and he sat serenely in his large chair under the mango tree. A talk about the Gurus was going on, and the new old man commented on it, and asked me how it was that I came to Bhai Sahib. I said that I have traveled much in India, met many Gurus especially in the Himalayan region, but not one of them made any impression on me. Even in my ignorance I knew that a Guru who is full of his own importance is full of the self; so I was not at all impressed by the big "I" in them. The only one who impressed me was Bhai Sahib because of his humility and his simplicity.

"Gurus are good, but the trouble is that they come on the platform to teach before they get rid of the self. One should not teach while there is still the desire to teach. This is the rule, but the Gurus are good. Who am I to judge anybody? . . .

"Before the self is gone, one is not complete; one is not perfect; one cannot make others perfect."

The old man laughed and I said again that the only one who impressed me was he, so I stayed.

"Why don't you say that your share was here, so you stayed here? Don't say the Gurus are not good; your share was not there . . . it was here. . . ."

He fell silent. The garden was still; there was no wind. I looked up at the sky and was speechless: curtains of gold, orange, crimson, covered it completely.

"Oh, look, look, please do look, how the Greatest Painter has painted the sky! No human being can reproduce these colors; one cannot paint them—they are dynamic light itself!"

"Yes," he nodded, looking for a few seconds, then began again to speak to the old man. But I continued to watch the colors changing shape, flowing into one another. Once more it was one of those rare, exceptional sunsets, and it occurred to me for a moment that sunsets, sunrises and rainbows played an important symbolical role in my life. Then I noticed something rare, never seen at any time in all my life: small, perfectly circular clouds stood motionless right above the bungalow, seemingly very low, only a few hundreds of feet away, but I realized it must have been higher; it was an optical illusion. They seemed about three feet in diameter, of purest, most incredible tender amethyst, or mauve, surrounded by all this orange and pink.

"Please look, this is very rare! I am old and I never saw anything like it before! Look at these little clouds of mauve! How unusual and how lovely!" I exclaimed excitedly. He glanced at them, a fine smile slightly curled his lips, then continued to talk to the old man who was not even a little interested in all this glory.

Watching attentively, I noticed to my surprise that they were not clouds at all, but perfectly round openings in the surrounding clouds . . . like little windows through which the blue of the sky was visible. The film of vivid crimson reflected by the clouds made the blue background appear as infinite, purest mauve.

They gradually changed, became pale blue; one could see clearly that they were holes, openings, but not clouds themselves. And then all of a sudden the whole garden, nay, the whole world seemed to glow with an incredible golden-pink light. Sometimes we see in dreams such glory and, if we are lucky, in rare sunsets. . . . I got up and went further away, stood by the door to take an eyeful of the golden garden in this strange ominous light. Him sitting there, the white garment glowing, his skin, all this Oriental scene, the disciples seated around him. It was incredibly lovely. The white walls of the bungalow, reflected and emphasized, deepened the effect. It was so much India. He looked like a golden Deva. I sat down.

"How beautiful you look in this golden-pink light; your skin seems to glow with it from within." As one sees in a dream, I thought, but I did not speak it out.

He gave me a glance, but his face was serious, and he looked far away into the blinking light shimmering with the setting sun. His strange eyes had an expression which I could not interpret, were reflecting faithfully the clouds and the sky and the colors. I did not know at that moment that the Greatest Painter painted the sky in Glory and bathed the garden in Golden Light, because a great Soul of a Golden Sufi was leaving this world forever. It was his last sunset, the last greeting . . . he would never see another one. Next day it was cloudy, and he would never have another physical body; it was his last. So Nature greeted her Great Son for the last time. . . .

I stood up to leave at my usual time.

"You want to go now?" he murmured.

"With your permission," I said, and he nodded briefly. My heart became quite small. . . . There was something . . . as if . . . as if some kind of regret in his voice. . . . Why? I felt disturbed. . . . It was his last evening and I did not know it. . . .

The night was cool. I slept fairly well. Woke up early; it was still dark. Felt such deep serenity, such bliss even physically, that I was thinking that perhaps this is the bliss they are talking about. . . .

And walking to his place amongst the busy morning traffic of cars, children going to school, cows wandering aimlessly, rikshaws driving at greatest possible speed, fighting dogs . . . and the sky was covered with white clouds, serenely sailing along. I was reflecting that the feeling of Nothingness is now not only in his presence. It stays with me. . . . I feel like that before God, before life; it seems to become slowly my very being. . . .

He was not out yet. I sat down and continued to think. The concept of ourselves and of our surroundings is of "I" and the not "I." That is: myself and the environment surrounding me, and my relationship to it creates causes which are called Karma, or one can call it actions . . . it does not really matter. And it is those relationships which are moulding our future. . . . But to me it looks differently: I see it now—FROM THE NOUGHT TO THE SOMETHING. It looks different, seen from a different angle.

He came out. His torso was naked, and he began to walk up and down on the brick elevation; then he sat down. The wife came and discussed something; the newspaper was handed to him by the newspaper man who came running through the gate. I brought his glasses. He began to read. Lately he was reading the paper every morning.

As he was leaving it, he probably wanted to know what was going on in the world. . . . I just sat there looking at him. The face of a Deva. His torso naked, brown and slender. What a graceful, beautiful human being. . . . A Muslim barber entered the gate. His chair was put in the shade of the mango tree, and the ceremony of cutting the hair and the beard began. For it was quite a ceremony and I loved to watch it. Today it was especially particular.

"A little here, and here, and here," he kept saying, pointing to the places he wanted to be cut or shaved either more or in a different way. I was amused. Poor barber, I thought . . . it lasts already over an hour. I wonder how much he intends to give him . . . I will pay for his haircut, I thought. I waited. It became hotter and hotter. The new tenant of the hut came and brought ten rupees. He told him to put it on the chair. When he left he said:

"There on the chair are ten rupees. Keep an eye on them that they should not be blown away and get lost; they are not mine." I said that I already was watching them. What did he mean: "not mine?" Was not the money of his tenant his? Now I know what he had meant. . . . He was going away tonight . . . the money was not for him anymore to dispose of. . . .

As soon as the barber finished, he came to the chair and sat down.

"How much is it? Please let me pay for it. It gave me such a pleasure to watch him doing it that I feel I should make a contribution."

He smiled, **"Put on the chair what you think he should get."** I did. He smiled again, and turning to the barber who was still putting all his paraphernalia away into a box:

"Here is the money for you." The barber left, thanking profusely.

"Oh, it is hot here! Why didn't you go inside?" He got up. I repeated that I enjoyed watching and was waiting till the barber finished to pay him, if he would permit it. He smiled.

"Oh, you forgot the black shoe polish I told you to bring the other day."

"I gave it to Munshiji the same day. I never forget what you tell me," I replied. We went into the room. He switched on the fan and went out but came back soon.

"I inquired about the shoe polish; those shoes are not comfortable if they are not polished properly. I really ought to get a new pair."

I was astonished. Why did he feel the necessity to check? It was unusual. After all it was such an unimportant matter. . . .

Soon I left. At home I was disturbed. But did not know why. Quarrelled with the landlord because he decided to paint my veranda, and the two men who were supposed to do it were looking into my window watching me and commenting on everything they saw in the room, including me, I suppose, instead of painting. And they made such a noise and laughed so much that it was impossible to rest; it was very hot. I was really angry, went to the landlord who was resting, got him up and he came with me, made a row, and the men began to paint at last. But the noise was even worse; I was really quite on edge. The room was full of dust; it was very uncomfortable. . . .

When I arrived about four p.m., he was reclining on the tachat talking animatedly, telling a story to his wife, sons and brother all sitting in the front room. I noticed nothing unusual. I remember I only thought he talks too much; it will do him harm. . . . At one moment we were asked to go out. Closing the door behind me I inquired from his brother if Bhai Sahib was not quite well. No, he said; somehow he does not feel too well. I thought that it might be an attack of diarrhea which he used to get sometimes in the rainy period. I was not really worried. After a few minutes the door was opened. I waited a little, then went to the door. He was squatting on the edge of the tachat holding his head with both hands.

"May I come in?" He gave me a cold look, not answering. I sat down. "Your brother told me that you are not too well." He turned his face sideways away from me and nodded quickly. But I managed to catch a glimpse of such compassion and tenderness, and it puzzled me. I kept quiet. His wife came in and sat opposite him looking at him with concern. They exchanged a few words in Hindi. Then I heard him say to her (simple sentences I understood in Hindi):

"I have great trouble with breathing." In fact his breathing was rapid and obviously painful; cardiac asthma, I thought, and became alarmed. I changed my place for I wanted to see his face, so I sat on the settee opposite, next to the wife. Babu was sent for the doctor. I could see he was obviously in distress; the body seemed to labor with each breath. I asked him:

"Shall I go to Dr. Ram Singh?" This was the heart specialist who treated him previously and helped him through all the previous heart attacks. He made an indefinite movement with his right hand. I was not sure how to interpret it. I think he meant: "What's the use?" I looked at the wife. "Yes," she said. So I got up quickly, went to Virendra who was doing his homework in the next room, and he immediately said that he is coming too. Actually he had to come for I did not know exactly where the heart specialist lived. I waited for a few minutes till he dressed, took a rikshaw and went to the medical college. He lived there in the compound, for he was the head of the Heart Department. I happened to look at my watch; it was ten to six. While going along, Virendra told me that he was worried—it was the third major heart attack he was suffering this year. I agreed that it was very worrying. I was worried, it was true, but somehow not too much. I had a stillness in me and a great peace, but this I realized only afterwards. In this very moment the only important thing was to get the doctor as quickly as possible. The journey seemed endless to both of us. The sky was grey with clouds, heavy with water. Dr. Ram Singh was at home, fortunately. He came at once, taking us in his car. When we arrived, Dr. Kant, the family doctor, was there already, and Ram Singh came to sit near Bhai Sahib, took out his instrument for blood pressure. I knelt behind him trying to see, but I could not see from where I was how high the blood pressure was. Bhai Sahib seemed a bit better and talked to Dr. Ram Singh. Then they all went out to consult outside, standing in the garden. Another doctor joined them, one of his disciples. I also left through the side door. I saw that he gave me a brief look while I was going out. Outside they all stood in a group in serious consultation; his sons and the brother were listening. Ram Singh was saying that it was a heart attack, and he did not like the look of it because it happens too soon after the last, recent and severe one in the middle of May, and this time the same left ventricle was affected.

"It is an attack all right. There is a cardiac asthma," he said to me.

I went back to the side door. Guruji was reclining, his elbow on the pillow, supporting his head with the right hand. I stood outside the door for a few seconds. My eyes, my face, must have expressed that all my being was crying out to him . . . my heart was full of anxiety. Without lifting his head he gave me a deep unsmiling look . . . lowered his eyes for a brief second and then looked again. It was the look of a divine lover. . . . My heart stood still as though pierced by a sword . . . I was so profoundly disturbed that I literally ran away back to the others, and Dr. Kant was preparing an injection which last time worked wonders. I was trembling somewhere deep inside. . . . Something did happen . . . my God, this look . . . a small voice was crying, crying . . . it was too terrible, and too sweet, I could not bear it . . . but I did not realize that it was his last look, and it was his special look for me. . . .

The doctor went inside and gave the injection. I sat outside with all others, and we were talking that now after this injection he will be better. Virendra who just came back from the room said that he was sleeping now, and I was telling Babu that in this case I will not stay here all night as I originally intended, but will go home. I will not be of any help anyhow. Suddenly we heard a strange sound like a kind of roar. Babu listened, I too.

"It is nothing," I said, "he only cleared his throat" . . . it sounded like that. Virendra stood near the door. I joined him. I noticed that his eldest son Ravindra was sitting on the bed behind him supporting him. After a few moments there was a commotion in the room.

I left the place where I stood for a moment, then came back, drawn by an invisible force. He was leaning on Ravindra's arm, but I heard somebody say that his head is too low; he should sit up, supported by the pillows. I could see that he made an effort to sit up, but I could not see well from where I was standing outside the door—did not want to go into the room, already several people were standing there. Virendra stood with me; his large dark eyes were wide open with anxiety.

"Father is not completely in his senses," he said in a low voice, "not completely conscious after the injection."

I looked at Bhai Sahib, half supported by the pillows. And I saw to my surprise his abdomen going up and down in a strange unusual way, working like billows. I pointed it out to Virendra.

"He is breathing with the abdomen," he answered, but I did not like it; I felt it was quite abnormal. Later, I was told, those were the last gasps. . . . The wife came into the room with several women. I saw him suddenly falling back heavily on Ravindra's arm. The wife took a look at him, uttered a piercing cry, and then threw herself on the bed weeping loudly. Virendra rushed into the room, took a look at him, came running back.

"He is dead," he cried, "he is dead!!"

I ran into the room. He was lying supine, heavy on Ravindra's arm. His face was as if swollen with effort and red. . . . I went out, dumbfounded. So many people were streaming in; they seemed to have appeared suddenly; they had not been here before. . . . Dead? I could not believe it . . . I felt deep peace . . . stillness . . . it could not be. He is not dead . . . not he. . . . No . . . how can he be dead? Impossible!! I stood there alone in my isolation amongst general commotion. Women began to howl like hungry wolves at the moon. Horrible habit that, I thought . . . such dreadful noise and so useless. . . . Be still you all. . . . He is not dead. . . . He cannot be. . . .

But he was. . . . I went into the room and looked at him. He was lying on his back now, hands stretched out along his body; he looked so tall, so slender. His face was severe, his lips a fraction open, but it was hardly noticeable. His eyes were closed. There was such a noise in the room. I went out. Like a lost sheep I walked near the mango tree, then I went inside. The wife cried helplessly, poor woman, an inconsolable, distressed sound of no hope. . . . I approached his tachat, bent down and kissed his already cold right hand, lifting it tenderly with both my hands. Goodbye, Sheikh. Never again . . . never again will I hear your ringing voice, your laughter. . . . Nobody will call me idiot, I will miss it. . . .

In the electric light his face seemed severe. I kept coming and going. . . . Somebody brought a small lamp which was put into the recess where he kept his books. The electric light was switched off. In the dim light his face assumed a strangeness, no more of this world. . . . I still kept coming and going. All was silent in the room now, full of mourning women with veiled faces crying silently.

I went in and knelt down at the end of the tachat. Pressed my forehead against his feet. Their coldness seemed to burn my skin.

"Goodbye Sheikh," I said mentally. My heart was aching with tenderness, the mind full of confusion. . . . A young doctor rushed in, a disciple or a relation.

"Are you sure he is dead?" he asked excitedly and began to press his chest with both hands, listening at the same time with the stethoscope. The wife made a movement with her hand.

"He is dead," she whispered, "no use. . . ."

The Sharmas came. He went inside and she sat with me for a few minutes on the tachat, outside. Went home about eleven. And cried myself to sleep. Heard midnight strike somewhere. . . . How will I live without you?? But in my heart was all stillness and eternal peace. . . .

Got up at four a.m. Had a cup of hot tea. Cried again but not much. Peace was with me and great vibrations in the heart.

Went there about five. Sat outside with others. When it became sufficiently light, I approached the side door and went inside the room. And to my surprise I saw that his face bore a smiling expression. A strange mysterious smile with closed lips. The mystery of *Pax Aeterna*. . . . It was so wonderful, so unexpected, that I could not take my eyes off his face. And my heart was beating so violently that I heard its beat in the whole of my body. . . . The tender curve of his lips . . . the beard which was cut yesterday with so much care and attention . . . his magnificent forehead. Never again, cried my heart, *finis*, the end. . . . Once more I kept coming and going, could not remain in the room. If I wanted to remain, I had to sit on the floor amongst all the women and I would not see his face. . . . So I kept coming and going, looking with hungry eyes, trying to remember this face forever, until my physical body would last. . . . This face so beautiful, so serene, so full of eternal peace. . . .

Went to the bank at Ravindra's request to get some money, then went home to have a bite to eat, cooked some spaghetti in milk, but could not eat. Went back and into the room, to look, to look, and to look. . . . And each time I looked the heart seemed to jump out of my chest and I was trembling . . . a kind of small, minute trembling inside the spine. . . .

The funeral would be about one, but it will be later . . . here nothing is on time. Many people were sitting outside on tachats and chairs; the garden was full with a milling, talking crowd. Then all the male members of the family went inside to wash him. We heard loud wailing and crying coming from the room. Then when he was dressed, the women were shepherded into the room. A great howling began. Durghesh and her husband arrived by taxi direct from

Aligarh. They began to cry loudly, practically running from the garden gate through the crowd. Mrs. Ahuja came. I helped her to get through the crowd into the room to show her his face. Somehow I managed to propel her and myself to the front, next to the tachat. His face was still the same—smiling, enigmatically tender, but already there was a kind of remoteness, a "going away". . . .

Prof. Batnagar said to me: "Courage, he is not dead; they make a noise for nothing." I smiled. Couldn't agree more. . . .

And it was the last time I saw his face (except for a fleeting glimpse when he was lowered into the grave). He was dressed in white kurta, and topi was on his head. . . .

We went out, and soon the wailing began again, increasing to a crescendo. A litter, a kind of a stretcher made of bamboo sticks, was prepared by the disciples in the meantime in the garden. It was taken inside; he was wrapped in a new white cotton sheath, and women kept wailing and wailing. Then he was carried outside by his sons and the nearest relatives. The Sharmas were there, so we went by car. Strangely, I don't remember the moment we reached *Samadhi*. But I clearly remember the grave. Two diggers were still inside throwing out large clumps of clay. I noticed that it was much deeper than in the West, and it had on the left side a niche, like a drawer, for the body to be put into it, which later was sealed off with bricks, before the earth was filled in. After a while the body arrived. There was such peace around, so much sunshine, clouds in the sky, the wide Indian plains and the wind. . . .

Sheikh, my Sheikh, never again . . . my Sheikh . . . Oooh. . . . They put the body on the ground beside the grave; some jumped into it supporting the stretcher, and some were lowering the body. "Take off the sheath from the face," somebody said, "the topi, the topi it is falling down!" It was adjusted, a glimpse of this serene face which after so many hours and the intense heat seemed fresh and only sleeping, and then it was all over, except for the sound of the moist earth being filled in. But I had time to notice that they put him into the niche and bricked it off. The grave diggers closed the opening, not very carefully I thought, jumped out, and then all the present began to shovel and throw earth, more and more of it. . . . Sheikh . . . Sheikh . . . , my mind kept repeating, and the sky was transparent with thin white clouds and the wind smelled good. . . . I took three handfuls—goodbye, this is for your body from me. . . . But you, for me, you will live forever, for always. . . . Took a little earth for H., blessed earth from a Saint's grave. . . . After that it was filled in quickly by the grave diggers. All remained there for a while, but as the Sharmas wanted to go, so I went too, though with much regret. . . . Was at home after four. Had something to eat . . . then was resting and crying and crying, and the vibration in the heart was very, very strong. . . .

84

Freedom

AND I WENT TO HIS HOUSE as usual, yesterday. In the night I slept fairly well though the vibrations were strong and persistent. Told all of them assembled in the garden that while I am here in town I will come every day, and everybody approved.

Was thinking in the morning that there is not much point to stay in this heat. I will go for a few months to the Himalayas to be alone, to find myself—but which self I didn't know, for can this nothingness be called "the self?" And then I will return to England to my work. . . .

Must write to H. for some money, so if I leave here by the 15th of August, there will be time to arrange all this. But where to go? Rishikesh, surely not, neither Darjeeling which is far too fashionable, far too worldly for one who seeks solitude. Somewhere . . . where it is beautiful, where I can be alone amongst the rocks, and the trees, and the mountains. A name came into my mind—rather a picture from a leaflet which I got once from the Tourist Office, showing a serene plateau and a chain of mountains. Almora district. That's it. But the name of the place? It begins with K . . . Kasali? Kosini? No, I cannot remember.

Prof. Batnagar came asking me what I intend to do, and I mentioned that I would like to go to the hills before returning to England. I will have to borrow some money for my return journey, so I can just as well live in the hills and try to save which will take some time.

"Where?" he wanted to know.

"I was thinking of Almora district," I said.

"Kausani? Why not there? Gandiji was there, and he said that it was the most beautiful place in the world." That's exactly the place I could not remember, I thought, and wrote down the address of a center where he thought that I might get a temporary accommodation and perhaps some help in finding a residence for a few months.

Wrote to H. for money and telling her about Guruji's death. Wrote to L. Wrote to the center asking for information and possible accommodation.

The garden is every day full of people now. We were discussing that we have great peace. All of us. We cannot grieve. He is with us. Such peace. . . . For the first time I really understood the Christ's meaning when he said: "I am with you always until the end of time." It means that this is the Gift of a Great Teacher when parting from his disciples.

25th July, 1966

YESTERDAY AFTERNOON WE WENT TO SAMADHI, in two cars, full to the brim with people. It was the third day, so they began to fill the grave with water . . . buckets and buckets of water. Incense was burned and prayers were chanted. At first I was puzzled but was told that it has to be done in order that the earth should settle before they put the stone over it. We were supposed to go at five p.m., but the cars were late so we started at six. I was squeezed in between Babu Ram Prasad and Babu who was talking in a loud voice all the time.

While water was carried from the well and poured over the earth to be sucked up immediately, I watched. Watched the sky and the plains and listened to the wind. The peace was unearthly. All those past days I hardly cried. Am full of such peace. And looking at the working man I was thinking that a great man of his time was gone from this earth, and his body will be surrounded by cold mud. . . . How will his death affect me? It is easier for me now. All I need to do is to keep being immersed in him. Disappear in Nothingness. . . .

"Can you drive out Jinns?" I asked Babu Ram Prasad yesterday.

"Of course!" he answered, his eyes shining like lamps. "I merge in him, then I can do anything!"

Here is the answer . . . and I feel that I can merge in him. I must practice to do it all day long, not only in the night, during the meditation. Then I will go on automatically. . . . Go with him, remain with him. Always.

When coming back from the Samadhi, in the evening, Babu Ram Prasad said in conversation that the color of Nakshmandia was yellow, and the color of Chishtia was rosy-pink. He had the two colors. And I thought of his last sunset, when he and the whole garden was bathed in gold and pink . . . and how beautiful he looked in this light. . . . A great Soul was leaving this world; signs were in the sky that he was going. A great heart, which was beating only for others, was tired . . . had enough. Apparently during the last Bandhara in Bhogoun he had said:

"I nearly finished my work; I still have some to do . . . but I have nearly finished."

27th July

WENT YESTERDAY TO THE SHARMAS for lunch. She told me that his sentence, **"There is nothing but Nothingness,"** had no connection at all with the question she had asked him that evening. And she wondered about it. It became clear to her when I told her that it was meant for me. And she was telling me that she was saying to him that Mrs. Tweedie has something now which was missing before— something was taken away from her. He laughed and said that it was quite correct. And then he added:

"It is difficult for them from the West. L. has an Indian temperament. She had to struggle less."

And yes, she too had noticed the very unusual color above Guruji's bungalow the evening before he died. And she called to her husband from the veranda:

"Krishna, come quickly and see the wonderful colors, right above Guruji's garden!" It was very startling.

28th July

THIS MORNING RAVINDRA was talking to me. He is upset because there is no cooperation and much jealousy. And he read one of the letters of his father in which he tells him to have courage . . . he is always with him. Later in conversation he told me that his father said once:

"The fate which is allotted to a human being cannot be changed."

After a while Babu Ram Prasad joined us, and he told us a story: Once they were all sitting with the Father of Guruji; many people were there, sitting on the *dharries*, and it was about ten p.m. At one moment he felt the necessity to go to a private place, so he got up and tried to open the door leading to the garden, which was locked. Ciacciaji (the Father was called so by everybody, it means "uncle") asked him:

"What are you doing?" He was always smiling and kind, but this time his voice was severe and abrupt.

Timidly I said: "I want to go to the garden latrine for I need to urinate."

"Don't go through this door, go inside," he told him. I never went inside to use the private toilets of his family. But I did what I was told and went. There was amongst the Sannyasis one old man who was a very old follower. So he dared to ask Ciacciaji: "Now, you prevented Babu Ram from going outside this door, but what about us? Babu Ram is allowed to go inside, but we are not allowed. What will we do?"

Ciacciaji laughed and said: "Oh, it is only for this moment; later it will be all right."

The old man asked: "Why?"

"Panditji, you will not understand," laughed the Guru. "It is because they are sitting outside."

"Who? They?" The old man wanted to know.

"Jinns are sitting outside." And if he would have opened the door and seen them, he would have been frightened.

I said to Babu Ram that, as far as I know, Jinns are invisible; it is not at all sure that he would have seen them.

"They are invisible," he answered, "but in the light of the Guru they become visible." He was fanning himself for it was very hot, his legs drawn up on the chair like Bhai Sahib, then he added:

"Those are great Gurus to whom even Jinns come for training. They are appointed by God to serve all creation. There is no propaganda; no official initiation is needed for appointment. If God wants, people will be attracted and will come. If God wills so. . . ." This is for me, I thought. This sentence comes to him from God . . . and I remembered his words of a few months ago:

"You must recognize me then, when I am not here anymore; I will come in many shapes."

                                                                    1st August

YESTERDAY ALL THE MALE MEMBERS of the family and disciples went to the Ganga to have their heads shaved, as it is the custom. I went too.

It was a cloudy, grey day; fresh wind was blowing. It was not raining. The Ganga was lovely. I never saw it so full. There is something about rivers, something so wide, so free . . . especially the Ganga, rolling along, grey, muddy water, swollen from the rains. The wind was blowing from the river. It smelled good. It was not deep near the bathing *ghat.* I saw men wading through to the sand island, and the water was not even to their hips. On the *ghat* itself was the usual activity—temple bells ringing, bathers dipping themselves into the muddy water. I saw a boy filling a bottle with this water. It was quite grey. I would not drink this stuff even if it were thrice holy. I drank it in Rishikesh though, but there it was different; there the

Ganga came out of a narrow gorge, still limpid, green, and dancing over the boulders. But here . . . brr. . . .

All the men sat in a sheltered place and had the barber working on them. I watched the activities of the *ghat*, looked at the river . . . it was so very lovely. Every river is lovely . . . but especially the Ganga . . . so large it is, with so many islands, and on the opposite shore, far away, one could see trees and houses. And the wind, the wind, of the wide distances, chasing low grey clouds, passing heavily, loaded with moisture. It is raining heavily in Dehra Dun and Hardwar: the Ganga is only a few inches below the danger level. Beautiful, beautiful Ganga. But how many villages it can destroy, how many people it can kill. . . .

I went home about ten a.m. Went to the doctor. My bladder is causing trouble. Went shopping. In the evening many people were sitting. The young Mohammedan from Bhopal was there, the grandson of the Grand Guru. He came out from the room where he stays with the cousin of Ravindra, and sat amongst us. Nobody spoke. Many were in Dhyana. He was in a high state, I could see it. His eyes were open in Samadhi, like Guruji's. And he kept looking at me with those eyes. I wondered if he was giving me something. There was a wonderful peace. I enjoyed this half hour.

This morning we went to the last ceremony at the Samadhi. Meditation. Prasad. The atmosphere was perhaps the most charged I have ever experienced in this place. I repeated and repeated *Iailahi*, could not do anything else, could not stop it, could not think of anything else. . . . We went there by truck. It was raining intermittently. Low, grey clouds were sailing majestically. The air was fresh, and I was thinking that when I go from India, who knows if, and when, I will see his grave again.

I returned by car with Ragunath Prasad and Poonam and some of the children.

This afternoon I have received the registered letter from H. with £40. Yesterday I got his photos. And also yesterday I felt suddenly that I was free. Those last photos of his—this wonderful face with the mysterious smile—I wanted to have them . . . they were my last important desire. Now I am free . . . what has remained? I am free to go, free as a bird belonging somewhere and nowhere, will do my duty and live so long as He wants me to live. . . . Sheikh, my Sheikh . . . I look at this wonderful face of yours, and my heart is beating and beating. . . . Never again will I see those eyes open . . . never again. . . . When I was looking at this face, coming and going like a restless soul, trying to drink it all in . . . never to forget this lovely tender expression of the smile—then too, my heart was beating and beating in a maddening tocsin. . . .

Sheikh, how sore I am. . . . Sheikh, my Sheikh . . . my gratitude will remain forever. . . .

2nd August

THE MONEY IS HERE. I can leave in a few days.

With Mrs. Sharma in the morning we went to Samadhi. Again it was a grey day with heavy clouds and slight drizzle. And the peace was such, deep and dense, that one had the impression that one can cut it with a knife. How I prayed. . . . It is the fifth time that I go to Samadhi, and it is going to be the last time until I come back, because I am leaving Thursday, the 4th of August, two weeks after his death. He died on Thursday too—it was the 21st of July . . . everything went very quick. I knew it was he who wanted me to go, he who wanted me to be liberated from the difficult conditions. What's the use of remaining? All the disciples congregate in the garden and are talking and talking. What's the use?

Yesterday in Guruji's garden I carried a heavy chair and fell down with it from the brick elevation on which he used to walk. Sprained my ankle and am a bit lame. Never mind, will be able to travel just the same, will bandage it tightly. The two Mohammedans come every day. I like them. They are very sincere. And the young one is very spiritual; one can feel it. One of the old disciples told us a story:

Bhai Sahib's father was asked by a newcomer to which caste he belonged. Even nowadays there are people in India who think that a Guru should be a Brahmin.

"I am," said Ciacciaji, "a washerman and . . ." he paused, "I am also a tailor and a dyer. As a washerman washes your garments and they become clean again, so I wash your hearts. Only to wash the clothes is easy, it does not take a long time; but to wash the hearts is difficult and it takes a long time. . . .

"As the tailor takes your suit and turns it inside out, the clean, new parts outside and the worn inside, so I turn the hearts and make them like new.

"As a dyer takes your faded garment, dips it into the dye and it looks new and fresh, so I make your hearts fresh and as good as new. So I am just a washerman, a tailor and a dyer. . . ."

Somebody came to him and said: "You have given me so much."

He replied: "Here is nobody to give and nobody to receive. The very fact that you came to me makes you entitled to get something. And if I don't give it to you, you will kick me with your boots till you get it. But it is not always the intention of the Almighty that help should be given 100%. If it is done, people sometimes turn against you. . . . Some help is given, then they come back for more, and the rest is done by and by in Satsang. The iron is put into the magnetic field till it becomes a magnet. If it is taken out too quickly, it loses its magnetic property and becomes iron again. So it is with Satsang . . . time is needed. . . ." Remember, God is in all men, but all men are not in God," he said on another occasion.

Somebody asked if Jinns can assume any shape they like.

"Yes," was the answer, "any shape at all. Beautiful or ugly, men or animal, any object, or flower, or plant . . . according to their wish at that moment. When they assume a human form, they are usually dressed in white, and the eyes are different . . . it is difficult to explain, but the eyes are not human. Also if they come to a Guru, the Guru never speaks to them. It is not necessary. He communicates with them by thought. If you notice something like that, it could be a Jinn."

While he was speaking, I remembered an incident which happened quite a while ago. Many of us were sitting with Bhai Sahib that day, but one chair to my left stood empty. Much talk was going on and people kept coming and going. Then I noticed that a young man sat in the empty chair. He was poorly dressed in white dhoti and kurta, and I thought that he might be a villager or someone from the province. He sat awkwardly on the corner of the chair. I thought that he must be a newcomer, but what struck me was his eyes. They were wide, very dark, and had a strange expression. Perhaps he is not quite normal or a little unbalanced . . . I got this impression—some unbalanced people have this non-human expression in their eyes. Women came to have their children blessed. Jagan Nathji was talking to me, and when I happened to look at the chair, it was empty. There was nothing unusual about it; many people came and went; one could not notice everything. I think it must have been two days later that I saw the same young man seated in the same place. This time I was a little puzzled, because I was looking in this direction a moment ago and there was nobody there. And nobody came through the gate; at least I saw no one. The young man spoke to nobody and kept looking at Bhai Sahib. Bhai Sahib was talking, explaining something. Strange, I thought. He is so polite to every newcomer; this young

man is a stranger, but Bhai Sahib took no notice of him, neither the
first time when he was here, nor this time. It was unusual. I began to
wonder if I should speak to him, to show some friendliness, was
reflecting if he understands English. I looked at him, his strange wide
dark eyes, then I looked at Bhai Sahib; shall I speak to him? I thought.
Bhai Sahib looked directly at me and there was a warning in his eyes. I
lowered mine and the next moment I saw the poet coming through
the gate. Bhai Sahib began to talk to him. I turned my head and the
chair was empty. This time I was surprised. He certainly did not go
out through the garden gate, and being clearly a stranger he could not
go into the inner courtyard; it was private; Guruji's family never
received strangers; they were rather reserved. But still even then, I
soon dismissed it from my thoughts, attributing it to some lapse of
my attention. I knew by now that my mind did not work well at all.

I told this story to the assembled disciples, asking if that could
have been a Jinn.

"Most certainly yes," said the disciple who was explaining about
the Jinns a moment ago. "The whole appearance which you describe
is typical of a Jinn who came to get something from Bhai Sahib.
That's why his warning look to you not to talk to him."

3rd August

I PACKED MANY THINGS. Yesterday had lunch with Sharma. Spent a
serene morning. Guruji's garden is so full of people and so much talk
is going on . . . useless talk . . . I will be going. It is so terribly hot.

What is the use of staying here without you, my Sheikh? I miss
your presence so much . . . what are all those people to me . . . talk,
talk, talk.

And my heart is empty and sore . . . I don't grieve, oh no, but I
miss you so much. . . .

4th August

WHEN I WOKE UP THIS MORNING there was a great sweetness within my
heart. As soon as I opened my eyes, I began my *Jap*. And this
sweetness is still with me. . . .

I said goodbye to his family. The brother told me that in a week or
two all will be swept away. And nothing will remain of the troubles,
and I should note each day in my diary, for many things will happen.

We will see if he is right. Yesterday afternoon I sat in the front
room and talked to the wife and Durghesh. The wife is changed:
much thinner, and the sorrow ennobled her; her eyes are completely

different. His light was in her eyes, and his tenderness. And I listened to the hum of the fan, the hum I know so well . . . this fan was in my flat, when I was the first time with him from '61 to '63. It witnessed all my agonies, my troubles and sometimes deep despair . . . . The sound of it was with me when I sat alone in the darkened room; they were playing cards in the next room. And I looked outside through the chik into the garden I know so well . . . the mango tree . . . the guava shrub . . . the lime tree so fragrant with blossoms or laden with green or yellow limes . . . the brick fence behind it, the neighboring bungalow just showing on the other side. Goodbye, it is all in the past already. From now on, great changes will be for me, a life of fire in the world. But at first there will be the silence of the mountains. . . .

Later Mrs. Sharma came. I left her talking to the women and went with Ravindra and the brother-in-law to see the marble stone for the grave. Snow-white marble, my Sheikh, for your grave. . . . When I come back, I will see it. It will be ready in two months, so they say; let's make it three, for we are in India and everything is slow. . . . And my heart was so full of HIM, His Infiniteness . . . *Iailahi* . . . for ever . . . forever, my dear Sheikh. Such is the longing that it is unbearable . . . but it is easier for me now . . . there is peace. The terrible tension I felt in his presence is no more. . . .

85

Love and Faith Become One

6th August, 1966

LEFT ON THE 4TH OF AUGUST at about 2:30. Had a good journey. Traveled in the second-class ladies compartment and could lie down all night. One woman with her children was in the compartment, but they slept all night and got out at four a.m. We arrived in Katgodam about seven. As soon as it became light I sat at the window and looked at the landscape. Approaching Katgodam it assumed already the northern aspect. The light was different, the haze in the air. I remember that I noticed that for the first time when I went to Dehra Dun six years ago.

Then I saw the first hills, the first ramparts of the Himalayas, the foothills which roll on for thousands of miles. How lovely they were, here right before my eyes in the northeast, the sun rising in pale gold and the grey sky behind them. . . . I never imagined that I will see them again, ever. . . . I thought that I will go back to England on completion of my training. It never occurred to me that I may see the mountains, because there was no desire to do so. But all is different now.

In Katgodam I had to wait more than two hours for the departure of the bus. And the old Mercedes bus (they seem to be all Mercedes buses in the hills, made in India, and so old that it is a miracle that they don't fall to pieces at every sharp turning they have to negotiate), climbed and climbed, cracking and moaning with every joint, wobbling along a very good road, if one considers how difficult the upkeep of roads is in the mountains. Landslides, avalanches, monsoon—they see to it that at certain times of the year the road is either damaged or completely destroyed. I partly remembered this road to Almora. Little bridges, pine forests, downs and dales and hills seen from different angles due to the sharp turnings all the way, every hundred yards or so.

The serpentine road seemed never to end, but at one p.m. we reached Almora. After a short interval we continued for another three hours, and about four or shortly afterwards we reached Kausani. Nobody spoke English and I had a job to make myself understood as to what I wanted. Finally they somehow managed to understand and implied that I should see Sarala Devi, Sarala Ban, as she is called here. Ban stands for "Banji" which means elder sister. I understood that she is English and that she lives on top of the hill about one mile away. At first I tried to tell them that they should send a man, and tell her that I am here, but then I saw that it was not a practical proposition, as they did not understand me, and God knows when the man would go and when he would return, so I said to the coolie: "Let's go!" Leaving my luggage behind in the tavern, we went up the hill. I noticed that climbing up a steep goat-path was unusually difficult for me. I really got weak in all those months of sweating. Was very breathless, could hardly keep pace with the man, and had to stop several times. At last we arrived at a group of houses and bungalows. While the man tried without success to persuade a little girl to call Mem Sahib, I went to the windows of the largest building where I saw somebody moving around. In a large room which obviously was an office, with many windows forming a large bay, was sitting a most extraordinary looking person. She was dressed in a short-sleeved, rough, hand-woven *kurta* and a kind of *salvaar* (baggy trousers) which, as I later saw, fitted badly and was really far too short. She sat cross-legged on a small carpet; a low table stood before her on which she was writing letters in Hindi, but this I saw later. A young man was seated at the typewriter in the background, also on the floor, a low table before him, Indian fashion. She had a kind, very intelligent face of pink complexion. She was old, and small of stature. Her hair was hanging down in a plait made to look longer with a band as many Indian women do. I saw that I was before an outstanding personality.

I told her that I have written, but she said that she had received nothing. The address Prof. Batnagar gave me, Sarvadaya Center, was not a correct one; if he would have said Gandhiji Ashram, everybody would have known what was meant; but as it did not mean anything to the postmaster, the letter was lost. Standing at the open window and talking to her for a while, I became more and more impressed by her unusual ways. In the meantime she suggested that I could sleep in the room above the cow-shed; the inmate of the Ashram to whom it belongs is at the moment in Delhi. We went there after the keys had been found. It was a delightful little room, all wood and glass windows. It was in the pine forest. So the coolie brought the luggage which was left down in the village literally at everybody's mercy—it was dumped in the tavern at the bus stop. This is the lovely part in this country of contradictions: one can do a thing like this and get away with it, amidst a huge crowd of onlookers and plenty of little boys standing around. I remember also that once in Dehra Dun I left all my belongings at the bus station amongst a milling crowd of coolies, children and people waiting for the buses going to various destinations: "My responsibility," said the employee who sold me the ticket at the bus office and disappeared closing the door. Strangely enough I was not worried and went for two hours to see the bazaar. When I came back, my belongings were still standing in the same place; a large bus was beside it, people crowding around to get in. They simply walked around my three suitcases and the bedroll on top of them, clearly obstructing the way; they stood alone, apparently unnoticed; nobody was looking after them. . . .

Things of India . . . this incredible country, where as soon as I appeared in the bazaar, no, as soon as they saw me approaching, all the prices went miraculously up. And one day I remember after I had asked at least at five places the price of tomatoes, and learned that they were everywhere at one rupee and a half-a-kilo, I bought some. Meeting Mrs. Ghose, she asked me how much I payed for them. When she learned the price, indignant, she went back with me to the vendor: she bought the same tomatoes for half a rupee, half an hour ago. . . . Mrs. Ghose released a torrent of indignation and I got my rupee back.

When the coolie was payed, I had a bath in one of the bath cubicles. Pumped some drinking water from the well with the help of the girls of the Ashram, and had some rest. The latrine was the "jungle," alias the pine wood; this was not too good . . . it can present some problems.

The prayers before the evening meal were lovely; they sang the second chapter of the *Gita* about the man who never gets upset. The bigger girls were spinning while singing, the storm lantern standing in the middle of the floor. The small ones were sitting in a row with their backs to us swaying gently. The darkening sky, the voices of children, the sound of the spinning wheels, it was all very moving . . . and later the increasing darkness behind the windows and the smell of the pines after the rain. The evening meal was gloomy, all seated in rows on a dirty long straw mat along the floor. Hard cold *pulkas* (unleavened flat pancakes) were distributed and some vegetables, of which I took little though I was hungry. Then a crowd of girls with a torch conducted me through a thicket to my sleeping place in the wood.

I was lying awake listening to the sound of the pines. And to the stillness. The SOUND was here again . . . the same Sound which I heard the first time in Harrow in my house. I remember I was very puzzled; then, I tried to get the note of it on my guitar. It took me a long time to identify it: it was the chord of middle D and middle F. But though on my guitar those were the correct sounds, later, in the Himalayas I heard the same sound supersonically at such a high pitch that I thought that I could not have heard it with my ears . . . and here was this SOUND again. Each time the wind stopped and complete stillness was reigning, it was clear, audible, loud. . . .

Gradually even the wind subsided, and it became completely still. Only this sound remained; it was like a lost friend, found again . . . something which belonged to me. D is the note of the second ray, and F is the sound of the green ray, the ray of the earth, but according to Guruji, green is the best possible color, the color of Realization of Truth. . . .

The peace was complete. But the meaning of the Sound I did not know. . . .

Next morning Sarala Ben came and brought me some *kitchery* (rice dish with peas). She looked quite extraordinary in her *salvaar* pinned up and a dirty *kurta*. She was planting some rugged willow trees near the water tank. They make water, so she was saying, and must be planted while it was raining.

Later I went for lunch which was just as gloomy, only there was daylight and a storm lantern as in the evening, giving so little light in the large kitchen that it was difficult even to see the food. A lovely, grey, very thin cat sat beside me, and I gave it my *dahi* which she licked up with such speed that it was amazing. In the afternoon there were people at Sarala's office and she told me that one gentleman, Jiva Bhai Patel, has perhaps the solution to my problem. He is in charge of Anashakti Ashram which was previously a Dak Bungalow situated on the opposite hill and which was given to Gandhi Memorial Fund by the Indian Government. There I could have one room with a bathroom attached to it, and she said:

"Of course, there you will have the full view of the snows and you will be practically alone." It sounded fine. It was raining heavily. But then it stopped. So I went to see the place. It was just right, on top of the next hill. And the road to it was a good one, a motor road halfway up the hill and a bridle path from there to the Ashram. So, we agreed that I will move the next day, weather permitting. And we all went to Sarala, Jiva Bhai, myself, and a Sannyasi from Shivananda Ashram, who was his friend and who was staying with him, and also another friend from the plains, a little fat man, very jolly and breathless. All was arranged; soon we had tea with Sarala, and I retired early. I did not want any supper, but did not miss the singing of the girls in the evening mingling harmoniously with the sound of the spinning wheels. . . .

Slept well. Cows did not smell much. Here in the mountains, cows are not at all smelly, and cow sheds are not offensive places as in the plains. From time to time I heard a cow moving below, and there was this fantastic stillness, typical of the Himalayas—this stillness which seems so thick and solid that one could cut it with a knife and which is like a sound, a continuous sound of the silence. . . . Silence . . . the absolute silence on windstill days has a sound, a tremendous sound, ringing all around. How still the forest can be on a windstill, foggy night. . . .

Waited next day for Jiva Bhai to send coolies, as promised. Coolies did not come. It was drizzling on and off. Had lunch in the Ashram. Sarala looked even more extraordinary in a green, roughly woven *kurta* and shorts of the same material. She was gardening as usual.

Immediately after lunch I went down. When going up the hill to the Anashakti Ashram, I met three boys midway seated near the roadway who were obviously waiting for me. They began to shout all together that Jiva Bhai has gone out and that they will bring my suitcases. I was perplexed. They were small boys; the suitcases were very heavy. But they said each of them is as strong as a man; so I took them first up to the Ashram; then the Sannyasi did some translations for us, and sent them immediately to bring the cases. I, in the meantime, went down to the village to get some provisions. It took quite some time to trace who has rice, which shop has potatoes and onions, and which one has salt, matches, and flour. I had to walk from one to another, backward and forward. When going up I met the boys, painfully walking up the hill with my heavy cases. I gave them three rupees each. They were satisfied and ran away happily. Two hours later a heavy rain started.

I was glad. I did well to hurry up in between two showers. . . .

9th August

SO I BEGAN TO SETTLE DOWN. And while unpacking and arranging my things, I was thinking that there would be eight months of serenity for me. Eight months of practically complete solitude. I will escape the English winter and will be sitting here enjoying the Himalayas.

On the 8th in the morning, at dawn, before the sunrise, the snows were clear for a brief half an hour. The pale yellow sky streaked with grey clouds behind the East was a glorious sight. . . . Himalayas . . . never expected to see you again, but here you are. . . . Right in front of me was Trisul. In Abbott Mount, Nanda Devi was right in front; here it is Trisul and the great, plump, enormous mass which has no name apparently.

To H. I wrote on the 7th, immediately; on the 8th to Christine, Ravindra, Joyce and Joan. It is raining every day. Fog. Bad weather. The pine air is balsam, and since I have been here, already on the second day I had no kidney trouble. Clearly the heat was responsible for it all.

9th August, Evening

AT LAST MY DIARY IS UP TO DATE NOW. In the afternoon went to Sarala Ban to pay the rent. They don't want to call it rent, but contribution to the Ashram. But for me it is the same, so I settled it. Scraped a bit of club moss from her water tank and got a plant with a large root, of *berberis vulgaris*. It was for kidneys; one makes a tea from it. Going down it was very slippery, nearly fell several times. And to fall on a steep hill is not much fun, as one can imagine. When I came home, it was nearly dark. I was glad of the man's shoes I bought in the village. They are huge, size 8, but very comfortable with thick wool socks. They are just the thing to tramp about in the hills; they will especially be useful in winter.

It is practically raining non-stop, all day long, and mountain fog is thick and persistent. August is a bad month; in September it should be better.

10th August

EVERY DAY IS THE SAME. Heavy rain and thick fog. The Ashram and the garden are on top of the hill; this is visible; but immediately behind is a thick, grey nothing. When the weather is like this in the mountains, it is depressing; one can see nothing and do nothing. At the moment I have an intense heart activity. From time to time every day, the heart is beating and beating, and I send a mental greeting to Guruji each time it happens. I do my *Jap* practically all the time. And the heart is beating and beating. . . . Guruji . . . you left me alone. . . . Why?

Why, Guruji, my dear . . . why? I am so alone . . . the longing, Guruji . . . the longing for you. . . .

Afternoon

SINCE THIS MORNING, very, very strong vibrations in the heart, so strong that at times it is difficult to breathe. The rain is hammering on my roof. Solid fog outside.

11th August

IT IS EXACTLY THREE WEEKS AGO, on a Thursday, that he died. In the evening after seven, I kept thinking of his last hours. He passed away at 7:20, so Virendra told me. And then the meaning of a sentence he told me not so long ago occurred to me:

"The time comes when love and faith become one and the same." It suddenly became clear that when the Master is no more, Love and Faith are one. Beloved, give me the power to remain forever under the shelter of my Sheikh. . . . And this thought filled me with a strange joy. A kind of security? My dear, dear Sheikh. . . . So many things became clear to me gradually. . . .

"When I am no more, many things you will understand. Now, you cannot understand, it is impossible for you." Not so many weeks ago he said that. . . .

Writing letters all the morning. . . . Good heavens, what vibrations I have, even the breathing causes difficulty. Why did you not take me with you? Why did you leave me alone? I don't want this world, and you know it. . . . Him I want. Only Him. And forever. . . .

14th August

IT IS JUST RAINING. That's all. The heart is so heavy, the longing infinite.

15th August

AND IT IS RAINING . . . bitterly cold.

16th August

I HAD TWO DREAMS, towards the morning, of which I remember very little. In both he was very kind to me, and in both he was about to die. In the last one, I remember, I told him:

"How will I live without you?" And he answered,

"The king dies and passes it over to the next one; this one dies, and it passes to the successor. That's how they do it in Windsor."

"But we are not in Windsor," I said.

"It is the *Param Para*; somebody has to remain alive," he said, getting up from his seat. And the atmosphere of both dreams was of terrible longing which remained with me all the morning. The heart activity was absolutely unbearable. In the afternoon it eased a bit, and there was much nearness and stillness and great peace. And a kind of sorrowful happiness. . . .

18th August

IT IS RAINING HEAVILY every single day with very short intervals. Thick mist is drifting over the hills or sitting tight on them all the time. I noticed that when I do the *Jap* intensely, the heart activity begins. And when I cry to Him, it becomes unbearable. . . .

20th August

IT IS FOUR WEEKS. It was four weeks yesterday. I went to bed shortly after seven. Suddenly great heart activity began. I got up and looked at my watch which I put into the recess of the window. It was 7:15. He was just dying, then . . . and I did much *Jap*. And I thought of him much. You promised, Master, you promised . . . and I am alone. . . . Please, keep your promise, Master, keep your promise! Felt much suffocation and I cried. And while thinking, all of a sudden I realized that, though it is only four weeks since his death, it all seems so far away . . . and even his death is already far away . . . and all I went through begins to lose its importance; the sting is taken out from it. After all, most troubles and sufferings were physical happenings only. It was the preparation for the future. The future could be now . . . now the Reality, the Effect of it all, will begin to emerge. . . . The Longing will take me to it, the ceaseless *Jap*. What he did was to clear the way. Only for that there was time. This was the only important thing, for time was short. The rest will be done now. I feel it. There are signs; the tremendous vibration in the heart is a harbinger of something. I keep remembering his words:

"When the Master makes the disciple like himself, the Master is in a deep state and the disciple. . . ."

"Is also in a deep state," I said.

"No," he answered. **"How can it be? The disciple has to learn how to go deep."**

And years before: **"You will see what vibrations will be when one realizes the Self. It is difficult to bear. . . ."**

Yes, he only cleared the way. There was no time to do more than that. All the suffering is far; it is moving away. And his death is far, and somehow not even important. He is alive. He is in my heart. My faith is taking me to him. Faith and love are the same thing now.

And before falling asleep and in the night, the longing was tremendous; so terrible were the vibrations I seemed to suffocate. And even now while writing it down I can hardly breathe. The heart is wild, going, racing, missing beats, stopping . . . racing again. Like waves in the ocean, on and off, coming and going, all the time. The reality is the *Jap*. The Longing. The Faith. The sweetness of resting in Him in deepest peace. . . . The physical world with its happenings is not important. To be in peace with Him is the only important thing.

"The destruction of the body cannot be something to grieve over. The Spirit is indestructible. It is an unbroken ever-flowing stream. Many bodies settle on it for a while and then disappear" (Vinoba, Talks on the *Gita*).

"The Self is impatient to pervade the world. It wants to encompass all creation. But we shut it up in a cell. So, we are not conscious of it. From morning till evening we are busy minding the body. Day and night we worry how fat or how thin our bodies have become. One would think that there is no other joy in the world. . . . but even beasts experience pleasure of senses" (Vinoba).

Yogic training is designed to release the Self. Gradually. Imperceptibly. It is a slow process. And don't I know how the changes take place, how the consciousness expands, the understanding grows, since I came to my Revered Teacher!

"The mind can be utterly serene; though action rages without: the heart can be tuned to produce unbroken music . . . (Vinoba). How very, very true. . . . And I know that this serenity, the peace, will remain with me—of this I am quite sure. It was his gift to us at his parting. . . .

86

Himalayan Retreat

24th August, 1966

THE DAYS PASS QUICKLY. Once again they pass quickly. When Guruji died, those two weeks before I left never seemed to pass. They dragged along with leaden boots, slow and heavy. . . . Now, once again, the time flies. . . .

I get up about six. Have my bath, then tea, and usually one pulka (*roti—chappathi*, a flat pancake) for breakfast. Watch the mist around the hills, always hoping to see the snows which sometimes are partly visible for a few minutes only, once here, once there, covered as they are by clouds and mist. This morning they are hidden completely by a thick curtain of fog. But the day is sunny, with a thin, sickly sun, like in England, seen through thin mist or high cirrus clouds. I read, write letters in the forenoon, and twice weekly go down to the village to do a little shopping. Cook something. Then a simple lunch. One cannot buy much in the village. Now I have nice tomatoes for at least one week. A tomato salad and *rotis* make a good lunch. Sometimes I have a grated radish to go with it . . . those large, white, very long radishes, so strong that tears come into one's eyes. They are very good for the kidneys and the liver. After lunch some rest. Then read or meditate. Then carry some stones for the Ashram garden wall to be built soon. Then read again or do something, mostly meditate. And then after six go out on the veranda and sit with the Sannyasi and Mr. Patel, and we have a chat until seven. Then we warm our milk and go to bed to our "Beloved." This is my day. Last Sunday we went three-and-a-half miles to see a friend of Patel who has an apple orchard. It was seven miles return, a lovely walk through the pine forest, part of it on a very steep hill. The Sannyasi and Patel walked on quickly, and I was breathless. Am not so young anymore, out of training, and weakened by the heat of the plains. We returned before dark. I was not much tired.

The longing is great. There is some resentment in my heart. . . . I hoped so much. . . . Prayed and longed and suffered, and . . . I am alone and I am nowhere. . . . There was a promise, Bhai Sahib . . .

but it was not said that it should have been kept right now . . . perhaps sometime in the future . . . who knows? . . .

"The time will come when Faith and Love are one. And then even Love will remain behind and only One will remain, and later this also will go, and nothing will remain."

Keep thinking and pondering. . . . I see the time coming when the One only will remain. And then it will go too. . . . I pray so much and do *Jap* all the time. God is much nearer than Guruji, like in London. One only will remain; it must become a permanent state, not on-and-off as it is now. . . .

Wake up about two every night. And the first thing to do is to listen for the Sound . . . if it is still there. It always is. Last night I cried, the heart was so heavy. Am so alone. . . how to reach you, my Beloved? I could reach you in London, when I was with Bhai Sahib, but now, sometimes I cannot. . . . Bhai Sahib . . . and where are you?? Cried myself into sleep.

And this morning the depression is great, and the loneliness and the longing. . . . Yesterday I looked at his photos. They never meant much to me—they were not him. The living man in Bhogoun, full of dynamism, and the dead face of utter serenity, his last Samadhi. . . . The love flared up like a sudden flame, and a strange feeling went with it, impossible to describe, which is perhaps a memory of this face, alive, dynamic, so deeply engraved within me. . . . The longing is intense and depressingly constant. And the loneliness . . . I will cry to Thee, and cry, and keep crying till the milk of Thy kindness boils up . . . says Rumi. During the conversation the Sannyasi told me that according to the *Shastras*, three things are difficult to get: A human birth, the desire for Realization, and a Sat Guru. . . . While he was talking, I was thinking how fortunate I am . . . I have the combination of all three. . . . Every Guru can take you to God, he was saying . . . if . . . you have enough faith. It is the faith which takes you there. The famous story of the Shudra (the lowest Hindu caste; an untouchable) woman, the Brahmin and his *yagña*:

A Brahmin was seated on the bank of the Ganga performing the *yagña* (a fire sacrifice). A Shudra woman approached him. He was annoyed.

"Be careful not to come near me, otherwise my fire sacrifice will be polluted," he said sternly.

"Maharaj," said the woman, "I will not approach you, but I see that you are a holy man; please give me a Mantra to be able to cross the Ganga. My son is seriously ill, and there is no boatman in sight to carry me across."

"Yes, yes," said the Brahmin, whose only thought was to get rid of her. "Repeat: *Ram, Ram,* and you will cross the Ganga."

The woman walked away full of faith, began to repeat *Ram, Ram,* and walked over the river. Having completed what she intended to do, she returned by the same means. The Brahmin was still sitting on the same place finishing his *yagña*. She waited till he finished, then she fell at his feet. He was astonished.

"Maharaj," she said, "you are a great Guru. I did as you have said and crossed the Ganga on foot." And the Brahmin was ashamed and did many more *yagñas* to atone for his intolerance. . . .

25th August

TODAY IS THURSDAY. Five weeks since you have gone. . . . It is strange that I did not suffer very much, strange that I don't feel that you are dead. You are more dynamically alive than ever . . . only for the moment there is great separation. I cannot reach you at all. . . .

Was that the last warning when you gave me the hint: **"When I put you in the mud, you will try to get out; the more the limitation, the greater the perfection will be. . . . If you want to commit suicide, show me how you are going to do it. . . . If HE does not want it, how will you do it?"** And he concluded that he was not only once, but very often in such a state. . . . It seems that all those hints are referring to the present state I am in now. . . . He disappeared from my sight . . . but God is near. . . . And it seems to me nearer and nearer. . . . I do my *Jap.* All the time. And the heart activity is tremendous. So much tenderness there is. . . . His Name is so sweet . . . and my being, my breath, my body . . . and my feelings are His.

When I woke up this morning, there was fear. I don't know why, just primitive fear at awakening. I dedicate it to you, I thought, and I will be free . . . immediately I was. The fear vanished as I began to do *Jap.* Everything I dedicate to Him—my pain of separation, my resentment, my longing, my love . . . everything. . . .

Such peace is with me, and a stream of love welling from the deepest depths of my being.

The jasmine flowers, which I plucked from the large shrub at the back of the house and put all over my bed and under my pillow, smell sweet and heavy. The snows, since yesterday, are covered with a curtain of mist. . . . Not white fluffy clouds, which assume the shape of the mountains, but just a screen of grey, a curtain of nothingness. But the days are sunny and warm. The Ashram garden is ablaze with marigolds, zynnias, cosmos. In the mornings and in the evenings at sunset, somebody on the opposite hill is practicing the flute. How lovely it sounds amongst the thickly wooded hills in the fresh mountain air. . . . A boy was waiting for Patel this morning, sitting on the veranda, and he began to sing—a devotional song it was. I listened, looking at the hills, the blue distances—so much sunshine, clouds, the azure sky, and the voice of the boy . . . and the heart was melting with the tenderness for Him, for His beautiful Creation. . . . Every movement of my heart to You. . . . All I think. All I feel. Enjoy through me . . . I am here for You, going back to You, wanting nothing but you, willing to do Your Will only . . . take my heart! It is full to the brim with tenderness for You!

26th August

LYING IN BED AFTER SEVEN, kept thinking of his last hours. And it occurred to me that I was the only disciple present at the moment of his death. I think it has a great importance. Only his eldest son was in the room; he was sitting on the bed supporting his father who actually died leaning on his arm. And Virendra, his youngest son, stood with me at the door. At that moment only his two sons and myself were there, nobody else of his disciples. Once, I remember that he told me how his Rev. Guru Maharaj died.

"And I was the only one present at that moment, neither my brother nor the others could come; they were away." And he smiled, obviously pleased, while telling me that. Naturally so, it was very human, for his Guru gave him everything. Actually, while dying, his Guru did send him away. And he saw him again after he died. Bhai Sahib did not leave a successor officially, nor did he leave anything in writing. But a few days after his death one of his disciples asked me:

"You were present at the very moment of his death?" I said that I was. "It is a great Grace of God," he said, and there was much longing in his voice and in his eyes. "It is a great satisfaction." I wondered why it should be called a satisfaction. . . . But now I begin to think that it might be a satisfaction, in some way. His last deep look . . . and the physical being which he was . . . I saw it go . . . the man was no more. . . . Was there a definite intention that I should be the only one stranger apart from the two members of his family? Was it the will of the Guru, or the Will of God? Of both I suppose.

To what extent did he get orders . . . how does it work? Who knows? . . . But there is a certain resentment in me, that he left me alone; he went, and I got nothing . . . nothing? I begin to wonder. . . .

27th August

A SPIDER WAS SITTING ON THE WALL above the bathroom door. And it did not move for about three hours, all the while I meditated. It was so lovely. Sitting on the wall, head down, all the eight legs spread out so symmetrically as to look like a perfect painting, or a piece of jewelery, not alive, almost too perfect. I moved during my meditation, sometimes my hands, or my head, or my legs. It did not stir. And I began to meditate on it . . . on the wonder and perfection of Him who created him so perfect, so beautiful, so rational. On Him whose substance manifests as a spider in this case. It was a large thing, with all its legs spread out, easily two inches or even more. The body not so big, perhaps three-quarters of an inch. And he was slender. He did not eat for a while, it was obvious. Perhaps he was preparing to hybernate, who knows? My heart was so full of his Creator, I had to share it with someone. . . . Patel's and Sannyasi's voices came from the veranda. They were discussing *Vedanta*. I opened my door and asked them to come into my room and see the spider. Patel was spinning as usual in the mornings, but the Sannyasi came in. Looked at the spider with a tender smile.

"Yes," he said, nodding slowly. "The loveliness of every manifestation of His. . . ." And he turned and went out. They picked up the conversation where it was interrupted.

28th August

I DREAMT THAT I WAS WRITING some verses. When I woke up in the night, I remembered them and wrote them down. The Sound was with me loud and clear. . . .

"Into my life you came like a storm of monsoon banging down
    from the eastern sky.
And you scattered me, like the wind disperses dry grass and
    the petals of flowers.
Out of myself you scattered me into Nothingness,
Beyond the Nowhere, beyond the Beyond. . . ."

Outside all was still. Some dogs were barking suddenly, and then silence again. Then a haunting voice of the barking deer . . . where barking deer lives, tigers and leopards are too, so I was told. Dogs began to bark in chorus down in the village. Then silence descended. Only the Sound remained.

SORTING OUT MANY THINGS within myself. Thinking a lot and remembering. How he was always pointing to the Truth, how in every way he was helping us all. . . .

For instance, I remember, it must have been sometime in January '62 that gradually I became aware that I was "seeing things." The world seemed transformed, full of light. The trees, the plants, every object had light around it—vivid light, sometimes static, sometimes dynamic and alive like in trees, plants, animals, but especially in people.

And the colors were of a purity, of a dynamism, luminous, like prismatic colors, and at the same time infinitely delicate, changing, flowing into each other, breathlessly beautiful. I saw an egg-shaped orange thing—its size must have been about two feet—jumping with lightning speed under the trees all around Guruji's garden. It could have been a nature spirit; I don't know. I saw lovely beings in the air: some had dragon shapes, some had a vague human semblance, but all were of wonderful colors, shimmering, made of light itself. But on the other hand I could see also black, horrid shapes, lurking in the dark corners or dirty places, sometimes attached to human beings or following them.

The world became a very interesting place to live. I came to know the thoughts of people, the reasons why they came to Guruji. I used to tell one of his disciples who sat near me: this one comes because his child is ill; this other one because he has a court case and wants some help and advice; that man on the right is ill and hopes that Guruji will heal him, and so on. . . . Of course I was delighted. Bhai Sahib did not take any notice of me, was talking to others, and I sat there full of wonder and delight, observing everything around me.

Then, one day, when he turned to me and said something, I took the opportunity and told him how pleased I was that only after such a short time with him I was progressing so fast.

"Oh?" he lifted his eyebrows, **"and why so?"**

I told him, describing in detail what I saw and telling him that I knew the reason why each one came to him.

He listened. His expression was that of slight irony; then he gave me a sideways look and turned away to speak to others.

I did not notice anything at that moment. Many interesting things always happened in his presence; people came and went, so I was not immediately aware that I didn't see anything else, except things of this physical world. Going home, I expected to see something as of late and watched carefully, but in vain. Thought that I was tired—this was the reason—and it will be all right tomorrow.

But when I woke up next morning and expected to see everything bathed in those wonderful colors, I was disappointed very much . . . the world was grey and ordinary . . . no more of this quality of wonder and beauty about it.

I waited. Not in his garden, not at home. Nothing. My disappointment was terrible. Then after three days of fruitless waiting, when he happened to look in my direction, I said:

"You took it away from me!"

"Of course!" he answered quickly. **"Just look at you! You were blown up like a balloon! Are you after Absolute Truth or are you after illusions? How will the self go if you continue like this?"**

I said nothing. But I remember well that I was resentful and sorry for myself.

I think, two or three weeks later, the fire began to flow in my body, and the ghastly visions which went with it and the suffering which it caused obliterated everything else. . . .

Yes. He tried to help every one of us. . . . And remembering it all now, a saying came into my mind. The mother of a friend of mine used to tell her when she was a child:

"From people to people, from Saints to God. And the Saints don't hang in the calendars on the wall, but are here with us, living with God and in God amongst people, helping them."

And didn't he say once that the Grace of God flows through a human being? . . . comparing God to a power house and the Saint to a transformer of this power.

5th September

HOW LOVELY IT IS when the sun is shining through the mist; it is like a painting of Turner. So many colors are in this misty, opaque light, and the deodars and the pines, here on the slope of our hill, look ghostly, unreal. It has just stopped raining. It was coming down heavily all night. It is clearing in the south already; patches of blue sky are appearing in between the clouds, and a slight breeze coming from the direction of the snows chases the mist down the slope, weaving it in and out between the pine trees. What a lovely place is Kausani. . . . And suddenly the sun comes out; the last patches of mist hurry past as if trying to clasp and clutch with long ghostly fingers the branches of the pines, and hide and linger in the crags, in the clefts between the hills. . . . How blue and clear are the distances . . . and now, now, as though by magic, the mass of Trisul appears as if suspended, resting on the white, soft mist . . . and vanishes behind the veil. No, not quite. Dimly it is visible, like in a dream. Just the outline, just a promise. . . . It is blinding white. Fresh snow fell on the heights. Near, so near are the snows. . . . For many weeks I was waiting for you to appear . . . like the Beloved you were obstinately hidden behind the veil . . . and like the Beloved you are suddenly, unexpectedly near . . . clear . . . sharp. So near, only to stretch out the hand to touch you. . . . Fifteen miles in direct line, as the crow flies, is not much. Now I wish I had a camera with me to photograph you in all your glory. . . .

Sannyasi is leaving today, and he was telling us about the tantric practices in a place near Calcutta where dead bodies and human bones are used for meditation and for all sorts of practices. He stayed there for a while, but he did not like it, so he said. I don't blame him. . . .

Am still thinking of the snows appearing like in a dream after the rain in the night. Now they are covered up once more. So completely, so thoroughly, that if one does not know that they exist, one could think that behind the nearest hill is nothing at all. . . .

But the fragrance of the pines is inebriating, and the rain hammering on the roof is a lullaby of the mountains . . . to be endured and accepted.

8th September

WOKE UP THIS MORNING with His Name on my lips. How imperfect I am . . . I still have interruptions, forget to call, to repeat His Name all day long. And when I remember, then I bow and ask His forgiveness. How tender is this feeling of love for Him . . . the loveliest, the softest feeling. . . .

It was raining all night. And this morning it is still pouring down steadily, as it can pour down in the mountains, unwaveringly, ceaselessly, and stubbornly, and thick mist is sitting tightly on the hills.

Wrote many letters during the last few days. Will go to post them if it stops raining. If not, they have to wait. Keeping a list of all to whom I wrote. Suddenly it is important; this represents now my work.

By repeating His Name all the time I am getting myself into a deeper and deeper state of peace. Nearness or not, the love seems to deepen, and somehow SOMETHING seems to change in my consciousness; but WHAT? . . . the mind cannot assess as yet. Later, perhaps I will know. . . . One usually comes to know later . . . or not at all. There is such a deep inner joy in repeating His Name with breath. It will become part of my being, I know. . . .

"First you do the mantra, then the mantra does you," and, **"and the time will come when love will remain behind and only One will remain, and then even this will go; nothing will remain. . . ."**

9th September

BY CEASELESSLY DOING J AP one is really the whole day in meditation. And it deepens and keeps deepening. Each repetition leaves a sweetness in the heart, like something infinitely dear . . . and becoming dearer, more precious all the time.

He prepared the Way and he went. . . . And now I just go to God—there is no other alternative. There is no other way at all to go (*Yajurveda*). . . . So simple really. Simple it is because the Way is clear. . . .

There is nothing but Nothingness . . . Nothingness in the triune, triple sense: Nothingness because the little self has to go; one has to become nothing. Nothingness, because the higher states of consciousness represent nothingness to the mind, for it cannot reach there; it is completely beyond its range of perception. Complete comprehension on the level of the mind is not possible, so one is faced with nothingness. And in the last, most sublime sense, it is to merge into the Luminous Ocean of the Infinite. I think this is how one has to understand it; that is how Bhai Sahib had meant it, when he spoke of Nothingness and of the One.

And then I see it increasingly as the consciousness expands and the understanding deepens: one begins to see Him in all and everything. There is nothing but He; one is surrounded by Him everywhere. . . . So one begins to surrender to life, to people, to things, as being Him, and Him alone. The tremendous implication of it is that one feels oneself to be part of it, but a tiny part of it, smaller than the smallest grain of sand . . . and still, this little grain of sand is necessary. To quote a great Sufi, Inayat Khan:

"The world would not be the same if you were not in it—a little note in the great Symphony of Life."

A note, just a note, contributing to the Harmony of Creation. So let us all be pure, ringing notes, never out of tune, singing His praise forever. . . .

87

Scorpion and Caterpillar

IT WAS VERY FOGGY THIS MORNING and it was raining until noon. I woke up with such a longing that I began to cry out of sheer, terrible longing, a kind of despair. . . .

Made a warm petticoat out of an old skirt. Prayed. Did *Jap*.

This afternoon there was, and still is, a large rainbow. Only its lower part was visible, growing out of the forest on the opposite hill to the left, curving towards the snows, hidden behind a thick, grey curtain of clouds. The part of the rainbow which was against the background of dark clouds was very vivid, exceptionally wide, and the yellow color was predominant. I thought of Guruji's words to Satendra: **"And the yellow color was gone. . . ."**

The yellow color is back again, Guruji, my dear, but you are no more. . . . No more in this physical world. But you are in my heart; and in the states of Nothingness, in the night during the deep meditation, you are with me. . . . But you are so different now that I don't even dare to call you "Guruji." You are just a Great Power, a whirlwind which sucks up my very being, leaving nothing behind but an empty shell. . . .

The day before yesterday it was seven weeks . . . there is some resentment from time to time. You went, my dear, and left me like this—alone. All I can do is cry to God. . . . Perhaps this is the purpose of it. . . I don't know . . . am so confused sometimes. And the heart is crying, crying . . . perhaps this was your intention. Perhaps it is exactly what I am supposed to do.

The rainbow is still there—very vivid in the small patch of sunshine on the side of the hill, as though growing out of the pine trees. . . .

11th September

I AM IN COMPLETE DARKNESS. I am in silence. My heart is crying for You. It is said that in silence and in darkness grows the seed. In all the Sufi books it is mentioned that after moments of great Nearness the heart is plunged in loneliness and even great depression sometimes.

Fell asleep in the afternoon for about two hours. It is not usual. And on waking up I heard myself saying to someone:

"And these meditations have been carefully translated by a friend who wishes to remain anonymous. They have been worded in such a way as to form gradual steps on the ladder of progress." And while completely awake, I thought: but those meditations are not for us. We trust in God and call His Name; that's how we progress. Did Guruji not say to us:

"On our line we trust in God only; we surrender to Him, and this is our Sadhana."

But the progress is gradual: the states of consciousness change imperceptibly . . . I can observe it clearly.

12th September

IT IS RAINING VERY HEAVILY this morning. I became disgusted when I looked out of the window about half past five. Solid, dense fog sat on all the hills. It just started to pour down as from buckets. And I was thinking that I have been here already more than one month, and I have never seen all the mountains clearly. Only some of them, and even this only sometimes. Bits and pieces of them, disappearing swiftly. And it seemed to me that they are a symbol of my life with Guruji: I always hoped so much, desired and longed for Reality. But all I got was a few bits and pieces sometimes, disappearing swiftly.

All was and is covered with thick fog. And every day I looked out, every day I hoped and prayed and longed. But elusive and invisible like snow, he gave me nothing to the last, except troubles, tests, heartache to no end . . . like those mountains. Every day at sunrise I look out, each time I hope . . . nothing. Grey fog. Thick clouds. For ever and ever, day after day. . . .

15th September

LAST NIGHT I WAS UNDRESSING in the semi-darkness; the mosquito net was already put up. Usually I don't throw my thick wool socks on the floor. Rats can touch them, or something creepy can find its way into them. I wear them over my stockings during the day; the floor is made of concrete, very cold, and it is cold in the shade during the day . . . especially now when there is hardly any sunshine left. But in the last two days I grew careless and threw them on the floor. There are no rats here; at least I found no evidence of them.

While taking the socks off, I saw in semi-darkness something large approaching the small carpet where my feet were resting. I quickly put my sandals on, searched for the matches on the table, found them, struggled to light one after another—they are all damp in the rainy season—all the time hoping that the thing should not creep away in the meantime. Finally I managed to light the small kerosene lamp. Took it to my bed. It went out. Lit it again. And then saw the thing. It was a baby scorpion. Still small, about two-and-a-half inches only, and light brown. It must have been of the same variety I saw in Italy; perhaps here in the hills they don't grow bigger. A fully grown scorpion—I saw one in Adyar—is about five to six inches long, jet black and very poisonous. But the small ones are quite poisonous too, and can cause much pain and a large swelling. It kept creeping away. At first I thought I'd leave it alone. The pretty little thing, when it saw me approaching with the lamp, raised its tail in a warning way. So I realized that I won't be able to sleep, imagining that it may creep up the wooden leg of my charpoy. It is true, I had my mosquito net which was a protection, but he could hide in the folds of it or in between the blankets and sting me when I was making the bed in the morning. So I got hold of a soft broom, trying to pick it up without hurting it. He in the meantime tried to hide in the corner between the door and the wall and attacked the broom vigorously. Small as he was, he had no fear—they have such courage, the scorpions. I managed at last to entangle him in the broom and threw him outside. He fell on the concrete steps and did not move, looking cramped and twisted. I went out. What a pity. So I killed him after all, unintentionally. I picked him up gently with the broom and threw him into the flower bed beside my door. As soon as he felt moist earth beneath him, he began to scamper away hurriedly. He was completely unhurt. He pretended to be dead in self-defense. It is not so easy to hurt a scorpion; it has quite a good armor, like a miniature lobster. I was glad. Creep away, little one, God bless you. May you not sting anybody, I hope. . . .

16th September

THE SUNRISE WAS ONCE MORE like a painting of Turner this morning, seen through the luminous mist driving up from the valleys, drifting in patches and stripes across the hill. One could just see the mountains, dimly, amongst swiftly billowing clouds, like in a grey-blue dream. It was lovely after a night of rain. The sun was warm. I enjoyed my cup of tea seated on my doorstep. And then I saw him: he was large, perhaps three inches long, very hairy, very thick, a caterpillar, of the most beautiful russet brown. He was walking rather purposefully on the ledge of the wall behind me towards the veranda. I was watching him; he was advancing surprisingly swiftly. You will be killed there; a crow or some other bird will get you; where are you going? What a large butterfly or moth it must be, to have such a large caterpillar; I wondered, what variety it could be? He was going and going, and from time to time he was lifting the front part of the body, checking if he could climb up. But the whitewashed wall was too smooth; he could find no hold with his little feet. Reached the pillar near the veranda steps and tried to climb up, but without success. I understood that there was an urge in him to go up, perhaps to pupate somewhere and be safe for the coming winter. In spring he will be a butterfly. Our garden was full of them, fluttering about in the sunshine. I took a folded newspaper and made him go on it and put him on a stone heap thinking that he will easily find a place there in a crack to settle for the winter, but he went again towards the wall and began to try to climb it unsuccessfully, falling back again and again. To help him I put him on one of the beams supporting the roof; surely he could find a good place there. But when after a while I went out, I found him lying on the ground, slightly dazed. He fell down obviously from this height, and thick and fat as he was, even cushioned by his hairiness, he must have hurt himself. Seeing me approaching he became energetic and tried again to climb up the wall. Such an urge to go upwards. . . . How can I help you? Where shall I put you? I put him again on the stone heap. But by that time he was clearly exhausted. For a few minutes he sat on a stone, his head hanging on one side, as a tired human being would do . . . then he began the fruitless attempt to climb the wall. An idea struck me: what about the tall cypress pine? It is so old, and has so many crooks and crannies to hide in the bark. There is a chance that a bird may get hold of him if he is foolish enough to expose himself, still, it is worth trying, though his urge made him oblivious of any danger, so it seems. Once more I made him walk on a folded newspaper. Then took him to the tree. The very moment he got the feeling of the bark beneath his feet, as if glad, as if relieved, steadily and rhythmically he began to climb upwards. I could feel the urge, the relief. I felt his hurry; up and up he went; he must be tired. His movements were slower than before. I hoped that he would have the strength not to let the bark go, to cling to it. Ten feet. Twenty-five feet. He was still going. There was, in between the two large branches, a crack, a hollow; that would be a good hiding place. But he ignored it; he was still going up. And suddenly it occurred to me that he was a symbol

.of spiritual life. . . . Caterpillars we are. One day we will all be butterflies. But in order to become a butterfly we have to go higher and higher to be able to transform ourselves somewhere in the darkness, in a secret hiding place. We have to go up higher and higher in spite of the dangers lurking around—danger of death, of falling down, of being killed, devoured by our passions and temptations. Up and up we have to go . . . and he, my caterpillar, what will he do when he reaches the very top of the tree, where there is nowhere to go except the void? Will he throw himself into the void full of sunshine, or will he creep into a nook somewhere in between the bark and old branches and hybernate there? My neck was aching, watching him, so high he was now, still walking upwards. By now he got hold of a small, thin branch hanging near the trunk, and he marched steadily on it. Probably, it was easier, his little feet could clasp it firmly. I went inside, washed up a few cups. When I came out, I looked on the ground around the tree, if by any chance he had fallen down. No, he was still walking so high that I could hardly see him amongst the shifting light and shade of the branches. He was still walking up. I confess I was full of admiration. Such an urge, such a persever-ance. . . . Then he turned a corner and disappeared behind a thick branch. He was lost from my view. Good luck. May you be successful in your tremendous urge. . . . What is this powerful instinct beyond your control which drives you on? Like me . . . this urge . . . beyond my control. We are brothers, little caterpillar, you and I. . . .

18th September

YESTERDAY I FELT SO MUCH IRRITATION. In the evening some children were shouting in unison, not far from here, somewhere in the hills. It was darkening. I was in bed already, and the endless shouting of what seemed to be the same sentence began to drive me mad. I started to pray. After a while it became completely dark and the shouting ceased. Probably they all went home. Here is no electricity, so when it becomes dark, walking can be a bit of a problem on moonless nights, so much more because torch batteries are not easily available.

Actually the whole day I was on edge, and when it happens, as usual, everything irritates me and disagreeable things happen more often than usual. Or does it only seem so, BECAUSE one is on edge? Is it He who is in everything who wants to test one's patience, just as Guruji did when I was mad with irritation caused by vibrations? I remember, dogs howled and barked near and far, children were unbearable, smells, heat . . . no end of irritation. Here too, last night dogs howled and barked in chorus. And in the hills sound travels far, echoing amongst the valleys in the pure and clear air. A child in the next farm only about two hundred yards away kept shouting for over an hour in the most irritating way: Mammy! The mother was working in the fields. A girl about eighteen was passing to and fro on the path opposite my door looking at me. I became suspicious, watched her and discovered that she went to steal a cucumber from the caretaker's farm, broke it with a stone, and hid half of it in a tree trunk down below near the steps which lead to the Ashram garden. She was eating the other half when I asked her: "What are you doing?" She did not expect it, said "Ji?," and went.

A thunderstorm was in the air. It was rumbling all around the heights. Clouds heavy laden with water came slowly, slowly, creeping from behind the hills in the southeast. Those were still monsoon clouds coming from this direction.

Told Patel about the girl. He did not understand my indignation and said that he can do nothing; it is the duty of the parents of the girl to do something. I tried to explain what I had meant, not for him to do something about it, but that it is wrong—it is stealing other's property. He shook his head.

"It is not the question of stealing; it is the desire, *Kama*; every kind of desire is so strong in the human being. It is a question of age in us to resist desire. At our age it is easy."

And I was thinking: is it? And wondered . . . but how right he was. How can I blame her? Who am I to judge? Am I so free from temptations? Didn't I too sometimes take something which I desired? And I put it out of my head.

About three p.m. tremendous vibrations in the heart began. I had the feeling of suffocation; heart was racing. So many vibrations I have lately, so many and so strong, but this time it was really bad. I was praying; there was nothing else to do. Was lying on the bed the rest of the afternoon listening to the heart and thinking of Guruji and doing *Jap*. Slept not too well. Patel gave the next room to soldiers to sleep for one night. There was a platoon doing some exercises in the hills. They kept talking with loud voices till late. There was a kind of rebellion in me, did not feel like doing my *Jap*. This morning I am alone. He is far away. *Jap* very difficult. And I became disgusted with myself. Told Patel, when he came out to do his spinning in the veranda.

"Well," he said, "why are you disgusted? It is good to be disgusted with oneself; it helps humility. But really there is nothing to be disgusted about. If you cannot do your *Sadhana*, leave it. It is the Will of God. It is God testing you. . . . All is His Will. What happens inside and outside us is His Will. So why the disgust?"

He was right, of course. And I put it out of my head.

88

The Snows and the Sound

19th September, 1966

ALL IS WELL. He is near. *Jap* is easy. I do it all day long, practically. And if my mind wanders or I forget to do it because busy with something else, I lead my mind back to it.

21st September

EVERY DAY IN THE AFTERNOONS there are thunderstorms and rainbows towards the evenings. Yesterday evening there was one, above the opposite hill, right in front. From a grey low cloud it seemed to drop, like a column of vivid colors right to the pine trees. And it stood there for nearly an hour in the fading evening light. Those rainbows are rarely complete; only a part of the complete arc is visible. They are seen everywhere, on the heights, across the valleys, or thrown towards the dimly seen snows, and they last an unusually long time, looking lovely, ethereal, out of this world. . . .

Vibrations are strong . . . and the Sound in the night very loud.

This morning I came out on my doorstep and just sat down. The snows. . . . Could not believe my eyes. . . . They were for the first time all clear. . . . Missed the early glow, because I did not wake up early enough, though waking up at one moment I saw the red glow in the sky but never thought that the whole range was in full view. Misra told me a few days ago that at sunset the snows show all the seven colors of the rainbow; it is a rare phenomenon and it can be seen only in this part of the Himalayas. I would like to see it, but I suspect that it might be an exaggeration. Until now the range was never clear in the evening. Let's hope it will be soon.

23rd September

I CAME TO YOU FOR TRUTH. . . . So much hope was in me, so much longing. . . . But you filled me with restlessness, threw me back into *Maya*, put all the appearances against you, shook me, emptied me, and then you left this world, leaving me with nothing to hold on to.

Did you? And what about this terrible longing, the great heart vibrations all day long? Practically all the time doing *Jap*, and I train my mind to do it better and better, and sweeter and sweeter becomes His Name. . . . And what about the moments of Nothingness, of Oneness, when all my being is merged in Something un-nameable? The body is cold and trembling, and the mind is not. Is it nothing to hold on to?

1st October

WHEN LARGE FLIES FIND THEIR WAY into the room and fly about with a loud hum, trying to find an exit, it is a sign of late summer. . . . This sound reminds me of days long ago far back in the shadows of memory. Half-forgotten memories of sunny days, freshly mown hay, the rattling sound of lawn cutters—summer . . . declining gently towards autumn. From the middle of August the flies kept coming into my room through the broken window-pane, sometimes in two's or three's humming about, and I listened to them gladly. Eventually they found their way out, and it was over.

Rain was falling all night. The day before yesterday we had a hailstorm towards the evening. As I stood on my doorstep before going to bed, the wind was blowing icy cold from the snows. But the night was windstill, very, very still. Even the crickets were silent.

Yesterday again we had a thunderstorm, and it was raining all night. At four a.m. when I opened my door, the air smelled strongly of pines. I looked up to the sky. High up above the deodars, a satellite sailed serenely looking like a large star. It went towards the northeast towards the snows. Orion, half hidden by the feathery clouds, was to the south dimly visible. Orion is now seen in the morning; when I was coming from the plains, he was rising in the evening.

A large, livid full moon was about to set in the west behind the hill. I began my breathing exercises. Patel was singing his *bajans* (hymns of praise) to the rising dawn as usual. It was cold, and the air was balsam, so fresh.

Made myself two mugs of tea. The sun was risen by now, but it was hidden behind a large bank of uniformly grey clouds. The snows were half hidden and somber. Suddenly I noticed a rainbow. It was like a straight column of vivid colors rising from the bank of grey clouds, right up like a flame, and the top of it was losing itself in the paleness of the blue sky. Here it stood, quite straight with all its colors, not far from the sun, still hidden behind the clouds. A rare phenomenon. It is a law of nature that the rainbow is always opposite the sun, never near or beside it. But here it was so vivid, so incredibly lovely and unexpected, standing firm, emerging from the grey of the clouds into the pale blue of the morning sky, losing itself there, fading away, becoming so tenderly faint. Rainbow, I thought, oh, thy beauty, how evident it is here. Rainbows have such a deep meaning for me, and here I see so many. And the yellow color is always the most luminous one. Now, when you are no more, my dear, the yellow color is never missing. I look out for it. . . . It stood there for more than ten minutes, then it began to fade only when the sun began to rise above the bank of clouds. But even then it did not go quickly but slowly, hesitantly becoming more and more aerial, incredibly lovely, hardly visible. And the yellow and the red still remained when all the other colors had gone.

My heart is glad today. I cry for Him and keep crying till the milk of His kindness boils up. . . . All day long I do *Jap*. Am full of stillness and peace. When the mind strays it is easily brought back. The mind returns gladly to His Name like a strayed child running to its mother with delight.

When the sun rose, still low on the horizon just over the edge of the opposite hill, the cosmos flowers looked transparent against the light. Permeated with luminosity they were—pink, red, white . . . and the rays of the sun shining in between the delicate, feathery foliage—it looked so lovely. The garden is a riot of flowers. Cosmos grows here wild in the hills, and marigolds too. They seem to run down in cascades, in yellow patches, down the hills. And everything grows so tall here, as if every plant wished to compete with the high hills. Marigolds, some of them taller than me. Cosmos, six, seven, and even eight feet high. When I stand amongst them, I am hidden behind a screen of star-like flowers. On one plant I counted fifty-seven blooms! And sunflowers nine, ten feet high. Our Ashram garden is lovely, and Patel planted the entire slope full of cosmos and marigolds, so the approach to the Ashram looks like a valley of flowers. . . .

2nd October

I WAS BORN TODAY FIVE YEARS AGO . . . and for the past ten-and-a-half weeks I have been an orphan already. . . . Why did you go and leave me alone, my dear? Alone? No! I do my *Jap* all the time. The heart is at peace. God is very, very near sometimes. And my heart is full of love for Him. Help me! I cannot do it alone! I cry to you for help. Do you hear me, my dear! Do you listen to me sometimes? To my longing, my endless longing and pain? Who knows? . . . Hear me, my dear! I am crying to you! I am an orphan after such a short time, a few years only. . . . Others enjoyed your presence for many, many years, thirty, forty years some of them. I was with you only two years and four months, and over two and a half years in England. . . .

Help me, help me, my dear!!

3rd October

THE WHOLE NIGHT I SUFFERED from headache. The first one since I have been here in the hills. Took two aspirins, but the head is still heavy and a dull pain is there. The snows are clear since sunrise. Swami Ananda told me the names of nearly all the peaks. I loved especially the Panchancholi; the five Pandavas and Draupadi; the dog leading, and Judishtra holding the tail of the dog went from there into the Heavens. The nicest story I have heard for years. . . . Actually from this mountain descends a large glacier; this was the road of the Pandavas, leading to Heaven.

6th October

LAST NIGHT I HEARD A STRANGE SOUND about three a.m. Auu, Auu— and the echo repeated softly and far away: Auu-Auu . . . I listened. All was still. Deep silence with the Great Sound in it. . . . Then again Auu-Auu—and the echo repeated Auu, Auu . . . it was not a dog. It was a wild creature; the sound came from behind the opposite hill. Again and again it came: Auu-Auu, at regular intervals. What could it be? A deer? No, the voice of a deer in autumn calling his female is rather like a kind of a roar. I listened, could not make out what it was, and decided to ask Patel in the morning. By now the dogs in the village began to bark in unison as well as the dog on the next farm. Now, I knew there will be no sleep for me anymore because this nuisance of a dog will continue to bark for several hours without stopping, and will howl in between. (It did.)

But in between the barking I listened as well as I could. It was lovely, this lonely sound echoing in the stillness of the hills. A wild creature is calling. A wild creature of God. My heart became so tender. I blessed it mentally. Whoever you are, lovely wild thing (all wild creatures are beautiful), whoever you are, I hear you, I listen to you, and I bless you. . . .

Patel, when asked, told me that it was a fox. Himalayan foxes are larger and taller than our breed, have tails like a dog, and do look like a dog of a sandy color, the fur not so long as our European foxes. So he told me. I would like to see one.

12th October

EVERY MORNING NOW, I get up long before sunrise. And I watch just the promise of dawn, coming up slowly in the east. Only a shade lighter is the sky, at first, but so faint that one has to look hard to notice it at all. The waning of the moon in the sky, every day getting smaller, every day its light more ghostly on the white walls of the Ashram . . . every day it is nearer the eastern horizon. And the sky is a blaze of stars. Nowhere, not even in the Indian plains where the stars seem so near, have I seen such a sky. Deep. Dark. And the stars, millions of them, like jewels, like winking lanterns. There towards the south, just above the hill, one beautiful object, large, shiny; it flashes blue and red as if signaling. Lovely. Orion is above my head with his sword and his dog. And the other day when I tried to find the Great Bear which I knew must be northwards, I discovered it just rising, standing on its tail above the snows. And not a sound. No more crickets or cicadas in the night. Only during the day. Sometimes, far away, there is a call of a bird, like the double sound of a small bell: ting-ting, ting-ting. That's all. But it is not so every night.

LETTER TO A FRIEND

Dearest,

This letter comes to you from a solitary retreat in the Himalayan hills. I am writing seated on my doorstep, facing the snows. The hills are clear this morning and last evening too. The whole range was coral pink, the glow after the setting sun dying gently away on the glaciers. And so near they seem . . . only fifteen miles away in direct line as the crow flies.

It is a glorious morning. The Ashram garden is a riot of color: sunflowers, zinnias, dahlias, and above all, cosmos and marigolds. The air is vibrating with the hum of the bees, and the crickets are busy filling the garden with the gay monotonous sound which seems to belong to the sunshine . . . sheer joy of living, bringing back to us childhood memories of summer days, blue sky and much hot, lovely sunshine.

Everything grows so tall here, as if the vegetation is trying to compete with the high hills around and the huge mountains. Sunflowers are nine, ten feet high. The one nearest to my door has thirty-two blooms and at least the same amount of buds. I did not count them, got fed-up counting. There are zinnias three, four feet high, and they become shrub-like here, covered with large blooms four inches across, looking rather like dahlias. And cosmos! Never have I seen anything like it! They grow wild here on the slopes, and in the clearings of the jungle and in our garden we must have several thousand plants; the slope leading to the motor road is covered with them: six feet tall, shrub-like with feathery foliage. On one plant I counted fifty-seven blooms. They come in five colors: crimson, white (four inches in diameter), deep pink, pale pink, and pink with crimson heart. Near the veranda, there is a marigold six-and-a-half feet tall; usually they are not more than four, five feet. Our Ashram garden looks like a valley of flowers just now.

The other day I went into the pine forest on the opposite hill and I had this impression. But actually it is not a valley at all; we are on a hill. The houses are built on a small plateau not so high as the surrounding hills. From here is an enchanting view into the three valleys. The valley of Garur (seen on the photo I enclosed here) with the snows behind it, then of Kausani and of Chenoda river. All around are high hills, the famous Kumaon Hills (Kausani is right in the midst of them), covered with pine forests at this altitude and jungle lower down on the slopes. The Ashram is at 6,075 feet above sea level. Kausani, a village of only one thousand inhabitants, is about six hundred feet below.

Once a week I go down to the village to do my shopping. It used to be a small expedition in the rainy season which is just about over now. All the paths became muddy and it was very slippery. The villagers seem to grow things only for themselves and are reluctant to sell anything. For the moment we get plenty from the Ashram garden. It is terraced, like all the cultivated land around, and the soil is good. We get even a certain amount of tea plants. The tea, fresh, only a few days old, tastes wonderful. It is of a very good quality; it is something in between Darjeeling and China tea. I mix it with Booke Bond and get a lovely drink. When there will be no more vegetables about the middle of November, then I will live on milk, rice, chappathies and dahl. Rice grown here is of excellent quality, and Himalayan wheat is sent to the hand-mill, and chappathies are lovely and soft. In England even when I bought the best flour from the health food stores, my chappathies were never really nice—far too many chemicals are added to flour; it makes them hard. Milk is also very good. Nowhere in India I dared to buy milk. It is so much watered down that it has a nasty bluish color and even loses the taste of milk. But here it is thick and creamy, lovely stuff. It is not cow milk, but buffalo milk. Water buffaloes are like outsize black cows, shiny, no hair on their bodies. Only on the very end of the tail they have a kind of small bunch of hair and that is all. When a herd of them wallows in the muddy rivers or pools, they look something in between a primeval cow and a hippopotamus. The milk is like cow's milk, only creamier and sweeter. What a heavenly thing it is, to drink a cup of cold milk seated on my doorstep at dawn. I seem to live on my doorstep lately, since the snows are clearly visible. During the rains they were always hidden for weeks on end.

My room is facing northeast. Every morning I am up long before sunrise. The green, livid transparency of the sky changes gradually into a pale yellow, the harbinger of dawn. It is perfectly still. The snows are somber, forbidding . . . no sound from anywhere . . . Nature is waiting. Then from the village below, sounds begin to come of life awakening. Children's voices, laughter, dogs barking, an occasional snatch of a song interrupted by voices. The sound of water running into the buckets, smoke begins to rise, the lovely acrid smell of wood fire. But the forest and the jungle are still. And then, all of a sudden, as if obeying the signal of an unseen music director, the birds begin to sing on the slopes and in the valley. At first hesitantly—it sounds so lonely, the soft modulation—one feels the bird is cold and hungry. Then all join in. As in the West the blackbirds are the first to begin. Here they have yellow beaks like our blackbirds. I was told it is the only part of the Himalayas where they have yellow beaks; as a rule it is black like everywhere in the hills.

And I sit and listen and the sky is orange now with shafts of light behind one of the peaks. One knows exactly where the sun will rise each day when one observes these shafts of light. Every day it is more to the south, every day a little more. And now the most dramatic moment arrives—the tips of the snows get the first glow. It is as if a Deva would light a crimson lantern on the tip of the highest mountain which is Nanda Devi (over twenty-five thousand feet), and one by one all the other tips begin to glow. The deep red light slides lower and lower, and in the meantime the tip of the peaks becomes coral-red, while at the foot of the mountain it is still deep red. Then as by a magic wand the whole range becomes coral-red, then deep gold, then brilliant yellow, and becoming paler and paler they will stand white, glistening, unreal in their purity, and all this at first against a livid, yellowish sky and later as though suspended in the blue. . . . Unreal. Colossal. Massive. And seemingly so light, so ethereal, that one can hardly believe one's eyes. . . .

The director of the Ashram, Jiva Bhai Patel, whose room is on the other side of the veranda, will be singing his *bajans*, morning hymns to the rising Surya (sun), and the air will be smelling strongly of pines, and a cold, cold breeze springs up coming from the glaciers.

A Canadian tourist came here a few days ago; he stood a long time contemplating the range and photographing it, and then he said in his broad Canadian accent:

"Well, I never imagined that mountains could be so high and that there could be so many of them. . . ." Actually one looks from here on 250 miles of an uninterrupted wall, peak after peak losing themselves in the distance.

The breeze is at first just like a sigh, hardly noticeable, smelling of snow and ozone, becoming stronger as the morning goes on, biting the cheeks.

The nights are mostly completely windstill. It was explained to me that it has to do with the climatic conditions; usually there is no wind after nine p.m., except when it is raining of course; then the rain of the monsoon will hammer mercilessly on the metal roof making a great noise. But when it happens to be windy in the night, rare as it is, it is lovely to lie in bed and listen to the pines. The wind is mostly on the heights; on our hill which is much lower the pines don't stir. But all around, coming from one hill or another according to the direction of the wind, one can hear the wonderful song of the wind in the pines increasing or decreasing. Himalayan pines have a very feathery aspect because the needles grow in bunches and are very long, eleven, twelve inches or even more. They are also of much lighter green than our pines, a kind of silvery sheen on them, and each bunch of needles is dark green just in the middle. So the branches have a dancing quality; they look very lovely standing stately all together near each other in the forest, or running gaily down the slopes to the rice paddies below. And in the wind they give a kind of hushed rustle like a raucous breath when the wind bangs down on them from the glaciers, or comes hurriedly blowing from the south, from the plains. Seems to be always in a hurry, brother wind. And clearly, distinctly, when one lies very quietly and listens, but not with the ears only, then one can hear the sound of *Om*, repeated, reverberating amongst the hills, coming from nowhere, and from everywhere around with the breath of the wind amongst the whispering pines. . . .

But the nights of perfect silence are even better. . . . There is something very special about the silence in the Himalayas. I never experienced anything quite like it. Not even in Switzerland which is full of lovely mountains. I mean the Sound. Has it to do with the special atmosphere? Or climatic conditions? Or the geological structure of the incredibly high mountains? I don't know. But everywhere I went, in Darjeeling, in Kashmir, on the border of Nepal, and here, of course, I heard it, louder than ever. The Sound, like a distant melodious roar. Something in between a supersonic whistle of a bat and the singing of the telegraph wires. It seems to come from afar, and at the same time it is very near, outside you and in the head. When the Silence is absolute, it has a Sound. I wonder if it works in the same way as with Light. It is said that Absolute Light represents Absolute Darkness. That's why God is called the Dark Light by Mystics and Rishis. I call it the Roar of the Silence, Nada, the first and the last Sound of Creation.

As soon as I arrived here from the plains on the 5th of August, I heard it. I woke up in the night. I didn't know what time it was; it was pitch dark; it had just stopped raining. Here is no electric light, so I couldn't see what time it was. I had a temporary accommodation in Sarala Ben's Ashram on the hill opposite, a small room above the cow-shed, right in the pine wood. As soon as I woke up in the night I heard it. And my heart was suddenly glad; it was like a greeting from the homeland. . . . There was this Stillness and the Sound. The silence is so compact, so dense, almost physically felt; it seems to descend on you, to envelop you; you are in it, lost, immersed in it, drowned, and there is nothing else beside it in the whole wide world. . . . This Sound is not the sound of the blood in our ears which is always with us and which we can hear when all is still. No, it is not. The sound in the ears is there, but the Other Sound is also there, very much so, deep, endless, eternal.

I was told by Yogis in Rishikesh that it is Nada, the first Sound of Creation, the Breath of Brahma, who can never sleep, can never rest, otherwise the Creation will disappear into Nothingness; and they also told me that one can hear it in the Himalayas much more easily than anywhere else in the world, because so many Rishis have meditated in those hills for thousands of years, creating thereby a spacially favorable atmosphere. Perhaps it is true, I don't know. But the Sound is true and very real. And it is impossible to say from where it comes, from all around, from very far and from very near.

Just in front of my door is a large bed of zinnias. And when I lie in bed and the door is open, at the level of my eyes are the vivid reds, oranges, yellows, pinks of the zinnias, and immediately above rise, as though growing out of them and suspended in the blue, Nanda Kunti, Trisul (the trident of Shiva), Nanda Devi (only the tip is seen, 25,800 feet), and Nanda Kot looking like a snow-white tent, perfect in its symmetry.

No wonder my heart is longing to remain here forever, so long as this physical body lasts. . . . I am so deeply happy here, of a happiness never experienced before. Prayer is easy and God is near.

I close with best wishes to you, and we will meet again in April '67.

My love to you

89

Seven Colors of the Rainbow

14th October, 1966

SEATED AT MY DOORSTEP WATCHING THE DAWN I repeated His Name
and what a consolation it is against all the ills, disappointments in
life, all the harassments to which the human being is subjected; just
to say His Name, call on Him, and the heart is immediately filled with
sweetness.

I tried to analyze this feeling. Perhaps I can say it is as if my heart
was carrying a sweet burden, the softest, sweetest pain. As if the heart
was wide open, full of helpless love. It is like a continuous call, like
one single note sounding ceaselessly, a call, a signal, transmitted on
and on. The Call of Longing.

And the sky in the meantime began to turn from this heavenly
crimson-orange into a purest, transparent gold. The snows were
glowing, and for a while I could not think, but was just looking.

Where was I? Oh, yes, like a sweet pain. Carrying a sweet burden.
And suddenly I remembered his saying:

"It takes time to make a soul pregnant with God." Good heavens,
this is it, I thought, struck by this idea like a revelation. This is it!
Pregnant with God! That's what he did all the time, nothing but
that. . . . Confused, perplexed, in the darkness I did not see it . . .
somehow expecting that I will "get" God from him. . . . Heaven
knows how I thought of it; as a sudden realization, I suppose . . . but
it was nothing of the sort. After purifying it, he put the seed into my
heart. And how apt is the expression "pregnant." He probably
translated it from Persian, I suppose. Pregnant is correct. Because He
has to be born within our heart. Born. Born within me. . . . It is
only a question of time. . . .

**"And the time will come when one wishes that twenty-four
hours should be twenty-five in order to love someone one hour
more. . . ."** And how his eyes shone when he said that.

Pregnant with God . . . my heart was overflowing with tenderness. . . . Guruji, my dear, yesterday it was twelve weeks. . . . And
I looked at your photos, and my heart was hot with sorrow. This face
. . . the high forehead. The beautiful strong hands. Guruji, my dear

. . . I wanted God so badly. And I still want Him just as I did then. I looked at this face once so dear to me. Him speaking, him in Samadhi on the lovely colored photos H. had made. The man alive, speaking, laughing or in Samadhi—and the man dead, the face which belonged not to him anymore, but to the body to be buried in a few hours.

Guruji smiling, seated behind the grave of his father covered with garlands of flowers during the ceremony of the nephew of Happy Babu. Guruji standing, tall, slender, all in white, like an ancient priest of days gone by, at the fire ceremony at the wedding of his son. And now . . . no more. . . . Now, only a tremendous Power to be reached in moments of non-being . . . a center of blissful energy, an answer to my cry for help, a merging in Something—but the man, the human being, is no more. How could I even think in the past that he deceived me? That I was left an orphan, that I would never reach him? He showed me the way to reach him through the divine love. Ungrateful wretch that I am . . . and this feeling, this feeling of sweetness and immense satisfaction when I call His Name and I feel His response, God's very being throbbing in the depth of my being! The magic of a *mantra*; each time I say it, it brings me nearer to Him. Literally so. But you, Guruji, you are something so different now from what you were then; looking at your photos, my heart is crying for you, yes, but somehow it is difficult to believe. . . .

And each time I say the *mantra* when going up the hill, I am suffering; with each step I say it, and my heart is so glad, full of unbelievable peace; it is beating so much, I feel a suffocation. . . . Guruji, dear Guruji, YOU DID NOT DECEIVE ME. You made my soul pregnant with God.

"People who are intended to realize God in this life have a sign on them." Rare are such souls for whom Vasudeva is all, says the *Bhagavad Gita.*

One gets from the guru what one wants: I came for the Absolute Truth. He made me pay the price for making my soul pregnant with God. . . .

"How much Grace of God you have received you will know only later, now you cannot understand," he said. Impregnated with God . . . Guruji . . . what do I owe you? How can I express it ever? How can I tell you, now, that I know?? Guruji, my dear. . . .

25th October
I AM WALKING MUCH NOW all around in the hills. The forest is still

damp but it is very lovely, and the snows seen from different angles look quite different, absolutely fascinating.

It is true that at sunset one sees here all the seven colors of the rainbow. Yesterday I saw it. And I nearly felt like crying because the Galloways who stayed here for three days and who left yesterday at one p.m. could not see it. One more day and they would have seen it. . . .

For the first time since I am here we had a perfect sunset. All the snows, the whole range up to Nepal, were very clear. At first they became pale golden yellow, and the three rows of wooded hills below them became of the most atmospheric amethysts and shades of mauve and soft violet. Then the snows became deep-gold and the hills indigo and misty blue. Gradually they changed into vivid coral pink, and the hills became of a misty-turquoise color, a kind of greeny blue. Then at last they are crimson, the light dying away slowly, slowly, and the hills become green. Of a strange, unreal green. The sky is all the time of an incredible transparency, pale greeny as if secretly shimmering with hidden light. . . .

And this morning we had a dramatic sunrise with immense curtains, gold, crimson and orange, displayed liberally all across the sky even as far as to the south. And then the sun rose, still invisible behind the opposite hill, showering with its oblique rays the snows which were cold grey a moment before, and now all of a sudden were bathed in a kind of brown light. It all appeared like an etching in sepia against the now completely grey clouds and the paleness of the sky in between.

Poor Galloways . . . I bullied them out of their beds at five a.m. to sit on the ridge and watch the sunrise. I used to bring the two easy chairs, drag them to the edge of the ridge, and all the blankets I could get hold of to cover them up. Poor pets, to be roused at such an unearthly hour. But I hope they found it worthwhile, the dawn chorus and the peaks lighting up, and I told them all the names of the different peaks, and there was the smell of the pines and the sounds from the village. I thought it was glorious; I hope they thought so too. . . .

28th October

I SAW A COMPLETELY *ROUND* RAINBOW. It was a rainbow circle as if glued to the edge of Trisul after a short shower. It was quite clear, and I think such sight must be rare. All the colors were there; it was complete. It was not very large, for if it were, it would disappear behind the snows. It just stood there and paled away.

1st November

THE SUNSET WAS LOVELY and different again, even if further from Panchencholi towards Nepal the snows were not quite clear, but half hidden behind the clouds, so delicately pink and fluffy. My glass mountain, Nanda Kunti, seemed to be made of pink crystal. Each time I look at her, she reminds me of the piece of music, "The Legend of the Glass Mountain." She gives the illusion of being semi-transparent; it seems as if one could see the sky behind, through her, owing to the color of the rock showing in practically vertical stripes in between the covering of the ice and snow. My lovely glass mountain . . . she is the first object I look at as soon as I come out of my door.

What is so particularly beautiful and startling is the afterglow. When the sun has completely disappeared behind the horizon, the snows become grey, frozen, so cold looking. Then after a short while they light up again. At first snow-white, shining against the greyish sky, blending with the palest pink and turquoise near the snows, and the whole dome of the sky becomes magenta pink. Then the snows become gradually golden. Not so vivid as at sunset, more subdued, more tender. The whole phenomenon is due to the reflection of the sky from the rays of the sun already beneath the horizon. And the gold deepens. And the sky becomes more and more greeny. Even the hills below partake of the afterglow, seem to radiate from within the soil, the trees as if illumined by golden-pink light. And then they become coral, and the snows in the meantime turn into deep crimson. And so they stay for a while getting deeper and deeper red. By now the hills below are veiled in grey-blue mist. And the sky too is pale grey with just a suspicion of turquoise above. . . .

And the glowing snows seem to be suspended in between the darker mist by which the hills are covered and the transparent greyness of the sky. Unreal, so fairy-like, so light, weightless . . . and then it is over. All at once it is all grey. Cold. Forbidding. It makes you shiver just to look at them. And one by one the stars appear.

8th November

THERE IS NOT MUCH TO SAY, so it seems. Strange isn't it? I have been here for three months. Sixteen weeks have passed since Guruji's death. So much happened within me, so much, so much. . . .

Slowly, gradually, ever so slowly, by degrees the world begins to look differently, to change imperceptibly.

Yes, the sunrises, the sunsets, the garden, the people, the whole of my daily life seems outwardly the same. I am nearly all the time alone, walk much, read books from the Ashram library. But the values have changed. The meaning underlying it all is not the same as before. Something which seemed intangible, unattainable, slowly, very slowly became a permanent Reality. There is nothing but Him. This of course is not a novelty to many of us. But at the beginning it was sporadical; later, of longer or shorter duration when I was acutely conscious of it. But now . . . the infinite, endless Him . . . nothing else is there . . . and all the beauty of nature which surrounds me is as if only on the edge of my consciousness. Deep within, I am resting in peace in His Heart. The body feels so light at times—as if it were made of the pure, thin air of the snow peaks.

I noticed that I am a bit breathless lately. Joan Galloway drew my attention to it, when she was here two weeks ago. I am sure it is not due to the altitude, which is not much, only slightly over 6,000 feet. It is true, when I walk up on some surrounding hills, it can be much higher; still, I think, it is not due to it. I think the heart Chakra is responsible for it. For my heart is humming incessantly its song to Him . . . the infinite, endless Him, all around . . . and like a fish in water I am in Him and have my being. . . . Wherever I try to look, there is nothing else . . . absolutely, nothing else. And neither can there be. Strange (or is it?), how this constant vision of the One deepening, increasing in one's mind, gives one eternal peace. . . . There is nothing to be worried at all. All is well with the world and with me.

Last week I saw the waning moon rise just in the depression of the two peaks: the nose of the Dog and the next peak. It rose out of the depression as out of a cup. Mysterious was its light, peeping beyond the range, ghostly, before it rose completely. The disc at first peeped out, then as if taking courage seemed to shoot up. Some music in the distance from a radio; a dog barked incessantly far away near the next hill. The sky was a shimmering movement of stars. The Milky Way was so clear, so dense with light. The Pleiades had just risen and stood above the next hill. Fancy that we belong to this constellation, so small and on the very edge of the mysterious Milky Way, forming part of this nebulous, rather small agglomeration of stars, there on the horizon, in the east. . . . Strange and rather difficult to conceive with the mind of an ordinary person like myself.

The day before yesterday I was watering the flowers with the hose. Below our plateau was stationed the car of the military wireless operator. The music was coming from there. The usual miauling of a childish female voice, so popular in India, squealing some silly songs from a film. This music brought memories, so vivid, so painful. Looking at the stream of clear water coming from the nozzle of the hose, I was musing. . . . Memories of the hot days in the plains. I seemed to be enveloped again in this acute feeling, a mixture of fear, hope, despair, hope again, the burning of the rebellious mind, the helpless feeling before him, my Master, who kept beating me down mercilessly. . . . So vivid, so real were those memories, the feeling, what a strange feeling it was . . . I did not realize it then. . . . Now I see what a powerful driving force it was. Something in its terrible intensity, richness and fear, did not really belong to this world of mortals. . . . This world of ours, I mean. . . . And I stopped watering the plants. Went to cook my meal in order to escape this banal and haunting music.

All the time I was with Guruji I heard something similar from one loudspeaker or another. From Deva Singh Park, at every wedding festivity, from the bazaar, across the Moti Jheel Park coming from afar, or so near that the ears were splitting. Intruding into my meditation, disturbing our meetings, or making my sleep impossible. . . . And now . . . now it made my heart ache with longing . . . for it brought memories back, rending my heart apart. . . .

Cried desperately while I was cooking. Tears were streaming down my face. The same intensity of the longing and despair, so terribly deep, so much a part of me that I was amazed. I forgot how intense the suffering was then; it nearly knocked me over now. . . . Yes, I must have forgotten it. And now remembering it clearly, I am astonished; how could I bear this intense burning, suffering, like fire consuming my body, unquenchable for years? . . .

After having eaten something, I was lying in bed crying and praying. How much I cried for you, Guruji. . . . How much, only you and God know. Had rarely a ray of light. And when I had, some poison was always hidden underneath. Had seemingly little kindness from you. Not much I had except this kind of pain which was unbearable, as I clearly see it now. And I did bear it all for the Sake of Him. . . . You who are all Justice, You whom I wanted so much and whom I still want more than ever now, help me to You! How I prayed! Could not stop.

And then the great vibration in the heart began and went on for hours. The pulse rate was 104; I listened to my heart. Prayed and prayed. Guruji, my only one Guruji; how I wanted the Truth, you know it! Even I, myself, have forgotten it, but you, you MUST KNOW. . . .

Tried to read. But of no avail. Went to bed not waiting for the dying light to spend itself on the peaks. Cried a little and prayed much and was already half asleep when the words of the prayer formed themselves in strange shapes of flames and became verses which I HEARD:

> For the sake of the love which I have for You,
> For the sake of the torture you gave to me,
> For the sake of my pining, my sorrow, my pain,
> Help me to reach You. . . .

> For the sake of my heart which was hurting so much,
> For the sake of my infinite longing—
> For the sake of my crying for years tears of love,
> Help me to You. . . .

> For the sake of my darkest months of despair,
> For the sake of the deepest surrender,
> For the sake of the hopeless endeavor and plodding,
> Help me to You. . . .

Fancy seeing it written with dancing flames and hearing it, I thought. Help my rebellious heart! I cried this time aloud. Something snapped in me and I fell asleep, sinking into it like a stone thrown into the water. . . .

9th November

THE GREAT SEPARATION IS HERE. And each time, the greater is the Nearness, the deeper, the more terrible is the Separation. Keep crying for Him. Crying endlessly. When I am so alone, it seems unbearable. Was wondering what to do, how to help my mind to remember Him all the time. Then an idea came into my mind: If I could only consciously see Him in everything, as in moments of Oneness. Absolutely in everything, see Him, literally SEE, then the Absolute Trust will be here. Absolute Trust; this is a great Grace of

God. . . . But the trouble is that I cannot induce at will those moments of oneness. . . . They come when they want to come. . . . It does not depend on me. . . .

10th November

MEMORIES COME CROWDING IN. . . . Unexpectedly I seem to hear his voice, remember his kindness. . . .

A moving episode stands out vividly as if carved in my memory.

It was a day with a sparkle in the air, a kind of trembling luminosity, a limpid transparence which in Spanish is called "dia luminosa."

He was already seated outside. An Indian village woman was talking to him.

She was small, very thin, her face was wrinkled, shrunken, as if dried-up by the merciless sun, the hot wind of the plains.

From the little Hindi I knew I understood that she was telling him her troubles of which she had many. An endless sorrowful litany of illnesses, misery, death of her husband, of most of her children, and now she was alone, useless, and nobody needed her, she had nothing to hope for, nothing to live for. . . .

And she came out with a question which seemed to burn, scorching her trembling lips:

"Maharaj, why did God create this world so full of troubles? Why did He create me to endure all those sufferings?"

I saw him leaning forward, a shimmering light in his eyes, the light of compassion I knew and loved so well. Soft was his voice when he answered:

"Why has He created the world? That you should be in it! Why has He created you? He is alone; He needs you!"

Never will I forget the broad, blissful smile on the lined, emaciated face when she was walking away. She went happy in the knowledge that she was not alone, not really, for God needed her to keep Him company because He too was alone. . . .

And never will I forget the utter admiration I felt then; only a very Great Soul could have expressed so simply and convincingly one of the greatest Mysteries to a childlike mind of a village woman—the Ultimate Metaphysical Truth: that He who is Alone and Perfect in order to realize His Perfection, He created the Universe. . . .

11th November

ONE IMPORTANT MAN CAME, one of the trustees of the Gandhi Ashram

Memorial Trust. So, there was lunch prepared for ten people and I was also invited. The caretaker prepared a good lunch. After lunch there was some rain. The sun came out immediately when it was still raining. I looked out for a rainbow. And here it was—very wide, all colors very vivid and clear, so bright. It began and ended both ends on the slope of our hill towards the north. And I noticed that it was a double rainbow, the second one above, and very faint. And the yellow, my dear, was the most prominent in both. . . . Since you have gone out of my life, the yellow color is NEVER missing!

12th November

VERY COLD THIS MORNING. After the rain the snows are azure and so near and so clear; every crag, every glacier, every rock is outlined sharply, in this clear bluish tinge. How incredibly lovely they are like this. . . . Writing, seated on my doorstep, I need only to lift my eyes to see the Panchencholi, majestic, enormous with its seven peaks, each peak bearing the name of one of the Pandavas, and the Draupady behind, and the smallest peak (the dog) in front. And the glacier which seems to reach nearly to the sky where all of them went into Heaven. . . . One after another marching into the Swarga Loka (Heaven). The dog leading and Judishtra holding on to the tail of the dog.

Last night I heard music after seven. For one moment I was thinking that there was some shooting, but then realized that it was fireworks. It must be Divali, the festival of Light. Got up and went outside. It was a dark, still evening. The valleys below looked lovely. Every house had many lights. Seen from here in the darkness it looked as if the sky full of stars was reflected below. It was a most poetical sight. The sky tremendous, so near, so full of large stars, and many little and big lights below. . . . Some small fireworks were seen, a bit of a noise and a flash or a small rocket. I walked up and down and stood looking into one or the other valley. . . . Lovely . . . People. . . . My heart was full of tenderness. All my feeling went out to them. They celebrate, have happy hours. . . . People. Hours of hope, hours of gladness, of light. And I went to bed doing my *Mantra*, praying for people, and soon went to sleep and slept well.

13th November

A FRESH WIND IS BLOWING FROM THE GLACIERS this morning. The peaks had some fresh snow. I learned that the Ashram will be closing at the end of December because the roads will be impassable when heavy snow begins to fall. There is also a danger of landslides. So I must make the most of the remaining time. Today it is fresh, it is bracing, it fills one's being with the joy of living.

Went for a walk after lunch about twelve a.m., up the hill, behind the Ashram. The wind from the glaciers, and the song of the pines were strong and continuous. Cicadas were busy too, filling the forest with their monotonous sound. Seems surprising that some of them at least are still alive at this time of the year. I could see five peaks on the Nepal side which are not seen from the Ashram. Big they were. Big stuff, I thought. One looked like a rectangular huge rock fallen on one side. The other one was smaller and the furthest to the east was like Nanda Kunti, my glass mountain, only much, much larger and more solid looking. The view was magnificent, and when walking along I had a glimpse in between the pines of the snows. I was filled with wonder each time how big and how near they are. Very old jungle mostly of mountain oaks was around. So old, crooked, full of hollows and holes, and many had all branches hacked off. Large rhododendron trees, branchless practically. Cut off by villagers desperate for firewood in winter. Pity. It must look magnificent in April when they flower. But rhododendrons must make a good firewood; they are all sorely mutilated. . . .

It was a dangerous climb. My large men's shoes were slipping badly on pine needles. In some places I could hardly get a foothold and had to scrape away the needles with the points of my shoes in order to be able to take a step forward. Sometimes I had to cling to trees or branches of the shrubs, and I was thinking that if I lose a foothold or stumble it could be the end of me. I would fall 100-200 feet, and there were not even many trees to hold onto on the slippery grass slopes mostly covered with pine needles. At one place I could not go further. "I am stuck," I said aloud, reflecting on what to do. Could not take a step forward so steep and slippery it was. So, I threw forward my wool jacket I had over my arm and crawled to a safer place on hands and knees. Later on the plateau it was easy. Sat a long time looking at the Ashram so pretty below, a doll's house, quite small, and the range of the majestic Himalayas. Came back at two p.m.

90

Chorus of Voices

WE HAVE A SPELL OF BAD WEATHER, cloudy and cold in the morning. I am praying. Doing *Jap.* And such peace is in me. My heart is glad calling His Name.

15th November

BLUE WERE THE HILLS this morning at sunrise, blue as blue could be. . . . And above Panchencholi a tiny pink baby cloud stood still. I am alone, crying for him.

It is a strange thing this Sound of the Silence. About ten I heard again the bark of the barking deer. It sounds lonely, free, defying. They say, where the barking deer is, there are tigers too. I never saw one. I think they are all exterminated. But leopards do live here. Only I never saw them either. They are night hunters; during the day they are in hiding. I roam so much alone. I rarely saw a monkey or a wild peacock, nothing else in my wanderings in the jungle.

But this Sound of the Silence. . . I sat still last night listening for a while. How still the nights are in the Himalayan hills. Not a dog was barking. Not a leaf was stirring. And as if from afar comes this sound, a kind of melodious roar on one note, one pitch, far and near, all around. But all around it is very faint, but from afar it is very distinct and loud. Listened to it for quite a while. Then went to bed. Did not sleep well. The sound was there all night; white lights were jumping before my eyes, and from time to time I heard a supersonic whistle in my left ear. I hear it lately very often. Towards the morning wanted to go out to listen to the sound outside. But dogs were barking in the village. When they stopped after a long while (when they begin it can go on for hours), I went outside once more and sat listening. It was a pale colorless dawn. The sound was there even when the cocks began to crow; only gradually as the world began to awake, it ceased.

16th November

WHEN THE SHAFTS OF LIGHT come obliquely from behind the clouds at sunrise, the snows have brownish tints and the hills below them are of all shades of mauves and blues. If I had to paint them I would do it in tender sepias and pinks. Later they become grey and gold with the patches of sunlight on the very tips. And the hills below are shrouded in bluish mist.

In the evening I could not fall asleep, had a kind of indigestion, pain in the stomach and in the bowels. Made myself vomit out all acid and bile. Realized that I had too much fatty food. Cannot digest it. Later, relieved, fell asleep. Dreamed that somebody played beautiful music in the void behind some clouds. How I love piano music when it is so soft and melodious. And I woke up with the sound of magnificent concert-piano music, my ears still ringing with it. What a pity to wake up, I thought. There was a constant supersonic sound, high, so high, not at all unpleasant.

The body was warm, comfortable; it felt good. It is wonderful to awake at the sound of beautiful music, drowned as in a warm bath of love. . . . I stretched out luxuriously and was deeply happy.

Watching the sun rise I sat for a while outside. This love. My God, what love! All the beauties of this wonderful nature around are very secondary, are just on the edge of consciousness; but deep, deep within there is this love and this is the ONLY REALITY—this love that digs deep into the heart its blazing abyss, this love that enwraps and exalts my whole being and the whole of creation as one. We are one, how very true; if only we could realize it, everything would be so very different. If only. . . . But how steep is the path that leads to this realization, to this supreme experience. We have to be emptied, made nothing, to be filled with thy divine love, with the purity of thy love, O God! Guruji, now I understand; I was emptied to be filled; I was made nought to be *human*. A steam-roller went over me and I was the better for it; but what managed to get up afterwards was something very different from the human being who faced you in 1961!

And in bed I was thinking that it does not matter if I stay in with closed eyes or go outside to watch the sunrise. . . . It is all in me . . . not outside me. I can be in a cave, in a prison, in eternal darkness, and it would matter little, if I had this glory within for ever. . . .

Was reflecting that this feeling of divinity has no pride in it; it is on the contrary a very humble feeling. It is: I am nothing before Thee. The body feels as weak as a kitten. The moments of oneness in the night strain it very much. This nearness is something! Too much for the physical frame.

I did all my work. Washed my woollies, sheets, boiled the milk, wrote in my diary. But all this is apart from me, has nothing to do with me, for I am resting somewhere in infinite peace. All the activities are on the outer edge of my perception, and it is not even a sacrifice to do those insignificant things. It is all in Him anyway. . . . And it is done for Him as an offering.

"Every position, every movement of the body is an act of offering to Thee," says Kabir.

How very, very true. . . .

17th November

SINCE I HAVE BEEN HERE IN KAUSANI, practically from the very beginning when the states of consciousness began to change considerably, I felt that I am nearing the end of the road. I mean the end of the road to the Real Home. There is nothing else to do. He takes over. When the devotee becomes His, everything ends there. Sure, I am only at the beginning of this state; there will be unavoidable ups and downs. But this is really the beginning of the end. But how long it will take me to the VERY END, who knows? . . .

This feeling of belonging to Him, every breath, every pore of the body, every thought, every little bit of me—is wonderful! There is such security in it, such tenderness, and it is Nothingness itself!

18th November

THE ENTIRE SKY was covered with small pinky-orange clouds and they looked very solid as if painted on with a brush.

19th November

I AM VERY BREATHLESS. The bending down, the slightest effort or even a quick movement sends me out of breath, hopelessly. It is such a helpless feeling. I wonder what it could be. Altitude? Hardly, 6000 feet is not very high. Age? Cannot be either; at 60. Something is wrong with my nose. Looks like a touch of sinusitis. Dryness of the mucus, some mucus seeping down from the sinus into the back of my throat. Hay fever? Perhaps. Deodars have been flowering since last month and there are still very many marigolds, though they begin to look a bit tired. The mountains have fresh snow this morning. I did not sleep well. Did *Jap*, prayed, the heart was so full of love for Him. Fell asleep towards the morning but at 6:30 was awake already. The sun was already in the sky and the snows clear and blue. Missed the sunrise. Never mind . . . the body felt tired, could hardly get up.

I wonder if it is those states of consciousness, the nearness, the tenderness, the love, the state of my heart Chakra which makes me so breathless. It could be one of these reasons. This tenderness is hard to bear. I feel giddy and the heart is beating and beating; it is as if it were wide open, belonging to Him and completely defenseless. And the feeling of belonging to him is tremendous; I feel like dissolving.

Yesterday afternoon it rained and hailed; the clouds were somber sitting tight on the top of the snows. This spell of bad weather drove off all the tourists, thank God. They were such a restless lot with their noisy children. One had hardly any peace at all. God knows why people must have so many children.

25th November

THE SKY YESTERDAY EVENING AT SUNSET displayed such tints of pastel pink and turquoise as I never saw before. Above Panchencholi it looked absolutely heavenly. And this morning at sunrise it was all sugar-pink sky. . . .

There are only two things in the whole Universe: The Lover and the Beloved. There is He and His Creation. And He loves His Creation. And there is the Soul and its Maker. And the Soul loves its Maker. . . .

26th November

SARALA BEHN TOLD ME that there was a terrific storm in the Himalayas last night. It was howling like thousands of wild animals. But the sky was clear and full of stars. I did not hear anything. Slept soundly. When I got up at four a.m., there was a sharp, cold breeze from the glaciers; the sky was clear; so I did not even suspect that there was such a storm only a few hours before, until she told me.

The sunrise was insignificant, all in pale yellow chrome tints.

27th November

SAT OUTSIDE FOR A WHILE. The moon is full. It was lovely and very, very still. The nights are mostly completely windstill. Before nine p.m. there was quite a bit of wind on the heights. Not on our hill which is much lower. The pines were singing. Sighing His Name. I listened to them, it was so lovely. But after nine all became silent. The pines and the cypress trees, patches of dark shadows, the snows of ghostly silver. It was about two a.m. I still sat outside. It was cold. At first a car could be clearly heard to go away amongst the hills on the road to Garur. On and off came the sound of the motor as it followed the hairpin bends, sometimes hardly audible, when it disappeared behind the hill, sometimes stronger, humming along. While the car was still audible, the noise gradually dying away fainter and fainter, I could not hear the Sound. Because the Sound is only heard in absolute silence. But when roughly about ten minutes one could not hear the car any longer, I heard loudly and distinctly the usual Sound. For a long time I listened to it. Not a leaf stirred; the dogs were asleep in the village. And the Sound was coming from afar, the usual melodious roar, and all around me, supersonically ringing, enveloping me in it. Like magic were the patterns of light and shade under the pines opposite my door on the path, and bright and full was the moon. Its light shone through the feathery foliage of Cosmos, making strange patterns on the soil. The snows looked ghostly and forbidding.

Later there was like a suspicion of a breeze coming from the direction of the snows. Not a wind, just a cold touch, like an icy breath, on my left cheek, as I was sitting facing the east. An icy touch which made my cheek prickle. I prayed so much. And went to bed praying. Thy Will be done, always. . . . It is such a bliss to do Thy Will only. To have no will of my own. I don't want to do anything else till the end of my days. . . .

28th November

AND THE MOON ROSE FULL, looking like a transparent white disc in the turquoise infinitude above the snows which were still coral pink after sunset. I sat on my doorstep. All was still. The Sound was there as always. Those still, romantic nights. Silence and the snows, ghostly patches of light and shade on the garden path, the moon shining through the pine branches. Not a Sound. Except that One. . . . And that ONE is beating in my heart. I am one with Him. And that ONE is taking me deeper and deeper, somewhere. . . .

29th November

LAST EVENING SOMEBODY WAS PLAYING the flute down below the village, shortly before sunset. And the sun was reflecting in the windows of the Lakshmi Ashram, high up on the opposite hill. . . . The sun reflected in the windows of a building always filled me with a strange, unearthly joy. Like a memory of some dreams, where all is grey and suddenly this sparkling, blinding light, reflecting the sun, represents hope and promise, though it is hurting the eyes. Listened to the flute, looked at the light, basking in this joy, so light, so incredibly lovely, so subtle. . . .

The sunset was once more of the seven colors. And I looked at it upside down and went to Patel and the Swami who was with him to do likewise. So they too looked at the mountains head down, and Patel was delighted how the colors seemed sharper, more clear this way.

I woke up this morning with this quiet joy. This wonderful lightness. All is HE. He is all; there is nothing else, and the song in the heart goes on and on. This Longing for something intangible, unattainable, is it fulfilled?

And it is a glorious day. The mountains are silver and deepest azure in the shade amongst the crags. The hills are clear; every tree is visible, bluish and deep green they are in the distance. It is rather chilly and my heart is dancing and dancing its dance with gladness to Him. . . . Oh, I know, loneliness will come again, for many days on end, there will be desperate longing, such a dark solitude, and the heart will be breaking with longing. I know it will be . . . but now it is not. Now is peace, a special peace, full of silent, deep gladness. . . . And what is more, it seems eternal, lasting forever, never ending, though my mind knows very well that it might end tomorrow, no, perhaps even in the next hour. . . .

Yes, it is a special joy. Tremendously deep, welling up from such depths which cannot be fathomed or ever explored. It is dynamic, full of hidden, incredible energy, but it is very, very still . . . like the eternal stillness of the Absolute. I imagine this eternal stillness, complete, unending, must be like this.

What a bliss is the smell of marigolds. Actually, I think they cause me some trouble; I have symptoms of hay fever. The garden is still full of them and chrysanthemums are all out. Many varieties are very unusual. I have never seen them anywhere before; first they are snow white and have an uncombed look; then later they turn crimson, then mauve; the colors begin to appear at first in the center petals and then turn completely crimson all over; and when they are faded, they are blue.

1st December

I AM NOT GOOD ENOUGH FOR JAP. I SIMPLY MUST do it uninterruptedly all day long. There was a storm in the night. It woke me up when the wind began to press against the bungalow. I don't know if it came from the direction of the snows or from the south. It lasted for about half an hour. And it ended as abruptly as it began. For a while the pines sang on the heights all around, but soon they stopped too. And this time I could hear the Sound in spite of the wind and the song of the pines.

2nd December

SOMETHING WOKE ME UP at about 2 a.m. I put on the winter coat and went out. The moon was in the waning stage. All was silent. A little icy breeze came from the glaciers which were in the shade silhouetted against the silvery sky. I stood only for a few minutes outside. It was too cold to sit. I knew now what did awake me: the Sound was different. For a while I could not make out what it was. It sounded like a chorus of voices, very high pitched, so high that no human voice could be like that. Strange voices, rising and falling, monotonous, as if composed of air, of the wind, of the atmosphere itself. Very beautiful, this chant. Human voices don't sound like that, not even from afar. But I was not sure. . . . Perhaps they were human voices after all distorted by the distance. No, they were not. From where? All the valleys were in darkness, everything was asleep. And the sound came definitely from the direction of the snows. I listened fascinated . . . what could it be? It was uncanny, it was great.

I went inside. Was freezing. In the room it sounded faintly, mingled with the usual distant roar.

3rd December

WROTE MANY LETTERS, all Christmas greetings. Will post them this morning. Cried last night, could not fall asleep for a long, long time. . . .

Why, oh, why? This pain in the heart. . . . But is not everything His Will? So I offer You this pain of mine, and until I am able to offer everything to Him, I am not completely surrendered. . . . The vibrations are too strong sometimes to bear. The body is under suffering. The mind stopped working and there was much giddiness. A sound of banal Indian pop music suddenly came from somewhere. And it enveloped me with memories of the hot time full of unspeakable torture. But was it not His Will too if I was tortured like this? Is not EVERYTHING ABSOLUTELY His Will?

4th December

AT SUNRISE a large bank of mackerel clouds was all along the whole

range of the snows. It stood low over the very tips and was of a lovely
pink. Trisul and the Wall did not become golden as usual but coral,
and the snows far away and the hills below were shrouded in bluish,
light mist. It all looked like one of those famous watercolors of
tender tints.

6th December

WAS THINKING THAT SOON I will be leaving here. Then I remembered
the Sound. I could not hear it. Went out. It was a still, warm night.
Sat down on my doorstep. There was such a silence; it was warm, the
sky so particularly luminous with stars. The snows, just a dark grey
wall on the near horizon. The Sound had changed. It was no more
like a melodious roar in the distance. It was so high, like many
electronic sounds, all flickering, crossing each other, mixed up, and
so high that it must be ultrasonic. I could hardly hear it; it was
difficult to follow. Signals from space? Music of the Spheres? Heaven
knows. . . .

8th December

THE SOUND HAS CHANGED for the last two days. It is "Electronic"
now. Slept till seven. Missed the sunrise. Do *Jap* all the time. Was
deeply lonely this morning. But soon a great vibration started. And
all day such peace . . . such stillness . . . can do nothing; only lie on
the bed and do *Jap* in utter inner stillness. . . .

May God give me the strength. May He guide me. In five-and-a-
half months my work will begin. To go on till the end of my life. His
work. Work, work, work, without expecting any result or reward or
any fruit. All is so still within the perfect Silence of Nothingness in
the heart. And *Jap* is easy, and goes on all the time.

10th December

ONCE MORE I HEARD THE SOUND as a magnificent chorus of unearthly
voices. I was told that the Sound sometimes manifests itself like this.
But now it is again as it was before: a melodious roar. Somehow I was
glad. It was as if an old friend had returned. I missed it; I don't know
why. . . .

11th December

LIKE A PERFUME RISING from the innermost center of sweetness is this
still joy. . . . All stillness, all peace. . . . And the heart keeps
singing His Name, singing as though to infinity in utter tenderness.

12th December

THE SUNSET WAS DIFFERENT this evening. Some small clouds were standing for hours in the afternoon just touching the tips of the peaks. They became pink. But the snows themselves remained grey; only the hills below became deep orange-pink. There must have been clouds where the sun was setting, in the west, behind the hill; they threw shadows on the snows. A little later the clouds moved away higher and those touching the snows became grey as if melting in the shade, but the snows remained coral. I sat outside. The heart full of peace and His Name . . . and I remembered when as a child I used to get up very early and stand at the window in my nightdress watching the Caucasian peaks getting pink, one by one at sunrise. Each time I experienced a deep feeling of wonder, of a joy so light, so ethereal, welling from within. I must have been about ten years then. Only now do I understand what this feeling was, comparing it to the present one I have now. Often I had this feeling, all peace, all joy; I did not know what it was, of course. I lost it while growing up and the world with its Maya closing tightly around me. Had forgotten it altogether.

There was no afterglow. The snows remained yellowish, livid. I closed the door to go to bed to pray. But after a few minutes I happened to glance out of the window while preparing myself to go to bed, and I saw that the snows were blue . . . I opened the door and went out. The sky above the snows was not pale grey as it mostly is, but of a transparent kind of wedgewood-blue; the hills below were of deep misty-indigo. But the snows were blue and remained so. It was lovely. I stood outside for a while, enjoying the feeling of deep peace. You are displaying your beauty because soon I will have to go, beautiful mountains. And very probably I will never see you again . . . not from here at any rate. . . . Then I went to bed.

91

Samarpan (Surrender)

14th December, 1966

WALKING A LOT AROUND THE HILLS, drinking in the beauty. The days are golden and warm. But the nights are bitterly cold. Soon, so I was told, the storms will begin; soon the weather will change. But now, I walk and look. Dug out a small pine tree, will take it with me to London. And many seeds from the plants of the Ashram garden. And the magic nights, the moon pale, mysterious light, reflecting on the white walls of the Ashram. And the flute player in the village. And the jungle and the smell of the pines.

I walk about much, so much. Loving the hills and the snows and the people. Soon . . . I will go. And there will be no regret.

The Sound is here always . . . I wonder if it will remain when I am not here anymore? Will I hear it in London or anywhere else? Who knows?

15th December

THE REALIZATION that every act, every word, every thought of ours not only influences our environment but for some mysterious reason forms an integral and important part of the Universe, fits into it as if by necessity so to say, in the very moment we do, or say, or think it—is an overwhelming and even shattering experience.

The tremendous responsibility of it is terrifying.

If all of us only knew that the smallest act of ours, or a tiny thought, has such far-reaching effects as to set in motion forces which perhaps could shatter a galaxy. . . .

If we know it deeply and absolutely, if this realization becomes engraved permanently on our hearts, on our minds, how careful we would act and speak and think.

How precious life would become in its integral oneness. And this, I think, is as far as the human mind and heart can go.

It is as far as *I can go* at this moment in time where I am standing now. And I think that this is the ultimate Goal of Mysticism. This experience can become only deeper as we progress; it cannot become *more*.

It is wonderful and frightening. The responsibility of it is terrifying and fascinating in its depth and completeness.

The perplexing insecurity of being unique and the profound consolation of forming part of the Eternal Undivided Whole, the knowledge that we all have the absolute right to it and can achieve the realization of this wonderful meaning of life: one is *quite simply* part of it all. . . .

The smallest grain of sand, myself and all else, part of the great magnificent chord echoing forever. . . .

This was, I think, what Christ had meant when he said:

"Let our eye be single."

To have a single vision of wholeness.

After this realization which comes upon one slowly like a thief in the night, we still look the same to others, behave apparently in the same way. But the inner quality has been transformed, has changed so much that the world is not the same again. Nor can it ever be the same.

This is as well as I can express it, but there is much more to it which can never be said, for no words exist to convey the full meaning.

I have to leave it at that.

For it is a perfectly balanced, mind-less state.

Glimpses of it I had increasingly already when with Guruji; especially in Part 2 the intelligent reader will find allusions to it scattered here and there, and one will be able to read in between the lines.

Very acute it became after Guruji's passing away, so that I couldn't reconcile the torment of the heat, the mangy dogs roaming the streets, stone-throwing children, the sweat, the smells; for they were *That* too. . . . And the only thing to do was to run away into the solitude. It was here in the stillness of the mountains that it gradually crystallized itself—no, crystallized is not the right word—it "distilled" itself from a different dimension into the waking consciousness.

From now on I will have to live with the Glory and the Terror of it. . . . It is merciless, inescapable, sometimes nearer, sometimes receding into the distance, but never far away, always just around the corner on the edge of perception; a throbbing, dynamic, intensely virile, intoxicating "Presence" so utterly joyous, boundless and free.

But "Presence" is not the right word either; I am helpless, I give up, I don't know how to express it.

For to put it in words seems almost a blasphemy. . . .

16th December

ALL I KNOW IS that the goal will be always receding, "for the Beloved can never be known."

17th December

THE GRASS AND THE FLOWERS are silvery with frost every morning. The garden begins to die gently.

Walking a lot. Sunny warm days. All around the hills there is a sound of bells ringing. Suddenly from around the bend will emerge a string of donkeys walking daintily on the narrow mountain paths, loaded with kerosene tins full of pine resin. This is the time of the year when the resin is collected.

When I first arrived in Almora in '61, I saw it; there every pine tree had a deep incision and under it a tin was fixed to collect the slowly oozing sap. They were slowly bleeding to death; some had already three or four wounds around the trunk, bleeding slowly. They had already hardly any needles at all; some were clearly dying. But still they sang in the wind, standing straight, the tall trunk looking russet in the sunlight.

And still they were friendly to human beings; they gave freely, while dying; there was no resentment in the tree.

Deodars (Himalayan cedar) are not friendly to humans, neither are chestnut trees (red Indians even say that one could get blind if one slept under a chestnut tree), but pines are so friendly. One needed only to come near it, to put one's hand on its fragrant bark, to feel that the tree does not mind you at all; quite on the contrary. . . .

You are bleeding, I was saying to them, and love was in my heart, when I sat under them looking at the crowns swaying high above me against the deep azure of the mountain sky. Many a time I just sat with them, relaxing in the fragrance, they singing around me, and deep was the oneness. I know; pine trees can love.

Here in the Kumaon hills not every pine is wounded, but many are. That's why we have the charming sound of bells coming either from one or the other direction of the slopes of the hills, the grey, patient crocodile of donkeys or mules, each a bell on its collar, a few foresters walking with long sticks beside. Often I stood aside and watched the fragrant procession pass by. The delicious strong smell of pine resin. The smell of animals and of men in their leather or wool garments. The forest around, the snows shimmering in the background, and the whisper and the song of the trees all around. . . .

Goodbye, days of peace, days of wrestling with myself. Days of incredible beauty of nature at its best, days of glorious states of consciousness wherein the divine heart within myself was the divine heart within the cosmos, when I knew the meaning of oneness because I lived it. Yes, Guruji, you did not deceive me. You pointed out the way and now the way has taken hold of me, fully, irrevocably.

And when the broken window pane was repaired and new glass was put in, for days my room smelled of fresh pine resin. The putty the workman used was made with pure pine resin.

It seems incredible that such a precious substance could be used to bind the putty; but it was, for here it is the cheapest binding substance, given to men free of charge by the generous pines who pay for it with their lives. . . .

29th December, 1966
Vedic Sadhak Ashram, Tapovan

LAST NIGHT THE SUN WAS SETTING serenely in the sea of clouds of liquid gold. We had a little rain during the night. But now the morning is clear with feathery clouds towards the north, the hills of Mussoorie. Here the sun is setting in the plains behind a line of trees or very low hills, going down in utter serenity, the colors of the sky dying away gently. I am here since the 21st December. Left Kausani on the 20th. The journey with several changes from bus to train in Kathgodam, then in Barelli, was tedious and long. Waiting a long time in ladies waiting rooms for the connections, and it was cold.

The last weeks in Kausani were very disagreeable. The Ashram underwent repairs and was being partly rebuilt. Noise, people coming and going, workmen all over the place; no peace at all. Patel arranged for me to come here; he is a close friend of Swamiji who is the director of Tapovan Ashram not far from Dehra Dun. It is a lovely place only 3,000 feet above sea level, so it is much warmer. It is very different from Kausani; no stately pine forests or dark deodar groves, but a thick jungle of mostly sal trees commencing on the slope of the hill behind the Ashram.

The sal tree is closely connected with the legend of Buddha; he was born under a sal tree, preached his first sermon amongst the sal trees in the Deer Park, and died in between two sal trees, his head to the north. It is not a very high tree, with large, roundish leaves, and it does not give much shade. But a forest of sal trees is lovely, has a fragrance and an atmosphere of its own. It is said that the sal tree has *Sat* and *Chaitanya*—intelligence and life. Its branches are not very outspread; the whole impression it gives is of a slender tree reaching upwards, rather like a poplar. Here we are on the first Himalayan foothills facing the endless plains of India towards the southwest. To the north rise abruptly the grey and steep hills of Mussoorie forming a plateau over 7,000 feet, on which this hill-station is sprawling around the smaller hills, covered with pines.

It is a rather large plateau and in the night the heights above seem to be adorned with rows of sparkling diamonds, stars fallen from heaven, the lights of the houses and of the street lamps.

In Kausani my room was facing the east; here my veranda faces the west.

This Ashram is a large one; it can accommodate many people. Most of the rooms are in the main building, quite at the bottom of the hill, where also the common dining room and kitchen are situated as well as several courtyards, and a temple where a perpetual fire is kept alive, and twice daily *Yagña Havan* (fire sacrifice) is performed with chanting of Vedic Mantras, reading of the *Vedas*, and where the daily *Kirtan* is held.

On the terraced slope of the hill are several very well built bungalows, each having one or two rooms. I have the smallest bungalow under an enormous peepul tree. It is an historical tree; when the Nepalese surrendered to the English (there are remains of a Nepalese fort on the top of the hill, two miles from here), all the women of fallen soldiers burned themselves alive on the place where the tree is now. *Sati* sacrifice, it is called, the burning of the widow. It must have been dreadful. One can imagine them all, young and old, walking voluntarily into the huge pyre singing mantras. There was a little brick temple to commemorate the event. The snake-like roots have completely enveloped and burst it asunder. And the tree itself grew all around it, and in the trunk one can still see embedded part of the small dome clinging as if growing out of the bark.

I measured the width of the trunk; it is forty-five feet in diameter. Peepul is a variety of a wild fig not fit for human consumption but very much liked by crows (saw it in Adyar), and especially bats. For a long time in the night I could not make out the noise which was going on in the branches of the tree; I thought they were monkeys. But one day when the noise was very bad I went out with my torch and shone it into the branches. Many dozens of fruit bats took off and flapping noisily vanished into the dark. They are called here the flying foxes; they have a wing span of about two feet, and during the day they sleep in the caves of the Mussoorie cliffs.

From my veranda the view is grand. To the right rise, like an enormous natural fortress, the hills of Mussoorie; lovely, rich jungle covers the hills immediately around the Ashram where even bamboo grows. Right in front is a dried-up bed of a river, all pebbles and boulders, and very low hills, like soft dunes covered with rich vegetation. To the South are the plains, and dimly visible in the distance the first houses of the suburbs of Dehra Dun. And at the back of the jungle rising up the hill one can hear foxes bark in the night and the hysterical laughter and the wild screams of jackals.

We are here only a few miles from Dehra Dun. As in Kausani there is here no electricity; we have candles or lovely old-fashioned brass kerosene lamps. Dehra Dun and Mussoorie have electric light. To go shopping is an expedition: one has to walk for over a mile in the dry river bed (I shudder to think what happens during the rainy season!), then stand on the road and wait for the bus which passes every hour, and takes one right to the bazaar in the center of the town.

The Sound stayed with me, in spite of the occasionally noisy nights filled with animal noises or the distant roar of the motor cars. Sometimes I heard a strange mournful singing all around my bungalow and I wondered if it was the mantric chant of *Satis* still resounding in the atmosphere when one after another they went into the fire. . . . And another strange phenomenon: I wrote above that a chanting of the *Vedas* is performed here twice daily. I attend the evening service, but in the morning it is too early for me. So I listen to the chanting from my veranda looking at the hills and the sky, the trees and the jungle. It is so uplifting.

But I soon noticed to my surprise that after the chanting has finished, and I see the Swamis dispersing to their dwellings, the chant is repeated, is going on softly in the atmosphere, in the air around, as if echoed, continued by some beings, some voices in the air. I found it lovely and moving and was waiting for it every morning, and it never failed to repeat itself. . . .

STAYED IN THIS ASHRAM until the beginning of January. Then had to go to the nearest branch of the agent of Barclays Bank which was two days journey from here; some muddle arose because of the transference of my pension. When I returned, I did not go to the Tapovan anymore but to the Shahanshah Ashram where I stayed till I had to go home to England.

This Ashram is at the other end of the plain of Dehra Dun, right under the steep rocks of Mussoorie. The dear Swami Govindananda,

Miss Asha and her delightful grandmother, and the *Kirtans*. Every evening when the sun was going down softly behind the houses of Dehra Dun in the distance, the lovely voice of Swamiji accompanying himself on the harmonium, my long walks in the sal forest around the hills, my heart so full of the words of Krishna in the *Bhagavad Gita*: "I am the fragrance of the earth, I am the brilliance of fire," etc. ringing in my mind. I lived at the bottom of the hill in the guest house; the Ashram was on the top of the hill; many steps were leading to it. The boy's school, Swamiji himself, and the whole atmosphere of the place with the Tibetan village just nearby. . . . I was so happy there, so deeply happy . . . and I stayed there till the end of March.

Had plenty of time to think, plenty of time to reflect. I knew that this diary has to become a book one day, though for the moment I was afraid even to look at it, for it was still burning inside me, hurting so much. . . . I knew that my life will be that of work for Him only, and I felt how fortunate I was: from now on I have nothing else to do but to sing the song of the Beloved until the end of my life. . . . What a wonderful prospect, how fortunate I am. . . .

8th March, 1967

THE RINGING SOUND of my friend, the Pachta, the Indian woodpecker is all the time in the air after the sun has risen. The lovely ash tree on the lawn in front of the bungalow where I stay is now yellow and dry, losing its leaves, and one seems to walk on a rustling, thick carpet. It remained bare for about a fortnight. Now it has new leaves once more, young, fresh, shiny, reddish at the tips. How I love this place . . . right against the Mussoorie mountain, on a hill with a splendid view to the Doon plain and such lovely walks all around in the sal forests, on the hill of the Bengali Ashram, nestling romantically against it with its white domed temple. Went to the lime stone quarry, about midway to Mussoorie up the hill, came back with the stone-cutter's truck, fully loaded with lime stones. The driver was excellent, but he drove rapidly, and the road is pretty dangerous especially with this load.

Passing days of great peace. . . . Praying so much. . . . Those are my last weeks in India. The air ticket is already waiting for me at the office of Air France in Delhi. Have the letter of confirmation. Wrote to reserve a hotel room, today. Will sleep one night in Delhi. It is going to be hot. Did not write into my diary for quite a while. What to say? Everything has been said, so it seems. Swamiji is very kind to me. He is a Yogi and a Bhakta. Gives me useful explanations about the *Gita*, the *Ramayana*, the *Vedas*. Something which is not in books, but he got it in his meditation and gave me the permission to use it in my talks. He has Yogic Powers. This *Raga* for rain, for instance . . . AND it DID rain, by Jove!

9th March, 1967

MY INFINITE ONE, asking for help I am . . . I am going to a life dedicated to Thee.

It is said that the river takes no rest, the wind knows no fatigue, and the sun can only shine and shine forever.

The child plays for the joy of playing. It does not think of the benefit; all its joy is in playing.

Yoga is falling in love, not a choice of a career. The brain can be compared to a computer; each Path of Yoga is a programming of the whole of the human being to a particular method how to reach Reality.

You have programmed me, my Revered Guruji. I will go on. I know that the states of Nearness will increase, will become more permanent, but also the state of separation will become more painful, more lonely the nearer one comes to Reality. This cannot be avoided; it belongs to this school of training. But it does not matter anymore; the memory of Nearness to Thee will remain and will give me strength to go on. I know I go back to a life of fire; for you, my dear Guruji, before accepting me, you have told me what to expect. And I said, yes, and sealed my destiny. I know health will fail me sometimes, I know I will be burned and it will not matter, for always, always, I will remember that I belong somewhere and that will give me strength to go on. I know one must not impose one's own experiences upon other people, for each of us is intensely individual, and experiences are unique for each of us.

I remember that after your death I felt like screaming only at the thought of returning to the West. Could not reconcile the states of oneness and the world around me. Solitude was the only way out. To be able to find myself again, which was not a self at all.

I know now, that I can never be alone anymore, for you are with me always. I know that God is Silence and can be reached only in silence. I will try to help people to reach this state, this is a promise, and I will keep it.

I know that there is nothing left TO DO for the devotee who has surrendered himself. For from then on He takes over and the will of the devotee becomes the will of the Beloved who is the only King of our hearts.

Love for the Unlimited is also unlimited; that's why our hearts have to be broken and become nothing to be able to accommodate the Unlimited.

All this I know. My life is offered to You. You take over.

And may God help me. . . .

Meditation

(TO BE DONE EVERY MORNING)

IN THIS MEDITATION we have to imagine three things:

1. We must suppose that we go deep within ourselves, deeper and deeper into our most hidden self. There in our innermost being, in the very core of ourselves, we will find a place where there is peace, stillness and, above all, love.

God is Love, says the Sufi. Human beings are all love, for they are made in His Image; only they have forgotten it long ago. When we love another human being, however deeply, there is a place in our heart where this beloved human being has no access. There, we are quite alone. But within us there is a longing, which is the ultimate proof that this place is reserved for Him alone.

2. After having found this place, we must imagine that we are seated there, immersed into, surrounded by the Love of God. We are in deepest peace. We are loved; we are sheltered; we are secure. All of us is there, physical body and all; nothing is outside, not even a finger tip, not even the tiniest hair. Our whole being is contained within the Love of God.

3. As we sit there, happy, serene in His Presence, thoughts will intrude into our mind—what we did the day before, what we have to do tomorrow—memories float by, images appear before the mind's eye.

We have to imagine that we are getting hold of every thought, every image and feeling, and drown them, merge them into the feeling of love.

Every feeling, especially the feeling of love, is much more dynamic than the thinking process, so if one does it well, with the utmost concentration, all thoughts will disappear. Nothing will remain. The mind will be empty.

It is a spiritual practice to control the mind, and also a useful exercise of will power.

After a while, when you practice it well, you cannot fail to notice that this place in the heart and your state of consciousness are one and the same. In other words, the spiritual locality where you find yourself equals your state of consciousness. It is called *loka* in Sanskrit, and it is a state beyond the mind. The mind can only understand things outside itself. In other words, *I* am here and *there* is the knowledge. That's duality. In the higher states of consciousness, known as *Samadhi*, you *are* the knowledge; there is no duality anymore. The understanding and you are one.

—Irina Tweedie
1986